FRANÇOIS TRUFFAUT
LETTERS

also published by Faber

La Petite Voleuse
Jules et Jim

François Truffaut

LETTERS

Edited by Gilles Jacob
and Claude de Givray

Translated and edited by
Gilbert Adair

Foreword by
Jean-Luc Godard

faber and faber
LONDON · BOSTON

First published in France in 1988
by Hatier, Renens
as *François Truffaut Correspondance*
First published in Great Britain in 1989
by Faber and Faber Limited
3 Queen Square London WC1N 3AU
This paperback edition first published in 1990

Photoset by Wilmaset, Birkenhead, Wirral
Printed in England by Clays Ltd, St Ives plc

A CIP record for this book
is available from the British Library

ISBN 0-571-14483-7

In memory of Helen Scott

Contents

Foreword by Jean-Luc Godard
page ix

Preface by Gilles Jacob
page xi

Translator's Note
page xvii

LETTERS 1945–84

Chronology
page 570

Index of Correspondents
page 574

General Index
page 576

Foreword

by Jean-Luc Godard

The article in *Arts*, no. 719, published on 22 April 1959, said 'We have won'; and then, a little further on, it concluded with the words '. . . for if we have won a battle, the war is not yet over.' I wrote that article, as pleased as Athos was by one of D'Artagnan's exploits. Our victory was the fact that *Les Quatre Cents Coups* had been selected to represent France at the Cannes Film Festival.

In those days there still existed something called magic. A work of art was not the sign of something, it was the thing itself and nothing else (and it depended neither on a name nor on Heidegger for its existence). It was from the public that the sign would come, or not, according to its state of mind.

Along the Croisette, bombarded with cheers, there came a strange trio: an elderly eagle whose broad-spanned wings were already greying, a young ruffian, awkward and pale, risen from the depths of a book by Jean Genet or Maurice Sachs and now holding the hand of an even younger boy who was to become the French equivalent of Pasolini's Ninetto.

Cocteau, Truffaut, Léaud. The elderly angel, Heurtebise, would whisper the passwords: look to your left, look to your right. Smile at the newspapers, smile at the newscasters! Bow to the minister! Slow down! Walk faster!

It was a good time to be alive. And the fame that lay ahead had not yet begun to weave the shroud of our happiness. For the war was a lost cause, precisely because of the hopes we invested in it (I mean that modern war between digital technology and human suffering, between what is said and what is not said because it is seen and recorded).

Why did I quarrel with François? It had nothing to do with Genet or Fassbinder. It was something else. Something which, fortunately, had no name. Something stupid. Infantile. I say fortunately, because everything else was becoming a symbol, the sign of itself, a mortal decoration: Algeria, Vietnam, Hollywood, and our friendship, and our love of reality. The sign, but also the death of that sign.

What held us together as intimately as a kiss – as when we used to buy our pathetic little cigars on emerging from the Bikini cinema on Place Pigalle or the Artistic, from a film by Edgar Ulmer or Jacques Daniel-Norman (oh Claudine Dupuis! oh Tilda Thamar!), before going to burgle my godmother's apartment to pay for the next day's movies – what bound us together more intimately than the false kiss in *Notorious* was the screen, and nothing but the screen. It was the wall we had to scale in order to escape from our lives, and there was nothing but that wall, and we invested so much of our innocence in the idea of that wall that it was bound to crumble beneath all the fame and decorations and declarations that lay ahead. We were devoured by Saturn. And if we tore each other apart, little by little, it was for fear of being the first to be eaten alive. The cinema had taught us how to live; but life, like Glenn Ford in *The Big Heat*, was to take its revenge.

These letters, from a young man tormented by the idea that he did not know how to write, demonstrate the victory of what is said over what is not said but seen. The pain that we inflicted, we inflicted through words, words, and more words, but the pain that we suffered remained of the cinema, therefore silent.

François is perhaps dead. I am perhaps alive. But then, is there a difference?

Preface

It is 6 February 1944 and dawn has still to break over Paris. A young boy steps out of a building at the corner of the rue de Navarin, no. 33, in the city's ninth arrondissement. Today is his twelfth birthday but he looks young for his age. A scrawny little fellow in his red and black check windcheater, his knees blue with cold from the icy wind that is blowing off Montmartre, he swings his satchel at the end of his arm. But there is, above all, something unusual about his eyes, which are dark, intense and full of expression.

He should, in the normal course of events, turn right at the end of the street and hurry off to the local school at no. 5 rue Milton. Instead, he turns left and, a few minutes later, slips into the courtyard of no. 10 rue de Douai. He whistles loudly, then, without waiting for an answer, climbs up the back staircase with its blacked-out window-panes. The kitchen door of a second-floor apartment is ajar. Another boy, older and stronger-looking, waits for him, a forefinger held to his lips, and leads the way into his bedroom. It is a quarter past eight. The older boy then grabs his own satchel, calls out 'Bye, mum!' in a deliberately loud voice and clatters just as noisily down the back stairs. Two minutes later, he sneaks back up the main staircase and into the flat again: nine empty rooms along a central hallway (empty, because his father, a betting man, has sold off the last of the furniture to settle his debts). There, back in his room, he finds his friend, on the bed, reading Balzac's *Le Père Goriot*, by the faint glow of a candle that must provide not only light but heat. It is so cold in fact that, far from undressing, Robert wraps himself up even more snugly, slips on a pair of gloves and, following his friend's example, settles down to read.

'Look, François.'

He shows him their latest prize: a classic of French literature with the familiar cream and black cover of the Fayard collection, purchased, for three francs and twenty centimes, in the rue des Martyrs, along with a packet of dried bananas. The book is Victor Hugo's *Hernani*.

These early years of diligent reading, punctuated only by the sounds that drifted up from the courtyard and the purring of Pompon, Robert's family cat, were the origin of François Truffaut's long love affair with the printed word.

Playtime would be later in the day, in early afternoon – 'Put a sock in it, we'll miss the newsreel!' – when our two truants would sneak into their local fleapits, the cinemas on the boulevards with their entrancing names: the Gaumont Palace, the Artistic (right on the rue de Douai), the Clichy, the Agora, the Pigalle, the Moulin de la Chanson, the American Cinema, the Cigale, the Trianon, the Gaieté-Rochechouart and the Delta, many of which would later, so very much later, become nightclubs or sex-shops.

Playing truant by day in order to discover Balzac and Hugo, slinking past the patrolling Germans by night in order to filch publicity stills of their favourite film stars, Jany Holt or Gaby Morlay, François and Robert lived rather more intensely than most schoolboys do.

And so was born a vocation.

And so François Truffaut – accompanied by his friend Robert Lachenay – made a surreptitious entrance into the history of cinema and also that of literature.

Exactly forty years later, a brain tumour brought his existence to an end, an existence dedicated to two passions, paper and film.

And between these dates there is what is called an *œuvre*: 21 feature films, 3 shorts, 10 books, 10 unrealized projects, 13 prefaces and literally hundreds of articles. And also what is called a life: the women he loved, who inspired his work, who bore him three children, three daughters.

The films of François Truffaut have made him a household name. But if these films, many of them now considered classics, were liked by the public, and if critics regard his book of interviews with Hitchcock as a seminal text, it has never been widely known that Truffaut was also an assiduous writer of letters. Indeed, in a period when most of us would rather telephone or telex or 'fax' than put pen to paper, Truffaut was undoubtedly one of the last of the great letter-writers.

The letters in this selection have been arranged in chronological order, from his first known postcard (written in 1945 at the age of thirteen) to the very last he ever wrote, in 1984, the year of his death. Replies have not, as a rule, been included. The sole exceptions to this rule are those replies which struck us as of significance in themselves; and to notably frequent correspondents (Robert Lachenay, Helen Scott . . .) we have allowed one reply apiece. Our primary aim was to concentrate on the personality of Truffaut himself.

The result is an exceptionally interesting, and primarily film-centred, correspondence. In it we discover Truffaut's extraordinary attention to detail, with regard to both his own work and that of the film-makers he admired and his constant need to explain both his work and himself. These letters, too, reveal the depth of his love for the cinema, even in his ferocity towards those whose conception of the medium he could not share, such as certain French directors of the preceding generation. Whenever he was not actually shooting a film, his entire life was organized around programme times and schedules. He could never resist turning down a dinner invitation if there happened to be an Orson Welles movie at the Cinémathèque or an early Hitchcock on television.

But he was also a reader – of novels, newspapers, trade journals, books on the cinema and star biographies. He would often read books unavailable in French, even if, given his poor command of English, it would be a slow and laborious process. It was reading, as he himself admitted, which had prevented him from becoming a juvenile delinquent and he remained a lover of books all his life. Part of his pleasure was purely sensual, the delight he took in the actual texture of books, in the shapes of words and letters: the literary *auto-da-fé* in *Fahrenheit 451*, with its tortured pages twisting in the flames, shows just how sensitive he was to books as physical objects. In a letter to Georges Cravenne, he writes: 'Run your finger along the spine of the cover and . . . ouch . . . ouch . . . go fetch a Band-Aid . . . .' 'If I did not make films,' he adds elsewhere, 'I would have been a publisher.' His fondness for the written word shows, too, in his handwriting, with its great, supple, curved letters reminiscent of Cocteau's. We have included a few extracts from his correspondence in facsimile to indicate the progress of that handwriting with the passage of time.

But none of this, interesting though it is, matters nearly as much as the humanity of the man as it emerges in his letters. 'My salvation,' he wrote to Jean Mambrino, 'will be that I "specialized" in the cinema very early on.' And indeed, through the letters, we monitor the development of his character from near-delinquency to accomplished artistry. This despite the fact that he can hardly be said to have come from a deprived background. His father, Roland Truffaut, was employed in an architect's office and was also a member of the prestigious mountaineering society, the Club Alpin. His mother, Janine de Monferrand, worked as a secretary on *L'Illustration*, the French equivalent of the *Illustrated London News*. François was initially brought up by his two grandmothers, the first in Paris, the second in the suburb of Juvisy where his paternal grandfather was a stonemason, principally of gravestones. He was a solitary boy, switching from school to school; top of the class in French, but hopeless at every other subject. Most of the time he would sit at the back of the class doing crosswords. Summer meant school camps at the seaside, at Binic or Les Sables d'Olonne. He ran away from home a couple of times, and did the odd job as a delivery boy or, very briefly, as an apprentice welder in the factory where Robert Lachenay worked. On one famous occasion, he and Robert stole a typewriter from Roland Truffaut's office and pawned it: the episode subsequently crops up in *Les Quatre Cents Coups*.

Soon Truffaut started attending film-society screenings, where he met André Bazin. He founded a film club which he called 'Cinémane' and which had only one session before going bankrupt. Eventually, he ran away again; he was committed to a reformatory at Villejuif, outside Paris; the rest is history. But what is less well known – and this comes across very clearly in the letters – is the fact that this young delinquent became, in the space of a few months, a highly regarded film critic. Bazin was an enormous influence, and a source of moral support, but Bazin alone could not have made Truffaut what he became. The missing link, as we see in his correspondence, was the Club du Faubourg. It is almost impossible, today, to imagine the enthusiasm and effervescence of such a club. All kinds of people, from wastrels to writers, from barristers to former ministers, were drawn to its meetings and debates. Truffaut dragged Lachenay along. He started making pronouncements about the cinema which betrayed an astonishing experience and self-confidence. Soon he was brandishing articles which he produced from a briefcase stuffed with newspapers and which provoked both admiration and notoriety. This, in turn, gave his confidence a further boost: it was at the Club du Faubourg that he began to work on his celebrated manifesto, 'A Certain Tendency of French Cinema'.

We owe an enormous debt of gratitude to Robert Lachenay who, just as we were on the point of completing this collection, came to us with bundles of carefully preserved letters; he had even kept the envelopes, without which letters are frequently impossible to date. Lachenay's letters are indispensable to understanding two critical but little-known periods of Truffaut's life: his teenage years and his experience in the army, about which, as Truffaut said, a whole book could be written. These extraordinarily frank letters take us, at first, on a grand tour of the ninth arrondissement in the company of two children, two little boys who one hopes won't grow up too quickly. But they do. And, as time passes, we discover what it was to be a critic in Paris in the fifties: 'I type with just the one [finger],' Truffaut writes, 'but that means I type harder and faster in accordance with the well-known law of mutual compensation which, so they say, makes one-armed men better in bed than those with two.' We learn of the misadventures of two young journalists eager to interview Alfred Hitchcock – the younger of them is Truffaut, the elder Claude Chabrol. The letters teach us all we need to know about the trials and tribulations of 'setting up' a film, the tantrums of actors and actresses, the reluctance of the money-men; they tell us, above all, about creative doubt.

Often, in the course of reading this correspondence, one chances upon the embryonic idea of one of his films. It may take no more than a simple anecdote to put us on the scent. 'There have been many, too many, deaths around me, of people I've loved, that I took the decision after Françoise Dorléac died, never again to attend a funeral, which, as you can well imagine, does not prevent the distress I feel from casting its shadow over everything for a time and never completely fading, even as the years pass, for we live not only with the living but also with all of those who have ever meant anything in our lives . . .' This extract from a letter to Tanya Lopert, dated February 1970, surely contains the seed of what was to become *La Chambre verte*.

Though Truffaut himself wished his letters to be published, and had arranged for a copy of each to be stored and filed, many were, of course, handwritten, and even he was not so obsessive as to make systematic copies of all of them. Many of his typewritten letters, moreover, contain handwritten postscripts. We therefore had to attempt to trace all the originals. Truffaut's family gave us permission to contact all his known and likely correspondents so that we might obtain letters in their original form; we also, of course, had to ask for permission to publish them. In so doing, we discovered just how much had been lost. Many of his friends – including those closest to him – had quite simply thrown his letters away. Others were lost. Saddest of all is the fact that André Bazin never kept letters. In still other cases, letters were, rightly or wrongly, judged too intimate for publication.

Our decision to publish Truffaut's letters was also, tragically, justified by the sudden death of Helen Scott, who had been one of his most frequent and regular correspondents.

During the 1960s, Helen Scott worked at the French Film Office in New York. This clever, devoted, discerning, difficult woman, with her occasionally ferocious sense of humour, became one of Truffaut's very dearest friends. She played a crucial role in conceiving and producing his book of interviews with Alfred Hitchcock. Over a period of ten years, they exchanged a voluminous correspondence, he from Paris, she from New York. Truffaut, incidentally, had asked Helen Scott to publish his letters to her, an initiative on his part which offered us additional proof that he would have approved of our undertaking. Helen had always refused to consider the idea, partly because the prospect daunted her and partly because she felt the letters were too fragmented to be of much interest. The fact is, however, that the charm of Truffaut's letters is precisely their quirky mixture of private and professional matters, a mixture of impetuous judgements, pseudo-indiscretions and carefully considered reflections on his craft. They do require – if they are to be fully understood – minimal annotation. Helen Scott was in a position to provide us with the notes we needed and she generously did so during the course of two long conversations just a couple of weeks before she died: without her recollections of people and films, the spirit of these little chronicles would be incomplete. And her death gave us an even greater incentive to ensure that Truffaut's other letters should be preserved. It encouraged us to urge all those concerned to contribute to the collective task of preserving François Truffaut's correspondence.

Gilles Jacob
January 1988

Translator's Note

For this English-language edition of François Truffaut's *Letters* I have chosen, on the whole, to respect the director's own frequently idiosyncratic syntax and punctuation, since it seemed to me that, by normalizing it, I risked diminishing the charm of what might be called his epistolary voice; only when there existed a very real danger of incomprehension on the reader's part have I taken the responsibility of radically altering the structure of a sentence or a paragraph. In the letters written during his adolescence, however, I felt it would be both tasteless and pedantic to attempt to transliterate his spelling errors (which were retained in the original French edition) unless they happened to be clearly intentional.

The dates within square brackets are those subsequently appended by the original recipients or else by the French editors; and square brackets within the letters themselves denote the relatively few passages which were removed at the request of the Truffaut family.

At Le Puiselet
(in the forest of Fontainebleau):
1 François Truffaut.
2 Roland Truffaut, François's father.
3 Bernard de Monferrand, Janine's brother.
4 Janine Truffaut, née de Monferrand, François's mother.
5 Denise de Monferrand, Janine's sister.

1945

To Robert Lachenay[1] *[25 June 1945]*

I write to you from St Brieuc. I'm cutting it short because the local train that connects St Brieuc with Binic is in the station.

I'll make it longer tomorrow

François

quick here it is

1 – Born in 1930, Robert Lachenay was Truffaut's oldest friend. See note 1, p. 119.

To Robert Lachenay *[Binic, 1945]*

My dear Robert,

I was really pleased to receive your two packages. Balzac has arrived safely. Don't send me any more magazines since I'll have to pay about 80F in postage to send it all back to you. I went to the post office with the empty box. My father is to send me 200 francs out of which there will be 80F for postage + 60F for the movies which I owe the headmaster that makes 140 francs.

Things are lousy and I mean really lousy! We went to see *A Thousand and One Nights!*[1] It's better than *The Thief of Bagdad*[2] but nothing to write home about. Just reading your cinema magazines makes me want to be in Paris as there seem to be lots of good films. Edward Robinson is all the rage at the moment since he's acting in 3 new films![3] I hope my letter won't find you still wishing it were last year. Should I send the magazines back to you at Le Tréport or in Paris? Try to be careful when bathing ~~on the nails~~ (it was a chum who wrote that).

I have to go as the peeryod of skoolwurk iz finnysht,

Lotz a luv,
Phronssouas your chumm.[4]

Discuss in your next letter my nocturnal and subterranean odyssey in the Métro the cause, the action, its consequence, discuss exactly how it happened that I slept in the Métro when we were at Ducornet's.[5] Because my chums refuse to believe me.

1 – By Alfred E. Green.
2 – By Michael Powell, Ludwig Berger and Tim Whelan (1940). In the footnotes, films are dated only when the date does not coincide with that of the letter itself.
3 – The three films starring Edward G. Robinson were *The Amazing Doctor Clitterhouse* (Anatole Litvak), *Manpower* (Raoul Walsh) and *The Sea Wolf* (Michael Curtiz).
4 – See Truffaut's own spelling in the facsimile opposite.
5 – Ducornet was the model for the teacher played by Guy Decomble in *Les Quatre Cents Coups* (*The Four Hundred Blows*).

To Robert Lachenay

[Binic, July–August 1945]

Dear Robert,

I can't help myself writing to you every day, do likewise. Was the chocolate good? I sévigne, you sévigne, we sévigne.[1] I go kayaking, I write five letters a day.

Write me! Write me!

François

1 – An allusion to the voluminous correspondence of Madame de Sévigné and possibly also to the chocolate firm 'La Marquise de Sévigné'.

To Robert Lachenay

Paris 18 [September 1945]

Dear Robert,

Oh! Oh yes! The Eiffel Tower is still there. You've got to read this letter carefully. Specially the underlined parts. I've been a Parisian for five days now. My first outing was for my 'Fayards' . . .[1]

The shop in the rue des Martyrs opposite the Médrano has tons of them I'm going there tomorrow. In the rue Mansard this afternoon I bought 36 classics of which the only ones you don't have are *Candide*, *Stello* (2 vols.),[2] *War and Peace* (8 vols.), *Histoire d'un merle blanc*,[3] *Premières Méditations poétiques*,[4] *Tartarin de Tarascon* 2,[5] and *Fromont jeune*,[5] that's to say 4 there are only 18 volumes that you don't have out of those I've bought and you'll be able to find them. I now have 295 books I need 90 more to complete the collection. My first and only film . . . so far has been *Félicie Nanteuil*[6]

ou à Paris ? tâches d'être prudent
en te baignant. ~~sur les clous~~
C'est un copain qui a
mis ça
je te quitte car leur deu
boulant ci fynyse
Tou a Coua
Phranssouas
ton caupin.

Raconte dans ta prochaine
lettre mon odyssée nocturne
et souterraine dans le métro
la cause, l'action, son résultat
Raconte exactement comment les faits
se sont passés quand j'ai couché
au métro quand on était chez
Ducornet.
Parceque mes copains ne veulent
pas me croire.

François Truffaut's handwriting at the age of thirteen (letter to Robert Lachenay).

yesterday I visited the Château of Versailles. I've been preparing a few surprises and presents for you to celebrate your return.

to keep me posted of your arrival place a red ribbon and a white ribbon on your balcony since I pass your house every day, I'll see them and I'll whistle. also since it's better to be safe than sorry, on the day of your arrival go to Thibaudat's[7] in Paris; that way since I go every day he'll tell me if you're back or better still write to him telling him the date of your return so he can tell me. But whatever you do don't put[8] any letters for me in your letter to Thibaudat.

I've been making plans for the two of us.

Write to Thibaudat as soon as you receive my letter

Claude Thibaudat 42, rue des Martyrs, Paris 9e

See you soon,

François

1 – As Truffaut himself was to write: 'The Fayard collection with its woodcut illustrations is of immense nostalgic value, associated as it is with the first third of the century and, for the grown-ups of today, conjuring up their parents' libraries, books piled up high in attics' (unpublished letter).

2 – By Alfred de Vigny.

3 – Alfred de Musset's *Le Merle blanc.*

4 – By Alphonse de Lamartine.

5 – By Alphonse Daudet.

6 – By Marc Allégret (1942).

7 – A classmate who was later to become the music-hall impressionist Claude Véga.

8 – The passages underlined in this book were those underlined by Truffaut.

To Robert Lachenay *[21 September 1945]*

My dear Robert,

Excuse these hurried words and this letter in pencil, it's not that I like you any the less . . . on the contrary what's making me write this letter in such a hurry is preparing the presents (I really can't hold my tongue!) that I'm going to give you when we celebrate your return. Your presents are all wrapped except 1 which needs a little box about 4 by 4 centimetres that I'm having a problem finding. I'm going to put the letter down maybe there's one (a box) in my mother's drawer. There we are a matchbox just what I need. This afternoon I went to see *Good-bye Master Chips.*[1] I go to Juvisy tomorrow I return Monday I'll drop in on Tuesday to see Thibaudat and you. Morning or afternoon. Don't come and see [. . .].[2] I believe you've written to Claude Thibaudat.

Latest Parisian pastime the Parachute Tower 25 metres high. You leap from the top in a Parachute. I don't know how much it costs. Latest invention of Parisian children. They no longer sell flowers or newspapers: they take a little bench a box with 2 brushes and 2 tins of wax and they shine the shoes of

d'autre part comme 2 suretés valent mieux qu'une,
tu iras le jour de ton arrivée chez Thibaudat à Paris
ainsi comme j'irai tous les jours il me dira si tu est
rentré ou bien mieux écris lui en lui disant
ta date de rentrée comme ça il me le dira.
Mais surtout ne m'est pas dans la lettre à
Thibaudat de lettres pour moi.
J'ai fait pour nous deux quelques projets.

25 centimes

Ludovic XVI

Napoléon I
empereur

2,5
Les maîtres
GOETE
WERTHER
Paris
FAYARD

Ecris à Thibaudat dès que tu recevras ma lettre

Claude Thibaudat
42 rue des Martyrs
Paris 9eme

A Bientot
François

Mais Oui!

F. Truffaut

Entrance. Franco-Roberto oui
Place Pigallo

mémorablement

Le sacré coeur l'arc de triomphe la tour eiffel sont toujours là

Letter to Robert Lachenay.

Americans, 1 customer = 25 francs, in 1 hour 10 customers therefore 250 francs![3]

Goodbye till Tuesday
François

1 – Sam Wood's *Goodbye Mr Chips* (1939).
2 – There is a word missing in the original letter.
3 – Vittorio De Sica made a film on precisely this subject, *Sciuscia*, the following year.

1946

To Robert Lachenay *[July 1946]*

Dear Robert,

As you see I'm not throwing all your money away on my sweetheart. As Proof: these 4 assorted postcards!

I received your parcel and your two letters with the 120F. You're too good to me! You don't say anything about the proposal I made you to get you to come here? Why?

I'm pleased for you (and for me) that the arms and munitions factory is doing so well.

You offer me three hundred francs a week: that's too much. 150 to 200 is quite enough. I'd prefer you to send me: if possible: 1 can of condensed Milk and a little butter since, as you know, I'm a big eater in the morning and since ration tickets for bread aren't necessary here I buy extra. But I want you, if you do send me that, to note down on a sheet of paper what I owe you for it, even for the food since if you send me something you can't sell it back to your father.

Send me what you can but 1 single can of milk, a little butter, sugar I'm sure you won't be able to, sardines and oh! DRIED BANANAS. Am I asking too much? I'm afraid so. But I'd prefer you to send me these even if it means sending me less money. But, I repeat, I insist you note down how much all of that is going to set you back. I wouldn't, though, want to owe you more than 1,000 to 1,500F when I return.

Monique is still well and she has . . . a sister, Nicole, 14½ years older! I'd like to have your opinion of: *The Wizard of Oz,*[1] *On ne meurt pas comme ça,*[2] *The Impostor,*[3] *Dorothée cherche l'amour,*[4] *The Spy in Black*[5] and *Weekend at the Waldorf.*[6]

Can you write me out a short review of these films. You really must be sick of me!

Don't forget whatever you do to send me the *Cinémonde* of 16 July. Your newspapers are very good, specially the article on Pierre Brasseur.[7] When I opened the parcel on the beach there were cries of joy when we saw Cyrano as we have to perform extracts from it on the 21st.

For 14 July we saw *Sergeant York*.[8] And next Sunday or Thursday we're going to see *Mission spéciale*,[9] that'll make a bit of a change from the duds we've been seeing.

If this continues, you'll have to send me a magnifying-glass to look at my vegetables.

On that goodbye and thanks,
François

1 – By Victor Fleming (1939).
2 – By Jean Boyer.
3 – By Julien Duvivier (1944).
4 – By Edmond T. Gréville.
5 – By Michael Powell (1939).
6 – By Robert Z. Leonard.
7 – French actor (1903–72): *Quai des brumes*, *Adieu Léonard*, *Lumière d'été*, *Les Enfants du paradis*, *Les Yeux sans visage*, etc.
8 – By Howard Hawks (1941).
9 – By Maurice de Canonge.

François Truffaut at the fairground.

The building in which François Truffaut spent his childhood,
33 rue de Navarin, Paris 9e.

CINÉUM

ASSOCIATION DES AMIS DU CINÉ-ART

(Association déclarée N° 8916, régie par la loi du 1er Juillet 1901)

Siège Social : 33, Avenue Pierre-1er de Serbie — PARIS (XVIe)

Membre Actif 1948-49 Carte N° 522

Mieur FRANÇOIS TRUFFAUT

33, rue de Navarin, 33 PARIS (9eme)

Le Président, Le Titulaire,

Cette carte rigoureusement personnelle, sera exigée à toute manifestation de

François Truffaut as an active member of Cinéum.

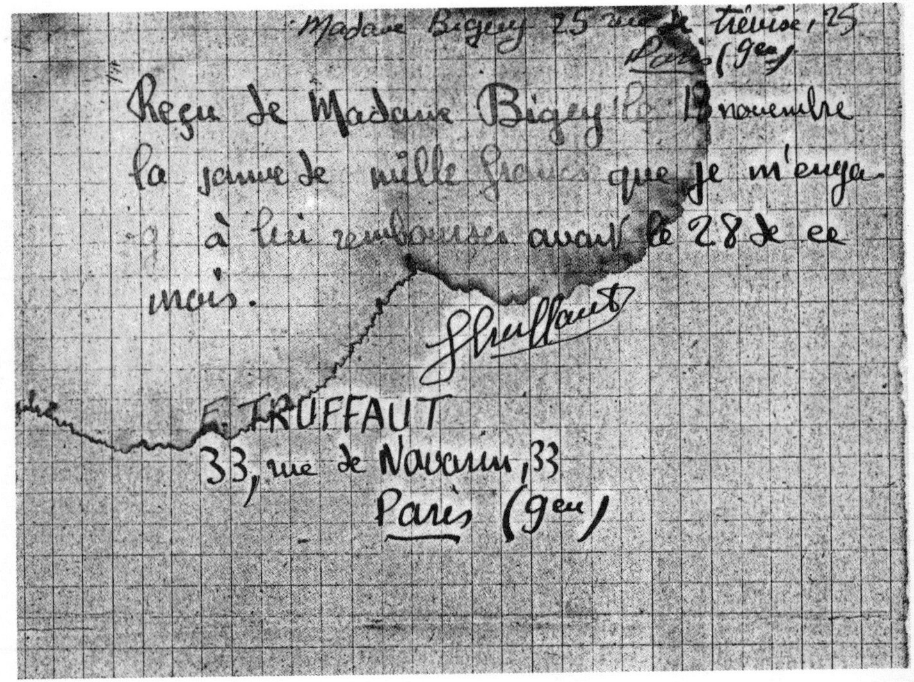

Madame Bigey 25 rue de Trévise, 25
Paris (9eme)

Reçu de Madame Bigey le 13 novembre la somme de mille francs que je m'engage à lui rembourser avant le 28 de ce mois.

Truffaut

F. TRUFFAUT
33, rue de Navarin, 33
Paris (9eme)

An IOU for 1,000 francs.

CENTRE D'OBSERVATOIN
DES
MINEURS DE PARIS

Villejuif le 16 mars 1947

Nom : Truffaut françois

Notes

Santé : Hum ! Hum ! Conduite : exemplaire

Travail : accompli Classe : ? ?

Cher vieux,

Si je tarde tant à t'écrire c'est premièrement que je sors à peine de l'infirmerie et secondement que j'attendais d'avoir une enveloppe, objet précieuse et rare entre tous.

Je te remercies des tes deux missives consécutives et de ce qu'elles contenaient. Arrête-là tes généreuse envois d'abord parce qu'ils te coûtent trop, ensuite parce qu'ils ne me servent que pour les timbres et un paquet de cigarettes hebdomadaire, car notre argent est déposé au greffe avec nos vêtements civils. Sache que je suis passé en jugement, que je ~~suis~~ vais être placé à Versailles dans un home de semi-liberté tout en travaillant au dehors. Je partirai incessament. Tu peux cependant m'écrire encore.

La vie actuelle n'est pas réjouissante. Quelle vie d'abnégation et de labeur! J'espère que cela ne durera pas et que l'usine ouvrira bientôt toutefois, je crois que cela est assez dangereux.

Ma mère vient me voir 1 fois par mois.

Je crois que cette année pour l'un et pour

N. B. Les visites ont lieu le l'autre sera peu brillante, cinémato-

31.3317 - Imp. adm. Melun. - C. 2494 - 1946 (C.O.M.) Madrid

Truffaut writting from the Villejuif reformatory.

1949

To Robert Lachenay

Villejuif, 16 March 1949

Dear old friend,

If it's been so long since I've written to you, it's firstly because I'm just out of the infirmary and secondly because I had to wait until I got an envelope, that most rare and precious object.

Thank you for your two successive parcels and for what they contained. You've been very generous but don't send me any more, first of all because they cost you too much, and also because they're only useful to me for the stamps and a weekly packet of cigarettes, since our money is deposited in the office of the clerk of the court along with our civilian clothes. You know that I've stood trial[1] and that I'm going to be placed in an institution in Versailles where I'll be free nevertheless to have a job outside. I leave any day now. You can still write to me, though.

Your life at the moment is not exactly rosy. What a life of toil and self-sacrifice! I hope it won't last and that the factory will open soon. Even so, I think it's rather dangerous work.

My mother comes to see me twice a month. I don't think for either of us this is going to be a vintage year, cinematically speaking; let's put our faith in 1950! Yes, I correspond with Claude Thibaudat who is beginning to 'get on' if I can go by the programme he sent me and the description of his theatrical activities. As soon as I leave for Versailles, I'll come and see you the first time I get out. I read *L'Écran* and *Ciné-Club*[2] regularly, thanks to the kindness of a movie-mad teacher here who belongs to all the film societies.

I don't need anything in particular except envelopes. So, if you can, send me a packet of cheap ones. Send them to me from Pontault[3] since parcels from Paris are prohibited.

Chenille[4] sent me my bound Cocteau and the book on Cocteau that I had lent to Gérald. That makes 2 survivors of the débâcle. I hope that Henry Poulaille's *Charlot*[5] will emerge safe and sound.

I leave you now and will post the next letter on Monday.

Very affectionately,

françois

My respects to your mother. Nothing for Gustave who declares that Chaplin is a buffoon. (Don't strangle him . . . Gustave.)

17 March Wednesday: I've just this minute learned that I leave tomorrow for Versailles. Expect a second letter immediately.

1 – Truffaut had run away from home to found the Cinémane film society which almost immediately became insolvent.
2 – French film magazines of the period.
3 – Where Lachenay was employed as a welder.
4 – A classmate whose parents ran a bookshop and stationer's.
5 – A book on Chaplin.

To Robert Lachenay

[30 July 1949]

Dear old pal,

Trip ghastly, weather so-so. The festival[1] starts this evening with Marcel Pagliero's *La Nuit porte conseil*. Cocteau arrived two hours ago. Photos and more photos, the beach in the style of Jean Vigo,[2] compositions *à la* Hathaway,[3] depth of focus *à la* Welles and perspectives *à la* Fritz Lang.

Write you a long letter Tuesday. Am nearly broke.

François Toréador

1 – Of Biarritz.
2 – French director (1905–34): *Zéro de conduite*, *L'Atalante*. His work was to have an enormous influence on Truffaut.
3 – Henry Hathaway, American director (1898–1985).

1950

To Robert Lachenay *[June 1950]*

Dear old squaddie,[1]

I received your last 2 letters at the same time. Since I got them at 2 o'clock in the morning when I came home, I read them before going to bed, so you are to blame for a ghastly nightmare about the army, soldiers, etc.

I'm leaving my room in the next few days and moving to a hotel in Villiers just 15 metres . . . from L—'s! Continue writing to me at the rue des Martyrs, I'll give you the exact name of the hotel and the number in my next letter.

I pay 3,500F a month and, as you pay in advance, I'll have to scrape it together tomorrow. The room is a little smaller than yours, but it doesn't have a mansard roof. There's a large window overlooking the courtyard and it's very light. There's lots of room for the books. I have an incredible amount of work, but I haven't forgotten you, bear with me a little for the magazines and clothes, I'll see to all of that in the next few days.

I won't always have so much work, for the moment it's lack of organization that makes me waste so much time. Yesterday I went to Michel Mourre's[2] trial; Ariane Pathé was there, feathers sticking out every which way; the case has been adjourned for two weeks, but his acquittal isn't in doubt. They read out a marvellous statement from the editorial staff of *La Tribune de Genève* and he (Mourre) explained his conduct with great sincerity; it was almost moving; I'll send you everything I write about it in various rags, since, now that I'm at *Elle*, all the small specialized magazines are clamouring for contributions from me; but I'm less and less inclined to write for nothing, as it's scarcely in my interest.

I'm still going to Hesdin on the 8th for the last 8 days of Bresson's shoot.[3] I'm going to take some more photos, I'll send you a print of each, as I can 'develop' free of charge at the magazine. Needless to say, I'll be taking some of Jacqueline from 'manifold' angles.

Give me lots of details on what you're reading. You should read everything, everything that comes your way, since it's wonderfully beneficial and I would sometimes like to be forced to read stupid books, thrillers, adventure stories, etc. I'm not joking, it can really be very instructive. In 3 days I'll be sending you the 1st parcel with 4 *Nouvelles littéraires*, 4 *Figaros*, etc. In 6 days: your glasses, *Paroles*[4] (mine) and some Fayards; in 8 days: 2 pairs of underpants, two singlets, some more Fayards. Gérald and Bielher will see to the parcels of grub.

Don't do anything foolish with your . . . oddball friend. I don't have your letters here (I'm at the magazine), so I can't reply point by point.

Last night I saw *The Picture of Dorian Gray*[5] at the Studio Parnasse,[6] it's not at all bad.

Enclosed is the programme of the Faubourg.[7] I saw *Le Corbeau*[8] (13th time) with M— and *Une si jolie petite plage*[9] (4th time) with L—. That makes at least 8 days I haven't seen Jacqueline, I dropped her a line telling her to come and see me or write to me but I haven't had any news.

I most certainly think your conjunctivitis comes from the welding. Here is the correct address for Chenille, don't fail to write to him:

André Chenille
Cartography Unit
SP-50-828
BPM-507

Correction: I'm sending you at the same time as this letter all the literary magazines since you left. To follow will be those of this week, then [. . .].[10] I no longer buy any film magazines, not even *L'Écran*. In any case you wouldn't learn too much from them since it's either publicity or propaganda.

Anyway, I'm in a rush, I'm going to take this letter down and the magazines.

yours,
françois

1 – Lachenay is now in the army. He did not desert but waited at home for the police to come and escort him to the barracks.
2 – French writer and scholar (1928–77). At the age of twenty-one this former novice monk (he had been expelled from a Dominican convent) ascended the pulpit at Notre-Dame on Easter Sunday and proclaimed Nietzsche's blasphemy: 'God is dead.' In the resulting scandal he was sent to an asylum, and later wrote a book about the affair, *Malgré le blasphème*.
3 – Of *Le Journal d'un curé de campagne* (*The Diary of a Country Priest*).
4 – Jacques Prévert's best-selling volume of poetry.
5 – By Albert Lewin (1945).
6 – A celebrated art-house cinema in Paris: every Tuesday evening it would hold a movie quiz, the winners of which received free tickets.
7 – A film society run by Léo Poldès, who also organized lectures and competitions in public speaking. The eighteen-year-old Truffaut was a regular attender and had already begun to make a reputation for

himself as a confident and often controversial speaker.
8 – By Henri-Georges Clouzot (1943).
9 – By Yves Allégret (1949).
10 – Illegible.

To Robert Lachenay

[14 June 1950]

Dear old Robert,

I came back from Hesdin to find your 2 letters. I saw Bresson, it was terrific. Yesterday I went to see *The Heiress*[1] with Jacqueline at the Agriculteurs,[2] that was Sunday, yesterday, in the evening. Afterwards we went to her place to have a bite, as her parents are away for 8 days, and I eat with her almost every evening. We talked until 1 o'clock in the morning and I got home almost drunk, as she had some Pernod and red wine. Janine lent her *Le Roman d'un tricheur*.[3] I have very little time to myself, but I'm going to see to your things; I'll see about the magazines. In any case, I buy them since I've got to read them – so why not send them on to you? In my next letter I'll send you 100F.

Gérald won't go to your place any longer because it's overrun with bugs. If you had any sense, you would throw out the carpet and the newspapers, put down some sulphur and, every week, clean the tiles with disinfectant, otherwise it will be unfit to live in. But you must do as you please.[4]

I have an incredible amount of work to do. Yesterday I had lunch with Ariane Pathé and Michel Mourre; I have to do an article on him.

4 or 5 articles on *Le Curé de campagne*, photos, telephone calls, 1 article on Mourre, appointments, talks at the Faubourg, spreads for *Elle*, I don't know how I'm going to manage, it's just too much.

I've also got to reply to Chenille and reply to Bazin.[5] I think L— and I will be going to spend 2 days with him, he lives 150 km from Paris. See you, regards.

Write to me at the Hôtel Dulong, 27, rue Dulong, Paris 17e. (L— is at no. 24, I'm at 27!)

françois

1 – By William Wyler (1949).
2 – A Parisian cinema.
3 – Sacha Guitry's novel, which he adapted for the cinema in 1936.
4 – Lachenay wrote in the margin of this letter: 'Where I am now, there's nothing much I can do about the bugs!'
5 – André Bazin (1918–58). Bazin was unquestionably the most famous French film critic and his influence has extended far beyond the frontiers of his native land. He was the *éminence grise* of the journal *Cahiers du cinéma* and the spiritual father of François Truffaut, whom he first

encountered at a film society. He helped the young Truffaut overcome a difficult adolescence and encouraged him to become a film critic himself.

To Robert Lachenay

[15 June 1950]
Thursday 1 p.m.

Dear old Robert,

I have a moment to myself, I'm taking advantage of it to turn my biro in your direction.

Robert Bresson on the one hand, Michel Mourre on the other have meant that I've had an enormous, and difficult, workload, since, with 5 articles on Bresson, I can't simply have the same article appear 5 times and I don't know what to keep for one newspaper or what would be suitable for another. Jacqueline told me a wonderful (and true) story.

About a year ago, she (Jacqueline) happened to be standing on the platform of a bus when a gentleman slowly put his arm around her waist while at the same time energetically playing 'footsie' with her. She discreetly puts him 'in his place' and, three days later, she goes to see her friend Janine (the one you know). Janine introduces her to her father: 'I'd like you to meet Daddy!', and said Daddy turns out to be none other than the gentleman on the bus. It seems he went terribly red, but not Jacqueline, you know her, she had no difficulty seeing the 'funny' side of the story. Ah! Those respectable bourgeois families!

Another story, not so funny, but just as true: I received a summons from the vice squad. On the summons was written: 'Case of X—' (X—, if you remember, was president of the Camping-Club de France, a club I liked less than the Black Chamber; X— had unwittingly helped me out with my first pay-packet from Simpère,[1] at the Bank of France. *Remember?*)[2]

Well, X—, a pillar of the Bank of France, the author of 14 books 6 of which have been translated into other languages, a respected member of the French Alpine Club, would take little boys off on camping trips and make them undergo 'ordeals'. On the pretext of 'baptisms' and 'totemizations' he tied them to a tree, had them whipped as a test of their 'endurance' and, at the psychological moment, would photograph them. He 'coupled' boys together. He had others undergo 'medical examinations', etc. After a complaint was lodged, he was arrested and they found more than 100 ultra-compromising photos.

They also arrested someone very high up in the Foreign Office (he once took me to the cinema in his car, do you remember? to see *Faisons un rêve*):[3] a prominent barrister, a friend of Cocteau, a friend of Schérer[4] as well, he was vice-president (no pun intended!) of the Quartier Latin Film Society!

It's like something out of the Marquis de Sade, Jean Genet and André Gide. What a business! The newspapers fortunately haven't got on to it. Since I've never had any reason to complain of X— nor of his set, I may perhaps testify in his favour. I'm going to get in touch (still no pun intended) with one of X—'s lawyers.

I won't go into detail about my visit to the filming of *Curé de campagne*, it would be too long and boring, I prefer to send you the articles when they appear.

L— sits her *baccalauréat* today. I'm as nervous as she is!

I don't know if I told you that *Le Roman d'un tricheur* is now in Jacqueline's hands. Actually, Jacqueline was under the impression that you had lent her Colette's *Chats*. I set her straight and she therefore thanks you. Her apartment is terrific. Her bedroom has an enormous bed in polished white oak; it looks like marble. Concealed lighting from 2 bracket lamps on the wall; a few books, about fifteen, 2 large curtains. On the pink bedspread, 2 children: a teddy-bear and a doll.

She made the carpet herself, 0.60 m by 1 m, it's sensational. It's like a black-and-white fur chequerboard – out of this world. The rest like your parents' place, fridge, cistern in the kitchen, etc.

Didier has broken off with Janine; for his sake I hope it's for good.

At the Faubourg, much as before: I'm getting ready for a public-speaking competition on 27 June. I have to speak for 5 minutes on Paris in 1950 and 5 minutes on an improvised subject that you're given at the last minute.

I am now very chummy with Genghis Khan and Bontemps,[5] especially his . . . charming wife.

2 o'clock already, I have to go to the Champs-Élysées, to *Ciné-Digest*, then to *Lettres du monde*. After that, at 4.00, appointment with Poldès and Genghis Khan in a bookshop at Saint-Germain-des-Prés; then I'll drop by the C.C.Q.L.[6] for 15 minutes to see Freddy and Schérer. Later, at about 8.00, I'm going to the Cité Universitaire[7] to see the foreign girls and find out how you say 'I love you' in every oriental language.

As you see, I have an extremely busy schedule. I wrote to Bazin, to Chenille, I saw *The Blue Angel*,[8] at long last, at the Cinémathèque, and a thriller – psychoanalytical, so-so. It's now 15 June and I've seen 4 films since the 1st, I don't even consult the cinema programmes!

But I read: I read the <u>3 Sartres</u> (*Chemins de la liberté*), *Pigalle* by René Fallet (who has just won the Prix Populiste, I predicted that 3 months ago!), La Varende's *Centaure de Dieu*, a contemporary Christian novel, plus some recent books, mostly novels.

I've been thinking I might come and spend a few days at Constance whenever you have 4 days' leave. Find out about the possibilities of accommodation, if I need a passport, how much it would come to, etc.

I've got to go now, I'll continue the letter this evening or tomorrow. 2.15 p.m.

Tuesday 20 June

Excuse me for having abandoned you for 6 days – I lost my notepad and these sheets along with it and found them in the *Ciné-Digest* office. Since Thursday, a lot of things have happened, most of them unpleasant:

1. Your mother and your grandmother went to the police, and the said police sent me a summons at 10, rue de Douai. But obviously, I don't live in the rue de Douai and I received the summons 3 days too late.

2. I returned the gramophone to your grandmother.

3. The concierges of no. 10 are on my side – they gave me your letter so I could show it to the police. The one mistake your concierges made was having told your grandmother, in the first few days, when she came to fetch the doormat, that it was Truffaut who lived there. Your grandmother believed it, repeated it to your mother, etc., etc.

This morning I received the letter your mother sent you. If I felt sure of myself, I'd sue her for slander, for calling me a homosexual, but I can't do it. All that's required is for you to send her a letter bawling her out and I'll do the same: bawling her out politely, straightening things out, for she doesn't give a damn how she treats people.

Not one single evening were we at your place. First of all it's completely unlit, then there are the bugs, and 3. I only ever see Gérald and Co. once a week, Sunday morning or Saturday.

I think it must have been Androuet who talked about orgies and gramophones, mixing the past up with the present, a stew that your mother took pleasure in spicing up to her own advantage. I've reread your letters, I can't find any queries I've left unanswered. The parcel containing most of what you asked for is ready, I'll send it off as quickly as I can. Jacqueline? She's fine, she asks me to say hello; and if you want to know why she doesn't write to you, I'm sure it's because she wants to leave you in the 'lurch' for a while just as you did when you wrote to us 3 weeks after you left. So she will be writing to you – when, I can't say – you know how stubborn she can be and how, when she gets an idea in her head, it can't be budged.

I'll be sending you some money, 100F at a time as far as my own means permit; I'll continue to send you the newspapers.

I've lots more to tell you, but this letter has to go off, otherwise I'll start again tomorrow and it will be another three days before it leaves.

So, your friend,

françois

The next scribble will leave on Friday evening.

1 – The firm in which Truffaut was briefly employed.
2 – Last word in English in the original letter.
3 – By Sacha Guitry (1936).
4 – Maurice Schérer, later known as Eric Rohmer, French film critic and director, born in 1920. The eldest of the group of critics who wrote for *Cahiers du cinéma*, he was the first to turn to film-making (in 1950).
5 – Two members of the Faubourg Club.
6 – Ciné-club du quartier Latin.
7 – Halls of residence for Parisian students, many of them foreign.
8 – Josef von Sternberg's *Der blaue Engel* (1930).

To Robert Lachenay

[28 June 1950]
Wednesday noon

Dear old friend,

I hope that by now you'll have received: 1. a thick parcel of newspapers; 2. a hurried note with 200F; 3. a parcel containing various things, including sunglasses, singlets, etc.

Yesterday evening, the public-speaking competition. L—, as I expected, got cold feet; she has an excuse, she's in a state over her oral exam.

As for me, I disappointed everyone because I assumed a pose of infinite lassitude, boredom and monotony, as though I were thinking 'what an idiotic subject': I came 3rd out of 11. You don't know the other winners. I got a bottle of Ricard, a set of beauty products and a pile of lottery tickets that I entrusted to Madeleine D— so I wouldn't lose them – which reminds me! tonight is the draw! If I win something, I'll notify you tomorrow! As for the Ricard and the beauty products, I'm making a present of them to L—'s parents since I go and have meals there all the time. I'm going there in half an hour's time, as Georges Juin is on the radio commenting on yesterday's competition – that's in an hour.

My room is larger than yours, larger than Didier's, it's like my parents' dining-room. There's a smaller bed than in the rue des Martyrs with a bedspread out of which I dream of making myself a dressing-gown: it's a material with mauve and orange stripes. There's a big chest of drawers with 4 drawers, a cupboard set into the wall, almost invisible, with 6 shelves (it's very large), a fireplace with little alcoves in which I can put some books, 1 table, 2 chairs, a sink, 2 mirrors and a large window overlooking the courtyard – something like this.[1] As you see, it's basic! Have you understood anything?

What I've seen recently: *La Porteuse de pain*: Maurice Cloche! Trade show. *La Règle du jeu*[2] (semi-complete version) 12th time. *Adam's Rib*[3] (trade show): first-rate comedy with Spencer Tracy and Katharine Hepburn. *The Lost Patrol*,[4] a joke, dreadfully dated. *Eugénie Grandet*:[5] a respectable Italian version – very Balzacian. *La Chienne*, the original version of *Scarlet Street*[6] with Michel Simon instead of Edward Robinson, Georges Flamment instead of Dan Duryea, by Jean Renoir, 1935.

And, last but not least, *Madame Bovary*,[7] made in Hollywood 1950, with Jennifer Jones, Van Heflin, Louis Jourdan and James Mason in the role of Gustave Flaubert! MIND-BOGGLING!

I don't have much more time. For your room, everything is more or less arranged. I can't give you any news of Gérald or the others, since I haven't seen Didier for 1 month and a half, and Gérald for 2 weeks – you're almost more likely to have news of them than I! My expenses are going to be enormous: my room, 500F on the 1st, yours, 1,500 on 15 July, L—'s birthday on 12 July, I'm going with L— to see Bazin for a couple of days, which will cost: trip 800F, hotel 400, grub 400, miscellaneous 400: total 2,000F. That's already 8,000 francs not counting my own food, transport, newspapers, cigarettes, movies, laundry, etc. The more you earn, the more you need.

And so, with that bleak picture of my life, I leave you and impatiently await acknowledgement of the newspapers and the registered parcels,

your pal,
F. Truffot

1 – On the letter Truffaut sketched in the plan of his room. See facsimile opposite.
2 – By Jean Renoir (1939).
3 – By George Cukor (1949).
4 – By John Ford (1934).
5 – By Mario Soldati (1946).
6 – By Fritz Lang (1945).
7 – By Vincente Minnelli.

To Robert Lachenay

21 July [1950]

Dear old thing,

Pleased to hear from you at last. Since my last letter, much has happened. Principally: there was a very real chance of my being in no condition to answer your letter, as I tried to kill myself and had 25 razor slashes in my

3/ Il y a une grande commode à
4 tiroirs, un placard encastré dans
le mur, quoi invisible muni de
6 planches (il est très grand)
une cheminée avec des petites niches
qui permettent de mettre des bouquins
voilà. 1 table, 2 chaises, un évier.
2 glaces et une grande fenêtre sur la cour.
ça donne ceci

Vue de dessus

évier
la commode
porte
la cheminée
grande chaise
table
le placard
le lit
la fenêtre

comme tu vois c'est simple!
As-tu compris quelque chose?

François Truffaut's handwriting at the age of eighteen (letter to Robert Lachenay).

right arm, so it was very serious. L— failed her *bac*,[1] but for her birthday she and I organized a huge party opposite her flat, there were more than 40 people including Claude Mauriac,[2], Schérer, Alexandre Astruc,[3] Jacques Bourgeois,[4] Ariane Pathé, Michel Mourre, the *tout-Paris* of journalism and 16 mm movies. There wasn't enough to drink and there were some grumblers: Bourgeois came without being invited and Claude Mauriac left because of him. The rest was like something out of *La Règle du jeu*. Intrigues, rows in the street, doors slamming, L— played Nora Grégor,[5] she switched 'Saint-Aubains' 4 or 5 times, I was Jurieu,[6] someone had to be the victim. In the morning, when I got home at 7 a.m., I crawled into bed and slashed my arm. About eleven o'clock L— came to see me, there was blood on the sheets and on the floor, she thought I had fainted, I was simply asleep, since I hadn't lost enough blood. She took care of me with a terrifyingly cool head, she boiled water, made compresses and bandages; for 2 days I was in bed with a fever. Now I'm like Frédéric Lemaître in *Les Enfants du paradis*[7] with a bandaged arm, I tell everyone I have a sprain. I don't think it's affected my handwriting too much, though.

2 days later, L— left for Monte-Carlo without giving me her address and without writing to me. I feel very alone. Her parents give me nasty looks; she was obliged to tell them all about it in order to look after me. Anyway, I'm trying to see new people, I never go out alone, I go out with Niko who failed his *bac* or with François Mars[8] who got a brilliant pass. I'm going to see Monique again, the girl in the rue Clauzel. I'm going to try and 'get over it'. That's why I don't find anything ridiculous about you and Jacqueline even though there's no comparison between Jacqueline and L—. The last I heard, Jacqueline had left her job, had taken up modelling fur coats and gone off on holiday. If she hadn't gone on holiday, I would have used her for 3 days in a 16 mm film[9] and invited her to the party where perhaps she might have defused the atmosphere. She sent me a postcard without giving me her address. As soon as she returns, I'll bawl her out and tell her to write to you.

I'm still at *Elle*, I'm conducting a survey among publishers at the moment, but I'm fed up with it all, I'd like to go off to a farm, just to sleep and rest physically and morally. Wait though, one thing has happened, I took my first photographs by 'flash-light' in the night-club Le Méphisto and one of my photos is to appear in *France-Dimanche*: Annette Poivre[10] and her daughter at the bar. It's good news, I don't know yet how much I'll be paid, but it was expensive, it cost me 1,600F for the bulbs. If they hadn't taken one of my photos, that would have been 1,600F down the drain. It's a real risk.

I'm sending you this very day 2 parcels of newspapers, one parcel of 9 and one of 11. Check to see that everything's there.

I have to leave now, I'm off to get some money from *F.D.*[11]

your friend,
françois

P.S. Depending on how much I get at the above, I'll enclose some money for you with this letter. F.

1 – Baccalauréat examination.
2 – The son of François Mauriac and the then film critic of *Le Figaro littéraire*.
3 – French critic and director, born in 1923, he is best known for his short film *Le Rideau cramoisi* and for an influential essay on what he termed *le caméra-stylo*.
4 – French film and music critic.
5 – The German-born actress who played Christine, the Marquise de La Chesnaye, in *La Règle du jeu*.
6 – André Jurieu, the aviator in *La Règle du jeu*, is in love with Madame de La Chesnaye, who flirts, however, with the foppish Saint-Aubain. The film ends with Jurieu's death.
7 – By Marcel Carné (1945). The character of Lemaître was played by Pierre Brasseur.
8 – French journalist and critic, he was one of the first (and only) members of Truffaut's Cinémane film society.
9 – This project came to nothing.
10 – French actress of the fifties: *Antoine et Antoinette*, *Copie conforme*, *Voyage surprise*, *Porte des Lilas*, etc.
11 – The tabloid newspaper *France-Dimanche*.

Madame Bigey to Private Robert Lachenay[1]

Paris, 30 July 1950

Dear Robert,

I received your letter of 25 July. Thank you for the good wishes you sent me on my birthday, that really pleased me. I hope your foot is better, except that, if there is a war, it would be advisable for you to spend your time in the infirmary. So it seems you are no longer training to become a sergeant or a corporal, well, so much the worse for you, since you had a unique opportunity to get away from being a labourer; what is a welder? It's nothing but a labourer, a foreman is the same, whereas in the army there are different ranks and, the higher your rank, the more you are paid: look at old Vejus, he has a brother who reached the rank of captain, a captain must be well paid, and besides in the army you have a good pension and when you are an officer, you can marry a girl with a dowry; when I was young, you needed thirty thousand francs to marry an officer, if my mother had lived, I could have married one, I would have liked that a lot, it would have been better than vegetating in this poverty and mediocrity; and besides in the army you mustn't get drunk and it's more pleasant to live with someone who never gets drunk than with someone who does. To come back to old Vejus, compared to his brother the captain who married a girl with a dowry and who is looked up to in the community today, well, I can tell you, old Vejus cuts a sorry figure indeed compared to his brother who has a motor car and some land. And I'll tell you something else: don't make fun of your superiors, for they might well decide to cancel your leave, then who would be worse off? My Robert, that's who. Put yourself in your superiors' place: how would you like some little smart-aleck answering you back, not much, eh? It's more prudent not to do it, since they can do much worse things to you than you can to them. If there's a war, it's all the layabouts and ruffians and bad boys like you and worse than you that are the first to be sent to the front and they have to go, otherwise they shoot them in the back. Try to change your behaviour and be more respectful and more disciplined, you'll be thought the better for it. When you come down to it, it's very big of them to let you have some leave, I think your superiors in the hierarchy have been very nice to you; they are only thinking of your own good, they thought you were intelligent and tried to raise you out of your working-class background. You on the other hand prefer to stagnate among the lower classes; an opportunity like this of improving yourself doesn't come along every day. Look at your father, he didn't turn down the chance to become an adjutant and during the war he had it very cushy, he didn't suffer the least little scratch; he had a horse for his little jaunts and an orderly for a servant. Now don't you think he was better off than if he had stayed a private? He had a very enviable position, one that was envied by a lot of people especially during the war, he was better fed and less at risk than a private. Now let's change the subject. Your grandmother is no worse, it's just that she is not getting any younger, that's what the matter is. It has been very sunny in Paris, we have had a good summer and it is not over yet, there is still August and September. Your chum Truffaut is a wicked rascal who must have taken a liking to your brown trousers for I can't find any brown trousers. That's where his great intelligence has landed you or, if you prefer, as you like to believe, his superior intelligence; we will have to lodge a complaint with the police. Many thanks for worrying about the health of the cats; they are very well, but I notice you are not very concerned about the health of your grandmother, it's obvious the cats come first . . . It strikes me that, without the grandmother, there would be no cats and that it's her health you should be worried about first. Well, my dear Robert, I will end by giving you a big kiss and hugging you with all my heart until I see you again without stripes; we would have preferred to see you wearing some, you would have dazzled everyone, whereas now you'll dazzle no one, unless they're dazzled because you haven't any.

Your grandmother, M. Bigey.

[Letter contributed by François Truffaut.]

1 – This letter from Lachenay's grandmother was published in the March 1955 issue of the monthly magazine *La Parisienne*.

To Robert Lachenay

19 August 1950

Dear old Robert,

Thank you for your letter and excuse me for having waited so long before writing. Your rent has been paid 1670F plus 300 (for the concierge). André was on leave again for 11 days. He's delighted with military service yet it hasn't improved him much, quite the reverse. He is more and more stupid, pretentious and 'affected'. But I couldn't not take him out, as he was alone (Gérald and Bielher are on holiday), so I took him to see *Lust for Gold*[1] (a bit like *Sierra Madre*), with Glenn Ford and Ida Lupino, *Man on the Run*[2] (a bad English film), *China*[3] (not bad Alan Ladd and the Japs), *Les Bas-Fonds* (Renoir), *Douce* (Autant-Lara[4] at the Studio Parnasse), *Raw Deal*[5] (English gangsters, not bad) and, at the Théâtre de la Huchette, a very good slapstick comedy, *Pépita*. I've seen tons of other films much like *Marthe Richard*, old pre-war films, the Légion d'honneur, etc., nothing that stood out. I'm reading a history of English literature, *Moby Dick* and *Le Sabbat*, by Maurice Sachs. Have you still got some money? Do you need a little? Didier would like to have his jacket back, you ought to return it to him. You haven't forgotten about the camera? Chenille is going to buy one for 364 marks, but you can get them for 200 marks.

Armand Piéral, a writer you must have heard at the Faubourg, one of the directors of Laffont, has sent me review copies of 4 recent novels including the latest Gr. Greene (*Ministry of Fear*).

I'm going to make a film in October; I have 25 reels of film, which makes 1 hour 40 minutes of material. Since my film will last about 45 minutes, I'll have more than enough. I've got the 16 mm camera and the cameraman, I've got all the actors. I need only a few costumes and a large room to serve as the dining-room, with a 40 amp meter for the lighting. I'll send you the script – it's the story of the communicant but with lots of changes. I'm going location-hunting tomorrow near the Charonne Métro station. I need a church that looks as though it's in a small provincial town. I'll have 20 communicants as extras and 4 real priests and nuns – the assistance of the Church. I'm supposed to be doing a 'documentary' on first communions. I hope to begin at the end of September.[6] At *Elle*, things are going well, except that it's the slack season, and there's not much work around. For the moment I've just finished an article on night-clubs in Saint-Germain-des Prés and now I'm looking for photographs of famous men as children (Jouvet when he was five, etc.).

You're coming to the end of basic training, from now on it will be easier. Chenille and everyone else say the same thing: 'The first 4 months are the hardest.' I saw Bazin at the sanatorium; I'm going to work with him on something that will earn 25 English pounds for the 2 of us, that's 13,000 francs each: a biography and complete filmography of Renoir. Bazin will be responsible for the text and I'll do the research, since Renoir made lots of films that he didn't finish or put his name to, and we've got to track them down. I'll be going to see Claude Renoir,[7] Pierre Renoir,[8] Braunberger,[9] etc. It's very interesting work. I have piles of newspapers to send you; it's very complicated, I have to take them to the office, buy some sheets of paper, borrow some glue from *France-Dimanche* and take the rolled-up parcels to the post office, it's a real expedition.

You may have read in the newspapers I sent you about Hermantier's[10] extraordinary success playing *Julius Caesar* in the Roman amphitheatre at Nîmes. Hermantier is the toast of the town. He has a major role in Duvivier's film,[11] as M. Pons, there's talk of him being entrusted with the Salle Luxembourg at the Comédie-Française. In any event he has really deserved his success.

I await a letter from you. Enclosed 2 enlarged photos: if you'd like me to keep them for you, send them back to me.

Cordially,
françois

1 – By Sylvan Simon (1949).
2 – By Lawrence Huntington (1949).
3 – By John Farrow (1943).
4 – See note 1, p. 100.
5 – By Anthony Mann (1948): in fact, the gangsters, like the film, are American.
6 – The film was never made.
7 – French cinematographer, born in 1914, the nephew of Jean Renoir: *The River*, *Le Carrosse d'or*, *Elena et les Hommes*, *Le Mystère Picasso*, etc.
8 – French actor (1885–1952), the brother of Jean Renoir: *La Nuit du carrefour*, *Madame Bovary*, *La Marseillaise*, *Pièges*, *Les Enfants du paradis*, etc.
9 – Pierre Braunberger, French producer, distributor and exhibitor, born in 1905. He produced numerous short films by the young directors of the New Wave.
10 – Raymond Hermantier, French actor, born in 1924: *Les Démons de l'aube*, *Prélude à la gloire*, etc.
11 – Julien Duvivier's *Sous le ciel de Paris*.

To Robert Lachenay *[August 1950]*

My dear friend,

Received your letter. If you can, and Chenille tells me it's possible, postpone your leave, in that way perhaps you'll be able to come for 3 weeks around Christmas. There are several reasons why:

1. In September, I won't be in Paris. I'm going for 12 days to Biarritz plus 3 days to Antibes, two days to Cannes, Nice and Cap-Ferrat to take some photographs.

2. These photos will earn me enough to buy some clothes, a jacket, a pair of trousers, a pair of shoes. I will have your velvet jacket cleaned and put both it and your trousers in mothballs. I have to be impeccably dressed for my job and a number of opportunities have slipped through my fingers because I wasn't well-dressed enough. You can see how important it is. In December I'll be able to feed you the whole time you're in Paris.

I'll write to you from Biarritz. At Billancourt I had lunch with the press agent of *Caroline chérie* and Martine Carol[1] who plays Caroline chérie. I'm going to do a large spread on it and Martine, with whom I quickly got on, has even agreed to write an article for *Elle*. I'll probably go to her apartment in the next few days to write it with her. She's a very nice person, the victim of stupid publicity, she really has talent. On the same occasion I made the acquaintance of Richard Pottier,[2] the director of *Caroline*, and 2 actors.

I saw Alfred Adam[3] at his home. He has a complete bound edition of Balzac and tons of books – he's very intelligent. It was he who wrote the play *Sylvie et le fantôme*. He lives at 33, rue de La Rochefoucauld. He gave me a snapshot of himself as an 11-year-old schoolboy with the *croix d'honneur*; the photo will appear in *Elle* with lots of others. I also made the acquaintance of Michèle Morgan[4] at the Gare de l'Est, where she was filming[5] with Jean Marais[6] and Jean Servais[7] (whom I had met before at the Club du Faubourg) under the direction of René Clément.[8] I had brought 2 chums along with me. There weren't enough extras, so René Clément asked them to be in the film. When they passed underneath the sound-boom, they deliberately talked about Truffaut so that my name would be heard in the film!

That's about all there is – and it's already quite a lot. You can write one more letter to me in Paris. I'll send you an issue of *F.D.* with 8 photos of Hitler 'rehearsing' his speeches and miming to a gramophone: they're as grotesque as those of Mussolini. Have you seen this issue?

Yours,
François

P.S. In *Caroline chérie* Alfred Adam plays a coachman who rapes her. She has five lovers including Jacques Dacqmine, Pierre Cressoy and Jacques Clancy. Her father is played by Jacques Varennes, etc.

1 – French actress and sex symbol (1922–67): *Voyage surprise*, *Les Belles de nuit*, *Adorables Créatures*, *Lola Montès*, *Les Carnets du Major Thompson*, *Vanina Vanini*, etc.
2 – French director, born in 1906: *Picpus*, *La Ferme aux loups*, *Meurtres*, etc.
3 – French actor and dramatist, born in 1909: (as actor) *La Kermesse héroïque*, *Un carnet de bal*, *Boule de suif*, *Sylvie et le Fantôme*, etc.
4 – French actress, born in 1920: *Gribouille*, *Quai des brumes*, *Remorques*, *La Loi du nord*, *La Symphonie pastorale*, *Les Grandes Manœuvres*, etc.
5 – *Le Château de verre*.
6 – French actor, born in 1913: *La Belle et la Bête*, *L'Aigle à deux têtes*, *Les Parents terribles*, *Orphée*, *Le Testament d'Orphée*, etc. His name is indissociably linked to that of Jean Cocteau.
7 – French actor, born in 1910: *Les Misérables*, *Angèle*, *Une si jolie petite plage*, *Du rififi chez les hommes*, *Thomas l'imposteur*, etc.
8 – French director, born in 1913: *La Bataille du rail*, *Les Maudits*, *Jeux interdits*, *Monsieur Ripois*, *Gervaise*, *Plein Soleil*, *Is Paris Burning?*, etc.

To Robert Lachenay

[29 October 1950]

Dear Robert

I am sorry, yet again, that this letter should bring you nothing but bad news. I don't have a penny. They have no money at *Les Amis de l'art* and I'd have to work for them for three months without being paid; they promise to pay me for these three months in February or March, which is to say 36,000 francs, I refused, as I've had enough of these long-term fortunes.

I went to the Reuilly-Diderot barracks to enlist before being called up; from there I was sent to the rue Saint-Dominique; from there to the law courts for a certificate of my police record. I won't have the latter document for another 6 or 7 days. I went to get my birth certificate, in a few days I go back to the rue Saint-Dominique and I'll probably be gone in a fortnight. I won't have any money before leaving and yet I owe my hotel around 6,000F plus 2,000F to the cleaners. I've got to be able to store my books and my few paltry belongings in your place, who has the key? Where is my father's camera?

Reply to me quickly on all these matters. Concerning my personal debts, I'll arrange for L— to pay them off bit by bit – especially since in January I'll have 12,000F which Bazin will be sending me as payment for the work on Jean Renoir.

I have 200 books to put in your place. I know they'll be safe there, particularly as you'll be back before I am.

I expect you to reply quickly.

I hope you are bearing up in prison.[1] You'll be out, I think, by the time you receive this letter.

Yours,
françois

P.S. Naturally I'm putting in a request for Germany. Gérald can pay the 1,500F plus 600F for the laundry. My yellow shoes are not unstitched, they're torn, behind, at the stiffening. So I need 2 pairs; I'll borrow some money to have the yellow ones repaired, then I'll have the black ones that are still wearable sent on to me.

1 – Lachenay served a short prison sentence during his military service.

François Truffaut's military service: enlistment, insubordination, discharge.

1951

To Eric Rohmer

[early January 1951]

Dear friend,

I forgot before I left to give you the sentence by Malraux to put at the beginning of my article on Pabst.[1] Here it is, I set great store by it. I would prefer you did not publish the article rather than publish it without this sentence.

> 'You, my friends from Germany
> around me, with their hangman's ropes, you
> who have perhaps just been struck down
> there exists between us
> what I call: love.'[2]
>
> Malraux

Thank you in advance. Around 5 January you'll receive a telephone call concerning what I gave to be sold to an antique dealer, i.e., a map of Paris in the reign of Henri IV and 2 trinkets. I'll accept whatever he offers, as he is extraordinarily kind and honest.

If he hasn't phoned you by 10 January, phone him:

> Monsieur Touret
> Antiques
> 75, rue des Dames,
> Paris XVIIe
> Métro Rome or Villiers
> Marcadet 36–26

He'll tell you what he's prepared to give for them and you can go and collect the money one day about 6 o'clock before going to the Cinémathèque, that way you won't have to make a special trip.

It's 10 minutes from the Cinémathèque and 5 minutes from L—'s flat and 5 minutes from Saint-Lazare (at the top of the rue de Rome). Keep what you want and send on the rest.

The original title of Pabst's film is *Duell Mit Dem Tode.*[3]

My enlistment is the result of my departure 6 months ago for Pontault, you can't say that I'm fickle or that I don't think things through.

To be continued.

1 – Georg Wilhem Pabst, Austrian-born director (1885–1967): *The Joyless Street*, *The Loves of Jeanne Ney*, *Pandora's Box*, *The Diary of a Lost Girl*, *Westfront 1918*, *The Threepenny Opera*, etc.

2 – 'Vous, mes amis d'Allemagne autour de moi, avec leurs cordes, toi que l'on vient peut-être d'assommer c'est ce qu'il y a entre nous que j'appelle: amour.'

3 – In fact, Pabst only supervised the film, which was directed by Paul May.

To Eric Rohmer

Wittlich, 7 January 51

My old fellow[1]

Though I haven't received a reply to my letter, I don't hold it against you, but I do urgently request you not to ignore this letter; what I am going to ask you is, for me and for the three years to come, vital.

I am here, at Wittlich, in hell; unbelievable discipline and overwork; I don't dare fall ill, since, as I'm doing field training, I'd be forced to accept promotion and leave for Indo-China. I therefore suffer martyrdom, crawling through the snow, lying flat on my face in the mud, forced marches with 32 kilos on my back and, if that weren't enough, topography, trigonometry, etc. I'll spare you the other stations of the cross. I have one chance of leaving Wittlich and not going to Indo-China; it's going to Baden-Baden as editor of *La Revue d'information des T.O.A.* (Troupes d'Occupation en Allemagne); I'll be paid 30,000F a month, get promotion, screw myself silly, smoke till it's coming out of my ears, in short, heaven on earth. I'm going to send in my request as soon as I've received what I'm expecting from you plus a note from *Elle*. You must, if you are my friend, type out for me or have someone type, in a single copy, on a sheet of paper with the letterhead of *La Gazette du cinéma*, the following note:

'I certify that Monsieur François Truffaut was a member of the staff of the fortnightly magazine, *La Gazette du cinéma*, from May to December 1950. He carried out for us a series of seven articles, and he wrote 22 reviews or analyses of films. We have nothing but praise for his contributions and he left *La Gazette du cinéma* of his own free will to do his military service.'

Signed – Eric Rohmer, 7 January 1951

Don't laugh, it's very important and I repeat, this document could be decisive in my posting to Baden-Baden.

It's now Sunday; I should say you'll receive this letter on Tuesday evening; as soon as you receive it, find a sheet of headed paper and have the statement typed either at Kaplan's or at Freddy's, but do it quickly, and send the letter off to me immediately. I need it before next Sunday.

thanks.

P.S. I've also written to *Elle* to ask for a similar statement, but it's better to be on the safe side.

If you make a film, don't forget that 'cinema is the art of the little detail that does not call attention to itself' and that 'cinema consists of having beautiful things done to beautiful women',[2] the rest is aestheticism.

Say hello to Rivette,[3] this letter is also for him, have him read it and don't forget that, on the other side of the Rhine, a friend is counting on you. If I die in Indo-China, it will be your fault! Hurry,

Yours,
Trufo

This new address is the right one:

2nd C.S.T. Truffaut François
1st Squad – 8th Battery
B.P.M. 526 A.S.P. 73 307

Write your address on the back of the letter and be quick!

1 – In English in the original letter.
2 – Truffaut is quoting Jean George Auriol, a French film critic.
3 – Jacques Rivette, French film critic and director, born in 1928: *Paris nous appartient*, *La Religieuse*, *L'Amour fou*, *Out One*, *Céline et Julie vont en bateau*, *Duelle*, *La Bande des quatre*, etc.

To Robert Lachenay

[8 January 1951]
Wittlich

Dear old Robert,

In a letter I received from L—, I found the letter you sent to me in Paris. I recently wrote you 2 letters, one from Idar-Oberstein, one from here; I'm pleased that it has sorted itself out. I was also amazed that you aren't making something of yourself, getting promoted so that, like Jean Genet, you can 'insult the insulters', each of us in his turn; you've just got to get promoted.

As for me, here, I'm very low, but hoping I won't have to stay that way.

'Eric Rohmer by his friend trufo'

Full kit in the middle of the night, scrambling through the snow and dumb ideas like that. And yet there's a deep meaning behind it all which escapes even the noncoms but which has a real value.

I haven't got much time, I'll write to you soon – it's free of charge, write me often, I expect a letter from you.

yours,
françois

Robert Lachenay to François Truffaut *[early January 1951]*

My dear old François

I had just made up my mind to write to you and call you an old bastard for having left me without news of you for two months, when I received your first letter. So there it is, the cinema and literature 'engaged' (and what an engagement) for three years in the forces of the IVth French Republic. I'm joking, but I don't feel much like it. François, here we are separated for three years, I can hardly believe it and I can't get used to the idea that I won't find François in Paris when I return. I wonder how I'm going to cope, how I'm going to live, how I'm going to get used to no longer seeing you, you and your briefcase, your papers, your glasses, your raggedy trousers, the holes in your socks . . . When I lost the apartment, nothing, my parents, nothing, when my father died, nothing, when I sold my books, nothing, when I went hungry, nothing, but now . . . Oh, I've had a hard life. One small consolation: if you leave for Indo-China or one of the colonies, you have the right to 30 days, I think, pre-departure leave (with pay), well then, if I'm still at Constance, come and spend a fortnight here or, if I'm in Paris, we'll have a whole month of chips, coffee, mustard, discussions, movies and books. I couldn't agree with you more. Many's the time I've said to myself, 'Oh! if only F. were here, we'd have some fun.' But you'll see, you start off by laughing and then you find yourself laughing less and less until you get angry and start insulting everyone, that's what's happening to me; at the beginning I thought everything was funny, everything was amusing, everything was good for a laugh and I'd find myself convulsed with laughter all alone and embarrassing everyone around me, but now it's been going on for too long and, at the slightest comment, the least little thing, wham! Writing to you, I've just remembered our fit of hysterics in a café, during my leave, when we were listening to a stall-holder talking about her Vitelloise or something of the sort, well, in my opinion, those were 'moments of a rare quality'. All alone, or with Gérald, Didier, Bielher . . . You should never have enlisted before being called up!

You ask me to tell you about myself. Here you are. Since I returned from leave, my situation has changed for the better. First of all I am now a secretary on the general staff, which means that I have a special position with all sorts of advantages where duties, work, accommodation and discipline are concerned; but that's not all, I'm coming to the most interesting part and there you'll see that my famous party and the influence of Jacqueline have had unexpected and far-reaching effects on me. You know that, in order to get her to pay more attention to me, and willing to make any sacrifice, I went as far as acting in a play. OK, well, at the general staff, I chanced upon a lieutenant of a higher calibre than most (though one day, when we were talking politics, I discovered that he had exactly the same opinions as I did at the age of 12 – armchair strategy – *Mein Kampf*, etc.), never mind, never mind, who wanted to set up a theatrical company. I introduced myself to him and with some others we put on a show (Max Régnier,[1] etc. oh! what, Max Régnier, the theatre, dear boy, the theatre), which was performed at Constance in the great Konzil chamber (a council was held there in 1414 to bring an end to the schism of the West – Larousse dictionary, page . . . from the schism of the West to Max Régnier – the sublime to the ridiculous). In short, we had an enormous success – stop – we go on tour – stop – your dad . . . (Through the little hole . . . through the little hole, through the little hole of the telescope[2] . . . try to guess.) Success so great that we've been to perform in manifold places, such as Lindau, Friedrichshafen, Mülheim (140 km from Constance), Fribourg, and there's a chance we'll be playing in Austria and at Dunkirk. The colonel of the regiment has become the company's honorary director and we are subsidized by the regiment (we don't care, Gut has the vouchers to pay for the sets, costumes and overheads). For 2 February we're preparing a new show which will be absolutely terrific. I'm acting for the first time in a play by M. Régnier (again! 'fraid so . . . the theatre, the theatre, what do you expect, all those who seek to educate the masses are leaving for Indo-China . . .) in which I play a little old man who strolls about the stage in his underpants (after being robbed by gangsters) and who goes to the police station to lodge a complaint, etc. and, in another role, a baron like Debucourt[3] in . . . what we saw at the Comédie-Française (*Un chapeau de paille d'Italie*,[4] I think). In short, this play that we haven't even performed yet is in demand all over Germany (yes, dear boy, Raimu[5] is furious, all over Germany). Perhaps we'll get to the 18th battery squad! As Didier would say, it's not to be sneezed at, this theatre lark, there are lots of advantages in it for me. First of all, a certain deference from and a special place in the regiment, in addition two afternoons a week for rehearsals (needless to say, we don't rehearse) and numerous, comfortable and even agreeable trips. What's more, wherever we go, we're entertained, pampered, warmly welcomed and comfortably lodged, I forgot to mention, we have a coach specially allocated to us. You see, as your father would say – I'm looking out for number one. But (exclamation mark), but that's not all, the best is yet to come. At Constance there is, for the general staff and the officers, a library of 4,500 volumes, strictly off-limits to NCOs and enlisted men. But, thanks to my lieutenant, I can have all the books I want, I just go to the library and mention his name. So since 1 January I've already read *Malatesta* (Month.)[6] – *Anthologie de la poésie lyrique* – *Les Fleurs du mal* – the poetry of Verlaine – *Clérambard*[7] – *La guerre de Troie n'aura pas lieu*[8] – and during December – *L'Histoire du cinéma* (Auriol), five or six other books on the cinema and about ten works of literature. Every week, I buy *Le Fig. litt.*[9] and *Les Nouvelles*[10] and every month *Historia*. As for the cinema, here are the latest films I've seen since I returned from leave; October: *La Symphonie pastorale* – *La Voyageuse inattendue* – *Letter to Three Wives* (Kirk Douglas) – *Mr Belvedere Goes to College* – *L'Aventure est au coin de la rue*; November: *Waterloo Bridge* – *At the Circus* – *Le 84 prend des vacances* – *Tarzan and the Leopard Woman* – *The Window* – *Fort Apache* – *Yellow Sky* – *Tangier* – *Prince of Foxes* – *Station West* – *Atoll K* – *Nancy Goes to Rio* – *La Beauté du diable* – *My Bill*; December: *The Street with No Name* – *L'Ingénue libertine* – *Le Soldat boum* – *La Route enchantée* – *Champion*; January: *The Major and the Minor.*[11]

As you see, it's thin, especially in quality. Now let's get down to some hard facts. On 15 January, I have to pay 1,880F in rent. Considering the money I owe her, my grandmother would rather hand my key to my dear mother than pay the quarter.[12] I wrote asking Gérald to take 2,000F to my grandmother, but she hasn't received anything and he hasn't replied to me. Without hesitation, I sold the marks I received in my last two pay-packets and sent 1,000F to B—, but I still have to send him another 1,000F. Which I can do when I'm paid on the 15th. I don't know how well off you are, but, if you could send me anything, it would be very welcome. Obviously, you mustn't leave yourself short. I'll scrape through again this time and even other times, I hope. But you, how did you make out, what did you do about your room, your books, your belongings and mine? Did you see Gérald, Didier and Bielher before you left? Did you go to their performance on 25 November? What's become of them? and Jacqueline? and L—? Is she going to wait for you like a Breton bride? You who enjoy writing so much, tell me about your life, and your misadventures since 22 October 1950, I'm not up to date on anything. Did you go and say goodbye to my grandmother? Not a chance! You were wrong. Did you repay your debts before leaving, like a man of honour? Hmm! Hmm! I enclose with my letter two photos of our first show. I ask you to send them back to me as I'd like to keep them as souvenirs.

I have just reread your letter, I've read all the books you lent me during my leave. Apart from *Les Liaisons*, which is all right, there's one which I thought was terrific and which is still in your briefcase at my place; I don't remember the title, but it's the story of a kid who has a slight hunchback and whose mother is a hairdresser. Do you know which one I mean? . . . As for *Haute Surveillance*,[13] I can't think what that might be! My plans? You ask me what my plans are. I don't have any except to pick up my life where it left off, any old job that pays, my books, movies, theatre (I'm going to go much more often) and music. But, alas, you won't be there. It makes me awfully sad, you know . . . Never will I be as close to anyone as I was to you. Let me hear from you very soon.

Robert

1 – French dramatist, born in 1907.
2 – Lachenay is quoting a popular French song.
3 – Jean Debucourt, French actor (1894–1958).
4 – Eugène Labiche's *Un chapeau de paille d'Italie*.
5 – French actor (1883–1946), described by Orson Welles as 'the greatest actor who ever lived': *Marius*, *Fanny*, *Faisons un rêve*, *César*, *Les Perles de la couronne*, *La Femme du boulanger*, etc.
6 – Henry de Montherlant.
7 – By Marcel Aymé.
8 – By Jean Giraudoux.
9 – *Le Figaro littéraire*.
10 – *Les Nouvelles littéraires*.
11 – By, respectively, Jean Delannoy, Jean Stelli, Joseph L. Mankiewicz, Elliott Nugent, Jacques Daniel-Norman, Mervyn LeRoy, Edward Buzzell, Léo Joannon, Kurt Neumann, Ted Tetzlaff, John Ford, William Wellman, George Waggner, Henry King, Sidney Lanfield, Léo Joannon, Robert Z. Leonard, René Clair, John Farrow, William Keighley, Jacqueline Audry, Nars Eric Kjellgren, Pierre Caron, Mark Robson and Billy Wilder.
12 – Quarterly rent.
13 – By Jean Genet.

To Robert Lachenay

[23 January 1951]
first letter

Dear Robert,

It's Sunday, I've just received your letter, I was happy, I no longer am – you'll find out why – and I'm also ill, I therefore have some time to myself; the infirmary was full, so they let me stay in my room, all I have is a rather bad case of flu which in the next few days could well develop into bronchitis or a severe throat infection.

I have a nasty piece of news to give you. In any event, I intended to tell you very soon, but your grandmother's letter precipitated things and I decided that, after all, it would be quite unforgivable to have you send off the camera and only then give you this news which is as painful for me to confess as it must be for you to learn.

All your books have been sold, mine as well needless to say. Because of what your grandmother contemptuously calls my superior intelligence, I could juggle every word in the French language and could easily prove to you and, who knows, convince you that my iniquity is a proof of my friendship,[1] that I'm wrong but that it's so easy to be right, etc., you know me by now.

Enough of words, terrified by what I'd done, I left; as soon as I receive my enlistment pay and the Indo-China money, I'll pay you back as much as possible,[2] I can't be more precise.[3] Only you can judge the depths to which I've sunk. Wait a little before writing, as I'd prefer a calm letter to a furious one.

Since I'm obliged to fill you in on the details that must be worrying you, you should know that I got into your room with my hotel key which I don't have any longer since I obviously don't have my room any longer. My books have been sold, a few of my film reviews are in your room, the little knick-knacks are safe[4] in L—'s flat (the spoon – the teapot).

My life since October? I finished the Renoir job for Bazin, the only thing I can pride myself on. It will bring me in 12,000F around May or June – I've lived by selling off my books one after the other. Yours I used to pay my hotel, which had lodged a complaint with the police and I couldn't sleep there any longer; so I slept one night at your place, and it was then that I decided to sell your books. I hope that my letter will reach you before Tuesday, that it won't prevent you from giving a good performance, and in that way you'll reply to it calmly on Saturday. With Gérald's letter, I do understand that you have every right to be sceptical.

to friendship,
françois

Another letter follows.

1 – Lachenay's scribbled comment on the letter: 'I doubt it.'
2 – Idem: 'Ha ha.'
3 – Idem: 'It's all too precise.'
4 – Idem: 'The word is well chosen.'

To Robert Lachenay *[26 January 1951]*

Dear old Robert,

I forgot in my preceding letter to enclose your two photos. Besides which, I felt the need to explain myself a little. It was obviously this business of the books which made me sign up both for the 3 years and for Indo-China. That's all I think I can say about it, so what I want to do now is reply to all the question marks you put in your 3 letters:

1. I realize now there weren't so many question marks after all. But I've decided to send you one of your own letters, the second one, so that you can recall the tone. When you return to Paris, I obviously won't be there. You'll go 2 years without seeing me and there's no guarantee that, afterwards, we'll be as we were before; you see how pessimistic I am.

I only have to look back, inside the wardrobe with you while your mother was drinking, glug glug, the times we played truant, the happy hours and also the sad hours, as Pétain used to say, the times, again and again, we'd borrow money from your grandmother, the Cercle Cinémane, the cafés, the first Naja cigarettes, Jo in the rue Lepic,[1] Bonamy, the woman in the delicatessen, the Trémolo[2] restaurant, the Mayol concerts, Ducornet in the rue [. . .].[3] So many things I doubt we'll ever see the like of again. One doesn't choose one's memories, insignificant moments remain etched in the mind, all of which means that, no matter how annoyed you are, and I can well understand how you might be, let's not fall out, we just have to work everything out and it strikes me that the deliberate sacrifice of 3 years and the choice of Indo-China prove how much it matters to me and should convince you that I no longer shrink from taking action. This letter, I hope, will prevent you from having stage fright. I know how much the public would lose. I've had *Elle* and Bazin send me references to try and obtain a posting to Baden-Baden, as editor-reporter on a magazine that you must have come across: *La Revue d'information des T.O.A.* If I succeed, I'll have a room in town, an open permit to travel around Germany indefinitely (I'll come and see you), in short, an incomparably better life than the one I'm leading here. I haven't been able to make a complete break with Paris and I write lots of letters (to 3 women who were in the audience at the Faubourg – to L— – Lorette – Schérer – Jacqueline P. – Chenille – to Geneviève S., Alain Resnais[4] (*Van Gogh*)[4] – Bazin – Niko – Thibaudat – François Mars, etc.).

I'm also writing quite a few articles (one of them will be appearing in *Lettres du monde*, I'll let you know when), etc.

You'd be doing me a favour by sending me my camera, as there are wonderful photographs to be taken in Germany; in addition, it would help me for Baden and I can have the negatives developed here at a nominal cost and, by photographing my mates, I get them to pay their share, so the others are almost free of charge. Speaking of photographs, I'm sending you one of me. I'll perhaps receive some parcels from the women at the Faubourg.

If there are lots of books at your disposal, see if there's Proust's *A la recherche du temps perdu* (16 volumes). It's a wonderful book and crucial to the future of the novel: Balzac and Proust are the 2 greatest novelists in the French language. One of these days, send me some *Figaro litt.* and *Nouv. littér.*: they're not sold here, this is a backwater. I don't know Péguy[5] at all, but I agree about Célou Arasca. You have *Les Joies de la tulipe*, and L— has read, by the same author, *La Côte des malfaisants*. You write to me of '. . . a strange charm' and L— in a recent letter: '*La Côte des malfaisants* is marvellous. What have you done with *Les Joies de la tulipe* which I'd so like to read?' Might you be made for one another . . . If you like, send that book to L— in your own name and ask her in exchange for *La Côte des malfaisants*, by the very same Célou Arasca. Besides, L— knows you and she has read one of your recent letters, since she takes care of the mail that comes for me at the rue Dulong. I'll have to end my letter here, since this time it's a long one and I am impatient as well as apprehensive to read your reply.

In spite of everything (I've done to you)

Your friend,
françois

P.S. That aside, Gérald's style surprises me: he writes quite well for a reader of Dale Carnegie and Dr Besançon.[6] 2. *La Gazette des lettres* has indeed changed: a *Digest*-style format and now a monthly; it's still very good; I've got the first 3 issues in Paris. L— will be collecting them for me, therefore for you as well.

1 – A costermonger in Montmartre who was friendly with Lachenay's mother.
2 – The young Lachenay would invite Truffaut to lunch in this Parisian restaurant and charge the bill to his father's account.
3 – Illegible.
4 – French director, born in 1922. *Van Gogh* was his first film, a documentary short on the artist made in 1948.
5 – Charles Péguy, French Catholic writer (1873–1914).
6 – Carnegie was, of course, the best-selling author of *How to Win Friends and Influence People* and Besançon the equivalent in France.

To Robert Lachenay

[27 January 1951]

Dear Robert,

Obviously, but pleasantly, surprised by your reaction. Is it the uniform that makes you so . . . carefree? Agreed, my letters were ridiculous (and, as I write, there's another, even more detailed one that you won't have received yet), but you know as well as I do that, in a situation of this kind,[1] one has to give the impression of being humble and even thick-witted, it disarms the enemy. I think it's too early yet for me to insert a hint of cynicism into my writing. I therefore remain on the defensive, still adopting a neutral tone from one letter to the next. (Oh! psychology when you have us in your clutches!)

At the same time as your letter I received one from a woman at the Faubourg replying favourably to my last letter which was more or less a declaration of love (my success, no doubt, is due to the fact that I wasn't sincere). As for my enlistment, I've discovered that the document I signed was only for provisional enlistment; finally, after a medical and a general examination by the squad, I've been accepted for 3 years and I sign the final document in 3 weeks, which is to say, in the 2nd half of February. I hope that this signature will be accompanied by cash, otherwise I'll go over to the enemy.

I forgot to tell you that I'm still writing to you from my bed; I was up for 3 days, then I was given an injection which meant another 4 days in bed and a numbed shoulder. I'm very impatient to hear from Baden-Baden.

I can't have any leave until after the 2nd squad (if I make it, since I do damn all) and the manoeuvres. That takes me to April. As it works out, I gain two months because I'll be going on leave at the same time as those who have been here since October or November.

As a volunteer, I had problems making friends with the guys here, but because of my position in Paris, the certificate from *Elle* and a few articles signed Truffaut, I was deemed worthy of their friendship.

By contrast, the fact that I enlisted has earned me the esteem and admiration of the officers, who wouldn't go to Indo-China for anything in the world.

Unfortunately, they've got it into their heads to make me an NCO and I'm forced to take command of the gunnery platoon,[2] in artillery, which doesn't exempt me from having to do the same boring old things and which I do very badly. When I say 'Platoon, at the word, forward . . . march,' no one moves, since only the officer cadet can hear me. For the moment they're teaching me how to shout. Since the day before yesterday I've been in bed, so it's been put off till Monday. I don't know anything tougher than arms drill at 7 o'clock in the morning. What do you think? I still don't know how to assemble a gun properly, but I'm not a bad shot with a Mauser at 200 metres and with a bren-gun at 30 metres. Target practice is the only thing I look forward to.

We should find out whether or not parcels can be sent from soldier to soldier, here in Germany, as I have a few books for you.

Before leaving I read *La Mort du petit cheval*,[3] it's not bad, but the raggedy young rebels, just as I was before Villejuif, are very 'thin' and, in sexual matters, H. Bazin is a cheat. Once he's said that he has never masturbated and that every woman falls hot and swooning into his arms, there's nothing more to say. I would have liked to write an article entitled '*La Mort du petit cheval* or the story of a cheat'.[4]

See if there are the 16 Prousts, I swear you'll be won over.

That's it for today.

Affectionately,

françois

P.S. At your place there's still *Fig. Litt.*, *Nlles Litt.*, *Chronique médicale* and *Histoire des papes*, I'm pretty sure that's all.

1 – On the letter Lachenay scribbled 'Stinker'.
2 – Idem: 'What a cock-up that must be.'
3 – By Hervé Bazin.
4 – Truffaut is alluding to Guitry's *Le Roman d'un tricheur*.

To Robert Lachenay

1 February 1951

Dear Robert,

Returning from Baumolder (north of Wittlich) where we spent 2 days on manoeuvres and cannon and tank gunnery demonstrations, I found your 2 letters.

You forgot to enclose that juicy letter you came across by chance. It's too late as far as my enlistment is concerned, I sign the main document any day now, but, because of the others I've already signed, I really can't get out of it; my papers for Indo-China are already at the medical unit for the injections. Here I'm still being made to take command, but I'm beginning to get the hang of it: 'If I've been on your back for the last week,' one lieutenant said to me, 'it's not to hassle you, it's to make sure you won't get killed in your first days in Indo-China.'

At Baumolder I ran into Bourget (from 5, rue Milton, he's at Idar-Oberstein) and Lemaire (same school, head like a skull, a chum of Pevel, both of them basketball players, rue Choron), another guy as well who used to live in the rue de Bruxelles and who remembers you; I didn't catch his name, he's Jewish and not very nice; you didn't tell me finally whether you share my opinion about *La Mort du petit cheval*. You must be blinded by love if you're reading the Paul Géraldy.[1] All things considered, I prefer Prévert even though I like him less and less.

I'm very tired, I'll continue this letter tomorrow!

2 February, late in the evening.

To come back to Proust: which 4 volumes are they? If it's *Un amour de Swann* or *La Prisonnière* or *Sodome et Gomorrhe* or even *Le Côté de Guermantes*, you can read them in any order.

If you read *Un amour de Swann*, you'll relive your whole affair (or lack of affair) with Jacqueline. I sold *L'Histoire de Louis XIII*.

The shirts are in your room (the 3 that are dirty I've put separate from the others). The records are still there. I finished the cigarettes. Along with *L'Histoire de Louis XIII*, I sold the *Plan de Paris sous Henri II* and the flintlock pistol; it's painful that you should have to learn this now, but that's it, there's nothing left to tell you.

You tell me it's an ill wind that blows no one any good and that the sale of your books will enable you to repaint your room; I confess it wasn't that noble thought that guided me, but, to be precise, I have to say that I too saw an advantage, a more subtle one: your military service will have made you a different person and perhaps you'll come back from it more enthusiastic about Ch. Péguy than about Louis Madelin[2] and, starting again from scratch, perhaps your library will take a completely different form? Balzac – Maupassant – Michelet – Proust . . . I've just remembered that it's one of the women from the Faubourg who has *Les Joies de la tulipe*.

Saturday in the small hours of Sunday.

Tomorrow is my day off, so I have no excuses. It's wonderful to be awake when everyone is asleep. There are no more NCOs; I am the only one in command. If there were a fire, I'd be the first to shout – I forgot the fire sentries!

Concerning my camera, make some inquiries, as it would obviously be much simpler for you to send it to me and I can't believe it's not permitted. I think we're going to be paid (5 days late) on Monday or Tuesday, along with some back pay since we get 15F a day now. So on Tuesday I'll be sending you some money with a letter, as much as I can afford, about 200F. For the moment I can't send you any marks, as I owe 5 or 6: in the squad, we have to buy our own pens, notepads, ink, etc.

I've had no reply from Baden. Can you give me the German address of the officer in charge of *La Revue d'information*?

My father asks me what I've done with the camera, I'm going to say that I have it here and I think he'll give it to me as a present.

Congratulations on your theatrical articles, but, hmm! it strikes me you're encroaching on my territory!

With this letter I'm sending you an amusing article that I wasn't able to sell anywhere. It's an attack on a ridiculous English film: *Odette*.[3] Let me point out a few witticisms that will help you appreciate its finer points:

1. L'enfant chargé de haine (an allusion to a novel by Mauriac, *L'Enfant chargé de chaînes*).

2. Une maison si peu fertile en guerriers. A deformation of Corneille's lines:

> 'Issus d'une maison si fertile en guerriers
> qu'ils y prennent naissance au milieu des lauriers'

3. Monsieur Robert (in Molière's *Le Malade imaginaire*: 'Et s'il me plaît a moi d'être battue!')

4. Sacher-Masoch (German professor around 1840, he had himself whipped by his wife, which is where the word masochism comes from, just as Sade = sadism).

5. Sarah Churchill: though the heroine of the film is French, she is . . . Churchill's daughter-in-law!

Tell me what you think of it and send it back to me, since I still have hopes of getting it published.

In *Raccords*, a de luxe magazine, the successor to *La Revue du cinéma*, there will be a special issue on Jean Renoir with 20 glossy pages by François Truffaut on *La Règle du jeu*.

I've sent to Bugat[4] (*Lettres du monde*) an article on 'Jean Genet, my fellow man', I don't know if it will appear *because*[5] the prevailing morality, etc.; it would be a pity, as I rate it highly. If you come across Genet's *Le Journal d'un voleur* (Gallimard, 330F), read it, it's wonderful and I'm not trying to be paradoxical or witty; it's simply overwhelming, a bit like J.-J. Rousseau (whom I haven't read!).

This headed notepaper is ridiculous, I know. The guys here are so stupidly militaristic that I'm naturally becoming militaristic myself; they say they detest the Germans and they sell them cigarettes; they see the army with civilian eyes whereas joining the army is like landing on the moon, a whole other world opens up to the curiosity of anyone capable of judging it objectively. If they really understood the lesson of the army, these guys would see everything quite differently when their m. service is over.

One learns that justice is nothing but a myth and that what counts is hierarchy, it's just the same as in civilian life, only more explicit. If you had done field training, you'd be a sergeant, I'm sure, because you're more willing to learn than I am, more authoritarian. We'll speak about all of this again. I enclose with my letter a programme from the Faubourg that one of the women sent me.

What is it you find fault with in my love life? I may lack Balzac's genius, but my love life is just as complicated as his, the objects of my affection being either sixteen or forty years old, with a few ambiguous relationships between these 2 ages; young women of good stock and widows; there's nothing else that matters and how heavenly to correspond with them, I could show you a collection of letters like no other! Jacqueline doesn't write to me any more, what an inconsiderate girl; I've dropped a number of pointless correspondents like Chenille.

But now I've really got to get some sleep and this time you can't criticize my letter for being too short.

Yours,
françois

Write the address correctly: 2nd C.S.T., it's us who get bawled out:
2nd C.S.T. (Gunner) François Truffaut
1st squad – 8th battery
S.P.73 307 B.P.M. 526 A.

1 – A once popular French poet and dramatist.
2 – French historian (1871–1956).
3 – By Herbert Wilcox (1950).
4 – Jean-Maurice Bugat, French journalist and film society organizer, born in 1921.
5 – In English in the original letter.

To Robert Lachenay

Mardi Gras 6 February 1951

Dear old Robert,

They've left us in peace for the afternoon of Mardi Gras – thank god – I keep feeling it's Sunday and, forgetting that it's Mardi Gras, I have the feeling we've been given a holiday to celebrate my 19th birthday which is today.

I've seen the post orderly, it's possible to send parcels from one military base to another if you pay the same postage as from France to Germany.

So, as soon as I have a little money, I'll send you a marvellous book, *The Picture of Dorian Gray*. I'll ask you to send me, along with the camera, *Haute Surveillance*, later I'll send you *Le Journal d'un voleur*, but only for a few days, as I constantly reread it and I'm making lots of notes on it. I'm sure my letter and your reply to mine of 3 February are going to cross each other in the post. You see how often I write to you, whenever I possibly can.

I'm upset that I haven't received any reply from Baden-Baden. If in your next letter I find the magazine's address, I'm going to try again. The address I wrote to was: *Revue d'information et de liaison des T.O.A.* 3, Kronprinzenstrasse, 3 Baden-Baden – is that the right address? Do you have the coded (military) address?

Field training is due to end in 3 weeks and then manoeuvres, then posting, but where to?

What have you been reading recently? Will you have a chance to read: *Le Lys dans la vallée* (Balzac), all of Jean Genet, Gide's *Journal*, *Le Journal d'un curé de campagne*,[1] *Les Grands Cimetières sous la lune* (Bernanos), *La Neige était sale* (Simenon) or *Gilles* (Drieu la Rochelle)? These are a few of the best books I've read this year along with . . . Proust of course. As for me, I'm learning by heart the salient features of the 105 HM A1 field howitzer, the bren-gun and the Browning 50 machine-gun, the duties of subordinates towards their superiors and how to prepare and supervise target practice. All of which is quite pleasant; being the hard worker that you are, you would make a success of it here, for I haven't your capacity for learning things by heart and remembering them . . . If you do 18 months, do the next field training (in May), you'll have the advantage of seniority and you'll be the kingpin.

Christ, where is your admiration for tactics, organization, order, discipline and asceticism (the camp bed, etc.)? Forget Prévert, think of Xenophon, Racine, Murat, Napoleon, Alfred de Vigny, General Hugo, even Rommel, believe in heroism and don't let yourself be fooled by the absurd outward show which is nothing but a shell.

Have you never noticed the difference between a private and a corporal, an officer cadet and a sergeant? At least let me have your opinion on the matter. Above all, you mustn't let yourself go; what's more, it's quite likely that, if you're really doing something useful in your own line, one of these days you'll be made a corporal.

I'll arrange to see you for a minimum of 2 or 3 days before leaving for Indo-China, it's important that you see me one last time in case I never come back, which wouldn't bother me too much. The little Germans were very polite for Mardi Gras. I'm almost getting nostalgic for the traditions I've so often jeered at.

I think too much, it tires me out. Write to me soon,

Your friend,
François

1 – By Georges Bernanos.

To Robert Lachenay

[16 February 1951]
Wittlich

Old friend,

Here, laboriously reconstructed, on a scale of 10/1,000, is a map of the French zone. As you see, we're at opposite ends. I received your 2 letters and the address of *La Revue d'information*. I've written to Col. Albert Moreau a curt but polite letter that should bring a prompt reply.

Meanwhile, apart from Resnais, Bazin is trying to help me, I received a letter from a civilian in Mainz, the director in charge of cultural affairs at the High Commission of the French Republic in Germany, who is going to recommend me 'in high places'; another guy, a lieutenant-colonel at the citadel in Mainz, is also going to write to me. If, with all these representations being made on my behalf, I don't obtain any satisfaction, I'll put a Mauser bullet in my head . . . after paying you back, of course.

I'm a little embarrassed by the expressions of friendship that you lavish on me, as I can't help feeling guilty and it's you, when all is said and done, who adopted the most Christian attitude (turning the other cheek).

In a week, it will be the end of field training and the examination. I'm the only one who isn't revising, I do damn all and this will cost me perhaps a few days in the guardhouse, since the squad lieutenant won't want to appear a fool in the eyes of the officers (major, captain, etc.) who are going to have us sit the exam, I'm not in the least scared, I don't give a shit, it's afterwards that all hell will let loose. Roll on my posting, for my life in the battery will be no joke though less tiring.

If I got the film posting, I would go to Mainz or Paris; I've come round to the idea of Paris, since my problems are working out. L—, to whom I'd stopped writing, sends me letters burning with passion (more or less) and, since I no longer have any feeling for her, it would be my turn to lead her a dance. On the other hand, such sadism is incompatible with the saintliness to which I aspire, the state of grace, the kindness and the charity.

'Why else does love bear wings
if not to fly?' (ter)[1]

I don't have your letter in front of me, I can't imagine what you might have asked me.

Did you receive the 4 issues of *Opéra*?[2] If so, I'll send you others as I receive them (from L—). As for the cigarettes, the guy is in the infirmary, so I won't know immediately if the Corfus can be sold, but, in any event, if they can't be sold, I'll smoke them myself and instead sell the African ones which are quite popular here, as they're not unlike our Gauloises Bleues. So, if you can send me the cigarettes (ask the post orderly about that), either I'll smoke them and, because I'll be buying less, will send you more money, or I'll sell them and send you the money.

Try to keep your 4 days' leave in reserve, because, after the field training and the manoeuvres, I might be able to ask for 72 hours, we could meet on neutral ground, Baden-Baden for example (equidistant from Wittlich and Constance). If you spend your life travelling, the time must pass quite quickly, more so in any case than when you're studying. I believe the 18 months or 15 months plus 3 months off are official; no?

You don't have to worry about your room, I haven't forgotten anything, except perhaps that L—'s mother has been using your coffee-pot and, given that she breaks 2 plates a week, she might well be capable of breaking the coffee-pot, and except also that I'm not sure if your little knick-knacks are in L—'s flat (the François I clasp, etc.). I don't recall having taken them to L—'s place, which doesn't mean they're lost, since maybe they never left my room. I'll give L— all the necessary instructions, but, as for your room, it's locked; it's been neither sublet nor sold . . .

I don't share your opinion of the army; every day I see officers whose intelligence and human qualities I admire, guys from the Polytechnique or the Centrale. You must have seen how the French equipment demonstrated at Baumolder dazzled the Americans. I'm all for this intensive rearmament, though it's a pity to be selling so much to America, but it alone has the manufacturing capacity, while we, we invent, and even if we don't profit from the genius of French engineers, it means that we have all the more glory. L— is going to send me *La Gazette des lettres*, I'll send it on to you and you must take care to keep every copy. No Saturday night or Sunday passes before the end of field training to allow us to revise, so I won't be seeing any more German films.

I very much admire *House of Strangers*.[3] Susan Hayward is terrific and so is Richard Conte. Ah! that walk up the staircase as the gramophone begins to play! How can you say the plot is weak? Personally, I find it rather literary, it could be a theme for a novel and it's very well handled. It's one of the films I most want to see again; but the cinema and me . . . that's another story (as R. Kipling used to say!).

Your friend,
françois

1 – From Beaumarchais's *Le Mariage de Figaro*, quoted by Renoir at the beginning of *La Règle du jeu*.

2 – A weekly arts magazine.

3 – By Joseph L. Mankiewicz (1949).

To Robert Lachenay

[February 1951]
Monday

Old Fellow,

Even though I wrote to you yesterday, I'm sending this off having meanwhile received your little note.

For Christ's sake, did you or did you not receive the 5 marks? I'll send the box back to you. If you are in love, don't wait to be cured before writing to me. I'm happy to know you're in love on condition that it works out better than with Jacqueline! Tell me all about your love affairs. Who exactly is Madame Tissot? What is she doing in Germany, how old is she, what sort of looks?

Try at least to sleep with her, or have I completely misunderstood what's going on? The squad has ended . . . badly for me. I'm still doing everything I can to get transferred. I found a copy of *Le Lys dans la vallée* again. I'm certainly going to enjoy breathing in that romantic atmosphere. If you are in love with a married woman, I'll have to send you the book, but write to me even though you're in love. Pay attention to your spelling if you write to Madame Tissot, I say that quite seriously, for I assure you it's important, especially if she's well-read, believe me.

That's all I have to tell you. Please note my new address, though it's still in the same barracks.

yours,
François

François Truffaut
Command Battery
SP.73 307 B.P.M. 526 A.

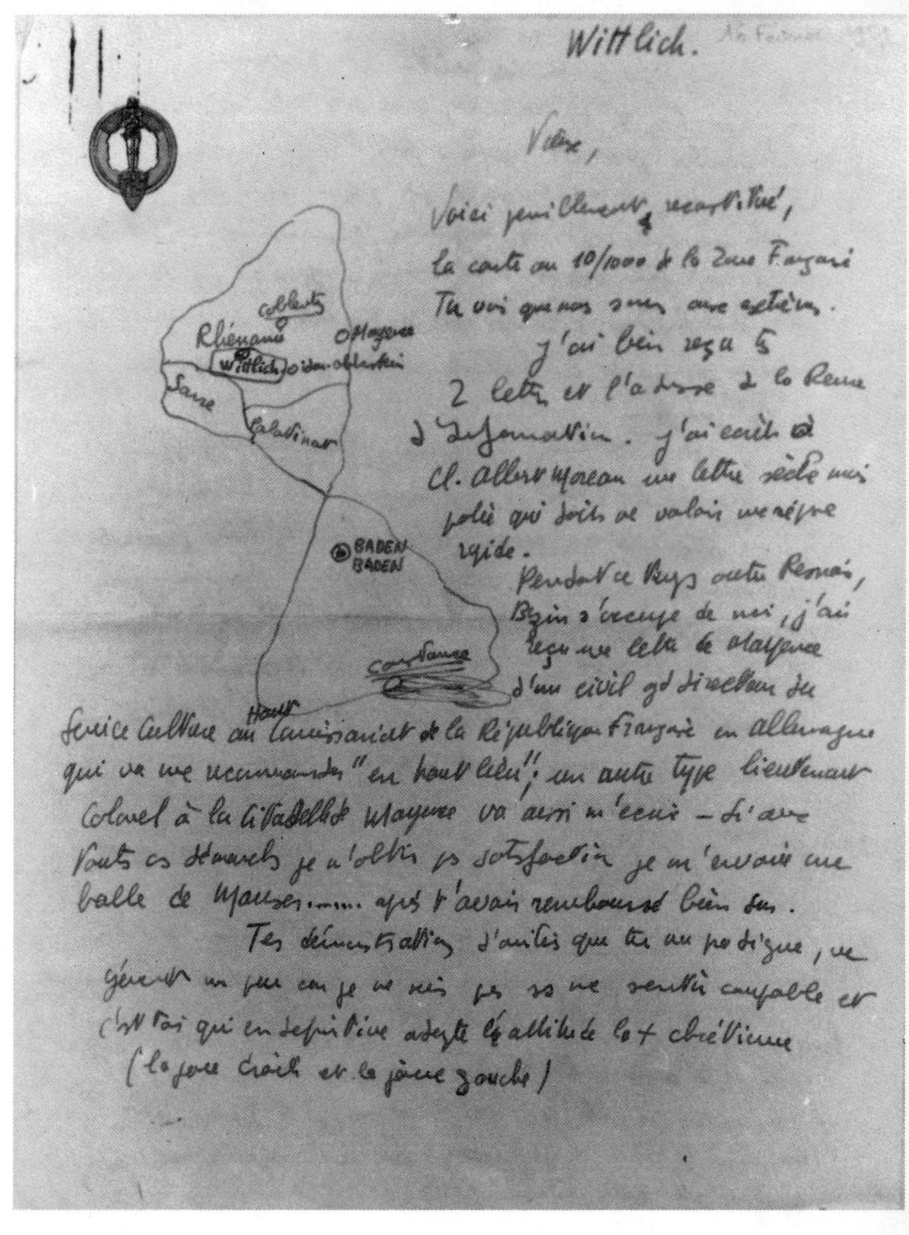

François Truffaut's handwriting at the age of nineteen (letter to Robert Lachenay).

To Robert Lachenay *[March 1951]*

Dear Robert,

I received your letter today. The distinction you make between humanity and individuals is spot-on, and yet the humanist is the one who loves the individual and not society. It's not surprising that Dostoevsky's novels bore you, they are novels of philosophy, like Balzac's, only more metaphysical; to read him with any real passion, you've got to read him by candlelight in a tiny room with maps on the wall and an ascetic's camp bed in a corner!

Try to read Gide's lectures on Dostoevsky, I don't remember who published them. They're a wonderful help in understanding him. By Dostoevsky himself try to read *The Gambler – The Eternal Husband* (the easiest to read).

I also agree about *Orphée*,[1] it's very flat, cold, glossy without being elegant and far inferior to *Le Sang d'un poète*.[1] It's *Le Sang d'un poète* as seen by Sam Wood![2] and photographed by Gabriel Figueroa[3] (a Mexican photog.). I hope you liked *Really the Blues*.[4]

Jacqueline has written to ask me for your address, which I had forgotten to put in my last letter to her. So she's going to write to you. I wrote to Genet and sent him a few pages I had written after reading *Le Journal d'un voleur* and *L'Enfant criminel*, and to my surprise I received an answer, I had addressed the letter care of Gallimard; he wrote me a very nice letter of thanks and sympathy: he told me to come and see him when I'm in Paris. His is a very good autograph to have.

On that I leave you. I will often write you short letters.

Yours,
françois

1 – By Jean Cocteau.
2 – American director (1883–1949): *A Night at the Opera, A Day at the Races, Goodbye Mr Chips, Our Town, Kitty Foyle, For Whom the Bell Tolls*, etc.
3 – Mexican cinematographer, born in 1907: *Maria Candelaria, La Escondida, Los Olvidados, El, Nazarin, El Angel Exterminador, The Night of the Iguana, Two Mules for Sister Sara*, etc.
4 – The autobiography of the jazz musician Mezz Mezzrow.

To Robert Lachenay *[12 April 1951]*

Dear Robert,

Received your letter very late. My bonus is on its way; I won't forget your money.

I was alone with the driver in the cabin of an army truck full of rifles – the truck overturned – the driver received a nasty blow to the head and I got one in the ribs – we're now resting before going to prison; him, for driving without a helmet, and me, for not having properly fastened the rifles which got scattered all over a muddy field – it was some Luxemburgers who noticed us and got us out of the mess.

Write to me at my new temporary address – I'm in the hospital at Idar-Oberstein.

Let me have news of you soon and my condolences for Simone, though the fact that she has a lover is in my opinion all the more reason for you to make known your feelings as quickly as possible . . . in writing.

françois

P.S. No news of Jacqueline.

François Truffaut
9.B. SP.84 025 B.P.M. 525.A

To Robert Lachenay *[8 June 1951]*

Dear old friend,

I hope that you've received my postal order for 4,000F. I would like to know. I'm in Paris until 18 June, then 1 week in Germany, then 1 month at Fréjus – departure for Saigon most likely at the end of August – drop me a line here at 27, rue Dulong. I won't be able to send you any money before I reach Indo-China, but I'll be sending you quite a lot from there. I saw Jacqueline who awaits your return with impatience and she isn't writing to you as she expects you to turn up any day now (sic). I'm all right; I'm sleeping with G—, she is therefore no longer for me the lily of the valley, pure and inaccessible. She lives in a dream half the time, it's no fun and I'm not in love with her; I'm using her, more or less unconsciously, to get my own back on L—.

I caught a glimpse of Chenille and I refused to see Gérald, Bielher and co-co.[1] I've been to the cinema a few times. I've seen Jean Renoir and Jean Genet; I went to the first night of Sartre's play,[2] that's all. It's not definite that I'm going to leave, since I feel I might desert, I'm thinking it over, let me have your opinion.

yours,
Truffaut

I've given you a rough idea of what's missing from your room. Don't think about it any more, I'll be sending you enough money so that you'll have absolutely no regrets about it – believe me.[3]

1 – In 'English' in the original letter: Truffaut presumably meant 'and company'.
2 – *Le Diable et le Bon Dieu.*
3 – On receiving the letter Lachenay wrote in the margin: 'Very difficult . . .'

To Robert Lachenay

[21 June 1951]
Wednesday

Dear old friend,

I am exactly where I was in the 1st barracks in Germany. During my 18 days in Paris I prepared the ground for a plan that will allow me to prolong my life or at least not end it you know where.[1]

Soon I'm going to find myself in the same situation as Jean Gabin at the beginning of that film set in Le Havre,[2] but in my case I'll have clothes, a job, friends I can trust.

I will await your return and help you to readjust. I want you to know that I have no belongings of yours outside your room. Bit by bit I'll buy whatever you need most and I'll help you as much as I can. Don't write to me, since I'll be in Fréjus in a few days, then I'm off to spend a few quiet days with friends who have a villa on the sea front, in a large town near Fréjus.[3] At which point I'll be in the same situation as Jean Gabin at the end of a film set in Algiers[4] (the ship leaves without him!). So, on 15 July, write to L— 1, rue Pierre-Brossolette, Courbevoie (Seine) and ask her for news of me, she will know all about it. Be very discreet, it would be better if you destroyed my letters, this one anyway, but don't forget, first, to note down L—'s address. I don't know if you'll approve of my decision, but I'm convinced it's the best solution.

Don't be thrown by anything that happens, trust me, I didn't take this decision lightly. See you soon.

very affectionately,
franchesco de Montferrand[5]

1 – In Indo-China.
2 – Marcel Carné's *Quai des brumes* (1938), in which Gabin plays a deserter.
3 – Cannes.
4 – Julien Duvivier's *Pépé le Moko* (1937).
5 – As one can see, Truffaut is extremely careful, in a letter that might have fallen into the hands of the military, to conceal or merely hint at his intentions and discreetly signs it with his mother's maiden name.

To Robert Lachenay

15 August 1951
Hôpital Villemin

My dear old Robert,

On the Saturday after you left I went to the Invalides with Bazin, his wife and L— to give myself up to the authorities. It was then that the guards, looking at my orders, discovered that I was not a deserter but AWOL, since, with leave or overseas posting, the deadline is not 6 days but 15 days. In my case, however, that made 14 days and 16 hours; that very same Saturday evening, at midnight, I would have been a deserter – which is to say, if I hadn't already given myself up. I said goodbye to Bazin and L— and I remained 8 days in the cells at the Dupleix barracks; then I was admitted to the Villemin hospital where I have to stay for about 1 month and a half, then I'll go to the psychiatric ward at Val-de-Grâce – my discharge on medical grounds is a real possibility.

Everyone is trying to help me, so I'm not at all anxious. If I'm demobilized, I'll live with the Bazins who want to look after me permanently [. . .].

I'm a prisoner here, but in a month's time a request will be put in for my release on medical grounds so that I can go to Val-de-Grâce.

I think everything is better this way. Living with the Bazins means material security as well as guaranteed and regular work (maybe at *Le Parisien libéré*).[1]

I'm working, I've written 60 pages of something that resembles Apollinaire's *Onze Mille Vierges*,[2] Sade's *Justine*, *La Princesse de Clèves*,[3] *J'irai cracher sur vos tombes*,[4] *Le Journal d'un voleur*, Sartre's essays, the *Confessions* of J.-J. Rousseau and Balzac, there's all of that in it, sometimes for better, often for worse, I don't harbour any illusions; it's of very minor literary value, but it's publishable and it's the first time I've got half-way through a book, therefore close to finishing it. I do believe that I'm going to do it this time, I'm going to bring it off. I forgot to say that it also resembles Diderot's *La Religieuse*. I'll type it out, with wide spacing, so that I can make sure the syntax and vocabulary are immaculate. I imagine it can only be published by something like 'Scorpion',[5] even though it deserves better.

It will also be very *Liaisons dangereuses*, XVIIIth century, libertine, both elegant and coarse. I'll need a pseudonym.

And you, what's become of you?
When do you get out?
Your plans?

Write to me. I've been cutting out lots of articles for you about Hitler with photos. Say hello to your friend the snailsman.[6]

Affectionately,
François

François Truffaut
3rd Médecine
Hôpital Villemin
8, rue des Récollets
Paris (10)

P.S. I think that, when you return, it would be best for you immediately to see about your grandmother's house.[7] You should convince her to live there and you yourself could travel back and forth from Andeville to Paris, etc., you see?

1 – A daily newspaper.
2 – A not infrequent lapsus: the title of Apollinaire's pornographic novel is not *Onze Mille Vierges* (or 'Eleven Thousand Virgins') but *Onze Mille Verges* ('Eleven Thousand Pricks').
3 – By Madame de La Fayette.
4 – By Boris Vian, though he published it under the pseudonym of Vernon Sullivan.
5 – A publishing house of 'controversial' books, most notably the Vian novel cited above.
6 – This was Bernard Largemains, whose mother sold oysters and snails at Boulogne-Billancourt. Largemains now works in the film industry as a construction manager.
7 – Madame Bigey had a house at Andeville in the Oise.

To Robert Lachenay

Monday (September 1951]
Andernach (18 km from Koblenz)

Dear old Robert,

My adventures aren't over yet; when I left the Villemin hospital, I once more tramped around for 4 days and this time I was arrested. Bazin was in Charentes and it was a situation no one had foreseen, so I had to return to Germany. I actually did return, but with 2 cops and handcuffs. My head is completely shaven *à la* Stroheim;[1] at the regiment I had a rather cool reception, fortunately I didn't stay long in prison (only 12 days) and they were forced to send me to the hospital.

Bazin is going to see about getting me transferred to the Ivry fort in Paris, to the film unit; I've been declared 'unsuited to the colonies' and I believe that the doctor here would like to have me discharged on grounds of 'mental problems and hysteria resulting from hereditary syphilis of a psycho-rachidian nature' or something of the sort.

You get out, they tell me, in 23 days – keep me informed – I'd like to have been there for your homecoming, since that would have been the best time for me to help you, I hope you'll manage to cope and I plan to be in Paris soon.

I rely on your answering me by return of post, I've been neglecting you so much I don't dare ask you to send me some books and yet I'm very unhappy in bed without anything to read.

Affectionately, your mate,
françois

François Truffaut
Hôpital complémentaire de l'armée André-Curtillet
S.P. 76.663 B.P.M. 515
P.S. I'm going to have myself photographed, I look like Fresnay[2] in *Chéri-Bibi*![3] Say hello to the snail!

1 – Erich von Stroheim, the Austrian-born director and actor (1885–1957), specialized in playing bullet-headed Prussian army officers.
2 – Pierre Fresnay, French actor (1897–1975): *Marius*, *Fanny*, *César*, *La Grande Illusion*, *Le Corbeau*, *Monsieur Vincent*, etc.
3 – By Léon Mathot (1938). Fresnay played the title role, a convict.

To Robert Lachenay *Tuesday 18 Sept. [1951]*

Dear old Robert,

I'm very happy this morning. I wrote to you yesterday, but your letter arrived this morning via the Villemin hospital, via the Invalides and via Koblenz – dated 2 September.

Very important: my spell in prison is nearly over – I will, nevertheless, be appearing before a sort of M.T.;[1] the regiment has given me 3 weeks to retrieve my greatcoat, my shoes, water-bottle, mess-tin, etc. I'm relying on you to help me avoid thirty days in the guardhouse and the 4 or 5,000F I would have to pay. As soon as you're in Paris, send it all to me – I'll send you money for the postage as soon as possible – thank you in advance.

2. When you are discharged, can you arrange to get a travel voucher for Andernach, near Koblenz (look it up on the map) and come and see me? In any case, you'll be going through Strasbourg afterwards. Look into it and give me a quick reply. This morning I received the mail that had been following me from Paris and 2 parcels of books: Nietzsche, Giono, Sartre, Barrès, Montesquieu, Cl. Mauriac and Faulkner. If you were to come and see me, I'd pass these books on to you, since I would already have read them

(about fifteen volumes). The photos are at a photographer's at the Porte Saint-Martin; I'll give you the chit, but though they must come to about 450F they're very good and I'll try to send you the money, if I have it. Do you want me to send you the chit?

I'm sure there are lots of things I'm forgetting to tell you. Anyway, don't forget to make every effort to come and see me, by passing yourself off as my cousin; I'm going to ask if you might spend 24 hours here and if you can give me a bag or an old suitcase or anything at all, since I've only got a briefcase, my suitcase is still in Paris, and it would be a pity to leave the books behind. When we've come to an agreement on this matter, I'll write to Bazin and ask him to find you some work if the factory is closed. He's very nice, you can depend on him; I could also have a word with Genet if Bazin can't do anything.

Write quickly.

friends as before,
françois

1 – Military tribunal.

To Robert Lachenay

[28 September 1951]
Tuesday morning
S.P. 50 034
BPM. 523

Dear old Robert,

Sorry about the misunderstanding: yes, they did hand over the Vaubourdolle classics[1] to me, I was taken by surprise, I didn't think you'd be coming so soon. If I'd had a chance to write you another letter, I would have told you how to go about it; instead of asking to see me, you would have asked for a pal of mine and everything would have worked;[2] well, better luck next time. I received your letter on Saturday.

I've entrusted 10 of the books to a mate who's getting discharged and who will be in Paris on Thursday 11 or 12 October; he will put the books in the left-luggage office at the Gare de l'Est and immediately send you the receipt in a letter.

As soon as you have the receipt, go and collect the books, since the left-luggage must cost 15 or 20 francs a day.

There are the 3 Sartre *Situations*, *Le Maître de Milan*,[3] *Un barrage contre le Pacifique*,[4] *Le Vin est tiré*,[5] *Histoire d'un fait divers*,[6] *Mirliton*, Montesquieu's posthumous *Cahiers* and *Introduction à une mystique de l'enfer*

(Claude Mauriac) – 10 books in all – I think they'll interest you. Also go to L—'s flat, she'll give you some books belonging to me and others belonging to Bazin (Brasillach's history of the cinema, etc.). I don't want to have books any more, so all my books, I have few enough, are yours now – it's not much compensation, but anyway . . .

If, by 15 October, the left-luggage receipt hasn't arrived, don't worry, it may mean that my mate has had to do extra time. It seemed to me there were lots more things I had to tell you.

Please send me, in a wrapper, any magazines you don't need and – I still don't have a bean, I'm waiting for some dough from L— – if you have a few stamps, send them to me.

I've had no word from Bazin, I don't know if he's back in Paris.

Will you have to do any extra time?

Koblenz, from my cell,
Thursday, 2 p.m.

I'm now resuming this letter that was started on Tuesday and interrupted, since they came to fetch me and put me back behind bars.

The delay is due to the fact that I've only just retrieved my paper, pencil and books. I reread *Les Lettres de mon moulin*[7] – a mixture of glibness and sometimes vulgarity yet there's talent there. Thanks to you, the shades of Shakespeare, Racine, Daudet, Pascal, etc. will hover about my cell and colonize my solitary confinement.

They continue to give me treatment; I have injections and I'm allowed a mattress, because they're intramuscular (my injections).

Write to me but be careful what you say, as the prison gates have microphones and binoculars.

very affectionately yours,
françois

François Truffaut
B.C. III
S.P. 73.307
B.P.M. 515

1 – A collection of classic texts for use in schools.
2 – Lachenay had paid Truffaut a visit but had not been allowed to see him.
3 – By Jacques Audiberti.
4 – By Marguerite Duras.
5 – By Robert Desnos.
6 – By Jean-Jacques Gautier.
7 – By Alphonse Daudet.

To Robert Lachenay

[1951]
Koblenz, Tuesday morning

Civvy bastard,

Received your letter and the stamps.

Boinard, whom you saw with me in the café near the Cinémathèque during your last leave, will come and see you on Saturday at 3 o'clock with about 20 books that are yours to keep (except for the Genets).

I recommend *L'Initiation à la musique*, *Le Passe-Muraille*,[1] etc. Anyway, you'll see.

I must confess that my optimism is a little clouded by all these mates in their civvy suits. I finally wrote to Bazin and asked him to speed things up, since I'm sick and tired of Germany.

I very much liked your observations on the similarity between doing military service and being a country doctor as seen by Balzac.

No, my novel will never see the light of day, I destroyed 40 pages and the 20 that are left will soon go the same way; I have more talent for film criticism.

Enclosed you'll find about fifteen aphorisms on cinema, the feminine art; those against which I've put a cross are the best, I wrote them after an enthusiastic reading of Pascal's *Pensées* – they meet with Rivette's full approval, Bazin less so, Schérer admires them – so I'm satisfied. Tell me what you think.

I've enclosed 3 stamps, since Bazin sent me some and I have the ones you gave me that you can't use in Paris.

Write to me often; I'm expecting a letter from Bazin, since I asked him what he could do for you; perhaps he'll send for you at the *Parisien*[2] – if you can't go, tell him so and keep me informed, also of what you're reading – it's true there was no reason for L— to send me money, but it was she who suggested it – I gave her such a bawling-out that she must be angry and she no longer writes to me. In any case, go and see her for the books.

affectionately,
François

P.S. Don't forget to be at home on Saturday at 3 o'clock.

1 – By Marcel Aymé.

2 – *Le Parisien libéré*.

To Robert Lachenay

[October 1951]
Wednesday evening

Dear old friend,

I can't express how I felt when I received your 500F and the stamps. I've been out of the guardhouse since yesterday. I'm still not A.D.L.[1] since for the moment I'm considered to be doing my service – so no pay so far – just tobacco (50 packets) if the captain agrees – you know how much I smoke, I can't sleep for thinking about it.

You'll forgive me for making pencil notes on your books, your classics, but ever since Genet I've learned how to read, and I can honestly state that I profit as much as I can from what I read – I was bowled over, yes, quite sincerely bowled over by Pascal's *Pensées*, only extracts, alas: Boileau seems very insipid by comparison, Daudet a teeny bit vulgar.

I got just as drunk in prison as in the rue Myrrha not so long ago,[2] I threw up in 2 cells, they bedded me down in a 3rd and if the officer on duty had been there, it would have cost me another 45 days; worst of all, I still bear traces of the binge. I wanted to shave with an open razor, my face is covered with nicks and I couldn't go to the infirmary, since we don't have the right to have a razor in prison. Oh well! My hair will grow back, my nicks will disappear and roll on civilian life. You remember Bourget who was at school with us – he's being discharged and he'll be bringing you a parcel of books, your classics plus Nietzsche plus 2 Gionos, etc.

Yes, I need all my army things: greatcoats (even without the buttons), shoes, mess-tins, water-bottles, braces, underpants, tie (beige); if there's anything missing, it will mean being confined to barracks and having my future pay-packets docked!

The airmail paper and especially the envelopes are very nice – you'll always know when it's a letter from old François. I'm going to adopt this paper and these envelopes, even if I have to sell my pack to do so. Next time I'll send you a copy of the best thing (!) I've ever written, 20 paradoxes or maxims or aphorisms on 'cinema, the feminine art' – the style fluctuates between Pascal and Radiguet.[3] On the lavatory wall, in prison, I read this charming verse:

> 'Love is kindled under trousers and put out under skirts.'

And this:

> 'Virtue becomes rigid when everything else has ceased to be.'

And to end (in ribaldry):

> 'If you were a flower and I a butterfly
> I'd spend my life sucking your bud dry!'

Enclosed is the chit for the photos. Try and collect them (about 300F) before the end of October, because I can't guarantee anything after that. When you go to L—'s flat, ask her for the following books: 5 thrillers, *Les Amitiés particulières*,[4] volume II of Genet, *Le Messie fou*,[5] *Mon Taxi et Moi*,[6] *Elle et Lui* (J. Duché), *Tous les hommes sont mortels*[7] – Bazin's books – Brasillach,[8] the big book on the movies by Lapierre[9] – the 2 vols. of Élie Faure's *L'Histoire de l'art*, a book on Proust, 5 issues of *Les Temps modernes*,[10] 2 Balzacs – *Les Fleurs du mal* – *Les Mal Partis*[11] – W. Scott's *The Talisman*. She'll lend you a suitcase. The best thing would be to ring her during office hours at DÉFense 25-40 Mademoiselle L—, and she'll tell you when you can go and see her in the rue Dulong. I'm eager to get those books back and know they're at your place. Write to me.

Regards and thanks,
françois

François Truffaut
B.S. III
SP. 73.307
B.P.M. 515

1 – *Au-delà de la durée légale* or 'Beyond the legal time-limit'.
2 – Truffaut and Lachenay had attended a memorable party in the shop owned by Jacqueline's father in the rue Myrrha.
3 – Raymond Radiguet, French writer (1903–23). He was the lover and literary protégé of Jean Cocteau.
4 – By Roger Peyrefitte.
5 – By Aimée Alexandre.
6 – By Alexandre Breffort.
7 – By Simone de Beauvoir.
8 – *Histoire du cinéma* by Maurice Bardèche and Robert Brasillach.
9 – *Les Cent Visages du cinéma* by Marcel Lapierre.
10 – The politico-literary journal edited by Jean-Paul Sartre.
11 – By Jean-Baptiste Rossi.

To Robert Lachenay

[30 October 1951]
Koblenz, Tuesday

Dear old Robert,

You obviously think I'm annoyed with you, but, you know, it's a bit ridiculous of you to fall silent again as you did when you left, and this time it's a real bore.

Yesterday I received the greatcoat. Thanks, but . . . What about the shoes? the haversack? the tie? the braces? L— stupidly didn't understand at all and sent me rubbish, but you, you know what a pack is and what a quartermaster is. I'll work something out for the other things, but I won't be able to get any

André Bazin, François Truffaut's 'adopted' father.

shoes – my pair of boots can't weigh more than 3 kilos, send them in 2 separate parcels if they're too heavy. It's a bore, I know, but better that than prison, for I've had it up to here.

I simply don't understand the way your attitude changed the day you returned to Paris. Did you receive the books from Boinard? And from Skulfort? I've got to know, because if you didn't I'll get back on to them.

Enclosed is some money, as much as I can afford, and 1 photo of me. Reply to me or explain whatever it is that you hold against me.

Have you been to pick up the photographs? Are you working? Have you seen Bazin? I hope to have heard from you by the end of the week. Did you receive the 2 parcels of newspapers I sent you?

Yours (nevertheless)
françois

To Robert Lachenay

[5 November 1951]
Andernach, Saturday

My dear old Robert,

I have received a letter from Bazin, who's furious with you, and he told me what was in your express letter.[1]

Obviously he can't understand, but I had no difficulty recognizing you in those four curt lines in which the concern for elegance, the poetic image and the precise and daring metaphor shows through your anger. Of course, I'd be lying if I said it didn't hurt my feelings; but, for all that, my friendship for you is in no way diminished.

This anger of yours I put down to the difficulty of readjustment, the fact that you have neither a job nor any books (and I'm to blame for the latter) and also the death of your mother.

Perhaps Jacqueline, too, has something to do with this inopportune wrath.

Whatever you may have written, did you receive everything I sent you? 2 parcels of newspapers, a letter with 4 photos of me and 500F. I entrusted the books to two guys, did they show up? I continue to receive newspapers, but I can't send you any for the moment, as I'm in neuropsychiatry, and I never get out of this bloody asylum. I'm sure I'm going to be discharged soon on grounds of irresponsibility and conscienceless behaviour. If I receive my back pay and I can change it into French currency, I'll send you some.

Write to me and fill me in on all the details of your life since you got back.

Don't write to Bazin, I'll see that he changes the poor opinion he has of you, but he could have helped you.

Quick, a letter.

still very affectionately,
françois

François Truffaut
H.C.A. André Curtillet
S.P. 76.663
B.P.M. 515

1 – On his discharge Lachenay had written to Bazin, informing him that he no longer wished to concern himself with Truffaut's welfare and asking Bazin to take over.

To Robert Lachenay

[7 November 1951]
Andernach, Wednesday

My old Robert,

I have just this minute received my shoes; most gracious . . .;[1] no matter how much I stare at them, they refuse to answer my questions; I ask them: 'You whom Robert's hands touched only a few days ago, what is he up to? Is he at the factory again? Is he seeing Jacqueline, Janine? What is he reading? etc.' The shoes clam up.

As for me, I'm not crazy yet, a fact on which I am, I believe, to be congratulated. I suppose, before depriving the army of my presence, I have to get to know all its different facets, and this one, though not the most attractive, is I think the most amazing.

The doctor in charge doesn't seem too convinced by my 'irresponsibility', but a letter from the War Minister, inserted in my file, will, I believe, suffice to allay his suspicions; just one more piece of bumf to come from Paris and there's more than a chance I'll be celebrating Christmas as a civilian.

And you? And Jacqueline, Janine, Didier and co? Is your concierge still as . . . talented? And does Androuet still sing Bacchus? And the pin-up girl opposite you, with her American truffallo-intellectual glasses? Have you joined the public library again? And the cinema? Have you seen *A Night at the Opera*?[2]

No, I never took your room for a cesspool, I'll have you know; why don't you use the will-power I know you possess, to react, to 'liberate' your anger and tell me the real reasons; examine yourself with all the severity and lucidity that you are capable of and let me know what the diagnosis is; no, it wasn't a Tartar who ate your sweets and I have never taken your room for a cesspool.

Remember the 'glug-glug-glug inside the wardrobe', the salted bacon that gave me such a thirst, the Bonamy delicatessen, the Trémolo restaurant, the Cercle Cinémane, a Sunday at Villejuif, an identity check in the rue de Douai, a Saturday at Andernach and days to come, as civilians, in Paris.

all my affection,
françois

Enclosed 7 photos of the dark days.

1 – Truffaut is imitating Charlie Chan's manner of speaking. (The effect is rather more perceptible in the French *merci* . . . *grandement.*)

2 – By Sam Wood (1935).

To Robert Lachenay

[12 November 1951]
Andernach, Friday

Dear old Robert,

I received your note and it has taken a great weight off my mind.

What never fails to surprise me in you is this combination of cold rationality and will-power with a sort of casualness, or recklessness, following some major upheaval.

You would greatly benefit from reading Sartre and you would often recognize yourself in those writings of his in which he extols rationality, unemotional intelligence, the triumph of the will, the permanent responsibility of man towards his actions, etc.

So it's very distressing that you and I should flare up in this way; the fact that an imbecile like Gérald is shocked is of no consequence, but when it's someone as nice and intelligent as Bazin, it's irksome, especially if you knew how well I'd spoken of you to him and how strongly I put it to him that he should try and help you out.

It would give me immense pleasure if you were to write him a note of apology, I know how painful it would be for you, but from the Christian point of view it's that very discomfort that constitutes both the punishment and the absolution. Obviously, that's just a theory, it won't be difficult and there's no need to write at length, especially since I've told him what little importance he should attach to the matter and that, if he knew you, he would not have taken offence.

I'd be very curious to know what you're reading and what you've bought. Why the devil are you depressed? Is it because, now that you've been discharged, your childhood is dead and buried? because another rotten life is beginning, so much more uncertain than the last? If that's the case, of course I understand, but would you prefer to be in Gérald's shoes or Bielher's?

Therefore rise up and walk! Make your way to some noisy café on the place Clichy and write me a long letter, go to the Cinémathèque one day and spend an evening with Rivette.

They're saying that half the French forces in Germany will be discharged on 15 January.

yours,
françois

P.S. That writing-paper of yours that also serves as an envelope is an excellent discipline for writing short letters, but, I beg you, make an exception in my case and tell me everything in detail. What about the photographs? *Opéra*? If only you had a few newspapers to send me . . .

To Robert Lachenay

[December 1951]
Koblenz

Dear old Robert,

Very touched by the present; Balzac is marvellous; *Les Comédiens sans le savoir* is marvellous. I hope you're buying the whole set. I recommend *Ursule Mirouet*, which is wonderful, and also *La Duchesse de Langeais*, a novel structured around an appointment missed by 10 minutes.

I'll soon be sending you a parcel of books and newspapers. I have to pay 700 francs for the water-bottle, you don't have it at your place? It would be less expensive.

Just one blow after another:

1. I haven't been discharged;

2. while I was pretending to be crazy (without success) at the lunatic asylum, a posting to Paris arrived for me, as journalist-reporter in the press office of the 46th Co. army service corps GHQ at the war ministry; no one had asked for such a posting which comes from a non-military register. The officers here arranged to have the posting cancelled; bunch of bastards; nevertheless I'm going to try and get it back through Bazin and the ministry, but there's no guarantee.

Write me a long letter, for the fates really seem to be against me; needless to say, I'll be spending Christmas here.

Thanks again, see about the water-bottle, congratulations on having dropped Gérald. Jacqueline? Is it really necessary? Wouldn't it be better to remain faithful to the memory of her dress on New Year's Day 1949–1950, her pink summer dress and her presence in your armchair with the lollipops and paying no attention to the piano?

And the music?

affectionately,
françois

To Robert Lachenay

December 1951
Koblenz, Saturday

My dear old Robert,

Forgive me writing 3 days late, but the post is very irregular.

I received, first, your Balzac at Andernach, then, here, your last letter, then the day before yesterday a letter that you wrote in a café about a fortnight ago, then the one with the parcel of classics.

More problems, more misunderstandings; do you remember Marc Rucart, who used to be Minister of Justice and is now a senator and speaks at the Faubourg? I put him in the picture and he replied with a letter praising me to the skies; meanwhile, it's Poldès's 60th birthday on 2 December (ah! the famous 2 December!),[1] so I write him a letter saying in effect, 'You are the Faubourg, the Faubourg is you, you were born together and if the Faubourg is no more than thirty years old, how could I wish that you . . .' and more of the same. Well, he is so taken by the letter that he has it read aloud at a dinner by a charming, ugly, old and very intelligent woman with whom I still correspond; the letter read (and applauded, I hope!), they start talking about me and Aimée Alexandre recounts my misfortunes, Marc Rucart throws up his arms and passes the following little note across the table to the above-mentioned lady: 'I was in Koblenz a week ago and I didn't know that Truffaut was there, I would have been so pleased to see him, I would have been so pleased to tell his superiors with whom I was staying what a high opinion I have of him.'

This note was sent on to me along with Rucart's proposal to help me, I wrote off to him at once, but there was no longer any point, because, since yesterday, I know that in 2 months at most I will be DISCHARGED. Some new documents, more urgent ones, have arrived from the departmental staff at the ministry and my enlistment is going to be annulled because of INACCURATE DRAFTING OF MY PAPERS: 1. I did not confess to having syphilis; 2. there was a misunderstanding over the choice of corps; 3. I am unsuited to the colonies, etc.

Also, as far as my medical history is concerned, it's more or less over, I've had my first negative blood sample.

I've now got a cushy job, I'm in charge of the library and I sell newspapers at the club, I really can't complain. For 1 month now I haven't eaten a single time at the canteen, I eat with the Red Cross girls at the club.

In this letter I'm sending you a thousand francs which you might use to buy *Julietta* by Louise de Vilmorin (Grasset) about 350 francs, and *Le Rempart des béguines* by Françoise Mallet (20 years old), Julliard, 300F. Read them and send them on to me. If you consider it a stupid way to use the money (which wasn't exactly stolen, here everyone semi-officially helps himself), do what you please with it if you need it for yourself.

I have Louise de Vilmorin's *Madame de . . .*; I'll send it to you.

In the next few days I'll send you some newspapers and 2 days after that some books; as for the water-bottle, I've found one, I now have my complete pack.

I landed a week in the guardhouse, I'll have done it by Wednesday, then I think I'll be sleeping out of barracks, as there's a nice, level-headed German girl at the club, Laura, who seems to have taken a fancy to me.

What about the girl next to you at table?

Don't send me anything else except the Fayard Balzacs, if you have any; on that note I have to leave you in the hope of hearing from you soon; I expect to be a civilian by February.

yours,
françois

By Balzac: *La Princesse de Cadignan*[2] and *Les Comédiens sans le savoir* are marvellous. Prévert: *Spectacle* – weak, very weak – 2 good sketches: 'With the family' and 'Clear for action', only the 1st could be performed in the army, maybe at Christmas . . .

1 – Truffaut is alluding to Napoleon III's *coup d'état* on 2 December 1851.

2 – Correctly, *Les Secrets de la princesse de Cadignan.*

To Robert Lachenay

Koblenz
Christmas, 25 December [1951]

My dear old Robert,

First things first: Merry Christmas, then Happy New Year, and finally, you treat me like dirt: you write to me at the André-Curtillet hospital! which I left a month ago! Haven't you been getting my letters from Koblenz? Did you receive the 1,000F? The parcels of books (at least one parcel of books containing *La Maison Nucingen*)[1] and one or more parcels of newspapers? My guess is that your letters to me, once they're written, are left lying about on the table for 1 week, then for as long again in your pocket; it's getting on my nerves, it's like two deaf men trying to communicate with one another (René Clair[2] – *Drôle de drame*[3] – *Un chapeau de paille d'Italie*.) 'The deaf,' said Cocteau, 'are more unfortunate than the blind.' You must know by now that I'm going to be in the guardhouse for a good while if Rucart doesn't intercede and Bazin fails; they (the Bazins) are darlings. Last night, 24 December, I received a telegram at 11 o'clock: 'Keep your spirits up – we're working on your behalf – Merry Christmas – affectionately – Janine – André.' Delighted to know you're reading Balzac. Have you forgotten my books? Or else send me the cash, as I'm broke.

A few recent thoughts: 'Gun holsters are of no importance',[4] 'That work is well done does not excuse the fact that it is work' and 'Women weep externally and men internally'. I'm also writing verse, alexandrines, often erotic, invariably about women.

With my letter I enclose an article by Sacha Guitry that you'll enjoy.

Write to me and this time by return of post so that there's no misunderstanding.

affectionately,
françois

François Truffaut
B.S.III
S.P.73.307
B.P.M. 515

1 – By Balzac.
2 – French director (1898–1981): *Entr'acte*, *Un chapeau de paille d'Italie*, *Sous les toits de Paris*, *Le Million*, *A nous la liberté*, *I Married a Witch*, etc.
3 – By Marcel Carné (1937).
4 – This prodigiously unwitty aphorism has rather more point in the original French, where Truffaut puns untranslatably on *tirer* (meaning 'to shoot') and *tirer à conséquence* (meaning 'to be of importance').

1952

To Robert Lachenay

[1st January 1952]
Koblenz

Dear old Robert,

I received your 2 letters together and this time I'm replying to them point by point; I haven't received a letter from you in which the name of Geneviève was so much as mentioned. No, since she sent me a letter in August lambasting me, I haven't replied to her. So what did you write on the envelope addressed to Jacqueline?

The best biog. of Balzac? What a question, for me it's always been all or nothing, especially where Balzac is concerned.

The 2 volumes of the *Vie de Balzac* by André Billy published by Albin Michel (I think) are interesting but insufficient; René Benjamin's *Balzac* is excellent but also, for other reasons, insufficient (in the Nelson collection and perhaps elsewhere as well); Claude Mauriac's *Aimer Balzac* is absolutely useless.

But there must exist something better for the Balzac 'specialist': Marcel Bouteron, Pierre Descaves, etc. In my opinion, my humble opinion, one should first have bought and read all of Balzac including the plays, etc. and one should even, before the biographies, have Balzac's *Correspondence* (at least 4 or 5 volumes), the letters to Zulma, Carraud, etc.

As regards the cinema, the same strategy, it would seem to me more interesting to buy the 20 issues of *La Revue du cinéma* (3,600F from Gallimard, but I can have them for 2,400), then there's the Brasillach, but only if you buy the 1946 edition updated by Bardèche rather than the pre-war one. Shorter, less biased, more complete: Sadoul's *L'Histoire du cinéma* (from Flammarion, 560 francs), best of all would be to wait for me, since I can lend you Bazin's books and you can compare; there you have it; do not under any pretext buy the Lapierre.

Today, New Year's Day – good news: the psychiatrist from Andernach was less of a bastard than I thought. Though he realizes that I am fully responsible for my actions, he concludes his report by saying that discharge would be desirable both from the army's point of view and mine, that my temperament, etc. Since, on FRIDAY THE 3RD, I appear before a board to decide whether I should be, as suggested by my regiment, temporarily discharged for physical and moral inaptitude – the question to be re-examined when the class to which I belong is recalled (in April 1952) – I have a 95 per cent chance of being discharged, and therefore in Paris by 12 January. I won't have to stay in prison because, in the meantime, Marc Rucart, senator and former minister, has interceded with General Noiret[1] (Guillaume's successor) and needless to say, tomorrow or the day after, the sentence will be mysteriously cancelled; it's in the bag; and that, my dear old Robert, is where you come in (hmm!): can you, on receipt of this letter, rush to the post office and deposit there, in my name and address, a parcel containing a shirt, a pair of trousers, a jacket or a windcheater – anything at all, provided it's CIVILIAN?

If it slips your mind, I'll be forced to ask my commanding officer's permission to leave in my uniform and hand it in when I get to Paris, but put yourself in my place, it's no fun having that awful travelling kit, and my prestige (!) in the eyes of my mates here is diminished, since, if I leave in civilian clothes, discharged, me, Truffaut the deserter, then the army, and more particularly the 32 RA, is made to look ridiculous, whereas if I leave in uniform, they won't believe it's true; it's not for me but against the army that I'm doing it, since, from now on, compared to me, Prévert[2] will seem like a regular noncom, a real old army pro.

What I'm trying to say is that, if you don't send me these clothes, it's not a matter of life and death, but in a sense they're indispensable. Can I rely on you for 9 or 10 January?

The 1,000 francs will serve for the postage. The shirt is less important; I have a roll-neck sweater – but the trousers and a jacket – thank you.

Yours, this time it's a cinch,

françois

1 – Commander-in-Chief of the French Forces in Germany.

2 – Jacques Prévert was famously anti-militarist.

To Robert Lachenay

[2 April 1952]

Dear old friend,

I can't make head or tail of your express letter; am I to understand that, having acted yet again on the spur of the moment, you told the landlord to go to hell?

1952

RENTE 3½%

A CAPITAL GARANTI

DE L'OR QUI RAPPORTE.....

'Dear old friend,

no paper on me – I'm going to the Post Office – enclosed 500F. don't invest it in the Pinay loan . . .

see you soon
yours
Truff

PS. I've unearthed a simple camp bed.'

If so, don't expect either thanks or congratulations from me; we had, as I recall, made provision for the arrears in rent and I was ready to pay up to 10,000 francs, and it would have been worth it.

Well, we'll speak of it further; it can't be helped if the damage is done – I'll try with Genet. Saturday is impossible; Rivette is coming to spend the day at Bry.

I'll see you Friday evening or drop you a line.

yours,
françois

To Robert Lachenay *[19 April 1952]*

Dear friend,

I didn't have a penny when I received your express letter; you must have borrowed from your G.M.[1] or someone else? I can't think of anything to tell you as I'm so fed up with everything. It's one of those days, more and more frequent, when I feel like ending it all. It won't happen this time, but I am more or less convinced that I won't be capable of holding out till the end of the year and what makes me think so is that I contemplate suicide with an extraordinary serenity – I will kill myself out of nonchalance, just letting myself go, the way I let myself go to sleep in the cinema with the great satisfaction of knowing that one could rouse oneself if 'one wished', but that one might just as well not.

Perhaps I'm ill or mad or neurasthenic, what do I know?

It's almost certain that Florent[2] has tuberculosis; he's at La Rochelle; we are all very down, write to me.

yours,
françois

1 – Grandmother.

2 – André Bazin's son.

1954

To Maurice Bessy[1] *[5 August 1954]*

Dear Monsieur,

[. . .] I would like to take this opportunity to thank you for having given me a job at *Cinémonde* and for having not yet sacked me in spite of the lengthy periods of absence that I arrogated to myself. No, I have not left *Cinémonde*, otherwise I would have given official notice. It has happened simply that I have been involved with several time-consuming activities (long articles – tape-recorded interviews – 16 mm films).

Unless you have any objection, I plan to come and see Michel Aubriant[2] in the next few days to ask him if he would be kind enough to consider keeping me at the disposal of the magazine.

My work at *Cinémonde* has been extremely beneficial to me. Everyone at *Cahiers* is agreed that I have made quite perceptible progress in my writing, which as far as I am concerned is due to the apprenticeship I have served in your establishment.

In the hope that you will find no reason to doubt my good faith, I beg to remain, dear Monsieur,

Yours sincerely,
François Truffaut

1 – French film critic and journalist, born in 1910, he was editor of *Cinémonde* for several years and director of the Cannes Film Festival from 1972 to 1977.

2 – French film critic and journalist, born in 1919.

To Robert Lachenay *[November 1954]* *Metz, Friday*

Old friend,

I learned by chance (and by Rivette) that your factory . . . I wanted to send you an express letter and then I left abruptly; I return Tuesday afternoon. I'll repay your 5,000F next week. We'll have to think of something.

In any case, you can always depend on me, even when I've reimbursed you in full. For Ophüls,[1] it's done. So everything is all right. Don't worry.

'bye, love, your pal,

françois

1 – See note 1, p. 82.

To Eric Rohmer

[November 1954]

Dear friend,

The people who run your hotel are swindlers; I telephoned in vain on Saturday, no one answered, ditto this morning. I saw Rossellini[1] on Saturday evening; so I added two brief questions and two long verbatim answers; you can check them later at the same time as we put in the titles.

Tonight at 8 p.m., 9, rue Christophe-Colombe, at Gaumont, there's a screening of *Joan of Arc at the Stake*.[2] Come alone please, the auditorium is tiny and Rossellini doesn't want lots of people.

till tonight, yours,

Truffaut

P.S. Wednesday 9 a.m., at the Cinéma d'Essai, *O'Kazan* (a Japanese film).[3] The same day at 2.30, Warner Bros. 5, avenue Vélasquez: *To Have and Have Not*.[4] 'Bye.

1 – Roberto Rossellini (1906–77), Italian director, father of the school known as neo-realism: *Roma Città aperta*, *Paisà*, *Germania Anno Zero*, *L'Amore*, *Viaggio in Italia*, *Il Generale della Rovere*, *La Prise de pouvoir par Louis XIV*, etc. He was much admired by the 'young Turks' of *Cahiers du cinéma*.

2 – Rossellini's *Giovanna d'Arco al Rogo*.

3 – Correctly, *Okasan* (*Mother*) by Mikio Naruse (1952).

4 – By Howard Hawks (1944).

To Eric Rohmer

[1954]

from Paris, Thursday evening,

You old son of a bitch,

Dear bastard, con-man friend, jerk of a brother, I would have you know that I've got a thousand bones to pick with you, to begin with, with . . . you'll soon find out. Let me tell you that I'm offering you the chance to redeem yourself; you have to lend me at once – and bring it yourself to *Cahiers* –

everything in that hideaway of yours that bears the slightest resemblance to film equipment: lamps, reflectors, wires, celluloid, money, etc.

So stop being such a pain in the arse and ring me pronto, here at *Cahiers*, tomorrow if possible or else you'll be hearing from me.

they all turn on their smiles for you here, but I won't be alone in despising you if you turn out to be incapable of doing your friends and acolytes a favour,

Ave, and hoping to hear from you soon,

truffaut

Les écrivains qui sont venus au dialogue de films ont observé les mêmes impératifs de la bassesse. Anouilh, entre les dialogues des Dégourdis de la 11 ème heure et Un Caprice de Caroline Chérie a introduit dans des films plus ambitieux son univers que baigne une âpreté de bazar, compromis permanent entre la noirceur de pacotille d'un Salacrou et la fantaisie de Giraudoux, sans oublier en toile de fond les brumes nordiques transposées en Bretagne (Pattes blanches) Jean Ferry, écrivain plus estimable, a sacrifié à la mode, lui aussi, et les dialogues de Manon eussent tout aussi bien pu être signés d'Aurenche et Bost: "Il me croit vierge, et dans le civil, il est professeur de psychologie!", et ceci, abject : "les femmes, elle se couchent toutes, il suffit d'avoir un bon matelas" (il tâte son portefeuille)

le blasphème a sa place dans Manon mais, c'est plus normal de la part de Jean Ferry, écrivain surréaliste. Michel Auclair et Cécile Aubry circulent dans l'église, elle, se mirant dans le bénitier, conversant dans le confessionnal etc....

Notons que cette forme de cinéma étant du cinéma de scénariste, la plus part du temps, tout demeure à l'état d'intention; rien ne vient se ficher sur l'écran et les audaces de ce cinéma qui se veut audacieux, ne sont qu'audaces de bandes sonores, ainsi dans Manon quand Michel Auclair crache à la figure de Cécile Aubry, il ne crache pas, on entend le bruit du crachat mais on ne le voit pas. Impuissance du metteur en scène à suivre son scénariste dans les voies merveilleuses de l'infamie.

Facsimile of François Truffaut's most famous article: 'A Certain Tendency of French Cinema'.

1955

To Ralph Baum[1] *4 February 1955*

Dear Monsieur,

You drew up a contract for me as 'trainee assistant' on the film *Lola*[2] for a period of five weeks at a salary of twelve thousand francs a month.[3] Owing to the fact that the film was delayed and that a regular second assistant was being paid only nine thousand francs a week, you requested me – contrary to normal practice – to return my contract to you, which I immediately did.

I do not know what you would now propose to me if I wished to remain on the crew, but I do know that, as the location-shooting in Nice begins on the 26th of this month, you would only have need of my services for fourteen days at most. For these two weeks I would be remunerated either on the official scale for trainees and, since I have to earn my living, I would be obliged to refuse, or at a slightly higher, and therefore non-union, rate which would be likely yet again to incur the resentment of the regular second assistant(s). I am therefore of the opinion that neither arrangement would prove wholly satisfactory and in the knowledge that I am not indispensable I have come to the conclusion that things will run very much more smoothly without me. By the same post, I am writing to Monsieur Ophüls to apologize and to thank him.

To you also I apologize and I remain, dear Monsieur,

Yours faithfully,
François Truffaut

1 – German production manager, born in 1908.

2 – Max Ophüls's *Lola Montès*.

3 – Correctly, twelve thousand francs a week.

Max Ophüls[1] to François Truffaut

17.2.55

Dear Monsieur Truffaut,

I do sympathize with you.

Your decision is quite natural. Nevertheless, I sincerely regret that we will not be able to work together. The 'bureaucracy' of this profession of ours is not conducive to the kind of collaboration that we might have enjoyed. You dislike that bureaucracy and so do I. It is too 'practical' for us.

But, believe me, you were a little too impatient. I was unable to give you any of my time before filming began. I know that, in the meantime, you felt isolated from the rest of the crew. But, once I was on the set, it would have given me great pleasure to know that you were at my side and to profit from your ideas. I think that the basic problem was that you arrived too late for this film. Next time, we will have to make use of you earlier, alongside the creators rather than their assistants. I hope that this is how Monsieur Rossellini will employ you.

I wish you many things for the time you are going to spend with him. I have the feeling, without being able to explain why, that you are going to be someone of importance in the art of the cinema and that your conversion – from film criticism to film-making – will go very smoothly.

I know that I would be happy to work with you again, for I know that we have much in common.

My best wishes to you and yours.

Max Ophüls

1 – German-born director (1902–57) of German, French and American films: *Liebelei*, *La Tendre Ennemie*, *Werther*, *Letter from an Unknown Woman*, *La Ronde*, *Le Plaisir*, *Madame de . . .*, *Lola Montès*, etc.

To Jean Mambrino[1]

[1955]
Saturday

Father,

I received your letter; thank you. I find it so perceptive, so remarkable, that I ask your permission to publish it in *Cahiers*, shorn nevertheless of the little phrase concerning Bazin. I am completely in agreement with you. If I spoke of the 'excessive severity which one might disapprove of', etc., it was merely to smooth the passage. At *Arts* I am often criticized for my enthusiasm, so, in order to be as laudatory as I please, I often have to pretend . . . Likewise, in the interview with Ingrid,[2] I refrain from taking sides and I even pose a few seemingly awkward questions so that no one will think I am in collusion with her . . . These are just the little tricks that a week-in week-out journalist has to employ . . .

Your letter is very persuasive; I cannot reply to it point by point as I am not competent to do so. Basically, I am very uninformed, very uneducated (I am not proud of the fact); I just have the good fortune to be blessed with a slight sense of and love for the cinema. That's all. That aside, any attempt at analysis in greater depth goes over my poor head; Bourdaloue? haven't read a word! As I hate the fact that I am self-taught, I try to 'learn' nothing, or almost nothing; my salvation will be that I 'specialized' very early on in the cinema . . . Chabrol[3] and the gang were very appreciative of your letter.

Awaiting your 'authorization', I wish to assure you of my respect and my admiration and also of the happiness I feel at knowing you.

françois t.

1 – Mambrino, a Jesuit writer, was born in London in 1923. It was through André Bazin that he met Truffaut in 1955 and started to contribute to *Cahiers du cinéma*. He continued to keep in touch with Truffaut throughout the latter's career.

2 – Ingrid Bergman.

3 – Claude Chabrol, French director, born in 1930: *Le Beau Serge*, *Les Cousins*, *Les Bonnes Femmes*, *Landru*, *Les Biches*, *La Femme infidèle*, *Que la bête meure*, *Poulet au vinaigre*, etc.

To Eric Rohmer

Tuesday [1955]

My dear friend,

I spent a long time with Rossellini yesterday; he left again for Barcelona this evening; I described to him our screenplay on the modern church. He's extremely interested; he has asked us to write it out as soon as possible. Ring me. The best idea would be to work two or three evenings at my place or more if need be. I'm depending on you and await your call; R.R.[1] returns Saturday or Sunday and he'll be expecting a final draft on the thing; there you are,

yours,
françois

1 – Roberto Rossellini.

To Robert Lachenay *[10 August 1955]*

Dear old friend,

I offer you five thousand apologies for my gruffness when you woke me up; I'm not a morning person.

Nevertheless I can only compare your virtuous attitude to the pigheaded stubbornness of a rural policeman: rules are rules. One neither accommodates nor compromises nor adapts: the letter of the law must be respected!

I quite realize that you sharpen and refine your scruples as much as I chip away at mine and 'flirt' with them, but you should, I think, allow me to be flexible. After all I've respected – scrupulously – the repayment dates and coughed up with good grace. I know that you are thinking: <u>if I let him carry on in this way, then he will indeed carry on in this way and tomorrow he'll be playing fast and loose with the finances of 'L'Ami des Livres',[1] just as he did yesterday with my own and the day before yesterday with those of my grandmother and my mother, so let us be clear, precise and strict in order to avoid any further recurrence of the tragedy of 4 September.</u> No, you needn't worry; there are limits to my nonchalance and the friends of books are my friends as you are too.

françois

1 – The bookshop in which Lachenay briefly worked.

To Robert Lachenay *[8 September 1955]*

from Venice, Wednesday

Dear old friend,

I'm writing to you from my bed where I've been laid up since Sunday with a raging tonsillitis that's costing me fifteen thousand francs in doctors, medicines and nurses, and is causing me to miss ten films, etc. etc. Luckily I'm getting up, since the festival ends on Saturday! I'm also lucky to have Laura for a nursemaid as she's turned quite maternal for the occasion and is becoming human at last.

I feel all the more guilty about you as I don't know exactly: 1. how much dough I should send you; 2. how much I've sent you already. This also irritates me since I suppose you'll have worked things out on the assumption that I would default on my debt. Oh well . . . I think it would be best for me to give up the idea of working with R.R. before he tells me himself that he can't take me to India[1] or something like that; I'm going to try to set up some short-film deal; don't write to me, as I think I'll be in Paris on Tuesday or

Wednesday. There's a chance, however, that I'll be leaving again to spend 4 or 5 days in Tours; I hope that 'L'Ami des Livres' hasn't taken you for a ride and that Janine Lesage isn't nagging you too much to marry her;

your friend,
françois

1 – For the film *India*.

To Luc Moullet[1] *from Paris, 19 December [1955]*

Dear friend,

Neither in its tone nor its form nor its content is your article on *Les Hussards*[2] right for *Cahiers*, even though it's not uninteresting. In short, I'm returning it to you.

I'm also returning the Ulmer[3] filmography which you will have to double-space with the titles of the films underlined twice and sc, act (and not ac) underlined once. A double underline means in small caps, a single in italics. Base it on the Hitch filmography in no. 39.*

You have made very few alterations to your article on Ulmer, we'll attend to that and submit our corrections and cuts for your approval.

We have had and are still having all sorts of difficulties with 'new' contributors** who take advantage of the fact that they occasionally write for *Cahiers* to ransack the stills libraries of distribution companies and use *Cahiers*'s name indiscriminately and create havoc all over the place.

That's why your joining *Cahiers* poses the moral problems that you can imagine; I'm sure we'll come to trust you, but you will understand why we are wary; come and see me before you leave for London and immediately after.

Cordially yours,
Truffaut

*You should also note the corrections we have made on the Ulmer filmography.

**In actual fact, they are not so much contributors as cinephiles who have failed to contribute.

1 – French film critic and director, born in 1937: *Brigitte et Brigitte*, *Une aventure de Billy le Kid*, *Anatomie d'un rapport*, *La Comédie du travail*, etc.

2 – By Alex Joffé.

3 – Edgar G. Ulmer, American director of Austrian origin (1904–72): *Menschen am Sonntag* (co-directed with Robert Siodmak), *The Black Cat*, *Bluebeard*, *Ruthless*, *The Naked Dawn*, etc.

1956

To Luc Moullet *[March 1956]*

Dear friend,

Bazin, before leaving Paris, instructed me to return your articles which are definitely unsuitable for *Cahiers* despite being very much in the style of the 'new criticism'.

With great regret I also enclose the filmography of Ulmer since it would be unethical, I think, to publish it separately from your critical text.

Dear Moullet, my very best wishes.

truffaut

To Luc Moullet *[March 1956]*

My dear Moullet,

I have just this instant received your letter and I am replying immediately, as it was so very friendly and revealed a Moullet I had not suspected, full of humour, relaxed and realistic.

In effect, your articles proved difficult to publish for the reasons you mention; I should have written to you at greater length to explain how things were done here, the articles we had all had rejected, etc.

An article with which I'm still not too satisfied, 'A Certain Tendency of French Cinema', took me several months to write and five or six complete revisions.

Yes, I admit it, we were a little scared of you. First because you are as (sincerely and violently) caustic as we used to be and there's something shocking about this eternal recurrence at *Cahiers*, this eternally recurring sarcasm, and it also seemed to us that you tended to go too far in both directions (adulation and loathing).

I didn't care for your making such pronouncements in the magazine as 'Resnais is not a serious film-maker' or 'Cottafavi[1] is the greatest Italian director since R.R.', as I felt I was seeing a caricature of myself (ourselves).

To come back to my first point: it's too early yet to publish any of your articles (write much more for yourself, discipline yourself, etc.), but we would be foolish to deprive ourselves of your remarkable erudition.

For Ulmer, there will be the review of the film by Domarchi,[2] the filmography and the still, and perhaps a biographical note that you can extract from your article that I returned to you.

An excellent idea: give me Ulmer's address.

Also, in the style of your note on Aldrich[3] (*Attack*), you might give us one or two typed pages, each month, on detailed little news items.

I saw *The Naked Dawn*[4] again, I totally share your opinion,

Very sincerely,
François Truffaut

1 – Vittorio Cottafavi, Italian director, born in 1914: *La Rivolta dei Gladiatori, Le Legioni di Cleopatra, Messalina, Le Vergini di Roma, Ercole alla conquista di Atlantide, I Cento Cavalieri*, etc.
2 – See note 1, p. 458.
3 – See note 1, p. 495.
4 – By Edgar G. Ulmer (1954).

To Odette Ferry[1] — *from Paris, 12 April 1956*

Dear Madame,

I have received your note.[2] For a month now I have been getting one first name wrong after another, in *Arts* and elsewhere; that's perhaps the drawback of working at night. In the next issue I am going to itemize my last six first-name mistakes and apologize to my readers. What makes it more amusing where Daniel Mann is concerned is that I had remarked the day before to Doniol-Valcroze[3] that several of our colleagues, because of that mistake, would not fail to draw parallels with *Marty*. Obviously, when one insults people, it's better to get their names right.

I have nothing against homosexuals in general and I am a great admirer of Cocteau, Nicholas Ray,[4] James Dean, Murnau,[5] Kazan,[6] etc. (they even say that dear Alfred . . .), but what irritates me in *The Rose Tattoo* is the smug and insulting misogyny, the contempt for women, the sense in short of homosexuality rampant, gloating, self-satisfied, the lewd exhibitionism of the most squalid night-clubs on the place Blanche. The campy style that amused me in *Artists and Models*,[7] for example, this time got on my nerves, camouflaged as it was by the intimidating label of intellectualism. Tennessee Williams is certainly a very talented writer and I am told that the play was much better . . .

Perhaps I should not have got as angry as I did, but I confess that I could not resist 'putting my foot in it' by 'saying out loud what others only . . .'

That said, after my review appeared in *Arts*, a few of my superiors, here[8] and there, received telephone calls from Paramount, which I find rather annoying. I am sure that you were in no way involved, and this is confirmed by your note, but, when a film by Hitchcock opens and I write three or four favourable articles (in my own fashion, but favourable nevertheless), no one seems to feel the need to express their satisfaction.* I hope to remain as independent as possible until the day arrives when I will give up writing criticism altogether in order to make my own films, a day which I hope is not too far off.

Thank you all the same for your note and please believe, dear Madame, that I am

yours sincerely,
françois truffaut

*And quite right, too!

1 – Odette Ferry was in charge of publicity at Paramount (France) from 1946 to 1968.
2 – In his review of Daniel Mann's *The Rose Tattoo* Truffaut had confused Daniel with Delbert Mann, the director of *Marty*.
3 – Jacques Doniol-Valcroze, French critic and director (1920–89). He contributed to Jean George Auriol's *La Revue du cinéma* and was co-founder and co-editor of *Cahiers du cinéma*. His films include *L'Eau à la bouche*, *Le Coeur battant*, *La Dénonciation* and *Le Viol*.
4 – American director (1911–1979).
5 – F. W. Murnau, German director (1888–1931).
6 – Elia Kazan, American director, born in 1909. It is difficult to know exactly what Kazan's name is doing on this slightly contentious list.
7 – By Frank Tashlin (1955).
8 – At *Cahiers du cinéma*.

To Jean Mambrino *[1956]*

Dear Good Friend,

Thank you for your interesting, long and very funny letter. Thank you again for all the compliments and even the criticisms, thank you finally for the slogans that could easily take up the whole contents page.

It's no secret, or scarcely one, that Eric Rohmer is none other than Maurice Schérer, but a new model, more direct and less allusive. And since we're talking of pseudonyms, you should also know that Jean-Yves Goute is Claude Chabrol's two-and-a-half-year-old son.

I sincerely believe that you should not harbour any resentment against Rivette for his stand-offish attitude towards you, and everyone else, for that

CAHIERS
DU CINÉMA
62 • REVUE MENSUELLE DU CINÉMA • AOUT - SEPTEMBRE 1956 • 62

'. . . when a film by Hitchcock opens and I write three or four favourable articles . . .'

matter. Rivette is my best friend; what's more, I believe that, of all of us, he alone is capable, at the drop of a hat, of stepping on to a film set at eight o'clock in the morning and directing a film for three months without getting into the most awful fix. He is as much a professional as though he had made ten films already. Also, you have to admit that, along with those of Schérer, his articles are the most comprehensive and the best that have ever been published in *Cahiers*. Rivette's problem is that perhaps all he has is strength, a brain rather than a temperament; I imagine him closer to Bresson than to Renoir. But there too I may be mistaken. Rivette's ideas on the films he wants to make, *La Porte étroite*[1] (in CinemaScope, I kid you not), *Le Bal du comte d'Orgel*[2] (in Technicolor), *Le Diable au corps*[2] (faithful to the book) and *On the Marble Cliffs*[4] (with 20 billion[4]), are first-rate, they have power and depth and beauty.

All of which, in my opinion, is rather more important than your petty quibbling over words. You argued in favour of the whole gang except Rivette, now I've argued in his favour alone: that makes us quits. [. . .]

I have to leave you now, as work awaits me, and it doesn't like to be kept waiting. Simenon will be receiving *Cahiers* no. 50 and, while I'm at it, the issue on Hitch.

Write to me soon,

respectfully and very cordially yours,
françois

1 – By André Gide.
2 – By Raymond Radiguet.
3 – Ernst Jünger's *Auf den Marmorklippen*.
4 – Old francs.

To Eric Rohmer

2 May [1956]

I'm very upset that your article didn't appear in *Arts*. I received a note yesterday from Aurel,[1] but he deliberately makes no mention of it. I'm writing to him at once to tell him what I think.

Were you perhaps too contemptuous or too 'oblique' with *Marie-Antoinette*?[2] Though what a putrid film it is!

Find a moment to write to me: have you seen R.R.? What exactly happened with Aurel?

You know that I'm very fond of you and that you can count on me more than ever despite all my hustling and bustling.

yours,
françois

1 – Jean Aurel, French director, born in 1925: *14–18*, *La Bataille de France*, *De l'amour*, *Lamiel*, etc. Aurel was at the time working for *Arts*.

2 – By Jean Delannoy.

To Eric Rohmer

from Paris, 29 May 1956

You must, as quickly as possible, contact Doniol. There's twenty thousand francs in it for you. I refer obviously to La Bruyère's *Caractères*.*

Doniol will be at *Cahiers* today Wednesday from 3.30 to 5 o'clock. Then he goes to the Pagode to present *Toni*[1] (at 5.30). You can go to the Pagode as he'll be there till 7.30. In the evening, you can call Doniol, from 9 o'clock onwards, at Chabrol's, where he'll be filming very late, on MAIllot 06.68. Be serious. I'm not sure that I'll be going tonight to the debate at the Bertrand, but no doubt you'll see Aurel there.

For *Arts* write a few lines, not too many, on the debate at the Bertrand cinema and a review of the Brooks[2] which opens at the Raimu, Friday, and I'll do short pieces on *Joe Macbeth*[3] and some other films.

The piece on Ingmar isn't urgent, since I'm doing one on the Hitchcock cycle.

Yours,
Truffaut

*Reread it attentively and very quickly in order to spare Braunberger the task (and with a short film in mind).

1 – By Jean Renoir (1935).

2 – Richard Brooks's *The Last Time I Saw Paris*.

3 – By Ken Hughes.

To Eric Rohmer

[1956]

Bang, crash! As far as *Arts* is concerned, *Le Mystère Picasso*[1] was reserved for Jacques Laurent himself no less, and I knew nothing about it!

If your review is already written and it's negative – or if you can 'negativize' it – perhaps it might appear here in *Cahiers* to offset Bazin's, which is too laudatory?

If not, well then, it's a lost cause, though I suppose I could offer it to *La Parisienne*.[2]

You can therefore extend yourself on Mauriac and *Nuit et Brouillard*.[3] As for me, I'll do at least two films, so everything is working out,

Regards,
truffaut

1 – Documentary by H.-G. Clouzot.
2 – French literary journal edited by the writer François Nourissier.
3 – Alain Resnais's short documentary (*Night and Fog*).

To Eric Rohmer

from Paris, this mild Sunday 56

There is, in fact, no point in your returning on the 26th. All that's required is for me to impart my know-how to you in a few pages. As far as *Cahiers* is concerned (cropping stills and copy-editing, dealing with the printers, proof-reading and page layouts), Bitsch[1] will be of great help to you. As for *Arts*, that will perhaps be a bit more tricky, unless you can get to the printers on Monday morning about 8 o'clock as I do every week. For the 'Selection' and 'Film News' columns, you'll be able to get some assistance from Bitsch – him again – but you will have to do the 'Reviews' column yourself unless I manage, before leaving Paris, to let you have one or two minor films in advance.

I'll also be leaving you a file of stills to illustrate my Venice articles; you only have to read *Le Figaro* every morning, or *France-Soir* in the afternoon, to guess what films I'll be speaking about in my 1st article, then in the second, and so on. I'll send quite lengthy articles from Venice so that you won't have to hunt up all sorts of 'Secrets'.[2]

In short, I'm sure everything will work out. Since there was a risk of Godard's cheque becoming void (?), I thought it best to have it paid into my account and spend the amount. In the meantime I have earned some dough and, if Jean-Luc were to have the good grace to return in the next few days, I'd be able to give him his 18,000 francs. Soon it will be too late, then too soon and finally just the right time again, by virtue of those financial cycles that imitate the rhythm of the seasons as well as the alternation of sunshine and rain. The Fritz Lang[3] is marvellous, and we saw *Monika*[4] again, which we also liked very much, Rivette most of all. There you have the kind of thing that fits in perfectly with Rossellini's grandiose projects.

One has only to put your letter side by side with mine to realize what a much better typist you are. Another victory of the educated[5] over the self-taught. And if you were also to beat me on speed, well then . . . True, I use my left hand neither for eating or for working.

Gervaise is Clément's best film. I wonder what you'll think of *The Bad Seed*, a nightmarish film by Mervyn LeRoy in which a ravishing little eight-year-old girl kills three or four people in cold blood.

Write to me soon, yours,

françois

1 – Charles Bitsch was a critic on *Cahiers du cinéma* in the fifties, an assistant to Godard in the sixties (on *Les Carabiniers*, *Le Mépris*, *Deux ou Trois Choses que je sais d'elle* and *La Chinoise*) and the director of two short films and one feature, *Le Dernier Homme* (1967–9).

2 – The magazine's gossip column.

3 – *While the City Sleeps*.

4 – Ingmar Bergman's *Summer with Monika* (1953).

5 – Rohmer, who wrote his doctoral thesis on Murnau, would continue to teach film even after he himself had become a director.

To Luc Moullet

from Paris, this mild Sunday 1956

My dear Moullet,

Yesterday I posted you a few *Hollywood Reporters* which should enable you to send us some Hollywood gossip before 26 August, the date of my departure for Venice. You are right about Boetticher,[1] it's easy to make mistakes if one isn't a specialist, but I do think you overrate him; if he had been a more talented director, *The Killer Is Loose* would have been a better film. We'll have to wait for *The Magnificent Matador*. After your letter, I reread Domarchi's article on Ulmer and I don't think that what you feared has happened. Perhaps it was you who made a gaffe in one of your letters? After an exchange of mutually flattering letters, Fritz Lang abruptly ceased corresponding with me, perhaps because I spoke too highly of *The Blue Gardenia*.

You mustn't think that I always judge films through my colleagues' eyes; Kyrou,[2] Labarthe[3] or anyone else. I dislike *Cela s'appelle l'aurore*[4] because it's badly acted: that's all there is to it. I like *Gervaise* because Maria Schell[5] makes me cry and *Monika* because it's the film every director ought to make when he's twenty. As for entrusting you with the review of a Buñuel film: agreed, provided you convince Doniol that you can do it. It won't be possible with *La Mort en ce jardin*, but as for *Archibaldo*,[6] if, as I suppose, you've already seen it, I commission you to do it in advance or at the very least to start working on it. (Personally I very much like *Archibaldo*.) *Elena*[7] won't be at Venice, but there will be *La Traversée de Paris*,[8] *Gervaise*, *Bus Stop*,[9] *Bigger Than Life*,[10] *Attack*, *Moby Dick*,[11] etc.

I suggest you send a little note of congratulations to Monsieur and

Madame Jacques Doniol-Valcroze, 41 rue de Douai, Paris (9e) on the birth of their son: Laurent. Because of this birth and the fact that the secretary is on holiday, I can't send you what we owe you: you'll get it when you return and, if need be, we'll lend you some money in Venice.

In no. 62, for which we did the page-setting ourselves and which, to all intents and purposes, represents a new Hitch issue without anyone having intended it to be, there will be, by you, some notes on the English Hitchcocks, some cinema gossip (a lot), the review of the Hungarian film and also of *Private Hell 36*.[12]

If you had stayed in Paris, you would have reviewed the Boetticher and the one about to come out (*The Magnificent Matador*) and also an amusing Allan Dwan (*Slightly Scarlet*, etc.), instead of which you'll be helping us cover the Venice Festival. Unfortunately, I haven't seen the two films by Stevens[13] that you mention; I know that Rivette likes *Something to Live For*.

I therefore expect to receive, before I leave, various things from you and if possible a well-documented article of three or four pages on De Mille.[14]

If, as may well happen in the autumn, I'm put in charge of the cinema section of a new right-wing weekly, a rival to *L'Express*, I'll ask you to help me and that way you'll earn a bit of money.

Regards,
François Truffaut

P.S. Thanks for the etymology of Redortiers-sur-Calavon.[15]

1 – Budd Boetticher, American director, born in 1916: *The Bullfighter and the Lady*, *Horizons West*, *Seven Men From Now*, *The Tall T*, *Ride Lonesome*, *The Rise and Fall of Legs Diamond*, etc.
2 – Adonis (known as Ado) Kyrou, French critic of Greek origin, born in 1923.
3 – André S. Labarthe, French film critic and director of television programmes on the cinema.
4 – By Luis Buñuel.
5 – Austrian actress, born in 1926: *The Heart of the Matter*, *Die letzte Brücke*, *Napoléon*, *Le Notti bianche*, *Une vie*, *The Brothers Karamazov*, *The Hanging Tree*, *Nineteen Nineteen*, etc.
6 – Buñuel's *Ensayo de un Crimen* (*The Criminal Life of Archibaldo de la Cruz*).
7 – Jean Renoir's *Elena et les Hommes*.
8 – By Claude Autant-Lara.
9 – By Joshua Logan.
10 – By Nicholas Ray.
11 – By John Huston.
12 – By Don Siegel.
13 – George Stevens, American director (1904–75).
14 – Cecil B. De Mille, American director (1881–1959).
15 – The region of the Basses-Alpes where Moullet was on holiday.

To Charles Bitsch *Venice, [September] 1956*

My dear old Charles,

I think the best thing would be to have nothing on Venice in this issue. It's very hard to obtain stills, Doniol does nothing but sun himself, Bazin does what he can on the jury, Domarchi runs around picking up nymphets, Moullet just laughs nervously. As for me, I've actually got lots of work for *Arts*.

We might, for example, simply reserve one page for the official prize-list followed by the personal choices of Doniol, Bazin, Truffaut, Bessy, Moullet, Lotte,[1] Salachas,[2] Moskowitz,[3] Chauvet,[4] Favalelli[5] and the like. Actually, all the films are good and deserve to be written about.

In my first article for *Arts* I'll be speaking about *Bigger Than Life*, *Toro*,[6] *The Ogre of Athens*,[7] *La Garnison immortelle* and *The Burmese Harp*.[8] If you go to the printers, make sure it's the least good stills that are eliminated, those of the last two films on the above list.

I hope that Schérer is hard at it. Bazin would like to be sent, as quickly as possible, either Domarchi's typed copy (to bring a moderating influence to it) or else the proofs (to make a few minor Sadoulian[9] cuts).

As regards the Dreyer[10] retrospective, there's only the collection from the Langlois[11] Cinémathèque plus a few dumb documentaries.

Which reminds me, Batala[12] is in fine fettle; his mating dances remain stubbornly platonic.[13]

Nuit et Brouillard is being bought, sold and exchanged like chewing-gum during the Liberation. D— and L— are getting fat and prosperous; their leftovers are selling like hot cakes.

Write to me at the Villa Laguna – Lido, or as before at box no. 412 in the press room.

love (to the men) and kisses (to the women).

françounnet

1 – See note 1, p. 131.
2 – Gilbert Salachas, French film critic and publisher.
3 – Gene Moskowitz, American film critic and journalist, for many years *Variety*'s 'Mosk'.
4 – Louis Chauvet, for many years the film critic of *Le Figaro*.
5 – Max Favalelli, French journalist and writer.
6 – By Carlos Velo.
7 – Nikos Koundouros's *Drakos*.
8 – By Kon Ichikawa.
9 – Georges Sadoul (1904–67) was perhaps the most influential French film critic and historian prior to the Bazin 'generation'.
10 – Carl Dreyer, Danish director (1889–1968): *La Passion de Jeanne d'Arc*, *Vampyr*, *Dies Irae*, *Ordet*, *Gertrud*, etc.
11 – See note 1, p. 442.
12 – The character played by Jules Berry in Renoir's *Le Crime de M. Lange* (1936) and used here as a nickname for the producer Pierre Braunberger.

13 – Notwithstanding Truffaut's remarks about the strictly 'platonic' nature of his overtures to him, two years later Braunberger would produce *Histoire d'eau*, a short film by Truffaut and Godard.

To Charles Bitsch

Venice, [September] 1956

My dear Charles,

My article for *Arts* is interminable (ten typed pages). I hope that Boussac will put two or three of them on the front page so that it won't be necessary to cut. I'm very pleased with my prose and I rely on you to protect it from the vandals with their red pencils.

All you have to do is reduce the number of stills, keep the news items brief, move them down level with the listings (which can always be thinned out as well) and publish only one still, from *Bigger Than Life*, for example.

By the same post, I'm writing to Boussac to recommend that he set my piece in small type and wait for you to get to the printers before letting his big fat many-fingered hands tinker with all of that.

regards, françois

P.S. It will help the page if you get to the printers before half-past ten.

To Charles Bitsch

Venice, Monday, [September] 1956

Dear Friend,

Received your note. Demonsablon[1] gets on our nerves and Domarchi is furious with him. Make it very clear to him: 1. that, now that the article on *The Man With the Golden Arm*[2] has been broken up, we're not sufficiently keen on it to have it reset; 2. that we already regret publishing the glossary, which was far too long; and 3. that given we accept only one article in five from Moullet, Siclier[3] and Labarthe, one in ten would be the correct proportion as far as he's concerned. Finally, refuse categorically to let him review *Scarlet*,[4] because he's a pain in the neck. Damn these demonsablative reviews that bore us to death!

Bazin is going to read *Le Fer dans la plaie* tomorrow and, as soon as he has, I'll return the article to you, much improved, I'm sure, since I happen to think that Bazin is right.

Thank you for taking care of *Arts*. I'm very impatient to see the issue, on Friday . . . Because of me, the last one was really bad, except for the review of *L'Olympia* which I read two days later and had completely forgotten!

We're having a lot of fun, much more than last year. Domarchi is in love with a tall, dried-up cow a little like Janine Lesage: Mademoiselle Nave. She glowers at him, while he endeavours to amuse her by sighing oh yes, oh yes! But she doesn't reply okai, okai![5] Hegel is now an open book to me.

Bigger Than Life wasn't an earth-shattering experience for anyone, and we even saw quite a few people shamelessly dozing. Very badly received. They should have put *Bus Stop* in the competition and invited Nick Ray or left him at home! Mason is a creep who's never heard of anyone called Ray;[6] he's very pleased with himself.

Until you've seen Braunberger cavorting about the beach in bathing-trunks, you haven't seen anything. But Pierrot is enthusiastic about my various scripts and seems to want to work with me. I speak very badly of *Le Coup du berger*[7] and very highly of *La Bruyère*,[8] that may help.

By the same post I am sending you two stills from *Gervaise*; if Schérer does the review in *Arts* this week, all you have to do is run the still of Schell over three columns and for my own article the one of Micheline Luccioni[9] (tell Schérer he has to say something nice about her). If the review isn't in this week, you'll have to publish the 2 stills or in any event the one of Micheline.

I'm going to try and see *Et Dieu créa la femme*[10] before the censors do, since it appears that . . . there will probably be a private screening here. It is, in any case, the most talked-about of the French films.

As for my article for next week, I'll send it or bring it with me on Monday, I'm not sure which. It also depends on Rossellini who arrives here on Thursday. Big Robert[11] is playing hard to get; he's no longer sure he'll be able to come.

I sunbathe next to Carlo Rim,[12] but we pretend we don't know one another which is sometimes amusing given that people try to introduce us three times a day, and we've got to make believe we didn't quite catch the name . . . Crazy!

As far as the Ray is concerned, on second viewing, it's definitely better than *Rebel*[13] because of the screenplay and the dialogue, which are extraordinary; obviously some of the scenes are a bit daft, but it's a great film about Robert, his first filmed biography.

For *Arts*, the stills that are essential? Jack Palance[14] over 2 or 3 columns (you'll find it at *Arts*), *Gervaise* and *Bus Stop*.

Love: to you, schérer, jacques, jeanclaude, marcorelles[15] (who is not a homosexual), claude, siclier, agnès (lots of love) and absolutely not demonsablob.

very affectionately,
françois

1 – Philippe Demonsablon, a critic on *Cahiers du cinéma*.
2 – By Otto Preminger.
3 – See note 1, letter dated late January 1979, p. 489.
4 – *Slightly Scarlet*.
5 – Truffaut's spelling.
6 – James Mason was both the producer and star of *Bigger Than Life*.
7 – An early short film by Rivette, which Truffaut in fact greatly admired.
8 – Jacques Doniol-Valcroze's short film *Bonjour Monsieur La Bruyère* was produced by Braunberger.
9 – French actress, born in 1925: *Édouard et Caroline*, *Rue de l'Estrapade*, etc.
10 – By Roger Vadim.
11 – Aldrich.
12 – French director and screenwriter, born in 1905: (as director) *L'Armoire volante*, *La Maison Bonnadieu*, *Virgile*, etc. His name is correctly spelt Carlo-Rim.
13 – Nicholas Ray's *Rebel without a Cause*.
14 – The star of *Attack*.
15 – Louis Marcorelles, French film critic and journalist.

To Charles Bitsch

September 1956
from Venice, Monday,

My dear Charles,

Instead of returning to Paris, I'm off to Rome. In an emergency, you can write care of Rossellini at Santa Marinella (Rome), Italy.

For *Arts*, you and Schérer continue to do the reviews, etc. In the next few days I'll be sending directly to *Arts* an article on 'Venice, Rome, Cinecittà . . .' 6 typed pages. Please see to the illustrations: head and shoulders of Clément, head and shoulders of Aldrich, and of Autant-Lara,[1] Aurenche and Bost.[2]

I'll be speaking about all sorts of things: the hilarious press conferences of Clément and Autant-Lara, my encounter on the beach with Aldrich, *Bus Stop* and what's happening in Rome, Anne Vernon's[3] intelligence, etc.

So there it is as far as *Arts* is concerned; have Schérer write the review of *Elena* leaving me the possibility of doing a 'secret'[4] after I've seen the film.

For *Cahiers*, here are the individual awards; enclosed in the file that the very sweet Madeleine Morgenstern[5] has just brought you, you'll find all the credits and a few stills; you'll also find the Aldrich file.

You may announce in 'Private Diary': 'After the screening of *Attack* at the Venice Festival, François Truffaut, on the beach of the Lido, put 60 questions to Robert Aldrich. The result of this convivial interview in our next issue.'

With the enclosed documents, you will be able to put together a good biography as well as a complete filmog. Also, you will have to get a scene from *The Big Knife* (the signing of the contract) translated into French. That will make for a spread on Aldrich: interview – *Big Knife* – filmography – the Italian reviews of *Attack*.

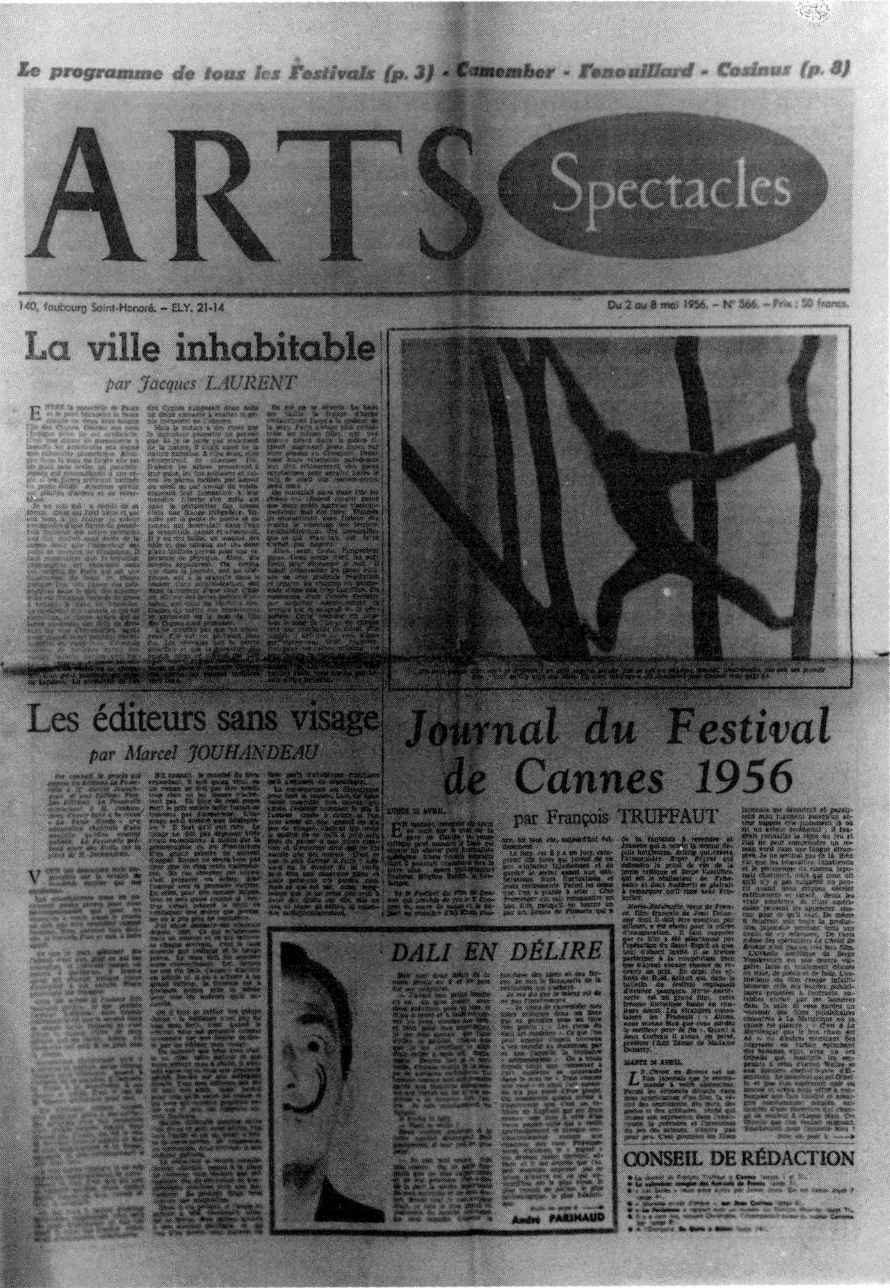

Le programme de tous les Festivals (p. 3) · Camember · Fenouillard · Cosinus (p. 8)

ARTS Spectacles

140, faubourg Saint-Honoré. – ELY. 21-14

Du 2 au 8 mai 1956. – N° 566. – Prix : 50 francs.

La ville inhabitable

par Jacques LAURENT

Les éditeurs sans visage

par Marcel JOUHANDEAU

Journal du Festival de Cannes 1956

par François TRUFFAUT

DALI EN DÉLIRE

André PARINAUD

CONSEIL DE RÉDACTION

Arts sends its special correspondent on the festival round . . .

I'm thinking of returning to Paris on the 18th or the 20th; I'm in a rush, a longer letter will follow.

best to everyone,
françois

P.S. Domarchi was magnificent and won everyone over including Anne Vernon. As for big Bob, I think it will be a good interview; four types of questions: 1. biographical; 2. film by film; 3. general comments on Hollywood,[6] etc. Plus 8 snap judgements on Brooks,[7] Hitch, Hawks, Fuller,[8] Mankiewicz, Lang, Ray, Ford, etc.

1 – Claude Autant-Lara, French director, born in 1903: *Fric-Frac* (co-directed with Maurice Lehmann), *Le Mariage de Chiffon*, *Douce*, *Sylvie et le Fantôme*, *Le Diable au corps*, *La Traversée de Paris*, etc.
2 – Jean Aurenche and Pierre Bost were screenwriters who often worked in tandem, most notably for Autant-Lara.
3 – French actress, born in 1925: *Édouard et Caroline*, *Rue de l'Estrapade*, *Les Parapluies de Cherbourg*, etc.
4 – See note 2, p. 93.
5 – Madeleine Morgenstern and Truffaut were married on 29 October of the following year.
6 – The schema prefigures that of the future volume of interviews with Hitchcock.
7 – Richard Brooks, American director, born in 1912.
8 – Samuel Fuller, American director, born in 1911.

To Charles Bitsch

[September 1956]
from Santa Marinella, Wednesday

My dear Charles,

I received your telegram this morning. The fact is that, pressed for time, I explained myself badly in the letter that Madeleine brought you. Sorry about the errors I'm making on this very dotty Swedish typewriter: no accents, no semi-colon, no apostrophe, and all sorts of useless signs: ú ú à % =& ^ ¨. To be honest, my mind is hardly on *Cahiers* here, in this antechamber to the Californian Eden. In short, no appendix for Domarchi, he'll have to go without!* As for the individual awards that Doniol lost, Janine Bazin has redone them after a fashion and no doubt you've got them already. Aside from sunning myself and warning the children that they'll be spanked if they don't 'go beddy-byes', I'm working on: 1. my article for *Arts*; 2. the wonderful interview with big Bob; 3. the memoirs of R.R.; 4. some ideas for films.

I hope that you are busy locating and getting someone to translate, or translating yourself, the scene from *The Big Knife*. It will also be necessary, after studying the Aldrich file, to pay a visit to United Artists.

For Christmas, I propose quite seriously the theme: 'Acting, the Mysterious Art'. With articles by Ophüls, Renoir, etc., questionnaires sent to directors and articles by actors: Anne Vernon, Stroheim. Something on Dean, some quotes and some terrific stills. I would personally write an article on 'How film-makers regard women'. There you have an issue that might be very popular, very good and win us some new readers. I'm thinking of returning to the fold at the end of this week or the beginning of next. I suppose that you're all working like Trojans, for *Arts* and for *Cahiers*, except Jacques who is taking things easy as usual. Rossellini is very enthusiastic about *Bus Stop* and explained three hundred marvellous details to me that I hadn't understood. For him, Logan is an American Rossellini and better than Ray. I'm so comfortable here that I haven't got the energy to go to Rome in search of Mireille Granelli![1] My first flight: I came from Venice by plane and you should tell Claude that he is right about *The High and the Mighty*:[2] it's a sublime film, no more, no less.

best to everyone,
françois

*Domarchi's article has had its appendix out!

Have Schérer type a carbon of his review of *Elena* for *Arts* and send the copy to me here by express letter. R.R. is very keen to read it.[3] Thanks.

P.S. I dined in Venice with Vadim[4] and tried to sell him on J.-C.,[5] without success alas. 'He's photogenic, but not right for us.'

1 – French actress of the fifties.
2 – By William Wellman (1954).
3 – Rossellini took a close interest in the critical reception accorded to films starring his wife Ingrid Bergman, the leading actress of Renoir's *Elena et les Hommes*.
4 – Roger Vadim, French director, born in 1928: *Et Dieu créa la femme*, *Sait-on jamais?*, *Les Liaisons dangereuses*, *Et mourir de plaisir*, *Le Vice et la Vertu*, *Barbarella*, etc.
5 – Jean-Claude Brialy, French actor and director, born in 1933: (as actor) *Le Beau Serge*, *Les Cousins*, *Paris nous appartient*, *Une femme est une femme*, *La Mariée était en noir*, *Inspecteur Lavardin*, etc.

To Eric Rohmer *[late 1956]*

Here is what it's all about: I can't deliver my usual article to *La Parisienne*. Nourissier has no objection to your replacing me.

You therefore have to deliver to him, by six o'clock tomorrow evening, a piece on the good films this year that have been undeservedly neglected, that haven't been too successful or haven't been talked about enough: *Amore*, *Fear*, *Lifeboat*, *The Night of the Hunter*, *The Saga of Anatahan*, *Nuit et*

Brouillard, *The Big Knife*, *Senso*, *The Trouble With Harry*, *Mr Arkadin*, *The Man with the Golden Arm*, *Smiles of a Summer Night*,[1] and, note well, as Nourissier thinks highly of it: *La Pointe courte*.[2] (The titles underlined are of films which haven't been covered at all by *La Parisienne*. The others were written about favourably but only in three or four lines each.)

1 – Respectively by Rossellini, Rossellini, Hitchcock, Charles Laughton, Sternberg, Resnais, Aldrich, Visconti, Hitchcock, Welles, Preminger and Bergman.

2 – By Agnès Varda.

1957

To Maurice Pons[1] *from Paris, 4 April 1957*

Dear friend,

Denise gave me your address but not your telephone number. I reread *Virginales* and I realized that the story entitled *Les Mistons* was perfectly suited to the film about which I spoke to you. If you are agreed, I would like to discuss the adaptation with you and explain to you how I envisage setting up the production from a financial point of view; rather than pin my hopes on the goodwill of some producer, I am going to try and film in a few weeks one of the seven or eight stories I have collected and then obtain the means whereby I might go on to film the others.[2]

If you telephone me quickly, I will take you to see, before Tuesday, a film by Ophüls, *Le Plaisir*, an exemplary adaptation, in my opinion, of three stories by Maupassant: *Le Masque*, *La Maison Tellier* and *Le Modèle*. And then I will describe or get you to read the other stories.

I believe that yours would be the most convincing from various points of view.

My private address is the Hôtel Royal-Montmartre – 68, boulevard de Clichy – Paris (18) MONmartre 22-91, but I can also be reached during the day here at *Cahiers*: ELY: 05-38.

very cordially yours,
truffaut

1 – French writer, author of the collection of short stories, *Virginales*, which includes *Les Mistons*.

2 – As Pons notes, Truffaut's proposal was, for the period, truly revolutionary and represented the true beginning of the New Wave.

To Robert Lachenay

Wednesday [1957]

My dear Robert,

I would like to leave my hotel before Sunday in order to go off for a few days to Noirmoutiers and free myself from the ball-and-chain of my financial problems. Then I'll be staying in the Palais-Royal at Charles's place until I leave for Cannes (1 May).

In July I'll be filming one of my sketches, entirely in the country, near a small town, maybe Andeville? Unfortunately, I am very broke and don't dare ask you how well off you are; if, however, by turning your pockets inside out, you were to find ten thousand francs going to waste, they would help me to observe the formalities of my departure, or should I say, my flight!

The essential problem is that of my books: are you willing, yet again, to store my library in your flat, the bookcase and all the books, until I find a flat of my own, which is to say, until I get married?

It's important that we get together as soon as possible to arrange having them moved: Saturday and Sunday; we might hire a new Jo from the rue Lepic whom we'd load up like a donkey and get rid of, once the job was done, by shoving him over the banisters of your stairway . . .

I hope you'll come and make the film with me instead of roaming the highways of Europe in the company of Largemains.

Ring me any hour of the night at my place or, after you get off work, here at *Cahiers*, the sooner the better;

yours, yours, yours, yours,
françois

To Charles Bitsch

[6 May 1957[
Monday, from Cannes, noon

My dear old Charles,

Thank you for your excellent letter; by the same post I'm sending some stills to you at *Cahiers*. For *Arts*, I would prefer you to use those from the good films: *Le Condamné*[1] (next week), *The Bachelor Party*,[2] *The House of the Angel*;[3] I'm beginning systematically to miss a few films: haven't seen *The Forty-First*,[4] haven't seen the Bulgarian film.

I'll be speaking essentially about *The Bachelor Party*, *The House of the Angel* (100% influenced by Astruc, *Le Risi cramoiseau*)[5] and *Guendalina*.[6]

Here is Cocteau's reply:[7]

1. Out of a need for a visual language.

2. It is not the cinematograph[8] which disappointed me, it is what prevents it from being free.

3. Poetry without the hint of a poetic style or of a poetic language.

4. It is often in short films that I detect the talents of the future (in those of Resnais and Franju, for example).

5. After *Orphée*, it is possible that I will cease to make films, unless I am ordered to (the only kind of order that matters, that which is issued by one's inner self).

And Carbonnaux's's[9] reply:

1. Landed up rather than arrived. Extenuating military circumstances.

2. Disappointed by its percentage of satisfied customers.

3. Absolutely nothing. If the thing were to happen, I rely on you to inform me of the fact.

4. Chaplin, René Clair, Tati and Fellini are a few of the hardest to forget.

5. No entry to under-sixteens. Direction Côte d'Azur.

There you are. Survey at an end.

I have a dreadful toothache, yet I'm going to write my long article before going to see the dentist; as regards this article, Parinaud[10] will just have to put up with it: I'm starting it in half an hour (it's 1 p.m.), I'll finish it, if the inspiration flows (a typed page-and-a-half an hour), tomorrow, Tuesday, at about 3 p.m.

Either I dictate it over the telephone to the exquisite Nisou on Tuesday evening or Wednesday morning, or I send it to you by post and you'll have it for Wednesday evening, which I'm sure will be time enough. That's it as far as *Arts* is concerned; and quite enough, too.

Jacques is a swine with regard to Ophüls (tell Jacques that Blain[11] is going to ring him when he returns to Paris in a few days, but make sure he doesn't speak to Blain about his wife;[12] she's delighted to be acting in *Les Mistons*, but he would prefer that she learn how to cook; for the moment *Les Mistons* is therefore a sort of exception; that said . . .

It's not very hot here, there's a lot of wind; the Chabrols are in good form, everything is going more or less well;

thanks again for everything (don't forget to shorten the caption to the photo of Agnès Laurent).

yours, yours, yours,
françois

P.S. Jean-Claude brille au lit, sins, grumbles and gives out autographs to their boobs.[13] I forgot to tell you that Nîmes is very nice and so is the countryside.

1 – Bresson's *Un condamné à mort s'est échappé*.
2 – By Delbert Mann.
3 – Leopoldo Torre Nilsson's *La Casa del Angel*.
4 – By Yakov Protazanov.
5 – Alexandre Astruc's *Le Rideau cramoisi* spoonerized.
6 – By Alberto Lattuada.
7 – To a survey on the cinema.
8 – Cocteau always referred to the cinema as 'le cinématographe'.
9 – Norbert Carbonnaux, French director, born in 1918: *Les Corsaires du bois de Boulogne*, *Courte Tête*, *Candide*, etc.
10 – André Parinaud, the director of *Arts*.
11 – Gérard Blain, French actor and director, born in 1930: (as actor) *Avant le déluge*, *Le Beau Serge*, *Les Cousins*, *Il Gobbo*, *The American Friend*, etc.
12 – The actress Bernadette Lafont, who was married to Gérard Blain.
13 – Truffaut is punning on *brille au lit* (which might be translated as 'is good in bed') and Brialy. Whatever allusions he is making in the rest of this obscure sentence are now beyond any hope of retrieval.

To Robert Lachenay

from Paris, Wednesday [1957]

Dear old friend,

Obviously you're surprised not to have heard from me, but as Bitsch gave you my address and telephone number: 61, rue de Grenelle, LITtré 04-18, I thought you would call me; for my part, I'm not too sure whether you're living at home or in the rue de Trévise.

I hope you're still free to come with us to Nîmes from 15 to 30 July; everything seems to be going well and my hopes are high.

I ought to relieve you of some of my books and belongings, but for that we'll have to get together.

You can call me; I'm very often at home and, in any event, there's always someone to take a message; we might see each other Saturday afternoon or Sunday.

yours,
françois

P.S. My wedding: November, this year.

To Charles Bitsch

[August 1957]
from Nîmes, Sunday
7 o'clock in the morning

My dear Charles,

Thank you for having forwarded the letters to me and for your letter as well; I've sent a telegram to Keigel's son[1] and another to Nick Ray (congratulations on Venice and get-well-soon for his syphilis). I've been here for 13 days, but we've only really managed to shoot 3 days and 4 half-days. Why? The variable weather, laziness, Provençal inertia and all that. On the other hand, I've been lucky enough, by sometimes sleeping over at Malige's[2] place in Montpellier, to put together a rough-cut as I go along, eliminating the bad takes and looking out for errors in continuity.

I'm shooting very quickly, sometimes without rehearsing, very often in a single take, occasionally two. This is (for me) the best method, since I can only see things clearly during the rushes and I'm free to start again and redo a scene three days later. It's going to be a very uneven film with terrible weaknesses and also some bizarre lucky breaks; by taking advantage of a real train in a little station in Montpellier, I shot 6 minutes of film (3 2-minute takes) in 20 minutes (between the train's arrival and its departure). Gérard left for real, Bernadette returned towards the camera crying her eyes out: cut!

That said, Gérard is, I think, very unhappy; he wasn't at the Actors Studious[3] for nothing and he's none too pleased to find Clément Duhour[4] when he was expecting Kazan; he bellyaches because I prefer Bernadette in high heels (he has a Toulouse-Lautrec complex) and because I have a tendency to place the camera too low rather than too high (which causes his nose to disappear). And then he's come to realize that Bernadette is completely at home in front of the camera and he makes a scene every day: 'If you make Chabrol's film I'll leave you, etc.' It has to be said that he finds it awkward filming with her, but so does she. He leaves Nîmes today and things will improve; it's a blessing I'm going to take advantage of by doing or redoing all sorts of things with her. Madeleine[5] arrives at noon, for two days.

The sore point is the photography. Malige has no taste, he's very finicky and works as though he were trying to win a prize; his lighting is an eternal compromise between what he likes (*Crin blanc*)[6] and what I like (*Le Coup du berger*). There again, the result is uneven, very good when the sky is overcast and I say, 'Too bad, we'll shoot anyway' (the station) and very weak when the sun beats down (the tennis court) and he takes advantage of my back being turned to try out the 'craziest' new little American filter. A curious film, in fact, a curious twenty minutes and a curious atmosphere.

That said, Malige is very nice and very well equipped. Best of all is

Bernadette; after every take, the refrain is 'Brigitte Bardot just won't know what has hit her!'

Claude II,[7] Robert[8] and Alain[9] could not be more co-operative and hard-working . . . The kids, who were chosen too quickly and on appearance alone, are uneven. Three out of five are very good.

The only film I've seen here, in the amphitheatre, was *En effeuillant la marguerite*,[10] which was so awful that it had us down in the dumps for 24 hours; the next day, the first screening of the rushes was very bad from nearly every point of view; the cinema was dreadful and another screening in a better cinema was much better and on the editing-table as well. But yesterday's rushes (street scenes, the blind man, the station, a tracking shot in a 2CV[11] of Bernadette and Gérard) are far more exciting.

I've decided I won't return to Paris until I have a rough cut with which I'm satisfied; that's why it will be quite some time before I leave the area. Here is my schedule: Gérard leaves this afternoon. Throughout the week I'll film things with Bernadette alone or Bernadette and the kids; I dismiss my crew (the 3 thieves) on Friday and leave for Malige's place in Montpellier to spend ten days (2 or 3 of them with Cécile[12] who is coming down) doing the editing (gratis). Gérard does his TV play on the 27th and returns here the following day; for 5 or 6 days, with him and B.B.,[13] I'll shoot the missing scenes (the cinema interior, the beginning and end of the 'big scene', a few street shots) and reshoot some others that are a little weak at the moment (in the amphitheatre).

In theory, therefore, I'll be returning to Paris around 6 or 7 September with a sturdy little film in rough-cut, ready to tackle the sound effects and the dubbing (very difficult), but all of that will be done under excellent conditions thanks to C.T.M.[14] which, in return for a 100,000F advance, is granting me credit for 7 or 8 months; that's why I feel like humming 'No, Pierrot,[15] you won't have my flower!'

In the street, chalked up on a wall, there was 'Vote for Poujade',[16] we didn't care for it and replaced it with 'Vote for Rivette'. Add to that homages to Louis Lumière, Jean Vigo, Hulot, John Ford, Dario Moreno[17] and Rossellini and you'll have some idea of the kind of unusual film this will be! . . .

Despite the tone of my letter, I'm not so very pleased with myself, though pleased not to be, since I can see very clearly (during the rushes) what isn't working and that's how I hope to be able to save the invalid that a film becomes from the 2nd day of shooting.

I hope you're all well and catching up on your sleep at Ermenonville. Has *Les Gigolos*[18] been 'registered'?[19] I haven't managed to speak to Lesaffre[20] who rang here 3 times without reaching me – why, do you know?

Obviously, Jacques may read my letter and in a few days I'll be submitting some stills of the film to his divinatory perspicacity; I'm pretty sure Gérard is going to 'bitch', but that's normal and to be expected.

Love to all, for you're the very best and I'm off to meet Cerise[21] at Nîmes station;

yours, yours, yours,
françois

P.S. *Arts* has become the least of my worries. A very good page this week; don't forget Laurel and Hardy; I would like Momo[22] to let his hair down a bit at Venice where he'll catch some nice little films. It wouldn't be a bad idea, when I return, to have your watch[23] appear before a medical board; let's hope it won't be definitively discharged! Don't fail to speak pejoratively of *Les Mistons* in order to help the pendulum swing in the opposite direction! Thanks.

1 – Léonard Keigel, a future director (*Léviathan*, etc.) and the son of the most important shareholder in *Cahiers du cinéma*.
2 – Jean Malige, the cinematographer of *Les Mistons*.
3 – In the original French, *l'Actors Studieux*.
4 – A little self-mockery on Truffaut's part: Clément Duhour was the producer of Sacha Guitry's last film, *Les Trois font la paire*, and he replaced Guitry as director when the latter fell ill during the shoot. Guitry had, in fact, died only a month before Truffaut wrote this letter.
5 – Madeleine Morgenstern.
6 – By Albert Lamorisse (1952).
7 – Claude de Givray, one of Truffaut's two assistants on the film, called Claude II to distinguish him from Chabrol.
8 – Robert Lachenay, production manager.
9 – Alain Jeannel, the other assistant.
10 – By Marc Allégret, with Brigitte Bardot.
11 – A French car, the Citroën Deux-Chevaux.
12 – Cécile Decugis, the film's editor.
13 – Bernadette (Lafont) Blain.
14 – A film laboratory.
15 – Pierre Braunberger.
16 – Pierre Poujade, the French populist demagogue.
17 – Spanish singer and (very occasional) actor, popular in the fifties: *La Femme et le Pantin*, *O que mambo*, etc.
18 – A screenplay by Charles Bitsch: it was never filmed.
19 – At the Society of Authors.
20 – Roland Lesaffre, French actor, born in 1927. From *Juliette ou la Clé des songes* onwards, he appeared in every one of Marcel Carné's films.
21 – Madeleine Morgenstern's nickname.
22 – Eric Rohmer's nickname.
23 – Bitsch had lent his watch to Truffaut.

To Charles Bitsch

from Montpellier,
Friday late August 57

Dear Carolus,

Thank you for your long and very witty letter; but, as the song says, I'd like to know more; you don't tell me if Domarchi is in Paris, if Rohmer is still

François Truffaut, Bernadette Lafont, Gérard Blain: filming *Les Mistons*.

leaving for Venice with or without the young bride, if the Doniols are on holiday and how the forthcoming issues of *Cahiers* are coming along.

I've only now begun to understand how the kids should have been directed and there's such a difference between what I was getting from them in the final days and what I got at the beginning of the shoot that I've completely got my confidence back; in spite of everything, it would be better to have no more than one in each of the sketches; one thing I'm certain of is that, where the kids are concerned, the soundtrack of *Les Mistons* will be simply extraordinary. When Gérard returns, I'll finish with him and Bernadette, then I'll treat myself to three extra days with just the kids. I filmed them tearing up a poster of *Chiens perdus*[1] and humming 'Colliers perdus sans clebs, tra la la, la la la, la la', to the film's theme song. Yesterday, taking advantage of Gérard's absence, I reshot all Bernadette's close-ups in the big scene by cutting after each phrase; since the opportunity arose, we shot 60 metres of film of a praying mantis killing a male and swallowing it: as I was directing operations with a twig that will be visible in the frame, I'll match it up with Bernadette grimacing in disgust and Gérard gloating sadistically; Painlevé[2] will be jealous and Bazin delighted; as for big Momo, he will cite the great Murnau of *Nosferatu*.

As for those who'll be directing Gérard in the future, I wish them joy; like Raimu, who wouldn't allow anyone to say 'merde' to him on the screen, Gérard refuses to wear a rucksack because James Dean wouldn't have, etc. I recognize nevertheless that I often sacrificed him to Bernadette, who is absolutely his opposite: she's better on the first take without any rehearsal, she's stimulated by the indications I give her once the camera is running, etc. Gérard's taste runs more to chalk marks on the ground, being timed to within an inch of his life, etc.

But I really can't complain about a shoot that was almost scandalously rich in lucky breaks and infinitely more tranquil than Kast's.[3] Sweet France, mean old cow of my childhood . . .[4] I had a visit from Maurice Pons just when the shooting had finished; it cost the company sixteen thousand francs for a first-class ticket on the 'Mistral'! Nor is he (or rather, he too is) none too happy: 'What? She rides her bike barefoot? What kind of ridiculous old bike is this? I wanted it chrome-plated and brand new! Who are these little guttersnipes? They're supposed to be *Les Mistons*?' Oh Lord, oh Lord! I've changed and cut and added lots of things with regard to the version you read, but I think it's better now.

Out of the question for Claude to house his company at the same address as mine, especially as I'm going to have to change addresses since I finally decided against using the sister-in-law of the guy in question as my continuity girl. If Claude is wealthy enough[5] to raise the capital of Les Films du Carrosse[6] from 1 to 5 million,[7] we might work something out!!!

I've just telephoned Parinaud who reassured me about the mistonerious little article.[8] I saw *Attack* in a dubbed version here and this afternoon I'm going to see *Dakota Incident*,[9] which I'm told is first-rate, Malige and Delsol[10] could not be more hospitable and there's an extraordinary atmosphere at their place: Jacques Simonot, the composer of Mistinguett's songs, with his boyfriend, and especially Louis Félix[11] himself, the begetter of *Amédée*, a charming Tartarin who keeps me doubled up with laughter all day long. He's here to write the shooting script of his next dud: *L'Inventeur*,[12] from a novel by René Lefèvre with Bardinet (whom Bresson wants for Lancelot), Frank Villard, Tilda Thamar, Pauline Carton, Jean Tissier and a few others.

His shooting script is so stupid I was in stitches when he had me read it; he deduces from this that it's going to be a great comedy. Madeleine writes to me that Jean-Luc has loosened up no end since he's been earning some money at Fox.[13]

Parinaud tells me that a film page without me is like a meal without meat (sic) and wants to have a long private talk with me when I return. Meanwhile, don't let yourself be taken in by him and don't forget that he's just like Doniol, hypersensitive to the fist on the table and the outburst of anger, whether real or faked.

As soon as I've found an envelope large enough, I'll send *Cahiers* a few pretty stills from *Les Mistons*, perhaps Gérard has shown you some? I still have to shoot the cinema interior, the beginning and end of the big scene, some pick-ups[14] and reshoot certain things with the kids and five or six pin-up girls whom I'll take on for the last two days.

I strongly advise you to read *Mythologies*[15] which is an admirable book and one from which all of us who write polemical and negative articles, like you and me, can learn a great deal.

It's been raining here since this morning and they tell me that the weather in Paris is very bad; write to me again, at length and with lots of details, and soon.

Thank Jacques for his letter. I'm going to send a note of congratulations to Momo who has beaten me to it, the bastard, yet again.[16] I'll try to catch up with him by taking double mouthfuls (hmm, hmm) and being the first to give birth!

P.S. I very much hope I haven't been put in the *Conseil des 10*.[17] I absolutely don't want to be in it,[18] it's not difficult to understand. When is the next issue due to appear? Have you had any word from Bazin, his address, etc.?

If you'd like to see Robert again, write to him at 10, rue de Douai, and invite him to spend a day with you at Ermenonville. Here it was Robert that everybody (the actors, the technicians, the locals) liked best.

Enclosed is a cutting sent in by a reader of *Arts*;

yours, yours, yours,
françois

1 – Jean Delannoy's *Chiens perdus sans collier* (1955).
2 – Jean Painlevé, French director who specialized in scientific films (1902–89): *L'Hippocampe*, *Assassins d'eau douce*, etc.
3 – Pierre Kast, French critic and director (1920–84), who was making his own first film, *Un amour de poche*, at the same time as *Les Mistons*. By an eerie coincidence, Kast also died on the same day as Truffaut.
4 – Truffaut's 'Douce France, sale chipie de mon enfance . . .' is a parody of Charles Trenet's popular dance song 'Douce France, cher pays de mon enfance . . .'
5 – Chabrol had just received the inheritance that would enable him to make *Le Beau Serge*.
6 – The production company which Truffaut founded and which was to produce (or co-produce) all his films. Its name was a homage to Jean Renoir's *Le Carrosse d'or* (1953).
7 – Old francs.
8 – In Truffaut's French, *l'articulet mistonnant*: i.e. a brief article on *Les Mistons* for *Arts*.
9 – By Lewis Foster (1956).
10 – See note 1, p. 241.
11 – French director, born in 1920. The film to which Truffaut refers is *Ce Sacré Amédée* (1955).
12 – The film was never made.
13 – Godard was at that period a press agent in the Paris office of Twentieth Century-Fox.
14 – Individual shots to aid the film's continuity.
15 – Roland Barthes's collection of essays had just been published.
16 – Eric Rohmer had just married.
17 – For many years a regular feature of *Cahiers du cinéma* in which ten critics would rate current films from * to ****.
18 – Having become a film-maker himself, Truffaut no longer wished to sit in judgement on his colleagues.

To Charles Bitsch

[September 1957]

My dear Carolus,

I saw *Œil pour œil*[1] and, probably like you and Rivette, I'm still reeling. To caption the article I suggest: 'With *Œil pour œil* André Cayatte[2] and Curd Jürgens[3] extend the frontiers of the grotesque on the screen'. Ridiculous can be substituted for grotesque, but the important thing, it seems to me, is to be merciless; you've got to shred to ribbons that rancid hotch-potch with its seasoning of bluff and naïvety. Slip this phrase in somewhere: 'Fernandel[4] is paid fifty million francs a film and it's only proper that Curd Jürgens should receive twice as much since he's twice as funny.'[5] When talking of Jürgens's performance don't fail to mention those of Pierre Blanchar[6] and Victor Francen[7] before the war and add that today 'there's virtually no one but our dear Antoine Balpétré who would dare to act in this fashion with his mouth twisted sideways and his leering eyes popping out of his head.'

'I have not seen *Bitter Victory*, but I know that Nicholas Ray was intelligent enough to cast him as a mournful cretin, the only kind of character he is fit to play. Vadim already realized that . . .'

1 – By André Cayatte.
2 – French director, born in 1909: *Au Bonheur des Dames, Les Amants de Vérone, Justice est faite, Nous sommes tous des assassins, Avant le déluge, Le Passage du Rhin*, etc.
3 – Curd (or Curt) Jürgens, German-born actor (1912–82): *Des teufels General, Les Héros sont fatigués, Et Dieu créa la femme, Michel Strogoff, The Enemy Below, The Inn of the Sixth Happiness, Lord Jim*, etc.
4 – French comic actor (1903–71): *Angèle, Un Carnet de bal, Regain, Le Schpountz, Fric-Frac, Topaze*, etc.
5 – This letter illustrates the influence Truffaut had on his friends, even on the articles they were writing.
6 – French actor (1892–1963): *L'Atlantide, Mélo, Crime et Châtiment, L'Homme de nulle part, Un Carnet de bal, La Symphonie pastorale*, etc.
7 – Belgian-born actor of French and American films (1888–1977): *Mélo, J'Accuse, La Fin du jour, Hold Back the Dawn, Tales of Manhattan, Madame Curie, The Mask of Dimitrios*, etc.

To Maurice Pons *from Paris, 2 October 1957*

Dear Friend,

Enclosed is a photograph: the father of *Les Mistons* surrounded by his children. I am unable to go and see Vasco[1] this evening, as Renoir has invited me to the dress rehearsal of *The Big Knife*.[2] But that doesn't mean to say I will not see the Jean-Louis Barrault production . . .

If I didn't contact you during the re-shoot of *Les Mistons*, it was because: 1. the shoot had to be wrapped up as economically as possible; I am deeply in debt; 2. the variable weather made it difficult to be sure of anything; 3. you would have found it very painful watching me at work, which, I should add, is quite natural.

I have now finished editing and started the sound-mixing; as far as the commentary is concerned, I would like us to work together to preserve your tone; nevertheless I am very afraid of showing you *Les Mistons*, since I am aware that I have not been faithful to your story; moreover, you are unaccustomed to seeing films in an incomplete form, which is an extremely demoralizing experience, even for professionals.

That said, I will show you the film before the 17th of this month, which is to say, before my wedding.[3] Prior to that, I would like you to consent to a little experiment. To illustrate the passage of the story that I like best ('In truth, we meant no harm, we were merely tormented by that childhood frenzy . . . frustration when confronted with love . . . which they do not understand and which haunts them . . .'), I have filmed about ten shots of girls in the street (walking), in the countryside (dancing), a kiss exchanged in a doorway with one of the urchins looking on, a poster of a pin-up girl with a sign: 'No admittance to under-sixteens', an obscene gesture, etc. I would like you, before seeing this section, to write two or three new sentences to follow on from 'we meant no harm, etc.' by developing the same idea. Here are the key words, or ideas, which might appear in succession in these two or three sentences:

a) kiss; b) pursuit (the idea of a chase or the word pursuit taken in its abstract sense: for example, the pursuit of love); c) hips or bearing or rump; d) convey, in a few words, the idea that the child laughs at love to conceal his own desire, that it's nothing but swagger; e) the word curiosity; f) the word walls in the abstract sense; for example, the wall one constructs around one's private life; giving the idea of movement, itinerary, awakening of desire; g) a young woman kissing a little child; h) the word censure (indispensable), the word rage or a synonym, the idea of impotence, the fist, the arm; i) impossible kisses.

I assure you I am not mad, merely persuaded that things can be safely left to chance (especially if one gives it a helping hand) and that these sentences, written by you in the abstract, will fit better than any which the images might suggest to you; not only does the film that I have shot not correspond to your style but it even contradicts it. Why so? Quite simply because my sensibility is at opposite extremes from yours and it is impossible to create something – a film, a novel, etc. – that does not absolutely resemble oneself. Reading *Les Mistons*, I was struck by about thirty images; I recognize them, but you will not recognize them. I can easily guess how painful it must be to feel that one has been adapted, which is to say, betrayed; I say all that to temper your disappointment when you see the film!

In any event, please accept my gratitude and my friendship,

F. Truffaut

1 – Georges Schéhadé's play *Histoire de Vasco*, which Pons had invited Truffaut to see.

2 – Jean Renoir directed Clifford Odets's play in the theatre.

3 – Truffaut and Madeleine Morgenstern were in fact married on the 29th.

To Maurice Pons *from Paris, 15 December 1957*

My dear Pons,

For my film to comply with the rules of the C.N.C. (Centre national du cinéma), it will be necessary for you to write me as soon as possible a letter (dated in the conventional fashion) in which you confirm that you agree to a short film being made of *Les Mistons* and bearing the same title, that you also agree to the terms of the contract as signed by me at Julliard concerning the purchase of the rights (and of which you should have a copy).

In effect, a contract between the publisher and the director is not valid for the 'Centre' unless the author's signature has been appended. This formality will allow me to compete for the 'quality subsidy' for shorts which will be decided in August 1958.

Given the problems I would have if I tried to continue, I am resigned to leaving *Les Mistons* as a short. It seems to me now that I ought to have entered it at Tours;[1] I regret that I missed seeing you before I left the Midi . . . I am happy that you do not seem disappointed by my 'illustration' of your work; as soon as I have sold *Les Mistons*, in January I hope, I will send you the percentage as agreed in the Julliard contract (which I don't have in front of me as I write).

Regards,
truffaut

1 – There was, at that time, an annual festival of short films at Tours.

To Charles Bitsch *from Paris, 31 December 1957*

My dear Charles,

Thank you for your best wishes; we naturally send you ours. I doubt if I can come and see you *because*[1] snow, and also work.

As you know, I'm going to shoot *Temps chaud*[2] in ten weeks in the Midi with the same crew as *Les Mistons* – possibly you as well? – and it will be a Pléiade–Carrosse co-production alternating between *Isabelle a peur des hommes*[3] and *Le Silence de la mer*,[4] in other words between the porn movie that is immediately snapped up in Belgium and Argentina and the respectable, ambitious, I say, good heavens, this is really something, sort of work that will be up for a *quality*[1] subsidy, no less, you get the picture.

For Pierrot,[5] it will be an ultra-'And God Created Woman in Black and White', for me a new *Diary of a Chambermaid*,[6] deliriously baroque in style.

Braunberger thinks it will be pretty to look at and tragic, I hope it will be harrowing and farcical, in short, we understand each other perfectly, as always.

Flaud[7] liked *Les Mistons* a lot as did Paul Graetz[8] who sent for me to propose that I work with Jean Aurenche on a screenplay about children . . . I put *Le Beau Serge*[9] top of the list of the ten best films of 1958, just ahead of *Temps chaud*!

I saw the finished version of *Charlotte et Véronique*;[10] it's terrific, even the interiors, even Nicole Berger.

In theory, the cast of *Temps chaud* will include J.-C. Brialy, Nicole Berger, Michèle Cordoue and the young fifteen-year-old promising newcomer whom I have yet to find.

I'm sure you have *very, very*[1] work, but, if you were to find the time to do a little work on re-editing the music of *Les Mistons* (did you take the reels with you?), that would be terrific.

Cheray,[11] who is on the short-film jury this year, detests *Les Mistons*, so we're off to a good start . . .

I leave for Montpellier next week to have a talk with Malige and go location-hunting with him for *Temps chaud*, a little house beside the sea, etc.

I took advantage of a lengthy bout of flu to read the script of *Le Beau Serge* which I thought was first-rate and so did Peggy (Peggy is Mado).[12]

To all of you we send our love and best wishes, write to me if you can, yours yours yours yours yours yours yours yours yours yours yours yours.

francesco

1 – In English in the original letter.
2 – This project was later abandoned.
3 – By Jean Gourguet.
4 – By Jean-Pierre Melville (1949).
5 – Pierre Braunberger.
6 – By Jean Renoir (1946).
7 – Jacques Flaud, director of the Centre National de la Cinématographie.
8 – French producer (1899–1966).
9 – The film about to be made by Claude Chabrol.
10 – A short film by Jean-Luc Godard; its more familiar title is *Tous les Garçons s'appellent Patrick*.
11 – Jean-Louis Cheray, manager of the Studio Parnasse cinema in Paris.
12 – And Mado was Madeleine Truffaut.

To Robert Lachenay *[December 1957]*
from Paris, Monday morning

Dear old friend,

I received your letter this morning just as, precisely, I was thinking of writing to you to inform you of a screening of *Les Mistons*, Wednesday evening at 7.00 on the dot, at Filmax, a little screening-room in the Ermitage building.

A few days ago I received an official producer's card in your name and for Les Films du Carrosse, a card I can entrust to you with a thousand recommendations; ideally, you might come to rue Saint-Ferdinand on Wednesday morning, about 9.30 or 10 o'clock, with, if you wish, a few belongings, files, boxes, who knows, a few books? We'd then go together to the Crédit Lyonnais, since I need your signature to open the bank account in the company's name; I already have one in my own name.

OK, I'll pay you back the five thousand francs and even help you make ends meet until the next shoot, which will be end of January, beginning of February. In a bookshop in your neighbourhood you'll certainly find Jacques Cousseau's *Temps chaud*, published by Corréa. That, in theory, will be our first feature film.

There would be no point in registering a screenplay on La Fayette, as it's not a new idea; there's already been a project by Sacha Guitry and also one by Gance;[1] neither of them ever came to anything . . .

If you have nothing to do on Wednesday afternoon, you could do *Cahiers* a great favour by helping Lydie, Maya and big Momo remove piles of the magazine from the rue du Trianon and put them in a car; they would like that . . . For ten days now Chabrol has been in the Creuse making his first feature on peasant life: *Le Beau Serge*.

I highly recommend a new American film: *Fear Strikes Out*.[2]

Yes, I'd like to come and visit my godson one of these days, yours,

françois

1 – See note 1, letter dated 20 October 1979, p. 500.

2 – By Robert Mulligan.

1958

To Robert Lachenay *[January 1958]*
from Paris, Thursday

Dear old Robert,

Our address is 27, rue Saint-Ferdinand, stairway D, 6th floor to the left as you come out of the lift. The telephone number is ÉTOile 81–89.

I almost always work there in the morning and I'd very much like to see you. Tomorrow morning, for example . . . Ring me and come with a few files. Also, I have to get you to sign certain papers for Films du Carrosse.[1] In the meantime, I am screening *Les Mistons*, absolutely finished, Tuesday evening about 6.00, on the Champs-Élysées. I hope you'll be able to come with whoever you like, the auditorium is very large and I'd like to fill it so as to have a better atmosphere.

Rivette, Rohmer, Godard, Doniol, Bazin, etc. like the film enormously, and I've also come to like it again, nearly all of it. The music is terrific, you'll see. A few days later, the film will be shown out of competition at Tours to two thousand people. I'm obviously very excited since the time is coming when I'll know what the immediate future holds for me: more sketches, a feature film or who can say? You might come and see me a bit more often, dammit, at *Cahiers* in the evening, here whenever you please. Madeleine is very fond of you and we are comfortably settled in. I'm counting on you to ring me very soon either here or in the afternoon at *Cahiers*.

yours yours yours yours yours yours yours yours yours yours yours,

françois

1 – When Truffaut became a director he did not drop Lachenay, who was the production manager on *Les Mistons*, then a partner in, and manager of, Les Films du Carrosse. He was the inspiration for the character of René Bigey in *Les Quatre Cents Coups*, assisted Claude de Givray on *Tire-au-flanc* and directed two medium-length films of his own: *Le Scarabée d'or* and *Morella*.

To Robert Lachenay *from Paris, 30 April 1958*

Dear old friend,

Enclosed is the ticket for the Pagode.[1] Have a nice evening. You found my note, I believe.

If you want to write to me, I'll be in Cannes at the Hôtel Suisse.

yours,
françois

P.S. Note down ideas, memories for Antoine's[2] running away. Dig out our letters, Villejuif, etc.

1 – A Parisian cinema.
2 – Antoine Doinel, the hero of *Les Quatre Cents Coups*.

To Marcel Moussy[1] *from Paris, Saturday 7 June 1958*

Dear friend,

This morning I received the package containing the proofs.[2] Thank you. I read the first story in one go: 'Henri Montel . . .' Fascinating; very close to what I'd like to achieve with *La Fugue d'Antoine* (working title) in which the point of view will tend to be that of the children (the parents being more stylized and the children more subtle). I wonder who will play the twelve-year-old Jean-Claude Montel on TV; the same actor?

What you'll find enclosed is the beginning of my film,[3] the first quarter of an hour, since there are going to be lots of things happening and it's going to go very quickly, like *Les Mistons*, but with quieter moments nevertheless. So that it gets off to an even stronger start, I think I'll give up the idea of the discovery of Antoine's illegitimacy and substitute something else: while playing truant, Antoine runs into his mother with a young guy, her lover. Since she spots him and doesn't say a word, the kid imagines a kind of complicity between them that blows up in his face at the first opportunity, which is to say, when the father comes to the school and slaps his son.

I haven't written the rest, but it's all in my head and I'd like to relate it to you in detail, if that's all right by you. After reading *Sang chaud* and your TV script, I'm convinced that you can be of immense help to this film which I'm confident I'm going to shoot in September; I know that you're a fast worker and that you have a sense of construction which I sorely lack. On the other hand, I think I really know the universe of twelve-year-old kids that I want to film. For this venture I'll be my own producer, but the screenplay has to be approved by the distributor who is none other than my father-in-law,[4] a fine, intelligent man such as one rarely encounters in his profession. On Tuesday evening I'm going to ask him to watch TV and have him read one of the three programmes whose scripts I have.

I'll see to it that, financially, your work on my film will be as well remunerated as would one of the other perhaps less interesting jobs that you'll be forced to turn down because of it; I'm impatient to know what your answer will be; I'll ring you on Wednesday morning;

very cordially yours,
Truffaut

1 – Moussy was co-adaptor and co-scenarist of *Les Quatre Cents Coups* and co-adaptor of *Tirez sur le pianiste* (*Shoot the Pianist*). Most of his subsequent work was done in television.
2 – 'These were the proofs of the published version of three TV scripts I had written.' (Note by Marcel Moussy).
3 – *Les Quatre Cents Coups*.
4 – Ignace Morgenstern, French producer and distributor (1900–61).

To Marcel Moussy

from Paris, 21 June 1958

Dear friend,

I hope that you are well and that René Clair is pleased with you; not so pleased, though, as to monopolize you for the rest of your life. I won't conceal my anxiety from you; you've understood everything about my film so clearly and so quickly that I can't imagine being deprived of your collaboration. Working on these memories, I have in a sense turned into a 'first offender'[1] again; I feel insecure and rebellious once more, overly vulnerable and completely isolated from society. It was Bazin who, ten years ago, straightened me out by becoming what you might call my guardian; talking to you, I felt at the same time guilty and rehabilitated, you are like Bazin in so many ways. Just as he helped me 'go straight' in life, you're going to help me make a film that will be more than just a whiny, complacent confession, a true film.

I've written out a thirty-page treatment which you will read when you return and which is very loosely constructed; let's just say that I've marshalled my notes in chronological order.

I still recall an introduction to René Clair by Cocteau on TV, which I liked: 'Our film-maker bears a poet's name: René Clair. René which means: reborn,[2] and Clair, which is to say: crystal-clear; look at this sign on the set of *Les Belles de nuit*:[3] "No admittance to outsiders". I got in under false

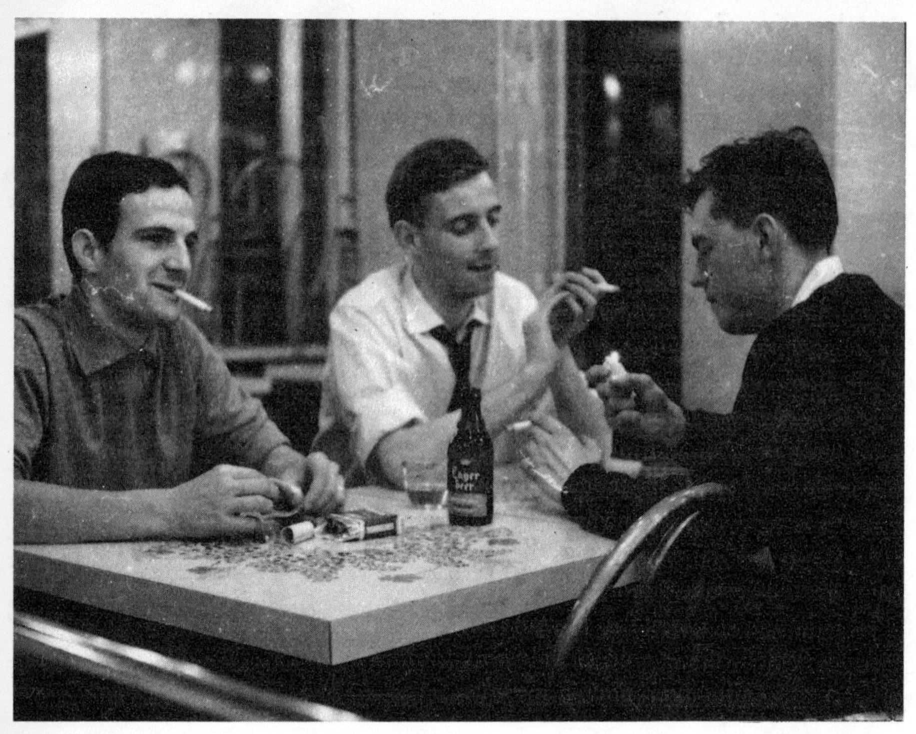

François Truffaut, Robert Lachenay and André Mrugarsky (Rivette's assistant cameraman on *Paris nous appartient*).

pretences and I invite you to follow me . . . etc.' As chance would have it, it was Bluwal[4] who directed that little scene about five years ago.

My best wishes to your wife and, for you, the devotion of your grateful admirer,

françois truffaut

1 – Cf. the letter to Lachenay, p. 13.
2 – Or *re-né*.
3 – By Clair (1952).
4 – Marcel Bluwal, French television director, born in 1925. He and Moussy had worked together.

To Marcel Moussy *from Paris, Thursday 26 June 1958*

Dear Moussy,

I can't tell you how happy your letter makes me; as soon as I received it, I turned down a short film on cancer, which is subsidized by the Dept. of Health and would have to be shot in August. We'll therefore be as free as air to work together. I've enclosed with this letter a copy of the scenario, which is still very much without a backbone. By the time you return, I will have drafted descriptive notes on the different characters, partly in order to see things more clearly myself. I admit that my strong point is making notes; I've scribbled several more pages of them.

Shooting can't start before 1 October, since my cinematographer is going to be Henri Decaë, who in France is the one I like best (*Les Enfants terribles*[1] – *Le Silence de la mer* – *Bob le flambeur*[2] – *Ascenseur à l'échafaud*[3] – *Le Beau Serge*). At the moment he is filming *Les Amants* (by Louis Malle), then *Les Cousins* (Chabrol) and won't be free till the beginning of October.

The shoot doesn't present any great difficulties, except for what takes place at the school, since I'm afraid I may have to use a playground here, a classroom there, and school gates somewhere else altogether; the enlistment of about thirty kids as extras poses a similar problem; none of that is very serious; I'm going to start right away trying to recruit the children.

8 July is a Tuesday; I'll be coming to your cocktail party, for which thank you. I hope we'll be able to start work very soon after that. My father-in-law quite likes the scenario, but he would prefer to sign the agreement after he has read the next version, which will be a little more developed, more 'dramatized', so that at the same time he can obtain the provisional authorization of the C.N.C. That said, I'll be in a position to release some money for any expenses that may arise and for the payment of advances on salary; with my father-in-law you have absolutely nothing to fear; he is just

about the only honest producer in the French cinema and, with *The Cranes are Flying*, which he bought pretty much on my advice, for peanuts, eight days before the Cannes Festival, he made the very best deal of his career.[4]

So everything is going well and roll on 8 July! My wife is expecting a child on 6 February next year, the exact date of my twenty-seventh birthday; on more or less the same day, I will have – touch wood – the master print of my film, for which, I inform you, I'm looking for a title; the ones I've thought of are too literary: 'The 400 Blows', 'The Awkward Age', 'The Four Thursdays',[5] 'The Little Pals', etc.

Thank you again, see you soon and best wishes,

françois truffaut

1 – By Jean Cocteau and Jean-Pierre Melville (1950).
2 – By Melville (1956).
3 – By Louis Malle (1958) (*Lift to the Scaffold*).
4 – Mikhail Kalatozov's film won the Palme d'Or at the 1958 Cannes Festival.
5 – From the French expression '*dans la semaine des quatre jeudis*', meaning 'when pigs begin to fly'.

To Marcel Moussy

[July 1958]
from Paris, Tuesday evening,
then Wednesday morning

Dear Moussy,

Thank you for your letter; I'm bursting with ideas that will justify the two or three things that shocked you. 1. The idea of illegitimacy has effectively been abandoned as a dramatic device, but one scene will show Antoine's mother visiting the C.O.M.D.[1] and explaining to her son the error of her youth, his father's forbearance, etc. 2. The father won't be a monster, even when he gives up his son to the police, since we'll indicate how Antoine (who went to a grammar school the previous year) finds it hard to adapt to the secondary school in which his parents have put him to prevent him from having to sit the same year twice over; the father makes frequent references to his joining the navy: 'I'll make a cabin-boy out of you yet, you'll see!' Moreover, the kid, for whom school has become purgatory, is keen to go to work, to earn his living so he can become free and independent. His father hauls him into the police station: a) because it was there that he reported the disappearance and after all the search has to be called off; b) let's not forget that it's the second time Antoine has run away. What's more, the father will be almost moving in his conversation with the police officer: 'I just can't seem to understand this kid any more, etc.' and the police officer only speaks in generalizations: 'Young people today . . .' All of that will have the atmosphere, which was just right, of your first TV programme, the one about the scooter.

You're right about the description of the school (even though it will be a very good part of the film, one of the most riveting). No doubt we have to start from there.

1. Antoine at school; things are not going well; 2. Antoine at home; things are also not going well (we have to show that one proceeds from the other and vice versa); 3. Antoine runs away for the first time; 4. Antoine at home, things are going from bad to worse, because of the lie and because of the ragging he gets at school as a result of that lie; 5. Antoine at school, also from bad to worse (because of the lie and the ragging, because of the atmosphere at home); 6. the friendship with René (Robert) who, however, informs on him (by going to his parents on his own initiative); this friendship with Robert (René), who is freer and wilder than he, leads to Antoine getting into trouble both at school and at home and so aggravates the situation. 7. Antoine runs away a second time; roaming about with Robert, at Robert's home; 8. theft of the typewriter; 9. arrest; 10. life in the institution; escape and end.

I hope the descriptive notes will be of great help to you; I can't deny your remarks are very justified and almost always correspond to an exaggerated simplification on my part of certain real events (for example: my father took me to the police station just as I have described, but I was fifteen and I had been working for a year in a grain merchant's; he collared me at a session of a film society which I had founded in the Latin Quarter and which was heavily in debt). It's therefore when mixing reality up with fiction that I make the most serious mistakes; you'll help me a great deal.

I rang up Judge Chazal, but I want to go and see him with you; it would be better; I hope you're filing everything I send you on the film, so we'll know where to find it all.

I'm forgetting the most important thing: I leave Paris tomorrow, Thursday, for Austria; it's just a short trip and I'll be back in Paris on Sunday during the day . . . I'll ring you when I arrive,

thanks again and very affectionately yours,

Truffaut

P.S. In theory, the definitive title will be *Les Quatre Cents Coups*.

1 – Centre d'Observation pour Mineurs Délinquants.

To Marcel Moussy *from Concarneau,*
Sunday 11 August 1958

Dear Moussy,

The first days of our holiday were rather depressing; set off without enthusiasm on Wednesday afternoon, slept over at Nogent-Le-Rotrou; rain and grey skies. The next day, from Nogent-Le-Rotrou to Rennes, with grey skies and rain; slept badly in bad hotels, started to miss Paris, etc. Third stage: Rennes–La Baule, the latter so depressing we didn't even stop; slept at Carnac, still rain and grey skies.

'To hell with this' we were beginning to mutter, and for two pins we'd have returned to Paris there and then. Then, just outside Concarneau, we chanced upon 'La Belle Étoile', a bourgeois paradise but a paradise nevertheless, a place of rest and meditation where you are very speedily relieved of all the cash that was weighing you down, in return for every kind of comfort and courtesy. As Madeleine, however, is still determined to 'do Brittany', we'll be leaving this quasi-Hawaiian haven to plunge ever deeper into Finistère and beyond.

Occasionally, I have a very vague memory of having quite recently produced a few pages for a film project; it was called, I believe, 'The Three Hundred Blows' or 'Five Hundred', what does it matter, the point being that you would skilfully get them into shape; if, by some miracle, or by some chance, you were to come across that little text when cataloguing your archives, I would not object in the least to your putting some flesh on our skeleton in order to make it presentable and inserting in its mouth a few of your very own 'fumetti'.[1] In any event, we'll be returning two or three days earlier than planned, which is to say, on Friday or Saturday, as I would like to see my friend Claude de Givray before his leave is up on Sunday and he sets off on *Summer Manoeuvres* that will be less bemedalled than some we know![2]

My wife embraces yours, while I shake your hand in a very manly fashion with all that such a gesture, given the circumstances, entails in gratitude and affection; and I also take this opportunity of suggesting that as soon as you've finished the dialogue we address each other as *tu*,[3] to make it easier for each of us to bawl the other out.

françois truffaut

P.S. I forgot to thank you for the article on *The Tarnished Angels*,[4] which was competent, instructive and constructive!

1 – The dialogue balloons in Italian comic strips.

2 – Truffaut is alluding to René Clair's *Les Grandes Manœuvres* (1955).

3 – The use of the more familiar form of address was to become increasingly rare in Truffaut's life.
4 – By Douglas Sirk.

To Marcel Moussy

from Paris,
Wednesday 24 Sept. 1958

My dear Marcel,

Thank you for the ending, which was as good as I expected it to be. In fact, I'll only start shooting on 3 November[1] and end on 3 January, without a break.

Rereading the script, I realize that what it lacks are actions, whether I planned them and forgot to put them in or I've only just thought of them; for example: when the kids are alone together, they rummage through the apartment and amuse themselves by dressing up . . . From now on I have to note down visual ideas, gags, etc., otherwise we'll end up with a film that we can't export because there'll be nothing but dialogue (an example: *Maxime*, by Verneuil[2] and Jeanson,[3] turned down by every foreign country; conversely: *Mon Oncle*,[4] a French-speaking American film). But we've already spoken about the scope for improvisation that I intend to give myself, though without distorting your ideas in the least.

I met Albert Rémy,[5] who is very nice and has agreed to 400,000F, which represents a maximum of twelve payments. I'm also talking things over with Colette Deréal[6] whom I will be seeing in a few days; I'm going to go to the Huchette[7] to see Cuvelier.[8]

I spent, with Madeleine, a weird Sunday at the publisher Buchet's place in Le Vésinet complete with the obligatory game of *pétanque* after lunch; there was Nadeau, Erval, Pierre Gascar, O'Brady, Cousseau[9] and I don't know who else; they were shifty, scheming, two-faced, flamboyant and boring beyond belief; the atmosphere was much more evil than the world of the cinema where there's less pretence.

Braunberger is having discussions with Buchet over the rights to *Temps chaud*: it looks certain to go ahead. I'm confident.

I'm going to buy a little car which will transport me about Paris until the spring; nothing to see at the movies.

The script will be mimeographed for 3 October, the day you return. Everything is going well, life is wonderful, regards to Yvonne from Madeleine and myself and for you all my affection and gratitude.

françois

P.S. The shooting of *Paris* . . . has been interrupted for a week because of

Betty Schneider,[10] who claimed she was ill and had to go to the country; but, in fact, she stayed on to begin rehearsing something or other with Yves Robert.[11] You might drop her a line telling her that you've heard good things about the rushes (from someone other than myself, naturliche!) . . . etc.

1 – In actual fact, Truffaut would begin shooting *Les Quatre Cents Coups* on 10 November and finish on 5 January.
2 – Henri Verneuil, French director of Armenian descent, born in 1920: *Le Mouton à cinq pattes*, *Maxime*, *La Vache et le Prisonnier*, *Un singe en hiver*, *Le Clan des Siciliens*, etc.
3 – Henri Jeanson, French screenwriter (1900–70).
4 – By Jacques Tati.
5 – The actor who would play Antoine Doinel's stepfather.
6 – The role of Antoine's mother was finally given to Claire Maurier.
7 – A Parisian theatre.
8 – An actor whom Truffaut did not use in the film.
9 – All of them literary critics or writers.
10 – The leading actress of Jacques Rivette's *Paris nous appartient*.
11 – French actor, producer and director, born in 1920: (as director) *La Guerre des boutons*, *Bébert et l'Omnibus*, *Le Grand Blond avec une chaussure noire*, *Un éléphant, ça trompe énormément*, etc.

To Marcel Moussy

late Sunday evening, 17/11/58

My dear Marcel,

The screening of all the material on Monday evening has been cancelled, since the editors have to begin chopping up the film to put the shots in chronological order. There will therefore be a good, real, interesting screening, with a provisional soundtrack, at the end of the week.

Concerning another matter, I've begun to notice that what I film in the morning or the beginning of the afternoon is better and more controlled than what I film later in the day when there are visitors; I have therefore decided not to allow any visitors until half-past six in the evening, as it bothers both the actors and the technicians. I myself feel ill at ease when people watch me working and I tend to rush things just to get them out of the way.

In the rue Marcadet it wasn't a problem given how cramped it was, but, at the Vermorels', I don't want anyone hanging about, in order to preserve the intimacy that I need; above all, the scenes with the two children have to be just right, then there's Flamand[1] and the Jollivet woman who won't be playing together but who are both very nervous.

I want you to understand; this film owes a great deal to you and I have no intention either of forgetting or concealing that fact, but the transposition to celluloid must be solitary and confidential, otherwise we'll have a film that is bland and cold, with neither tension nor warmth.

The stage hands and the electricians, the camera crew and the assistants all have a specific job to do and they aren't watching me when I speak to the kid; the feeling that I'm being watched paralyses me; what's more, I've fallen behind and it will be easier for me to catch up if there are fewer of us on the set.

If you're afraid of my changing the script, I don't mind promising to telephone you before making a drastic change to any given scene, so that we can work it out together, even though from now on it'll be more a matter of adding than of cutting.

Don't be angry with me and write,

your faithful friend,
françois

1 – Georges Flamand, who plays M. Bigey in *Les Quatre Cents Coups*.

The Truffauts and the Moussys at the Colombe d'Or.

1959

To Robert Lachenay *from Paris, 14 March [1959]*

Old fellow,

Rohmer needs the clapperboard to shoot a little film (4 days) produced by Chabrol; obviously, you'd be his assistant?

Drop by *Cahiers* any day in the late afternoon with the clapperboard; thanks.

yours,
françois

To Lotte Eisner[1] *[May 1959]*

Dear Mademoiselle Eisner,

I will probably not be in Cannes on the day of the Cecil B. De Mille screening, but *above all* I am incapable of speaking in public on a given subject.

I only know how to reply to questions. Honestly, what you ask of me is physically impossible.

This in no way lessens my affection for you, Langlois, Meery[2] and the Cinémathèque.

Forgive me and believe me when I say how very touched I am by your liking for *Les 400 Coups*.

yours sincerely,
Truffaut

1 – French film historian of German origin (1896–1983). A specialist in German Expressionism, she worked closely with Henri Langlois and was head archivist of the Cinémathèque Française from 1945 to 1975.

2 – Truffaut has contracted the name of Mary Meerson into Meery. Mary Meerson was Henri Langlois's companion for many years and continued his work at the Cinémathèque.

To Georges Franju[1]

from Paris,
Tuesday 10 August 59

My dear Franju,

Here is *Fire in the Flesh*.[2] It's just occurred to me that our telephone call this morning was rather vague, and perhaps you meant a completely different book?

This one – I don't recall having spoken about it to Aznave[3] – did tempt me for a while, then I realized I would end up making a 'Franju pastiche' with, necessarily, Charles A.[3] and Edith Scob.[4]

I'm shocked that *Les Yeux sans visage* is not going to Venice. I'm eager to see it finished: it was my only film as an 'apprentice'.

amiamiamitiés,[5]
Truffaut

1 – French director (1912–88): *Les Yeux sans visage*, *Thérèse Desqueyroux*, *Judex*, *Thomas l'imposteur*, etc. In 1936, with Henri Langlois, he co-founded the Cinémathèque Française.
2 – Novel by David Goodis about a pyromaniac. Truffaut, of course, subsequently filmed Ray Bradbury's *Fahrenheit 451*, about a fireman whose job is burning books.
3 – The singer and actor, Charles Aznavour, who had just appeared in Franju's *La Tête contre les murs*.
4 – Actress-mascot of Franju's films.
5 – Truffaut is conflating the words *ami* (friend) and *amitiés* (friendship).

To a journalist

Paris, 13 August 1959

Dear Madame,

Your letter reached me while I was on holiday and I did not reply to it immediately since I did not have at hand the issue of *Le Film français* in which you published the survey in question.

1. The four points in the 1st paragraph concerning the minimum crew correspond neither to factual reality (as far as *Les Quatre Cents Coups* is concerned) nor to my own ideas on the subject. How do you explain the similarities between Camus's[1] statement and mine: 'most often imposed by stars and directors'?

2. In interviews I have always refrained from expressing myself in a dogmatic manner and with the kind of pretension that characterizes the three points of the 4th paragraph devoted to 'corrupt' and 'wasteful' practices.

3. For the same reason I would be incapable, when speaking about actors, of saying: 'We will therefore go looking for actors where we know we can

find them and they will have to understand that something has changed.' The tone is quite simply worthy of Poujade.

4. If the risk of 'technical perfection' were that it 'left nothing but an impression of coldness', then Rembrandt, Baudelaire and Mozart would be so many frigidaires!

5. 'Besides, I went over my initial budget because I found myself confronted with realities of which I had been unaware.' I am certain I could not have said such a thing to you given that the film cost 37 million whereas the budget was 46 million!

6. I could mention several films costing 40 million (or less) which did not cover their production costs.

7. But what particularly shocked me and seemed to me to warrant a protest concerns the 8th paragraph devoted to the quality subsidy. Every sentence in it misconstrues what I said, the most flagrant example being 'the problem of a criterion' to which I absolutely do not subscribe.

Having been a journalist myself, I know how articles are written, rewritten and truncated, which is why I have never had any rectifications published. But *Le Film français* is not just any journal and it is not read casually by the public but attentively by professionals. That explains my letter to Maurice Bessy when I was mistakenly informed that the text of this survey was to be reprinted in *Cinémonde*.

Though you have not asked me, I could point out nine or ten mistakes in the article published in *Cinémonde*, starting with the directors' biographies and ages, but that is obviously less serious.

I would have you know nevertheless that I did not marry 'the daughter of my worst enemy' and that you might have allowed such an idiotic suggestion to remain the 'exclusive' of its originator, Monsieur Claude Brulé of *Elle*.

With regard to *Le Film français*, the only film magazine besides *Cahiers* which interests me, I have simply resolved in future to grant it an interview only on condition that I can reread the text before it is published.

With regret that our points of view are so divergent, I remain, dear Madame,

Yours sincerely,
François Truffaut

1 – Marcel Camus, French director, born in 1912: *Orfeu negro, Os Bandeirantes, Le Chant du monde, Le Mur de l'Atlantique*, etc.

To Charles Aznavour *from Paris, 16 August 1959*

My dear Charles,

I must have missed you by just a few days on the Riviera. The work is going ahead. A first draft is finished that I'm going to put aside in order to rewrite everything by myself; clearly, it will be a documentary on timidity.

I'm very pleased to be making a film with you and I hope we'll see each other very soon. Constantin for his part is working for us.

Naturally, we'll change the dates if that would suit you; since we'll be finishing the film with the exteriors in the snow, it would be wonderful to celebrate Christmas all together in the wilds; when do you return to Paris?

regards,
F. Truffaut

P.S. I've had *Fire in the Flesh* delivered to Franju. That is the novel we spoke about?

To the organizer of a film society *Paris, 22 December 1959*

Dear Monsieur,

Having reflected on the matter, I regret to have to reply to you in the negative.

I am unable to sponsor your film society:

1. Your 16 mm programmes oblige you to screen only dubbed versions of foreign films, which I regard as counter to the spirit of a film society.

2. I find the artistic level of the films selected by the F.L.E.C.C. extremely low and unworthy of a film society wishing to develop the cinematic culture of its members.

Before making a decision, I took the liberty of drawing a pencil score through every film which I would regard as substandard and I realized that too few remained and that such a veto on my part might reasonably strike you as excessive.

Moreover, your activity extends to areas other than the cinema and I cannot approve of the choice of personalities whom you envisage inviting to your debate on popular music.

I do regret this, believe me, but, just as I wouldn't make a film from a screenplay I was unhappy with and with actors not of my choice, so I cannot sponsor an undertaking whose ideas are so distant from my own.

Happy New Year and best wishes from

François Truffaut

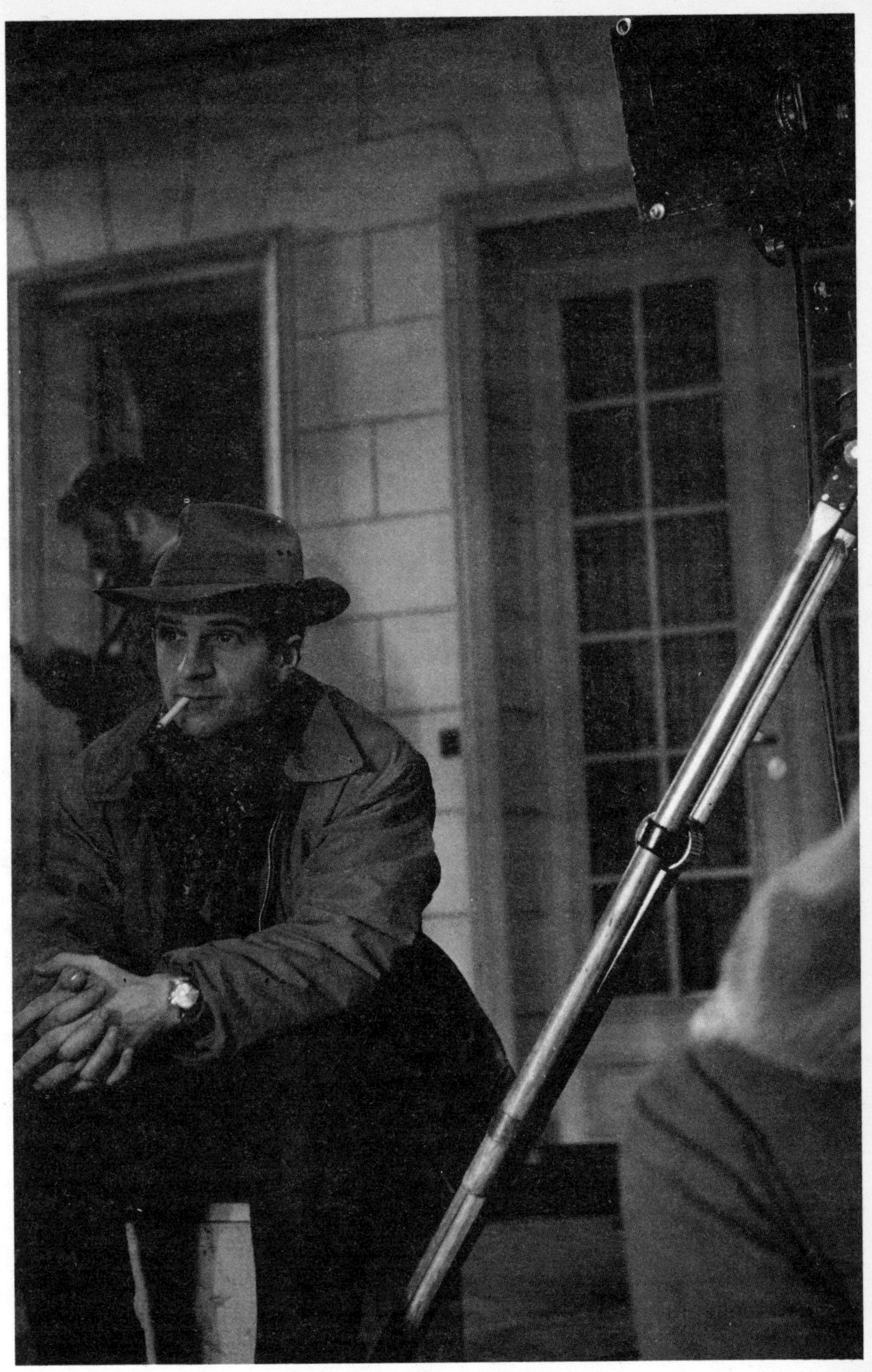

Filming *Les Quatre Cents Coups*.

1960

To a young screenwriter *Paris, 29 February 1960*

Dear Monsieur,

I read your script which I greatly liked but which strikes me as too personal to be filmed by someone other than yourself; naturally, it's nowhere near perfect, but, if you wish, I will have Raymond Devos[1] read it to see his reaction.

Do not suppose that I was disappointed by your second film; if I was more critical, it was simply that the element of surprise no longer came into play and that I had liked the first one so very much.

It is my belief that you have now served your apprenticeship and are ready to tackle a professional film. I am prepared to produce a 35 mm short of yours, supplying you with both the financial backing and a small crew for one week (5 or 6 complete days of shooting). The technicians, who are very good, are the same ones I had on *Les 400 Coups* and *Le Pianiste*, and I am certain that everything will go off well. The essential thing is that we agree on the script, that everything is sufficiently prepared and that you have actors you can trust.

You could actually reuse certain elements from your two 16 mm films since there is no relation between the kind of audience the second film might have at the Studio Parnasse and the kind that a 35 mm short would have.

It might even be worth considering the possibility of abandoning the second 16 mm film altogether.

To come back to your new project: it has many points in common with *Paris nous appartient* which you probably admired; but even if you were influenced by it, it's in the most positive sense of the word. My only fear is that you lack Rivette's experience, his resourcefulness and his judgement, not to mention the fact that he required no less than two hours twenty minutes to avoid the schematicism that is the primary danger of this sort of subject-matter.

That is why I had the feeling that your script was too short, too underdeveloped, and that one or more of the four characters would necessarily suffer.

If I had more time at my disposal, I would praise the overall script in more precise terms and criticize certain details with greater severity, but that, it seems to me, is beside the point; I sincerely believe that you should completely revise and restructure the script in such a way as to favour a single character with whom we would identify from the beginning to the end of the film, the others appearing only in the background. I am quite aware that this would be the opposite of what you wish to do, but I would also remind you that it was by focusing on an investigation and an individual investigator (Betty Schneider) that Jacques Rivette managed to show us as many places, people and walks of life as he did without ever toppling over into caricature.

I don't know if these few words correspond to the 'enlightened opinion' that you tell me you need, but I would like to offer you my very best wishes,

François Truffaut

1 – French radio, television and music-hall comedian who made a brief but memorable appearance in Godard's *Pierrot le fou*.

To Helen Scott[1] *from Paris, Tuesday 29 March, late in the evening. Letter reread, corrected and posted 30 March 1960*

My dear Helen,

You mustn't think your letter irritated me (the one with the explanations). It was a letter (mine, I mean) dictated to Lucette;[2] rereading it before I signed it, I realized that it was too impersonal, which is why I hurriedly added the few handwritten lines. But you were right to bawl me out, since I do have a tendency to take the easy way out by dictating a few letters every morning to 'expedite matters at hand' and so prove to myself that I am a *big business man*,[3] a *self-made man*,[3] a man of *first class quality*,[3] and goodness knows what else.

In short, thanks to you, I'm going to turn over a new leaf, I'm going to get back into the habit of personally typing a few letters at home, and my friends from the provinces or abroad will start wondering why I've become so affectionate and will never suspect that they owe it all to Helen Scott, my dear Helen.

Since I'm at home, I don't have your letters in front of me, which is why my reply won't be too methodical, unless I decide to finish it tomorrow at the office . . .

Naturally, you'll soon be receiving the documentation on *Le Pianiste*.

Speaking of Oscars, you really don't think we might be in with a slight chance for 'best original screenplay'? Yes, Godard is having a great success and I'm very pleased for him. For Cannes? At the moment it's between *A bout de souffle* – *Le Dialogue des Carmélites* – *Le Trou* (outside the competition) – *Paris nous appartient* – *L'Amérique vue par un Français*.[4] Tomorrow I'll try and have stills of these films sent to you.

I went to London for the opening of *The 400 Blows*;[3] I think it's doing well, but I haven't had any news, because there's no distributor, no press agent and above all no Helen Scott. Don't think I'm out to flatter you, but I realize more and more – three days in Copenhagen, I'm just back – that one very rarely comes across people of your competence on that tortuous path that leads from the editing-room to the cinema auditorium. The number of impecunious middlemen who live off directors they don't know and films they despise! Take Copenhagen, I didn't want to go; they begged me, the cinema was brand new, they had paid a lot of money for the film, etc., etc. So off I go, the cinema manager has left for the weekend, there was a press conference scheduled at the same time as another, more important one at the Theatre Royal, in short, a tiring and absolutely pointless trip.

The editor of my film, Cécile Decugis,[5] 27 years old, has been sentenced to five years in prison for having rented in her own name an apartment which served as a meeting-place for the F.L.N. We'll have to try and get her out, but it won't be easy. I've had to hire another editor, which is why I've fallen behind. All that, as well as Jeanne Moreau's son's accident,[6] has forced me to put off my next film, *Le Bleu d'outre-tombe*,[7] for a year. I'm tired, I'm demoralized, I have more and more doubts as to the point of making films. My only pleasure is playing with my daughter[8] who's turning into someone very special. So I'll stay home all year long, playing with her and reading, reading more and more, because I'd given up reading. Also, I'm going to take tap-dancing lessons, not to launch a new career *à la* Fred Astaire but because I'm not relaxed enough and too fidgety.

I've had no news of Patrick Auffray.[9] Jean-Pierre Léaud's[10] life has taken a turn for the better, since he no longer lives with his parents; he's got a room of his own with some people who have six children and a large bungalow in the suburbs, he's catching up with his schoolwork in a special school that seems to suit him and he spends every weekend with us; he's to be the star of Julien Duvivier's next film, *Boulevard*.

Films? There are a lot of bad ones: *Pantalaskas*, *Une fille pour l'été*, *Plein Soleil*, *L'Eau à la bouche*, *Le Huitième Jour*, *Normandie-Niemen*, *Le Bossu*, *Les Loups dans la bergerie*, *Sergent X*, *La Main chaude*, *Classe tous risques*,[11] etc. I liked *Le Testament d'Orphée* (which should do well in N.Y.

as a curiosity), *Les Yeux sans visage*, *Le Bel Age*[12] and especially *A bout de souffle*. This week I'm going to see *Suddenly Last Summer*,[13] which has just come out.

I went to see Jérôme[14] in Bordeaux immediately after the accident; it was terrifying, that pale little boy with tubes up his nose and inside his mouth, he seemed lost; he came out of the coma after fourteen days; every day, he gets more of his memory back, it's amazing. I'm returning to Bordeaux at the end of the week to see him again.

You know how fond I was of Max Ophüls; his son[15] is in Paris, I'm going to try and pull a few strings to help him with his first film, *Le Retour de Casanova*, from a novel by Schnitzler, an excellent subject. I'm also producing two shorts, one on the love life of insects, in colour, the other from a poem by Cocteau, *Anna la bonne*, which Claude Jutra[16] will direct. There will be an American version of the latter which I'll send you so that you can sell it in N.Y. Is that O.K.?

Thank you for all the American articles. Our friend (?) Frankel[17] did indeed write to me, but to ask my permission to represent Moussy and myself in Hollywood, if Oscar there is. The little devil didn't mention the plaque.[18] My father-in-law, Ignace Morgenstern, accompanied by his wife, leaves next week for New York, since he would like to help his brother set up a small hardware business. I've spoken to him about you and I think there's a good chance you'll meet him; he's going to see about the plaque and about overseeing the box-office returns, etc.

Here, to amuse you, are the names of some future young directors who will be starting their first films in the next few months, selected from among those I believe in: Marcel Ophüls (*Le Retour de Casanova*)[19] – Jacques Demy[20] (*Lola*) – Jacques Rozier[21] (*Les Dernières Semaines*[22]) – Jean-François Hauduroy[23] (*Le Noeud coulant*)[19] – Claude de Givray (*Tire-au-flanc 60*)[24] – Paul Gégauff[25] (*Une partie de plaisir*).[26]

Jacques Rivette is finishing his heroic *Paris nous appartient* which is marvellous; I won't be going to Cannes this year, because I'll be busy finishing my own film, the music and the sound-mixing; moreover, they saw enough of me there last year; and finally, it would smack too much of self-publicity. I may be a whore, but I'm the coquettish, crafty, subtle type who keeps his hat and shoes on (I wish I knew how to draw so I could illustrate that image).

I think again of the list for Cannes: *A bout de souffle* and *Les Carmélites* are considered the favourites, followed by *L'Amérique vue par un Français* and *Le Trou* (outside the competition since Becker is dead and the film isn't doing very well). But there's also talk of Lamorisse's *Le Voyage en ballon*[27] (which may not be finished in time) and *Les Petits Chats*,[28] a piece of 'poetic' crap on the so-called mysterious and supposedly fantastic world of childhood, for God's sake. The odds on *Paris nous appartient*? I'm too prejudiced in its favour to be able to rate them. There are your seven titles, to which you can add for the record Chabrol's *Les Bonnes Femmes* (remarkable, so they say). In all likelihood, the films that are rejected for Cannes will have a good chance of representing dear old France, land of my childhood, at the Berlin Festival,[29] not to mention the fact that *Tirez sur le pianiste*, directed by a good friend of yours, will perhaps be a candidate for Berlin where it can be hooted at in German which, after so many years of American occupation, may well be considered a triumph.

Jean-Claude Brialy, who has been in bed for six months because of displaced vertebrae, is getting up in the next few weeks. In Switzerland Godard has started his new film, *Le Petit Soldat*, about torture. Moussy is going to direct his first film: *Saint-Tropez Blues*.

Do you know the date of *Hiroshima*'s[30] opening in N.Y.?

I've spoken rather a lot about myself. The TV script that you wrote, which one is it? Have you had it translated into French? I'd like to read it and even, if you wish, show it to some TV people in France or to some producers. If you relinquish the rights to it for N.Y., won't you be retaining them for Europe? Naturally, we'll continue to keep in touch, but if possible I'd like the devoted service to work both ways and I'd very much like to help you as much as I can, don't hesitate to ask me any personal favours, anything you want me to do for you, especially since, having resolved to make myself voluntarily unemployed, I'm going to have some time on my hands!

We've moved from the rue Saint-Ferdinand to 15, rue du Conseiller-Collignon, in the 16th arrondissement, yes, my dear, and you may write to me either here or at the office. Do you need any French books, or magazines, or documentation? Did you read the novel of *Les 400 Coups*? What do you think of the scenes that were cut from the film or else weren't shot? How are the Lassalles?[31] And Genet's play, *Le Balcon*, tell me, did you see it?

I'm still thinking of this business of the Cannes selection which bothers me since it also bothers you, and what I suggest is this: if you tell me when the deadline of your bulletin is, I can telegraph the titles of the favourites to you at the last minute, as I'm likely to know more in the next few days, before the end of the week.

It's getting late, dear Helen, and my fingers are numb from typing; I should say finger, since I type with just the one, but that means I type harder and faster in accordance with the well-known law of compensation which, so they say, makes one-armed men better in bed than those with two; I'm not too happy about ending on such a trivial image, especially as I am again impotent to illustrate it (another ill-chosen word, guess which), but that's the way it is.

You know, I think a lot of you, and frequently too; it reflects no credit on me, because you are one of those people who aren't easy to forget; for me the name Scott used to evoke the Antarctic, now Scott is New York, yes, even more than Ivanhoe. So if Scott is New York, then la belle Hélène is Paris, you see how we're linked to one another. But I seem to remember that you didn't care for puns, for the sort of woolly wordplay indulged in by those mercurial minds, of a slightly feminine, slightly childlike cast, for whom the consonance of words takes precedence over their profound meaning, etc., etc. There is one thing I've noticed, though, that quite sincerely disturbs me: my letter is written in less good French than yours.

I thank Chicago and its fogs since we got to know each other better because of them; the ice was broken, we confided in each other and so became, I hope, friends,

françois

1 – Helen Scott (1915–87) was working at the French Film Office (F.F.O.) in New York when Truffaut suggested that she collaborate with him on a book of interviews with Hitchcock. Apart from translating these interviews, she was involved with marshalling the material and writing the book itself, which became a best-seller, notably in the United States. She remained one of the director's closest friends until his death.

2 – Lucette de Givray (the wife of the screenwriter and director Claude de Givray) was for many years Truffaut's personal secretary at Les Films du Carrosse.

3 – In English in the original letter.

4 – Respectively by Godard (*Breathless*), Philippe Agostini and le R(évérend) P(ère) Bruckberger (*The Carmelites*), Jacques Becker (*The Hole*), Rivette, and François Reichenbach (whose film was finally titled *L'Amérique insolite*).

5 – She was also the editor of *A bout de souffle*.

6 – He suffered a fractured skull in a car crash.

7 – This film was never made.

8 – Laura, Truffaut's eldest daughter, was born in 1959.

9 – The young actor who played René Bigey, Antoine Doinel's best friend, in *Les Quatre Cents Coups*.

10 – French actor, born in 1944. He was discovered by Truffaut for *Les Quatre Cents Coups* and continued to play Antoine Doinel in *L'Amour à vingt ans*, *Baisers volés*, *Domicile conjugal* and *L'Amour en fuite*. He made two further films for Truffaut, five for Godard and also worked with Glauber Rocha, Jean Eustache, Jacques Rivette, Bernardo Bertolucci, etc.

11 – Respectively by Paul Paviot, Edouard Molinaro, René Clément, Jacques Doniol-Valcroze, Marcel Hanoun, Jean Dréville, André Hunebelle, Hervé Bromberger, Bernard Borderie, Gérard Oury and Claude Sautet.

12 – By Pierre Kast.

13 – By Joseph L. Mankiewicz.

14 – Jeanne Moreau's son.

15 – Marcel Ophüls, German-born director, born in 1927: *Le Chagrin et la Pitié*, *A*

Sense of Loss, The Memory of Justice, Hôtel Terminus, etc.
16 – Canadian director (1930–87): *A tout prendre, Comment savoir, Mon Oncle Antoine*, etc.
17 – Dan Frankel, American distributor.
18 – Frankel had kept for himself the New York Critics' Award won by *Les Quatre Cents Coups*, and Truffaut wished to retrieve it.
19 – This film was never made.
20 – French director, born in 1931: *Lola, La Baie des Anges, Les Parapluies de Cherbourg, Les Demoiselles de Rochefort, The Model Shop, Une chambre en ville*, etc.
21 – French director, born in 1926: *Adieu Philippine, Du Côté d'Orouet, Les Naufragés de l'Île de la Tortue, Maine-Océan*, etc.
22 – This was to become *Adieu Philippine.*
23 – French director.
24 – This was finally titled *Tire-au-flanc.*
25 – French screenwriter, born in 1922. He frequently worked with Chabrol.
26 – Gégauff's script was eventually filmed by Chabrol in 1974, with Gégauff playing the leading role.
27 – *Stowaway in the Sky.*
28 – By Jean Villa: it was shot but never released.
29 – At that time the Berlin Festival was held in June.
30 – Alain Resnais's *Hiroshima mon amour.*
31 – The previous year Martin Lassalle had played the leading role in Bresson's *Pickpocket.*

To Georges de Beauregard[1] *Paris, 14 May 1960*

Dear Monsieur,

Opening the latest issues of *Le Film français* and *La Cinématographie française*, I was surprised to find my name mentioned as supervisor on your next film, *Lola.*[2]

I am very flattered by the honour which this appointment represents, but, alas, I have to decline it as, apart from the fact that I have no recollection of signing a contract with your company to that effect, my own commitments at the time the film will be made would prevent me from undertaking the work involved.

In the case of *A bout de souffle*, the participation was genuine, since I had written the script four years before and had several times been on the point of directing it myself. In the present case, however, I consider Jacques Demy to be a better technician than I am, and I have, moreover, no desire to be anyone's 'supervisor' or 'technical adviser'.

In any event, such an arrangement would not make sense since the presence of a supervisor or technical adviser is required by the Centre only when the film in question is to be made by a young director who has been refused the dispensation for a first film, which would not be the case with Jacques Demy as he has directed at least three shorts (I had only one behind me when I obtained the dispensation for *Les 400 Coups*).

I would therefore be grateful if you would remove my name from

FRANÇOIS TRUFFAUT

vous souhaite une belle année,
bon pied bon œil, une générale
par trimestre, et vous invite à
voir
PARIS NOUS APPARTIENT
le vendredi 6 janvier à 21 heures
au Club Publicis,
merci
ft.

'FRANÇOIS TRUFFAUT wishes you a happy new year, the very best of health, a new show opening every three months, and invites you to see PARIS NOUS APPARTIENT on Friday 6 January, 9 p.m. at the Club Publicis,

thank you

ft.'

subsequent announcements appearing in trade journals or any other kind; otherwise I will be obliged to do so myself.

cordially yours,
François Truffaut

1 – French producer (1920–84).

2 – Directed by Jacques Demy.

To a screenwriter

from Paris, 22 June 1960

Dear Monsieur,

You do me too great an honour in asking my advice; I have never written a shooting script and I never know where I'm going to place the camera 1 hour before I begin shooting, which is to say, before seeing the actors move through the set. I am therefore bowled over by the work you have put in and open-mouthed with admiration.

I have never been able to understand flashbacks; that's why I can't make head or tail of my new film,[1] in the middle of which there's a long sequence set in the past. Consequently, I understood nothing of your 'subject', which I read all the way through a few months ago, and, skimming, a few minutes ago.

Films resemble the people who make them, which is why you need have no worries about yours; I don't like reading screenplays, especially when they are full of mysterious abbreviations; invite me to come and see the finished film and then I'll have no hesitation in telling you what I think of it,

cordially yours,
François Truffaut

1 – *Tirez sur le pianiste.*

To Helen Scott

from Paris, 21 August 1960

Dear Hélène,

I received your two letters but went on holiday for a few weeks, resolved to read but not to write. I really was very tired and all I wanted to do was play with Laura whom I normally don't see enough of: I took 40 photos of her a day, in black and white, in colour, and also filmed her. Finally, I returned to Paris to add a few final touches to *Le Pianiste* which has had a very poor reception from the public in spas like Vichy, Deauville and Biarritz. It's been withdrawn from circulation until it opens in Paris, most probably in October; its career depends now on the Paris critics and first-run audiences. Even so, don't think I'm downhearted, because failure stimulates me just as success terrorizes and paralyses me. All I think about now is *Jules et Jim* which will be a very difficult film to make but may turn out extraordinary. I've been offered – by the inevitable Raoul J. Lévy[1] – a very fine American novel, Ray Bradbury's *Fahrenheit 451* (in paperback, read it in English). But I'll shoot it in two years.[2]

I'm going to write to Elie Wiesel[3] in the next few days: everything you tell me about him appeals to me; would it be possible for me to read *Le Jour* in manuscript or in proof before it's published in French? There's also Goodis,[4] tell him again how much I like and admire him. When Lucette said to me one evening, 'Helen Scott leaves tomorrow at eight,' I understood eight in the morning and it was only the next day that the misunderstanding was cleared up; but there was also the fact that, being sentimental myself, I distrust overt sentimentality and prefer not to clear up misunderstandings. As far as I was personally concerned, I therefore considered that you had left: don't begrudge the way I pander to my own self-image; our friendship is more epistolary than verbal, as you would surely agree since I sometimes send you long letters.

The new edition of *Down There* is to be titled *Shoot the Pianist*, like the film. Braunberger is on holiday and no longer seems to have the slightest interest in *Le Pianiste*, which Malraux likes a lot and had designated for Venice. It seems the Italians refused it for some bloody silly moral reasons. Too bad for Shapiro whom we could play off against Davis, who's also interested.

On the subject of literature and in reply to the relevant paragraph in your letter, I'll have you know, my good friend, that from September to the end of the year I'm going to write a weekly article on the movies for *L'Express*. Perhaps I can retain the American rights and send you a copy each week via Lucette. What do you think?

Why don't you describe the 'unforeseen' activities that have been taking up all your time since you returned? I would like you to become, whether thanks to me or not, very rich, so you can afford to spend three months of every year in Paris. But working as much as you do for others should not blind you to the fact that you are a very exceptional individual, capable of producing books, articles, reports, TV programmes, scripts, etc. Don't fail to send me copies of your prose, should the occasion arise . . . O.K.?

La Nuit[5] is a finer book than *L'Aube*,[5] but only by virtue of its subject-matter. I helped Grimblat[6] a lot with the script of his first film,[7] which he's going to make with Eddie Constantine.[8] *Le Petit Soldat*, which is really terrific but loathed in certain quarters, has not yet been passed by the censor. If you'd like to do a favour to some film-buyer in New York, call his attention to a French film which could do very well in the U.S.: *Paris nous appartient*!!!!!!

My father-in-law left this morning to spend 3 weeks in Moscow (a pleasure trip); Claude de Givray, a civilian at last, will also be writing for *L'Express* (film reviews) and is preparing a military farce which I will supervise, a burlesque comedy that will be better, and better paced, than *Mon Oncle* and its extraordinary success in the States will owe a lot to you!!

I've bought a very fast car at whose steering-wheel I bear an irresistible resemblance to James Dean, but my wife is not too keen on the comparison.

Everyone in Paris sends you love and I go along with Paris on that,

françois

1 – French producer (1922–66).
2 – In fact, he shot it six years later.
3 – French writer, born in 1928, winner of the Nobel Peace Prize in 1987.
4 – David Goodis, American thriller writer, the author of *Down There*, on which *Tirez sur le pianiste* is based.
5 – By Elie Wiesel.
6 – Pierre Grimblat, French director, born in 1926.
7 – *Me faire ça à moi.*
8 – American-born actor of (mostly) French films, born in 1917: *Ça va barder*, *Lemmy pour les dames*, *Lucky Jo*, *Alphaville*, *Lions Love*, *Die Dritte Generation*, etc.

To a Danish correspondent

Paris, 1 September 1960

Dear Mademoiselle,

I acknowledge receipt of your synopsis for a thriller, but I do not understand why you sent it to me.

You ask me 'to submit it to my production agent', but I do not have a production agent and I do not even know in what such a job would consist.

You also point out that you are 'only interested in selling the synopsis', but I neither buy nor sell synopses nor have any intention of becoming a middleman.

You go on to praise 'the sensitivity and subtlety of tone which makes French films first-rate artistic productions' and you believe that 'a French writer would be more qualified than you' to develop the screenplay whose action, as you also recognize, does not have to take place in California.

In these circumstances you must understand my amazement. You wish to sell me or have me sell the screenplay of a thriller whose buyer will be free to alter the setting, the plot and the characters and will have to write the adaptation and the dialogue himself.

There must be about a dozen detective stories on a par with yours being published in France every day; some of these novels become films, but films which are rarely the 'first-rate artistic productions' you refer to in your letter.

I therefore regret that there is nothing I can do for you and remain

Yours sincerely,
François Truffaut

To Jean-Pierre Mocky[1] *5 Sept. 60*

My dear Jean-Pierre,

The films I like are those which bear no resemblance to any others, therefore I am a fan of *Un couple*.

I'm sorry we're no longer the friends we used to be. We first met at Fox, through Chabrol, I believe. You liked having lunch with me, and we would chat away for hours at the *Paris* café.

I have never said anything nasty about you no matter what you may have been informed; what I thought of *Les Dragueurs*, both good and bad, I told you in person, so I've never understood your attitude, as though you were avoiding me.

Our last relatively friendly meeting dates back to the evening of 22 January 1959, my daughter had just been born and you were filming in the passage du Lido. I avoid like the plague those people I don't like and who don't realize it, but, as far as you and I are concerned, it would seem to be the other way round. Forgive me for being sentimental, but I was moved by the serious scenes in your film and I laughed a lot at the others. You've achieved an extraordinary tone; every one of the supporting roles is magnificent and the best of all is the guy who kisses Mayniel[2] in the nightclub. Véronique is very good this time, and I adore your chum Hofman.

I'm eager to show you *Le Pianiste* which has met with more or less the same difficulties, but, with the sort of films we make, I find that if friends like them, it all seems worth while.

Un couple makes an impact because it's a film in which, obstinately, only one thing is spoken about, in this case the zigs and zags of the libido; you are entitled to feel pleased with yourself, except that I know that's something you're temperamentally incapable of,

very cordially yours,
f. truffaut

1 – French director and actor, born in 1929: *Snobs*, *Un drôle de paroissien*, *Solo*, *L'Albatros*, *L'Ibis rouge*, etc.
2 – The actress Juliette Mayniel.

To Helen Scott

from Saint-Paul-de-Vence,
26 September 1960

My dear Helen,

I've just left Paris to take refuge here, alone, in peace and quiet, in order to work on *Jules et Jim* and nothing else. In front of me I have your long letter of 30 August and the shorter one of 9 September.

I didn't manage to agree with the editors of *L'Express*, since, there like everywhere else, they let their art, music and literary critics get on with it, but everyone has to have his say on the cinema. I told them, in so many words, to stuff it. In any case, I realized it's very difficult for me to write about other people's films, good or bad; a number of old directors are unemployed because of the 'New Wave' and it would be tasteless for a lucky young devil like me to be talking about them, etc., etc.

Even so, the 'New Wave' is insulted more and more each week on radio, TV and in the newspapers; I even have the feeling that the industry itself is closing ranks. I don't have a persecution complex and I don't want to start speaking about a conspiracy, but it's now quite clear that films by the younger directors, as soon as they stray ever so slightly from the norm, come up against a barrier erected by the exhibitors; it's happened to Mocky and Queneau[1] with *Un couple*, to De Broca[2] with *Le Farceur* and also with *Le Pianiste*, to which I added a few final touches; because the film had a poor reception this summer on the beaches, the first-run cinemas on the Champs-Élysées have all turned it down. It has to be said that, this year, there's a plethora of major French films which seem to have settled in for a long run: *La Vérité*,[3] *Zazie*,[4] *Et mourir de plaisir*[5] and *La Française et l'Amour*[6] (an abject film). Braunberger doesn't take the situation very seriously and believes we should wait for the opening of Cayette's film[7] which will make Aznavour a star; I think he's right. *Le Pianiste* seems to be doing very well in Canada and the distributor never stops asking for new prints. But it was partly to escape from Braunberger and his daily cascade of publicity stunts that I holed up here; he doesn't even know where I am! Wiesel must have spoken to you about my letter; he replied to me and sent his new manuscript which I'm going to start calmly reading tomorrow.

As for *Fahrenheit*, which was proposed to me by Raoul J. Lévy, nothing has been settled as yet, since the rights are very expensive; nevertheless, I'm going to buy them together with Raoul J. so that he won't be able to change either his mind or his director! But my next film, in any event, is *Jules et Jim*, a hymn to life and death, a demonstration through joy and grief of the impossibility of any sexual combination outside of the couple. The shoot has been fixed for 1 April 1961, because the two leading performers, Jeanne Moreau[8] and the German Oskar Werner,[9] are doing theatre work all winter.

As soon as I return to Paris, I'll send you the photo of Laura that you requested; she walks, she talks, she telephones, she flirts a bit, but she's a girl . . . In fact, she's in love with me, which gives me a lot of influence over her so that I'm able to dissuade her, even now, from going to too many parties.

Tell that old buffoon Bosley Crowther[10] that the Japanese actor in *Hiroshima*[11] came to Paris to dub himself into French (the film was shot without sound, therefore postsynchronized in a recording studio). He didn't know any French at all during the shoot, but they taught him the dialogue by heart, phonetically. Resnais had spotted him in a bad Japanese film shown in Paris under the title *Christ en bronze*.[12] I haven't got in touch yet with your chum Françoise Prasche, since I'm delaying that delightful moment the way children take for ever over a dessert they've been longing for.

As for Avedon,[13] he's a young buffoon and so is Robbe-Grillet,[14] but I like the photo of me because it makes me look like an Italian-American gangster from New York. I'm very pleased you're friendly with Goodis whom I continue to adore; tell me if he still resembles the old photograph that I've enclosed, from the dust-jacket of the Série Noire edition of *Le Pianiste*. (Exhibit No. One!)

Grimblat is very taken up with the preparation of his first film *Me faire ça à moi* (provisional title), with Eddie Constantine; I did a little work on the screenplay (without putting my name to it); it will be a very whimsical film and totally Hitchcockian given the nature of the gags. But I'm going to pester him on your behalf and show him the part of your letter that concerns him. He believes he's hugely in my debt, since I didn't want any money for my contribution to his script; though usually so brilliant, he was paralysed with fear; it was his wife Marion, mine Madeleine and myself who typed the whole thing out during the holidays, but we had lots of fun doing it. I'm sure that he'll be very forceful on the set, totally in command of the situation, a subtle visual stylist, and that, thanks to him, we'll finally see a good film with Constantine.

You must be surprised to hear that I'm going to do nothing till April; in fact, de Givray will be shooting *Tire-au-flanc* (the rights to which we are in the process of negotiating) in January and February, somewhere in the French countryside, if we find an old, disused barracks. I'll be supervising, in an official and also very real capacity, the shooting of this comedy in which I have enormous faith; the humour will be visual, very dense, very international, very young, acrobatic and choreographed. And that's not all, my sweet! In addition, the stage-hands, electricians and actors will all be gagmen and a bonus will be awarded for each gag suggested to and used by the director; it will be the first collective film comedy since Mack Sennett.

You probably know that *Le Petit Soldat* is totally banned and that a member of parliament has demanded that Godard, who is Swiss, be expelled from France. If the producer attempts to sell the film abroad by giving it Swiss nationality, his producer's card will taken away from him.

Things aren't going well in France. Along with Resnais, Doniol and Kast, I signed Jean-Paul Sartre's statement on insubordination[15] (in favour of all those soldiers who are deserting in Algeria and also those French people who are aiding the F.L.N.). I'm probably going to be charged, which was another reason for leaving Paris, to gain a little time and think things over. Everything is rotten, everything stinks, long live Castro.

Paris nous appartient comes out in a few weeks (without Mingus's music) at the Cinéma d'Essai and the Ursulines. If it doesn't do well in these two cinemas, it means it won't do well anywhere; I'll keep you informed and send you a set of stills.

Jutra's little film (*Anna la bonne*, from Cocteau's poem) is very accomplished; it lasts 8 minutes, but the English version won't be ready until the end of the year. I produced another little film lasting 7 minutes, *La Fin du voyage*, which, since it has only music and sound effects, no words, is easily exportable; it concerns a child and his relation to water, in the sink at home, in a public fountain, a stream, a river and the sea, from a model yacht made out of paper to a fishing trawler; it's a bit silly, but pleasant and quite poetic; I'm trying to soft-talk Clouzot[16] – here at the Colombe[17] – into buying it and showing it with *La Vérité*, a film lasting just over two hours.

I think Bernard Aubert's[18] film *Les Lâches vivent d'espoir* is going to get an export licence (to compensate for the ban on *Le Petit Soldat*); in America it would probably go down very well (the love of a black student for a white Parisienne), it's sweet, generous, naïve, sympathetic and unpolished.

It's true, I don't write often, but, as my grandfather used to say, 'Y'can't beat a loafer once he gets down to the job.' So even if you wait a long time for my replies, they're well worth waiting for. That's something that had to be said. As you can imagine, these epic letters aren't written at a single sitting, which is why a cheerful paragraph may follow on from some outpouring of bile.

I'm so serious-minded at the moment that I flew down to Saint-Paul, leaving my beautiful car in Paris.

As for Milton Bracker, damn all. Out of sight, out of mind.

In Paris, I put aside, to send to you, one of the ads for *Le Pianiste* so Goodis can see that his name is mentioned on it in very large letters, as well as the title of the book. In the next few days I have to show the film to Marcel Duhamel,[19] the director of the Série Noire imprint and therefore the French publisher of the book; perhaps he'll republish it or liquidate the stock? I'm also depending a little on the records that are due to come out with the two songs from the film and Delerue's[20] music.

In a few days Marcel Ophüls is going to start filming a short on *Matisse ou le Talent du bonheur*, which is, I think, destined for American TV; it's the first of a series on painters. That's one whose quality I can guarantee. Jeanne Moreau wants to become her own producer, because she's tired of always being exploited, always being hard-up. Her first film as producer-cum-star? *Madame Bovary*, no kidding, and I'm seriously pushing Ophüls as director; it might work . . .[21]

Agnès Varda[22] has shot a sequence of *La Mélangite*, it's rather beautiful if a trifle hieratic. The film can't really get under way until we've found an Italian co-producer, which won't be easy, believe me, given the screenplay, which is first-rate but terrifying. We have high hopes for March 61 . . .

Lamorisse's *Le Voyage en ballon* is very boring and very stupid, even for kids. It's dying the death in Paris, which is no more than it deserves when you consider Lamorisse's cynicism. Let's hope the Americans are no more stupid than the French. One very fine French film is Pierre Kast's *La Morte Saison des amours*, on the sexual relationships of two couples; it's unflashy, intelligent, moving and remarkable (and still unreleased).

The most eagerly awaited French films, about which I can tell you nothing, are *Zazie* – *La Vérité* – *Lola* (by Jacques Demy, Varda's husband) – *Une femme seule*[23] (by Astruc) – *Os Bandeirantes* (by Camus) – *Candide* (by Carbonnaux).

Those friends of mine who have seen *Le Farceur*[24] were very disappointed, but I have enough faith in you to expect something good.

Resnais has started his new masterpiece in Munich, *L'Année dernière*,[25] one doesn't have to be a fortune-teller to predict something sublime. Florence Malraux is his assistant on the film; she put her father[26] in a frightful situation by signing the call for insubordination that I mentioned to you earlier.

Since I know so many young guys who haven't done anything yet but are very capable, the idea came to me – whatever you do, don't mention this – of producing a sketch film, each episode of which would be directed by a newcomer under my supervision. I'm still looking for the theme; I thought of six short stories by Edgar Allan Poe, because he's a genius and because the *Tales of Mystery and Imagination* are truly works of mystery and imagination, and Baudelaire's translations are magnificent. I haven't made up my mind yet, but it strikes me as something worth trying, since short films are all very well but they're hard to sell. Another possibility would be for each sketch to be shot by a newcomer but supervised by a different, established director: Godard, Malle, Astruc, etc. That would give the venture a fraternal and even slightly polemical, anti-old wave aspect that I would rather like. After all, we've got to fight and take advantage of the fact that the door is ajar to allow our mates to get a foot inside before it's too late.

from Saint-Paul, Saturday evening 1 October

I'm resuming this letter a few days later. I'll post it tomorrow at the aerodrome, because I'm returning to Paris. Politically, events have worsened considerably in the last few days. If you read French newspapers, you will know that the 'artists' who signed the manifesto in favour of insubordination are henceforth on an official black list; banned from speaking on radio and TV, from acting in subsidized theatres, etc. Where the cinema is concerned, it's very complicated (fortunately), since there's talk of refusing our films the financial aid that all French films automatically receive, as well as the various quality subsidies or advances on box-office returns that already exist. It's Malraux who has the responsibility of carrying out this punitive action, Malraux whose daughter Florence signed the manifesto as did Alain Resnais whose assistant[27] she is; and, for the cinema, there was also Pierre Kast, Jacques Doniol-Valcroze, Claude Sautet,[28] myself and, among the actors, Simone Signoret, Danielle Delorme, Roger Pigaut, etc. It was, in theory, Sartre who wrote the text, which was also signed by Françoise Sagan, Louis-René des Forêts (one of whose novels you received), Marguerite Duras, etc. For my part I tried without success to get Jeanne Moreau to sign (she was a long time making up her mind) and Louis Malle (his family prevented him). In short, it's a real mess!

All this has obviously upset me and prevented me from concentrating on my work. If I could speak English, I'd seriously contemplate trying my luck in America, but I have a terrible complex about languages; there might also be opportunities in Italy where I have lots of friends. I'm both discouraged – because every day brings new charges and threats and the problems of my own military service are bound to be exploited by the right-wing press – and stimulated, because they only have to prevent me from making films to remove all my doubts on the subject. The 121 signatures became 144, then more than 400, and now the police are making house-searches to prevent it from spreading; a lot of teachers have signed, which may mean their dismissal. A funny atmosphere.

It's going to become very awkward for me as official supervisor on *Tire-au-flanc* and my fear is that they'll cancel the grants for the shorts I've produced. Will I have to make *Jules et Jim* outside France?

Jeanne Moreau came to spend a few days here, at the Colombe, since she's very tired; Raoul Lévy also turned up and, naturally, he who was Godard's no. 1 adversary on *Le Petit Soldat* no longer speaks to me about signing the *Fahrenheit* contract with all of this going on; it's not that he's wicked or reactionary, he's just anxious to maintain good relations with the authorities, especially as he's a Belgian of Russian origin!

I'm going to end this letter now even though it doesn't have a very optimistic finale. I'm looking forward to being reunited with my daughter tomorrow evening, then my wife, my Paris mates who are all very nice, my lovely little car and all my worries.

I've read two-thirds of Wiesel's *Le Jour*, which is abominably grim; in effect, it's quite close to what I'd like to film, but also when you come down to it a bit too close to *Hiroshima*; this guy Wiesel is more heart-rending than sympathetic; I mean that he must be frightful to live with, endlessly moaning and groaning over himself, but I admire him a lot and I'll write to him next week, as soon as I've finished.

Ask me for anything you want, books, etc. Lucette is back from holiday.

Lots of love and kisses,

françois truffaut

1 – Raymond Queneau, French novelist, poet and essayist and also the screenwriter of *Un couple*.
2 – Philippe De Broca, French director, born in 1933: *L'Amant de cinq jours*, *Cartouche*, *L'Homme de Rio*, *Les Tribulations d'un Chinois en Chine*, *Le Roi de cœur*, *Chère Louise*, etc.
3 – By H.-G. Clouzot.
4 – Louis Malle's *Zazie dans le Métro*.
5 – By Roger Vadim.
6 – A sketch film by Henri Decoin, Jean Delannoy, Michel Boisrond, René Clair, Henri Verneuil, Christian-Jaque and Jean-Paul Le Chanois.
7 – *Le Passage du Rhin*.
8 – French actress, born in 1928: *Touchez pas au grisbi*, *Ascenseur pour l'échafaud*, *Les Amants*, *La Notte*, *La Baie des Anges*, *Chimes at Midnight*, *The Last Tycoon*, etc.
9 – Austrian-born actor (1922–84): *Lola Montès*, *Ship of Fools*, *The Spy Who Came in from the Cold*, *Fahrenheit 451*, etc. He died just two days after Truffaut.
10 – Then the film critic of the *New York Times*.
11 – Eiji Okada.
12 – By Minoru Shibuya.
13 – The American photographer Richard Avedon.

14 – Alain Robbe-Grillet, French novelist and director, born in 1922: (as director) *L'Immortelle*, *Trans-Europ Express*, *L'Homme qui ment*, *Glissements progressifs du plaisir*, *Le Jeu avec le feu*, etc. He wrote the screenplay of *L'Année dernière à Marienbad.*
15 – Le Manifeste des 121.
16 – See note 1, p. 254.
17 – The Colombe d'Or hotel.
18 – Claude Bernard-Aubert, French director, born in 1930: *Patrouille de choc*, *Les Tripes au soleil*, *Le Facteur s'en va-t-en guerre*, etc.
19 – See note 1, letter dated 15 October 1962, p. 201.
20 – Georges Delerue, French composer, born in 1925. He wrote the music for nine films by Truffaut: *Tirez sur le pianiste*, *Jules et Jim*, *L'Amour à vingt ans*, *La Peau douce*, *Les Deux Anglaises et le Continent*, *Une belle fille comme moi*, *La Nuit américaine*, *L'Amour en fuite* and *Le Dernier Métro*.
21 – The film was never made.
22 – French director, born in 1928: *La Pointe courte*, *Cléo de 5 à 7*, *Le Bonheur*, *L'une chante, l'autre pas*, *Sans toit ni loi*, *Kung Fu Master*, etc.
23 – The film was finally titled *La Proie pour l'ombre*.
24 – By Philippe De Broca.
25 – *L'Année dernière à Marienbad.*
26 – André Malraux was de Gaulle's Minister of Culture.
27 – And later wife.
28 – French director, born in 1924: *Les Choses de la vie*, *Max et les Ferrailleurs César et Rosalie*, *Vincent, François, Paul . . . et les autres*, etc.

To Louis Malle[1] *from Paris, Tuesday 25 [October 1960]*

My dear Louis,

Zazie bowled me over; it's a madly ambitious and hugely courageous film. I would like to have laughed louder and more often, but I was often moved by the manipulation of the image, by the close-ups against a background in motion, etc. My favourite shot? Albertine crying. My favourite performer? The sublime Catherine Demongeot. My favourite scene? The arrival of the militiamen with the enormous heads.

I've rarely wanted a film by someone else to succeed as much as I do yours, since what Zazie is saying – to anyone capable of reading between the lines – is: *Mon Oncle*, my arse, *Ballon rouge*,[2] my arse, *awful Negro*,[3] my arse, etc.

I had returned my invitation to the première, as I mixed it up with last Thursday (I was in London). If the mistake can still be rectified, I'd very much like to see the film again on Thursday evening by reclaiming my invitation, as on Friday I'm going into hospital for several days; if not, then I'll see it later, one Saturday evening with the ordinary-Parisian-cinemagoer,

very affectionately,

F. Truffaut

1 – French director, born in 1932: *Les Amants*, *Zazie dans le Métro*, *Le Feu follet*, *Le Souffle au cœur*, *Lacombe Lucien*, *Pretty Baby*, *Au revoir, les enfants*, etc.
2 – By Albert Lamorisse.
3 – Truffaut is referring to Marcel Camus's *Orfeu negro*.

To an aspiring screenwriter *Paris, 14 December 1960*

Dear Monsieur,

I have read *Les Cloches de Bâle*,[1] and the story that you have adapted from one of the episodes of the novel might well constitute a film, and even a very good film, but only on condition:

1. that Monsieur Aragon agrees;
2. that a producer acquires the rights to the novel;
3. that the said producer offers the film to me;
4. that I agree to make it;
5. that I choose you to write the adaptation.

As you see, it makes better sense for me to return your manuscript and advise you now to try writing an original screenplay.

With thanks, dear Monsieur, I remain

Cordially yours,
François Truffaut

1 – By Louis Aragon.

To Helen Scott *from Paris, 27 December 1960*

Dear Hélène,

Happy new year and good health. My wish is that this year you work just a tiny bit less for other people and a tiny bit more for yourself, that your boss at the French Film Office gives you a free hand, that the visitors from France who pass through New York are charming and kind, less than me, though, so as not to overshadow the memory of my visit, that Kennedy names you minister of the movies and that men give you . . . what it is you want from them.

[. . .] Above all, don't concern yourself any further with *Le Pianiste*; I suppose Braunberger has been too greedy, but that's his funeral. I'm asking you to forget the film, draw a line through it and think of nothing but *Tire-au-flanc*, by my mate de Givray, and *Jules et Jim* (which starts at the end of March). Though it had a mediocre first-run in Paris, *Le Pianiste*, thanks to some very intelligent reviews, has not disgraced me. Madeleine thanks you for the little book; did I tell you we're expecting a little brother for Laura (round about July)?[1]

I agree with you about Camus[2] who's a sentimental cretin; as far as he's concerned, Negroes are good for nothing but dancing and this from someone who thinks he loves humanity. Loving it as he does in the abstract, he doesn't truly love any individual human being, thereby demonstrating how utterly barren and absolutely vapid his mind is. He resembles – with respect – American left-wingers *à la* Dassin,[3] the type who discover at the age of thirty-five that everyone, on this earth, should have enough to eat. He can only make a film if he's 5,000 km away from his native land, far from the judgement of his own people, surrounded by 'inferiors' for whom he personifies the 'witch-doctor with the camera', and the fact of being bitten by mosquitoes deludes him into thinking that he's risked his life. He imagines that his adventure is visible on the screen whereas, on the contrary, it all works against the quality of the film; good films are ones that are made in ordinary rooms, with one's backside on a chair.

As you see, I'm entirely of your opinion and I can hardly bring myself to forgive poor Camus for reaping all the glory while *The 400 Blows* had to be content with the crumbs!!!

Can you obtain for me as soon as possible the address of the brilliant young New Yorker John Cassavetes,[4] the director of *Shadows*? There's a lot of talk about him Paris where his film is due to open any day now and I know a French producer who wishes to make him a proposition; first of all, the address. Then the film will open in Paris and, if the proposition is confirmed, I'll explain the whole business to you in detail, since at that point you might perhaps meet Cassavetes?

What's happening about *Hiroshima* and the Critics' Award? When does *A bout de souffle* open? *Le Voyage en ballon* is horrible (the same argument as against Camus), *Zazie* is a half-success or a half-failure depending on how you look at it and the only really good new film (which hasn't opened in Paris yet) is Jacques Demy's *Lola*.

I've fallen quite a bit behind with my work on *Jules et Jim*; anxiety is setting in, I'm petrified with fear; I'll send you a copy of the dialogue at the end of January.

love,
françois

P.S. I've taken out a subscription for you to an absurd magazine, *Haute Société*, starting from no. 3 in which there appeared a very amusing article on *Le Pianiste*. Would you like a subscription to *Cinéma 60*?

1 – It turned out to be a little sister, Eva.
2 – The director Marcel, not the writer Albert.
3 – Jules Dassin, American director, born in 1911: *Brute Force*, *The Naked City*, *Night and the City*, *Du rififi chez les hommes*, *Never on Sunday*, *Topkapi*, etc.
4 – American director and actor (1929–89): (as director) *Too Late Blues*, *Faces*, *Husbands*, *A Woman under the Influence*, *Gloria*, *Love Streams*, etc.

1961

To Helen Scott

from Paris, 9 January 1961
11 o'clock

Dear Hélène,

Thank you for your latest letters.

In effect, Jeanne Moreau will be in New York around the 20th of this month, with which boyfriend I couldn't say. I spoke to her about you and she would like nothing better than to see you; perhaps you'll be disappointed in her, since I've noticed you continue to labour under quite a few illusions about performers, actors and stars. Can you imagine the kind of mentality that's needed to do a job like that? It means endlessly boosting yourself above other people, which basically comes down to belittling them; it starts off as a vocation, a quite sincere form of ambition, to be just as good as the next man, then better than the next man, then doing in the next man; stars are sad creatures, but there's something sickening about their sadness. Stars suffer because they're constantly being harassed; when they're no longer harassed, it's even worse. They work eight hours a day cutting themselves off from humanity and then claim to be able to express all human feeling. I tell you, there's not one of them any better than the others.

Varda? She's with Jacques Demy, the father of *Lola*. Godard will perhaps be going to New York on the 23rd, in any case, it's a possibility, as he's finished shooting. There's no question of my father-in-law buying a cinema in NY, nor of me either, except, perhaps, if the enclosed bit of news turns out to be true: that Jerome Robbins wants to make a ballet out of *Les 400 Blows* and that it earns me enough. I'm relying on you to clear up the mystery!

2 p.m.: I've just had lunch with Godard. He confirmed that he'd like to go to New York with his inamorata, Anna Karina,[1] but on condition that he's invited; he has the feeling that Shapiro[3] and Unifrance[3] are going to go back on their word that they'd pay for the trip. If he is invited, he'll be at your disposal for anything you might arrange. Thanks for Cassavetes' address, I'm going to forward it to the French producer concerned.

Congratulations and many thanks for your bulletin.

Naturally, as regards *Tire-au-flanc*, I've been telling de Givray for months now that he has to include some long, funny scenes without dialogue. I haven't seen *L'Ours*[4] which has been the flop everyone expected it to be; in the graveyard of telegraphed pseudo-poetry it's buried beside *Le Voyage en ballon*, *Terrain vague*,[5] *Os Bandeirantes*, *A cœur battant*,[6] *La Proie pour l'ombre*, *Une aussi longue absence*,[7] *Moderato Cantabile*,[8] *St Tropez Blues*, etc.

I liked *La Morte Saison des amours*, *Les Grandes Personnes*,[9] *Lola*, *La Pyramide humaine*[10] and *Les Lâches vivent d'espoir*, but only the last two (and especially the last one, which is anti-racist) would have any hope of success in the US.

X—? I've practically fallen out with him, since he called on my services a lot for his first film but was deplorable on the set; the film will be dreadful.

I agree with you about *Le Passage du Rhin*, which is, all the same, less bad than Cayette's other films.

I'm at war with Vadim who has stolen someone else's film, the one with Bardot that Jean Aurel had been shooting for 3 days;[11] you'll hear talk of it in certain newspapers, but not in *L'Express* which is shielding Vadim and prefers not to speak about it. I received a new prize from Austria for *Les 400 Coups* and, for *Le Pianiste*, the prize of the Nouvelle Critique (Paris), but only the future matters and during the next few weeks you'll be receiving documentation on *Tire-au-flanc* and *Jules et Jim*, as well as some production stills from *Le Pianiste* that we are having printed especially for you.

Don't give way to the unspeakable Bracker[12] since I send you

a thousand kisses,

françois truffaut

1.– Danish-born actress, born in 1940. Under Godard's direction she appeared in *Le Petit Soldat*, *Une femme est une femme*, *Vivre sa vie*, *Bande à part*, *Alphaville*, *Pierrot le fou*, *Made in USA* and one episode of *Le Plus Vieux Métier du monde*.

2 – American distributor.

3 – The organization (known in the United States as the French Film Office) responsible for promoting French cinema abroad.

4 – By Edmond Séchan.

5 – By Marcel Carné.

6 – Jacques Doniol-Valcroze's *Le Cœur battant*.

7 – By Henri Colpi.

8 – By Peter Brook.

9 – By Jean Valère.

10 – By Jean Rouch.

11 – *La Bride sur le cou*.

12 – Milton Bracker, a *New York Times* journalist based in France.

To Helen Scott *Saturday 11 March 61*

My dear Helen,

I have your recent letters in front of me; knowing that the shoot of *Jules et Jim* is just one month away, you will perhaps forgive my silence. I was very touched, as was Madeleine, by your words of sympathy after the death of my father-in-law; my mother-in-law has taken it very hard; finding oneself alone, after thirty years of married life, is really an ordeal. Fortunately there's Laura, who's more and more high-spirited. My father-in-law had started discussions with the distributors about *Tire-au-flanc* and *Jules et Jim*, but nothing had been settled; it's up to Berbert[1] and myself to carry on, but, apart from the fact that 'we're not up to the job', the people we're dealing with are trying to take advantage of the situation, so much so that we're worn out by so many inconclusive meetings.

Claude de Givray has finished *Tire-au-flanc*; it's not as good as expected, but very much better than expected, and I can confirm that the French cinema boasts a great new comic film-maker; the screenplay was constantly improved and enriched; you'll be seeing it soon, I hope.

Godard has just got married in Switzerland. He'll soon be making a film with Jeanne Moreau: James Hadley Chase's *Eva*,[2] for the Hakim brothers. The films jockeying for position for Cannes are either bad ones backed by the government: *La Princesse de Clèves*,[3] *Monsieur Sorge*,[4] *Taxi pour Tobrouk*,[5] etc. or good ones like *L'Année dernière*, *L'Enclos*[6] and *Une femme est une femme*[7]. . .

There are a lot of good films in Paris at the moment, but they are harming each other's chances because they're all too similar or else have too many of the same faces and are set in the same sort of surroundings: *Les Grandes Personnes* (interesting), *Le Farceur* (a real success in a tiny cinema), *L'Amant de cinq jours* (De Broca's best film, it's doing very well), *Lola* (by Jacques Demy, remarkable but people have been staying away despite very good reviews), *La Récréation* (by Moreuil), very graceful, a minor success, *La Mort de Belle* (Molinaro, pleasant). Life is becoming hard for the young French film-maker! I'm all for your becoming *my exclusive agente dame*[8] in nouillorque,[9] but I'm going to ask Berbert how he thinks it should be arranged.

Now, just about to start my third film, I'm suffering from a dreadful bout of nerves; it can be put down to a mixture of pride, vanity, ambition and a number of other sordid but also irresistible factors: what I would like for *Jules et Jim* is the most complete success imaginable, not just the kind enjoyed by *Le Pianiste*. Naturally, since my father-in-law is no longer with us, I have the extra responsibility of not throwing away his widow's money, and that matters to me. There's also the fact that I dream of producing films and purchasing equipment, all of which will demand energy and success.

You're going to receive some production stills from *Le Pianiste*, some stills from *Tire-au-flanc*, the script of *Jules et Jim* and so on and so forth.

Would you like some other books, or anything?

I am, dear Hélène, very affectionately yours,

françois truffaut

1 – Marcel Berbert, the production manager of Les Films du Carrosse. Whether as line producer or executive producer, he remained one of Truffaut's most loyal colleagues until the latter's death. As with Serge Rousseau and Jean-Louis Richard, Truffaut entrusted small parts to him in a number of his films.
2 – It would finally be filmed by Joseph Losey in 1962.
3 – By Jean Delannoy from a script by Cocteau.
4 – By Yves Ciampi.
5 – By Henri Verneuil.
6 – By Armand Gatti.
7 – By Jean-Luc Godard.
8 – In 'English' in the original letter.
9 – Truffaut's pseudo-phonetic spelling of New York.

To Pierre Lherminier[1]

Paris, 21 June 1961

My dear Lherminier,

Of all the names (assumed or not) mentioned in *France-Film Cinéma Nouveau*, yours is the only one known to me and in such a way that it is with complete confidence that I send you this rectification:

'I began shooting *Jules et Jim* on 10 April and since then I have not once had the opportunity of going to the cinema and I have still not seen Henri Colpi's film *Une aussi longue absence*.

'Even if I had seen it and detested it, I would never have made a remark as stupid as that which is attributed to me by an item in the latest issue of *France-Film Cinéma Nouveau*:

' "I no longer attach the slightest value to the official award which I received in 1959 for *Les 400 Coups*. I find it unacceptable that my film should be placed on the same level as the horrible production by Henri Colpi!"

'I am anxious to send you this disclaimer as I have nothing but admiration for Henri Colpi as an editor and a director of short films.

'In case you suspect this disclaimer to have been prompted by caution and cowardice and also to justify the epithet of 'pseudo-*enfant terrible*' that you have bestowed on me, I wish to point out that I have indeed regarded as "horrible" a number of prize-winning films at Cannes, notably *Moderato Cantabile*, *Friendly Persuasion*,[2] *Ballad of a Soldier*[3] and *Orfeu negro*, but that there was, for all that, no question of my not attaching "the slightest value to the official award which I received in 1959 for *Les 400 Coups*", one award I continue to regard as well deserved.'

I rely on you, my dear Lherminier, to publish this rectification and remain cordially yours,

François Truffaut

1 – French film journalist and editor.
2 – By William Wyler.
3 – By Grigori Chukhrai.

To Joseph Bercholz[1]

Paris, 25 July 1961

Dear Monsieur,

I am told that you phoned me several times at the office. Your flattering insistence is such that I prefer to explain to you in writing the reasons that lie behind my definitive refusal to direct one of *Les Sept Péchés capitaux*.[2]

First reason

As I told you several times, I consider that the time required to prepare, shoot and edit such a sketch is quite out of proportion to the running time it would have in the film as a whole and, if I had accepted the assignment, it would have been with the intention of devoting at least six weeks of my time to it, which is materially impossible since I was obliged, a few days ago, to confirm to Cinédis that the master print of *Jules et Jim* would be ready by the end of October.

Second reason

From the very first moment we discussed the project I was struck by a contradiction between your urgent wish to have me participate in the film and the time you had let elapse before making your proposal; in other words, if you were so determined to engage me, why did you summon me when there remained only a single sketch to be assigned, 'Anger' (even if, after my refusal, you offered me 'Pride' which, I think you should know, Yves Ciampi[3] still believes has been allotted to him)?

I can assure you that if, at the beginning, you had offered me any sketch out of the seven, six or even five, it would have been extremely difficult for me to extricate myself, since then the proposal would have been much more attractive.

Third reason

As you know, Chabrol, Godard and I are very fond of employing '*la politique des copains*',[4] which is to say, of helping, by means of an opportunity such as this, certain friends of ours, in whom we believe, to establish themselves. I was disappointed, however, that during the course of our discussions you systematically rejected the names of Marcel Ophüls, whose short film on Matisse you have not seen, and Claude de Givray, whose *Tire-au-flanc 61* you nevertheless assured me you had liked. Furthermore, I know that Pierre Kast, for whom I have great respect, would like to film 'Pride' and had a very good idea for the sketch.

Fourth reason

As you yourself were honest enough to tell us from the outset, there was, between the sketch conceived by Audiberti[5] (for 'Pride') and the one on 'Sloth' which Jean-Luc Godard will shoot, a similarity of situation which could well be detrimental to the film; but, because Jacques Audiberti and I had decided to abide by that initial idea, there was no question of our starting all over again.

There you have, dear Monsieur Bercholz, the four reasons underlying my refusal; I am prepared to acknowledge that not one of them, if taken separately, would be absolutely conclusive, but when taken together they force me to reply as I do, both firmly and a little sadly, since one takes no pleasure in refusing an attractive offer.[6]

Please do not hold my frankness against me, as I was very touched by your perseverance.

Yours sincerely,
François Truffaut

1 – French producer, born in 1898. Though his enormous output belonged squarely within the French 'tradition of quality' which the critic Truffaut had attacked in *Cahiers du cinéma*, the fact that he had produced Renoir's *Elena et les Hommes* was perhaps sufficient to 'redeem' him in the young film-maker's eyes.

2 – *The Seven Deadly Sins*, a sketch film.

3 – French director, born in 1921: *Les Héros sont fatigués*, *Typhon sur Nagasaki*, *Le Vent se lève*, etc.

4 – Or 'the policy of helping one's friends'. Truffaut's phrase is a parody of *la politique des auteurs* (in English, 'the auteur theory') of which he had been one of the most vocal advocates.

5 – Jacques Audiberti, French poet, novelist and dramatist (1889–1965).

6 – Ultimately, the *politique des copains* would be well represented in *Les Sept Péchés capitaux*, the seven sketches of which were directed by Molinaro, Godard, Demy, Vadim, de Broca, Chabrol and the dramatist Eugène Ionesco.

To Jean Mambrino *from Paris, 28 October 61*

My dear friend,

It's after a delay of five weeks that I'm replying to your very kind letter. As it happens, I left the Molkenrain about ten days before you arrived there and, overwhelmed with work, I did not reply to the letter announcing your arrival. Forgive me.

As for the young man you tell me about, I'm sorry but there's nothing I can do for him. Because of the way we shoot, in real interiors and in the street, it would be impossible to have a trainee around, however actively involved. In my films two-thirds of the crew spend all their time on staircases (when we're filming in a room) or in a café (when we're filming outside). I receive several requests a week from people wanting to be trainees, which unfortunately I regularly have to refuse, and you will understand that I feel obliged always to use the same assistants; they have wives and children, I know their problems, and they don't work the whole year round.

If he isn't too penniless, advise him, until something better comes along, to make some amateur 16 mm films or even 8 mm; a short film can be made for thirty thousand francs; one does the editing oneself, that's how we learned, Rivette, Godard and myself. A little film of this sort, if successful, constitutes the best possible introduction to an interesting producer like Braunberger.

Jules et Jim has really exhausted me. I was right to wait before shooting it, since it was, of my three films, the most difficult one to make. Though it has a very salacious theme, it's a film I believe to be profoundly moral, if on no other evidence than the frightful melancholy that emanates from it. It's the third time this has happened to me: starting a film under the impression that it's going to be amusing and discovering as I go along that the only thing that saves it is its melancholy. Jeanne Moreau is, I think, really very good and the Austrian actor Oskar Werner is extraordinary. Delerue has written a very beautiful musical score. We begin the sound-mixing in a few days.

Godard is very dismayed by the failure of his latest film; he had decided against *Mouchette*[1] and is looking for a project for Anna Karina who in a few months has become his sole reason for living. If an idea should come to you . . . I believe – and so does he – that it would be to his advantage to adapt a major novel. Rivette is putting the finishing touches to a magnificent adaptation of *La Religieuse*.[2] The Christmas issue of *Cahiers* will be devoted to criticism.

I recently saw some very fine films including Michel Deville's[3] *Ce soir ou jamais* and especially Jacques Rozier's *Adieu Philippine*. Next week Varda will be showing *Cléo de 5 à 7*. Do you still like films as much as you did?

I'm going through a Hitchcockian period; every week, I go and see again two or three of those films of his that have been reissued; there's no doubt at all, he's the greatest, the most complete, the most illuminating, the most beautiful, the most powerful, the most experimental and the luckiest; he's been touched by a kind of grace.

I'll be coming to Metz next year for the opening of *Jules et Jim* whose cause I intend to plead in city after city, by sheer hard work, since, for Les Films du Carrosse which hasn't exactly made a fortune out of *Le Testament d'Orphée*,[4] *Paris nous appartient* and four short films, it more or less represents the last chance, along with, fortunately, de Givray's *Tire-au-flanc 62* which looks promising.

A little note with more news about yourself would give me great pleasure,

yours faithfully
françois truffaut

1 – Georges Bernanos's novel was eventually filmed by Robert Bresson in 1967.
2 – From Diderot's novel.
3 – French director, born in 1931: *Adorable Menteuse, Benjamin ou les Mémoires d'un puceau, Bye Bye Barbara, Péril en la demeure, Le Paltoquet, La Lectrice*, etc.
4 – Jean Cocteau's last film (1960), which Truffaut helped produce.

To Helen Scott

Paris, 9 November 1961

Dear Helen,

No, it wasn't just out of politeness that I told you how impatient I was to see Stanley Kramer's film on Nuremberg;[1] it so happens that for two months now I've been reading lots of books on the subject, on Hitler, and particularly the first-rate American book on the 3rd Reich (Shirer?).[2]

Speaking of which, and to cut this rather sensitive matter short, let me draw your attention to the documentary and emotional interest of a new French film entitled *L'Enclos*.

Madeleine is preparing to write you a very long letter.

There's nothing new on *Le Pianiste*, and once again I want you to understand that the fate in America of *Jules et Jim* and *Tire-au-flanc 62* matters much more to me. I know that *Marienbad* has been bought with an advance of 75,000 dollars.

Could you find out what the distributor paid for *La Notte*[3] (Jeanne Moreau's latest film)?

Nevertheless, concerning *Le Pianiste*, if the people from Astor[4] would like to have a try-out or a preview, it would be very easy for them to obtain on loan the print with English subtitles that you saw in Montreal, by asking the distributor: André Pépin – Art Films – 418, St-Sulpice – Montreal I – who would be delighted to entrust it to them for a few days.

I don't know if Resnais has left Paris, in any event I can't possibly show *Jules et Jim* to anyone before 25 November.

I'm going to photocopy the page of your letter concerning Grimblat and send it to him; he's rather masochistic and your insults may well stimulate him.

I'm sending you, by the same post, the documents I told you about in my last letter: two recent interviews, one of them unfriendly (*Cinémonde*), the other very friendly (*France-Observateur*).

Yesterday I received your nice new letter; as for the collage of interviews, it's a wonderful idea which really appeals to me; so I'm going to send you a publication on Resnais from Lyon which was put together more or less on the same principle.

And the book on the cinema and war, when is it going to come out? I'd like to have the list of directors who sent in replies; then I'll select the 5 or 6 most important ones and ask permission to publish them in *Cahiers*.

Paris nous appartient is finally opening here, in early December, at the Essai-Agriculteurs cinema. I'll send you any interesting cuttings. Enclosed you'll find a rather swell handout. If you'd like any more, there's no problem. How many?

Patrick Auffray will make an appearance in *L'Amour à 20 ans*;[5] it's a real bore for me to have to do this sketch; I would have preferred to emerge from *J. et J.* with my virginity renewed; I haven't prepared anything; I haven't any script, any notes, any ideas, I'm empty, dried up, sterile. I've put off starting it several times; I'll have to shoot in January at the latest. I would have liked to follow *J.J.* from country to country, this will partly prevent me from doing so.

Did you finally get to meet Aznavour?

Varda's film *Cléo de 5 à 7*, is excellent, very influenced by *Lola* and by Godard, yet of unrivalled visual beauty; but in my opinion the best film still to be released is *Adieu Philippine*, wonderful, funny, moving and simple.

When I come to N.Y. I'll bring with me *Tire-au-flanc 62* (which opens in Nice in a week's time), *Paris nous appartient* (with English subtitles!) and *Jules et Jim*, also subtitled under my wife's supervision.

By that time we'll also have a version of *Le Scarabée d'or*[6] with an English commentary (also a German version). As you see, at Carrosse we think 'internationally'.

I sent Norman McLaren[7] Queneau's book (*Poèmes*): no reply. To Claude

Fournier and his wife a novel: no reply. They're a funny lot, the Canadians!

The Tin Drum[8] follows and I'm going to think of two or three good new books,

love,
françois

1 – *Judgment at Nuremberg.*
2 – William Shirer's *The Rise and Fall of the Third Reich.*
3 – By Michelangelo Antonioni.
4 – An American distribution company.
5 – *Love at Twenty*, a sketch film whose directors, apart from Truffaut, were Renzo Rossellini, Shintaro Ishihara, Marcel Ophüls and Andrzej Wajda.
6 – Robert Lachenay's short film produced by Les Films du Carrosse.
7 – Canadian director and animator (1914–87).
8 – By Günter Grass.

To a future ex-film-maker

Paris, 13 December 1961

Dear Monsieur,

I acquainted myself with the script you sent me and frankly I found it to be of no great interest: the ill-digested influence of Godard and Antonioni, a dearth of personal ideas, in short, nothing that struck me as 'necessary' or, at any rate, urgent.

In fact, I am rather shocked that you should be thinking of setting up a new project even though the first has been interrupted. It is not on account of my 300,000 francs that I say this, since I harboured few illusions when I lent it to you. But however you now manage to justify your actions to yourself, it seems to me that a number of technicians and actors who put their trust in you have been taken for a ride and that the fact of attempting to set up a new film instead of finishing the first represents something of a betrayal of them.

Anyone can make a film, good or bad; anyone has the right to try his luck; but in an area such as this, in which there is an element of risk, material success (by which I mean, getting as far as the master print) and artistic success go hand in hand.

When I saw a rough cut of [. . .], I quite liked the faces of the actors I saw on the screen, but I deplored, even if I didn't see the point of telling you so, the incredible flatness of the *mise en scène* and, above all, the lack of any personality, despite the fact that it was a project undertaken by two people rather than one, by two friends.

I repeat, I helped you on a matter of principle and also because you assured me that with 300,000 francs you would see the film through and would certainly be able to pay for the dubbing and post-production work on credit.

Moreover, I am convinced it would have been possible for you to do so, as

Jules et Jim, 1961.

several of my friends have demonstrated. There are, in Paris and the region around Paris, a number of small laboratories and studios prepared to work on credit . . . I am certain that you allowed yourself to disperse your energies, that you constantly rubbed people up the wrong way and that your dedication remained 'relative' by comparison with Rivette's which was total.

In a sense, leaving the film unfinished constitutes an act of cowardice towards yourself since it spares you from having to examine your conscience and so, as I believe, reaching this conclusion: [. . .] is not a good film.

I have all your letters in front of me and what I detect in them is a chronic reluctance to face up to your responsibilities and a habitual tendency to set yourself up as a victim: you are anti-militaristic yet you are in uniform, you are against the Algerian War yet you practically have one foot on the boat; and, being a left-winger, you blame the dirty capitalists who cheated you for the fact that your film is unfinished. If you were on the 'right', it would doubtless be the fault of all those Jews who infest the film industry.

This is a very severe letter, but it seems to me that the passionate desire for self-expression that you display does not permit such a degree of irresponsibility.

Yours attentively,
François Truffaut

To Charles Aznavour

from Nice
Saturday 16 December 1961

My dear Charles,

One thing we share, I believe, is the fact that we live for our work. And that's why our paths so seldom cross.

That evening a few months ago when I saw and heard you at the Alhambra I was really enthusiastic and the idea occurred to me of suggesting that we make another film together, one in which you would sing. Nothing is harder to bring off in Europe than this kind of thing, which the Americans frequently do very well.

I'm in Nice, I'm working in a hotel room on a sketch for Jean-Pierre Léaud;[1] I've been listening to your latest LP which is very good and the idea has started to excite me again. What I have in mind is quite a realistic film, similar in tone to those scenes in *Le Pianiste* in which you play opposite Nicole Berger, a psychological film but in the most basic sense as the action would be reduced to 60 minutes, not including the songs; unless, unless we managed to devise a means whereby certain songs would advance the action instead of holding it up . . .

For the people in the industry the objection will be that this kind of film can't be made in France, because a dozen dubbed or subtitled songs would be unacceptable to non-French-speaking audiences. I personally think we would have to envisage an American version for all the songs, since you have no problem singing in English.

If the idea appeals to you, then at the beginning of January I'll have to show you an old Doris Day film, *Leave Me or Love Me* (I can't guarantee that the title is correctly spelt)[2] in which she sings about ten songs. She's brilliantly partnered by James Cagney; the film is superb, it's the biography of a celebrated American singer of the twenties.[3]

To come back to the film we might make, I see it as very simple, almost a documentary on the world of the variety theatre, the recording industry, etc. We would have to show a singer's career, the early hardships, the tacky little productions, the rise to fame and, parallel to that, his love life which at first is normal, then stormy, then back to what it was. Many singers are bad actors, some are good actors but become unphotogenic as soon as they start singing, which isn't your case! I also saw a little kinescope[4] on TV showing you, as I recall, singing 'Je me voyais déjà', what an impact it made.

As you know, I work slowly and never rush things; if such a film appeals to you, I don't mind waiting several months for you and taking my time over the preparation.

Apart from that, I've read the first version of *Pulcinella*, which is very good indeed; I return to Paris on Wednesday and would be happy to show you *Jules et Jim*.

yours,
François Truffaut

1 – For *L'Amour à vingt ans*.
2 – There is nothing wrong with the spelling, but the correct title of Charles Vidor's 1955 film is, of course, *Love Me or Leave Me*.
3 – Ruth Etting.
4 – A precursor of the video clip.

To Helen Scott

from Paris,
Wednesday 20 December 1961

Dear Helen,

This before leaving Paris for a few days' rest in the Midi: I received your latest letters. No word from Resnais since he returned.

Paris nous appartient: the print, which was very well subtitled, was a success at the London Film Festival.

It's the same print I'll be bringing with me to N.Y. in February. The film opened last night in Paris in the tiny Agriculteurs cinema. The reviews have been mixed, but very good in the most important journals, such as *L'Express* . . . For the foreign market, Rivette has agreed to cut 15 minutes, which will bring the film down to 2 hours. I'll ask Lucette to send you the publicity material and the good reviews as they come in.

Tire-au-flanc 62: it's already out in Marseille, Nice and Toulon with fair success; but it would have been better to open it in Paris first, since the absence of stars in an ostensibly unambitious film has a very negative effect in the provinces; there weren't enough preliminary articles. Opening in Paris, in theory for Christmas.

Jules et Jim: certain intellectuals are enthusiastic (Queneau, Audiberti, Jules Roy and my film-director pals!). Women cry, a lot of men get pissed off. It's my first deliberately boring film (1 hour 50 minutes). Frankly, because of the three actors, it holds up better than my previous films. The French and foreign critics will find it easier to defend than *Le Pianiste*; the public will find it a bit more commercial, but less so, of course, than *Les 400 Coups*, which was the kind of success I know I'll never achieve again.[1] The important buyers (Germany and Italy) are very pleased with the film, as are the Siritsky brothers[2] who are bringing it out in January at the Publicis-Vendôme, after Bergman's *The Devil's Eye*.

At the same screening that Resnais attended before he left, there was Frankel, in Paris for a few days, who greatly liked the film and says he's interested in buying it. He claims to have lost a little money on *400 Coups* and wanted that to be taken into account as regards *Jules et Jim*. In the end we didn't discuss figures; he's going to make us an offer one of these days. Between you and me, he's perhaps waiting for it to open in Paris, which doesn't bother me. I'm more or less certain we'll have a favourable reception from the critics and the first-run public, so we've nothing to lose by waiting.

Braunberger confirmed that Astor still haven't signed the contract for *Le Pianiste*, what a bunch of jokers!

L'Amour à 20 ans: I shoot the sketch with J.-P. Léaud on 15 January; it will be finished on the 28th. On the 29th the Vadim 'libel' trial;[3] I'll probably lose, but honourably so.

In February, *go west*![4] In fact, that nice Monsieur Pépin is in financial difficulties and hasn't honoured his contracts; so there isn't much chance of *Jules et Jim* opening there before N.Y.!

I hope you'll find the time to read all the books brought by Resnais and the time, too, to write to me. I'm a little demoralized at the moment, as always at the end of a film; there's the tiredness and also a slight bitterness about the disproportion between the work one has put in and the worries one has had, on the one hand, and the arrogance and condescension of the money-changers from the Temple on the other.

Marienbad is going to have a very good first run here; I consider that such a success, for a film like that, retroactively justifies the project, even if originally one felt there was something gratuitous about it.

We're all delighted here by the failure of *Tout l'Or du monde*[5] and even Clément's *Quelle joie de vivre!*, which is vulgar and conventional.

In a few days I'll be writing to give you my opinion of Kramer's *Nuremberg*. Would you please take out a subscription for me to the magazine *Show Business* and arrange with Lucette about payment? I posed for some colour photographs for them along with Cynthia Grenier,[6] as it turned out; it seems she's rather ill, which makes her a nicer person . . . !?

I'd be pleased to help organize a little Parisian jaunt for you any time you like, on one pretext or another.

I received a very kind letter from Robert Hughes;[7] I'll settle things with him. Jeanne Moreau detests *Les Liaisons dangereuses*[8] and she'll refuse to put herself out for the film just as she did with *La Notte*. She told me on the telephone that she'd like to come with me and publicize *J. et J.*, but one has to take her promises with a pinch of salt.

As regards Victor, the drummer,[9] it's you I blame, because he's a good-looking guy, very funny and very nice.

I find infinitely appealing the prospect of a film co-produced with Astor; why not *Fahrenheit*, shot in N.Y. with Paul Newman?

Hoping to see you very soon, dear Helen,

love,
françois

1 – Truffaut in fact achieved even greater success with *Le Dernier Métro* (1980).
2 – Jo and Sammy Siritsky, French distributors.
3 – See the letter to Helen Scott dated 9 January 1961, p. 159. When, at the request of the film's producer, Roger Vadim agreed to take over the direction of *La Bride sur le cou* from Jean Aurel after just three days' shooting, Truffaut violently attacked him in print. Vadim then sued for libel.
4 – In English in the original letter.
5 – By René Clair. As one may note, the quarrel between the Ancients and the Moderns was so intense at this period that the young directors of the New Wave actually took pleasure in the failures of their predecessors. Even today, this somewhat sadistic attitude is recalled with bitterness by certain unforgiving members of the older generation.
6 – American journalist, later based in Europe.
7 – American film critic and writer.
8 – By Roger Vadim.
9 – Aznavour's drummer.

Production still from *Jules et Jim*.

1962

To Helen Scott *from Paris, 13 March 62*

Dear Helen,

All right, I'm a louse. I haven't written to you these last few weeks because the stew I've got myself into at home was becoming too well-seasoned by 'mutual friends' [. . .].

As far as you are concerned, I knew I had no reason to fear anything indiscreet or ill-intentioned on your part, but, in the state of extreme irritability in which I found myself, I began to regret having taken you into my confidence from the start, especially when I found references in your letters to things you had heard from people around me, that on such-and-such a day I was sad, on such-and-such a day I was happy, etc. There's no distance at all between the mental strain which I've been under for months and a feeling of outright persecution. I hated absolutely everyone; I'm slowly coming out of it, but I'm still quite disgusted with everything.

Having made it up with Madeleine, I'm going to take this trip with her, but the prospect doesn't excite me; in fact, what we need are real holidays which we'll be taking immediately after.

I am emerging from *Jules et Jim* as though from some humiliating failure and I cannot seem to understand why.

I'll write to you again tomorrow on 'business', this is the letter of a friend. I'm very happy that I'll be seeing you again soon, happy too that it will be after a few days of sunshine and relaxation at Mar Del Plata and Rio, which will allow me to offer you a less wretched, less pathetic image of myself,

yours a thousand times,
François Truffaut

To Robert Laffont[1] *Paris, 25 April 1962*

Dear Monsieur,

Thank you very much for having thought of me to direct *The Desert of the Tartars*[2] which I read when it first came out, 12 or 13 years ago, I think. I had the good fortune of making the acquaintance of Armand Piéral who took an interest in me and used to obtain important books for me.

I have not reread it since, but my memory of it is still very precise, and I sincerely believe that it does not correspond to my temperament which is much more realistic and I would even say much more homespun. So convinced am I of that fact that I recently turned down film projects as tempting as *L' Etranger*, from the novel by Camus, and Kafka's *The Castle*.

The Desert of the Tartars would need to be filmed by a more intellectual director, like Alain Resnais (who would probably refuse), or else a 'visionary primitive': I am thinking of Georges Franju, who would certainly accept, or even, and this would be a shrewd compromise between Resnais and Franju, Agnès Varda; you may have seen her film *Cléo de 5 à 7*, which is both visually very beautiful and very intelligent, poetic and intellectual.

The Cottafavi option is worth considering, since he is a director who is probably overestimated by the young 'Macmahonians',[3] who praise him to the skies, but at the same time underestimated by Italian producers who force him to make films of pseudo-biblical hokum.

I was very pleased to receive your letter which I found on my return from America, since, by one of life's coincidences, it so happens that in New York I had an idea for a book which I would like to do (it concerns the cinema) and which I was planning to propose to you first.

I leave in a few days for Cannes where I will be staying until the end of May. I do hope that we will be able to get together when I return and that you will keep me informed of any developments in *The Desert of the Tartars*, since indeed, more so than with any other film, the choice of director for this project and of a leading actor are crucial.

Yours faithfully,
François Truffaut

1 – French publisher (notably, of *Le Cinéma selon Hitchcock*, which is doubtless the 'idea for a book' mentioned by Truffaut in this letter).

2 – By Dino Buzzati.

3 – A sectarian group of film critics and enthusiasts with a particular penchant for 'virile' action movies.

To *France-Observateur*[1] *Paris, 30 May 1962*

Monsieur,

I have received your circular inviting me to renew my subscription. I have no intention of doing so, and if it interests you to learn the reason for my dissatisfaction, a mere glance at the cinema page of *France-Observateur* in the last three months will enlighten you.

Nevertheless I have a very pleasant memory of our meeting one evening, at the Théâtre des Champs-Élysées.

Best wishes,
François Truffaut

1 – French news journal.

To Alfred Hitchcock[1] *Paris, 2 June 1962*

Dear Mr Hitchcock,

First of all, allow me to remind you who I am. A few years ago, in late 1954, when I was a film journalist, I came with my friend Claude Chabrol to interview you at the Saint-Maurice studio where you were directing the post-synchronization of *To Catch a Thief*. You asked us to go and wait for you in the studio bar, and it was then that, in the excitement of having watched fifteen times in succession a 'loop' showing Brigitte Auber and Cary Grant in a speedboat, Chabrol and I fell into the frozen tank in the studio courtyard.

You very kindly agreed to postpone the interview which was conducted that same evening at your hotel.

Subsequently, each time you visited Paris, I had the pleasure of meeting you with Odette Ferry, and the following year you even said to me, 'Whenever I see ice cubes in a glass of whisky I think of you.' One year after that, you invited me to come to New York for a few days and watch the shooting of *The Wrong Man*, but I had to decline the invitation since, a few months after Claude Chabrol, I turned to film-making myself.

I have made three films, the first of which, *The Four Hundred Blows*, had, I believe, a certain success in Hollywood. The latest, *Jules et Jim*, is currently showing in New York.

I come now to the point of my letter. In the course of my discussions with foreign journalists and especially in New York, I have come to realize that their conception of your work is often very superficial. Moreover, the kind of propaganda that we were responsible for in *Cahiers du cinéma* was excellent as far as France was concerned, but inappropriate for America because it was too intellectual.

Since I have become a director myself, my admiration for you has in no way weakened; on the contrary, it has grown stronger and changed in nature. There are many directors with a love for the cinema, but what you possess is a love of celluloid itself and it is that which I would like to talk to you about.

I would like you to grant me a tape-recorded interview which would take about eight days to conduct and would add up to about thirty hours of recordings. The point of this would be to distil not a series of articles but an entire book which would be published simultaneously in New York (I would consider offering it, for example, to Simon and Schuster where I have some friends) and Paris (by Gallimard or Robert Laffont), then, probably later, more or less everywhere in the world.

If the idea were to appeal to you, and you agreed to do it, here is how I think we might proceed: I could come and stay for about ten days wherever it would be most convenient for you. From New York I would bring with me Miss Helen Scott who would be the ideal interpreter; she carries out simultaneous translations at such a speed that we would have the impression of speaking to one another without any intermediary and, working as she does at the French Film Office in New York, she is also completely familiar with the vocabulary of the cinema. She and I would take rooms in the hotel closest to your home or to whichever office you might arrange.

Here is the work schedule. Just a very detailed interview in chronological order. To start with, some biographical notes, then the first jobs you had before entering the film industry, then your stay in Berlin. This would be followed by:

1. the British silent films;
2. the British sound films;
3. the first American films for Selznick[2] and the spy films;
4. the two 'Transatlantic Pictures';[3]
5. the Vistavision period[4]
6. from *The Wrong Man* to *The Birds*.

The questions would focus more precisely on:

a) the circumstances surrounding the inception of each film;
b) the development and construction of the screenplay;
c) the stylistic problems peculiar to each film;
d) the situation of the film in relation to those preceding it;

e) your own assessment of the artistic and commercial result in relation to your intentions.

There would be questions of a more general nature on: good and bad scripts, different styles of dialogue, the direction of actors, the art of editing, the development of new techniques, special effects and colour. These would be interspaced among the different categories in order to prevent any interruption in chronology.

The body of the work would be preceded by a text which I would write myself and which might be summarized as follows: if, overnight, the cinema had to do without its soundtrack and become once again a silent art, then many directors would be forced into unemployment, but, among the survivors, there would be Alfred Hitchcock and everyone would realize at last that he is the greatest film director in the world.

If this project interests you, I would ask you to let me know how you would like us to proceed. I imagine that you are in the process of editing *The Birds*, and perhaps you would prefer to wait a while?

For my part, at the end of this year I am due to make my next film, an adaptation of a novel by Ray Bradbury, *Fahrenheit 451*, which is why I would prefer the interviews to take place between 15 July and 15 September 1962.

If you were to accept the proposition, I would gather together all the documents I would need to prepare the four or five hundred questions which I wish to ask you, and I would have the Brussels Cinémathèque screen for me those films of yours with which I'm least familiar. That would take me about three weeks, which would mean I could be at your disposal from the beginning of July.

A few weeks after our interviews, the transcribed, edited and corrected text would be submitted to you in English so that you might make any corrections that you considered useful, and the book itself would be ready to come out by the end of this year.

Awaiting your reply, I beg you to accept, dear Mr Hitchcock, my profound admiration. I remain

Yours sincerely,
François Truffaut

1 – British-born director (1899–1980).
2 – David O. Selznick, American producer (1902–65). Having invited Hitchcock to Hollywood, he produced three of his earliest American films: *Rebecca*, *Spellbound* and *The Paradine Case*.
3 – Transatlantic Pictures was a small independent company which produced

Hitchcock's *Rope* and *Under Capricorn*.
4 – Hitchcock made five films in this wide-screen format: *To Catch a Thief, The Trouble with Harry, The Man Who Knew Too Much, Vertigo* and *North by Northwest*.

To Helen Scott

Paris, 2 June 1962

Dear Helen,

I am going to reply as scrupulously as possible to the dozen letters that I have in front of me. Not only have I read them – which you always refuse to believe – but I've also taken the trouble to file them, if not in chronological order, at least in the order in which they arrived in France.

Thank you for all the articles.

I received the viewfinder from Goodis, unfortunately it's a really rudimentary one, and now I understand why, if they treated him as badly as that, he hasn't a pleasant memory of Hollywood!

In accordance with your instructions, I was very friendly with the Americans at Cannes, but, as I was on the jury, they realized that I was very busy and none of them pestered me, not even Archer.[1]

Harvey[2] was very kind since he continued to make reassuring noises, even though I imagine he's a little disappointed with the results.

As you probably know, the English critics were also quite favourable and the box-office figures in London are satisfactory.

I can reveal to you that it was very much thanks to me that Sidney Lumet's film obtained a prize at Cannes.[3] When I was in New York, Maternati[4] had made the mistake of telling me that Preminger[5] (whose behaviour is as odious as ever) was determined that the prize for best actor should go to Charles Laughton.[6] So my first job on the jury was to foil his evil designs and Laughton's trip was cancelled.

I have to say in all honesty that Lumet's was the best of the three American films.

As far as *Fahrenheit* is concerned, you probably know that everything is going quite well and we're in the process of negotiating the rights. We took advantage of Maternati's stopover in Paris to give him a very small part of the deal, and I think he and Congdon[7] will be getting together when he returns.

It suits me that Bradbury won't be collaborating on the adaptation and I'm probably going to work with Marcel Moussy.

We should be shooting the film around the end of this year, probably with Jean-Paul Belmondo.[8]

I've completely given up the idea of trying to get Paul Newman, since it's too important a script to be shot in English with my poor command of the language.

The idea of filming in English still tempts me, but with a more lightweight script, speaking of which, I must tell you that I read *Love in Connecticut*; it's a quite well-written comedy which could easily be improved and in which Jean-Pierre Léaud, even in a year's time, would be terrific.

I'd like you to read it and I'll give you the references:

Original screenplay by Maxime Furlaud, 121, East 17th Street – New York 3, N.Y. Gramercy 3-8167.

If you meet the author, you might let me know if he's a pleasant and flexible kind of guy, and if you have the feeling I could get on with him.

What would be amusing for the scenario is if we had Jean-Pierre Léaud speaking English scarcely better than I do and having endless recourse to the titles of famous American films. I'm dying to know what you think.

Did you receive the first consignment of records? A second one, also consisting of odds and ends, went off a few days ago, and one day I'll send you something better.

I wasn't able to read Miller's[9] play since it hasn't been translated into French, but Madeleine and Moussy, who read it carefully, tell me it's rather dated and actually very boring, and both of them are against my pursuing the matter.

Don't tell our friends Simon and Schuster what I've just said, but, if you should see them, try and find out what they think of the play.

And while we're on the subject of Simon and Schuster, convey my warmest regards to Elizabeth Sutherland.

The Cannes screenings of *L'Amour à vingt ans* were a great success and, as you perhaps know, the film has been bought for the United States by the people at Seven Arts,[10] so you'll probably be seeing it in a month's time.

Dear Helen, I come now to the essential, and you'll soon get over your disappointment at not working with Bradbury and me if my other project works out. I refer to the book of interviews with Hitchcock that I spoke to you about.

You'll find enclosed the letter I'm sending to Hitchcock. I want you to make sure he receives it as soon as possible, along with an English translation which, it seems to me, is indispensable.

Here is his address: 10957 Bellagio Road, Bel-Air, Los Angeles 24, Calif. Check to make sure I've got it right, it's essential we avoid going through that very unpleasant agent of his, with whom I exchanged a few bitter-sweet words on the subject of *The Birds*.

I don't want this Hitchcock project, if it comes off, to force you to give up your trip to Europe if you've persevered and succeeded in your idea of attending the Locarno Festival. That's why you have my permission to alter the dates in the letter so that they fit in with your own availability, the essential point for me being that it takes place before the middle of September, since, if it were later than that, it would clash with the preparation of *Fahrenheit*.

Dear Helen, I impatiently wait to hear from you and – forgive me – even more impatiently to hear from Hitchcock, since it's all linked together.

Warmest regards,
François Truffaut

1 – Eugene Archer, a film critic on the *New York Times*.
2 – Cyrus Harvey, American distributor (Janus Films).
3 – *Long Day's Journey into Night* won an award at the 1962 Cannes Festival for the performances of its four leading players, Katharine Hepburn, Ralph Richardson, Jason Robards Jr. and Dean Stockwell.
4 – Jo Maternati, the director of the French Film Office of New York.
5 – Otto Preminger, Austrian-born director and actor of American films (1906–86): (as director) *Laura*, *Fallen Angel*, *Whirlpool*, *The Moon is Blue*, *River of No Return*, *Bonjour Tristesse*, *Anatomy of a Murder*, *The Cardinal*, etc.
6 – For his role in Preminger's *Advise and Consent*.
7 – Don Congdon, Truffaut's literary agent in New York.
8 – French actor, born in 1933: *A double tour*, *A bout de souffle*, *Moderato Cantabile*, *Une femme est une femme*, *La Sirène du Mississipi*, *Stavisky*, etc.
9 – Arthur Miller.
10 – American production and distribution company.

To Helen Scott

from Saint-Paul-de-Vence,
Wednesday 20 June 1962

My dear Helen,

It's true, I'm a sod. After my telegram, which was sent at least a week ago and ended with the words 'letter follows', I dropped you like an old cotton sock (I can't bear nylon). As always, if Madeleine isn't to blame, then you are. In fact, I dictate all my letters to Lucette except those addressed to you, since I haven't forgotten the ticking-off you gave me after my first visit to New York on account of a letter that was too impersonal.

I've received all of yours, including the most important one that was posted to Antibes, a town twelve kilometres away, or fifteen more like. I am, to be sure, merely a *young director*,[1] but after all the Colombe d'Or is the most famous de luxe bordello in the Alpes-Maritimes!!!

Thank you for the documents on Balthus; he's my favourite contemporary painter, and my idea is to make an extremely simple and respectful short on his work, showing the paintings without any pyrotechnical camera movements or pretentious commentary; if it works out, we'll have to get one of our photographer friends in New York to take some first-rate 'slides' of the paintings that are there, whether privately owned or at Pierre Matisse's. We'll speak further. There's no point in chasing after the other documents.

Your holiday. I'm waiting to hear from you about that. For the moment, we have no plans to leave Saint-Paul which suits us perfectly. I'm doing a little work on the Hitchcock project and a little on *Fahrenheit*, Marcel Moussy (my collaborator on *Les 400 Coups* and the director of *Saint-Tropez Blues*) will come and work more intensively with me around the beginning of August. Then he'll work alone while we go off on our Hitchcockian caper. All of that will go like clockwork. If you come to France, you will, naturliche, come and spend a few days with us. In fact, I'm spending a week or two here, which is very good for the health of my marriage. I don't cook up trips for myself, I just don't turn any down. For example, I leave in two days' time to spend 4 days in Berlin with Jean-Pierre Léaud, since *L'Amour à 20 ans* is opening the festival.

In about ten days I'll be going to Rome with Jeanne Moreau to hold a press conference in protest against the banning in Italy of *Jules et Jim*. Then, to Spoleto (150 km from Rome, the temple of pure theatre, as seen at the end of *Vie privée*),[2] where we'll be presenting *Jules et Jim* and seeing a play staged by Rossellini, *Les Carabiniers*, which Godard happens to be adapting for his next film.

There's also a possibility, later, of presenting *Jules et Jim* in Stockholm, but that's not certain yet.

And while I'm at it, *happy birthday to you.*[1]

Hitchcock. I was a little annoyed by your scepticism on the matter; for my part, I never doubted for a moment what his answer would be.

Here is the text of his telegram:

'Dear Monsieur Truffaut – Your letter brought tears to my eyes and I am so grateful to receive such a tribute from you – Stop – I am still shooting *The Birds* and this will continue until 15 July and after that I will have to begin editing which will take me several weeks – Stop – I think I will wait until we have finished shooting *The Birds* and then I will contact you with the idea of getting together around the end of August – Stop – Thank you again for your charming letter – Kind regards – Cordially yours – Alfred Hitchcock.'

I've asked Lucette to send you the three most important issues of *Cahiers* devoted to Hitch, but I've forgotten to tell her the most important one of all. When I pass through Paris, I'll also send you some of the articles I wrote about him in *Arts*. For the moment I'm reading the novels he adapted for the cinema. *The Birds*, by Daphne du Maurier, is only a short story in the style of Bradbury; it looks very promising.

Your idea of transcribing the tapes as we go along is first-rate, but I would have thought difficult to do. As far as the tape recorder is concerned, would you advise me to bring one from Paris or else buy (or rent) one in New York? The choice of a tape recorder is important, because it mustn't be an ordeal for me to transport it, yet we have to be able to record for a long time without changing tapes. Make some enquiries, maybe Bachman[3] will know? Another important thing, in the course of the interviews, will be to take notes each time Hitch says something important and the tape recorder isn't switched on, whether because he's invited us to have a bite to eat or I'm in the process of changing the tape or setting up the machine.

By the way, you don't think the guys from Bleecker Street[4] would have some non-European documentation on Hitch? If they have, read through it and tell me what it is before sending it to me. Actually, I'm not short of material, it would just be to add some finishing touches.

I'm very excited by this project and I've already chatted sufficiently with Hitchcock to know that I won't be disappointed; his talent is not of an instinctive nature like Preminger's, for example; he's really the guy who has given the most thought to cinema as both spectacle and style. Just as the short on Balthus is little more than a pretext to enable me to take a long, calm look at the paintings without wasting my time as a film-maker, so this book on Hitchcock will only be a pretext for me to educate myself.

Love in Connecticut. It was via Jeanne Moreau's agent that I got the script (CIMURA is affiliated to MCA). I told them I had quite liked it, no more than that. I agree we shouldn't make any further move, especially as I'm more excited than enthusiastic; what I saw in it was the chance to combine several ambitions of mine: to make a new film with Jean-Pierre Léaud before he grows up, to make a film in America, to learn English and to make a comedy. Of course, I won't be absolutely faithful to the script and maybe I won't even be faithful to its spirit; for me the actor (because he is specific) will always take precedence over the character (who is abstract). I would prefer a film to change its meaning along the way rather than have an actor ill at ease. Jean-Pierre wasn't the character I had intended for *Les 400 Blows*. What worries me in Furlaud's script is that the boy is too sure of himself, he knows in advance that he's going to seduce the woman; what I would do is make him more crafty and at the same time more timid, he would 'make his play' with cunning and naïvety, he would gradually worm his way into her bed rather than seduce her; I'm not mad about the monstrous little kids in the background, they're too cartoon-like. If Jean-Pierre has to speak impeccable English, then it isn't possible (because he's bone-idle) and I'd find it much less amusing. As you see, we're not getting off to a good start. Our only meeting of minds is Barbara Bel Geddes[5] whom I had also thought of. No, if this business ever comes to anything, it will be necessary for the writer to agree to spend three weeks with me revising his script, then he'll have to swallow his pride and accept that, when we start shooting, a whole third of his script might be replaced by improvisation!

To end this talk of *Love in Connecticut*, I'd be happy to meet the writer when I come to N.Y., but I'd very much like to know why the deal wasn't made with Renoir. Was it he who pulled out or the producers, or what?

As regards the illustrated book you've been asked to do, I'm only now beginning to understand what it's all about and what sort of material I have to send you. Let me know if there's still time, I can try and get one of my assistant directors on the job because we'll have to chase all over the place to dig up some interesting production stills and amusing little anecdotes, and all before the offices close for the holidays, that is what you're talking about, isn't it?

An aside regarding Goodis. Could you ask him whether or not the contract he or his publisher signed for *The Burglar*[6] allows for the possibility of remaking it one day? It's the only book that would induce me to do another thriller in the style of *Le Pianiste*.

Thank you for the material on Bradbury, which is very useful and very good. So, *Fahrenheit* started out as a short story entitled *Fireman*. This business of the title is a real pain in the arse and I'm unable to announce the film because of it. I thought of a kind of international title, *Phoenix* or *The Phoenix*, and I'd like to know, despite your lack of any commercial sense, what you think of it.

The Losers is an excellent idea, especially as a play for TV. Don't give up. At first there's genuine humility involved in not doing things, then self-regarding humility, and finally a kind of pride, which is to be avoided since it's one of the seven deadly sins.

Delighted to know that *Le Pianiste* is finally opening in N.Y.; congratulations on the idea of the intimate little cinema, that was the best solution; let's hope it's a good print and that they haven't cut anything. Let me know.

As regards Harvey, what you say is probably true, but you know that Astor's offer wasn't any better and the other distributors weren't coming forward; we didn't have much choice. What's more, even if the comparison that you make with *Marienbad* is favourable to *Jules et Jim*, Resnais's film is so special that people are more curious about it. Mine is a good film that one can see, his is a curiosity that one has to have seen. I'm sure that's the way people perceive them. In Paris and the provinces *Jules et Jim* is doing far better than *Marienbad*, but that certainly won't be the case abroad; in Germany, in Italy (and for good reason!), in London, etc., *Marienbad* will have more paying customers than me. As the Siritsky brothers (the exhibitors) say in Paris: 'Resnais is a sexy name.'

However, I'd be lying if I said I wasn't disappointed by the shortness of the run at the Guild. The trouble with the film is that it has all the disadvantages of a controversial work with none of the advantages; I sometimes wonder whether, in the advertising, we shouldn't exploit the idea that 'This film has been banned in Spain, Italy, Colombia and Portugal, etc.'

I was in Paris, but not in the office, when Wiesel phoned. I was leaving the next morning for Saint-Paul. If he's still angry, tell him to go to hell.

If there's a record of *Le Pianiste*, send it to me. Has Astor had the books reissued? It's too late for me to think of writing a text; let's place our trust in Gilmore la douce[7] and in providence. Let me know what people like Penn,[8] Lumet, Darach,[9] etc. think of *Le Pianiste* when they've seen it. I hope Penn will have a prize at San Sebastian.[10]

I agree with you about *A bout de souffle* which is heart-rending, but I assure you that one day you'll be amazed by *Le Petit Soldat* and *Vivre sa vie* which that arsehole Halliday[11] doesn't want on the pretext that Karina didn't move him! I saw *Vivre sa vie* again the other day and, my God, I don't often cry in the cinema . . .

You write more than I do, but your letters are terribly incomplete: tell me what Congdon and Furlaud thought of *Le Pianiste*. Why did you like *Guns in the Trees*[12] better the second time?

What is scandalous is that you talk to me about a screening of *Tire-au-*

flanc that disappointed you without telling me a) how many people there were in the auditorium; b) whether or not the audience laughed; c) the reactions of Diener,[13] MacGregor[14] and Maternati; d) why you were disappointed; e) whether or not there's any hope of selling the film in N.Y. Don't forget that the fate of that film in N.Y. means more to me than that of *Le Pianiste*. I'm exaggerating, but only slightly. What I want above all is to make you realize how disappointed I am and how important it is that you write at greater length in your letters when it concerns Carrosse business. I'd prefer your letters to be less frequent but longer, with lots of precise details and judgements.

For example, I no longer remember very clearly which records I sent you and I repeat that the real consignment will come later, but it would please me (and at the same time help me) to know what you liked the best; tell me 'I was disappointed by this singer, intrigued by that one, bowled over by the other one . . .'

The same with your reading (did you read Goodis's *Down There*?), etc. I'm sure you've recently been reading tons of things by Bradbury and you haven't told me about them.

I'm now going to end this little domestic squabble which has been simmering for a long time but was unleashed by your two laconic lines on *Tire-au-flanc*. I'm quite aware that what you were implying is that the film is crap and I'm willing to listen to any opinion even if it doesn't correspond to my own. Personally, I think the film has its weaknesses, especially towards the end, but I consider it inventive, very fresh and very true to life, occasionally quite poetic and rather cruel, superior at any rate to the average French comedy: Dhéry[15] and even the heavy-handed Tati. There you are, I've said my piece.

Well, I really think, this time, I've covered all the ground. First and foremost among our preoccupations is HITCHCOCK, second, *Le Pianiste*'s own little career, third, what's to become of *Paris nous appartient* and *Tire-au-flanc*. If David Diener doesn't want to handle *Tire-au-flanc*, would the boys of the Bleecker agree to take it? As regards Hitch, try nevertheless (before me) to sound out Miss Sutherland, since it's from there that all my complexes emerge. Even if I never had any doubt that Hitch's reply would be favourable, I'm not convinced that Simon and Schuster are going to leap at the project with enthusiasm and it would help to reassure me on that point, if only in my dealings with the French publisher. Then we'll have to peddle the book to the Italians and the Germans. I've calculated that our Hitchcock expedition will cost around 3,500 dollars which I'll have Les Films du

Carrosse advance me; that represents our travelling and accommodation expenses; to that, I think, we'll have to add the salary of the stenographer or stenographers who'll decipher the tapes and type out the texts. Then, as far as you yourself are concerned, we'll have to agree either on a fixed salary or a percentage cut (whichever you prefer), for don't forget that it's going to mean work, a lot of work. In my opinion, we'll earn no more than two thousand dollars from the French edition of the book. Hence the need to arrange something in New York.

Can you for the moment let me know what a return ticket from New York to Los Angeles costs? It will help me in my accounts. Thanks.

I'm now going to terminate this interminable letter, especially since I'm not sure I'll be able to find an envelope large enough to post it in. If I didn't type like a brute, I might, as you do, use both sides of the paper, but it's impossible.

I'm going to ask Lucette, before she goes on holiday, to send you the French reviews of *L'Amour à 20 ans*, which opens on Friday evening at the same time as the presentation at Berlin, and which you're bound to see in N.Y. some time during July.

In the next few days I'm also going to send you the book that Chabrol and Rohmer wrote about Hitch.[16] It's remarkable, even sublime in places, but a little too intellectual, as Crowther would say.

I send you a thousand kisses, dear Hélène, and all sorts of expressions of affection and gratitude, because, if I didn't have you, I'd never have contemplated, or set in motion, half of my American activities and particularly not the Hitchcock book, the idea for which came to me during our meetings with journalists in New York.

your faithful Truffaldino*,
françois

*Truffaldino: a servant in the *commedia dell'arte*, a sly hypocrite and liar.

P.S. This morning the telephone hasn't stopped ringing from Paris. I learn that Arthur Penn received 2 prizes at San Sebastian and I'm delighted. Then, *Jules et Jim*, in French, will open the Spoleto festival on the 25th, which is to say, next Monday evening. I'll therefore go directly from Berlin. The Italian intelligentsia, novelists like Moravia, film-makers like Rossellini, are putting up a real fight against the censors; so I hope everything will work out. I'll be back here, in Saint-Paul, around the 28th or 29th and what I hope to find is a single letter from you, but one that's long and precise and full of details.

As for *Le Pianiste*, you may be sure that any journalists you can get to read the interview on the film in *Le Monde* will write about it less stupidly than the others. And coming back to *Jules et Jim*, is it already being shown in different neighbourhoods or is that only later?

Look after yourself and give Renée Bord[17] my love.

1 – In English in the original letter.
2 – By Louis Malle.
3 – Gideon Bachman, American film journalist.
4 – A group of film buffs who ran an art-house cinema in Greenwich Village and published, at irregular intervals, the *New York Film Bulletin*.
5 – American actress, born in 1922: *I Remember Mama, Caught, Panic in the Streets, Fourteen Hours, Vertigo, The Five Pennies*, etc. She is doubtless best known, however, as Miss Ellie in the television series *Dallas*.
6 – Filmed by Paul Wendkos in 1957.
7 – Noelle Gilmore, who had dubbed and subtitled many of Jean Renoir's films.
8 – Arthur Penn, American director, born in 1922: *The Left-Handed Gun, The Miracle Worker, Bonnie and Clyde, Mickey One, Alice's Restaurant, Little Big Man, Night Moves*, etc.
9 – Brad Darach, a film correspondent on *Time*.
10 – For *The Miracle Worker*. In fact, Anne Bancroft was named best actress, Patty Duke (who played Helen Keller) received a Special Mention and the film was awarded the International Critics' Prize and the Catholic Office Prize.
11 – American distributor, the partner of Cyrus Harvey at Janus Films.
12 – By Jonas Mekas.
13 – David Diener, a New York publicist and the American distributor of *Paris nous appartient*.
14 – Duncan MacGregor, the manager of the Paris cinema in New York.
15 – Robert Dhéry, French actor and director, born in 1921: (as director) *Les Branquignols, La Belle Américaine, Allez France!, Le Petit Baigneur*, etc.
16 – *Hitchcock*, published in 1957.
17 – Maternati's secretary.

To Helen Scott

Paris, 5 July 1962

Dear Helen,

I have before me your brief letter of 21 June and the big, thick letter of 24 June (being in Paris, I lack only your most recent letter which arrived at the Colombe d'Or).

I won't be shooting *Fahrenheit 451* before March 1963, since Belmondo, who has agreed to make it, won't be free before then. That enables me to put back the dates I had indicated to Hitchcock till 31 October.

You must understand that, in matters concerning the cinema, dates are always put back and never brought forward, so it's out of the question for me to ask Hitchcock to rush through his last ten days of shooting even if it means massacring a few more birds and editing the film any old how! You'll find enclosed a copy of the letter which I'm sending him this very day, and I'm certain that, between the two deadlines, he'll choose the one that's further off.

François Truffaut in Helen Scott's apartment.

By the same post I'm sending you the little book by Rohmer and Chabrol, which in my opinion is quite remarkable; if you don't have the time to read it all, even though it's very fascinating, I recommend the third chapter: 'The American Period' (II).

The best of the *Cahiers* issues devoted to Hitchcock are out of print, which is a good omen for our undertaking, but it means you'll have to wait a little longer, since for the moment I'll have to keep the single copy of each of these precious issues to help provide me with questions.

The publisher Robert Laffont is in complete agreement on the principle of the thing, but in France publishers very seldom offer an advance, except when it concerns a commission, which is why the 750 dollars we may receive from Simon and Schuster would come in very handy for offsetting some of our travelling expenses.

Naturally I have no objection to the book coming out in *paperback*.[1]

I realize now that our bilingual recording method will be of enormous benefit in all matters of publication, since, as soon as the tapes are transcribed, we'll have a book in two languages requiring practically no translation (simply a scrupulous revision of the French), which couldn't be better.

When talking to American journalists, I came to realize that, even though Hitchcock is very popular in America, he's only understood very superficially and, above all, he's considerably underrated as an artist by the critics.

In France, on the contrary, he's been supported, especially on the part of *Cahiers du cinéma*, by a major critical movement, though one that's a little too excessively intellectual, and what we have to achieve in this book is something between the two, something closer to the truth and above all very exhaustive.

The book will open with an introduction which I will write after the event and which won't exceed between 20 and 25 typed pages, then the interview proper which will sometimes have the tone of an interview – a very short question and a lengthy answer – and sometimes the tone of conversation, when I will express certain ideas of mine to prompt him to react or express his own ideas. It will be a very detailed and chronological work:

1. the British silent films;
2. the British sound films;
3. the first American films for Selznick and the spy films;
4. Hitchcock as producer-director;
5. the Vistavision period; the films in colour;

6. the recent period, from *The Wrong Man* to *The Birds*.

The questions would generally focus on:
a) the circumstances surrounding the inception of each film;
b) the development and construction of the screenplay;
c) the stylistic problems peculiar to each film;
d) the situation of the film in relation to those preceding it;
e) Hitchcock's own assessment of the artistic and commercial result of the film in relation to his initial intentions.

There would be questions of a more general nature on good and bad scripts, good and bad characters, different styles of dialogue, how to direct actors, the art of editing and the development of new techniques; and these would be interspaced among the different categories to prevent any interruption in chronology.

In my opinion, the interest of the book will lie in the fact that it will describe in a very meticulous fashion one of the greatest and most complete careers in the cinema and, at the same time, constitute a very precise study of the intellectual and mental, but also physical and material, 'fabrication' of films.

I'd like everyone who makes films to be able to learn something from it, and also everyone whose dream it is to become a film-maker. There you have it as far as Hitchcock is concerned.

David Goodis wrote me a letter and I realized that he liked the subtitled *Pianiste* less than when he couldn't understand anything and believed the film to be more faithful to his book.

As for *The Burglar*, he omitted the essential point, probably because he doesn't know: namely, for how many years were the literary rights signed over to the producer or distributor? It's possible they were sold outright, as often happens in America, in which case it would be possible for me to make the film in a few years' time by conveying my wish to do so to the *big boss*[1] at Columbia, assuming I'm in their good books at that moment.

Don't forget to tell me when *Le Pianiste* opens and to send me the marvellous article by the wonderful Gilmore, your sole rival.

Diener will receive any day now – if he hasn't already – the print of *Paris nous appartient*. Keep me informed.

Love in Connecticut. Let's not speak any more about it for the time being. As for the New York–Los Angeles flight, we'll be travelling, if you have no objection, in 'economy' class, but on the fastest airline nevertheless, since with our shared brilliance we certainly ought to be able to earn 144 dollars for 7 hours' work.

I'm delighted to hear from you how well *Jules et Jim* is doing throughout the country.

I've heard a lot of talk about Marcabru's[2] article, but I haven't read it and I haven't made any attempt to obtain a copy for myself. Madeleine told me it was extremely spiteful, yet he appears to have written a very good review of *L'Amour à 20 ans*, and that one I'm going to read as soon as possible!

I don't think I'll be going to Vancouver, since I can't spend my life travelling, except if it ties in with my stay in the U.S.

You're very unfair about Resnais, and the incidental music at the T.N.P.[3] has often been wonderful.

Regarding *Tire-au-flanc*, I'd like to remind you that I had predicted the screening would be a failure, since I had begged you not to see it in a preview unless there was a full house. Diener, MacGregor and you acted just like the distributors in Paris who think they're smart enough to judge an unfinished film or a comedy in an empty cinema, and who are now kicking themselves, since I'd like to mention in passing that in France *Tire-au-flanc*, perfunctorily distributed by Rank, will do as well at the box-office as *Jules et Jim* (still in France) and maybe even slightly better. This remark brings the *Tire-au-flanc* chapter to an end; the best thing would be to send the print home as soon as possible.

Don't forget that there's also *Le Scarabée d'or* to come, which MacGregor wanted to show to some television people in the hope of generating a series of 13 films, and also *La Fin du voyage*. I'd very much like these two films, which together make up a running time of 40 minutes, to be screened quite soon to Diener, MacGregor and if possible Cyrus Harvey so that we know where we stand.

I hope my letter has answered most of your questions and your worries, even though I imagine that, as far as Maternati is concerned, an absence of 10 days at the end of September is no more convenient than the one which you planned for the beginning of the month. You must tell me what the situation is.

You ask me again how we'll proceed after the recordings and I confess I still haven't got it absolutely clear in my mind.

Since the main chunk of work will be the transcription itself, I think it would be better to have it done at my expense by some specialized agency in

New York. Such a thing must exist. Find out about it and also about the rates they charge so that your work will consist only of carefully rereading the English version before submitting it to Hitchcock and also checking the accuracy of the French translation.

On the question of your remuneration, I'm going to think about it a bit in order to make it fair, financially attractive to you and also, since there's always an element of chance in this kind of undertaking, proportionate to the book's success. It shouldn't be difficult for us to come to an agreement.

françois

1 – In English in the original letter.
2 – Pierre Marcabru, French theatre and film critic.
3 – Théâtre National Populaire.

To Helen Scott

Friday evening, 20 July 1962

My dear Hélène,

Following on from our telephone call yesterday.

Only now do I understand that I was wrong to shuffle the dates around, but you must believe I thought I was doing the best for everyone concerned, you included. I believed that if it was imperative for you to keep the dates as close as possible, there wasn't much chance of the same being true for Alfred and that the ideal solution was to give him the opportunity of suggesting the date that was furthest off. In that way, according to my calculations, your colleagues would have returned from their holidays and there would be no problem with the F.F.O.

No, I have no wish to do the book with Gilmore! Let's be patient and wait for Alfred's next letter and pray to our respective gods that it will all mesh together perfectly.

I've asked the *Pianiste* publishing house (Royalty) to send you some records of 'Framboise'[1] (sung by Boby Lapointe) and the music from the film. What's happening about the opening? Aznavour is soon going to be spending a few days in New York before joining Albicocco[2] and Marie Laforêt in Guatemala for a shoot.[3] Would you like me to ask him to tell you when he'll be there? Do you think some important journalists would be interested in meeting him?

I'd be very pleased to receive two or three copies of the book in English, and also Gilmore's article.

Concerning *Jules et Jim*, an interesting piece of news: the novel[4] is going to be brought out in English by a publisher in London: John Calder, 17, Sackville Street, Piccadilly, London W1. Would you tell the Janus people who may well decide to have some copies sent over or else enter into association with an American publisher-cum-distributor? To be honest, I know nothing of such matters, but perhaps something good may come of it. What do you think? The book has also been translated into German and Italian. That makes me very proud with regard to H.-P. Roché's widow.[5] Since yesterday morning I've been sole owner of the rights to *Fahrenheit* and I'm starting to get the jitters. I still don't know how to 'set up' the film as a commercial proposition; it's that aspect of the business that really pisses me off. My company, Carrosse, can co-produce a third or a half of the film, but no more than that; who can we get into bed with? *That is the question.*[6] Thanks to the success of *Jules et Jim*, there's no lack of offers, so it isn't really a problem, but, as soon as I get moving on it and discover that Belmondo is asking for a salary of 60 million, it gets my back up and makes me want to change professions. In fact, I'd like to be able not to concern myself with all of that and even not to hear about it, but then I'd no longer be free as a film-maker and wouldn't be able to choose my own actors . . .

Hitchcock: Have you received Chabrol's little book? I've enclosed some rather uneven articles that I once wrote about the Master! As for the American contract, there was nothing so very urgent about it, but I'm pleased all the same that you've arranged things with Simon and Schuster.

As far as you yourself are concerned, I propose the following: that you receive 10% of all moneys accruing to me from the book throughout the world, from both publishers and magazines. In the event of the book doing very badly in America, even worse in France and elsewhere, I will nevertheless guarantee you 600 dollars whatever happens; if you consider this offer inadequate, tell me very frankly.

I won't be deducting from that the costs of travelling and accommodation in California; that will all be paid for by Les Films du Carrosse since I'll be taking advantage of the trip to see Bradbury, look around Hollywood, etc. *L'Express* has asked me to do an article on Bradbury when I return, etc.

I come back to the translation problem you spoke to me about in your letter; the text will necessarily be better in English since Hitchcock will be speaking in English; all he has to do is correct the text that we'll be sending him after an initial correction that you and I will make. The question of the translation into French is more problematic, in so far as your simultaneous translation of H.'s answers will perhaps need to be revised by you on paper to make it more faithful to Hitch. But, that apart, the transcription of the tapes will provide us with a text in two languages. It therefore won't be a book translated into either French or English. I hope, this time, I've made myself clear.

What remains vague, I know, is how we'll proceed immediately after the Hitch trip. I don't know yet whether I'll be able to stay on in New York or have to return to Paris at once. In my opinion, the tapes should be transcribed in New York by a woman who does that sort of thing professionally (ask around, there must exist agencies of this kind). The important question is this: how long will this woman (or this agency) need to decipher and type out 20 or 25 hours of bilingual conversation? That's what it comes down to. Then you and I will go over the French text very closely and make a few corrections. You'll transfer our corrections on to the English text which will then be sent to Hitch so that he can make whatever cuts he might desire. When he sends us back the approved text, the book will be more or less finished. At that moment I'll get down to the introduction, which will probably come to about twenty typed pages and will have to be translated into English by you. I see the whole book as being rather long, exhaustive, the story of a very complete career and covering every aspect of film-making.

Thank you for having gone to the trouble of translating the piece on Bazin even though I can't help feeling somewhat embarrassed when I reread it; all that was too intimate to be put into an article. One of these days I'll write a short story entitled *My First Kiss* which will be very amusing. Try and see *L'Amour à 20 ans* (Seven Arts) as soon as possible and tell me what you think.

I've sent off a letter of agreement to the boys in Bleecker Street. There were several points in my letter of 5 July to which you didn't reply: *Le Scarabée d'or*, etc. Incidental music at the T.N.P., etc.

The French films in the running for Venice are *Vivre sa vie*, *Adieu Philippine* (both of them brilliant), *Le Repos du guerrier*[7] and *Les Dimanches de Ville d'Avray*.[8] In fact, in my opinion, it's Orson Welles's *The Trial* which will carry off the Golden Lion.[9]

The screenplay[10] of Resnais's next film, *Muriel*, is very beautiful, very simple and very moving.

Dear Helen, your last letter wasn't as nice as it might have been, but since you yourself are, everything is as it should be and I do understand how my playing around with the Hitch timetable might have put you out. When the time is right, I'll undertake to write half a dozen begging letters to Jo

Maternati which will soften his heart and make him accept your escapade with me.

I assure you that one of the reasons I believed the Hitchcock project was possible is my conviction that Hitchcock is going to fall in love with you at first sight; he's never ceased to be slightly anti-American, he'll be won over by your European (continental!) vivacity and especially your humour.

No, I don't want you to limit yourself in your letters to matters of direct concern to me, you know how much I like having your opinions on records, books and films.

I've thought of something for which now might be just the right time: a French Cinema Week in New York in the autumn, during which the priority would be to show the French films that have been bought but not screened, like *Lola*, *Une femme est une femme* . . . What do you think?

Since poor Hallyday didn't care for *Vivre sa vie*, it was MacGregor who carried off the prize; I'm impatient to learn your reaction to the film, which hasn't opened anywhere yet but which I think is going to do very well everywhere. I went to see it again the other day with Jeanne Moreau and we blubbed three or four times.

I won't send you any classical records from Paris because they're 2 or 3 times more expensive than in America, but in the autumn I'll really get down to selecting a lot of old and new French songs, and you'll be over the moon.

I hope you enjoy the very best of health, I embrace you because I love you and I trust we'll see each other very soon,

françois

Levine's[11] people are very eager for me to come to New York for the opening of *L'Amour à 20 ans*. If it's at the same time as my planned trip, they'll pay for the airline ticket, which is not to be sneezed at. Regarding my financial proposal, my fear is that you won't tell me frankly how you feel, which would be stupid of you.

Monday morning: this morning I received an adorable letter from Sutherland.

1 – 'Avanie et Framboise'.

2 – Jean-Gabriel Albicocco, French director, born in 1936: *La Fille aux yeux d'or*, *Le Grand Meaulnes*, *Le Coeur fou*, *Le Petit Matin*, etc. He was married to the actress and singer Marie Laforêt.

3 – That of *Le Rat d'Amérique*.

4 – By Henri-Pierre Roché, a neglected writer to whom Truffaut's film brought belated (and virtually posthumous) fame. He was also the author of *Les Deux Anglaises et le Continent*, which Truffaut would film in 1971.

5 – Roché died before being able to see Truffaut's film.

6 – In English in the original letter.

7 – By Roger Vadim.

8 – By Serge Bourguignon (*Sundays and Cybèle*).

9 – As it happened, Welles's film did not go

LETTER *from* **FRANCE**

French Film Office • 654 Madison Avenue, New York City

TRUFFAUT MIS A NU

Il est divinement pénible d'être la femme d'un génie

Confession par Madeleine Truffaut

Mon père et mon ami par Jo Matemoti

TRUFFAUT, LE MORALISTE par Gideon Bachmann

François Truffaut, the pseudo-editor of *Letter from France*.

to Venice, and the Golden Lion was awarded *ex aequo* to Valerio Zurlini's *Cronaca familiare* and Andrey Tarkovsky's *Ivan's Childhood. Vivre sa vie* won the jury's Special Prize.

10 – By the poet and novelist Jean Cayrol, who also wrote the commentary to Resnais's *Nuit et Brouillard.*

11 – Joseph E. Levine, American producer (1905–87).

To Alfred Hitchcock

Paris, 17 September 1962

Dear Mr Hitchcock,

First of all, I must ask you to forgive me for having waited so long before writing to you. From Cannes my wife and I telephoned Claridges in London, but unfortunately the day after your departure for New York.

At the same time as this letter I am sending you a telegram, as I prefer that you receive my letter translated into English by Helen; after my recent exchange of letters with Peggy Robertson,[1] I have had the impression there is no one at Columbia capable of translating faithfully from the French.

The transcription of our interviews is proceeding very smoothly both in New York and in Paris. I am very pleased with what I have read so far, but I do believe nevertheless that – if you are of my opinion that the book should be both complete and unflawed – it would be a good idea if we were to converse again into a tape recorder for a day or a half-day in order to deal with a few general questions which have been neglected.

A few days ago I saw *Vertigo* and *Rear Window* again and, in the light of our conversation, I naturally noticed many new things in them. *Vertigo* is the more sentimental, the more poetic, but *Rear Window* is perfection itself. I very often think about *The Birds* which I am impatient to see again. I have a great desire to know the film by heart, and, with regard to that, I wonder if I might ask a favour of you. When the film is dubbed into French, I would like to be present at the sound-mixing, but I would not think of asking Universal-Paris's permission until I had yours.

You entrusted me with some rather old, therefore very, very precious, photographs. I am sending them back today to Peggy Robertson along with an extra set, as I had new prints made of them.

On the subject of music, I thought of something that might be interesting. It would be to issue a record, 'Alfred Hitchcock Presents Bernard Herrmann,'[2] which would consist of the music from *Harry*, *The Wrong Man*, *The Man Who Knew Too Much* and *North by Northwest* interspersed with the kind of little introductions that you alone know how to do: music to strangle by, music to faint by, music to bury bodies by, etc.

To bring the record up to date, you could even include a few of the synthesized sounds from *The Birds*. What do you think of the idea?

I know there would be an audience for such a record in France, but I cannot speak for America and as for Japan . . .!

Dear Mr Hitchcock, the fact that you agreed to the idea of the book I took as an expression of your confidence in me; I spent a fascinating week with you, one that proved very rich, very lively and very instructive. It was also a great pleasure to make the acquaintance of Mrs Hitchcock.

Our dinner in Paris – of which, I confess, I was rather afraid – went off very well and delighted all our guests.

I will continue to correspond with Peggy Robertson on all material questions relating to our book, but from time to time I will take the liberty of writing a little note to you in the hope of seeing you again very soon.

I remain, dear Mr Hitchcock,

Yours very sincerely,
François Truffaut

1 – Hitchcock's assistant.
2 – American composer (1911–75). He composed the scores for seven films by Hitchcock (*The Trouble with Harry*, *The Man Who Knew Too Much*, *The Wrong Man*, *Vertigo*, *North by Northwest*, *Psycho* and *The Birds*), two by Truffaut (*Fahrenheit 451* and *La Mariée était en noir*) and numerous other films from *Citizen Kane* to *Taxi Driver*.

To Marcel Duhamel[1] *Paris, 15 October 1962*

Dear Monsieur,

I made the acquaintance in New York of David Goodis for whom, I believe, you share my admiration.

Through a screening of *Tirez sur le Pianiste*, Henry Miller became a friend of his and an enthusiastic fan of his books.

That pleased me for Goodis's sake, as it has to be said that the situation of the thriller-writer in America is not an enviable one. Lost in the shuffle, ignored by the American intelligentsia, maltreated by his publishers who insist on happy endings, compromises, cuts and title changes, poor Goodis consoles himself as best he can.

He is very happy to know that he has admirers in France and very proud of the fact that some of his books have been translated by Série Noire.

He gave me four novels as yet unpublished in France.

Since I don't read English, I was unable to ascertain what they are like, but my wife very much enjoyed them. I take the liberty of forwarding them to you on Goodis's behalf in the hope that you will read them and possibly include them in your list.

I trust that I am not imposing on you and wish to convey my very warmest regards,

François Truffaut

1 – Born in 1900, Duhamel was the founder of the Gallimard imprint *Série Noire*, which specializes in thrillers.

To Helen Scott *from Paris, 18 October 1962*

My dear Hélène,

No, no, no, I am absolutely not sulking and I've been meaning to write to you for about ten days now, at length as I always do when I get down to it.

At the moment I'm going through a period of low morale, for no particular reason, I might add, since things are fine with Madeleine and the two girls are wonderful; like some civil servant, I come home every evening at 6 o'clock and play with them for a couple of hours. For the same reason I no longer go to the office in the mornings.

I've therefore no cause to be depressed; business is not too bad; in spite of the crisis that is looming, I'm one of the five or six directors whose next film people are prepared to back and *Jules et Jim* continues to do very well in France, Belgium and Italy.

You're right when you say I want everything, but for the moment I don't even know myself what it is I lack.

It's perhaps Hitchcock's bitchiness which is contagious, because, in fact, I react to the failures around me as though they were humiliations: *Eva*, for example, which as an English-language film was so important for Jeanne in America, etc., etc. In fact, I repeat that everything is going well for me, but what a mess our profession is in. To be sure, my pals in the New Wave had too many hopes pinned on them, Chabrol more than anyone, but the old wave has made a mess of things as well; the producer of *La Fayette*[1] will lose 600 million on that film alone, and Raoul Lévy, even though he was scandalously indemnified by the Centre[2] and by Fourré.[3] And the Hakims are making one failure after another: *The Eclipse*,[4] *Eva*. In your last two letters you don't speak about your health; will you need another operation or not?

As regards Linda,[5] Lucette is handling everything and all is going well. Don't worry about the expenses, we're within the budget, everything is fine. I'm very optimistic about it. I'm reading the French text as it's being transcribed (not expensive since it's being done by Lucette and Yvonne). When it's finished, I'll leave Paris to edit it all. What will be difficult, I fear, is the work you'll have to do; I hope you'll be able to find the necessary time. Frankly, it's going to be a good book, both funny and informative.

I hope Hitchcock and Robertson will reply to my latest letters, the ones you translated; for the moment, damn all, but I've heard from Odette Ferry who has just returned; I believe Alma[6] was ill which upset their holiday plans.

As for *La Mort du cygne*,[7] it's quite a complicated business tracing it back to its origin. It was a French film shot in 1937, it's no longer in theatrical distribution but a small television company bought up the rights for French (and perhaps foreign) TV screenings. The company is called Télédis. Now, it appears that the scenarist was the writer Paul Morand, but obviously one no longer knows what type of contract he had at the time (obviously no one then had any thought of TV).

As you know, I'm always happy to be of service to Hitchcock; he wants us to set about buying the remake rights as though for our own company, it's feasible and naturally we'll make the contract over to him without taking any profit. In short, we're at his disposal and we'll be careful not to make a move in our inquiries until we receive his instructions.

If he's agreeable, it's Berbert who will open the discussions and, as soon as we have an indication of the price being asked by the people who own the rights, we'll cable him for his decision.

I still haven't sent Congdon the description of the book, because I find doing that as much a bore as writing a synopsis of *Fahrenheit*, but of course I'll get down to it soon.

What do you think of the Awards Dinners? I leave you to judge. Tell me what I ought to do.

Incidentally, you didn't speak about that nice guy who wrote me in English to tell me of his pianistic enthusiasm[8] and whose letter I gave you so that you might kiss him for me.

Also, I'd be very happy to receive 5 or 6 copies of the Bleecker Street *N.Y. Film Bulletin*. You might also send one to Renoir in Calif.

In Paris, *Vivre sa vie* is doing quite well, moderately so, less well than I thought it would, and it would probably have been better to wait before bringing it out in N.Y.

In fact, if I didn't write to you earlier, it was because I'm doing a lot of work with Moussy on *Fahrenheit*. I have the impression that, by the time we start shooting, I'll have had other ideas and made more radical changes, but for the moment it's not too bad. Quite faithful to the book, but much more realistic and closer to home. Doubtless because of Hitchcock, we've endeavoured to create, if not suspense, then at least a fairly constant tension; there's more violence than in the book, a more physical, more immediate sort of violence, and also more humour.

Pessimistic forecast: a nation getting ready to say yes to de Gaulle is a nation that doesn't give a shit whether its culture disappears or not, and therefore doesn't give a shit about *Fahrenheit*.

Optimistic forecast: books are solid, visible and tangible objects; everyone knows them, everyone has them, buys them, lends and borrows them. Therefore, everyone is capable of being moved by a film that shows books burning in extreme close-up.

That's my state of mind, dear Hélène, before going off to see my daughters again, since it's 5.30.

No, I wasn't sulking; on the contrary, I miss you already and my dream would be to return to Hollywood, not to start all over again, but to continue our work with the Master,

see you very soon, a thousand kisses,

françois

P.S. 1. I never see Linda in Paris, since she doesn't speak French, I'm very much the family man at the moment and it would be no fun for either of us, given what I know about her.

2. I read a very good American script: *Daffy*; I'll keep you posted.

3. Apart from the Léonide Moguy,[9] what have you seen? *La Mort de Belle*?

1 – By Denys de la Patellière.
2 – Centre National de la Cinématographie.
3 – Michel Fourré, the first director of the CNC.
4 – Michelangelo Antonioni's *L'Eclisse*.
5 – The transcriber of the Truffaut – Hitchcock tapes.
6 – Alma Reville, Hitchcock's wife.
7 – By Jean Benoît-Lévy.
8 – Presumably, his enthusiasm for *Tirez sur le pianiste*.
9 – *Les Hommes veulent vivre*.

1963

To Helen Scott

from Cannes, 14 January 1963

My dear Helen,

It all started on the day you criticized me for a letter I had dictated to Lucette. Because of that I've got into the habit of writing you either long letters or none at all.

For several months now I've been working extremely hard, without a break and on one thing at a time.

I'm in Cannes, at Saint-Michel, with Madeleine and the children, but I work all day here, at the Hôtel Martinez, on the *Fahrenheit* script with Jean-Louis Richard.[1] There was already a first version which I did with Marcel Moussy but it wasn't much good; so with Richard I'm starting again from scratch; I get along much better with him than with Moussy and the work is better too.

Before this, we spent a month and a half together writing the script of *Mata-Hari* which he'll be directing for Jeanne Moreau; it is, I think, a good strong script, both funny and sad, exciting from beginning to end. I'm working as hard as I am because I'm nervous about 1963. I'm going to shoot *Fahrenheit* in June and I would like to edit the Hitchcock before that, if possible.

As you requested me to do, I spoke about you to Unifrance, not to Jérôme Brierre but to Robert Cravenne. He already knew of your situation through Desdoits,[2] who just happened to be in Paris. He said he might be able to commission you to write some articles on film shoots 'with an eye to the U.S.', but that the work wouldn't be regular. He added, 'Obviously I could speak to my brother about her.' (His brother is Georges Cravenne,[3] *public relations number one*,[4] who has worked for Zanuck,[5] Preminger, etc.)

17 January 63

I'm resuming this letter today; I'm in Paris for 48 hours.

Madeleine has received your letter; no, the idea of your living in Paris doesn't worry me. I used to live from one day to the next and it was just like that. For several years now I've begun to worry about the future and, naturally, the future of other people; Claude de Givray, for example: his two films did well, yet no one is offering him a 3rd. Jean-Pierre Léaud: no projects except for his military service. Robert Lachenay: nothing on the horizon.

You have a strong but paradoxical personality; I think, for example, that you would have too strong a personality to occupy a position like Peggy Robertson's with Hitch, yet it would be the ideal solution.

You're condemned either to do interesting work for mediocre people whose mistakes you manage to correct by doing their job as well as your own, or else to work beneath your capacity, as a secretary, for example.

There's also the fact that the kind of job that attracts you and that you do best is typically American.

Of course I'll speak and go on speaking about you to the people around me but, if they're serious, they don't take me seriously when I discuss facts or figures or anything other than films.

Finally, it's with Deutschmeister (Franco-London Films) that I'll be co-producing *Fahrenheit* and its star will be our friend Aznavour, yes indeed. So a date has now been fixed: June.

I really can't tell you if I'll have the time in March to dictate to Lucette the French text of the book on Hitch or whether it will have to be put off until August, with all the problems which that will entail (delaying on *The Birds* . . .).

Madeleine, who will be replying to you, I hope, is very well as are the little ones, my life is less and less frivolous, more and more domestic and hard-working.

I think that, after *Fahrenheit*, I'll give up adaptations in favour of original screenplays, which are unquestionably easier to do! Before getting down to *Fahrenheit*, Jean-Louis Richard and I wrote the script of *Mata-Hari* which he will direct with Jeanne Moreau. (I can see I'm repeating myself!!!)

The work was easy and pleasant and I think the result is very good, especially for Jeanne who needs a real success to silence some increasingly mean attacks on her from the newspapers (*because*[4] *Eva* and even *The Trial*).

Dear Hélène, I leave you now and I expect to hear from you, in detail,

love,
françois

P.S. I'll have 3 undisturbed days in Tel Aviv to see Jérôme Brierre and I'll talk to him a lot about you, naturliche.

P.S. Congdon got 3,500 dollars, which is perfect. Richard Davis can go to hell (!).

1 – French screenwriter, actor and director, he worked on the scripts of four of Truffaut's films (*La Peau douce*, *Fahrenheit 451*, *La Mariée était en noir* and *La Nuit américaine*) and acted in *Le Dernier Métro* and *Vivement dimanche!* He was married to Jeanne Moreau, whom he directed in *Mata-Hari, agent H 21* (1964).

2 – See note 1, p. 510.

3 – See note 1, p. 308.

4 – In English in the original letter.

5 – Darryl F. Zanuck, American producer and studio executive (1902–79).

To Charles Aznavour

from Paris, 18 January 63

My dear Charles,

I was there last night, I just made it and was very happy to have done so, I'm off again tomorrow morning.

I'm working hard on *Fahrenheit* and, in a month (mid-February), I think the script will be more or less ready.

The preliminary discussions with Deutsch went very well, I believe everything is going to work out. The current situation calls for prudence and I think we'll have to give up the idea of shooting in the Midi in order to save between 12 and 15 million francs.

I'm going to visit the tower blocks of Sarcelles, Meudon, Antony, etc. I think of you a lot while writing the script, Montag will be quite a strong character, I believe, better than in the novel.

I'm very pleased that you're looking forward to this new collaboration.[1]

Jeanne Moreau, with whom I lunched, is coming to hear you in the next few days.

As I did after the evening at the Alhambra, I thought yesterday that one day you ought to take the risk of doing a *Love Me or Leave Me*[2] (with Cagney and Doris Day) or something along those lines, we would have to listen to Gardel's[3] tangos . . .

regards,
françois

1 – Truffaut was thinking at the time of casting Aznavour as the fireman hero of *Fahrenheit 451*, Montag. Later both Peter O'Toole and Terence Stamp were considered and the role was finally given to Oskar Werner.

2 – Cf. the letter to Aznavour dated 16 December 1961, p. 171.

3 – Antonio Gardel, Argentinian singer and musician, born in France and killed in an air accident in 1935.

To Helen Scott *from Paris, 18 January 63*

Ma belle Hélène,

Once I start writing to you, I can't stop. How painful it used to be for me to write to you by hand!

I've just been rereading all your letters since 22 October and I've ticked off the points that have been left in suspense (as Hitch would say).

1. Linda, the salary, the invoices, the expenses, etc., I just don't want to know about all that. All money matters have to be settled between Lucette, Berbert and yourself. Do you need some more money?

2. Neither Besh nor anyone else is interested in *Fahrenheit*. Even with Deutschmeister, nothing has been signed; since the current situation is catastrophic, we're going to try, once we've made a deal with Deutsch, to do a co-production with Italy. I hear nevertheless that Janus is beginning to show signs of wanting to come into the deal or buy the American rights . . .

3. I would have been delighted to see the Seavers.[1] If you have their address in France, give it to me. I think Madeleine would also very much enjoy meeting them.

4. You tell me about your chats with Melville,[2] but what did you think, think, think, I say, of *Une femme est une femme*? I'm less concerned than I used to be by what this or that person thinks of films, even so I'm still amazed at your systematic reluctance to offer an opinion. What do you think of *Teruel*,[3] *Une femme est une femme*, *Lola*, *Longue Absence*, etc.? I would like to know. For my part, I haven't seen *Ville d'Avray*. I was disappointed by *The Trial* and *Eva* . . . I go to the theatre a lot.

5. I'm impatient to read Bogdanovich's[4] prose, even in English. Since an old friend of mine, a Russian lady, who used to send me parcels when I was in the guardhouse, is now utterly penniless, I'm getting her to translate some English articles by Hitchcock that Peggy sent me. She's written tons of books that have all been turned down. She sent a short novel to Julliard letting him believe that she was a young woman of 25; he published it; she made the mistake of dropping the mask too soon, he withdrew it from circulation. Since then, he's died!! If it would amuse you to read it, I'll send it to you one of these days . . .

6. I haven't seen X— for ages; his new film is dreadful; he's the only guy who can pride himself on having got the better of me through intensive flattery.

7. Agreed, I'll tell Lucette to send you copies of the correspondence with Congdon.

8. I'm going to talk to Micheline Rozan[5] about you.

9. I'm pleased to hear that Y— is detestable. The other day, in a restaurant, a guy with the face of a thug calls me an arsehole and says he's going to beat me up. The waiters pull us apart just as he's about to belt me one (he was very big and very fat and very strong) and I discover that he's the husband of Ludmilla Tcherina[6] who holds me responsible for the 500 million he lost. He was a bit drunk . . . I'm therefore very impatient to know whether the film[7] is doing well in N.Y.!!!

tenderly yours,
françois

1 – Janet and Dick Seavers, publishers at the Grove Press.
2 – Jean-Pierre Melville, French director (1917–73): *Le Silence de la mer*, *Les Enfants terribles*, *Bob le flambeur*, *Le Doulos*, *Le Deuxième Souffle*, *Le Samourai*, etc.
3 – Raymond Rouleau's *Les Amants de Teruel*.
4 – Peter Bogdanovich, American director (and former critic), born in 1939: *The Last Picture Show*, *What's Up, Doc?*, *Paper Moon*, *Daisy Miller*, *Nickelodeon*, *Mask*, etc.
5 – Actors' agent.
6 – French actress and dancer, born in 1925: *The Red Shoes*, *The Tales of Hoffman*, *Sign of the Pagan*, *Oh Rosalinda!*, *Les Amants de Teruel*, etc.
7 – *Les Amants de Teruel*.

To Helen Scott *[February 1963]*

My dear Hélène,

I was rather irritated by the letter from Sutherland concerning her lack of confidence in me with regard to the book; I had a very strong impression that her somewhat ill-judged note was the result of conversations between you; that's why I am sending you a copy of my reply, which I trust will set her straight once and for all. As you know, I bristle when people try to put me on the spot, because it happens too often, in my work, that pressure is put upon me. The matter is now closed, at least as far as I'm concerned.

In answer to your letter of 22 January:

1. The *Fahrenheit* script is going slowly but surely; it's becoming more and more clear to me that I won't be able to tackle the Hitch before the end of the year.

2. I'm also sorry to have to disappoint you on the question of your coming to watch the shoot, but it's impossible from a practical point of view; I have a crew that's very light yet still too heavy for my liking; what you like best in my films, the interrogation of Antoine, Nicole Berger's confession, Jeanne Moreau crying with Oskar, all of these were achieved between Coutard[1] and

myself, after kicking everyone out; I wouldn't want to treat you in that fashion; actors don't like to feel that someone's watching them; being on a shoot means subjecting yourself to harassment fifteen times a day; you're pushed aside, you're made fun of, you're left behind when there's a change of location. And above all you're bored, you don't understand anything, you spend all your time waiting around and you learn nothing at all. Madeleine almost never comes.

3. For the production's publicity, I'm not saying no, but Deutschmeister uses the same people all the year round, since it produces 4 or 5 films one after the other; because of the crisis, we're determined to make the film very economically, the idea is open to discussion, but I know that Deutsch will be against such an expense . . .

4. I talked to Micheline Rozan about you; there had been a misunderstanding, since what she's looking for is a very wealthy company for which she would be the correspondent in Paris!!!

I interrupted my work on *Fahrenheit* to spend five days in Israel; it was a very pleasant trip. I saw Madeleine again when I returned to Paris; we treated ourselves to a few plays and films before leaving again for the Midi, for the two girls and the work at hand. I hope to finish *Fahrenheit* by the end of February. As soon as I do, I'll send you a copy of the script in spite of your negative (and unconstructive!) reaction to *Jules et Jim*.

This time, I think, you'll appreciate certain long scenes which have no dialogue and are therefore '*cinématiques*', as Hitch would say courtesy of Scott's translation.[2]

On the subject of *Le Pianiste*, Braunberger has engaged a lawyer in New York who seems to be making things hum; what's regrettable is that the film won't be on in March when Aznave is the toast of New York; I believe Sinatra is going to give him a lot of support.

The '*jules* and *pianiste*' record is very bad. Thanks all the same. You irritate me by prejudging *Mata-Hari* when I took the trouble to explain to you that it was a very good screenplay, specially conceived to be of help to Jeanne . . .

I come now to your new letter, the one dated 31 January. I cannot possibly come to N.Y. for the Hitch retrospective. At some time or other Hitch's shows[3] will be shown in France, perhaps on Channel 2.

How did you find *L'Amour à 20 ans*? I'm going to dictate a note to Lucette concerning the financial arrangements for the Hitch book. I didn't much care for Chabrol's *Landru*, but I very much liked *Le Petit Soldat*, from which the ban has finally been lifted, and an Italian film which you will also like, *Il*

Posto.[4] *Hatari*[5] is also a very fine film; along with Hitch, Hawks is the most intelligent director in the States.

Thanks for the Robert Burns[6] which landed on my desk, from you and Archer. He is someone I'm avoiding because of his bad review of *Paris nous appartient*. Madeleine is nevertheless going to read in English his script of *The Wild Palms*[7] which I received.

Look after yourself, write to me often, I send you a passionate kiss since, between us, passion is compulsory,

your truffaut,
truffle

1 – Raoul Coutard, French cinematographer, born in 1924. He was director of photography on numerous films of the New Wave, notably five by Truffaut (*Tirez sur le pianiste*, *Jules et Jim*, *L'Amour à vingt ans*, *La Peau douce* and *La Mariée était en noir*). He did not work on *Les Quatre Cents Coups*, however: the cinematographer responsible for lighting 'the interrogation of Antoine' was Henri Decaë.

2 – The correct French word for 'cinematic' is *cinématographique*.

3 – Truffaut is referring to the television series *Alfred Hitchcock Presents*.

4 – By Ermanno Olmi.

5 – By Howard Hawks.

6 – A brand of cigarillo.

7 – Eugene Archer had written an adaptation of Faulkner's novel.

To Don Congdon[1]

Paris, 27 March 1963

Dear Mr Congdon,

Thank you first of all for the copies of *Fahrenheit 451*, which have been of great use to us, since, as you probably know, film producers and distributors take a different view of a script according to whether or not it has already appeared between hard covers!

Regarding the Simon and Schuster clause, I agree with you that it is acceptable only if the publisher is willing to risk losing the whole of the advance which he has given.

When you informed me that other publishers might be prepared to offer better advances than Simon and Schuster's, it was my wish nevertheless that the deal be made with them, since I felt in a sense morally obligated to them or rather to Elizabeth Sutherland who is a really charming person. Now, however, I consider that I am no longer bound by such an obligation, and if the other offers still hold good and Simon and Schuster refuse to adjust the clause to our satisfaction (which is to say, to forfeit the totality of the agreed advance), well then, I am wholly favourable to the idea of changing publishers.

My experience as a young producer has taught me that when one has a project of adapting a novel for the cinema and, for whatever reason, it comes to nothing, one loses the whole of the sum paid for the rights and there is no question of the publisher paying back even half.

That little paragraph is specifically intended for our friend Elizabeth Sutherland!

I wish you to know that, for me, the two most important points concerning the book, which will be translated into English by Mrs Helen Scott, are:

1. that Mr. Hitchcock retain the right of approval on the book's cover and layout;

2. that the book be offset, which will allow us to place the stills anywhere in the text.

In the hope that you will soon have completed negotiations with Simon and Schuster or another publisher, I remain

yours cordially,
François Truffaut

P.S. In the *Times* I was described as a *'Gallic Salinger'*. Would Miss Sutherland refuse a manuscript from Mr Salinger?!

1 – American literary agent.

To Alain Peyrefitte[1]

Paris, 25 April 1963

Monsieur le Ministre,

Perhaps this letter will surprise you. We would certainly have greatly preferred to ask you to grant us an audience, but, for the present, we have chosen to write to you to let you know of our distress and our hope.

We have been informed that, in a few hours, you are to decide the fate of a film which we hold very dear and by which we were all extremely moved. *Le Joli Mai*[2] impressed us as a crucial film for a period in which, as you remarked last year, 'the means of exerting pressure on the individual conscience have become so numerous'. With a degree of personal sympathy which we find profoundly touching, our friend Chris Marker[3] has allowed dozens of alienated, bewildered, anxious, impassioned and sometimes baffled men and women to speak their minds. It was also you who said: 'It is the plurality of points of view, the confrontation of different opinions, that will safeguard the fundamental liberties of our citizens.'

Your remarks, it is true, applied to the press. But we believe in a cinema of personal expression. And Chris Marker is, in our opinion, one of its most brilliant exponents. Liberty, in the cinema, encounters certain great and formidable obstacles. Beyond the economic pressures exerted by commercial interests, it seems essential to us that a whole range of intellectual currents should find expression on the screen.

We do not regard the cinema as an underdeveloped sector of culture. What applies to the press should, we believe, apply equally to the cinema. Several years ago there emerged a new kind of film-going public. Their responses are those of individuals. They judge. They have become adult. Now, when you are about to decide the future of a difficult and ambitious film, a film destined for this new breed of spectator, we wished to tell you how important we feel that decision will be since on it depends to a certain extent the future of the French cinema.

We are convinced, Monsieur le Ministre, that you will forgive the liberty we have taken of acquainting you, with confidence, of our anxiety: the fate of *Le Joli Mai* rests in your hands.[4]

Yours sincerely,
François Truffaut

1 – Then the Minister of Information.
2 – By Chris Marker.
3 – French director (principally of documentaries), born in 1921: *Lettre de Siberie*, *Cuba Si!*, *La Jetée*, *Le Fond de l'air est rouge*, *Sans soleil*, etc.
4 – Peyrefitte authorized the release of *Le Joli Mai*, including three sequences to which the state censorship board had objected.

To Helen Scott *[April 1963]*

My dear Helen,

This time again I'm replying to you within a couple of hours, almost as though I had done something to you for which I wanted to be excused – and yet it isn't so!

What I regret is the failure of the screening of *The Birds*: I'm absolutely flabbergasted and also really upset, since I've been living this film for months.

The fact is that, in the film, the plot is such an obvious pretext to keep people waiting patiently between each attack that there is a disproportion between its 'psychological' side and its spectacular side. In other words, one doesn't give a damn whether the boy is going to succumb to the girl's advances, whether the mother is going to accept her daughter-in-law, etc. Remember, it was the first thing he told us in the car, as we were driving to

Universal: 'The problem with this kind of story is making the characters sufficiently interesting,' and he mentioned Stanley Kramer's[1] film *On The Beach*[2] as an example of a failure because of the characters.

The major weakness of *The Birds* is the male character and there, really, Hitch's misanthropy did him a disservice; it's too obvious that he despised the character and subsequently the actor playing him; since, on top of that, the girl is portrayed as rather swanky and upper-crust, etc., it makes for a couple with which audiences have no particular desire to identify. I have the feeling that, if *The Birds* doesn't have the success they hoped for, Tippi won't be doing *Marnie*.[3] This contempt that Hitch has for actors and, in spite of himself, for his characters is his only present handicap and, oddly enough, it's also what has happened to Renoir, Rossellini and Hawks. Each of them does what he can to conceal it, but it's obvious with all of them, as soon as they reach their 55th year.

It's the only thing which is capable of diminishing the complexes that Hitchcock's brilliance gives me, knowing that I at least am able to make the public feel sympathy for a young kid who steals everything he can get his hands on, for a selfish little coward of a piano-player, for a turn-of-the-century bitch who sleeps around, you see what I mean. Making a film with an idiot like Rod Taylor[4] . . . God, I'd be bored out of my wits . . .

The fact remains, though, that I would be proud to make a film like *The Birds* one day.

Now, I reread your letter and I see that the screening was for journalists only and it's true that Hitch has more of a feel for what the public expects than what critics expect: I would have liked to know who was present at the screening.

It's possible – and desirable – that a public screening of paying customers would show that Hitch was right about the film, with the whole cinema responding to it as one without feeling that there were any longueurs. The argument of yours that really worries me concerns the ending: critics, as a rule, think that we explain things too much and the public that we don't explain enough. If, on this occasion, the critics are reacting like the public (on this precise point), it's rather disturbing.

I don't know if you've seen *Psycho* again. Every time I see it, I'm shocked by the psychiatrist's final explanation, I find it unbelievably pointless and superfluous; if Hitch put it in, however, it's because it was necessary.

I've just called the Siritskys, they're very pleased at the idea that it's working out for them.

There was nothing in your letter that replied to any points raised in mine, apart from my request for information concerning the screening of *The Birds*.

Yet another complaint; you don't tell me, always that incredible modesty of yours, what you – you, Helen – thought of the 3rd screening.

Naturally, I understand that, thinking of me, you were above all attentive to the reaction in the cinema (speaking of which, were there any screams, or noises, or damn all?), but, all the same, there are shots which you hadn't seen before because they hadn't been ready (the descent of the birds over the town after the fire, the children coming out of school, the final shot) and above all that famous electronic soundtrack that we didn't hear. Please tell me all about it and anything else you might have heard about the screening in the meantime.

You're mistaken when you refer to 'the American public's indifference to your idol'; that wasn't the public. If the newspapers have already begun to speak about the film, give me a few details. By the way, you've rather let me down as far as the press cuttings of *L'Amour à 20 ans* are concerned. There was only the *Times* and one other: there's no need to send everything, just enough to give me the general idea: Crowther? the *New Yorker*? Winston?[5] that nice old hairy-chops and his wife? I'm delighted with '*the Gallic Salinger*'!

As for *Fahrenheit*, I'm not too demoralized by the general lack of enthusiasm here, since I've taken a major decision (please don't tell anyone about this): if I don't receive the conditions I want from the distributors and if Deutschmeister backs out, I'll put the film off for a year, I'll send you the script in French so that you can translate it into English and I'll come to New York and try to set up the film with some small-scale American producers like Ely Landau[6] or Levine or United Artists, with the idea of making it in English and if possible in America. All things considered, I'm quite pleased with the script.

If you aren't overworked at the moment, I would like to ask you, as a favour, to reread carefully the book in English: in a couple of weeks I'll send you the script so that you can really compare the plot and the characters, O.K.?

3 o'clock: lunch break with my friend Coutard. He says hello. Jacques Rivette and Godard also looked in. The latter was complaining that you haven't replied to his most recent letters; he acknowledges that he had previously left several of yours unanswered. In fact, he'd like to know what old MacGregor is getting up to with *Vivre sa vie*, which, I have to tell you,

has been a real commercial success here in France and in several other countries.

I'm not convinced by what you say about Hitch concerning *Jules et Jim*, since, on the contrary, it was to be expected that he wouldn't like it. At best, he probably thinks that, of its type, it's not bad or that it deserves its reputation, but he cannot genuinely like a film which was shot in ignorance and defiance of the laws which he himself has been laying down for thirty-five years to keep audiences on the edge of their seats. For that matter, he's obviously a puritan and therefore opposed to any favourable depiction of adultery, etc.

Since you tell me that you sometimes reread the interviews, I have to tell you I had a very pleasant surprise when looking through them the other day. First of all I realized, after having put it all aside for three or four months, that it makes for fascinating reading.

Secondly: it will be very easy to put into shape. I'll dictate it all to Lucette and it will go directly on to the typewriter. Whenever I change something or shift some passage or cut it out, I will also dictate a 'note to Hélène Scott concerning page 18 of tape 7', etc. I'll be keeping a very conversational style, including even a few doubtful usages.

I would like you to translate in the same casual fashion, even if it means keeping colloquialisms and possibly vulgarisms. The only scruples you should have concern the strictly technical sections (there aren't too many of them, as it turns out) where you ought to get the assistance of some bilingual film type like Sidney Lumet who would be delighted to help you.

There are two things I'd like you to realize:

1. it's very pleasant work,
2. it's very easy work,

let me add, 3., that you'll do it very well and undoubtedly better than anyone else.

Finally, it's obvious that if Hitchcock takes it all as seriously as we think he does, he'll go over the final version very thoroughly.

Speaking about the book, my rather insistent letter to Sutherland is maybe going to rebound on me and you have my permission to take a certain wry satisfaction in my plight. In the event, I have learned that she is having an escape clause added to the contract under the terms of which the publishers may decide against publishing the book if they are disappointed by the manuscript; in that case, we would have to return half the advance or some such arrangement. Congdon, very sweetly, is furious about this and would prefer to say no, particularly as there are still other publishers interested. As usual, I'm going to leave it up to him, specifying all the same that if he obtains a bigger advance elsewhere, he can tell Simon and Schuster to go to hell, and this time I won't have any feelings of guilt since they themselves will have brought about the situation with this new demand of theirs!

My departure for Japan has been put off until Thursday. Madeleine is treating herself to a little four-day trip to London [. . .].

In fact, I've been encouraging her to take this trip, which has been put off ten times, since it's a very good idea: she's going to be shown around by Richard Rood or Round[7] whom you must know and she'll be seeing all the shows she could never drag either me or her mother to, like *My Fair Lady*, *West Side Story* and all that, plus a few cashmere sweaters, etc.

The little girls are very well and are very cute and adorable. For the moment they get along and are beginning to be able to play together.

You often write to me, I know, but never at the same length as I do or with such an abundance of detail, you must agree.

Don't take advantage of my trip to Japan to stop writing to me; I'm still concerned about: a) your new job; b) what is to become of *The Birds* in America; c) the Aznavour show and the influence it might have on *Le Pianiste* and *Fahrenheit*, etc., etc.

lots of love,
françois

Postscript:

The only point which I forgot to answer: yes, I saw *A Taste of Honey*[8] at Cannes and I liked it a lot. It was at my insistence that the girl who plays the leading role[9] got a prize.

2. I've sent the little thing you'll find enclosed in order to prove to you that in the U.S.A. you can buy bras very cheaply in comparison with the one you bought in Montreal for 50 dollars.

3. Jean-Luc Godard told me that, in New York, *L'Amour à vingt ans* is doing very well at the box-office. Is that true?

4. So that you won't drop me, here is my address in Tokyo:

Shinagawa Prince Hotel
Tokyo

or, for telegrams, to Unifrance-Film: telegraphic address Film France Tokyo.

5. In case it should be useful: Charles Aznavour, Hotel Americana, Seventh Avenue, New York (U.S.).

1 – American producer and director, born in 1913: (as director) *The Defiant Ones*, *Inherit the Wind*, *Judgment at Nuremberg*, *It's a Mad, Mad, Mad, Mad World*, *Guess Who's Coming to Dinner*, etc.
2 – The first film to have portrayed the end of civilization after a nuclear holocaust.
3 – In the event, Tippi Hedren did play Marnie in 1964.
4 – Australian-born actor of American films, born in 1929, and Tippi Hedren's leading man in *The Birds*.
5 – Arthur Winston, then the film critic of the *New York Post*.
6 – American distributor and producer.
7 – Correctly, Richard Roud (see note 1, letter dated 7 November 1968, p. 330.)
8 – By Tony Richardson.
9 – Rita Tushingham.

To Charles Aznavour

Paris, 3 July 1963

My dear Charles,

I made a very careful study of your film treatment and, though I do find it fascinating, I have to decline your offer to direct it.

It's a marvellous theme and one that could make for a marvellous film, as happens each time the cinema presents the portrait of a man who interests the spectator.

What I'm afraid of, the problem I don't believe I'm capable of solving, is the uniformity of tone between the scenes that are 100% documentary, those that are 50% documentary and those that are pure fiction. I must be honest with you: this film tells the story of your life, you wrote the screenplay, you will be the leading actor and probably the producer, the songs will be your own; all of that guarantees the authenticity of the project but risks depriving you of the necessary distance to make a success of it.

I know very well that you would trust me to direct 70% of the film, but the other 30% would always worry me. I couldn't help, for example, having an idea on such and such a song, quite possibly on the speed at which it should be sung, on how it should be sung and how it should be filmed!

Or, to take another example, if I had to interpolate a song into a film, out of ten songs I would choose the three fastest ones and, from those three, I would choose the best and the shortest. I saw an extract from *Pourquoi Paris* on television and it seemed to me that the choice of 'L'amour c'est comme un jour' was, in filmic terms, a mistake.

I realize that we would agree on the need to create a character who was not too calculated but, on secondary matters, it would be difficult to avoid areas of disagreement, as is always the case in any collaboration where the material is autobiographical for one of the collaborators.

You have a great idea there, but the film will be <u>your</u> film and you might even think of directing it yourself, in collaboration with a director of photography and a technical adviser, after getting someone to write a very good script under your supervision.

It certainly gives me no pleasure to admit that I'm not the man for the job, because it's an exciting project. Out of friendship for you and because of my interest in the subject, I'd like to suggest that you keep me informed of further developments in the script so that I might possibly draw your attention to certain risks or points of detail, if you think my opinion would be useful to you,

Yours,
François

To Helen Scott

from Paris,
Thursday 18 July, 1963

My dear Hélène,

I'm only now replying to your letter of 10 July because of these damned French strikes . . .

Concerning the book: I'm keeping your comments very carefully to examine them later, all at once. I agree with you on the need to create a 'sustained rhythm', but, on the other hand, if at present there's a lot of journalistic material on Hitch, what the public lacks is information on his early work and the English period. Lots of magazine articles have been published on his American films . . . as you see, it's swings and roundabouts, but all the same we'll take a close look at all of that. Then again, there's always the risk of Hitch himself wanting to cut certain passages, so, for the moment let's keep everything. O.K.?

As regards the other point, I'm determined that the form of the book be very rigorous, so I reject at the outset your idea of a collage of stills captioned with Hitchcock's own comments, because that would create confusion.

Whenever we start to discuss a new film, I'll arrange to have it preceded by a particularly significant still to jog the reader's memory. The caption for that first still will be in very small type and sum up its plot in a few lines. The subsequent stills will correspond exactly to Hitchcock's own comments on the film. I've got it all very clear in my head.

I didn't ask a question about the business of the lovebirds on their perch in the section on *The Lodger*, as I realized 1. that it would break the rhythm of what he was saying; 2. that it isn't really the same thing and 3. that it would only be interesting if we were able to illustrate it, and after all there was no question of having a still from *The Birds* that early on . . .

As regards the money, I learned that Janus owes us nothing. Since Pépin, in

Montreal, is in debt, I've sent him a very firm letter asking him to straighten things out. So I think I'll be able to send you 1,000 dollars by the end of this month, as an advance on your share, let's say rather the beginning of August . . . What you ask me concerning Allen[1] is absurd and contradictory. If, as you would like, I write to tell him that you are representing me, me and not him, he will be able to use that as an argument to engage you on *Fahrenheit* and only on that film. Also, I don't want any confusion between the Allen business and the Hitch book where money is concerned, we mustn't mix it all up, Berbert shares my view.

I'm very pleased to hear your morale is high. Don't worry about the dough. I can't have any money paid to you directly by Pépin because we'd lose the export subsidy, but even without considering Pépin, we should be able to send you 1,000 dollars at the beginning of August.

I leave the day after tomorrow to begin the new script[2] with Jean-Louis Richard. It will be very easy to write because very close to life; the film will be very outspoken, quite shameless, rather sad but very simple. We'll write it quickly, shoot it quickly, release it quickly and, I hope, quickly get our money back.

Muriel is very good, completely Hitchcockian, but in the most subtle sense; strange to say, the film it resembles most is *The Birds*! *Le Mépris* is one of Godard's best, in the line of *Vivre sa vie*, serene, tranquil, and melancholy.

– As for Allen, we'll see how things turn out . . .

– *Camera Obscura*:[3] I'm giving it up completely because of the new script.

– Hitch: I've received permission to publish *The Birds* in *Cahiers* . . . I await the material.

– The book is practically finished. You'll be receiving the last chapters.

– I'm exhausted, but I'll feel better next week at Cannes.

Work well, don't get discouraged before you reach the end, look after yourself, don't do too many things at once, love,

françois

1 – Lewis Allen, American producer, born in 1922. He would produce *Fahrenheit 451* in 1966.

2 – *La Peau douce* (*Soft Skin*).

3 – An unrealized project based on Nabokov's novel.

To Helen Scott *from Paris, Monday 9 September 1963*

My dear Hélène,

I have had your letter in my hand for half an hour and now, without further delay, I'm going to answer it, after having looked at it for a long time and even vaguely read it!

In actual fact, this will be one of my last letters before I start shooting my next film, *La Peau douce*.

By the same post, I'm sending you the script of the film. I ask you at once:

1. not to let anyone read it, nor even to describe it to anyone;

2. not to speak of it as an 'autobiographical' film *à la 400 Coups*, but of a fictional work inspired by various *crimes passionnels* . . .

3. to read it yourself and, if possible, at a single sitting, without watching television at the same time . . .

4. to give me your impressions as soon as you have read it.

Actually, I think you'll like it, because it's concrete, realistic and closer to life than *Jules et Jim*; there's something in the script that resembles you or resembles your way of seeing things. I'm not saying this in order to 'condition' you in its favour, it's just an impression. Any detailed or general criticism will be given my full attention, as you know.

As you also know, this is a transitional film, before *Fahrenheit*, a film made for a specific purpose, to get Carrosse back on its feet again with a production that runs no very great risks at the outset and has a good chance of making more money than *J. et J.*

Nevertheless, all these notions on adultery have been running through my head for so long that perhaps no one will notice how rushed the whole project has been. The structure, too, strikes me as being tighter and firmer than in my earlier films. In fact, I now no longer think of anything but the film and making a good job of it. The three actors are Jean Desailly, Nelly Benedetti and Françoise Dorléac. Raoul Coutard behind the camera, Delerue for the music, etc. At the beginning, as you know, Carrosse was to be the sole producer, then my mother-in-law lent me Sédif's[1] state subsidy (25 million), repayable on the first sales. She had been to see Fellini's *8½* and, like you, had been knocked sideways. Ever since, she has so admired me that she prefers to invest and risk her subsidy rather than lend it. So it will be a Carrosse – Sédif film. Curious, eh? I too was very disturbed, moved, impressed, and influenced by *8½*. . . Anyway, here we are, embarked upon a new adventure. I'm horribly nervous and, at the same time, extremely impatient.

We begin shooting around 15 October.[2] No question of my coming to New York before. I'll come at the end of December or beginning of January, either for *Fahrenheit* and our book or exclusively for our book. I'm delighted at the idea of spending several days of intensive work with you, perfecting the French version. In the meantime I won't be dropping it altogether, since I'll be busy collecting stills from each of the films in order to have the most complete documentation possible. All goes well.

I'm glad you saw *Rope*, but as usual flabbergasted that you didn't see fit to write even half a dozen words on that marvellous film!

Now, I shall answer your letter point by point:

– Berbert is going to find out tomorrow what happened to your dough which was sent off several days ago. Send us a telegram as soon as you receive it.

– Yes, I'll give a warm welcome to your Terence MacCartney Filgate. How could he have read the English script of *Phoenix* without Allen knowing? I could send you the translation which I received, but only if you ask me to, because: 1. It's badly typed, with a typeface that's too small and on transparent paper which has been blackened by the carbon. 2. I'm afraid it will delay you in your translation of the crowing of the (Hitch)cock. 3. I would prefer you to read *La Peau douce*. 4. You already know the script of *Phoenix* and the translation isn't likely to change much.

On the question of New Wave publicity. I had a very interesting lunch with two people from *Life*, a certain Mr Kaufman and a charming, beautiful and exciting woman named Madame Libert; she's going to be speaking to the major directors all over the world, Bergman, Fellini, in short, she's not doing it by halves. They asked me a whole lot of questions while we were eating, without taking any notes, but lots of photos and even some 16 mm (non-commercial) film, I didn't really understand what it was all about . . .

Independently of that, lunch with another woman, Betty, from *Time* magazine; I understood even less of what she wanted, especially as she seemed completely exasperated by having to do a job that was so obviously beneath her. I let her pick up the bill . . .

Wonderful news, the job with MacGregor; they are much more reliable people than our friend Allen whose fate hangs on that of the two duds he backed, the Peter Brook and *The Balcony*.[3] Speaking of which, how is *Lord of the Flies* doing?

You could perhaps make up with Archer by putting the idea in his head that Jeanne still wants very much to work with Arthur Penn and that both of them are keen on *The Wild Palms*. It would be the most reasonable outcome for that tired old project, except if Archer is still full of resentment . . . and vanity, etc.

The Arthur Penn story is very simple. He shot a week with Lancaster and everything was going very well.[4] Then two more days with Lancaster and that, too, seemed to go well. Then there was the failure of *The Leopard*[5] in New York, the bad reviews, and, overnight, Lancaster started making disparaging remarks about 'art movies', etc. The next evening Penn was informed by his agent telephoning from New York that he was no longer on the film but that he would be paid his salary. Then Frankenheimer[6] arrived and he's someone Lancaster can manipulate as he pleases: a close-up of me here, now a tracking shot of me, etc. And the film took on a new dimension, it became a major production . . . Penn went back to New York in rather low spirits; I dined with him and his wife. For the moment, Jeanne is trying to extricate herself from the project, but it's not yet certain whether she'll succeed, as they're putting a lot of pressure on her and she's already spent the dough she received . . .

I haven't seen Bernie Willens,[7] but Berbert has. Whenever Berbert mentioned your name, Bernie would look up at the ceiling and Berbert felt he was pissing in the air!

You ask me about Jean-Luc. Here too, he never stops talking about going to New York. I see a lot of him. He hopes to make *La Bande à Bonnot* for the Hakims around the end of October, but it may not happen.[8] His ideas of forming a production company are amusing, but I remain sceptical all the same. The important thing for him is to get out of the fix he's in. I think you'll like *Le Mépris*, which is very simple, luminous, sad and beautiful, in the line of *Vivre sa vie*. You know that, in America, Godard won't have his name on *Le Mépris*, because everywhere, except in France, the film will be re-edited by the ignoble Levine and the infamous Ponti.[9]

The Birds opened a few days ago and it isn't liked. I know now, but not from you, that it's been pretty much a failure all over the world and in Hitch's career. Long live *Marnie*, naturally.

I spoke to Arthur Penn about my theatre projects and he offered to intercede for me with Inge[10] concerning the performance rights for *Picnic* which I would like to stage with Belmondo, Marina Vlady,[11] Albert Rémy and a few other geniuses I know . . . I don't really want to burden you with this or distract you from the Hitchbook, but if you should ever meet Penn in the street . . . you might just remind him of that . . .

To finish with the Hitchbook, I'm pleased that you're pleased with the result, I'm going to send a little note to the Master to keep him patient for another few months. My dream would be for this book never to come out and for you and me to spend a month together every year bringing it up to date, adding new questions and conducting new 'interviews' with the maestro, in short a few weeks of Hollywood holidays every year.

Is there anything from Paris you need: books, newspapers, magazines, records, caramels?

Write to me at the same length as I did to you before I start shooting and immediately after reading *La Peau douce*,

lots of love,
françois

P.S. Two omissions:

a) Claudine won't be going to New York now because of my film.

b) Allen has sent the latest cheque; I'm amazed. On the other hand, the director's contract is unacceptable as it currently stands. We're going to make some counter-proposals; that means it's likely to drag on for several weeks more.

1 – The film company of Ignace Morgenstern, Truffaut's father-in-law, who had died two years before.
2 – In fact, on 21 October.
3 – By Joseph Strick.
4 – The film in question was *The Train*, on which Frankenheimer replaced Penn for the reasons detailed by Truffaut.
5 – By Luchino Visconti and starring Burt Lancaster.
6 – John Frankenheimer, American director, born in 1930: *The Young Savages*, *Birdman of Alcatraz*, *The Manchurian Candidate*, *Seven Days in May*, *The French Connection II*, etc.
7 – New York impresario.
8 – The film was never made.
9 – Carlo Ponti, Italian producer, born in 1910.
10 – William Inge, American dramatist and screenwriter (1923–73).
11 – French actress, born in 1938: *La Princesse de Clèves*, *Adorable Menteuse*, *L'Ape Regina*, *Dragées au poivre*, *Chimes at Midnight*, *Deux ou trois choses que je sais d'elle*, etc.

To Helen Scott *from Paris, 15 October 63*

My dear Hélène,

This last note before 1964! Excuse my long silence.

I appreciated your comments on the script of *La Peau douce*. I took note of your criticisms, especially those concerning the character of the girl. Also, I interviewed three air hostesses (the perks of the profession!), and that enriched the script with 50 extra details. I included your idea of the stain on the piece of clothing, but at a different point in the film (when he makes his escape), which therefore ties up with the idea of the suit coming back from the cleaners at the very end. Impossible to cast Rémy as Clément, he is too nice, too sympathetic. I've chosen a more incisive type of actor whose name won't mean anything to you: Ceccaldi.[1]

FRANÇOIS TRUFFAUT

Samedi 19 octobre 63

Ma chère Hélène,

ce petit mot pour vous montrer que le trac rend mon écriture toute tremblante, et pour vous demander de m'écrire dès que possible.

Votre lettre me sera remise un soir, juste avant les rushes. Je l'ouvrirai pour voir si elle est épaisse et longue et je la lirai tranquillement à la maison avant et après le dîner,

je vous Kiss,

f. t.

'My dear Hélène,

This little note to show you that nervousness has made my handwriting go all trembly, and to ask you to write me as soon as possible.

'Your letter will be handed to me in the evening, just before the rushes. I will open it to see if it's thick and long and I will calmly read it at home before and after dinner,

je vous kiss,

françois'

Thank you for the *Times*, it came at just the right moment. I've given MacCartney Filgate permission to watch 5 days of shooting.

That's enough about *La Peau douce*.

I spent two weekends in Brussels[2] to see or see again 16 English Hitchcocks, some of them for the first time: *The Pleasure Garden* (the one whose 1st day of shooting he describes), *The Farmer's Wife* and *Bon Voyage*.[3]

So I saw again *The Lodger*, *The Ring*, *Champagne*, *The Manxman*, *Blackmail*, *Murder*, *The Skin Game*, *Rich and Strange*, *Number Seventeen*, *The Man Who Knew Too Much* (1st version), *The 39 Steps*, *Secret Agent*, *Sabotage* and *Young and Innocent*.

This will enable me to make considerable changes to the first section where you felt, rightly, that I didn't intervene sufficiently.

What I might do, for example, is summarize the plot in my first question, before each film . . . ?

I'm going to spend an evening soon working on that with Jean-Louis Richard who saw all these films with me.

Drop me a line and let me know how you're getting on with the book (what stage you've reached) and how you're getting on from the point of view of money and work.

It won't be easy for me to write to you for the next 8 weeks, but if you have specific questions to ask me, I'll be able to dictate a line or two to a secretary during the shoot.

Madeleine and the girls are well, so am I, but the cinema is not.

Tell me all,

love,
françois

1 – Daniel Ceccaldi, French actor, born in 1927. He was later to play Antoine Doinel's father-in-law.
2 – At the Cinémathèque Royale de Belgique.
3 – One of Hitchcock's least-known films, a propaganda short produced by the British Ministry of Information in 1944.

To Luis Buñuel[1] — *Paris, 15 November 1963*

Dear Monsieur Buñuel,

Two years ago a lady sent me a screenplay written by hand in an exercise book. It concerned an old, true story about a case of incest in Andorra.

Though it was a rather naïve and melodramatic effort, there could nevertheless be detected in it real strength and beauty. And remembering that your film *El* had been based on a sugary, sentimental romantic novel, and finding in Madame Pauline Charles's screenplay a vaguely Mexican quality, I took the liberty of giving her your address in Mexico.

Furthermore, I advised the lady to type out her screenplay, as a manuscript is easily lost. She therefore had it typed especially for you and she has now written to me again to inquire whether you have received the screenplay, what you think of it and also whether you might return it to her or arrange to have it returned since it's the only typed copy.

I do hope that this will not be putting you out too much.

I am enclosing a copy of the lady's letter, as it is rather charming and will allow you perhaps to reply to her yourself . . .

I have heard from Jeanne Moreau that your shoot is going very well[2] and I greatly regret not being able to come and visit you. When you have finished, it would please me very much to have a chat with you and I am impatient to know how you feel about working with Jeanne, in view of the conversation we had several months ago on the terrace of a café at Saint-Philippe-du-Roule.

I remain, dear Monsieur Buñuel,

very faithfully yours,
François Truffaut

1 – Spanish director (1900–83): *Un chien andalou*, *L'Age d'or*, *Los Olvidados*, *Nazarin*, *Viridiana*, *Belle de Jour*, *Le Charme discret de la bourgeoisie*, etc.
2 – *Le Journal d'une femme de chambre*.

To Helen Scott *[late November, early December 1963]*

My dear Helen,

Lucette told me that you wrote to her and that you were, as I can imagine, distressed by the death of Kennedy. I'm dashing off this little note to you at top speed and I haven't even written the scenes for tomorrow. In the end I find that writing the dialogue of a film from one day to the next makes me very nervous and yet it's what Godard does every time.

I received your latest and very sweet letter. The one before had annoyed me, because it contained some old complaints tarted up as new, complaints about the book: that I was too sycophantic and over-generous with praise, that Hitch was unbearably conceited . . . I know all that, which is why in our work together, we'll both have the same goal in mind and therefore achieve it. When one is fully cognizant of the nature and degree of a risk, then the risk ceases to exist. I know, for example, that the risk with *La Peau douce* is that I'll end up with an unsavoury film, therefore it won't be unsavoury, it's as simple as that . . .

I'm pleased you've finished the book. Now all you'll have to do is reread it a couple of days before I arrive and we'll finish it standing on our heads. I won't have as much time at my disposal as I would wish, because of the enormous amount of work involved in the editing, dubbing and post-production of *La Peau douce*, but we'll work something out nevertheless.

This film shoot has been much less pleasant than the others, it's been very tough, difficult and demoralizing. Jean Desailly, who will be on the screen throughout, doesn't like the film or the character or the story or me. So our relationship is cold and insincere.

Françoise Dorléac[1] is charming and talented and behaves as well as Jeanne. The other one, Nelly Benedetti, starts tomorrow and, there being no indelicacy to which I would not stoop, the domestic quarrels of the Lachenays will take place in my own apartment in the rue du Conseiller-Colignon.

I'm worn out, almost. In fact, you wouldn't recognize me, as I'm nothing but skin and bones. I'll have such an unpleasant memory of this shoot that I'm going to have a terrible fit of nerves before the next one.

What are you going to live on now?[2] Couldn't Elizabeth Sutherland ask her bosses to find you something, or our friend Dick Seavers?

Roll on next year, which will take both you and me off in a new direction, maybe the same 'new' direction, the same old job on that bloody *Fahrenheit*?

Keep writing to me,

lots of love and kisses,

françois

P.S. Thanks for the records. I saw *Muriel* again, it really is Resnais's best film. You are the only American capable of liking it, make an effort, go and see it again.

P.S. Would you like to receive some stills from *La Peau douce*?

P.S. Have you listened to Jeanne Moreau's record, do you like it?

1 – French actress (1942–67): *L'Homme de Rio, La Peau douce, Cul-de-Sac, Les Demoiselles de Rochefort*, etc. She was Catherine Deneuve's sister.

2 – Helen Scott had just left the French Film Office.

To Helen Scott *17 December 63*

My dear Hélène,

It's midnight. I'm calmly seated in my office in the rue Quentin-Bauchart, since we're going to do some night shooting, in a restaurant near here, of the film's final scene: Franca, with her rifle, goes to kill Pierre.

In the film it takes place during the day, but, as the restaurant doesn't have a closing day, we are shooting at night, without showing the windows.

I hope to finish by Christmas with the full crew and by 31 December, completely. We have had a very difficult and exhausting shoot. Dubbing from 12–31 January. A short trip to New York at the beginning of February for just 8 to 10 days. *La Peau douce* finished by 30 April.

I had a brief word with Allen one evening and I'm still unsure of him despite his signature on the contracts and his word of honour.

What I'm afraid of is that he'll make me film *Fahrenheit* on the smallest possible budget, a cut-price version, whereas I would like to make a rather lavish, rather spectacular film to help audiences accept the idea of the 'book-men'. I'll be seeing Allen and his wife at greater length when they return, at the beginning of January.

Contrary to what I first supposed, I couldn't possibly have had MacCartney Filgate on the shoot, since there were four of them and the set was too small, well, it's just too bad.

At the request of Universal's publicity department, (and maybe it was one of Alfred's own ideas), I dictated to Lucette a little note in answer to the question: 'Why did you stop your film work for a year (!!) to write a book with Mr Hitchcock?' I'm sending you a copy of my reply. It is deliberately hyperbolic (excessive in praise) because, it seems to me, it was a question of doing a Alfred a favour, publicity-wise, but, in view of the fact that it was intended as a puff, I'd like to show you that it will be easy for me to write a preface to the book that will be precise, analytical and will prepare the reader for the style of the book.

What annoyed me in one of your recent letters was your idea of getting Simon and Schuster to have a preface written by some neutral American, Lillian Ross, say.

I'm not unhappy with *La Peau douce* in relation to the script. All the ideas that were there have been given flesh and been reasonably well filmed. The character of Nicole became much more interesting as we progressed, thanks to Dorléac and also to the fact that, before the film, I interviewed 3 air hostesses.

Franca has less moral authority than I had hoped, since the actress Nelly Benedetti has absolutely no sense of humour.

Fortunately, she's beautiful, sexy and above all very good in scenes of violence and conflict. The marital scenes 'where things aren't going well' are better than those 'where things are going well'.

I changed the little ten-year-old boy of the script to a little seven-year-old girl, little Sabine[1] from *Jules et Jim* . . . She was perfect . . .

Desailly . . . He has to carry the whole film! [. . .] He was very good as the middle-class man trapped by circumstances. I portrayed him as highly strung, almost on the edge of a breakdown in order to avoid: a) insipidity; b) conventionality.

It's taking a very big risk *vis-à-vis* the public, because I don't think they're going to find him very sympathetic . . .

Besides which, the distributors have turned the film down because of him . . . In the end, I did a deal with the Siritskys who've coughed up very little money but who will handle the film quite well, at least I think so and hope so.

Jacques Bar,[2] who arranged a meeting for me in his office one morning with Jane Fonda whom I had been refusing to see since her arrival in Paris (a little pose of mine that's very complicated and would take too long to explain), would like to make a film with me.

I gave him Goodis's book, *The Burglar* (in French, *Le Casse*), because I'd like to adapt it notwithstanding the film, which you've seen, that Wendkos made of it.

So he (Jacques Bar) will be expecting to meet you and Goodis. I hope it all works out. I would like Belmondo, I've been wanting to work with him for a long time.

Allen didn't say a word about the script you described to me, *Clyde Barrow*, but I managed to get some *France-Soir* comic strips on the subject, very interesting.

Now there would be an interesting part for Jane Fonda . . . Maybe . . .

I think of you a lot during this pre-Christmas period which, as I know, only adds to your loneliness; your little Paris pal can only hope that it passes quickly and smoothly. When I was a child, I dreaded these holidays, for the same reasons, I hated my family, I was bored by my family . . . I hope you haven't too many financial problems, let me know all about that and also your current work schedule.

Give me more news, since, despite what you believe, I do a job that leaves me with lots of time on my hands; we only work 8 out of 24 hours. I am not sleeping at the moment and I have nothing to do between each set-up, each scene, each take, each shooting day, and I am impatient to hear from you.

I give you a very special kiss for the end of the year,

françois

1 – Sabine Haudepin, French actress, born in 1956.

2 – French producer.

To Robert Lachenay

Thursday 26 December 63

My dear Robert,

More than the gift itself, I'm moved by the choice, which is to say, by the instinct, the discernment that guided you. It's the ideal gift, the one really designed to give me the most pleasure; every three months, I would postpone buying it for myself and I wanted it desperately.

All sorts of images come back to me involving the two of us with Sacha Guitry, especially this one: having run away while my father was at the Club Alpin, I made a date with you at the Champollion cinema . . . and we sat through *Le Roman d'un tricheur* several times,

all my gratitude and my affection,

françois

1964

To Helen Scott

Sunday, 1 January 64

My dear Helen,

I hasten to wish you a happy new year before coming to the bad news.

Madeleine and I are separating. [. . .]

La Peau douce was painful to make and, because of the story, I now have a loathing of marital hypocrisy; on that point I feel total revulsion at present.

The situation is less horrendous than it was two years ago, since Madeleine will remain on good terms with me, and our friendship is absolutely indispensable, above all because of the children.

There you have it in a nutshell. I'll go into greater detail when we see each other, next month, I hope.

I return to your last letter in order to change the subject of the conversation.

I don't know if there was much point to your taking the trouble to translate the little piece on Hitch. Anyway, if it's already done, too bad and thanks.

Concerning the book:

a) I don't want to reread it for the moment. I'll wait until we're just about to see each other again so that everything will be fresh in my mind.

b) I've started chasing up the stills again. The ones to be found in Paris are often disgusting duplicates. I'll persevere, nevertheless. When we're in New York, we'll have to get in touch with some competent people at Simon and Schuster to discuss the quality of the illustrations. Then we'll have to go to the majors themselves to consult their stills archives and get them to make prints of the photos we like.

Still concerning the book. If Hitchcock goes on to make *Marnie*, then *Mary Rose*,[1] we'll no doubt have to add a few pages to make the book really up-to-date when it's published. I'd very much like it to come out at the end of this year in New York (Elizabeth S. was speaking of a 7-month schedule for the publisher!).

As far as English is concerned, don't worry; I won't be learning a word before the first day of shooting.

Don't tell me I have to know English in order to shoot this film since I'm making the film in order to learn English. All the same, there's no reason why you can't buy me the pack of cards you mentioned!

La Peau douce? The title has no special meaning. It has a slightly sensual connotation, but it isn't a *double entendre*. On the other hand, the contrary French expression 'la peau dure' does have a double meaning. To have a hard skin means being able to withstand life's misfortunes.

As regards America, Janus is the company which is most interested; they're due to come to Paris this month. We'll be asking a little more from them than for *Jules et Jim*, namely 50,000 dollars without any penalty in the event of censorship cuts and, naturally, a guaranteed minimum.

As you say, X— is a jealous cretin; yet another grudge from Cannes; when I was a critic I demolished one of his films. Two years ago, as a member of the jury, I defended his film against *Divorce Italian Style*,[2] but I know he believed I hadn't defended it; he can go fuck himself, if he hasn't already done so.

I'm waiting for the Allens[3] to return in the next few days. I decided to stand up to him on the question of the film's budget, as I recently saw *The Balcony*,[4] which is the most pathetic, ugly and badly produced film in the United States since the invention of the cinema. I'll start by demanding that none of the crew who worked on *The Balcony* be involved in *Fahrenheit*!

I haven't seen the issue of *Life*, but I must tell you a very funny thing. Three months ago, the people from *Life* spoke to me about this issue in which they were going to have a 6-page spread on me!! For a week they followed me everywhere with a photographer: at home, with the family, at the office with the whole staff, in the editing room with the editors, in shops with Françoise Dorléac, it all took place ten days before I started shooting; later, they visited the set several times.

One day the very charming girl who was handling this at the Paris end, Nadine Libert, Russian-born, married to an American, said to me, 'The editors of *Life* in New York would like even more photos.' I said 'OK', given the importance of the thing, and we made a date to meet. Then Nadine rang Lucette: 'It's not worth it, they've looked at the photos again and they've got enough.'

Then, a few weeks ago, Nadine sent me a very sweet note of apology; because of a long article on Hitch, the first illustration for which would be one of the photos of the three of us together while were were taping the interviews, the thing on me will be very much shortened, it'll no longer be a *close-up*,[5] etc.

The whole business is amusing *because*[5] the 'irony of fate' and so forth. I'm always very philosophical about such things as I tell myself that the moment hasn't arrived yet but that it will come. I didn't want to tell you about this article, precisely out of superstition and also so that you wouldn't think that I was stealing a march on you in New York!

I agree with you that we should consider the possibility of reactivating things with Wasserman.[6]

The film by Grimblat and Reichenbach[7] comes out in a few months in two small cinemas, because it was turned down by all the others. I don't want to see it, since I know that it will be very confused and incoherent but visually beautiful.

I saw *Tom Jones*[8] this afternoon with Madeleine; I didn't care for it; jokey but insincere.

In one of your recent letters you told me that you were sending me that particular issue of *Life*. Not a sausage!

It's a good idea to speak to Jacques Bar about *Bonnie and Clyde*. I think you might also draw his attention to the William Irish book which I spoke to you about some months ago and which has already been filmed at R.K.O. I can't seem to recall the title; can you get that information for me? It would be a nice story for Jean-Pierre Léaud . . .

I am now just starting the editing. I rather like the film. There are only two things worrying me:

1. It's too long and at present comes to 2 hours 30.
2. The leading character risks alienating the 'general public'.

That apart, it's impossible, I think, to be bored and there's nothing squalid about it.

Best wishes, dear Helen, until we meet in February,

françois

P.S. Monday: I have just received this morning by post the *Clyde and Bonnie* script via Allen's office, with a letter from Elinor Wright. Claudine Bouché is going to read it.

1 – Hitchcock long wished to make a filmic adaptation of J.M. Barrie's play, but the project remained unrealized.
2 – Pietro Germi's *Divorzio all'Italiana* (1961).
3 – The producer Lewis Allen and his screenwriter wife Jay Presson Allen.
4 – Produced by Lewis Allen.
5 – In English in the original letter.
6 – Lew Wasserman, head of Universal Studios.
7 – *Les Amoureux du 'France'*.
8 – By Tony Richardson.

To Helen Scott *Saturday then Tuesday [January 1964]*

My dear Helen,

'Letter follows' . . . here it is. You know that, with *La Peau douce*, we'd like to try our luck at Cannes. Besides which, even if the film isn't selected, it will have to be ready by then to be screened in the market so that we can sell it abroad. At the moment the film is far from having enough 'coverage'.[1]

So we'll have to work steadily on the editing throughout February and March. I won't be taking on anything else, no meetings, no interviews, no visitors, just editing from morning till night.

To be honest, I don't like doing several things at the same time. First, I have to finish *La Peau douce*. Then, finish the book with you. Then, *Fahrenheit*. I've asked Allen, if we shoot in Toronto, to let me do the editing in Paris so that I won't be stuck over there for ever. I'm very tired and my dream would be not to have to work for several months, but I know perfectly well it can't be done. I'm caught in a trap.

I've rented an apartment in the avenue Paul-Doumer, not far from home. I'm beginning to get organized. A Spanish woman, Carmen, does the housework and takes care of everything. My relations with Madeleine are fine, we go out together every week. What really hurts is not being able to see the children every day, but there's no one to blame for that but myself.

It's you I'm worried about. It occurred to me the other day that the satisfaction of working on *Fahrenheit* was making you lose sight of the fact that we're talking about a 16-week assignment at most: the preparation and the shoot, unless Allen takes you on permanently. He's nicer than Maternati, but the same basic type, which is to say, someone you won't be able to respect, who will sense that you don't and resent you for it, he won't be the tough, virile and yet affectionate boss you need! I'm joking, but it's true nevertheless. Your stubborn insistence on doing *Fahrenheit* and the fact that no one in New York knows what your real situation is, I find all of that as distressing and childish as your determination to find a job in Paris last year.

Give it a lot more thought. Why not have a word with Sutherland who is leaving S & S[2] to work on a magazine or Dick Seavers or some others?

I've had *Clyde and Bonnie* read by two or three friends here: everyone is enthusiastic and assures me I should make the film. I'm going to ask Claudine Bouché to go through it for me scene by scene before making up my mind. I slightly regret having already involved Jacques Bar and Lewis Allen, since it's such a simple and inexpensive film to shoot that I could have produced or co-produced it myself, with the backing of a company like United Artists.

Please explain to me your precise relations with the writers of the script and how it happened that they asked you to read it. Are they themselves the screenwriters or is there someone else? Did they offer it to anyone else? Do they want to sell it to a producer? Were they commissioned to write it? Was it their own idea to offer it to me? . . .

After your telephone call last night, I have nothing to add; once more I advise you to be cautious; think hard about your future this year and look after your leg.

all my love,
françois

1 – A term which applies to the amount of footage shot to 'cover' the requirements of a particular scene in a film.
2 – Simon and Schuster.

To Helen Scott

[22 February 64]
from Paris, late on Saturday night
while my assistant editors
are falling asleep over the moviola

My dear Helen,

I've been neglecting you a little these last few weeks. It's because of the film which, on account of our deadline, is being finished in a panic. I still haven't seen it complete. The other day, I saw an hour and a half of it and at the end the characters hadn't yet arrived at Rheims for the conference! So it was too long, rather boring, full of repetitions and with a variety of bloopers, in short a horrendously disappointing screening.

Since then I've cut it and tightened it up, and I hope I've improved it.

One simply can't write a script in 22 days, even with apparent ease, without it being affected. I think the *Fahrenheit* script is more precise and polished, but, even so, I'm determined to take a long, hard look at it before I start shooting. There's nothing more idiotic than shooting scenes that subsequently wind up on the cutting-room floor: that represents so many working days and millions of francs down the drain.

It was obviously when reeling from the blow of that first, disappointing screening of *La Peau douce* that I wrote to Allen (I've had a copy of the letter sent you) to curb his wife's enthusiasm as far as the additional dialogue of *Fahrenheit* is concerned.

Speaking of Allen, I wasn't very hospitable to them when they were in Paris because it coincided with my separation from Madeleine. Explain to them, because it nagged at me after they left.

'First of all, I have to finish *La Peau douce* . . .' (Production still: François Truffaut, Suzanne Schiffman.)

In one of your recent letters you criticize me for having lent Yvonne[1] some records that took you 'five months to find'. In fact, that too was because I was living in a hotel at the time and didn't have a record-player!! No, I hadn't received the issue of *Life*, now I have, for which thank you. Speaking of which, there's another record I'd very much like to have, the one with the music from *Vertigo* (Mercury M.G. 20384). Thank you in anticipation.

Next week I'm going to have you sent the two books you asked me for: *Les Mots*[2] and *La Force des choses*.[3]

I won't speak to you about *Bonnie and Clyde* until I've read the script in a French translation that's being done now. Then I'll send a detailed note to the writers of the script in case they start taking it in another direction from the one I want; unless I'm disappointed by it and decide not to do the project.

I thought it was a slip of the tongue when you told me that Eleanore[4] was married to *Tom Jones* who is having such a success on Broadway at the moment!!!!!!!?

With the help of Jean-Louis Richard, I've been working on the first volume of the Hitchbook, by which I mean, we interpolated synopses of each film in each first question. It's an enormous improvement, you'll see. Next week I'm off to London for two days and I hope to bring back lots of stilis from the early films, because, up till now, I haven't had everything I had hoped for. It's very important that the book be lavishly illustrated, since it's rarely the case with film books.

As regards *Tom Jones*, I'm glad you didn't like it, but even more glad that you did like the only scene I liked as well, the erotic dinner with the redhead. Great minds really do think alike!

With Madeleine, things are all right. I'm often at the house and, as I have rented a rather large apartment, it's very easy for the children to come and see me with the nanny. So, as far as that's concerned, I suppose it could be worse. I'm leading a very monkish existence, if only because of the work I have on my plate. We continue editing late into the evening and also on Sundays.

What's new in Paris? Cayatte's two-part film,[5] which is atrocious, is a complete flop. *Le Mépris* has done very well. Jacques Demy's film, *Les Parapluies*,[6] which is wonderful, you'll love it, has just opened; no one knows yet if it's going to be a success, but I think it will be. No one in America has bought it, but I'm sure that, in a first-run cinema in New York, it would appeal to everyone who knows French, as well as that great mass of people who pretend to know it.

It's a splendid film, really, and it will make you cry even more than mine do! *L'Homme de Rio* is due to open next week, a guaranteed success, the best thing De Broca has ever done. I'm certain it will do well all over the world, and it deserves to.

Jean-Luc has just started a new film,[7] untitled as yet, with Karina, Frey[8] and Claude Brasseur.[9]

I still haven't seen *Le Journal d'une femme de chambre*,[10] which is my main competitor for Cannes along with the René Clément film[11] . . . 'But we've talked enough about me; how did you like my latest film?'

Seriously, I'm very upset about your foot and I'll spare you all the classic jokes, e.g. 'What do you write with now?'[12] Send me your latest medical bulletin.

As for Aznavour, there's nothing I can do, since: 1. at the moment he's never in Paris; 2. I've turned down one or two films with him and, more important, he imagines that I would never consider making *Fahrenheit* without him, even in America. So there's nothing to be done there. If the job with Aznave materializes, don't be fool enough to turn it down on the grounds that I'll be coming at the same period; we can always work things out, as you well know, and I'm sick of Paris.

My dear Helen, I hope I've covered all the questions that concern the two of us. Let me know how you are, in both your health and your work.

I forgot to tell you that Alexandra Stewart[13] left very suddenly to make Arthur Penn's new film[14] in Chicago. The actress who was supposed to do it, Yvette Mimieux, became unavailable at the last moment. Penn remembered Alexandra whom he had vaguely met on *The Train* and about whom I had spoken to him. He rang me in Paris to ask me what I thought of her. I was very encouraging though I did point out that I was a close friend of hers, therefore could not be completely objective, that not everyone in France regards her as an actress of the first rank, but that . . . under Penn's direction . . . In short, it worked and I'm glad.

Standing beside Penn, there was some assistant who also talked to me, but I didn't understand much of what he said, could that have been the Morgenstern who is married to Piper Laurie?[15] Do you think the film will be any good?

I'd very much like to receive some photos of a girl from New York: Kitty Saint-John – 1430 Midland Avenue – Bronxville – New York 8 (apartment 1-C).

Relax, she won't be my Tippi, I won't be signing her up to an exclusive contract, but in *France-Soir* I saw an extraordinary publicity still of her, when she was in Paris. Would you try and get in touch with her – or her agent – and obtain about ten photos and some information?

I kiss your foot, my dear Helen, in the hope of hearing from you very soon.

françois

P.S. On Wednesday evening I'm seeing the complete *Peau douce* with Delerue. The following day, I leave for London. I'll drop you a line to let you know whether, once and for all, the film is a dud or not.

POSTSCRIPT

Sunday

My dear Helen,

In one of your letters you mentioned the existence of shops that specialize in old film stills and also your collector friend.

In order to gain some time, could you not ask your friend if he has any stills from Hitchcock's films?

As for the shops, you might ask the lads in Bleecker Street to make inquiries in these shops.

a) Are the photos filed or loose?

b) If they are filed, is it by film or by director or by company or by year?

When I'm in New York, it just might mean that we could save some time.

I've noticed you've never been terribly troubled by this whole question of stills, but you can take my word for it, it's a very important and very difficult one.

I continue my close and meticulous rereading of your letters and I answer one small point: no, I have no intention of shooting *Bonnie and Clyde* in France, at any rate not for the moment.

I'll wait till I've read the script in French (in a week's time) to tell you more.

Do you think I ought to write to Hitch to explain why the manuscript has been delayed and indicate a date to him, some time around the middle of April?

I've reread your last four letters and I don't believe I've left anything out, so, I give you a big kiss and say, see you soon,

françois

1 – Truffaut's secretary.
2 – By Jean-Paul Sartre.
3 – By Simone de Beauvoir.
4 – Elinor Jones, the agent who had taken an option on *Bonnie and Clyde*. There had been a misunderstanding between Truffaut and Helen Scott, owing to the fact that Truffaut had confused a Broadway musical of which Elinor Jones's husband was the producer and the opening of Tony Richardson's film in New York.
5 – *La Vie conjugale*, which consisted of not

one but two films, presenting the same narrative from the point of view, respectively, of a husband and a wife.
6 – *Les Parapluies de Cherbourg.*
7 – *Bande à part.*
8 – Sami Frey, French actor, born in 1937.
9 – Claude Brasseur, French actor, born in 1936. He was the son of Pierre Brasseur and Odette Joyeux.
10 – By Luis Buñuel.
11 – *Les Félins.*
12 – The French expression *écrire avec son pied*, or 'to write with one's foot', means 'to write badly'.
13 – Canadian-born actress, born in 1939: *Exodus*, *Le Feu follet*, *La Mariée était en noir*, *La Nuit américaine*, etc.
14 – *Mickey One.*
15 – American actress, born in 1932: *Has Anybody Seen My Gal?*, *The Mississippi Gambler*, *The Hustler*, *Carrie*, etc.

To Paula Delsol[1]

Saturday 11 April 1964

My dear Paula,

Cannot possibly become a member of the jury you mention; besides, since my one and only experience as a juror, at Cannes two years ago, I made a promise to myself that it would be the last time. Naturally, I'd like to have seen you and Malige again, and in the atmosphere of Montpellier, of which I have such fond memories.

It's just occurred to me: I have to tell Paula what I'm doing in New York and, thinking about it, I realize that I have no idea myself. As a result of making depressing films, I am becoming completely neurasthenic. Everything disgusts me, I'm fed up, exhausted, completely drained. What scares me most is losing my enthusiasm for work, for that would really be the end; I'm sorry to be writing to you like this, I hope you will get great satisfaction from your own work this year and that you are all happy at home.

kisses to you and also to little Bernard,

your friend,
françois

1 – French director: *La Dérive*, *Ben et Bénédicte*, etc.

To Helen Scott

Thursday 28 May 64

My dear Helen,

Nothing very new to report. After having been closeted with me for 4 tender and violent weeks, I imagine you found my letter a little dry and aloof, but you were kind enough not to complain.

I've put down in front of me again your letters of the 13th and 15th of May which I read the first time around with an eye that you know all too well, grim, glazed and inattentive, like that of a dozy turbot.

Page 1 of your letter of the 13th, nothing to reply, page 2, I learn that you've been to see *La Peau douce* for the third time, well well, that's very nice.

Ah! One question: I don't think I've given you a report on the Cannes press conference,[1] which was lousy.

Because the actors were there, it was a free-for-all of photographers and TV cameramen with a lot of stupid questions and evasive answers. For example:

Question: Why did you choose that title?

Answer: We couldn't think of any other.

Laughter.

Dear little Lew Allen sent me a kind little note.

Concerning the Algonquin: I am really annoyed that I haven't received any mail and especially the letter from Jeanne. Where on earth could they have forwarded those letters?

Have your efforts to get the subtitling job on *Les Parapluies* led to anything?

In front of me, your 2nd letter, that of 15th May.

I'll skip the soft soap, my importance as an artist, four films, etc.

How far have you got with the subtitles of *La Peau douce*? Have you come up against any problems?

I received two charming postcards from Texas, from the writers of *Bonnie and Clyde*. I'm going to send them the comic strips.

I haven't got the courage to write to Renée Furst,[2] as I'm too tired and dispirited. The film, in its first run in Paris, is heading for a second wishy-washy week and this morning in *L'Express* there was a very unfavourable review. I had decided not to let myself be discouraged, but the accumulation of bad reviews (even after Cannes) and bad box-office results has ruined my peace of mind.

I'm dying to leave Paris and have a rest, I'm tired,

love,
françois

P.S. I know that you're discreet, tactful and all that, but <u>be careful</u>, in your discussions with Madeleine, not to make any <u>casual</u> references to past, recent or current flings that she doesn't know about. She's still very important to me and, as she is very crafty, she pretends not to give a damn in order to get the lowdown on me.

1 – For *La Peau douce.*

2 – An American press agent.

To Maurice Bessy

from Paris, 29 June 64

My dear Friend,

The new layout of *Cinémonde*[1] is much better, clearer and sharper, your editorials are very interesting, but . . . but . . . I am dismayed not to have found, for nearly six weeks now, the cinema crosswords that made me forget the poor quality of TV programmes on Tuesday evenings.

On Thursdays there are the crosswords of *Ciné-Revue*[1] which are obsessed with terrorism and puritanism; have a look at them, they're a scream,

yours,
Truffaut

1 – French film magazine.

To Helen Scott

from Paris, 3 July 64

My dear Hélène,

Scribbling this little note in haste before I leave for the Midi, then Rome. Have had in front of me since this morning your delightful letter of 29 June. Happy birthday. Next year you'll begin the second half of your life.

1. I'm sweating a bit over the dialogue for *Mata-Hari.* I'm half-way through.

2. The Hitch book hasn't made the slightest headway.

3. I'm in the process of selling my soul in Italy and very expensively; set your mind at rest, unpurse your lips, it's only a sketch to be filmed for Dino De Laurentiis,[1] I need the money to buy myself an apartment . . . I haven't signed yet and for the moment it's our secret . . . I am to introduce Soraya[2] (a great celebrity in Europe) to the screen!

4. For *Fahrenheit*, I'm quite prepared to wait. An affirmative word from Peter O'Toole will rekindle my enthusiasm and I'll get going. It's a magnificent subject that mustn't be rushed.

5. Pub-li-ci-ty – Did you receive the little profile of me that appeared in *Réalités*? It seems to me an American magazine might buy it and publish it,

that would be very good, no? eh? Another, similar article will be appearing soon in *Lui*.

6. Thank you and (in anticipation) bravo for the subtitles of *La P.D*.

7. I'm still impatient to have the meeting with Steph. Phillips.[3]

8. I received the wonderful photos for *Bonnie and Clyde*. It's all very exciting.

9. No, I absolutely don't regret telling you about Madeleine. As of now, I fail to see how we can start over again. I have to straighten out my life, get to know the children better, that's all.

10. I perhaps forgot to tell you that *Mata-Hari* (co-produced by Carrosse) starts shooting on 15 August. It's the best news of the moment,

kisses to last the whole summer,

françois

1 – Italian producer, born 1919.
2 – The second wife of the Shah of Iran.
3 – Stephanie Phillips, an American agent.

To Franco Brusati[1]

Paris, 17 July 1964

My dear Franco,

As you know, after our last session together, Y— and I went to see Soraya who turned down the story of the child and the singer. I can't really blame her, as it wasn't suitable for her at all.

On top of that, I had gulped down an enormous glass of tomato juice that was probably too cold and made me feel ill all evening and all night, and I realized that the Roman way of life was not for me. I felt discouraged, tired and above all in need of a holiday. I therefore sent a telegram off to Dino to tell him that I had decided against filming the sketch.

I have sent Soraya a note of apology, since I don't know what reason Dino might have given her for my withdrawal. You will find a copy enclosed with this letter.

It was a great pleasure for me to make your acquaintance and work with you and I trust you will keep in touch. [. . .]

I hope the work goes well.

Very best regards,
François Truffaut

P.S. I am sending you Soraya's book since it is unavailable in Italy.

1 – Italian director, born in 1922: *Pane e Cioccolata*, *Dimenticare Venezia*, etc.

To Helen Scott *21 July 1964*

My dear Hélène,

You appear to be dropping me like an old sock, was it something I said – or did?

I seem to recall having written to you, two weeks ago, on the eve of my departure, no?

One piece of good news, I've turned down the sketch with Soraya. I had accepted because of the money (thirty million = $60 thousand), but the story by O. Henry that I wanted to film was not for sale and the ones they offered me were unworthy of the major international talent that you were the first to recognize (which is not to say you were the only one!).

In short, I sent a telegram off to Rome and I went to stay with Jeanne Moreau in the Midi to finish the dialogue of *Mata-Hari* and take a rest for the first time in two years.

Then, I ensconced myself in the Martinez at Cannes and every day I would go out and play with my two adorable, exquisite, bewitching, etc., little girls.

Madeleine and I have decided against getting together again, but things were fine between us. In short, my recent life has been peaceful, pleasant and frankly happy.

I thought that perhaps this business with Soraya shocked you because of Allen and because of the fact that I've been keeping you waiting? Here's my excuse: I suddenly saw myself with a large sum of money that would enable me to buy an apartment in the Muette, since I'm a little too far from the children at present and would like to be closer to Conseiller-Collignon.

I'm off again in the next few days. The children are going to Gstaad in Switzerland. I'm going to fetch them at the airport, in Geneva, and take them to Gstaad by car, then I'll return to Cannes or La Garde-Freinet.[1] This time I will definitely get down to the Hitch book.

My dear Helen, if the clue is *young French boy director*[2] in 7 letters, then the answer is BASTARD, but, between two cross words, send me a kind little word . . . or rather, between two drunken binges since that's your *new hobby*.[2]

Lucette is taking her holidays at home, Yvonne has settled in, Claude de Givray is making a film on prostitutes, *L'Amour à la chaîne*, Berbert has gone to present *La P.D.* at Karlovivary[3] where the Reds are, *Mata-Hari* begins shooting on 17 August, there's Hitchcock all over the Champs-Élysées: *Spellbound*, *Rope*, *Rebecca* . . .

I think of you, as this letter demonstrates, and I send you my love,

françois

1 – Jeanne Moreau's house in the Midi, referred to earlier.
2 – In English in the original letter.
3 – Correctly, Karlovy Vary, a film festival held every two years in Czechoslovakia and alternating with the Moscow Festival.

To Don Congdon *Paris, 19 August 1964*

Dear Mr Congdon,

This letter concerns neither *Fahrenheit* nor the *Hitchcock* book, since these two projects are progressing slowly but surely. It relates to a third matter. I would like to buy the film rights to a novel entitled *The Bride Wore Black*. It was the first novel by William Irish whose real name is Cornell Woolrich. The book was published in the United States in 1940, but I do not know the American publisher.

I asked our great mutual friend Helen Scott to reconnoitre the terrain and she succeeded in tracking down the man, whose address is as follows:

Mr Cornell Woolrich
Sheraton Russell Hotel
37th Street & Park Avenue
New York City

Helen was very disappointed that my name meant absolutely nothing to Mr Woolrich, who, however, informed her that:

1.This novel is the only work of his never to have been bought by Hollywood (which cannot be entirely accurate, as Irish is above all, like Bradbury, a very prolific short-story writer).

2. Irish has no objection to our acquiring the rights, but he does not know how much to ask for them and moreover does not have an agent.

3. He reads French sufficiently well to decipher a letter of mine.

What I am now proposing, dear Mr Congdon, is not that you become Mr Irish's agent, but on the contrary that you represent me in my dealings with him, if you think it might be possible.

I will delay writing to Mr Irish until I have received a reply from you on that particular point.

What Marcel Berbert and I would like is a simpler and more advantageous contract than the one for *Fahrenheit 451*. Why 'simpler' and more 'advantageous'?

a) Simpler, because I wish to buy the property outright, without any question of a gross or net percentage, since such a clause would complicate subsequent negotiations with the various backers involved in the setting-up of a film.

b) More advantageous, because William Irish, though probably more famous than David Goodis (the author of *Shoot the Pianoplayer*),[1] more famous too, perhaps, than your friend Charles Williams, is less well known as a writer than Ray Bradbury.

c) One last, and very good, reason why this contract should be more advantageous to us than the *Fahrenheit* one is that, this time, you would be representing the buyer and not the seller!

On the *Shoot the Pianoplayer* deal I was only the director, but I believe the producer acquired the rights to the book at a very good price. I am leaving Paris, but, in the next couple of days, Marcel Berbert will send you either a copy of the contract for *Shoot the Pianoplayer* or details concerning our exact requirements.

In any case, as soon as you have received this letter, you might let us know by telegram whether or not it would be possible for you to negotiate on our behalf.

In the hope that your answer will be favourable, I send you, dear Mr Congdon,

My kindest regards,
François Truffaut

1 – The American title of *Tirez sur le pianiste*.

To Helen Scott *Wednesday 19 August 64*

My dear Scottie,

Life is wonderful. I leave Paris tomorrow morning for Cannes to meet my 2 daughters and Mado on their return from Gstaad. That aside, I've been feeling rather low these last few days, especially since they started shooting *Mata-Hari* last Monday. I was happy for J.-L. Richard but I envied him as well, because I adore the script and also the notion of the 'designing woman', as Alfred would say! Just as Raoul Lévy would take off all over the world when he was producing a film, so I'd like to get as far away as I can from this shoot where I feel useless and in the way.

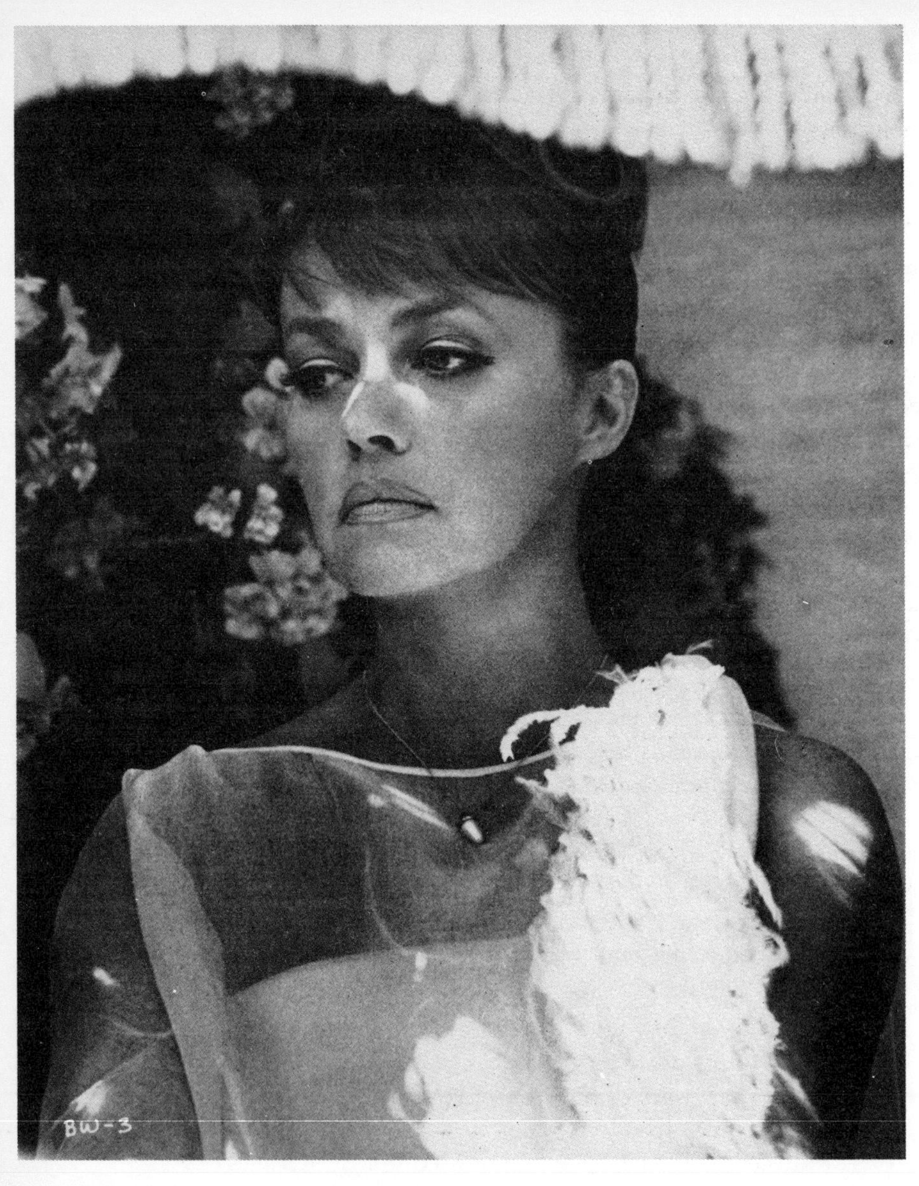

The bride . . . (Jeanne Moreau in *La Mariée était en noir*.)

Everything is going well, the film will be first-rate and set Carrosse back on its feet again.

The other day I called off the Canadian trip, partly because of our New York–Paris conversation, but mostly because Jeanne, who's broken off yet again with her pansy couturier, needed my help.

We left to spend a few days at her place in the Midi and were blissfully happy, which is why our return and the start of this film which is going to keep us apart has made me so melancholy. Only to you can I talk about this, because, in Paris, there's absolutely no question of my confiding in anyone about Jeanne, not even Jean-Louis . . . As always, the same problem confronts me, to put up a fight or not to put up a fight, to allow things to happen or force them to happen, pessimism or optimism, living for the future or for the immediate moment, wanting something or not, etc. Life's not all a bed of roses and there are moments of loneliness, yet even so I am experiencing an intensity of feeling such as I haven't known since the Chicago-New York period which you witnessed, but this time it is more genuine, more reciprocal, less 'manufactured' on my part.

Naturally, for both Jeanne and myself, this is all leading up to the desire to work together as soon as possible, which explains my interest in the novel *The Bride Wore Black*. Speaking of which, I have a couple of things to ask you:

1. read the book as soon as possible and give me your opinion, even if it should be negative.

2. talk to no one about either the project or Jeanne's involvement in it (not even to Congdon).

I was speaking of coming to N.Y. in Sept. *because*[1] festival. In fact, I'll come for the opening of *L.P.D.* except if Allen has some news on *Fahrenheit*.

I'm sending you copies of several American letters which will make you understand:

a) that I want to curb the enthusiasm of Elinor Jones.

b) that I have castigated Allen.

c) that I am getting under way on *Mariée en noir*.

I agree with you that we should leave Rugoff[2] and Peppermaïs[3] in peace, particularly as we've finally received both the money and your brilliant subtitles.

I'm pleased to hear that you're in better health and happy to have left Allen's office. I hope things can now be patched up with Maternati . . .!?

It's already the 19th and I haven't heard a word from Allen. I hope he'll call me in Cannes so that I can visit O'Toole in Ireland. I feel the time has come to play that card, that very important card.

I finally received the *Fahrenheit* script and I notice that Jay[4] has kept her name on it. I'm having it translated immediately. If it's bad, I'll insist that Jay's name be completely removed. No, but really! Try and read this new version. Why don't you meet Mattewson[5] to find out more about how the script has been juggled around?

Dear Hélène, I send you a passionate kiss and wait impatiently to hear from you,

francesco

1 – In English in the original letter.
2 – An American distributor, who had just bought the American rights to *La Peau douce*.
3 – Truffaut is making a little bilingual pun on the name Peppercorn (from the French word *maïs* meaning 'corn'). Peppercorn was Rugoff's partner.
4 – Jay Presson Allen.
5 – Truffaut is in fact referring to Richard Matheson, the American science-fiction writer and scenarist.

To Nicole Stéphane[1]

Paris, 31 August 1964

Mademoiselle,

At the end of April you telephoned me to propose that I direct for you a film version of Marcel Proust's *Un amour de Swann*.[2]

I was, according to you, one of the few, one of the very few, directors capable of successfully handling so ambitious a project.

I immediately informed you of my scruples and reservations, but I did not want to turn it down definitively until I had reread *Du côté de chez Swann*. I therefore asked you if I might have a few weeks to think it over and I was supposed to call you at the beginning of June.

In fact, I did not call you and the weeks went by. Why? Having reread *Du côté de chez Swann*, it was perfectly clear to me that I should not have anything to do with it, that no one should. Even so, though it would be sacrilegious to adapt Proust for the cinema, there is something terrible about uttering the words: no, I'm sorry, I'm not interested. Which explains my silence.

In the last four years I ought to have become hardened by having been obliged to turn down *Voyage au bout de la nuit*,[3] *Le Grand Meaulnes*,[4] *L'Étranger*, *Le Bal du comte d'Orgel*,[5] *Le Chant du monde*[6] and other such masterpieces, and yet it is not so. Though a refusal was necessary in each case, it cost me dearly.

Rereading Proust convinced me that only a butcher would be prepared to film the Verdurin salon and it was brought to my attention that, without your having been worried too much by my silence, you had meanwhile sought out the services of just such a butcher, René Clément, who, demonstrating anew that shameless vulgarity so characteristic of him, leapt at the chance with not a moment's hesitation.

Mademoiselle, I wish you no ill; I admired you, as an actress, in *Le Silence de la mer* and even more so in *Les Enfants terribles*, and I am not unaware that you are a courageous producer, but you must understand that I cannot possibly wish you every success in this new project.

Be that as it may, please find here, even if belatedly, my answer: I cannot, in 16 mm any more than in Cinerama, make a film of *Un amour de Swann*.

Yours attentively,
François Truffaut

1 – French actress and producer, born in 1928.
2 – A film version of *Un amour de Swann* was finally made twenty years later, produced by Nicole Stéphane and directed by Volker Schlöndorff.
3 – By Louis-Ferdinand Céline.
4 – By Alain-Fournier.
5 – By Raymond Radiguet.
6 – By Jean Giono.

To Elinor Jones[1]

Paris, 7 September 1964

Dear Madam,

As I promised you in my last letter, I have had the new script of *Bonnie and Clyde* read to me in French.

I thought all the modifications were excellent and I continue to think that it's an excellent script. I am, unfortunately, obliged to reply to you in the negative, for the following reasons:

1. The film *Fahrenheit 451* has just been postponed by a year (for shooting in summer 1965). But, as far as Lewis Allen is concerned, *Fahrenheit* must be the first film I make in America.

2. Before *Fahrenheit 451*, I have an idea for a film that I would make in Europe with Jeanne Moreau, and I do not wish to have too many projects in the offing as I never make more than one film a year.

I took the liberty of letting my friend Jean-Luc Godard read *Bonnie and Clyde* and he, too, greatly liked the script.

He makes far more films than I do, being a very fast worker at every stage: preparation, shooting, editing.

I do not know how you feel about offering him the chance to direct the film. I am convinced that he would be absolutely the man for the job, he speaks English fluently and what he might well give you is an American *Breathless*. His sensibility is totally attuned to that of David Newman and Robert Benton.

He is at this moment at the Venice Festival, and I believe that, in ten days or so, he is due to go to New York directly from Rome. Helen Scott will know where to find him if you wish to see him.

I am sorry to be giving you, this time, a negative response as far as I am personally concerned, but I do not think that I have caused you to waste too much time, nor have I broken my word, since I had always made it clear that I would only make my final decision when the second version of the script was finished.

I would like you to know that, of all the scripts I have turned down in the last five years, *Bonnie and Clyde* is by far the best, but I hope that you will fully understand my reasons and that David Newman and Robert Benton will also understand them.

I will almost certainly be in New York at the beginning of October for the opening of *La Peau douce*, and I would be delighted to see you again.

Very sincerely yours,
François Truffaut

1 – See note 4, page 240.

To Henri-Georges Clouzot[1] *from Paris, 28 September 64*

My dear Georges,

I almost wrote to you twice, first before you started shooting and again when the film was shut down.[2] Since then I have been thinking about you a lot and now, as I am about to leave on a trip, I see no reason to hold back.

I simply wish to tell you how sorry I am to hear what has happened to you and that it takes no great effort of imagination for me to put myself in your place and share your feelings.

There is also the fact that I recently saw *Quai des Orfèvres* and *Le Salaire de la peur* again and admired both of them enormously, and also, at the Cinémathèque, the thrill of *Le Corbeau* whose dialogue I knew by heart when I was thirteen and which I went to see again the other evening in an

8/9/1964 – 10^{h}30 BAL 49.83

JEAN LUC GODARD HOTEL EXCELSIOR
LIDO VENISE

TA BELLE PETITE FEMME MARIEE
RESSEMBLE A UN GRAND MELANGE BIEN
HOMOGENE STOP JE LUI SOUHAITE MEME
SI PAS NECESSAIRE LA PEAU DURE POUR
CE SOIR STOP RECOIS EN PARTICULIER
MES AMITIES GENERALES FRANÇOIS

508H221

Truffaut wishes Godard luck for the 1964 Venice Festival screening of *Une femme mariée*.

unbelievable state of curiosity and anxiety. It's a masterpiece, a film that hasn't dated in the least, it's perfect and profound and subtle and powerful.

When we first met, in 59, I was too shy to talk to you about all that and about what *Le Corbeau* had meant to me, from every point of view.

We are not exactly friends, but we know each other a little and this letter is intended simply to let you know of my loyalty, my sympathy and my admiration.

Naturally, my wish is that everything, your health first of all and then your work, will take a favourable turn as quickly as you yourself would wish,

and I am, dear Georges,

your faithful
Truffaut

1 – French director (1907–77): *Manon*, *Les Diaboliques*, *Le Mystère Picasso*, *Les Espions*, *La Vérité*, *La Prisonnière*, etc.

2 – The film in question was *L'Enfer*, left unfinished when Clouzot suffered a coronary thrombosis during the shooting.

Helen Scott to François Truffaut *24 November 1964*

The Diary of a Woman of Letters

or

How François Truffaut Torments the Women Who Work for Him

Extracts from letters and telephone conversations between H.S. and F.T. from 1963 to 1964.

H.S. – I realize you're busy, but . . .

F.T. – Françoise D. is wonderful!

H.S. – May I remind you that . . .

F.T. – Françoise D. has been a terrible disappointment to me . . .

H.S. – My work schedule depends entirely on yours . . .

F.T. – Anna Q. has chubby knees . . .

H.S. – Don Congdon and the publishers ask me to remind you that . . .

F.T. – . . . What I don't like about you is that you're always trying to rush things.

H.S. – Hitchcock is getting older by the minute. Let me remind you that, as of now, I'm completely free to work on the book, and that I would prefer not to accept other commitments until we've completed the revision . . .

F.T. – I'm off to Stockholm. I need a change . . .

H.S. – Hello, François! Lewis Allen is prepared to send me to Paris to speed up work on the screenplay. We might take advantage of that to get the Hitchcock out of the way . . .

F.T. – Have you taken leave of your senses??? Let's be serious now!

H.S. – I want you to know that Hitch is not at all satisfied . . .

F.T. – Well, do give him my best . . .

H.S. – . . . And if, as you advise, I go back to the F.F.O., we'll have a serious problem on our hands when the book has to be revised . . .

F.T. – Be reasonable, Hélène! All in good time!

H.S. – I'm overworked, exhausted, and worn out by my job at the FFO . . .

F.T. – And I'm sure you'll find Francine very sweet, even if her right foot is considerably larger than her left eye . . .

H.S. – And, what's more, I'm in love, and I wanted you to share all the emotion I'm feeling . . .

F.T. – Dear friend, please find enclosed a copy of my letter to Congdon on the subject of *The Bride* and another to Lewis Allen . . .

H.S. – Oh joy, how wonderful to relax on my own! How I love these weekends in the country!

F.T. – I have just completely revised the Hitchcock and I am very impatient for you to get to work. This is an urgent job . . . we don't want Hitchcock to think we're stringing him along. [. . .]

To Helen Scott *from Paris, Friday 27 Nov. 64*

My dear Helen,

Your little dialogue was very entertaining, and never let me hear you say again that I don't appreciate your witty observations!

I have made what I consider to be a very intelligent response to Peppercorn's grievances concerning the fiasco of *La Peau douce* in NY: a full page of advertising, paid out of my own pocket, in *Le Film Français*! (In fact, my euphoria about Canada, Sweden and England has been vindicated.)

I've had no word from Lewis and I imagine he's very upset at having to tell Jay I want her name to be removed. Whatever you do, don't tell Lewis that I find it all a big joke, that would be a mistake. Let him worm his way out of it by himself. I agree with you about the flaws of the film *Eva*. Of Demy's three films *La Baie des anges* is the one I like least, even though . . . Lucette and

Yvonne have only just finished typing out the Hitch. Don't concern yourself about it.

As for the young Englishwoman, I'll judge for myself. You describe her profile and her nose, not a word about her knees . . . Don't trouble to raise your eyebrows, given that you're going to be unfaithful to me for a whole week with Demy.

In London I met up with X— who was feeling a bit lost; two very pleasant days together and more recently two days spent motoring around, with Y—, who is charming, in Grenoble, where I screened my 4 films to two thousand students. Thanks to the fact that I unburdened myself in *La Peau douce*, I behaved very well with Y—, taking her everywhere and introducing her to everyone. She was very nice, very lively, cheerful, beautiful and anything else you care to mention. The fact remains that there's still nothing serious in my life and that my critical attitude towards others, which has now moved beyond obsessiveness to outright madness, prevents me from falling in love. I almost don't even regret the interlude with Z—. I know that when I talk to you about these ladies and their backsides, I'm actually only speaking about my own, well, that's just your hard luck, get your own back by describing Harrisson's[1] knees to me.

Let me know once and for all whether you receive, yes or no, *Cahiers du cinéma*, either at home or the office, so that I can arrange things if necessary. Don't ask me to do any favours for Harrisson, I won't. I would like you to read, in the latest issue, the first in the new format, the interview with Hawks so that you can see that he's as intelligent as I say. There you are.

Mata-Hari is almost finished. As I told you, I have a lot of faith in it and I'm depending on it to make me a rich man in three months' time, to enable me to buy an apartment, etc.

You ask me why on earth I'm going to Stockholm . . . I'm going for three days, round about the end of December, to further the success of *La P.D.*, to attend the closing ceremony of a homage to the French cinema which ends with *Jules et Jim*, to meet Kenne Fant[2] and Ingmar Bergman. When I return, I'll go to Cannes and spend Christmas there with Madeleine and the little ones.

The major resolution I have made for 1965 is that I will improve the quality of my professional life. Less travelling, fewer appointments at the office with people who waste my time, less time wasted, fewer letters to Helen (no, I'm just kidding) and no more all-consuming projects like the book.

Like Resnais and the Americans, I'm going to put three or four screen-writers (like Moussy, Gruault[3] and de Givray) to work on ideas for films that

I'll be keeping in reserve for myself. If the project comes to nothing, I'll pay them a kill fee, and two or three times as much if the film is made, and I'll see each of them, separately, once a week, to develop the structure. The kind of sessions I had on *Bonnie* with the two boys. Here's what these projects are: 1. *L'Enfant sauvage* [*The Wild Child*] (the story of the wolf-child I told you about); 2. *La Petite Voleuse*[4] (like Ingmar Bergman's *Monika*, the flowering into femininity and flirtatiousness of a young delinquent girl, a female *400 Blows*); 3. a story in the style of *Le Pianiste* or *Bande à part* for Jean-Pierre Léaud, perhaps one of Goodis's early novels; 4, a comedy-drama about a young couple who separate then are reconciled, for, possibly, Romy Schneider[5] and Belmondo; 5. and finally the film I've been speaking about for a long time in which all the action would unfold in a school.

There you have five projects, at least two of which will be under way by next month. All this is confidential. I tell you because I tell you everything, but mum's the word.

The situation in France is very depressing; Bresson, Resnais and a lot of others are finding it impossible to set up their projects, even Clouzot is stuck.

I may have forgotten to tell you that Paddy Chayefsky[6] sent me a very nice note after having, I think, spoken to you, as did, quite recently, Stanley Kubrick, who very much liked *La Peau douce* and spoke well of it to me, at the same time attacking the American critics who hadn't liked it.

[. . .] I do nothing with my new-found freedom yet I have the impression I couldn't do without it. It will soon be almost a year since we separated and we had got used to each other, each in our own way, and our little quirks and tics have only got worse. I cannot see any way out and I find it all very painful. I'm not asking you for advice, I know that in this particular instance it would be pointless.

I still manage to spend quite a long time with the children on Thursdays and Sundays, but my life isn't well-organized enough to have them sleep over at my place on Wednesday and Saturday nights as I would like. I absolutely have to get an apartment that's larger and closer to the rue Collignon, with some kind of live-in housekeeper whom I would employ full-time so that I wouldn't be obliged to dine out every night.

I forgot to tell you I came down with quite a bad dose of flu recently, I was bed-ridden and Lucette arranged to rent a TV set for me. You know a thing or two about loneliness too, don't you?

I think I ought to end this letter before it becomes too depressing! That apart, all is well. It's just a pity that 'that' is the real heart of the matter.

Dear Helen, I send you a tender kiss, because I love you,

françois

1 – Harrisson Star was a film production manager who had worked with Arthur Penn. He was a close friend of Helen Scott.
2 – Swedish producer.
3 – See note 1, p. 338.
4 – For many years Truffaut worked on the screenplay of *La Petite Voleuse*, which he would have filmed had he not fallen gravely ill. The film was finally made in 1988 by Claude Miller.
5 – Austrian-born actress (1938–82).
6 – American screenwriter (1923–81): *Marty*, *The Bachelor Party*, *Network*, *The Hospital*, etc.

To Helen Scott

Sunday [December 1964]

My dear Catherine,[1]

It's been a very long time since I've sat down at the typewriter. Now where were we?

Louis Malle's film:[2] I've heard nothing new, as Jeanne is on holiday in Tripoli. All I know is that United Artists told Brigitte and Jeanne that there would, in any case, be someone in America responsible for giving the newspapers 'three stories' a day, you see the sort of job it would be, promoting news items, rumours, etc. What's more, Jeanne and Brigitte have insisted that Christine Brierre[3] also be taken on, but for the moment U.A. don't see eye to eye with Christine over the question of money and, as Christine will have to give up two other films for the Malle, she's determined not to give way. There you have it. But she confirmed to me that she wouldn't be taking your place, she would be there in addition.

I have just completely revised the Hitchcock and I am very impatient for you to get to work. How are we going to do it? We'll see. If you remain at the FFO, the only way would be to explain everything to Korda and Don Congdon so that someone from Simon and Schuster could do the work under your supervision. There are new passages to be translated (about 25 typed pages), quite a number of corrections to be both translated and marked up, some structural changes and even a few cuts. It's not a lot of work, but it is urgent, if we don't want Hitchcock to think we're stringing him along.[4]

In 3 days' time I'll dictate to Lucette my notes explaining the changes.

Thursday

I've received your letter of the 17th. Today I've brought myself up to date with the US: Don Congdon and Lewis, and I'll be sending you copies of these letters.

Cahiers is doing very well, as you can see for yourself. They're all at work preparing the Christmas issue. The article in *Arts* was stupid and spiteful, of absolutely no interest.

Speaking of the young English girl in *Atlas*, you don't mention what really counts, I mean her knees, her buttocks, her cheeks, her nose, you see how incorrigible I am!

Harrisson's enthusiasm for the book doesn't surprise me, it pleases me. Apart from Eisenstein's book, *Film Sense and Film Form* (which has never been translated into French), there's been nothing quite so important.

Arthur Penn, who films every scene from twelve different angles, out of ignorance, can learn everything from such a book and the same applies to Huston, Wyler, Stevens, that's what you'll understand one day!!!

I realize that you would prefer Toronto to Stockholm, but as for myself, I tend towards Lewis's solution, because his problem is not going to be easy, believe me.

Do you think that my attitude to 'Jay' is:*

a) sadistic
b) justified
c) excessive
d) hateful
e) vengeful
f) logical
g) funny.

I worry about the tone you adopt when you speak to me of Harrisson. In effect, by getting carried away (that's not the right word), by becoming 'warm', you're just asking for trouble. You're both too warm at the same time, whereas between you and me, it's more a question of alternating currents or the principle of Archimedes. Be careful, apply the brakes, try to be as frosty and sophisticated as a Hitchcockian heroine, don't come on too strong and don't allow yourself to get over-excited – actually, what I've just said is a load of nonsense.

Marnie has bombed here even though the 'fans' are happy. In fact, every film is a flop at the moment, *Monsieur de compagnie*[5] (very weak) [. . .], *La Ronde*,[6] etc.

I'll write to you again next week.

hugs and kisses from the heart of a pure 3-way love affair,

regards to Jim,
Jules Truffaut

*Delete where inapplicable.

1 – An allusion to the character played by Jeanne Moreau in *Jules et Jim*. Truffaut is comparing Helen Scott's situation to Catherine's, caught between two men, the first, Harrisson (Jim), a friend of Helen's, the second, Truffaut himself (Jules). Thus, in

the letter's envoi, he writes 'regards to Jim' and signs himself 'Jules Truffaut'.

2 – *Viva Maria!*, with Brigitte Bardot and Jeanne Moreau.

3 – A press agent.

4 – Compare with Truffaut's final little 'speech' in Helen Scott's imaginary dialogue on p. 255.

5 – Philippe De Broca's *Un monsieur de compagnie*.

6 – By Roger Vadim.

To Helen Scott *from Paris, 16 December 64*

My dear Helen,

I leave Paris tomorrow morning for my Scandinavian trip: Denmark, Norway, Finland and Sweden. It's going to be like de Gaulle's tour of South America: a different country every day, speeches, newspapers, visits to studios, etc.!

I return to Paris on Tuesday the 22nd, during the day, but I leave again the following day to rejoin Mado and the children in Cannes where I'll be resting until 4 January. Rest in a relative sense, since I have quite a few books and screenplays to read, without counting the Hitchcock preface.

Note the following carefully: from Monday 11 January I'm going to study English, oui, oui, yes, six hours a day for six weeks, that's to say until the end of February. It's a sort of crash course in small groups. It costs 300 dollars and Lewis needn't worry, I'll be paying for it out of my own pocket!

So there's no question of my leaving Paris before March, no question either of going to Mexico City at the end of January, something I haven't yet dared to tell Jérôme Brierre[1] who has managed to have *La Peau douce* (which hasn't yet been sold in Mexico) entered in the festival.

The English classes are from 9 o'clock in the morning (ouch) until 1 o'clock in the afternoon (hell) and from 2 o'clock (shit) to 4 o'clock (phew). I won't be feeling too lonely as Géret,[2] an actor whom I seem to remember your liking in Buñuel's *Le Journal d'une femme de chambre*, will be taking the same course.

I'm giving you all the details, as it has been the big event of the day at the office, and talking about it as much as possible will help me to go through with it. I hope I won't be tempted to play truant. So there you are.

I was amused by everything you tell me about Demy and his paratroopers. I agree, he's an odd fish.

Fahrenheit: I worked for a week with Claude de Givray on improving the French script. It's now more or less finished. It's being typed out and you'll receive it by the end of the year. Naturally, I will be very wary of Spiegel[3] if he should get involved in the project, for I'm certain he won't approve the script as it is. Like *La Peau douce*, though not for the same reasons, *Fahrenheit* is one of those films that everyone will see differently and want to tamper with and change: not enough science fiction or too much science fiction, too weird or not enough, not sufficiently a love story or too much of a love story, in short the only way I can have any peace in such a situation is to tell everyone to go to hell. If you can think of another way, let me know.

I'm forgetting the most important point: For once, thank God, we see eye to eye. I would like you to be the translator of *Fahrenheit*. So that you don't spend too much time on it, I suggest you translate only the dialogue. As far as the rest is concerned, the shot-by-shot description, since this job has already been done once, all you have to do is copy it out again.

The Hitchcock Book: Lucette is at this moment tidying up the manuscript specially for you, in order to make it very easy to tell at a glance the passages that we've changed. It will be a piece of cake.

Timing: Your idea of coming to Paris to work is not bad. If you were to come in January, you could work part of the day alone and then with me from 5 o'clock onwards, when I return from school . . . That would be the ideal solution, unless I'm worn to a frazzle by the lessons and am in the foul mood that you know all too well!

The awful thing is that the book and the script are equally urgent. What should I give priority to?

If your trip to Paris in January or February (or both) is out of the question, either because of the F.F.O. or for money reasons, we might arrange for me to return to New York at the beginning of March to practise my English and work with you, but, until then, we can only hope that lots of things will have progressed.

Lewis: Your letter arrived just in time, because this very day I had to deliver *Fahrenheit* to Frechtman; I cancelled the appointment . . . speaking of which, Lewis was very cavalier about not having written to me; all I received was a note from Stephanie[4] concerning the medical which I'll be taking at the beginning of January (between the 4th and 11th) and a copy of the Swedish costings. As far as removing Jay's name is concerned, I won't give way and I suppose that's why Lewis no longer writes to me personally.

Jeanne: I'm delighted with the publicity Jeanne has been receiving in America; it will also benefit *Jules et Jim* and *Mata-Hari* (with which I'm really very satisfied and which will be finished by the beginning of January).

I agree with you about your creative potential and you have my full confidence; so I'm delighted with what you tell me of your collaboration with Harrisson and am not at all sceptical.

Fourth and last page. I've fallen a bit behind as I have to attend a dinner in honour of Dreyer, 76 years old, who has come to Paris to present his latest film.[5]

I'd better bring this to an end now: don't put yourself out for my daughters, they're spoiled rotten, you mustn't buy them anything, believe me.

As regards *L'Amour à 20 ans*, I refuse to fall into that crude trap of yours which consists of asking me to send you a print solely for the pleasure of screening it for Harrisson while you hold his hand in the dark! Nevertheless, you've unwittingly given me an idea. If Embassy can do nothing with the whole film, I might suggest that they specially distribute, as a supporting programme, my own sketch which, separated from the others, could make some money if it were to be shown with *Le Pianiste* or *Jules et Jim*. I'm going to think it all over between now and January.

I can make the same criticism you did: you do not scrupulously reply to the various questions I put to you in my letters, to take a single example, the one concerning *Cahiers du cinéma*'s new format.

To conclude. If Allen seems favourably disposed to your coming to Paris, given that you will end up dividing your time between *Fahrenheit* and the book, I might be able to squeeze some money out of Carrosse to help pay your expenses . . . ha ha . . . Seriously, though, it's an idea worth considering, on your side with Lewis and mine with Berbert. What's more, I would make some office space for you in my apartment in the avenue Paul-Doumer; well, in any event, we could always work something out.

I wait to hear from you; love,

happy new year
françois

1 – From Unifrance-Film.
2 – Georges Géret, French actor, born in 1924: *Le Défroqué*, *Week-End à Zuydcoote*, *Compartiment tueurs*, etc.
3 – Sam Spiegel, American producer (1901–85).
4 – Stephanie Sills, Lewis Allen's assistant.
5 – *Gertrud*.

1965

To Serge Rezvani[1]

[1965]

My dear Serge,

I'm not alone in thinking you should, one of these days, get down to writing a book: poems? prose? fiction? childhood memories? what does it matter, but think about it!

You know how I adore stimulating work around me, doubtless in order to give myself the clear conscience of an activist and stir things up. Well, anyway . . . it's an idea . . .

I'll end like poor Albert Camus whose car went too fast,[2] by suggesting that you toss and turn on your bed of grief until you find the least uncomfortable spot; in other and simpler words: look after yourself,

love and kisses,

françois

1 – French singer, song-writer, painter and writer, he played in *Jules et Jim*, which also featured one of his songs, 'Le Tourbillon'.

2 – Camus was killed (as a passenger) in a road accident.

To Danièle Rezvani

[February–March 1965]
Saturday (nothing doing)

My dear Danielle,

There's been nothing but good news from Jeanne;[1] yet, all the same, she watches every morning at her attic window for the arrival of the postman from Santa-Cruz who might be bringing her news from Europe. She very much needs to receive letters and, like everyone 4,000 miles from home, she imagines that all sorts of things are going on in her absence. Don't disabuse her and write to tell her how and why you've become a blonde and Serge has been made sub-prefect of the Alpes-Maritimes, why the only thing that could be saved from the fire at La Mourre was the stewpot of the Chinee cook (imported from Monaco) and everything that's been happening in the Bas-

Var and the Haut-Var. A good long fat letter weighing half a pound is just what she needs with one of Serge's drawings concealed on the back of the stamp.

I've had good news of you from Carlojean and little Maroulier[2] and things are going well for me too; long time no see, or so I find, and I'd be very happy to pay you a visit, maybe for Easter?

Thinking of you,
françois

1 – Jeanne Moreau, who was in Mexico filming Louis Malle's *Viva Maria!*

2 – Jean-Louis Richard and Carla Marlier.

To Helen Scott

Paris, 22 March 1965

My dear Helen,

I am immediately replying to your letter of this morning, but I cannot be much more precise than when we spoke on the telephone:

1. No, I haven't really quarrelled with Lewis and I didn't bawl him out as he deserved. It was all rather vague since, as you recall, he pretended to have learned about the delay by ringing Kindberg from our office; all that happened was that Lucette, who had heard Lewis's comments, and several of the comments he made a few hours before, led us to believe that he had known about it all along.

I simply demanded at that point that we go and see Stamp on the very next day, as I wished to make sure:

a) that Stamp wanted to make the film;
b) that he would prefer to make it with Spiegel rather than anyone else;
c) that he would agree to wait a year.

We got the answers to these questions when we had a talk with Stamp, and the very fact that he is now refusing to make Arthur Penn's film[1] as well as Litvak's (*The Night of The Generals*), both of them also produced by Spiegel, is all in our favour.

Everyone who has seen Wyler's film *The Collector*, whether they like it or not, agrees that Stamp is a revelation, etc, etc.

The most pessimistic scenario would be to imagine that, no agreement on *Fahrenheit* with Stamp and Spiegel having been signed by the end of May and Wyler's film being ridiculed at Cannes like *The Soft Skin* last year, the whole deal would collapse through general indifference! That's the worst hypothesis!

2. Lewis's trip to Paris was not as pointless as all that since we were able to clear up the situation as regards the numerous screenwriters of the film who will all have to give up their percentage of the profits in the event of a deal with Spiegel. In other words, the last thing to be worked out is my own contract so that Spiegel can be faced with a clear-cut situation and can buy out the others without any problems.

In reply to the different possibilities concerning your immediate future, you must obviously be wary of anyone who says to you, 'If you're in Paris, you could work on this or that project.' People like that are first cousins to Lewis Allen, and usually less nice.

I haven't done anything yet about the subtitling of *Mata-Hari*, because it doesn't only involve Carrosse and I'll have to get in touch with Lépicier,[2] who has just returned from abroad.

Jean-Luc Godard has decided against going to New York this time, but he told me that he's written to arrange for you to do the subtitles of *Une femme mariée*, even if someone else has already been considered, and, as for his new film[3] with Eddie Constantine, it hasn't opened yet in America.

Hitchcock: I take your point regarding page 207 of the manuscript. You are absolutely right and it will have to be cleared up.

At the end of *North by Northwest*, in the last shot of the scene on Mount Rushmore, Eva Marie Saint is suspended in space and Cary Grant pulls her up by the arm, but this gesture immediately fades into another, similar gesture in the sleeping compartment of a train with Cary Grant this time pulling Eva Marie Saint up on to his bunk.

It's immediately after that shot that the train enters the tunnel and the words 'the end' appear.

George Hamilton's extraordinarily indiscreet remarks about X— are certainly going to cause some sparks to fly. If any other newspapers pick up the story, I suppose that X— will deny it, which is the only thing one could do.

I'm very pleased you're seeing such marvellous films. Don't fail to reread the chapter on *The 39 Steps* before seeing the film again, and take a good look at how the meal with the Scottish farmer was shot if you ever want to take my place on *Fahrenheit* should I fall ill.

Send me Pauline Kael's[4] book, since only a rave review of me will motivate me to read some English. [. . .]

1 – *The Chase.*
2 – Eugène Lépicier, co-producer of *Mata-Hari.*
3 – *Alphaville.*
4 – The film critic of the *New Yorker.*

To Jean Vilar[1]

Paris, 2 April 1965

Dear Monsieur Vilar,

I have not had the pleasure of being introduced to you, but we have, from Jeanne Moreau to Georges Géret, not to mention Micheline Rozan, so many mutual friends and I have such great admiration for your work that I feel I know you personally.

I am writing to you on a theatrical matter, more precisely a manuscript to read: *Blood* by Helen Hessel.

Helen Hessel is an elderly lady, probably in her seventies, whom I have never met but with whom I have been corresponding for the last three years, as she was the model for the heroine (Kathe) of Henri-Pierre Roché's novel *Jules et Jim*, of which I made the film.

She is of German nationality and is a woman of letters. She translated *Lolita* into German.

Not long ago she sent me the manuscript of this play and I liked it very much.

For me, however, while it's already no easy matter 'visualizing' a screenplay, for the theatre it's even worse, and I would be quite incapable of hazarding a guess as to the critical and commercial success of this play whose theme is the advent of Nazism as observed and experienced by a Jewish family in Germany. There you have it.

I well know the kind of panic we are thrown into when, up to our ears in work, we receive urgent requests to read manuscripts. I know the fear of being inundated, the fear of being swamped, which is why my initial thought was to ask you whether you had time at the moment to read the manuscript, but finally I preferred to gain time and send it to you enclosed with this introductory letter.

If you are overworked and you do not think you will be able to read it now,

From left to right: Danièle Rezvani, Serge Rezvani, François Truffaut, Jean-Louis Richard, Carla Marlier.

I ask only that you let me know and I will have the manuscript picked up at the Théâtre de l'Athénée.

In the hope that I have not imposed on you, I remain, dear Monsieur Vilar,

yours in admiration,
François Truffaut

1 – French actor and theatre director, born in 1916. He founded the Avignon Festival, was director of the Théâtre National Populaire and appeared in such films as *Les Portes de la nuit*, *Les Frères Bouquinquant*, *Les Eaux troubles*, etc.

To Helen Scott

Paris, 3 May 1965

My dear Helen,

I received, in effect, while holidaying in the Midi with the children over Easter, a telegram from Spiegel which reads as follows:

EAGERLY LOOKING FORWARD MEETING WITH YOU ON *FAHRENHEIT* END OF MONTH – HOPE CAN REARRANGE MY COMMITMENTS KINDBERG AND FLY TO EUROPE FOR OUR TALKS – STOP – WILL BE BACK IN TOUCH WITH EXACT DATE AND PLACE SOONEST – WARM REGARDS – SAM SPIEGEL.

You therefore know as much about it as I do. When I see Spiegel, I'll know if the deal is getting to a contractual stage. The discussions I'll be having with him will bear solely on questions of dates, actors and script, since all matters relating to money will be thrashed out by our lawyers, but, as I've told you several times, these won't – of this I'm certain – present any problem.

You have my assurance, needless to say, that one of the first requests I'll make of Spiegel will concern taking you on at the same time as the deal is signed.

Obviously, it can all still collapse if, for one reason or another, Spiegel loses interest in the project, but, depending on how *The Collector* is received at Cannes, we'll see whether Stamp's acceptance will be enough to set it up again with another company, United Artists, for example.

You don't mention in your latest letter how you're getting on with the Hitchcock manuscript.

For my part, I recently got down to the preface which is horrendously difficult to do. I hope to have it finished by the end of this week so that I can send it off to you at the beginning of next.

Where this text is concerned I am absolutely without vanity and will be prepared to accept all your criticisms and those of Don Congdon, to whom, by the same post, I'm sending a letter, a copy of which you'll find enclosed.

Allen is barking up the wrong tree if he thinks the negotiations with Spiegel are taking forever because of my contract or my demands. In reality, it's Spiegel who is dragging things out probably because he is very busy, because he's very sure of himself, because he suspects that Stamp and I would prefer that the deal be made with him and because, knowing that Lewis Allen's position is growing weaker by the day, he gets a certain sadistic satisfaction out of it.

I realize from a recent letter from Lewis Allen that he has only just noticed that the rights are about to expire, and, since he refers to a 'secretary's' mistake, I cannot help wondering if Stephanie Sills's disappearance from the Broadway stage isn't directly linked to this oversight!

That's it for today, my dear Helen,

françois

To Helen Scott *from Paris, Wednesday 19 May 1965*

My dear L.N.,

No, my life is not filled up with all the things you imagine or even a few of them. I simply didn't want to write to you before finishing the preface I promised to Don.

Here it is, then. I sweated almost a month over it, no doubt because I was out of training and for all sorts of other reasons.

I think the beginning, about the frozen tank, is heavy, top-heavy and heavy-handed. I think the best section is the middle and I don't know what I think of the end which is perhaps too personal and which I don't want to upset or displease Hitch.

Naturliche, I'm very impatient to have your opinion and your criticisms. I know that, for the French edition, this text, if slightly revised in 2 or 3 months, will do very well.

I don't know if it's what Simon and Schuster wanted and especially Don, who is hoping to have some extracts published in magazines.

As it comes to about 30 pages, perhaps all that need be done for magazine publication is to have it shortened. You will probably complain that, once again, I've been too flattering, it's for you to judge. You will agree nevertheless that I've made an immense effort:

a) to be clear;
b) not to use – and therefore to spoil – extracts from the book;
c) to argue points through;
d) to be easily translatable.

Apart from my Scott, I intend to solicit the opinions of:

a) Madeleine, who is an even sterner critic of my work than you;
b) Aurel, an intelligent Hitchcockian;
c) Claude de Givray, a critic and friend.

Their opinions will prompt me to make a few little changes and there we are.

I have to know very soon what you think of the text and the date by which you think you'll have translated it.

If you are, as I am, in two minds, you may read the piece to Don so he can tell you whether it corresponds to what he was hoping for.

Then: I suggest you write to Hitch to ask him: a) when he'll be able to read the complete material; b) when he'll be able to give us a couple of days to bring the book up to date.

Next week, during my convalescence (see below!), I'm going to reread the text of the interviews, now that I'm relieved of that worrisome preface, and I'll be jotting down a few notes to compare with yours.

MY LIFE: I've been living for 3 days now in the rue de Passy, on the 10th floor with a terrace overlooking Paris. It has an (Eiffel)[1] tower window.[2] It's a beautiful apartment with 5 rooms including one for my daughters and a lav just for you. I'm renting it unfurnished, which means that I have my own furniture, some fine antiques, beautiful lamps, crockery, bedding and so on.

Lucette is now looking for a maid-cum-cook for me.

In a couple of weeks Carrosse will have new offices 200 metres from the old ones, rue Robert-Estienne (between rue Marbeuf and the Champs-Élysées). My office will be magnificent, bookshelves everywhere, Japanese wallpaper, Spanish furniture, a little divan (hmm!), all mod cons, a little bar.

I leave tomorrow morning, Thursday, to spend just 2 days at Cannes, even though I learned (only yesterday) that Terence Stamp would not be going. I knew he hadn't liked either Wyler's film or the girl,[3] but I would never have thought him so strong-willed.

In fact, Allen has as usual got the wrong end of the stick, since, if Kindberg and Spiegel are coming to France, it's for no other reason than to see *The Collector* in Cannes, of course!

Next Monday, a surgeon is going to extract a wisdom tooth which is growing (sideways) inside my filthy gob. Which explains the convalescence at home for a few days.

Then, from the 1st to the 18th, I'm off to London to study English 3 hours a day with a lady teacher and a tape recorder. I'll fill up the time by going out with Stamp, to the theatre and cinema.

As you see, I'm planning my life as though Spiegel and Kindberg didn't exist, since I don't want to live in weitting for them.[4]

After several sessions with me, my friend Jean Gruault has started writing the script of *L'Enfant sauvage*, which will be a stupendous film.

'And where does Scott come into all of this?' I hear you say. I haven't forgotten her, no, besides she's unforgettable, but you must understand, my dear L.N., that I'm unable to do anything for the moment because of this whole business of *Fahrenheit* and also, I have to admit, because of my difficulties in learning English.[5] For 3 weeks now I've been taking lessons, just 1 hour a day with Jill Popplewell, who was our teacher on the famous course.

I agreed to Stamp's suggestion to study it in London for 3 weeks because it's not going to cost me too much, because it will bring us closer together and because he's going to make a simultaneous effort to learn French. Moreover, I'll be able to pop over every weekend to see my little girls.

I saw my parents again, both of them together, at a lunch at my mother's place. She thought *La Peau douce* was a little less vulgar than *Jules et Jim* and my father is seeing the film next week. I put that in to amuse you a little!

So, take careful note: I am having my operation in the afternoon of Monday the 24th and then I return to my apartment in Passy, the number is: MIRabeau 57-93. You can ring me there Monday evening or Tuesday any time during the day,

I enlace you
I embrace you
how I love you
dear Hélène
from you to me
just once a month
I disappoint you
signed françois[6]

1 – Truffaut had always been extremely fond of the Eiffel Tower: two of the apartments in which he lived overlooked it and he owned a large collection of miniature Eiffel Towers (it is with one of these that Fanny Ardant brains an unknown aggressor in *Vivement dimanche!*, just as it is a shot of the Eiffel Tower which opens *Les Quatre Cents Coups*).
2 – Truffaut's original phrase, *fenêtre sur tour*, is a pun on *Fenêtre sur cour*, the French title of Hitchcock's *Rear Window*.
3 – Samantha Eggar, Stamp's leading lady in *The Collector*.
4 – In 'English' in the original letter.
5 – Though he made several more or less serious attempts to study English – by means of courses, tutors, 'total immersion' sessions, etc. – Truffaut never learned to speak the language fluently.
6 – For the original French of this little piece of doggerel, see facing page.

To an admirer of Georges Brassens

Paris, 31 May 1965

Dear Monsieur,

I am replying a little belatedly to your letter, as it pains me to have to disappoint you, but I have no great admiration for Georges Brassens's work, even if I know it quite well.

The songs of his that I like best are those of his records no. 4 and no. 5 or, to be more precise, those from *Porte des Lilas*:[1] 'Au bois de mon coeur', 'La Noce', 'L'Orage', etc.

What I don't care for in Brassens is the division of the world in two: pacifists and warmongers, intelligent and stupid people, poets and bourgeois, lovers and cops, and, where style is concerned, his is so calculated and laborious that you can guess what the rhymes are going to be one verse ahead.

My preference is for Charles Trenet, Boby Lapointe and Bassiak.[2] They are the three actor-singers whom I admire.

Hoping that I have answered your questions, I remain regretfully but cordially

yours,
François Truffaut

1 – By René Clair (1957), it starred the singer Brassens.
2 – 'Bassiak' was the pseudonym of Serge Rezvani.

Cela, c'était pour vous divertir un peu!
Donc, ~~notes~~ notez bien ceci: je me fais opérer lundi 24 dans l'après midi et ensuite je rentre chez moi à Passy dont voici le numéro:
MiRabeau: 57-93
Vous pouvez m'y appeler lundi soir ou mardi toute la journée,

je vous enlace
je vous embrasse
comme je vous aime
ma chère Helène
de vous à moi
une fois par mois
je vous déçois
signé François

To Elinor Jones *Paris, 18 June 1965*

Dear Friend,

I received your telegram for which thank you. But before accepting your invitation to come to New York to discuss *Bonnie and Clyde*, I would first like to raise several points of some importance to me.

In fact the successive delays on *Fahrenheit 451* have caused me a great deal of concern, and to add to all that there have arisen some very serious problems relating to the film *Mata-Hari* of which I am one of the producers.

That is why your proposition concerning *Bonnie and Clyde* has come at just the right moment, provided, as I told you, that we will be able to start shooting this summer.

In fact, the screenplay is in pretty good shape and most of the locations have already been found. We should be able to prepare the film quite quickly and easily.

Please forgive me for immediately bringing up the subject of money, but this does seem to me an opportune moment to do so. As director of *Bonnie and Clyde*, what I would like is a salary of $80,000 plus 10% of the producer's net profits.

The second point of my letter concerns Helen Scott, whom I wish to have as my personal assistant. I would like her to be officially engaged on the same day that I myself am and for the duration of the shoot. She is to receive the same salary as that which was negotiated for her collaboration on *Fahrenheit 451*.

The third point concerns the role of Bonnie which I would like to entrust to my friend Alexandra Stewart, with whom I have long had the desire to make a film. As far as I am concerned, she would be ideal for the character. She is an Anglo-Canadian, totally bilingual and capable of assuming any accent with extraordinary ease.

I trust her both as an actress and a friend, and she would represent for me, in addition to Helen, another reassuring presence, since it is very important, in this my first English-language film, that I have around me people with whom I can get along and whose confidence I have, whether it be technicians or actors.

If you are in agreement on these three points, I will be able to come to New York whenever you wish to discuss the other important matters, which are:

a) the male lead. I think we might offer the part to Terence Stamp whom I greatly admire and who hopes to play Montag in *Fahrenheit 451*. But I will not speak to him before hearing what you have to say and, moreover, as he has very definite ideas on his career, it may be that he will prefer to do

Fahrenheit and not *Bonnie and Clyde*. There is still a question-mark over that.

b) the choice of cinematographer-cum-cameraman, who must be someone very pleasant and up-to-date, since, myself apart, the speed with which we shoot will depend essentially on him. He doesn't have to speak French, but he does have to be competent, easy to get on with, fast, receptive to new ideas and well-disposed to what you in America call 'The New Wave'.

c) David Newman and Robert Benton. I would be very pleased to re-examine the script with them before shooting starts, and it would be very useful if they themselves were able to follow the shoot, in the event of our wanting to make some minor alterations as we proceed.

There you have it! If you have any ideas concerning actors for the film, I suggest you send some photos to me as soon as possible. In any case, we will have a chance to discuss that in New York, since, as I told you, I am prepared to come whenever you wish.

In the hope of hearing from you very soon, I send you my warmest regards.

François Truffaut

To Helen Scott

from Paris, Saturday morning
7 August 1965

My dear medallist,[1]

Tomorrow morning, Sunday, I'll get up at the crack of dawn to give la Givrette[2] this letter and the Hitch intro, botched but finished in time! You will note, all the same, that I've cut the bit about Hollywood war movies, added a note on Renoir and patched up what's essential.

Actually, Yvonne hasn't had time to reread the text and maybe some errors have slipped through the net. What's more, some tiny details have been changed which perhaps you won't even notice. So, Monday or Tuesday, we'll be sending you:

a) a list of corrections, if necessary, of the typing errors.
b) a note dictated by me, drawing your attention to any detail which may have been changed.

I wasn't at home last night when Lewis telephoned from N.Y. Perhaps he had read the letter in which I asked him to pay you $3,000 (not the advance but a simple reimbursement of expenses) or perhaps he wanted to talk about Universal. [. . .]

Jeanne is very determined to do *La Mariée – The Bride Wore Black* – and has persuaded Oscar Lewenstein (Tony Richardson's[3] Berbert) to buy the rights for us. So, after Lewis Allen, my next boss will be Tony Richardson. One day I hope to make a film for the producer Claude de Givray and his associate producer Helen Scott of France.

And that, dear medallist Helen, is the news on this rainy Saturday. Next Thursday, with Jean-Louis Richard, I start the script of *Un jeune homme à Paris* (a working title inspired by *A Young Man in Boston*).

Take care of yourself. Near Montreal or elsewhere, try to breathe in some good country air, best wishes to my father Rossellini if he really is in Montreal, look after Claude de Givray, regards to Juneau, to the Cadieus[4] and Jutra, don't besmirch the chaste and virtuous reputation of the Queen Lisbeth Hotel, but try and find yourself some little old septuagenarian (as our mutual friend would say) and accept a kiss from me on your medal,

françois

1 – Helen Scott had just received the medal of the French Liberation for acts of resistance during the war.
2 – Lucette de Givray.
3 – English director, born in 1928: *Look Back in Anger*, *The Entertainer*, *A Taste of Honey*, *The Loneliness of the Long Distance Runner*, *Tom Jones*, *The Charge of the Light Brigade*, *The Border*, etc.
4 – Pierre Juneau and Germain Cadieu were the organizers of the Montreal Film Festival.

To Helen Scott

[August 1965]

My dear Helen,

I have your letter of 11 August in front of me. I'm annoyed with myself for not having spoken to you more often about Roberto, my Italian father. In fact, his name had been mentioned in Nouillorque, in connection with the Mon Réal festive,[1] but I thought he would stand them up as he often does. Otherwise there are several reasons why I would have spoken to you about him: a) knowing both of you as I do, I didn't doubt you'd take to each other; b) I would have asked you, when speaking to him, not to mention Hitchcock. Too late. Now that you know the man, his extraordinary presence and so on, you will understand, I hope, 3 years on, why I didn't appreciate Hitchcock's (funny!) story about Ingrid's twin daughters and why I was irritated to hear you repeat it.

For that matter, since I'm in a sermonizing mood, let me add that, if you were actually to read *Cahiers* instead of 'wittily' bitching about it, you would have discovered Roberto twice a year, thanks to some wonderful interviews. To continue bawling you out, I haven't forgotten how condescending you were last month when I talked to you about *Francesco – Giullare di Dio*.

In short, I'm trying to pick a pointless fight with you; the truth is that I fall in love with people through films while with you it's the opposite. Obviously you're the one who's right since people are more important than celluloid.

But Roberto is one of the great intellects of the century and, if I find something good about him to send you, I'll do so.

I'm writing to you solely to answer your letter, since otherwise I have nothing new or special to tell you.

Fahrenheit: I'm pleased Lewis is doing something about your $3,000; he's in London at the moment and he told me he had seen you, but did he sign the cheque or not?

I'm not as optimistic as you about the film and for me you'll always be 'gullible Helen'. Universal hasn't signed and we haven't advanced any further from last year.

Naturally, I think you should leap at the chance if Lewis takes you on and we'll calmly sit down and discuss all these important translation problems.

In an interview, Gore Vidal said that he was getting ready to work on the script for *Fahrenheit*, but I had told Lewis NO when he mentioned him to me! It's always the same old story.

The intro: If you ask me to add a sentence on Rossellini, I'll resign! [. . .]

The Bride Wore Black is getting under way, but because I'm superstitious I'm not ready to tell you exactly how. I hope for an answer by the end of August.

Like you, I'm full of anxiety about Hitchcock. Patience, patience.

Your letter was really very sweet and though I regret having begun mine so aggressively, I'm afraid I didn't have the energy to throw it into the waste-paper basket and start again.

Why has Midge not replied to the letter I wrote her in English? Maybe she couldn't make head or tail of it, including the signature.

If my second-last thought is for her, the very last one is just for you and I send you my love,

françois

1 – The Montreal Film Festival.

To Helen Scott *from Paris, Friday 20 August nineteen hundred and sixty five*

My dear Helen,

Thank you for your letter and also for not holding the stupid criticisms of my earlier one against me.

Roberto! He was, just as Jean-Luc is, quicker than anyone else, more alive, more intelligent, more enterprising and, of necessity, more quickly disillusioned with the cinema. He would take 60 days to make a film, then 40, then 20, and you know the rest: the failure of the whole cycle with Ingrid, a brief resurgence with *Il Generale della Rovere*, more failures and, running through it all, his increasing aversion to 'fiction', his attraction to pure documentary, etc.

Today his activity consists in obtaining enormous sums of money from the great financial powers of Europe (steel, foodstuffs, meat-packing, pharmaceutical products, etc.) with the intention of promoting a kind of filmed encyclopaedia: the history of steel, the history of food, the history of medicine, etc.

The enormous budgets of the Italian educational system, educational films and television stations, as well as UNO and UNESCO, have all been coopted.

If Roberto wasn't the man he is – sincere and brilliant – one might describe it all as a huge confidence trick, a mammoth deal or else the biggest cultural swindle of the century, but it isn't so.

It is true, however, that he is turning out a series of cultural artefacts which, from the point of view of the industrialists who make it possible, constitutes a camouflaged exercise in public relations. To the extent that his backing comes from various European governments, either with subsidies or by their giving him access to their TV channels, there can be no question of his criticizing the established order, the laws of society, etc.

In fact, Roberto, a non-practising Catholic, is above political allegiances, above all such labelling, above the crowd, but it's easy to imagine the attacks that could be levelled against him from left-wing sociologists, the day the whole undertaking is analysed for public opinion.

That's what it's all about. I've only spoken about the ambiguous side of his character, because I think you yourself saw the very genuine positive aspects.

All this is between you and me. Roberto, who is not very highly regarded in France, tried to involve me and Carrosse in the business, but I already had so many problems that I pulled out. For several weeks I was afraid there would be bad feeling between us but, as it turned out, he took it very well.

I'm sending you a little book on Roberto; there's an article in it by me, page

199, and reminiscences by Cocteau, Godard, Renoir, etc. Keep it, I'll buy another.

On the other hand, I would like to retrieve a few of the articles on R.R. that I recently sent you, those on which I have written 'Return to Truffaut', because I'm still rather obsessive about my papers!

To finish with R.R., he's a man who needs an enormous income since he has to support about 11 children, including the daughter of Ingrid and Dr Lindstrom whom we glimpsed one evening at Hitchcock's . . .

He has a great need of love, of absolute devotion, but he's something of a tyrant and terribly disorganized. You can have a professional relationship with him, but beware whenever the subject of money comes up. It's true. It's not that he's avaricious, on the contrary, but he simply has no business sense in spite of all his wheeling and dealing.

I'm not very happy with this description which is both too long and too short and now strikes me as unfair, but try all the same to get the picture!

This evening I leave for Cannes to see my little darlings. As a result of spending day after day in the swimming pool, Laura has an ear infection. At the beginning of September we're going to have her tonsils and adenoids removed, early enough so that she won't fall behind in school.

Jean Gruault has finished a first version of *L'Enfant sauvage* which is not bad, will be easy to improve and will make for a superb film.

With Jean-Louis Richard I've begun the script for Jean-Pierre Léaud, who will play a young journalist; it will be both cruel and funny, in the tone of *L'Amour à 20 ans*.

With everyone on holiday, I have no news of *Camera Obscura*. As for Patricia Highsmith's *Deep Water*,[1] it's Raoul Lévy who owns the rights and he would like to direct it himself one day, with Jeanne! Nevertheless, he doesn't know of my interest in it and it's possible that one day I'll carry off the prize.

Lewis Allen had the brilliant idea of having Linda and Clarisse (in *Fahrenheit*) played by the same actress with two different hair-dos. That would solve all the problems that have been plaguing me for so long about their figures, their ages, their looks, etc. I gave my approval to the idea and, my goodness, how wonderful it would be if it were Julie Christie. Lewis keeps asking me to go to London and visit the studios, but I keep putting it off to teach him to manage without me and to let him see that my scepticism is ever alert.

I wouldn't be too surprised to see him turning up at the Saint-Michel Résidence[2] tomorrow or the day after!

I inform you of the arrival in America of:

a) Jean-Luc for the N.Y. Festive.

b) Eugène Lépicier who is going to try and sell *Thomas l'Imposteur*.[3]

I would like you, starting now, to spread some positive rumours about *Thomas l'Imposteur*:

– 'They say it's Franju's best film.'

– 'They say it's the best film ever based on Cocteau.'

– 'They say the film is bound to beat the box-office record set by *Tom Jones* in America.'

– 'They say Godard, Resnais and Truffaut put together couldn't have made such a magnificent film . . .'

I leave you to come up with other rumours.

Seriously, though, don't do the dirty on the charming Eugène who is depending on your influence to get back on his feet.

The loves of truffaut

1) Nothing to report
2) Nothing serious
3) A little renewal of affection
4) I'm going to answer Midge's *sweet letter*.[4]

More about Roberto: I've just come across a text entitled *Rossellini Year 49*, 82 typed pages. It's a '*mémoire*' (a thesis) by a student of IDHEC.[5] I am what is called the 'supervisor' of this thesis, which is to say, that some day soon I will have to 'defend' it in front of the school's profs. So send it back to me as soon as you've read it. Thanks.

I'm impatient to receive the snapshot of you. It already has a place waiting for it on the wall.

Jean-Luc's new film is genuinely new. The very height of novelty! Compared to it, all those he made before were as linear as *The Bridge on the River Kwai*.[6] But once again it's superb and quite different from usual. Even he could not take improvisation any further than he has done this time. Now everyone is wondering what he can possibly do next.

You mustn't think that *Alphaville* will do any harm whatsoever to *Fahrenheit*.

I thought that at Montreal R.R., who loathes aesthetes, would have made some kind of protest or other against *cinéma-vérité* or something else and, since you don't mention it, I suppose he managed to 'hold himself in'? Am I right?

I now interrupt this marathon letter, hell, what a marathon it is! since I'm going to try and persuade Lucette to have lunch with me, which would be a first for us, since we started working together in 1958.

That's that, Lucette and I had a bite to eat in the little Italian restaurant next door: scampi, escalope, cheese and coffee.

I've just lit up a good cigar and I'm wondering if there's anything I've forgotten to tell you.

Claude's[7] two latest films have come out in his absence: *Un mari à prix fixe* (Roger Hanin, Anna Karina, in the style of an American comedy) and *L'Amour à la chaîne* (prostitution from a sociological angle). There have been lots of good reviews for both films, so much rejoicing among the families concerned and de Givray's stock rising on the Champs-Élysées.

Could you send me 3 copies of *The Bride Wore Black* and Sterling Hayden's[8] autobiography?[9] I saw again *Johnny Guitar*[10] which has been revived with great success and I assure you that it's a film of exceptional poetic sensibility.

You will like it as it deserves to be liked the day that you have the privilege, the good fortune, the delight, the pleasure, the honour and the joy of seeing it with me.

Have you skimmed through or glanced at Audiberti's book *Dimanche m'attend*?

I had lunch yesterday with Nadine Libert and our relationship is moving towards real friendship. Sitting opposite her, I once more become timid and gauche, and, as she seems to have no intention of throwing herself at me, our relations are going to settle into a routine of chastity which I am not yet prepared to describe as dispiriting.

Jeanne, who is exhausted, often rings me up to assure me that, despite Richardson Tony's kindness, I'm still the one with whom she prefers to make films. In short, like me, her dearest hope is that Oscar Lewenstein succeeds in buying the rights to *La Mariée*. [. . .]

Could you please ask the dear little fellows in Bleecker Street for two or three copies of the *Bulletin*, the one whose cover is of me sitting with Jeanne on the bench in *Jules et Jim*?

Inside the *Bulletin* there is a photograph of old Renoir and young Truffaut seated side by side. If this photo still exists, could they lend it to you? It's all for Janine Bazin's TV programme on me. Thanks.

I would have liked to write you a twenty-page letter, but, honestly, I believe I've covered everything.

Of course, if I had to put in writing all that you mean to me, we'd very soon have exceeded the Hitchcock manuscript, but, frankly, what would Congdon and Korda say?

Now the ball is in your court. I'll be back here on Wednesday morning; so you won't have any excuse not to reply to me pronto except if the Hitch introduction drains you of all your strength,

love,
françois

P.S. Let's pretend you're still at the F.F.O.: Resnais's shoot with Yves Montand (*La Guerre est finie*) slightly delayed *because*[4] a few little pre-censorship problems (the day-to-day life of a Spanish militant in Paris) – Shoot of *La Religieuse* (Rivette, Diderot, Karina) imminent – Bresson shoot: *Au hasard, Balthazar* (the story of a donkey from birth to death) in progress – Varda shoot: *Les Créatures*, Catherine Deneuve, imminent – Polanski-Dorléac shoot[11] wrapping up in England – Demy's film, *Les Demoiselles de Rochefort*, has fallen through *because*[4] cash – Medical bulletin: Jacques Tati has flu, Demy is ill, de Broca has displaced vertebrae, Truffaut is out of work.

1 – Filmed in 1981 (as *Eaux profondes*) by Michel Deville with Isabelle Huppert.
2 – Madeleine Morgenstern's apartment above Cannes.
3 – By Georges Franju.
4 – In English in the original letter.
5 – See note 1, letter dated 3 November 1967, p. 313.
6 – By David Lean.
7 – De Givray.
8 – American actor, born in 1916: *The Asphalt Jungle, The Star, Johnny Guitar, Doctor Strangelove, The Long Goodbye*, etc.
9 – *Wanderer*.
10 – By Nicholas Ray (1954).
11 – *Cul-de-Sac*.

To Gérard Oury[1]

4 Oct. 65

My dear Gérard,

I may have seemed rude to you the other evening at Maxim's when I failed to acknowledge the compliments you paid me and I would now like to clear up the unease I still feel about it.

I very much liked *Le Corniaud* which I saw in a cinema in Cannes, where it opened 'at the same time as in Paris'. I had the opportunity of saying so to Robert Dorfmann with whom I had a long chat one day at Orly and it was a little foolish of me not to tell you yourself.

In fact, intimidated by the kind things you were saying to me, I felt it would be difficult to respond to compliments with other compliments and then there is the enormous success of your film which makes one feel curiously awkward about voicing one's admiration; I'm sure you understand what I mean; there is a tendency for every such colossal success, whether it be *Bonjour tristesse* (the book),[2] *Patate* (the play),[3] *Goldfinger*[4] or *Le Corniaud*, to invalidate the very notion of criticism. It becomes stupid (because almost meaningless) to speak ill of it, but the high regard in which one holds it may appear insincere if one tries to express it.

It's a curious phenomenon and, at the same time, I believe every artist must dream of reaching such a point; I mean the point at which 'opinions' are meaningless (Prévert with *Paroles* or Chaplin with all his films).

In short, I didn't dare say to you: 'And *I* liked *Le Corniaud* very much,' for fear that you would think: 'He feels he's obliged . . . ,' etc. It's all very curious, very complicated and, believe me, I would prefer to be simpler and more direct, especially with someone as congenial as you.

best wishes,
Truffaut

1 – French director and actor, born in 1919: (as director) *Le Crime ne paie pas*, *La Grande Vadrouille*, *Le Cerveau*, *La Folie des grandeurs*, *Les Aventures de Rabbi Jacob*, etc.
2 – By Françoise Sagan.
3 – By Marcel Achard.
4 – By Guy Hamilton.

To Alfred Hitchcock

Paris, 5 October 1965

Dear Mr Hitchcock,

I am sorry to disturb you just as you are about to begin shooting your new film, but I have a few questions to put to you concerning our book *Interviews with Alfred Hitchcock*.

I imagine you have finished reading the manuscript and I am naturally very eager to know your opinion.

1. Do you think that the text can now be delivered to the publishers in New York and Paris?

2. If such is not your opinion, I imagine that you would like to make some changes in the text or perhaps cuts, or on the contrary add a few extra paragraphs? In which case, would it be possible for you to dictate these changes to Miss Peggy Robertson or would you prefer the work to be done next time we meet?

3. If you are more or less satisfied with the book as it stands, we still have to complete together the first half of the final chapter, which is to say, everything concerning *Marnie*, *Torn Curtain* and perhaps *RRRRR*.[1]

This next meeting poses a problem of dates, since there is a possibility that I will begin shooting *Fahrenheit 451* in London around the beginning of February, which is to say, at the same time, I believe, as you will be finishing *Torn Curtain*?

4. If you are satisfied with the book, my only problem will be to convince the publishers in New York and Paris to let us insert the three hundred film stills, frame enlargements and production stills which will provide a graphic illustration of your comments.

At present, the publishers are afraid that if the book is so lavishly illustrated it will become too expensive.

Dear Mr Hitchcock, I know that your time is extremely valuable and I do not expect you to answer this letter, but perhaps Miss Peggy Robertson could telephone or write to Helen Scott to let us know what you think?

I hope that I will have the pleasure of seeing you again quite soon, I wish you good luck on *Torn Curtain* and I ask you to convey my very best wishes to Mrs Hitchcock.

Yours truly,
François Truffaut

1 – One of Hitchcock's projects.

To Bernard Gheur[1] *Paris, 22 October 1965*

Dear Monsieur,

I very much appreciated your text, *Le Testament d'un cancre*, and I suppose you have sent it to me more for literary than cinematic reasons.

I suppose, too, that you have been influenced by writers for whom I also have a great admiration, such as Cocteau and Radiguet, but it is your personality and sensibility that make the work what it is.

Naturally, I think you should develop the themes that are already present, the central character, give it much more breadth, escape the confines of the short story and undertake a real novel.

In which case, *Le Testament d'un cancre* might be regarded as a summary of the last third of the book to be written, you are capable of it, and I sincerely believe you ought to do it.

Most cordially yours,
F. Truffaut

1 – Belgian writer, born in 1945. Encouraged by Truffaut, to whom at the age of 20 he sent a short story which was to become *Le Testament d'un cancre* (published in 1970), he later wrote *La Scène du baiser* and *Retour à Calgary*. Gheur continued to write to Truffaut at irregular intervals; and the latter, without ever meeting him, took the trouble to read his manuscripts out of both generosity and a love of literature. The case of Bernard Gheur is indicative of the attention and assistance given by François Truffaut to certain aspiring young directors and writers.

To a young screenwriter

Paris, 22 October 1965

Dear Mademoiselle,

I received your letter of 12 October and I apologize in advance for not being able to boost your morale.

In the current French cinema there are a great many directors, old or young, talented or not, who are looking for work or for money, or for a producer, or a co-producer, or a distributor, or a subsidy from the C.N.C., or a star who might be available, but very few of them are looking for scripts.

Among the handful of directors who are fortunate enough to work regularly, it's virtually the same story. Don't forget that there still exists, among producers, distributors, bankers and even those members of C.N.C. committees whose function it is to subsidize 'quality', that age-old prejudice in favour of adaptations from famous or best-selling novels and, conversely, a suspicion of anything that has been typed out and subtitled 'original screenplay'.

What happened to you with your adaptation of Hector Malot will happen to you again and again unless you decide once and for all never to undertake a commission without first having signed a contract.

Don't forget that the film business is full of pirates, and it costs them nothing to have some intellectual write a hundred pages in good faith and then have these read by any number of people, everyone is briefly in seventh heaven and the script is a lost cause as far as the market is concerned.

I have never gone into the statistics of the question, but if, out of the hundred films that the French cinema produces in a year, you managed to find ten original screenplays, you would soon discover that these ten original screenplays had been written specifically for a star or a location, or a combination of elements, and that, whatever the circumstances, these ten screenplays had been commissioned by a producer. Well, then?

There remains the theatre, or else, still in the cinema, another approach which would consist of first proposing the idea to a director or a star, or a producer, and then possibly collaborating on the treatment with the person concerned.

I think I have covered the question from every angle. Do excuse me for being pessimistic,

and accept my very best wishes,

François Truffaut

To Guy Teisseire[1] *[autumn 1965]*

My dear Friend,

I was a little embarrassed and regretted not having agreed with you on an arrangement from the beginning. I hope you aren't disappointed.[2]

Obviously, it was difficult to proceed in the usual manner, as there's no question of my starting the film before 1967 and I'm not even sure that I'll be able to make it then.

In fact, it's above all by chatting to you that I learn things and it's perhaps from that point of view that we'll reconsider the question when the time comes, which is to say, working together for 2 weeks at regular hours, if you're free at that time and if it would interest you.

For the moment, I've got to put all of that aside because of my other commitments for 1966.

Before leaving Paris for London where I'm going to be living for several months, I'd like to have lunch with you and talk everything over again,

let's ring one another if you like between now and then,

best regards,

Truffaut

1 – French journalist, film critic and novelist, born in 1934.

2 – 'At that period Truffaut was planning a sequel to the adventures of Antoine Doinel, which eventually emerged as *Baisers volés* [*Stolen Kisses*], but was initially to have been set in the world of the press. Doinel was to have started out as a dogsbody on a daily newspaper; and Truffaut, knowing that I had just spent 5 years in the "general information" bureau of *L'Aurore*, had suggested that he and I work together on a few scenes in the life of a tyro journalist. Truffaut subsequently decided against making Doinel a journalist: in the version written by Claude de Givray and Bernard Revon he became a detective . . .' (Note by Guy Teisseire).

To Tony Walton[1] *Paris, 15 November 1965*

Dear Tony,

I am at present carefully rereading the script of *Fahrenheit 451* and also the novel. I still haven't given any very precise thought to the film's costumes, but here, at any rate, are a few of my initial impressions and I won't fail to write to you again as soon as I have some new ideas.

As far as Julie Christie is concerned, we'll model the costumes as closely as possible on the clothes she actually wears, since she tends to dress in a very contemporary style. I feel, however, that we might distinguish between Linda and Clarisse[2] by choosing glossy materials (satin, silk, etc.) for Linda and dull and unglossy materials for Clarisse.

Speaking of glossy materials, I have always thought that Carole Lombard's gown in *To Be or Not to Be*[3] was the most erotic woman's costume ever to have been seen in the cinema. It happened to be a long gown, which has nothing to do with what we're looking for, but I'm referring to the material's consistency, its texture.

As a general rule, one might also say that Clarisse will be dressed more like a young girl and Linda more like a woman, or else that Clarisse will wear pleated skirts and Linda preferably straight skirts or dresses.

What we want to avoid above all are costumes that are excessively bizarre, so we don't fall into the trap of facile freakishness, I'm thinking in particular of the magazine photos that currently show Ursula Andress in *What's New, Pussycat?*[4] and *The Tenth Victim.*[5]

We are completely in accord, then, on the idea that the visual principle of the film will be contemporary life with just a slight twist; what this will mean in practice is that there may be one strange detail in any given image but never two.

For the men, the same thing: contemporary life ever so slightly modified, mainly having to do with jacket lapels. Their outfits should make one think of clothing in Eastern European countries, with the jackets vaguely hinting at the tunics of Russian soldiers.

We should, however, avoid the danger of any too close resemblance or confusion between the civilian costumes and the firemen's uniforms.

Concerning the firemen, two points:

1. their uniforms;

2. the asbestos outfit resembling a diving-suit in which the one who burns the books is clothed. His colleagues stand around him and help him put on this kind of diving-suit in the way that a toreador is helped on with his

costume or an archbishop is enrobed. There should be the suggestion of a ritual.

Rereading the book, I came across a detail I had always missed, the idea of the number 451 being very visibly embroidered on the uniform of every fireman. It will help people familiarize themselves with the title and the meaning of the title.

That's it for now, my dear Tony, I'll send you another letter in a few days.

I leave tomorrow for a day's work with Oskar Werner, which will give me another opportunity to pore over the script, and you may depend upon receiving my next letter in six or seven days' time.

Everything in London is progressing satisfactorily and sometimes I even have the impression that the film is going to be made! I'm very pleased to be working with you and wish you all the best,

François Truffaut

1 – English costume designer.
2 – The two roles played by Julie Christie in *Fahrenheit 451*.
3 – By Ernst Lubitsch (1942).
4 – By Clive Donner.
5 – Elio Petri's *La Decima Vittima*.

To Helen Scott

[1965]
Wednesday afternoon

My dear Helen,

I'm happy to know that you're in better health and determined to lose some kilos; you know I don't care for scrawny women, but I know that slimming is good for one's health . . .

I haven't had any news from Lewis since his return to N.Y. and though I congratulate myself (and congratulate <u>him</u> and congratulate <u>you</u>) on the 3 thousand dollars, for me that doesn't mean the film will be made.

I'm worried about Hitchcock; we're definitely not, either of us, his favourite people at the moment. I think you ought to call Peggy and speak to her about my anxiety and my concern to know how things stand.

Naturally, it would be possible to postpone the linking interview in December until after the *Torn Curtain* shoot, but why is Hitch taking so long to give us his approval on the text?

Which reminds me, can you send me a copy of *Torn Curtain* since it's based on a novel? If you don't know the name of the author, I would think that Yougine Archer[1] or Androu Sarris[2] must know it.

If you receive twice over, from Jean-Luc, then from Eugène Lépicier, the perfume you requested, don't complain. Ever since the Drafield-Trenet incident,[3] I've decided to send you everything in duplicate; it'll be just your bad luck if I slap you one day!

I'm in a bit of a state today, I saw my very first mistress again, the first girl I ever lived with, in 1948, M—. She's no longer much to look at, just like me, and she's been in prison, 3 children, streetwalking and a bit of everything. She lives in Marseille. I'll go and see her in October to tape an interview with her on which I will base the scenario of *La Petite Voleuse*.

I'm working hard at the moment with Gruault on *L'Enfant sauvage* and with J.-L. Richard on *Un début dans la vie* (Jean-Pierre Léaud as a journalist).

So, if I also manage to finish *La Petite Voleuse*, I'll have 3 original screenplays behind me before starting on *Fahrenheit*. Which explains my current professional well-being.

Jean-Pierre Léaud has just walked into my office, so I'm going to interrupt this letter.

Time is running short. Lépicier is going to drop by to fetch this letter and also the reimbursement of your expenses = $100 lent to me and the 3 copies, etc. If that's not all right, let me know. Write to me as soon as possible and above all as soon as you have spoken to Peggy Robertson (even a telegram to Carosfilms to reassure me if it turns out that Hitch isn't angry after all and still likes us)!

lots of kisses,
françois

1 – Eugene Archer.
2 – Andrew Sarris, American film critic (notably, of *The Village Voice*) and exponent of the Auteur Theory.
3 – Drafield, an American distributor, had lost a Trenet record that Truffaut had entrusted to him for Helen Scott.

To Alfred Hitchcock

18 November 1965

Dear Mr Hitchcock,

Thank you very much for having found the time to reply to my letter while you were in the middle of a shoot.

Thank you also for having so scrupulously reread the manuscript of the book. Helen and I found all of your corrections to be extremely pertinent and we have transferred them on to the French version.

Given that what Helen and I did was merely a journalistic exercise and that it is in reality a book by Alfred Hitchcock, we see no reason not to admit that we adore the book, to the point where it pains us to have to part company with it. Our dream would be to get together with you every year to 'update' the manuscript, continue improving it and keep it for ourselves!

Perhaps you have already had occasion to deliver a film to the distributors with a certain regret . . .

At present, we are going to send everything we have done to the American and French publishers and work on the illustrations which are both very numerous and very directly related to the text.

I begin shooting *Fahrenheit 451* in London on 10 January and I think that Helen and I will be able to come and see you immediately after the shoot, which is to say, at the beginning of April.

I imagine you will be in the process of preparing your next film . . .

In London I met Bernard Herrmann who will be writing the score for *Fahrenheit 451*. We had a long talk together about you and I feel that, in him, you have a great and genuine friend.

Odette Ferry has just sent me this morning the French translation of *Torn Curtain*. I plan to read it this evening.

I will end this letter with three questions:

1. Do you think you will be able to see Helen and myself at the beginning of April so that we might conclude our interview on: a) *Marnie*, b) *Torn Curtain*, c) *R.R.R.R.* and d) your future projects?

2. Can you now let us know the nature of your appearance in *Torn Curtain*[1] (to complete the footnote on *Lifeboat*)?

3. What exactly was the role of Jack Warren in *Torn Curtain* (and *Spellbound*)?

Since the preparation of *Fahrenheit 451* was done at M.C.A., Helen and I took the opportunity of screening several of your TV films.

I greatly liked *The Jar*, *The Story of Diaz* and best of all *Four Hours* which you yourself directed.

In the hope that your new film will give you nothing but satisfaction, I remain yours very sincerely,

François Truffaut

1 – In *Torn Curtain* Hitchcock is to be seen holding a baby who has a little 'accident' on his trouser-leg.

1966

To Serge and Danièle Rezvani *from London, 4 January 66*

Dear Danièle, dear Serge,

No problem, then. Jean will have the key to my apartment, he'll give it to you and there we are. The exact address is 53, rue de Passy. Explain to your friends that they have to walk up to the first floor, then take the lift to the tenth. There, my name is at the side of the door. The telephone number is MIRabeau 57-93. There's very little food left (a few cans of sardines), it's there to be eaten and there's some champagne: a) under the telephone; b) under the kitchen sink; c) in the refrigerator. As far as everything else is concerned, doors, cupboards, crockery, I'll leave you to discover all of that for yourselves.

There's a woman, Yvonne, who during my absence has been coming in for an hour or two a week, but she won't come after 15 January, except if you want her to. If so, all you have to do is speak to (or with) Madeleine whom you'll always be able to reach at home, TRO. 00-75, since Yvonne is the family's cleaning woman.

I very much regret not being able to have you invite me over to dinner one evening during my stay; I would have loved to play the role of the crabby guest who never stops complaining; but Jean will do it very well.

To be honest with you, the apartment is not without its drawbacks; being divided into two parts, it's difficult to heat, especially in the corridor and bedrooms. On certain winter nights, one has the impression of sleeping on Wuthering Heights, you'll see.

I suggest you have separate bedrooms, since the place lends itself to such an arrangement and also, because of the disposition of the rooms, you could easily settle in for a month and a half without ever meeting each other . . .

Finally, there are your plays which I'm dying to read. The Easter holidays strike me as a suitable time for getting to know them. *Fahrenheit* will be finished, for better or worse, and I'll be completely relaxed.

I don't know if Jeanne or Jean has spoken to you about my wish to have you collaborate on the episode in *The Bride Wore Black* that concerns painting. One of the male characters is a painter. First we see an exhibition of his recent work, then Jeanne becomes his model as a kind of Diana-the-huntress and kills him with an arrow at the end of one of her sittings.

It's all rather eccentric, but interesting. Perhaps the idea of painting a few parodies and pastiches would amuse you or perhaps it would make you uncomfortable, I don't know . . . I've already spoken about it to Oscar Lewenstein and he liked the idea. We'd arrange it so that it could all be done at home and you wouldn't need to come to London, except if you wanted to.

I start shooting in a few days and, writing to you, I've momentarily forgotten my nervousness.

If I think of anything else you need to know about the apartment, I'll write to you again, but probably it could be done just as easily on the phone with Jean.

Thank you for your very funny letter, sorry about last Sunday, see you soon and lots of love,

françois

P.S. There are quite a few books in the apartment, so there's no point in bringing any from the Midi; I hope you'll read some old Audibertis and, if you're not familiar with it, Gide's *La Séquestrée de Poitiers*.

To Odette Ferry

Paris, 17 June 1966

My dear Friend,

Here is the latest news concerning the interviews with Hitchcock.

At Laffont the French text was quite carefully reread by Loys Masson and I am now in the process of rechecking the corrections he made, most of which were very sensible and have made the book somewhat simpler and less heavy.

Michael Korda, from the New York publishers Simon and Schuster, has written to tell me that Herman Citron, Hitchcock's agent, telephoned him to say that Mr Hitchcock was unhappy with the English text. After reading it, Hitchcock had sent me a little note, which I quote verbatim: 'I think you have done a wonderful job.' (That was six months ago.)

He did ask us to make a certain number of corrections which we immediately marked up on both versions (English and French).

It was not until two months later that Peggy Robertson, telephoning from Pinewood, mentioned to us that Hitchcock found the style insufficiently colloquial.

Given that I undertook the project out of admiration for him and with the aim of fostering a better appreciation of his work, it has always been my wish that the book be of service to Alfred Hitchcock and I would naturally like him to be absolutely satisfied with it.

The question of money has obviously never been a priority with this book, but I would be rather annoyed to have to write off all the money I have invested in it over the last four years, amounting to more than four million francs (the tapes, the transcription of the tapes, the typing-up of the successive drafts, the translations, the airline tickets, the stills collected from all over Europe, many of them frame enlargements, the filmography, etc.). I beg you not to discuss this aspect of the problem with Hitch, but I mention it here to show you what a blow it would be to me if the book were purely and simply to be cancelled, without forgetting the participation of Helen Scott which represents weeks of unpaid work.

I hope the situation is not that serious and that Hitchcock merely wants the style to be thoroughly revised, but, in that case, who will do it, when, how and will it still be possible to publish by Christmas, since it was because of the possibility of bringing the book out during the holiday period that I was able to persuade the publishers to agree to three hundred illustrations?

I believe Robert Laffont has already sent the first five chapters to the typesetters and obviously I will now have to restrain his eagerness and tell him to call the work to a halt, considering that I don't know the answer to the following question: are Hitchcock's reservations on the book concerned solely with the style of the dialogue, therefore with the American version, or are they meant to apply to the French version as well?

You will understand with what impatience I await your reply,

yours,
Truffaut

To Odette Ferry

Paris, 20 June 1966

My dear Friend,

I was infinitely relieved by your letter, which I received this morning, since for several days I was in an extremely pessimistic frame of mind, as you must have noticed from my last letter.

I am pleased that Hitchcock likes the dummy[1] and the introduction (I immediately marked up the corrections on the French version), and pleased above all that our final meeting has now been fixed.

So, around 25 July, immediately after I finish the sound-mixing, I will leave

'I start shooting *Fahrenheit 451 . . .*' (François Truffaut and Julie Christie.)

for New York with Helen Scott to complete the first half of chapter 15, the one dealing with *Marnie*, *Torn Curtain* and the new projects. So all is well.

Nevertheless, Michael Korda (from Simon and Schuster) is naturally very eager to obtain Mr Hitchcock's approval of the manuscript in writing. That is why there still remains the question of whether Hitch wishes to read or have one of his assistants read or reread and correct the definitive version, and I would be grateful if you would now put that question to him.

The second point concerns the title. In French, *Le Cinéma selon Alfred Hitchcock* strikes me as being clear, precise, since it does not suggest too strongly the idea of a book of reminiscences or memoirs (which Hitch wanted to avoid most of all), and yet rather more commercial than *Entretiens avec Alfred Hitchcock* would have been. What will now become of the expression *Le Cinéma selon Alfred Hitchcock* in English is a question to be thrashed out between Hitchcock and Michael Korda, and perhaps you will have your own suggestion to make?

There's a third point which seems a bit silly but to which Robert Laffont attaches great importance: the question of obtaining permission to reproduce stills from the films. Last year, when publishing an illustrated book on Gérard Philipe,[2] he found himself having to pay the producer Paul Graetz for the use of stills from *Le Diable au corps*[3] and *Monsieur Ripois*![4] Even though I have assured him that no American producer would have the nerve, he wants to be protected and I think we could easily obtain letters from Paramount, Warner Bros. and Universal giving us unconditional permission, but the situation naturally becomes more complicated with the old pre-war English films, the Selznick productions, etc.

Rober Laffont is determined to have the book out by 16 November and I'm delighted that he is being so dynamic. I don't know whether things will go as quickly at Simon and Schuster, but I tend to think they will become more enterprising as soon as they have Hitchcock's go-ahead.

Within the next forty-eight hours we'll be sending the English manuscript, complete with Hitchcock's corrections, to Michael Korda, and I am going to ask him to have a second copy made at once for Hitch so that the contact between Simon and Schuster and Herman Citron, Hitchcock's agent, can proceed without interruption.

I am pleased by what you tell me of the film and am also very impatient to see it.

Thank you again for your very kind letter of this morning,

best wishes,

Truffaut

P.S. I will be in London from Sunday the 26th to the morning of Wednesday the 29th and will call you at home on 4 July as agreed.

1 – A publishing term for the mock-up of a book's layout.
2 – French actor (1922–59): *L'Idiot*, *La Chartreuse de Parme*, *Une si jolie petite plage*, *La Beauté du Diable*, *La Ronde*, *Fanfan la Tulipe*, *Les Grandes Manœuvres*, *Montparnasse 19*, etc.
3 – By Claude Autant-Lara (1947).
4 – By René Clément (1954).

To Don Congdon *Paris, 28 July 1966*

Dear Don,

I received your letter of 8 July but am still waiting for your answer to one precise question: since the Simon and Schuster edition is three to five months behind the French one, how will you proceed on the matter of selling extracts to American magazines and, most important, when will they publish them?

Last Tuesday Hitchcock granted us the final interview that we required and we covered *Marnie* and *Torn Curtain*. At this very moment in London a Frenchwoman and an Englishwoman are working on the transcription of the last tape.

The book will therefore be absolutely finished by the end of August and ready to come out in France by the end of November.

Hitchcock told us that he was willing to sign the letter of agreement and we telegraphed Michael Korda to draw up this letter himself which Hitchcock will sign as soon as he receives it. As far as that's concerned, then, all is well.

Concerning *Fahrenheit 451*, Universal, whose first European film it is, wants to launch it with a lot of publicity in Paris. I asked, and Universal agreed, for Bradbury to be invited at their expense, but, as you know, the problem with him is flying. Could it not be possible for him to come to Europe by boat and couldn't you persuade him of the importance of the trip?

Here is how we see things. He could come to Venice for the evening of 7 September and remain at the festival until the 9th, which is to say, the day on which the prize-winners are announced; then he could go to Milan where his Italian publisher would organize something with the press and with Universal's help; then he would come to Paris where, on 15 or 16 September, the film will be premièred at the Théâtre Marigny with Julie Christie, followed by a reception, dinner, etc.

Leading up to that day a series of interviews might be organized both by Universal and the publisher Denoël; and finally Ray could return – by boat again – or, if he wished, travel via London where Universal would again organize something with the press and publishers.

Let me add further that I've asked for the novel, from now on, to be automatically sent to all the French and Italian film critics. It will also be distributed to the eight hundred guests attending the Paris première at the Marigny.

As you can see, I'm endeavouring to make sure that all the publicity surrounding the film be centred on the novel and on having it read by as many people as possible. This is in my own interest, since, as the film is very strange, its strangeness will be easier to accept once one has consulted the book, but obviously it's also very much in the interest of the book itself, one I have so long admired.

So it's up to you to see whether you can persuade Ray and naturally whether his own schedule will permit such a trip, which will mean his being away from Los Angeles for about four weeks. He should have received the official invitation from Universal sometime in the last few days, but perhaps he won't have replied to it immediately.

As regards the piece which you requested me to write for the new Simon and Schuster edition of *Fahrenheit 451* (what a small world it is!), I think that in about ten days' time I'll be able to give you between 12 and 15 typed pages consisting of the English translation of a few extracts from a shooting diary I wrote from day to day for *Cahiers du cinéma*. If this piece is too long, it will be very easy to cut by retaining only what you consider to be interesting. Naturally, the passages I've chosen are those in which I speak of Bradbury or the book or anything that relates to the shooting of scenes which appear in both book and film. I should think I'll be able to send you all of it around 12 August. Will that be enough?

I'd be very pleased to accept the fee of 100 dollars that you mention, since it would enable me to split the money between the two people who have been translating the diary into English.

I hope to hear from you soon on all these matters and send you my very warmest regards.

F. Truffaut

Oskar Werner, from Henri-Pierre Roché to Ray Bradbury . . .

To John Huntley[1]

Paris, 14 September 1966

Dear Mr Huntley,

I have in front of me your letter of 1 September in which you ask me to let you have a copy of the tape recording whose text will appear in bookshops under the title of *The Cinema According to Alfred Hitchcock*.

In fact, this recording comprises forty hours of magnetic tapes which are very difficult to listen to, since the simultanous translation overlaps Mr Hitchcock's voice and my own. There exist two copies of the recording, one of which is in Mr Alfred Hitchcock's possession and the other in the possession of Mrs Helen Scott in New York.

Nevertheless, I would be prepared to send you the material now that everything has been transcribed, but I cannot let you have it just yet, as I intend to impose a prior condition. Here it is: the British Film Institute holds the sole surviving prints of three of Alfred Hitchcock's earliest films, *The Mountain Eagle* (1926), *Downhill* (1927) and *Easy Virtue* (1927). These three films are in such poor condition that they cannot be put through a projector and yet historians are permitted to view them on a moviola at the risk of irreparable damage to the perforations.

Here is my proposition: I will deposit with you, with Mr Hitchcock's permission, the forty hours of recorded interviews when you are able to assure me that the British Film Institute has made dupes of the three above-mentioned films in order to safeguard a 'unique material which would be of enormous interest to film historians'.[2]

Yours sincerely,
François Truffaut

1 – John Huntley worked at the British Film Institute.

2 – In English in the original letter: the phrase quoted is from Huntley's own letter.

To Alfred Hitchcock

Paris, 19 October 1966

Dear Mr Hitchcock,

Our book, *Le Cinéma selon Alfred Hitchcock*, is to be published on or about 20 November in Paris, which is to say, more or less concurrently with the release of *Torn Curtain*. The publisher, Robert Laffont, thought of organizing a launch party, but I cannot see that such a gathering would have much sense given that you will not be present.

I proposed another idea which I submit for your approval.

Instead of sending journalists review copies, we would invite them to collect these copies during an organized homage to you held one afternoon at the Cinémathèque of the Palais de Chaillot.

There would still be the obligatory drinks party, but it would be preceded by an hour-long screening of extracts from several of your films which I myself would very carefully edit together, with your permission.

To simplify the problems of authorization from the various distribution companies, we would content ourselves with one British film, *The Thirty-Nine Steps*, using the Cinémathèque Française's own print (the scene of Madeleine Carroll and Robert Donat handcuffed together).

Then there would be three of the Paramount films:

a) *Rear Window* (the ending of the film from the moment James Stewart telephones Raymond Burr to force him to leave his apartment).

b) *The Man Who Knew Too Much* (the scene of the concert at the Albert Hall beginning with Doris Day entering the foyer).

c) *Psycho* (the shower murder, Anthony Perkins mopping up the bathroom and the car sinking into the swamp).

Then two Universal films:

a) *The Birds* (from Melanie Daniels's arrival at the schoolhouse to the end of the scene).

b) *Marnie* (the psychoanalytical session at night).

In this way, we would only be dealing with Paramount and Universal and I think these 60 minutes would make quite an impact.

Naturally, if I briefly touched on the idea when talking to our friend Ascarelli, I have made no official request to either Universal or Paramount, since I wished to have your reaction first; the screening will of course be exclusively reserved for film critics.

If you should happen to like the idea, the second question I wanted to ask you concerns *Torn Curtain*. Do you think we ought to end the screening with an extract from *Torn Curtain* or not?

For practical reasons, it would be impossible to organize the screening before the book's actual publication and, because of that, I cannot yet know whether *Torn Curtain* will have opened in Paris the week before or be due to open a week later.

On all matters concerning the launch of the book, Robert Laffont will be getting in touch with the publicity department at Universal and I am sure that, together, they will come up with a number of excellent ideas. The book will be sold, for example, at the box-offices of the first-run cinemas in Paris showing *Torn Curtain* and also *Fahrenheit 451*.

I am very impatient to know what your answer will be, and impatient, too, to hear you announce your 51st film. My very best wishes to Mrs Hitchcock and yourself,

Yours very sincerely,
François Truffaut

To Robert Hakim[1]

Paris, 16 November 1966

My dear Robert,

I went as planned to see Jean-Paul Belmondo this morning, and we had a long talk about *La Sirène du Mississipi* [*Mississippi Mermaid*].

He greatly liked the novel, the characters and the plot.

The only reservation he indicated to me concerned the character's age, which is indeed more advanced in the book. I believe I set his mind at rest on this point by explaining to him how I saw things, and he then expressed his wish to make the film with me. I told him how important it was for me that we begin shooting in January or in any event before 15 February, and that seemed to suit him.

Having mentioned several details from the book, I was left in no doubt that Jean-Paul Belmondo had read it very attentively. I told him that the adaptation would follow the book quite closely and he showed no desire to delay his acceptance until he had read the script, which would in any case be physically impossible since we will have to begin pre-production in two weeks and I plan to write most of the dialogue during the shoot, as I have almost always done in my French films.

I have long wished to make a film with Jean-Paul and I believe this desire to be mutual; which is why I am convinced that everything will go smoothly if you and he can come to an agreement on financial matters.

I will ring you tomorrow to find out how everything went,

Yours sincerely,
F. Truffaut

1 – French producer, born in 1907. Though he and his brother Raymond were initially to produce *La Sirène du Mississipi*, it was finally made by United Artists and Les Films du Carrosse.

To Bernard Gheur *Paris, 9 December 1966*

Dear Monsieur,

The first part of your novel arrived safely and I took the liberty of noting in pencil the words and expressions that I found jarring as I read through it. In effect, the thing is to maintain a style that isn't yet completely natural to you and to write gracefully within the framework you have adopted, and that's not so easy. I apologize for playing the professor.*

I am unable to grant you the interview you request as I have just started a screenplay which has to be delivered by mid-February and I can't accept any appointments between now and then.

I will always be pleased to hear from you,

cordially yours,
François Truffaut

*But I do seriously urge you to continue, possibly by aiming for greater simplicity wherever there would seem to be no overriding call for preciosity.

1967

To the Centre National de la Cinématographie

Paris, 30 January 1967

Dear Mademoiselle,

I have received the documents which you sent me concerning various honorary titles, but I have not filled in the questionnaires, as, to be honest, the prospect of being honoured in this way makes me rather uneasy.

I have no hesitation in accepting the awards which are bestowed on my films, but it's quite a different matter when it's a question of my role as a citizen, one which I have never been able to assume, as my name is not even on an electoral list. You will therefore understand that, lacking as I do all sense of civic responsibility, it would be hypocritical of me to seek some national honour.

I am naturally flattered that the directors of the Centre National de la Cinématographie thought of me in this context and, with regret, I remain

Yours respectfully,
François Truffaut

To Charles Bitsch

Wednesday [1967]

My dear Carolus,

It was impossible for me to read through your script again.

I think you ought to do a little revision yourself, trim some of the provisional dialogue, clear up 3 or 4 problems likely to worry the Commission (the business with the cave at the end, for one) and indicate in a prefatory note that the dialogue will be worked out later during rehearsals with the actors, before you begin shooting. In short, the thing is to demonstrate an aesthetic criterion with a view to greater verisimilitude, etc.

I'll go on working with you sometime in April. Keep it up and good luck,

yours,
françois

To Jacques Ledoux[1]

Paris, 6 February 1967

My dear Ledoux,

I received your press releases, prospectuses, questionnaires, etc. concerning the experimental festival, but, as I didn't feel they concerned me, I have to confess that they went straight into the waste-paper basket.

Now I'm consumed by remorse, the more so as I've just seen a 16 mm film lasting thirty minutes directed by Djurka, a Hungarian sculptor who has lived in France for about ten years and is married to Bernadette Lafont. It's a magnificent film relating in a very simple style a narrative that's easy to follow, inspired by the story of the parish priest of Uruffe: the young priest who gets his servant pregnant, stabs her at eight months, delivers the child himself, stabs it as well and grants absolution to his two victims. In fact the film mostly describes the events leading up to the fatal day and, though very personal, is shot in a direct, neutral style recalling both Dreyer and Buñuel. It is, in short, an ideal film for your festival. How should I go about having it sent to you?

I await your reply with impatience and hope you'll take the opportunity to let me know how things are with you. Did you receive the Hitchcock book I sent you? Have you met Skolimowski[2] and Jean-Pierre Léaud who are in your part of the world?

Hoping to see you very soon,

François Truffaut

1 – The late Jacques Ledoux was curator of the Cinémathèque Royale de Belgique and the organizer of the Festival of Experimental Film at Knokke-le Zoute.

2 – Jerzy Skolimowski, Polish director, born in 1938: *Walkover*, *Deep End*, *King, Queen, Knave*, *Moonlighting*, etc. He was filming *Le Départ* in Brussels with Léaud.

To Théodore Louis[1]

Paris, 7 April 1967

Dear Monsieur,

I read your script, *Le Secret de Peaussenac*, and, its title having made me fear some rather old-fashioned mystery, in the style of the thrillers which used to be published by 'Le Masque', I was surprised to discover quite the finest script I have ever read in the 8 years I have been receiving them, certainly the best from outside the industry, which is to say, not written by a director.

The idea is a remarkable one, remarkably handled and developed, and the whole thing is extremely powerful.

The technical indications, in the left-hand margin, are exactly what they should be and nothing remains but to shoot the film.

Perhaps the only reservation I would make concerns the fact that there is too much dialogue, which means that there will be too much material to film, and I would suspect the script is considerably longer than the running time of an average feature (90 minutes); yours must come to somewhere between 110 and 140 minutes.

I come now to practical matters. In view of the quality of your script, you would need a major director. Major directors, as a rule, find their subject-matter themselves, or else adapt it themselves, or have the work executed under their supervision; but they rarely use something that is already complete and was sent to them unsolicited.

On the other hand, a merely average director would probably not succeed in making his producers accept such a subject, and, even if he did, the result would probably be very inferior to the quality of the original material. That is why I find it difficult to be optimistic about your script.

There is always the other possibility which would consist in offering it to those actors capable of playing the part of Monsieur Peaussenac; there too, however, we come up against a problem, since 55-year-old French actors tend not to be stars and are therefore unable to impose a screenplay of their own choosing – except for Jean Gabin,[2] who would simply not understand the story.

In Belgium, there might also be the possibility of having the script read by André Delvaux,[3] who directed *L'Homme au crâne rasé* and would seem to me very capable of making a success of it, with the same leading actor. How would you feel about that idea?

As far as France is concerned, I am still at a loss; yesterday I gave the script to my agent, Gérard Lebovici, in whom I have complete confidence, and when he has read it we will have a talk together and explore the different possibilities.

I cannot make you any promises given all the difficulties I have indicated, but I will nevertheless do my utmost to have the story read by anyone who might be able to do something with it.

I trust you have other copies of the manuscript.

I suggest we write to each other each time a new development arises.

Thanking you very much for having given me the opportunity of reading such a fine story, I remain

Yours very cordially,
François Truffaut

1 – Louis was for thirty years the film critic of *La Libre Belgique*. In *Domicile conjugal* (*Bed and Board*) Truffaut had Daniel Ceccaldi 'quote' a line of dialogue from the script of *Le Secret de Peaussenac*.
2 – French actor (1904–76): *La Bandéra*, *La Belle Équipe*, *Les Bas Fonds*, *Pépé le Moko*, *La Grande Illusion*, *Quai des brumes*, *La Bête humaine*, *Le Jour se lève*, *French Cancan*, etc.
3 – Belgian director, born in 1926: *Un soir, un train*, *Rendezvous à Bray*, *Belle*, *Benvenuta*, *L'Œuvre au noir*, etc.

To Georges Cravenne[1]

Paris, 18 August 1967

My dear Georges,

I very much appreciated Yvette Camp's[2] presence on *La Mariée*. She was, at one and the same time, efficient and discreet, exacting and patient, sweet and sympathetic and liked by the entire crew, a good choice therefore. As you know, I attach a great deal of importance to the idea of keeping the murder plot of the film a secret so that the public won't feel bludgeoned by the publicity slogan: 'Jeanne Moreau kills five men', and holding that whole aspect of the film in reserve as a surprise for when it opens.

There has been a single lapse, a single blot on the copy-book, but a big one: a complete synopsis of the screenplay in *Ciné-Revue*, obviously concocted from a shooting script that was handed over to Monsieur Fougères, but by whom? There's the mystery! I don't take it too seriously because:

1. We've finished shooting.
2. We're now in August and few journalists read *Ciné-Revue*.
3. The summary is so badly done that one has no desire to read it carefully.

All the same, I find it hard to swallow.

'Since the death sentence does not exist in schools, Dargelos was expelled' (Jean Cocteau).[3] I don't want to have anyone expelled, but I would like to know the name of the person who, either at 'Georges Cravenne Ltd' or at United Artists, disobeyed the order of silence so that in future I might, quite simply, be on my guard against him or her.

The second point of my letter concerns the film's publicity brochure for which you were responsible. I invite you to take a look at it and tell me if you aren't first of all offended by its ugliness! Now let's open it together: the paper is of poor quality, the text badly laid out, the typeface banal and old-fashioned, the printer's ink faded and the typing erratic.

There are literals everywhere, typing errors clumsily corrected (instead of the page being retyped). I recommend that you cast your eye over the second-last page, the one dealing with Raoul Coutard.

Now close the brochure again, run your finger along the spine of the cover and . . . ouch . . . ouch . . . go fetch a Band-aid if, like the rest of us, you have just fallen victim to that lethal stitching.

I therefore ask that you no longer distribute this brochure – particularly as it's now 'out of date', the film being more or less finished – and that you and I completely rethink the publicity material.

And there you have it. If I take the liberty, my dear Georges, of making these comments to you, it's because we will be working together, I hope, right up to the – tricky – moment when the film opens and mainly because I know how scrupulous you yourself are and how insistent on work being well done.

I'd very much like to get together with you as soon as possible and draw up our new battle plan, since releasing a film is equivalent to joining battle; until then, I remain cordially yours.

François Truffaut

1 – French journalist then publicist, born in 1914. It was he who conceived the notion of the 'Césars', the French Oscars.

2 – A press agent.

3 – From *Les Enfants terribles.*

To Roger Régent[1] *23 August 1967*

Dear Monsieur,

As I meant to tell you the other evening, I have just read an early book of yours, *Cinéma de France*, with enormous pleasure. I relived my youth, my discovery of the cinema, in chronological order. I had the impression of seeing again *L'Assassinat du Père Noël,*[2] *La Duchesse de Langeais,*[3] *Madame et le Mort,*[4] *Le Baron fantôme,*[5] *Douce,*[6] but I also discovered from your descriptions that I had seen films whose very titles I had forgotten: *Pension Jonas,*[7] *Cartacalha,*[8] *Madame Clapain,*[9] *La Ferme aux loups*[10] . . . In short, a nostalgic and uplifting read; I took lots of notes as I went through it. If you do not mention *Paradis perdu,*[11] *Le Grand Élan*[12] and *Mademoiselle ma mère,*[13] 3 films I remember, it's probably because they were made before 1940 . . .

As a book, *Cinéma de France* is simple, precise and extremely well done. It's a pity you have not extended it further, for example from 1946 to 1959. In fact, what I am most in need of is a history of the French cinema from 1930 to 40, as there exist very few works on that period. I am convinced that this kind of narration, more chronological than critical, is the best format: if I were a publisher, I would reprint *Cinéma de France* with more stills, notes and documents. There . . .

Last year I sent you an unpleasant letter concerning the Cinéma des Champs-Élysées, this one makes up for that one, besides which I'm going there this evening to see that wonderful film *North by Northwest*!

Yours sincerely,
François Truffaut

1 – French journalist and writer (1904–89).
2 – By Christian-Jaque (1940).
3 – By Jacques de Baroncelli (1941).
4 – By Louis Daquin (1943).
5 – By Serge de Poligny (1942).
6 – By Claude Autant-Lara (1943).
7 – By Pierre Caron (1941).
8 – *Cartacalha, reine des Gitans*, by Léon Mathot (1942).
9 – *Le Secret de Madame Clapain*, by André Berthomieu (1943).
10 – By Richard Poitier (1943).
11 – *Le Paradis perdu*, by Abel Gance (1940).
12 – By Christian-Jaque.
13 – By Henri Decoin (1937).

To Alfred Hitchcock[1]

Paris, August 31, 1967

Dear Mr Hitchcock,

Before answering your letter, I wanted to finish the shooting of *The Bride Wore Black*. The picture is now in the cutting room and will be turned over to United Artists, completed, on November 15th.

Since I was working in the French language and especially since there was no Oskar Werner to contend with, the shooting was much more pleasant and harmonious than that of *Fahrenheit 451*.

The production set-up was efficient and the actors so cooperative that we were able to wind up the shooting eight days ahead of schedule, thereby cutting the eight hundred thousand dollar budget down by one hundred thousand. Though this saving is not, in itself, tantamount to success, the United Artists people are obviously rather pleased.

I can tell you that Jeanne Moreau's willing attitude, quick wit, consistent good mood and her whole-hearted solidarity with the picture make her an ideal actress to work with. Since she hates to see herself on the screen and trusts the director completely, she never even bothers to look at the rushes. On the set, she's willing to give a fast or slow performance, to be funny or sad, serious or zany, to do whatever the director asks of her. And in case of disaster, she stands by the Captain of the ship: with no fuss, no bother and no singing of 'Nearer, My God, To Thee . . .' she will simply go down by his side.

'. . . an ideal actress to work with'. (Filming *La Mariée était en noir*.)

I agree, of course, that the two Richardson pictures you mention[2] were not exactly helpful to her reputation, but hope that the picture she made with Peter O'Toole, *Catherine the Great*,[3] and *The Bride Wore Black* will serve to wipe away whatever damage there was.

The danger for her in *The Bride* is that the role she plays is simply too wonderful; the character, a woman who dominates men and then kills them, is too 'prestigious'. To counter-act this, I asked Jeanne, as in *Jules and Jim*, to play the role with simplicity and a familiar manner that would make her unexpected actions plausible and human. As I see it, Julie Killen[4] is a virgin, since her husband was killed at the church on her wedding day. But this information is not spelled out in the picture and will have to remain a secret between Jeanne Moreau, you and me!

The five men who played with her turned in excellent performances and if anything is wrong with the picture, it must be attributed to an error in the construction of the script.

Your comments in respect to the episode with Morane, the father of the little boy, were invaluable and I did my best to make him more plausible. It's too early to tell whether I was entirely successful and this may turn out to be one of the weaknesses in the story.

My next two pictures are:

1) *Stolen Kisses*, a small-budget film about the first loves of a young man in Paris, starring Jean-Pierre Léaud, the young actor for *Four Hundred Blows*.

2) *The Wild Child*, a picture I mentioned to you, the story of a deaf-mute child who was discovered at the age of eleven, living an animal-like life in the woods.

If things work out according to plan, both pictures will be made in 1968.

I called Odette Ferry today and learned that you had delayed your film because of problems with the script. Have you found a script-writer? As you know, I am very eager to know more about this new film of yours. Judging by your brief description in one of your recent letters to me, it should be a tremendously exciting picture.

The Paradine Case and *Rebecca*[5] which are now being re-released by the Siritzky brothers throughout France are both doing very solid business everywhere.

I am impatient for the American publication of *Cinema According to Alfred Hitchcock*; you will remember that my initial aim in undertaking [it] was not to make the best-seller list, but to influence and shake up the smug attitudes of the New York critics. It is geared towards the specialists and the growing audience of film buffs and undoubtedly closer to the books by Igor Stravinsky or the *Journal* of Paul Klee than to the memoirs of Svetlana Stalin. Despite this note of warning, it's reassuring that Robert Laffont seems very pleased by sales in France and Canada.

Dear Mr Hitchcock, in the hope that I shall soon be hearing good news of your 51st,[6] I ask you to convey my very best regards to Mrs Hitchcock and remain

Most faithfully yours,
François Truffaut

1 – Save for its final paragraph, this letter was written in English.
2 – Tony Richardson's *Mademoiselle* (1966) and *The Sailor from Gibraltar* (1967).
3 – Or, in America, *Great Catherine* (Gordon Flemying, 1968).
4 – In reality, the character's name is Julie Kohler.
5 – Two early Hitchcock films, made in 1948 and 1940 respectively.
6 – Fifty-first film.

To Gilles Jacob[1]

Paris, 17 October 1967

My dear Gilles,

Thank you very much for the copy of *Sight and Sound* and I am extremely proud to find myself speaking English so well.[2]

What worries me nevertheless is our (for me) unexpected appearance in *Cinéma-Billard*,[3] since one expresses oneself differently depending on whether one is speaking to foreigners or to one's own compatriots. I therefore ask you to see if there's still time for me to correct the text, particularly the paragraph concerning Godard (where you recycled an article I had written for *Les Lettres françaises*, one that specialists know too well for it to turn up again in an interview), and also for the paragraph on Lelouch's activities, which might lead to confusion. If it's too late, it can't be helped,

and, in any event, very best wishes from

françois

1 – Jacob, born in 1930, met Truffaut for the first time in 1949, when he asked him for an article on Renoir for the magazine *Raccords* which he had just founded. A film journalist from 1963 to 1975, he is now the director-general of the Cannes Film Festival and one of the editors of this book.
2 – A translation of a Truffaut–Jacob interview had just been published in the English film journal.
3 – Truffaut is referring to the French film journal *Cinéma 67*, whose editor was Pierre Billard.

To a student of IDHEC[1]

Paris, 3 November 1967

Dear Monsieur,

I have received your project. It is absolutely impossible for me to be your supervisor, since, having had no secondary education, I received no university training and do not even possess the vocabulary that would enable me to read the books to which you will be obliged to refer.

I have a very poor knowledge of Albert Camus's work. I have read one play, *Les Justes*, which I thought execrable, and, two years ago, *L'Etranger*, of which I was offered the chance to make a film. As a novel, it seemed to me inferior to any one of the two hundred written by Simenon. None of that is of the slightest importance, it means only that, even if Camus has not helped me in my work, he is helping you in yours and, by virtue of your authoritative knowledge of his career, you will be able to write a good thesis. You understand now why that thesis will have to be supervised by someone other than myself, why not Bernard Pingaud?

Since, in the letter he sent me, the director-general, Rémy Tessonneau, expressed a certain scepticism with regard to your project, I prefer not to answer him personally, having no wish to add grist to his mill. I therefore ask you to explain my refusal to him.

I am sorry if I have disappointed you and remain notwithstanding

Yours sincerely,
François Truffaut

1 – Institut des Hautes Études Cinématographiques, the celebrated French film school founded by Marcel L'Herbier in 1943. Its most successful graduate has been Louis Malle.

To Pierre Lherminier

Paris, 27 November 1967

Dear Friend,

I haven't seen Yvonne Baby[1] since Sadoul's death and I don't know her present state of mind concerning the book, but I'm going to send her a copy of your letter.

I did receive the *Renoir* by Pierre Leprohon,[2] but I didn't much care for it. Jean Renoir made 35 films, Leprohon likes only 13 of them. Without going into detail, this would seem to indicate that he was perhaps not the man for the job, as after all I'm not alone in thinking that Renoir is the greatest film director in the world. Decidedly, Renoir has been unlucky with the books written about him: this one coming on top of the libellous issue of *Premier Plan*[3] and the ridiculous monograph by Cauliez! I'm quite aware that Leprohon himself is a sincere and scrupulous man, but his lack of humour means that he is out of sympathy with a third of Renoir's work.

I can't help wondering if the only means of doing justice to Renoir, aside from the book it seems he himself is preparing, would be to publish a *Jean Renoir* by André Bazin and his friends which would consist of all Bazin's articles as well as those of Rivette, Rohmer, Doniol-Valcroze and myself, but that's an old project and I believe you considered it with Janine Bazin . . . As far as Bergman is concerned, it's hard for me to say more: all I know is that he himself is coming to France in May (the Cannes Festival, press conferences, etc.), as he places enormous importance on the launch of his new film.[4]

Cordially yours,
François Truffaut

1 – Baby, a French journalist and novelist, was Georges Sadoul's daughter-in-law.
2 – French film historian, born in 1903.
3 – French film journal.
4 – *Hour of the Wolf.*

1968

To Jean-François Hauduroy[1]

15 January 68

My dear Hauduroy,

Excuse me for not having returned your call the other day. I am absolutely swamped by work . . . In less than 3 weeks I have to start shooting my film[2] . . . I don't have the definitive script, or the actors, or the locations.

In actual fact, I practically never dine out because of plays to see, films and evenings in front of the TV set and especially because I prefer to talk to only one or two people at a time. Here I am having to own up to my little quirks! I'd like to have lunch with you at the beginning of April, as soon as I've finished shooting, if you have no objection,

kindest regards,
Truffaut

1 – Assistant director, then director.

2 – *Baisers volés*.

To Gilles Jacob

Monday 15 January 68

My dear Gilles,

I very much enjoyed lunching with you and your wife; in retrospect, I had the impression that I outstayed my welcome, but it was most agreeable. Thank you for *Premier Plan*, which is invaluable despite its second-hand articles . . .

Benjamin[1] is breaking all records, so there is no chance of bringing *La Mariée* out before the end of March or beginning of April. By then I'll have finished *Baisers volés* which I start on 5 February and you'll have seen *La Mariée* at a private screening. I therefore suggest 1. that you wait until I give you a ring for the screening of *La Mariée*, 2. that we have dinner together one evening after the shoot, 3. that we do the interview then. O.K.?

yours,
françois

1 – Michel Deville's *Benjamin, ou les mémoires d'un puceau.*

To an agent

Paris, 1 February 1968

Dear Monsieur,

It touches me greatly to learn that Mademoiselle X would be pleased to have a role in my next film, the more so as your letter specifies that she is very 'commercial'. If I may judge from your letter, from the way it was typed and laid out, and the condition in which it arrived, complete with documents, I should say that Mademoiselle X might best be offered the role of an illiterate slut. You will understand perfectly by taking a good look at the package which you addressed to me and which I am sending back by return of post so that you will be able to appreciate its tact and refinement.

I remain, dear Monsieur, most cordially yours,

François Truffaut

To Luc Moullet

[1968 or 1969]

My dear Moullet,

You've put me on the spot with your request: 1. I didn't want to read any more screenplays, 2. I never get involved in the affairs of my actor friends.

Your screenplay is good but, in my opinion, unrealizable with the means at your disposal. If the continuity outline and budget had been properly drawn up – as well as a work schedule – you'd realize that it would take between 100 and 120 working days to shoot all the material. It's not only a film of intention but also a film of execution, so why begin by trying to be Etaix?[1] Would you make *The General*[2] with the miniature railway of the Bois de Boulogne zoo? Particularly as you're much better at filming interiors (*B et B*[3] – the steak – the ending of *Les Contrabandières*) than natural locations. That's my advice . . . As for Jeanne Moreau, it's completely out of the question, but I'd prefer you to find out for yourself, via Jean-Louis Livi, since, if I were to speak to her about it, it would be like Marcorelles telling Janine Bazin: 'You remind me of Jean-Paul Sartre . . . physically, I mean' (authentic, or rather historical, as Abel Gance used to say).

yours,
truffaut

1 – Pierre Etaix, French actor and director, born in 1928: *Le Soupirant*, *Yoyo*, *Tant qu'on a la santé*, *Le Grand Amour*, etc.

2 – By Buster Keaton and Clyde Bruckman (1927).

3 – *Brigitte et Brigitte*.

To Alfred Hitchcock

Paris, 19 February 1968

Dear Mr Hitchcock,

I really am very sorry not to have written to you sooner about *Frenzy*, but I was determined to give you a detailed account of my impressions of the script, scene by scene; unfortunately, we started shooting my latest film, *Stolen Kisses*, rather earlier than expected.

Then there was the whole business of the Cinémathèque Française,[1] about which I am sure Odette Ferry has told you and which has taken up most of my time when I am not shooting.

Here then is my report on *Frenzy*, and I must ask you to forgive me if, at times, I sound like someone who has made 50 films preaching to a young underground film-maker!

You know how much I respect, admire and esteem you; you know, also, how intimately familiar I am with your films, but I consider that, as a script represents simply one stage of the completed work, one should be able to criticize it sincerely and frankly, even if none of my criticisms strikes you as justified.

Frenzy certainly contains the germ of a great film, a film of the stamp of *Shadow of a Doubt*, *Strangers on a Train* and *Psycho*, which is why I am in no doubt whatsoever as to the final result.

Report on the script

1. I very much like the beginning of the film on the New Jersey Flats as well as the presentation of the President and his family.

2. The presentation of Willie is excellent. Many people will probably tell you that he reminds them of Perkins[2] in *Psycho*, but I think he could just as easily be a relation of Bruno[3] in *Strangers on a Train* or Uncle Charlie.[4]

3. The scene in New York's Shea Stadium also seems to me perfect.

4. The following scene with Willie Cooper and his mother does not seem quite satisfactory at this stage of the script, but it would be hard for me to explain why. Perhaps it will work better when it has been given some dialogue.

5. The scene with Willie and Caroline in front of the United Nations

Henri Langlois visiting the shoot of *Baisers volés* (1968).

building sounds extremely promising and I know it will work very well, as always when you depict a high-minded criminal explaining his ideals.

6. The other scene which complements the one in the graveyard strikes me as equally promising.

7. Then there comes the murder in Central Park and there we know we'll have a brilliant scene with the *Hitch touch*[5] working a hundred per cent.

8. Now, I can't help wondering whether Willie's relationship with his mother is quite right, since we so quickly have the impression she suspects her son that I am afraid it subsequently becomes very hard for us to believe in the idea that she might wish to help the police in their inquiries – even in the hope of proving her son's innocence. This is the only important reservation I would make about the script, but I must say that it has persisted through several detailed readings. Given the business about the roses whose thorns have been removed by the florist, the injury on the hand and the newspaper article, the public will be left in no doubt whatsoever about what Miriam really believes.

9. I think the scene of the rehearsal in the theatre will be first-rate.

10. The episode in the artists' studio also strikes me as first-rate except for the single point that Patti falls for Willie a little too easily and too arbitrarily; naturally, the notion of her obsession with him can be established by the acting and the dialogue.

11. The next scene, in which Patti takes Willie home and we unexpectedly discover that she has a boyfriend there, seems to me very good.

12. I also like the scene at Miriam's with all the people from the theatre.

13. Patti's murder on the boat strikes me as excellent. Of course, there does rather seem to be an insistence on sex and nudity, but it does not worry me too much because I know that you shoot such scenes with real dramatic power, and you never dwell on unnecessary detail.

14. The following scene with Willie and Miriam is perfect.

I begin to wonder if, from this point on, the script is perhaps just slightly too predictable.

15. For instance, I think the audience will expect to find the police at the studio and I wonder if it might not be an idea to show Willie also expecting to find the police and being a little hesitant about going there. You might show the contradictions in his behaviour. I do see that you have adopted another solution, with the imaginary voice-over in the stairwell, but I am not sure that I completely understood what you were trying to do.

16. The next scene between Willie and Miriam bothers me a little because

it is simply too explicit. The spectator might feel the action has ground to a halt. Also, it reinforces Miriam's suspicions even further, which might pose a problem later.

17. The scene with Miriam at Willie's father's house does not seem to me to be right yet. It seems to be there for the sole purpose of conveying information to the audience and what makes it disappointing is the passive attitude adopted by Willie's father. I can't quite see the point of the scene anyway; it has neither a beginning, a middle nor an end and I do think that, if we are to see the President at this juncture, we will expect to see him again for a third time.

18. Similarly, I am not sure about the scene between Miriam and Lieutenant Hinckel. It raises a question which we discussed in the book (Simon and Schuster, pages 76 and 77) about showing a collusion (or even a love affair) between a character from the police and a character who is intimate with the murderer. I am afraid the audience will find this scene very hard to take.

a) because Miriam's doubts as to her son's guilt are not, at this stage, believable;

b) it is not plausible that she should agree to help the police, even if it is a matter of preventing further murders. I do know, of course, that all scripts contain scenes which are not really comprehensible until the dialogue is written, or even until they are shot, edited and inserted into the film, but I have difficulty imagining how this scene might work. I know that there have been other, similar scenes in your work (and this is what we discussed on pages 76 and 77), but, in your previous films, the unease which they might have provoked was compensated for either by a romantic element or by the fact that the degree of kinship was a lesser one (uncle and niece) or, then again, by references to Nazism; in *Frenzy*, the plot is more simplistic: a mother agrees to help the police set a trap for her son.

I would not be so insistent on this point if I felt it to be an essential element in the narrative. But, in fact, I don't. I know you want to make the mother's part a very real and active one, but I am sure there is another way of going about it, even if you are afraid it might make the plot a bit more complicated.

In fact, I cannot help wondering if the second half of *Frenzy* may not be a little too simple.

I think the reason for this lies in the fact that this is an original screenplay. When you adapt a novel, even if it is distilled to its bare essentials, subsidiary scenes always survive which, even if they might appear odd or unexpected, do enrich the finished film. In this case, we have only the main, essential plotline and I worry that such directness, which is so effective in the first half, might make the second half a trifle banal.

19. Of course, I do admit that the film picks up again as soon as Julie Cook arrives on the scene, but wouldn't it work just as well if Miriam too thought that Julie was a reporter?

20. I do like the way you develop the romantic relationship between Julie and Willie and I feel that these will be very good scenes. The character of Willie becomes genuinely moving as he gradually falls in love with Julie. (My negative feelings, however, about the Miriam–Lieutenant Hinckel scenes remain unchanged.)

21. Now comes the scene in the car when the cop checks Willie's driving licence and, as it stands at the moment, the cop's reactions seem very exaggerated, but I am sure that this can be rectified during shooting.

22. Willie has gone to so much trouble to shake off the police who are chasing him, that the arrival of the inspectors is a bit of a disappointment.

23. In the last scene, the idea of breaking the news to Miriam when she's on stage is intriguing but I don't think it's quite right yet. I assume you want the plot to go very quickly at this point, but that is a pity because the ending would be crueller and more ironic if, for example, the policeman were to decide not to tell Miriam the news until she had calmly finished her performance or part of her performance, in other words, there could be a relation set up between her work as an actress and the news which she is about to receive, which she is expecting to hear and is afraid to hear (on the same principle as in the wonderful scene no. 9).

A note on characterization

I know that the quality of the characterization will depend on the final script, but I will nevertheless give you my first impressions.

a) I don't really like the character of the father (there's either too much or not enough of him), the character of Milton Korfe (who does not yet come across clearly) or Patti (insufficiently detailed) or Hinckel (unless he turns out to be as interesting as Arbogast).[6] (Do you call him Hinckel because it was Chaplin's name for Hitler in *The Great Dictator*?)

b) I very much like Willie, Miriam (despite my one reservation), Caroline and Julie.

Naturally, if you are not too upset by these criticisms, I should be delighted to read the next version of *Frenzy*,[7] and I am sure that, even as I write, you have already solved most of the problems which I have mentioned.

I trust also that you have got a good cast in mind. Willie will be a great break for somebody.

And those, Mr Hitchcock, are my thoughts on reading *Frenzy*.

The Bride Wore Black won't be coming out in France until April because the Paramount film *Benjamin* has been such a hit.

I will not be sending you a copy of my script for *Stolen Kisses*, which I am shooting at the moment, because it is just a nostalgic, romantic comedy, budgeted at 250,000 dollars and largely improvised!

My next project is a more important one, *Waltz into Darkness*, adapted from a book by William Irish, with Catherine Deneuve and Jean-Paul Belmondo. I bought the rights to the book from Fox and I am hoping to make it for United Artists. I have written a first draft of my adaptation which I'll send you as soon as it has been translated into English, within the month.

I hope Mike Korda will soon have some good news about the Hitchbook for me; I see the reviews have been very good and I hope sales do as nicely.

I hope that the length of this letter is some compensation for its tardiness and I look forward to hearing from you soon.

Please give Mrs Hitchcock my best regards.

Yours very sincerely,
François Truffaut.

1 – In February 1968 the Minister of Culture, André Malraux, appointed a managing director to take over the administration of the Cinémathèque Française from Henri Langlois. Langlois refused to accept this appointment and was supported by a large number of famous figures from the film world, as well as French film fans represented by *Cahiers du cinéma* and Truffaut; there were also student protests. In the end the government gave in.
2 – Anthony Perkins, who played the murderer Norman Bates.
3 – Played by Robert Walker.
4 – The character played by Joseph Cotten in *Shadow of a Doubt*.
5 – In English in the original letter.
6 – The detective played by Martin Balsam in *Psycho*.
7 – Hitchcock eventually made *Frenzy* in 1970 but its screenplay bore little resemblance to that analysed by Truffaut in this letter.

To Jean-Louis Bory[1] — *Paris, 14 March 1968*

My dear Jean-Louis Bory,

I would like to clear up a point relating to me in your note on the 'Langlois affair' published in *Le Nouvel Observateur* on Wednesday 13 March.

It concerns the 'Face to Face' between Pierre Moinot and myself announced in your issue of 6 March and which you say was adjourned at the request of Pierre Moinot.

The course of events was as follows: the idea of the 'Face to Face' was proposed to me by *Le Nouvel Observateur* on 1 March and I withheld my answer until 7 March, since I first wished to observe proceedings at the 5 March meeting of the Cinémathèque's board of directors, of which Pierre Moinot has been president since 5 February and on which I sit as an associate member, i.e. representing both the government-appointed administrators and the friends of Henri Langlois.

When it became clear to me, on Thursday 7 March, that Pierre Moinot was not keeping the promises he had made to us 48 hours earlier, notably that he would be the sole administrator of the Cinémathèque until the extraordinary general meeting called for 22 April, and that Messieurs Barbin and Mallet were continuing to run the Rue de Courcelles,[2] I let you know via a telephone call from my secretary that there was no further question of my accepting the 'Face to Face'. It was on account of that same duplicity that I refused to join the committee of 'advisers' of which there had been talk in the few days leading up to the meeting.

It is my belief that, if one sincerely wishes the reinstatement of Henri Langlois and the departure of his 'successors', the only effective form of struggle exists within the Committee for the Defence of the Cinémathèque Française, of which Jean Renoir is honorary president and Alain Resnais president.

One can join this defence committee either as:

a founder: 500F

a benefactor: 50F

or a member: 5F.

The aim of the defence committee (whose address is 7, rue Rouget-de-Lisle, Paris 1er) is:

1. to re-establish the full and proper administration of the Cinémathèque;

2. to do everything in its power to instil respect for the integrity of the Cinémathèque and its freedom. Thus its activities will not cease with the reinstatement of Henri Langlois in his position as artistic and technical director, a reinstatement demanded by the entire film industry.

Since I have no doubt of your loyalty to the cause, I know you will publish this letter in the next issue of *Le Nouvel Observateur*.

Yours sincerely,
François Truffaut

1 – French novelist, film critic and broadcaster on the radio programme *Le Masque et la Plume* (1919–79).

2 – In which the offices of the Cinémathèque Française are located.

To Guy Teisseire

[15 March 1968]

My dear Guy,

Your piece 'New Confrontation at the Cinémathèque'[1] is remarkably precise and lucid. If Langlois is reinstated, it will be thanks to articles like that. We must hold out till 22 April, since, as became clear to me at the last board meeting, the only thing these people are afraid of is the press,

bravo and keep it up,

françois

1 – In the newspaper *L'Aurore*. 'Truffaut was particularly alert to the need for a right-wing newspaper to champion Langlois's cause. All at once it transcended the strictly political debate within which attempts had been made to contain the affair.' (Note by Guy Teisseire)

To Alfred Hitchcock

Paris, 4 July 1968

Dear Mr Hitchcock,

I wish to thank you very much for your letter of 17 June and I am most touched that you took the time to look at *The Bride Wore Black*. Your analysis of the film was extremely indulgent and you will certainly have noticed that the New York critics mention your name a great deal in their reviews. I think that in one sense it is quite justified because I do owe you a lot and in another sense unjustified because the story is in fact rather different from those which tend to interest you as a film-maker.

On the whole, the New York reviews have been quite good and the box-office as well.

As far as *Frenzy* is concerned, I am not sure that you should abandon the film as it contains a number of tempting features. There were obviously numerous problems to be solved in the second half, but also numerous fascinating scenes throughout the script.

I will certainly be very happy to read *Topaz*[1] in French if you can send me the Canadian edition. The reference you make to *Notorious* is very interesting. I had imagined something closer to *The Man Who Knew Too Much*, but in fact it will perhaps fall somewhere between the two films.

Jean-Luc Godard, François Truffaut, Louis Malle: Cannes, May 1968.

'We urgently request you to attend the press conference of the Committee for the Defence of the Cinémathèque at 3p.m. on 18 April in the Salon des Champs-Élysées 44 Champs-Élysées during which will be debated prior to the general assembly on the 22nd every aspect of the Langlois affair very cordially François Truffaut'

ORIGINE	NUMÉRO	NOMBRE de mots	DATE de dépôt	HEURE de dépôt	MENTIONS DE SERVICE	Timbre à date
≡≡≡ PARIS	568310	60	15	1925 =<≡		

<≡ NOUS VOUS PRIONS INSTAMMENT DE BIEN VOULOIR ETRE PRESENT <≡

A LA CONFERENCE DE PRESSE DU COMITE DE DEFENSE DE LA CINEMATHEQUE

AVRIL A 15H AU SALON DES <≡ CHAMPS ELYSEES 44 CHAMPS ELYSEES

AU COURS DE LAQUELLE SERONT DEBA-<≡TTUS AVANT L ASSEMBLEE GENERALE

DU 22 TOUS LES ASPECTS) DE L AFFAIRE LANGLOIS BIEN CORIDALEMENT

= FRANCOIS TRUFFAUT =<≡

N° 701

64 1101. 2 35 004 3
421286

Pour toute réclamation concernant ce télégramme, présenter cette formule au bureau distributeur

VOIR AU VERSO la signification des principales indications qui peuvent éventuellement figurer en tête de l'adresse.

I know that you plan to engage several French actors. The first victim of *The Bride Wore Black*, Bliss (Claude Rich), who caught your eye, unfortunately does not speak English. On the other hand, the father, the third man, Morane (Michel Lonsdale), speaks it perfectly, being the son of a British subject.

Helen Scott will have sent you some photos and a tape recording of the voice of Claude Jade, the 20-year-old girl who plays the heroine of the film which I've recently completed, *Stolen Kisses*; she is eight years younger than Catherine Deneuve, has something of Grace Kelly–Joan Fontaine about her and, from what I know of the novel *Topaz*, would be suitable for one of the roles.[2]

If I can be of any possible help to you with regard to the film, do not hesitate to ask me.

In reply to what you tell me about Henri Langlois, I believe you will soon have the opportunity of showing your esteem for him, as a foundation is to be established in the USA in aid of the Cinémathèque Française, and all contributions to it will be tax-deductible. I also believe that Langlois will then ask you to give him prints of some of your films. All of that will be finalized in October and we have the impression that in future the government will ease up on Langlois.

I spent a few days in New York and I learned that the Simon and Schuster edition of the Hitchbook had sold 100,000 copies, which is excellent. I hope that sales of the British edition will be no less satisfactory.

Hoping to hear from you soon, I beg you to convey my best wishes to Mrs Hitchcock and remain

Yours very sincerely,
François Truffaut

1 – By Leon Uris. In the event, Hitchcock filmed *Topaz* before *Frenzy*.

2 – Hitchcock did engage Claude Jade for the film, though not Lonsdale.

To Lucette de Givray[1]

Sunday 1 September 68

My dear Lucette,

[. . .] Next Friday I go down to Cannes again, as Laura is having her adenoids removed; Madeleine thinks that she will have a speedier recovery there than in Paris, and I've promised her a little camera as soon as she is better.

The press screenings of *Baisers volés* are going very well, with unhoped-for success; if the public response is similar and the film makes its money back, then one of these days I'll be asking Claude[2] and Bernard[3] to help me continue the series: Antoine Doinel's married life (hmm, hmm . . . more and more difficult), Antoine the family man, etc.

My dear Lucette, I'm going through a period of soul-searching; it's now ten years since we started working together. [. . .] It has meant a great deal to me to know that you have been at my side during these ten years and seven films. I'm always so afraid of fouling up in my work that I've probably acquired a much thicker skin; I've become selfish and have sacrificed many precious things around me. On the pretext of protecting my films, which I've always treated as though they were children in danger, I haven't been attentive enough to other people's problems and yet I realize that yours have come to a head this year. But you do know, even if I have never spelled it out, that your integrity, your honesty and your delicacy have allowed me to succeed in my work and have made life very pleasant for me in this office where, along with Marcel,[4] who has also been with me for ten years, we make a good trio.

There you have it, dear Lucette. I wish you lots of courage, to Geori[5] I send a kiss and to you all my affection.

François

1 – See note 2, page 141.
2 – De Givray.
3 – Revon.
4 – Berbert.
5 – Claude and Lucette de Givray's son Georges.

To Richard Roud[1]

Paris, 7 November 1968

My dear Richard,

The evening that *Baisers volés* is screened in London[2] I will be somewhere on the Ile de la Réunion on the third day of shooting *La Sirène du Mississipi.* But I would very much like to know how the film is received, which is why I'd be extremely grateful if, the day after the screening, you could drop me a line at Les Films du Carrosse where they will forward the letter to me.

Also, the young actress in the film, Claude Jade, would be available and very happy to attend the screening, providing, naturally, it's possible for you to invite her . . .

As for Jean-Pierre Léaud, I don't know whether he will be free since he is due to make a film with Pasolini[3] as soon as he has finished the one he is

Antoine Doinel's married life: '. . . hmm, hmm, more and more difficult . . .'

currently making with Djurka. But if you would like him to be present, you should get in touch with Madame de Givray at Les Films du Carrosse.

As for Jeanne Moreau, she is, as I told you, filming in Czechoslovakia. You can write to her at the Alcron Hotel: Stepanska U1, 49 in Prague 1, or care of Gérard Lebovici, 37, rue Marbeuf, Paris 8e.

I very much hope that the English public will like *Baisers volés* and that it will wipe away the unpleasant memory left in that country successively by *Fahrenheit 451* and *The Bride Wore Black.*

If the opposite happens, I will keep such wishes for my future films, for one must never give up hope.

I hope you won't mind keeping me informed about all this and remain affectionately yours,

François Truffaut

1 – American journalist, film historian and biographer of Truffaut (1929–89). For many years the director of the New York Film Festival, he published studies of Ophüls, Godard, Straub and Henri Langlois.

2 – At the London Film Festival, of which Roud was then the director.

3 – Pier Paolo Pasolini, Italian poet, novelist and director (1922–75). The film in question was *Porcile.*

To Serge and Danièle Rezvani *Friday 15 November 68*

Dear Sernièle,[1]

Impossible rencontrer Jelinek[2] because I am going to the Reunion Island in few days. I had very disappointed with Corsica country because of exigences of my scenario. We are stay in Reunion Island jusqu'à Noël. We hope come back on your beautiful french Riviera for Noël and shooting of *Sirène du Mississipi* continue à Nice (Musée Masséna transformed by us in hospital, why not?), with Naviplane on airport and after that, we will shoot à Antibes (place Jacques-Audiberti) and Aix-en-Provence for one or two weeks, after that Lyon and Grenoble because the happy end in the snow juste like *Pianist.* That's all. Si vous correspondez avec la chère Jelinek, dites-lui my admiration et le plaisir que j'aurai à la voir à partir de mars 1969.[3]

Now, see here, it looks as though we're not going to be getting together again for some time, eh? That will be for your Volume 3 and my Opus 8. Your next one I hope to read in manuscript, I'd like that a lot.

Jean has become a real Czechoslovakian Jew, and everyone I've spoken to adores your new book (everyone you've spoken to as well, I hope). I can imagine how thrilling it must be for you to roam the world with your typewriter in your hand; that's what I call living free and living out your

Mon cher Claude Berri

j'ai vu les → GAULOISES

bleues et ça m'a laissé

complètement → CELTIQUE

amitiés,

François

Wordplay on Michel Cournot's film *Les Gauloises bleues* (1968).

freedom, it's the dream of the tap-dancer who steps in off the street, prances about on the stage and leaves as he arrived, without any props, humming a tune. I would have expressed these thoughts much better in English, but I was afraid of boring you!

I seem to recall that your 3rd book will cover the period between the 1st and the 2nd. Am I right?

If you also write letters, I would have you know that everything addressed to me at 5, rue Robert-Estienne is promptly sent on to me and that I reply with alacrity and good humour.

Look after each other and look after yourselves. I think of you often and with great tenderness.

If I knew how to write, I wouldn't be playing the fool behind my big Mitchell 300;[4]

love,
françois

1 – Truffaut has conflated the names of Serge and Danièle. The first paragraph of this letter is exactly as he wrote it.
2 – The French writer Henriette Jelinek.
3 – 'If you write to dear Jelinek, convey to her my admiration and the pleasure I will have in seeing her from March 1969 onwards.'
4 – Truffaut's film camera.

To Helen Scott *Friday 29 Nov 68*

My lovely soft Scottie,

The enclosed document[1] will prove to you that I find myself thinking of you several times a day . . .

I swagger around, but, as you well know, I'm in a blue funk, three days before filming, with the same old fantasies of pulling out: 'What if Catherine were to break a leg . . . what if Jean-Paul were to have a sore throat . . .' In short, once again they're going to have to drag me screaming and kicking to work, it's la Shife[2] who will drive me on by booting me up the backside.

My first observation: you don't write to me very often. Observations 2, 3 and 4 make the same point. Yet I'm sure that you've got lots of things to tell me and that you're taking advantage of my absence to be seen at all the cocktail parties.

That moron X— hasn't put in an appearance, and so I don't have the strength to begin on Monday the diary of the shoot that you will naturally refuse to translate until it's guaranteed that a shower of $ will pour down on Mrs Rezwick's little girl[3] who is nevertheless so pure, soft and absorbent.[4]

If you were the Scott I knew in 1960, you would have settled all that with a few telegrams to Don, but there we are, this is 1968.

If you were the Scott of 1964 (the Scott of the Hitchbook), you would make it your job to find out, on Thursday the 5th, what sort of reception *Stolen Kisses* had at the London Film F . . .; anyway, be yourself, be the valiant Scott of Paris and don't let yourself be harassed any longer by anyone, not even me. Which reminds me, what's new with Jean-Pierre Rassam?[5] Where is Claude B.?[6] What's he doing? I miss you with your little pot-luck dinners of stale ham and yesterday's bread and a nice glass of lukewarm lemonade. When I see a salad on the table, I cry out: 'How can I have this salad if my Scottie's fingers haven't been sloshing around in it?!'

Deep down, I'm certain that you've thrown me over for a bouncing Czech, some run-of-the-mill douche-douche[7] or that old young rival of mine from North Africa. When I left it, no. 1, rue de la Pompe[8] was not far short of turning into a brothel, maybe you claim to have gone into partnership with Madame Claude . . . ?[9]

Dear Scott, write to me, type to me, the sooner the better, the sooner and the longer, as I've nothing to read. The entire crew arrives tomorrow.

Je vous kiss comme je vous love et je vous adresse mes best regards hitch-coquins,

françois

1 – An advertisement for Scott toilet paper.
2 – Suzanne Schiffman became Truffaut's continuity person on *Tirez sur le pianiste*; his personal assistant on *Fahrenheit 451*; his first assistant from *L'Enfant sauvage* onwards; and his co-scenarist from *L'Argent de poche* onwards (excepting only *La Chambre verte*). She worked in close collaboration with him from 1960 until his death.
3 – Helen Scott's maiden name was Rezwick.
4 – Another allusion to the "pure-soft-absorbent" qualities of Scott toilet paper.
5 – French producer.
6 – Claude Berri, French actor, director and producer, born in 1934: (as director) *Le Vieil Homme et l'Enfant*, *Le Cinéma de papa*, *Le Maître d'école*, *Tchao Pantin*, *Jean de Florette*, *Manon des sources*, etc. He was Rassam's brother-in-law.
7 – Jean Douchet, film critic and lecturer.
8 – Truffaut's address at the time.
9 – France's most celebrated brothel-keeper.

1969

To Charles Bitsch

Aix, 14 January 1969

My dear Carolus,

I find it very thoughtful of you to propose that my name be mentioned on the credits of your film,[1] but I don't believe it's justified. I gave you a helping hand, as I myself have had occasion to ask for one before or after shooting one of my own films.

For example, Rivette was instrumental in sorting out my ideas before *La Mariée était en noir* and Aurel after the shooting of *Fahrenheit*.

One day when I find myself in trouble, perhaps it will be my turn to ask you the same kind of favour and I know that you won't hesitate.

With *La Sirène du Mississipi*, when all my regular collaborators were taken up by television or by their own projects, I was left alone with the viewfinder in my right hand and the novel in my left; fortunately for me, it was Jacques Doniol-Valcroze's viewfinder and a novel by Irish (I wonder what the opposite would produce!).

I hope that everything ends well and that I'll see you very soon,

Happy new year,
françois

1 – *Le Dernier Homme.*

To Costa-Gavras[1]

the last day of February 1969

Dear Monsieur,

We met once, at the television centre, with Jean-Claude Brialy who introduced us.

I wished merely to let you know that I saw *Z* and that I liked it very much; it's a film that manages to be logical, beautiful and useful, which is the hardest thing to pull off.

I saw it at an ordinary evening performance at the Français, the public applauded at the end, it was nice to be there and feel that one was in complete agreement;

best of luck for the future, keep up the good work and accept my warmest regards,

François Truffaut

1 – French director, born in Athens in 1933: *Z*, *L'Aveu*, *État de siège*, *Missing*, *Betrayed*, etc. He was president of the Cinémathèque Française from 1982 to 1987.

To Jean-François Adam[1] *Paris, 13 May 1969*

My dear Jean-François,

I read your script[2] while recording the music for *La Sirène* and I'm pleased that you gave it to me because I believe I can help you guard against a considerable danger: the script, if it is shot as written, would make for a film with a running time of not less than 180 minutes (3 hours) and probably more.

I do understand your wish not to handle each scene in the spirit of contraction and synthesis usually adopted in the cinema but, on the contrary, to film life as it's lived, with all its uncertainties, its hesitations, its repetitions and random acts. It's not unlike what happens in the last reel of *Hiroshima mon amour* (but only the last reel) as well as in Resnais's other film, *Muriel*.

Given that the effect of such a style, such a premise, will be to make each scene three or four times longer (in relation to the traditional cinema), in the event of your wishing to make a feature film not exceeding 100 or 120 minutes, you would have to cut the script to half the length of this one.

You probably think I'm exaggerating and that there will always be time to rethink matters on the editing-table. That might well be the case if you had a free hand and unlimited credit. If such isn't the case, you run the risk, once the film is finished, of leaving on the cutting-room floor the equivalent of three or four weeks of filming which might more usefully have been spent on perfecting what had to be retained at any cost.

If you have a friend who works as a continuity-girl, ask her to do you a favour by meticulously timing the script.

You'll be flabbergasted by the result, and the next stage will naturally consist of reworking the whole script in such a way as to render it filmable.

I also think that this moment of astonishment ought to coincide with the costing, which might be done simultaneously with the timing. As it has been written, I would consider the film impossible to make under the conditions which currently exist in French cinema, unless you really are more realistic than I think you are and your intention is to follow the example set by Jacques Rivette with *L'Amour fou* (in actual fact, *L'Amour fou* contained only two interlinked sections, both of them very simplified, which is why he was able to shoot a film lasting 4 hours 15 minutes in four weeks at a cost of 60 million).

You are perhaps thinking that I haven't mentioned the essential point . . .

I became very interested in Mathieu, also in Jeanne, not much in the neighbour and not always in the minor characters. It's a very sincere piece of writing, very personal, often moving and much too private to judge on a critical level. All of that is your concern, but I only hope that you will take note of my objection on the question of the running time. It's true that, in a first film, one would like to get absolutely everything in, but seldom as much as in this case! Given the stage you have reached, the problem of the running time strikes me as absolutely crucial.

As you know, I have at present scarcely the time to meet you, but I would always be pleased to hear about *Mathieu*.

Very cordially yours,
François

1 – French director (1938–80): *M comme Mathieu, Le Jeu du solitaire, Retour à la bien-aimée.* He was Truffaut's assistant on *La Peau douce.*

2 – Of *M comme Mathieu.*

To Gilles Jacob — *Wednesday 20 May 69*

My dear Gilles,

I've read your book,[1] the first novel by a cinephile that isn't about the cinema, perhaps . . . Compared to our mutual friend's,[2] it's twice as thick, has an identical cover, also the Venice Festival . . . hers had an *engagé* quality, yours seems rather *dégagé* . . .

Seriously, what I liked about it was its simplicity and its lively pace; in tone it resembles Bergman's sentimental pre-1960 films, the ones I prefer. I didn't read it *à la* Kennedy[3] and I assure you that that great man (?) would not have noticed that the 6th line on page 121 was quite clearly missing. We'll speak further of it. The interview with Cathe de Neuve[4] was by far the best piece of journalism about her, *Life*'s included; she was very pleased, I hope she told you so.

I'll show you *La Sirène* in a fortnight; I begin the sound-mixing tomorrow.

See you very soon,

françois

1 – *Un jour une mouette*, Éditions Grasset, 1969.
2 – Yvonne Baby's novel *Oui, l'espoir* had also been published by Grasset in 1969, which is why the covers were identical.
3 – Truffaut is referring to the speed-reading method employed by John Fitzgerald Kennedy.
4 – Catherine Deneuve.

To Gilles Jacob

Sunday 13 July 1969

My dear Gilles,

Even if you don't like *La Sirène*, keep in touch! I return to Paris at the end of August, beginning of September. The work here,[1] far from the telephone, from interruptions, from newspapers, and even from holidaymakers, is going well. Perhaps you've started a new novel?

My regards to your wife and my very best wishes to you both,

françois

My address: 'La Garde' Pont-Mort (63).

1 – The filming of *L'Enfant sauvage*.

To Jean Gruault[1]

1 August 1969

My dear Jean,

I am half-way through *L'Enfant sauvage*; it's all going quite well, considering that I didn't properly prepare this shoot, which is so much more difficult and special than the earlier ones; I am sticking very closely to the screenplay; I am rereading Itard and have retrieved a few details such as 'Victor's invention of the chalk-holder'. The script is well-constructed. Forgive me for having not let on about my taking the role of Itard, I was determined to keep it a secret until the last minute and I hope you won't be disappointed by my amateurish performance.

I'm going to send you some stills of the film; come and see us when we shoot at the Institut des S. et M.[2] at the end of August.

Have a lovely holiday, best wishes to the entire Gruault tribe,

see you soon,

françois

1 – French screenwriter. With Truffaut he wrote the screenplays of *Jules et Jim*, *L'Enfant sauvage*, *Les Deux Anglaises et le Continent*, *L'Histoire d'Adèle H.* and *La Chambre verte*.

2 – Institut des Sourds-Muets (Institute for the Deaf and Dumb).

To Gilles Jacob

Toledo, Friday late October 69

My dear Gilles,

I am resting in Toledo[1] and making notes for the next film, *Domicile conjugal*. I received the interview with Brigitte B.[2] and have no desire to reply to it because of three rules which I have laid down for myself:

1. never agree to become a member of a jury,
2. never 'reply' to newspapers,
3. never take legal action.

Brigitte is amusing, impulsive, but not very clear or logical; in fact, even when I was discussing *La Sirène* with the Hakims, there was never any question of her; it was during the filming of *Belle de jour*,[3] the brothers would swear by no one but Catherine. My differences with them concerned the choice of the man, they wanted Alan Bates or Delon,[4] I favoured Jean-Paul. I broke with them and two months later I realized that the Hakims had been bluffing all along and that they did not own the rights to *La Sirène*! These belonged to Twentieth Century-Fox which was trying to get rid of them; I bought them for 20 or 25 million by borrowing from 3 people and I need hardly tell you that, if Brigitte had known what she wanted, she would have bought them more quickly and more easily than I! These last few years Brigitte has offered me four or five ideas or scripts that I've turned down (including the famous *A cœur joie*,[5] which was originally called *Prologues*), but it would never cross my mind to mention that in an interview, as I would consider it to be in poor taste. That said, I bear her absolutely no ill will. There you have, if not the truth, at least my truth; actually, I quite enjoy this kind of imbroglio, when, as a result of something made public, one comes to realize that 80 people have being toying with the same idea without knowing it so that one could almost write a book about it *à la* 'rosebud'.[6]

There, my dear Gilles, is my version of the affair (abridged, but I'll fill you in on the details when we see each other). I'm going to shoot *Domicile conjugal* in January, even before *L'Enfant sauvage* comes out (in February), after which, from April onwards, I've decided to have a long rest until 1971.

Give my regards to everyone, first to your wife, to Yvonne[7] if you see her,

'Even if you didn't like *La Sirène*, keep in touch . . .'

to Billard[8] and (why not?) to Charensol,[9] the ringmaster of the 'Mask and Pen Circus', and then try to write a new book,

cheers,
françois

1 – Where Buñuel's *Tristana* was being filmed.
2 – In which Bardot complained that Truffaut had advised against offering her the leading role in *La Sirène du Mississipi.*
3 – By Luis Buñuel and starring Catherine Deneuve (1967).
4 – Alain Delon, French actor, born in 1935: *Plein Soleil*, *Rocco and His Brothers*, *The Eclipse*, *The Leopard*, *Le Samouraï*, *Borsalino*, *The Assassination of Trotsky*, *Un Flic*, etc.
5 – By Serge Bourguignon (1967).
6 – Truffaut is, of course, alluding to *Citizen Kane* and the fact that, in that film, Kane's motives are interpreted differently by different acquaintances.
7 – Yvonne Baby.
8 – Pierre Billard, French journalist, born in 1922.
9 – Georges Charensol, French journalist, film critic and art critic, born in 1899. He was a regular broadcaster on the arts programme *Le Masque et la Plume*.

To Bernard Gheur

Paris, 29 December 1969

Dear Monsieur,

I am at this moment finishing one film, *L'Enfant sauvage* and about to start another, *Domicile conjugal*, and it's really impossible for me to deal personally with every manuscript I receive, even when it happens to be a film project.

That's why I will be unable to read your novel before the month of April 1970.

I have a friend in whom I have every confidence and who lives in Brussels; he is a teacher, I believe, and at the same time a man of letters and a real cinephile, his name is René Micha. I suggest you write to him, mentioning my name, and ask his advice. Here is his address: 74, avenue Louise – Brussels 5.

If I have in any small way encouraged you in your work, I don't regret it, as there is nothing sadder than unfulfilled dreams and first novels abandoned as soon as they are begun.

I am returning the first manuscript to you without having found the time to read it and I will also return the revised manuscript unless the April date does not strike you as being too far off.

Regretfully but cordially,
François Truffaut

1970

To Claude Lelouch[1]

Paris, 13 January 1970

My dear Claude,

Last Saturday I met Abel Gance who asked me to have a word with you about the situation of his *Napoléon* (the real title will be *Bonaparte*) and, not knowing whether I would be able to reach you by phone, I prefer to write to you.

It concerns his two versions of *Napoléon* (the silent and the one with added sound), the rights to which he has been buying up so that it is now available for screening all over the world, in the cinema and on television. As he wished to make a genuinely new version, he completely re-edited the film with scenes which had been cut and others newly shot. To finance this work, he received considerable support from André Malraux who had funds released, not, it seems to me, from the C.N.C., but directly from the Ministry of Culture. The departure of Malraux occurred when Gance was half-way through his work. He therefore still has a few shots to film and some screening-room and laboratory work to be done. I believe he is looking for about 40,000 dollars.

If, when this work is complete, there emerges the truly great film that we can imagine from what we've seen over the years in mutilated versions at the Cinémathèque, and if that film will then be available for the whole world, cinema and television, it would definitely represent a very good deal.

Abel Gance is 81 years old. He is extraordinarily youthful for his age, strong and healthy, and his reputation abroad, in America and Japan for example, is much higher than we can possibly imagine.

In short, he feels that you are the man for the situation, but he is reluctant to call you directly.

Let me know how you feel about all this as soon as possible so that I won't have to keep him waiting.[2]

If you are interested and would like to contact him directly, here is his address: 22, rue de l'Yvette, Paris 16e – Telephone: JAS 76-34. During the day, he is often to be found at C.T.M. – GRE 40-37.

I am relying on you to reply quickly and remain

yours,
François Truffaut

1 – French director, born in 1937: *Un homme et une femme*, *A nous deux*, *Édith et Marcel*, *Les Uns et les Autres*, etc.

2 – 'Thanks to François Truffaut, I was able to meet one of my favourite film-makers and help him complete his life's work' (note by Claude Lelouch). In actual fact, Gance's own *Bonaparte et la Révolution* (as the sound version was finally titled) has been superseded by the reconstruction of the original silent version by Kevin Brownlow and David Gill.

To Lydie Mahias[1]

Wednesday 14 January 70

My dear Lydie,

You know the *Cahiers* situation. Éditions de l'Étoile = 200 shares! J. D.-V. and I hold 25 shares each. We're on the lookout for new partners who might be interested in buying 1, 5, 10 or 15 shares at 120 thousand old francs each. Will you think about it? What would be ideal is for you to buy an enormous stack of shares, thereby becoming the majority shareholder and returning to *Cahiers* to tweak their ears and rule the roost;[2] that's my dream but, between that and doing nothing at all, a reasonable solution ought to be possible,

affectionately,
françois

1 – Lydie Mahias worked at *Cahiers du cinéma* before serving as continuity person and production manager on Truffaut's films. She was his assistant on *L'Homme qui aimait les femmes*.

2 – Daniel Filipacchi, a French publisher who had become the majority shareholder in *Cahiers du cinéma*, was unhappy with its editorial policy and eventually sold off his shares, causing publication of the magazine to be briefly interrupted. To his original letter Truffaut had attached a newspaper cutting on the '*Cahiers* situation'.

To Jacques Doniol-Valcroze

Paris, 22 January 1970

My dear Jacques,

Here is my answer to your questionnaire:[1]

1. a) In April 1959, my first film, *Les Quatre Cents Coups*, was banned to under-16s, but two weeks later, because it had won the Prix de l'Office Catholique du Cinéma, the ban was lifted.

b) In 1960, *Tirez sur le Pianiste* was also banned to under-16s (or perhaps 18s), a ban which was lifted not long afterwards because the film's producer, Pierre Braunberger, managed to pull some strings. The point of contention on that occasion was not the overall thrust of the film but a single shot of Michèle Mercier[2] sitting on a bed, her breasts bared. Pierre Braunberger undertook to cut one of that beautiful actress's two breasts (which struck me as technically a very difficult thing to do) and everything was settled in the corridors of the Ministry.

c) In 1962, *Jules et Jim* was banned to under-18s, a ban which was lifted four years later thanks to a change of distributor and the cachet of several international prizes.

2. I cannot agree to lend you the shots that were cut because of the problems involved in tracking them down but also because I know from experience that a montage film consisting of censored sequences runs the risk of producing the opposite effect from the one desired, in other words, of seeming to justify censorship and, at any rate, of provoking its spectators to reactions of excessive ribaldry.

3. I will not be taking part in the press conference organized by the S.R.F. since I will be shooting until the end of March.

4. I cannot agree to take part in an interview which would be interpolated in the montage film for the reasons which I explained in paragraph 2 and which concern the unintentionally comic effects of a such a film.

5. Obviously I do not approve of the manner in which the Board of Censorship currently functions:

a) because it is not genuinely impartial;

b) because, despite what is widely believed, the members of our profession do not constitute a united front and, when they include film-makers as embittered as Henri Calef[3] or as paranoid as Jean-Pierre Melville, accusations of vote-rigging may sometimes be directed at an unexpected quarter.

The Board of Censorship, so they say, is the watchdog of the nation's morals. However, to take just one example, I can inform you that, a year and a half ago, I met one of its members in a brothel. Even though I have no direct contact with the censorship board, I happened to know this particular senior official because he had been among Henri Langlois's opponents at the time of the Cinémathèque affair (March 1968). Thrown into confusion at meeting me under such circumstances, he began to stammer and inquired about my impressions of India, at which point I realized that he had mistaken me for my colleague Louis Malle.[4]

I relate this anecdote merely to show that the members of the Board are themselves not beyond reproach and that there exists one weapon which the government cannot sell to any foreign power, and that is subterfuge. Just as the intellectuals of certain countries are obliged to fill jotter after jotter copying out censored books by hand, so there exist several kinds of subterfuge by which one can evade, either partially or totally, the law of the scissors. These subterfuges are practical, easy to apply, and if I do not care to list them here, you will understand why.

Such would be the solution adopted by any film-maker considering the problem from a concrete, practical point of view. I am well aware that the aim of the S.R.F. is to lead the struggle on a theoretical level, but, there too, I believe in the necessity of practical solutions.

If I were to level a criticism at the S.R.F., it would be that it demonstrated a lack of realism at the very beginning of its existence. Rather than demanding the impossible, which is to say the total abolition of censorship following the events of May 68, it could at that time have asked for, and obtained, the establishment of a lower age limit from under-18 to under-14. That would have been a reasonable demand to make in the climate of reform initiated at the C.N.C. by André Holleaux, but it was not done, and I now come back to my practical proposition.

I propose the setting-up of an Anti-Censorship Board comprising film-makers, journalists and public figures. The members of this commission (which would have to be allocated an office, a staff and a budget) would undertake to give maximum publicity to all the more outrageous decisions of the censorship board. This might consist of publishing in a magazine the dialogue of, and stills from, some censored film sequence, then disseminating such material to foreign newspapers, radio and television stations – in short, it should be run like a kind of specialized agency.

If this were done in a serious fashion, we would eventually reach the point where the members of the Board of Censorship would begin to feel that, as the proverb has it, the game wasn't worth the candle.

1 – A questionnaire from the Société des Réalisateurs de Films (The Society of French Film-makers).

2 – French actress, born in 1939.

3 – French director, born in 1910: *Jéricho*, *La Maison dans la mer*, *Les Chouans*, *Les Eaux troubles*, etc.

4 – Louis Malle had indeed directed *Calcutta* in India, but in 1969. Even if the dates do not entirely coincide, the anecdote is an amusing one.

To Tanya Lopert[1] *[February 1970] Monday evening*

My dear Tanya,

There have been many, too many, deaths around me, of people I've loved, that I took the decision, after Françoise Dorléac died, never again to attend a funeral, which, as you can well imagine, does not prevent the distress I feel from casting its shadow over everything for a time and never completely fading, even as the years pass, for we live not only with the living but also with all of those who have ever meant anything in our lives.[2]

Your father gave me a great deal of help and support these last five years; I enjoyed our frequent meetings in Paris and also in Monte-Carlo; I saw him for the last time at the Hôtel Georges V on the day of your wedding, and I also liked very much talking to your mother whose ideas on life and the cinema are always so enthusiastic and generous. Tell her that I am thinking of her, tell her that I feel close to all three of you, tell her that I will often think of your father and believe me when I say that I remain

affectionately yours,
François Truffaut

1 – French actress, whose father, Ilya Lopert (born in 1905, a film producer and distributor, then head of United Artists in Europe) had just died.

2 – In this letter can be seen the germ of *La Chambre verte* (*The Green Room*).

To Bernard Gheur *Paris, 13 May 1970*

Dear Monsieur,

I am delighted with the news you send me and I think your novel will be in good hands at Albin Michel. I have not read it yet, only dipped into it, and would be very happy to write a short presentation text.

However, as there is a certain elegance of style and you have been kind enough to ask my advice from the beginning, may I propose, in your own interest, that you revise your manuscript one more time.

Let me know if I have your permission to read it with pencil in hand, since I would like to underline or circle words or parts of phrases that seem to me to ring less true. If the answer is yes, I will return to you the copy in my possession by the end of this month.

It's because I feel I have a small stake in your project and because it's my wish as much as your own that it be well received that I take the liberty of making such a suggestion.

Reply to me soon,

cordially yours,
François Truffaut

To Bernard Gheur *Paris, 2 June 1970*

Dear friend,

I read your novel very attentively and with real pleasure and I noted in pencil a number of corrections. These are suggestions, do with them what you will. In general, they correspond to your desire for greater pace and fluidity.

I am certain that Albin Michel's positive reaction to your manuscript will stimulate you considerably to undertake its rewriting.

When you decide the time has come, I'll reread your manuscript, putting myself this time in the position of a reader, and I'll write the little introduction if you still wish it.

Very sincerely yours,
François Truffaut

P.S. I very much liked Jean-Marc, his relations with the others, the characters of the women, but I didn't have the time to read it at a stretch. I was hurrying to make the corrections; next time I won't deprive myself of the pleasure of the ordinary reader. Very best wishes,

fr.

To Richard Roud *Wednesday 3 June 70*

My dear Richard,

I am writing to confirm my intention to come to the New York Festival and introduce *L'Enfant sauvage* if you yourself so wish it and United Artists as well.

For the moment, they don't know what they are going to do with the film in the United States. They want to distribute it themselves in certain countries, Japan, Spain, and sell it in others: Italy, Germany . . .

For the States, they are waiting to view the 'mixed' version that Helen and I have put together: subtitled dialogue, dubbed commentary. I think that would be the best version for America.

In the meantime, my literary agent, Don Congdon, is endeavouring to have the illustrated screenplay published in English, for September, either by Grove Press or Simon and Schuster.

If I'm determined to give special attention to the American release of *L'Enfant sauvage*, it's because I want to efface the negative impression left by *La Sirène* (the *mermaid*!).[1] I haven't forgotten that you were the first to have seen, liked and defended *Le Sauvage*.

For the moment, I have no further film projects; I am going to publish or have published several books including Bazin's on Renoir, which is superb. I'd very much like to hear from you soon.

regards,
François Truffaut

1 – In English in the original letter.

To Bernard Gheur *from Paris Wednesday 17 June 70*

My dear friend,

I reread your manuscript with a great deal of enjoyment, now I think it's just right. With no pencil in hand, I found it both gripping and touching. I hope everything's going to work out for you. Here is the brief foreword; send it on yourself to Albin Michel, but only if you consider it suitable; I'm always afraid of the reaction of literary critics: 'What does this film-maker know about it, etc.'

Let me have news of you,

yours,
François Truffaut

To Paul Vecchiali[1] *11 or 12 August 1970*

My dear Vecchiali,

Thank you for having thought to send me the note before embarking on your film.[2] I hope it will be as good as *Les Ruses du diable*, but also better understood and accepted. I remember liking the script but finding it a little obscure, that was two years ago . . . Have you revised it? Vecchiali the

TELEGRAMME — VOIE TELE FRANCE

NNNN ZCZC PSW948
FRPA HL UWNX 063
BEL AIR CALIF 63 29 210P

LT
FRANCOIS TRUFFAUT
NUMBER 5 RUE ROBERTESTISNNE PARIS8 (VIA WUI)

MON CHER FRANCOIS
JAI VISIONE LENFAND SAUVAGE QUE JE TROUVE MAGNIFIQUE JE TE
PRIE DE MENVOYER UN AUTOGAPH DE ACTEUR QUI JOUE LE DOCTEUR
IL EST FORMIDABLE JE DESIRE CET AUTOGRAPH POUR ALMA HITCHCOCK
FES YEUX ETAIENG INONDES DE LAMES CE FILM

CFM 5 8

PAGE 2/13

DIT ELLE EST LE MIELLEUR DE TOUS CHEUX CE TRUFFAUD AFFECTION
PROFONDE

HITCHCOCK

'MY DEAR FRANÇOIS
I SAW THE WILD CHILD WHICH I THINK MAGNIFICENT PLEASE SEND ME THE AUTOGRAPH OF ACTOR WHO PLAYS THE DOCTOR HE IS WONDERFUL. I WISH THIS AUTOGRAPH FOR ALMA HITCHCOCK HER EYES WERE BATHED IN TEARS THIS FILM SHE SAYS IS THE BEST OF ALL THOSE BY TRUFFAUT PROFOUND AFFECTION

HITCHCOCK'

François Truffaut in the role of Dr Itard (*L'Enfant sauvage*).

producer must not be allowed to go bankrupt on account of Vecchiali the director!

It's difficult enough for us to have our vision of things, our sensibility, accepted, without compounding that difficulty with the less noble one of a narrative construction which we regard as crystal-clear simply because we conceived it, but which proves hard to follow for people seeing the film for the first (and last) time. It's as a friend that I write this and also as someone whose wish is to see you recognized and appreciated and free and independent and sought-after and lionized and with lots of projects in the offing,

yours,
françois tr.

1 – French producer-director, born in 1930: *Les Petits Drames*, *Les Ruses du diable*, *Femmes Femmes*, *Change pas de main*, *La Machine*, *C'est la vie*, etc.

2 – *L'Étrangleur*.

To the President of the High Court *Paris, 8 September 1970*

Monsieur le Président,

I had made arrangements to testify on 8 September at the trial of the distributors and vendors of *La Cause du peuple*.[1] Having postponed my departure to the United States until 10 September, I cannot once again adjourn the trip, which is why I am now sending you this written testimony.

In the first weeks of June, I had read that the newspaper *La Cause du peuple*, of which Jean-Paul Sartre had just become editor, was being systematically seized even before the authorities had read the articles it contained. I learned also that the police were apprehending, arresting and prosecuting the vendors of the newspaper and sometimes even its readers, if they should happen to have at least two copies in their pocket or in the saddlebag of a moped.

I knew, again from having read it in *Le Monde*, that one court of law, that of Rennes, I believe, had for a while refused to prohibit distribution of the newspaper.

All of which clearly demonstrated that, in order to persecute a newspaper, the Minister of the Interior did not hesitate to commit acts that one can only call illegal.

I have never engaged in any political activity and am no more a Maoist than I am a Pompidolian,[2] being incapable of any feelings towards a head of state, no matter who he might be.

I happen simply to love books and newspapers and to hold very dearly the idea of the freedom of the press and the independence of the law.

It also happens that I made a film entitled *Fahrenheit 451* which portrayed, in a highly critical manner, an imaginary society in which the state would systematically burn every book; it was therefore my wish that my ideas as a film-maker and my ideas as a French citizen be in accordance.

That is why, on Saturday 20 June, I decided to sell the newspaper *La Cause du peuple* on the public thoroughfare. It was there, in the street, that I met other vendors, among them Jean-Paul Sartre and Simone de Beauvoir. Many passers-by took an interest in our activities, my pile of newspapers rapidly melted away and, when a policeman appeared in front of us, I had the pleasure of offering him two copies of *La Cause du peuple*, which he accepted, thereby leaving himself open to prosecution. A photograph, taken by a passer-by, will confirm the truth of this statement. After ordering us to disperse, the policeman then asked Jean-Paul Sartre to accompany him to the police station, which the writer was quite willing to do. Naturally, I followed behind, as did Simone de Beauvoir, other vendors and a few curious pedestrians.

If the policeman asked Jean-Paul Sartre, instead of me, to accompany him, it was patently because I was wearing a white shirt, a dark suit and a tie, whereas Sartre had on a crumpled suede windcheater that had seen better days. There was already, therefore, at the vestimentary level (as one says nowadays), a discrimination being made among the vendors of *La Cause du peuple*, those who seemed to be selling it as a means of earning their living being more liable to prosecution than those of us who were doing it on principle.

What happened next only reinforced this impression, since a pedestrian, recognizing Sartre, shouted at the policeman, 'You're surely not going to arrest a Nobel prizewinner!' At which point, we were astonished to see the policeman release Sartre's arm, begin to walk more quickly, draw ahead of our group and rush off at such a speed that it would have been necessary to start running in order to catch up with him. That was all the proof we needed that there did indeed exist a double standard, and that one is more likely to be arrested if one happens to look like a fishy customer, or rather a fishy vendor.

I can only conclude this testimony by advising my colleagues, the vendors of *La Cause du peuple*, to wear their Sunday best every day and refuse the Nobel Prize if ever it is offered to them.

Such, Monsieur le Président, are the facts that I would have related at the hearing of 8 September.

François Truffaut

1 – Two vendors of *La Cause du peuple* had been arrested and imprisoned in June 1970.

2 – I.e. a supporter of Georges Pompidou, then President of France.

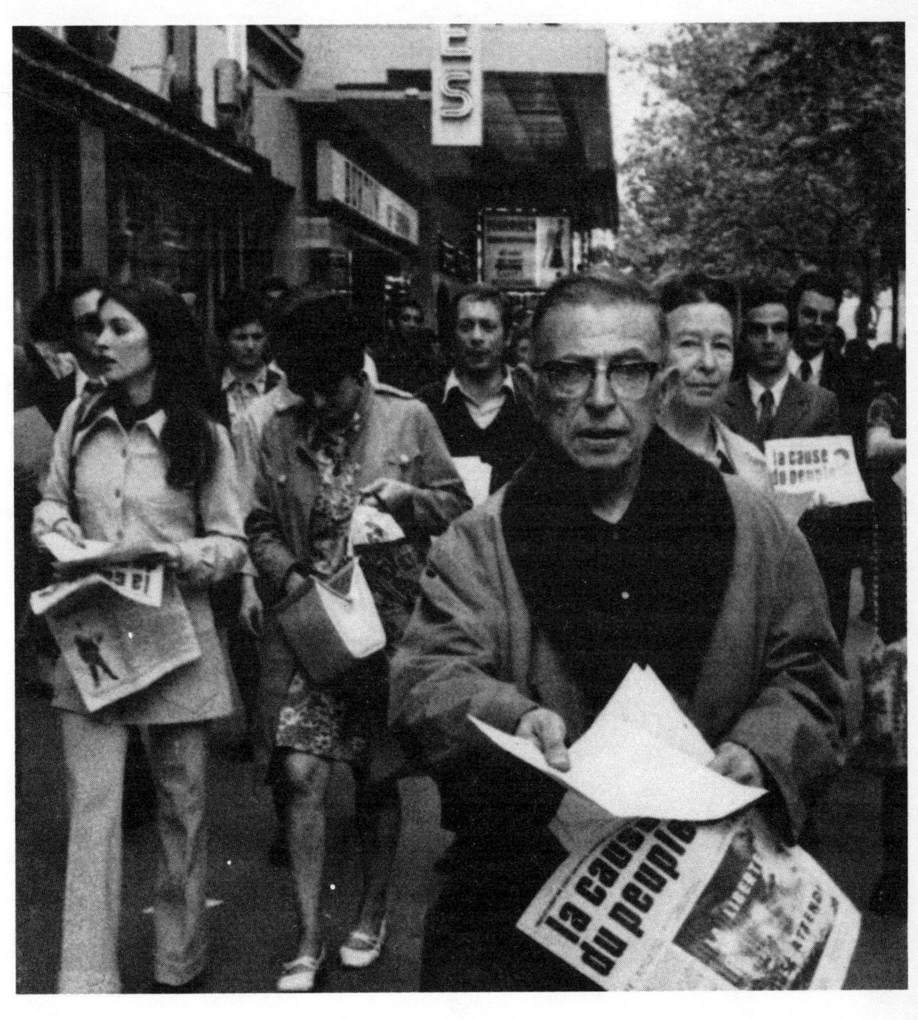

Jean-Paul Sartre, Simone de Beauvoir and François Truffaut: 'Such, Monsieur le Président, are the facts . . .'

1971

To Lillian Ross[1]

Paris, 22 January 1971

Dear Lillian,

Thank you very much for sending me the book *For Esmé, with Love and Squalor*[2] which I read with a great deal of pleasure.

Unfortunately, I cannot consider it for a film adaptation, as, at this moment, in the French cinema, several directors are exploring the theme of a love affair between a young French woman and a German soldier during the period of the Occupation. Since *Hiroshima mon amour* the theme had not been dealt with, but it appears that it will be abundantly so this year. Curiously, one readily accepts the idea of several novels telling the same story in the same year; by contrast, when it is a question of several films, it somehow becomes less acceptable.

Quite apart from that, the story I would like to film on the subject of the Occupation[3] would not include a German soldier, since I feel almost certain that I would be incapable of bringing off such a character.

I was very pleased to receive and read the book and I would like you to tell your friend Salinger how much I admire him and how proud and grateful I am that he should have thought of me.

I am returning your copy of the book, I hope I have not damaged it.

With my very best wishes,

yours,
François Truffaut

1 – American journalist, the author of *Picture*, a memoir of the filming of John Huston's *The Red Badge of Courage*.

2 – By J. D. Salinger.

3 – This would become *Le Dernier Métro* (*The Last Metro*) in 1980.

To Roger Diamantis[1] *Paris, 5 April 1971*

Dear Monsieur,

I have read your thesis[2] on my films with a good deal of attention and interest. As you will see, I have made copious notes in the margins, sometimes to clarify or correct a point of detail, sometimes in order that your line of thinking should be easier to grasp for your future readers.

I think it would be in your interest to provide the reader with references for every quotation, whether from interviews or extracts from my films published in a book or a periodical; it would also be helpful to know in greater detail the context of each of the scenes you have chosen to analyse, as their meaning is sometimes unclear when taken out of context.

I cannot, at present, grant you the interview you request in order to complete your work because I am about to embark on a new project and would, in any case, find it very hard to discuss the theme you have chosen for your article because my method is to approach such matters indirectly, via the camera.

I will, however, attempt to assist you as much as I can, by providing you with the information you are looking for.

Les Mistons

You should obtain a copy of the script, which was published in the 4th issue of *Avant-Scène*, together with the script of Jacques Demy's *Lola*.

In addition, you ought read the short story by Maurice Pons, from which the script was adapted, published in *Virginales* (Julliard).

You might also make a comparison between the theme of *Les Mistons* (five children persecuting a courting couple), and that of *La Mariée était en noir* (a woman assassinates each of the four men responsible for her husband's death).

Les Quatre Cents Coups

I am going to send you, by separate post, a text we didn't include in *Les Aventures d'Antoine Doinel*[3] (Mercure de France), but which will be in the American edition. This is a list of characters, drafted before the script was written. You will certainly find this of interest, particularly regarding Antoine's mother.

Antoine's bed is a small day-bed, one of whose arms has to be folded back so he can go to sleep at night. When this is done, the little bed blocks the entrance to the flat so that, in the scene where Antoine's mother comes home

From left to right: Eva Truffaut, Matthieu and Guillaume Schiffman, Laura Truffaut and Jean-Pierre Léaud (*Les Deux Anglaises et le Continent*).

late (after Antoine and his father have dinner alone), she has to clamber over the boy's bed to get into the adjoining room; at that moment, her legs are illuminated by the light on the landing, until she has closed the front door behind her.

In the other scene to which you refer, after she has dried her son in the bath, she carries him into his parents' bed, but this is an exception, since it is already morning and it has all happened after the scene in which Antoine has spent the night wandering the streets of Paris. A point should be made of the fact that, during this scene, she tells Antoine about her younger days, and about her first and unhappy love affair with a young shepherd . . . during her summer holidays.

You are quite right to point out that, on a several occasions, Antoine's glance wanders to his mother's breasts. In the same way, later in the reformatory, he stares at the hat his mother has put on specially for the occasion.

Please also note, during the scene in the police station, the arrival of the three prostitutes, each of whom makes a remark on how filthy police stations are, and note how the three remarks were specifically chosen to remind the spectator of fairy-tales (Goldilocks and the Three Bears, for example).

On the subject of gender confusion, you will note that Antoine and René greet a priest with 'Bonjour, Madame', just as Antoine will reply 'Oui, Monsieur' when Delphine Seyrig asks him if he likes music.

Tirez sur le pianiste

There are three women in the film.

Michèle Mercier, who lives on the same floor as Charles Aznavour and is also a prostitute (her dialogue includes several references to clothes).

Nicole Berger: the downtrodden wife who throws herself out of the window.

Marie Dubois, who is an orphan – the girl with whom one could make a fresh start.

These three characters represent the three types of women any man might come across in his lifetime; just as the five men in *La Mariée était en noir* represent five different modes of male behaviour in their relations with women.

La Peau douce

You were quite right in your remarks about Françoise Dorléac's character but you are perhaps less perceptive on Franca and her clothes.

Fahrenheit 451

You don't mention this film at all, even though there are a couple of scenes in it which illustrate your thesis.

When Linda, the wife, swallows the sleeping-pills, male nurses give her a blood transfusion and warn Montag that next day she will have a voracious sexual appetite and, accordingly, she sets a trap for him by hiding behind one of the walls of the apartment.

La Mariée était en noir

In this film, the plot needs no explanation, so the dialogue is free to concentrate on notions of male–female relationships. Julie, who symbolizes vengeance, dresses up to seduce her victims before killing them off.

She dresses in a white outfit with feathers for Claude Rich, a black cape for Michel Bouquet, in the style of a whore for Daniel Boulanger (the scene in the garage), as Diana, the goddess of hunting, for Charles Denner, the painter – and she kills him, appropriately, with a bow and arrow. This last detail is an allusion to a book by Pierre Klossowski, *Le Bain de Diane*, published by Jean-Jacques Pauvert.

In the scene during which Julie is detained for questioning, there is a moment when she senses that Jean-Claude Brialy is staring at her legs and she pulls her skirt down to cover her knees. (Though it is a colour film, Jeanne Moreau's costumes are either black or white throughout.)

Baisers volés

I draw your attention to the following points: when Antoine Doinel is released from the guardhouse he pauses for a moment outside a classroom where a sergeant-major giving a lecture makes a comparison between approaching a live explosive and accosting a woman.

Then you have the first brothel scene, with two different girls.

When he is working as a night porter in a hotel in Montmartre, during the adultery scene the husband begins ripping his wife's underclothes before throwing the flowers on to the bed where he has found her with another man.

One of his first assignments, when he becomes a private detective, is to tail a woman in black stockings and later, at the garage owned by his future in-laws, he tells them about his latest investigation, which is the story of the nanny who neglects her charges in order to work in a strip-club where her costume is that, precisely, of a nanny.

When Delphine Seyrig enters Antoine Doinel's room to seduce him, the pictures on the wall are reproductions of paintings by Balthus (Pierre Klossowski's brother).

Since you are interested in the relationship between love and death, I draw your attention to the conversation between Antoine and one of his colleagues at work (*Les Aventures d'Antoine Doinel*, Mercure de France, pp. 206–7).

La Sirène du Mississipi

My intention, with this picture, was always to be very specific about the couple's physical relationship. The script turns the usual clichés upside down since Jean-Paul Belmondo is as petrified as a young virgin, whereas Catherine Deneuve is a woman with a past. In each successive scene, the audience is made very well aware of the stage reached in the couple's physical relationship.

After Michel Bouquet's death, when they are both on the bed, she asks him to take her fully dressed; later, in Lyon, at night, he warns her over the entryphone of his return from Réunion and she gets out of bed and dresses quickly, just because it's him. There you have the main difference between this scene and the one you mention from *La Peau douce*.

I won't list the things that might interest you in *Domicile conjugal*, because it's a more recent film and you will find the script in *Les Aventures d'Antoine Doinel*.

You have chosen a very interesting subject for your thesis, but I have no wish to comment on it in any depth. I think it would be in your interest to work with a friend on giving the piece a more literary or scholarly style.

In any case, I should very much like to read it when you have made some further progress.

I trust that this will have been of some assistance to you,

Yours sincerely,
François Truffaut

1 – French film distributor and exhibitor.
2 – An unfinished thesis (entitled 'Cinema and Psychoanalysis in the films of François Truffaut') which Roger Diamantis undertook for the École Pratique des Hautes Études, under the supervision of Christian Metz.
3 – The published scripts of *Les Quatre Cents Coups*, *L'Amour à vingt ans*, *Baisers volés* and *Domicile conjugal*.

To Jean Hugo[1] *[1971]*

Dear Monsieur,

With my friend, the scenarist Jean Gruault (together we adapted Henri-Pierre Roché's novel *Jules et Jim* and Dr Itard's report on the wild child of Aveyron in *L'Enfant sauvage*), I have for several weeks been examining the possibility of making a biographical film about Adèle Hugo[2] and in particular the long episode of her love for Lieutenant Pinson.

I did not attempt to contact you before, since, for the moment, our work is still at an exploratory stage, and it often happens that we plot out a film only to abandon it – especially if it should concern a true story rather than a novel.

My great desire was to have got in touch with you through Louise de Vilmorin, of whom I was very fond . . . alas[3] . . . Then Maître Matarasso suggested himself, but I asked him to wait for a while, since I felt that, for you to be able to express an opinion, it was important that you read a fairly complete outline. In the meantime, I made the acquaintance of Mrs Frances V. Guille,[4] with whom I had been corresponding, and she told me that she had already spoken to you about the project; that is why I felt it necessary to explain why I am approaching you so belatedly.

By the first half of February I will be able to send you a first draft of the screenplay in the hope of receiving your general agreement on the project and, of course, any comments you might wish to make on what we have done.

Concerning the moral and legal questions between you, Mrs Guille and ourselves, I suggest we ask Maître Matarasso to represent our respective interests in the matter.

There only remains for me to tell you how passionately involved Jean Gruault and I have become with Adèle in the course of our collaboration; and, hoping I will soon have the pleasure of meeting you, I remain, dear Monsieur,

Yours very sincerely,
François Truffaut

1 – Born in 1894, a direct descendant of Victor Hugo, Jean Hugo was a celebrated and innovative stage designer.
2 – *L'Histoire d'Adèle H* (*The Story of Adèle H*).
3 – The novelist Louise de Vilmorin had recently died.
4 – The biographer of Adèle Hugo.

The four ages of Antoine Doinel.

To Jean Gruault

Thursday 8 April 71

My dear Jean,

We haven't been able to reach you by phone: I wanted to tell you that I've received from Jean Hugo a very encouraging letter. His only reservation concerns the flashbacks to Guernsey (the physical depiction of Hugo), he would prefer that we show only photographs but, even on that point, he's not categorical, it can still be negotiated.

I'm going to reread very attentively scripts no. 1 and no. 2 and make notes so that you can do a little more work on them. Jean Hugo's letter has made me very happy, for this film matters a great deal to me.

love,
françois

P.S. I return to Paris next Wednesday.

To Jean-Loup Dabadie[1]

7 May 71

My dear Jean-Loup,

I don't have the time to give you as detailed an account of things as I would wish. The discussions with Columbia for the Série Noire novel[2] are dragging a bit, as they've become wary of French producers since *Le Cinéma de papa*[3] and especially *Juste avant la nuit*[4] (Génovès), but Lebovici assures me the deal will go through. In any event, we won't waste any time and will start working together from 15 August, on that idea or another one.

Don't have any worries about the way I use improvisation in my work; I'm forced to do so for lack of time, and because of the amateurism of the people I usually work with; it was the script of *Louise*[5] that made me want to work with you, as I had the impression of reading for the first time a French script filmable as it was. If together we can give it a balanced structure (2 to 3 weeks), and I then leave you to flesh it out, taking a look at it once a week or (if you prefer) only when it's finished, we'll arrive at something that I'll be able to film without having endlessly to patch it up or fill in the gaps. That's what I want and what I need. I don't have an 'auteur' complex, I'm not the kind of director who brushes aside or ejects or forgets the writer who got the script into shape. I think *Le Chant de la sirène* is the right material for the two of us or else it might equally well be the film about shooting a film.[6]

Have you already moved out of the rue Vineuse? How are Marie and the fruit of her loins: And Philippe,[7] alone in the country with his omelette? And

Sautet, between two of those slaps that his characters give each other? It would be nice if you could find a moment to let me know how you are. If you're going to see Charles Trenet or Raymond Devos, I envy you.

I'm back in Paris on 7 June and am shooting there until 10 July (more or less). The work is going well, I don't think there has been a falling-off of the film[8] compared to the script and it may even be an improvement on it, thanks to the English accent and also thanks to the actors who are so well cast and so convincing that they manage to make almost everything work; their youth gives an edge to everything and plays no small part in the result on the screen; I hope you won't be disappointed despite the necessary cuts (the weather, the running time, money, etc.). In January, you saw me when I was at my lowest ebb; now things are fine.

regards to the 2 of you,
françois

1 – French screenwriter, dramatist and novelist, born in 1938.
2 – A project which came to nothing.
3 – By Claude Berri.
4 – By Claude Chabrol and produced by André Génovès.
5 – Philippe De Broca's *Chère Louise*, with a script by Dabadie and De Broca.
6 – Truffaut was already thinking of *La Nuit américaine* (*Day for Night*).
7 – De Broca.
8 – *Les Deux Anglaises et le Continent* (*Anne and Muriel*).

To Marcel Berbert

Tuesday 19 July 71

My dear Marcel,

In a moment I leave Paris for Antibes, Nice, etc. As you know, I am more comfortable with the written than with the spoken word, so I am taking advantage of your absence to thank you for everything. At the beginning of the year, Carrosse was really getting stalled, you helped me, discreetly but very effectively, to remedy the situation; I hope that everything will go smoothly from now on and that we won't have cause to regret the adventure of *Les 2 Anglaises*.

See you in September; and, once again, all my gratitude and friendship.
françois

To Nestor Almendros[1]

from Paris, 10 September 71

My dear Nestor,

I am sending you – to entertain and amuse you – a little brochure on culture in Cuba.[2]

I hope all is going well for you and Barbet;[3] when I make a film far from Paris, my slogan is 'If we make a bad film, it's not serious since we'll have had a good trip . . .' I don't know whether Barbet shares that view!

This evening I spoke to Rohmer, he has agreed to wait for you until 10 or 15 March,[4] which will enable us to begin working together in the Midi at the beginning of January.[5]

This evening there's a screening of *Les 2 Anglaises* at the Ponthieu (before the dubbing which starts next week). Because of that, I'll be continuing this letter tomorrow to tell you how it went. The 8 or 10 people who saw it in Nice (for example, Jean Aurel, Jean-Loup Dabadie, Jean-Louis Richard . . .) think it the most beautiful of my films, because of the photography.

I share their opinion; it's the first time in one of my films that there's been nothing ugly on the screen, at any moment;* in fairness, I ought to add that the sets and costumes also help. The present, more or less definitive, running time is 2 hours 13 minutes, and no one seems to get bored.

In Antibes, where I spent 7 weeks, I worked on the editing at the Victorine studios and made a start on two screenplays: the one on the cinema that I spoke to you about, the story of a film shoot, with Jean-Louis Richard. We'll be able to make it together, I hope, in September and October 72, actually at the Victorine.[6] The other screenplay, obviously, is *Le Chant de la sirène* which will be retitled *Une belle fille comme moi*, with Bernadette Lafont (script by Jean-Loup Dabadie).

I'm ending this letter now and will resume it tomorrow afternoon. Goodnight, Nestor.

*There was also nothing ugly in *L'Enfant sauvage*.

11 September [1971]

My dear Nestor,

The screening yesterday evening went off well. Georges Delerue adores the film, he's starting to write the music. There was also the scriptwriter, Jean Gruault, who was very moved, Gérard Lebovici, Serge Rousseau, Christine Brierre, Levert,[7] Cambourakis, etc., all of them very pleased as was Jean-Pierre Léaud. The two or three pick-ups I need will be done with Lafaye, as Rivière is on a shoot.

1 – Spanish-born cinematographer, born in 1930. He worked on nine of Truffaut's films.

2 – Though born in Barcelona, Almendros spent his youth in Cuba.

3 – Barbet Schroeder, French producer and director, born in 1941: (as director) *More*, *General Idi Amin Dada*, *Maîtresse*, *Barfly*, etc. Almendros was filming Schroeder's *La Vallée* in New Guinea.

4 – For *L'Amour l'après-midi*.
5 – The film in question, *Une belle fille comme moi*, would finally be photographed by Pierre-William Glenn.
6 – As with *Une belle fille comme moi*, Pierre-William Glenn would be the director of photography of *La Nuit américaine*.
7 – René Levert, the film's sound engineer. He worked on eight films by Truffaut.

To Jean-Loup Dabadie

Sunday [1971]

My dear Jean-Loup,

My daughters are watching Jerry Lewis on TV, I'll have some peace and quiet for a while. I didn't telephone you, mainly because I like the idea of your work progressing without me.

My return was disturbed by the theft of one of my suitcases: my car in the street with the hood up, locked for the night, its rear window sliced out with a razor; so I lost about twenty books (some Sartres, some books on the cinema) – the documentation on my Victorine script – the Marcel Aymé (*La Vouivre*) and some scripts, a manuscript on Chekhov, a few tapes, nothing irreparable or irreplaceable but all bloody inconvenient.

You aren't missing anything by being away from Paris. I've returned to my suite at the George V (for 8 months now I've been subscribing to Pierre Doris's[1] principle: 'Better to weep in a Jaguar than in the Métro').

Don't feel obliged to see *Le Sauveur*[2] in spite of the girl; it's somehow both pretentious and unambitious. I got more pleasure out of *Smig, Smag, Smog*,[3] which is as manipulative as can be but cunning and lively.

My problems with Columbia are being smoothed out; I haven't seen Bernadette;[4] I watch little Jade, I don't say a word to her; since I do think she may be a bit too young; [. . .] I'm considering, now sit down before you continue reading, I'm considering playing the role myself;[5] I have never spoken to you about such an idea even though it occurred to me when Bernadette was staying at our villa; that said, I haven't entirely made up my mind yet, since either a more obvious idea might come to me or else, at a certain moment, I might realize that the narrative contains scenes that would be difficult to play for the non-actor I am. I don't want to make X—s[6] mistake, but I have to admit that playing the austere Dr Itard gave me a great deal of pleasure and at the same time the impression that I was completely dominating the shoot; I see in this idea the same opportunity to call the shots by giving myself the role of an investigator; I know that I would be impassive and that a contrast would therefore be set up between Bernadette and myself, the danger being of a too developed sense of realism or rather of reality; in any event, I would value your opinion if you felt free enough to give it to me, and no decision will be taken before the script is finished.

I'm now beginning the dubbing of *Les Anglaises*, so I won't be able to reread the book for another week; there was a screening of *Les Anglaises* with Gérard Lebovici, Serge Rousseau,[7] Aurel, Georges Delerue and Jean-Pierre Léaud, it seemed to make a favourable impression and, since then, there have been a few little improvements to the editing. Thank you again for your comments, they were very helpful.

Jeanne is in great form, she has really taken to office life – editing the current affairs programme. I think that Philippe[8] is getting a move on at last; it seems to me that the possibility of the young Rumanian from *Bof*[9] represents a real advance on the various Brunos: Pradal, Garcin, etc. (I would remind you that, in *Bof*, the boy was dubbed into French, so his accent was lacking. But he had all the requisite youth, virility and innocence.) I saw the photo of the young (Argentinian) golf champion, not bad either; Jeanne has managed to track him down, he lives in Rome.

In the end I didn't write to Philippe, but I'll speak to him about *La Poudre*[10] when I see him. Resnais and Florence gave me a copy of *Portnoy's Complaint*[11] which had been in their car for ages, I accepted it thinking of you, so it's rather like an indirect gift.

I can hear my daughters laughing. I'm therefore going to leave you now and have a look at Jerry. Until later.

6.30 = Jerry is finished, replaced by Luis Mariano in *La Belle de Cadix* (. . .). At about 7 o'clock I intend to watch Maurice Pialat's[12] serial, *La Maison des bois*, which it seems is remarkable.

Jeanne has asked me to accompany her on Wednesday to Reggiani's[13] première, she has time enough to change her mind from now until then, I'll tell you all about it.

I'm very happy to know both of you, I hope I'll soon be able to let you see me as I used to be, rather more cheerful; work well but not too hard, take advantage of the end of the holiday, as far as our film is concerned, there's no rush; let me repeat that I feel very confident and that the beginning of our collaboration confirms in my mind that you are a true professional sensitive to the really important matters, etc. When we speak about the cinema, we are speaking about the same thing.

As I recall, you return in about 8 or 10 days' time; you can write to me at the office, 5, rue Robert-Estienne, Paris (8), but don't ring me since I'll be at Billancourt all day (or else at the Hôtel George V: 225.35.30, early in the morning but too early for you and in the evening maybe, maybe not).

Regards to both of you (I suppose that Clémentine[14] is no longer there), hoping to see you soon,

françois

1 – French comedian.
2 – By Michel Mardore.
3 – Correctly, *Smic, Smac, Smoc*, by Claude Lelouch.
4 – Truffaut had not yet made up his mind to cast Bernadette Lafont in *Une belle fille comme moi* (*A Gorgeous Bird Like Me*).
5 – The role of the sociologist in *Une belle fille comme moi* was finally given to André Dussolier.
6 – A director who acts in his own films.
7 – See note 1. p.448.
8 – De Broca.
9 – By Claude Faraldo.
10 – *La Poudre d'escampette.*
11 – By Philip Roth.
12 – French director, born in 1925: *L'Enfance nue, La Gueule ouverte, Loulou, A nos amours, Sous le soleil de Satan*, etc.
13 – Serge Reggiani, French singer and actor, born in 1922.
14 – Dabadie's child by his first wife.

To Eric Rohmer

[1971]

I know that you no longer care to write about films, but this time I must insist, and here is why. As you know, Janine Bazin no longer does her TV programme, with all the attendant financial hardships . . .

I've suggested to Éditions du Cerf that they publish a collection of Bazin's pieces on Chaplin, with an emphasis on the 'revivals'; they have agreed in principle but only if someone well-known writes a piece on *A Countess From Hong-Kong*.[1] I know how much you adore the film, I can organize a screening if you wish to see it again. If you say yes, the book will go ahead, and a good thing too, so let me have your answer.

yours,
françois

1 – By Chaplin (1967).

1972

To Jean-Loup Dabadie

4 February 1972, Friday evening

My dear Jean-Loup,

Here are my notes and suggestions concerning the song; see what you can do if you have: a) the time, b) the patience, c) the inspiration. I would like the 'bitch' aspect to be brought out more strongly; I know that your angle is psychologically realistic (the girl who's been around and now sings something sentimental), but I think the public would be disappointed.

Sam's[1] song was very good and we're guaranteed a laugh with every subtitle, the same thing ought to happen when the American public reads the subtitles of Camille's[2] song.

We'll speak on the phone; I'm very happy with just a week to go before I take the plunge, Denner[3] did a magnificent reading for me and I trust every member of the crew; thanks again for everything.

françois

NOTE TO JEAN-LOUP DABADIE

concerning the song for *Une belle fille comme moi*

I'm going to speak with all the self-confidence of someone who doesn't know what he's talking about, but since you encouraged me to criticize the song, that's exactly what I'm going to do.

I've already explained to Jacques Datin that, without wanting it to parody a contemporary beat, I was afraid that the melody I heard gave a rather dated impression (perhaps I was influenced by Jean-Loup's singing style, which is very 'Johnnie Hess').

Now for the lyrics: I realize there's no question of relating the plot in a song, but, all the same, it does seem to me that it ought to describe or complement the character of Camille, who has a strong personality: a shameless bitch . . . disingenuous . . . totally vulgar and cynical . . . all of that would be brought out by lyrics that were less trite and more *risqué*.

The song will be heard after 1 hour 15 minutes of running time, and if

Bernadette resembles a little girl doing her party piece, the public will feel let down. The character has got to remain strong.

For the first verse, I suggest you cut out all the negative expressions: 'Not in forest deep, nor on mountain steep, not even in Kam—chatka' and substitute some positive elements, i.e. Camille's own description of herself.*

By contrast, I'm very pleased with the bridge passage: 'I lost my watch, etc.' even if it doesn't correspond exactly to what I described.

These comments are not dictated by any box-office considerations of what makes a hit record or by the way a Nicoletta is launched . . . or Ewa or anyone else, but I do believe nevertheless that if the song becomes better for the film (and in the film), it will also be better from the point of view of radio coverage.

I fully realize that, in its present form, it can easily be sung by Bernadette, but I don't see any objection to the composer and lyricist taking more of a risk from that point of view.

When Bernadette–Camille arrives on stage for her song, she should either take our breath away or make us laugh, but not leave us cold.

François Truffaut

P.S. Would there be anything to stop you attempting a version in slang, in the style of Pierre Perret[4] but for a woman?

*Something like 'I'm pretty and full of wiles, as my lips are ripe with smiles, etc.', but obviously less feeble . . .

1 – The character played by Guy Marchand in *Une belle fille comme moi.*

2 – The character played by Bernadette Lafont.

2 – Charles Denner, who plays a rat-catcher in the film.

4 – French popular singer.

To Odette Ferry

6 February 1972

Dear Friend,

Here, a little late, but my new shoot starts tomorrow, is a letter for Hitch and a copy of my request for a rectification from Mr Samuels, the anti-Hitchcockian. I am quite taken aback by the reaction of our great friend;[1] even knowing how vulnerable he was, I believed him to be totally indifferent to the printed word, but it isn't so. His reaction is perhaps also that of a friend who feels he has been betrayed; which obviously touches me a great

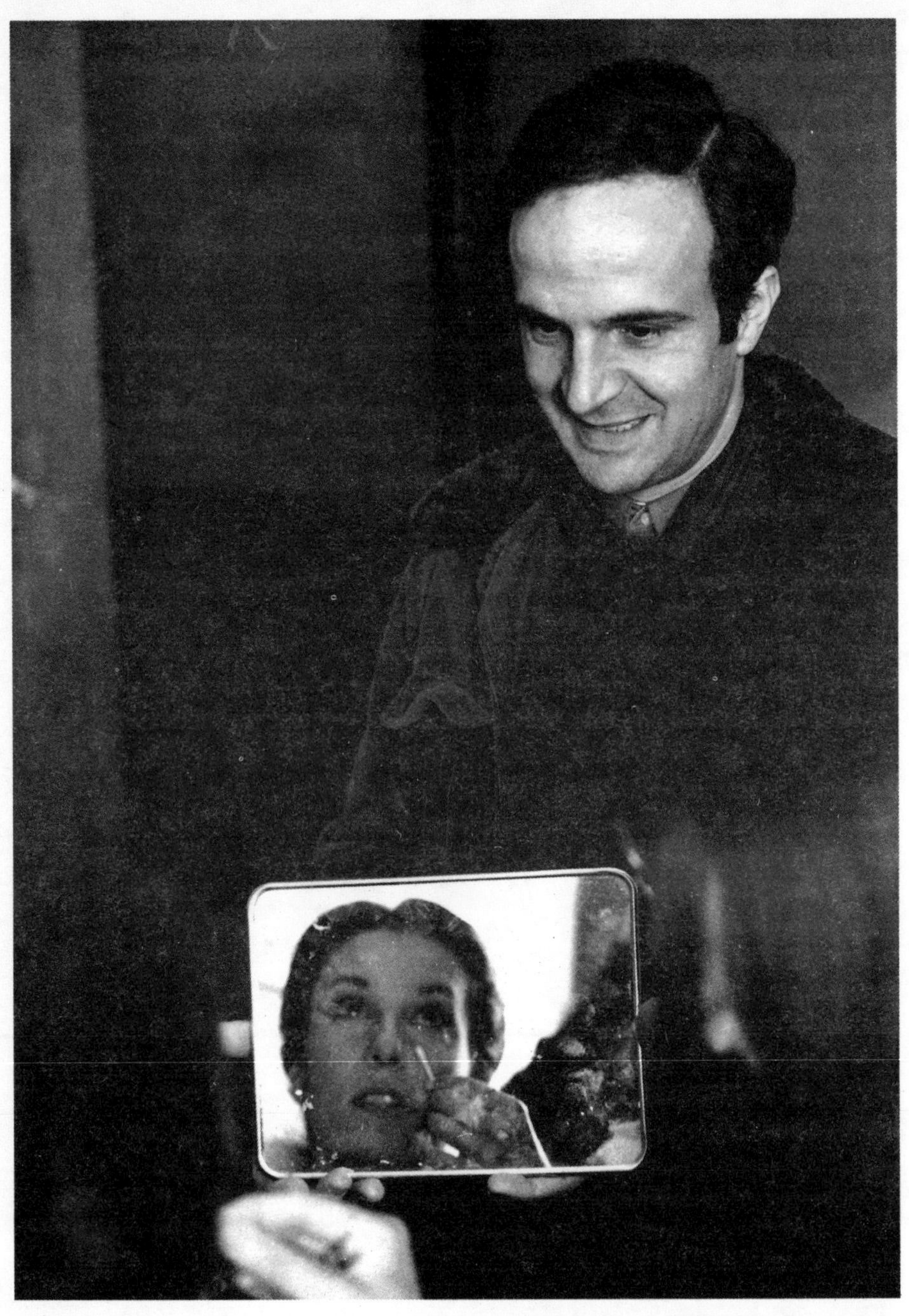

Truffaut reunited with Bernadette Lafont, the heroine of *Les Mistons*, for *Une belle fille comme moi*.

deal. I hope that my letter won't be hard to translate and that it will succeed in convincing him, I hope, too, that Mr Samuels will play fair.

Yours sincerely,
françois

P.S. I return to Paris on 15 April.

1 – Truffaut had been interviewed by an American journalist, Charles Thomas Samuels, who had falsely attributed to him a slighting comment on Hitchcock. The latter had taken offence.

To Helen Scott

Sunday 13 February 72

My Scottie,

I am thinking of you on the eve of this new shoot.[1]

I regret having spoilt our last evening together, on Saturday, by once or twice needlessly losing my temper, I was doubtless a bit nervous, I no longer am in the least thanks to the peaceful week I spent here before starting . . . tomorrow.

I realize how disgustingly I behaved to you since, whenever you turned away from me, I forced you to look at a close-up of Marthe Keller[2] on the other side of the room! Speaking of close-ups, I'm going to enjoy gazing at my own mug on TV tonight.[3]

I have the impression that Labarthe intends to cut what I said on the programme about Mike Nichols,[4] and also the shot I chose of Candice Bergen[5] laughing, I'm a little annoyed about it, but there's nothing I can do.

Let's you and me take advantage of these two and a half months of enforced separation by reverting to our Franco-American, by which I mean epistolary, relationship, with you praising *french movies*[6] and me *Hollywood pictures*;[6] in actual fact, I haven't been to the cinema, I'd rather smoke a cigar in front of the television set every evening. Thanks to the large apartment I've rented right in the centre of town,[7] I've never been so well organized on a shoot. Marie[8] is with me, which means I can invite the actors to dinner here as they arrive; we can rehearse the scenes in advance, release the tension, etc.

Bernadette is in great form and I'm very pleased with the casting. Tell me what's happening in Paris, tell me about Berri, the Club Lelouch,[9] Pialat, Liliane Siegel's sister and Michèle De Broca,[10] tell me all about your evenings and outings. Try and see something of Mado, I swear that she loves you for yourself alone and not for your dollars. I've asked Christine Brierre to send you the press-book of *Une b. f. comme moi* because there's a piece by me in it, with certain pretensions to humour, written in the hope of taking your mind off your allergies.

I've had an enlargement made of that pretty snapshot of you, I'll be sending you a print later, I look at you every evening.

My dear Scottie, the beginning of each year is our anniversary, twelve years ago you were waiting for me, furiously waving your arms, behind the glass enclosure of N.Y. airport, I kiss you because I love you,

your frenchie,
françois

1 – Of *Une belle fille comme moi.*
2 – Swiss actress, born in 1945: *Marathon Man*, *Bobby Deerfield*, *Fedora*, etc.
3 – On a programme about Truffaut by André S. Labarthe and Janine Bazin.
4 – American director, born in 1931: *Who's Afraid of Virginia Woolf?*, *The Graduate*, *Catch-22*, *Carnal Knowledge*, *Silkwood*, *Working Girl*, etc.
5 – American actress, born in 1946: she was one of the stars of Nichols's *Carnal Knowledge*, which had just opened in Paris.
6 – In English in the original letter.
7 – Béziers.
8 – Truffaut's housekeeper for many years, she died after the shoot of *La Nuit américaine.*
9 – Claude Lelouch's Club 13 in Paris, a lavishly appointed screening-room and meeting-place for film-makers.
10 – French producer, born in 1927.

To a petitioner

Béziers, 13 March 1972

Dear Madame,

Since you charmingly insist that I add my signature to the list of those who have signed the Manifesto for Survival, I find myself obliged, other than by silent abstention, to inform you of my disagreement with its text which is, in my opinion, completely woolly, vague and insipid and bristling with too many capital letters.

As for the list of signatories, with all those Presidents and former Ministers, I think it sufficiently eclectic and prestigious not to have need of my name.

I would certainly have shown greater interest in the Association of Friends of Edith Piaf with which, I gather, you were formerly involved.

I am sorry to have to disappoint you, but I beg you to accept the best wishes of

François Truffaut

To Odette Ferry *Béziers, 13 March 1972*

My dear friend,

I am forwarding to you the reply that I received from Charles Thomas Samuels, in reference to the misunderstanding over Hitchcock. I rely on you to have him[1] sent a copy of this letter which I hope will reassure him.

Naturally, Mr Samuels is playing with words when he says that the sentence-cum-question was directly transcribed from the tape; in my opinion, Mr Samuels lumped together one of his questions and one of my answers, thereby obtaining a statement more closely corresponding to his own ideas on the subject.

You might also tell Hitchcock, even though he generally takes little interest in his earlier work, that two friends and I have made a deal with Rank for the French distribution rights to *The Lady Vanishes* and *The 39 Steps*. Naturally, it will be extremely embarrassing for me if I suddenly become very rich by distributing these two Hitchcock films, but, if such turns out to be the case, I'll use the money to promote Hitchcockian studies!

As you know, I am most impatient to see *Frenzy* and I hope you'll be able to screen it for me when I return to Paris around 15 April.

Cordially yours,
françois

1 – Hitchcock.

To Nestor Almendros *Paris, 10 May 72*

My dear Nestor,

This last shoot has exhausted me and I leave Paris for a fortnight's rest in Normandy.

Notwithstanding my admiration and affection for you, I'm going to make my next film[1] with the same camera crew (Glenn,[2] Bal,[3] Khripounoff[4]) in addition to a couple of others, since we're going to shoot with 3 and sometimes 4 cameras. I had a lot of difficulty getting this film financed – because of the subject – so I'm going to simplify it in order to shoot it in 6 weeks with the enlarged crew; the work is not the same as that which we did together on *L'Enfant* or *Les Anglaises*, it's a different type of project.

I hope you understand my reasons and do not doubt my wish to work with you again; if *L'Enfant sauvage* and *Les 2 Anglaises* are, of all my films, the two most visually beautiful, it's thanks to you, something I haven't forgotten.

I'd like very much for us to have lunch together at the beginning of June if you're in Paris and, in the hope that our friendship is still intact, I sign myself

yours sincerely,
François Truffaut

1 – *La Nuit américaine.*
2 – Pierre-William Glenn, French cinematographer and director, born in 1943. He has worked with Rivette, Truffaut, Costa-Gavras, Tavernier, Losey, George Roy Hill, Pialat, etc.
3 – Walter Bal, cameraman.
4 – Anne-Claire Khripounoff was replaced on the film by D. Chapuis and J.-F. Gondre.

To Jean-Pierre Aumont[1] *from Paris, 16 June 72*

My dear Jean-Pierre,

Forgive me for jumping the gun as regards our friendship and dropping the 'dear Monsieur' before the 1st day of shooting.

I was enchanted to read your *Souvenirs provisoires*,[2] I noted several things that you might relate in the film; the 'Duse-and-a-half'[3] for example; in the train, my fellow passengers saw me screaming with laughter as I read the story of Marcel L'Herbier[4] and the beef hash . . . wonderful![5] If I add, finally, that Maria Montez[6] was one of the idols of my film-going youth, you will understand the emotion I felt throughout the last 100 pages; it's a fine book, superbly written. I have ordered ten copies so that my friends can read it and also some of those participating in the film.

So everything is going well, Warners has signed; the only risk would be a repeat of what happened to *La Condition humaine*[7] at M.G.M., which is unlikely given the modesty of the budget, the speed with which we'll be filming, etc. The French title: *La Nuit américaine*. The English title: *Day for Night*. The women: Jackie Bisset, Valentina Cortese, Dani, Alexandra Stewart. The men: J.-P. Aumont, Jean-Pierre Léaud, Mario Tisu (for the role of the producer . . . probably),[8] François Truffaut(!).[9] The filming begins: 23 September[10] at the Victorine.[11] (For publicity purposes, the names will be listed as indicated in my letter; I hope that will be satisfactory.)

The film will be announced in *Le Figaro* and by various agencies during the month, you can put it about as soon as you like. I very much enjoyed meeting Valentina Cortese,[12] a real character, extremely feminine and very funny. So there you have it, I'm looking forward to making this film, I would even say it's particularly special to me, but I don't want the shooting to be a solemn affair, because Renoir is right: 'One should have a good time when making a film.' I am very happy at the idea that we are going to work together, happy and confident; between two songs by Jacques Brel drop me a line, it would give me pleasure as I complete the sound-mixing on *Une belle fille comme moi . . .*

very cordially yours
François Truffaut

1 – French actor, born in 1911: *Jean de la Lune*, *Lac aux dames*, *Maria Chapdelaine*, *Drôle de drame*, *Hôtel du Nord*, etc.
2 – Aumont's memoirs, published in 1957.
3 – An untranslatable anecdote which puns on *Duse* (the great Italian actress Eleonora Duse) and *douze* (meaning 'twelve').
4 – See note 1, p. 422.
5 – Unfortunately, Aumont himself did not consider the story wonderful and even quarrelled with Truffaut over whether he should tell it in the film. In the end it was not used.
6 – Spanish-born actress of American and European films (1918–51): *That Night in Rio*, *Arabian Nights*, *Ali Baba and the Forty Thieves*, *Cobra Woman*, *Tangier*, *The Exile*, etc. She was Aumont's second wife.
7 – The film, based on André Malraux's novel, had been cancelled.
8 – The role of the producer was played, in fact, by Jean Champion.
9 – As Ferrand, the director.
10 – In fact 25 September.
11 – The studio at Saint-Laurent-du-Var.
12 – Italian-born actress, born in 1924: *Thieves' Highway*, *The Secret People*, *The Barefoot Contessa*, *Le Amiche*, *Juliet of the Spirits*, *The Legend of Lylah Clare*, etc.

To Jean Gruault

26 June 1972

My dear Jean,

I agree with you 100% about F—, he's a painful, paranoid bore; I only brought up your name because I was sick and tired of hearing him say, 'There aren't any good screenwriters in France . . .', etc.

I'm happier to know that you're at work on *Julien et Marguerite*; I have completely finished *Une belle fille comme moi* and I'm off to spend 8 or 10 nights in the Midi then return for the colour-grading; I don't know if I'll be back for 14 July, but Berbert will give you 1 or 2 Xeroxed copies of (the abridged version of) *Adèle*.

I shoot *La Nuit américaine* from 23 September to 15 November. Next year, 1973, I'll shoot nothing at all, but I'll be working actually with you to establish the definitive scripts of *Adèle* and *Julien et Marguerite*. Have a good rest, my regards to the 4 Gruaults, hoping to see you soon,

love,
françois

P.S. *Les 2 Anglaises*:
*huge success in Stockholm and Helsinki (semi-short version, 2 hours).

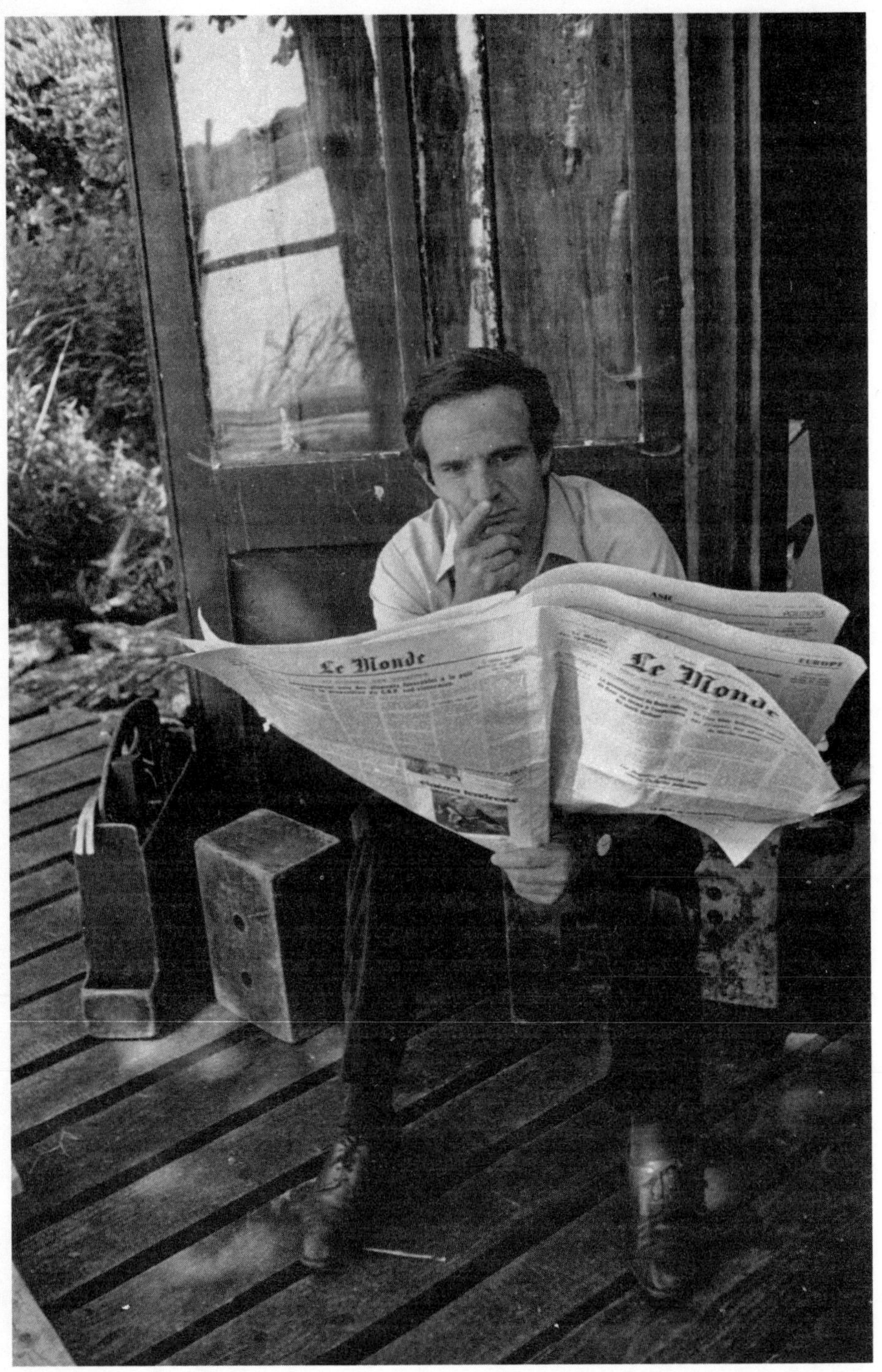
Le Monde
Le Monde

*Tokyo release in August, the distributor enthusiastic and confident (the short, so-called Anglo-American version: 1 hour 45). Title: *Sentimental Education*.
*sold in America to Janus Films (distributor of *400 Coups*, *Jules et Jim*, *Pianiste* and *Peau douce*). September or October release.

To the producers of *Les Dossiers de l'écran*[1]

Paris, 27 June 1972

Messieurs,

Scheduled on three separate occasions during the last year and cancelled twice, my film *Fahrenheit 451* is finally to be the subject of *Les Dossiers de l'écran* on Wednesday 5 July.

You invited me to participate in the debate which is to follow the screening, and I accepted in the hope that the discussion would bear on the film's subject, which is to say, the banning or burning of books and the whole idea of free speech.

Since I am only the director of *Fahrenheit 451*, which was an English production, it is not within my power to prevent you from screening the film, but you will understand that I no longer wish to take part in the programme. After reading the press release in which you justify the cancellation, last Sunday, of Janine Bazin and André Labarthe's programme *Vive le cinéma*, introduced by Maître Kiejman,[2] I don't even feel like asking, on live television, why the publication of books as interesting as *Le Dossier noir de la police* (Éditions du Seuil) and *L'Affaire du bazooka* (Éditions de la Table Ronde) have never been mentioned in any literary programme. I believe, however, that deliberately passing books over in silence is equivalent to burning them; I am prepared to bet that the word 'censorship' will not even be pronounced during the debate which follows the screening of *Fahrenheit* and that the real questions will be completely glossed over, so obvious is it that French television is still being run by pyromaniac firemen.

Since a replacement will have to be found for me in this debate, allow me to suggest that you invite Maître Kiejman in my place, as he is an expert in both books and films, banned or not.

As for myself, I wish to have no further contact with the Dossiers Noirs of television.

Yours . . . (expletive deleted by self-censorship),
François Truffaut

1 – A French television programme in which the screening of a feature film is followed by a debate on the particular issue which it raises.

2 – French barrister, born in 1932. He has specialized in cases involving the arts and the media.

To Robert Florey[1]

Paris, 25 August 1972

Dear Monsieur,

I would like to offer you my very sincere thanks for having sent me the article from the *Los Angeles Times* which otherwise would certainly have escaped my notice. By coincidence, I am at present reading your book *Hollywood année zéro*, which I find absolutely fascinating. I suppose you correspond regularly with Maurice Bessy, but should you ever need any French books for your documentation or anything else for that matter, I remain at your disposal.

Very sincerely yours,
François Truffaut

1 – French director and film historian (1900–79). He emigrated to the United States in 1921, where he made *The Cocoanuts*, *Murders in the Rue Morgue*, *The Desert Song*, *The Beast with Five Fingers*, etc., and was associate director on Chaplin's *Monsieur Verdoux* in 1947. He wrote several film-historical studies of early Hollywood.

1973

To Andrzej Wajda[1] *Paris, 8 February 1973*

My dear friend,

I recall with great pleasure our collaboration on *L'Amour à vingt ans* and our meeting in Paris, but it is really impossible for me to participate in the film on Chopin, as I have decided to keep my distance for as long as possible from French television, in any case for as long as it adopts policies so detrimental to French cinema. It is not your problem, as I imagine and hope that the situation is better in Poland, but for the moment I cannot possibly change my attitude.

That said, I am certain that Monsieur Barillé[2] can easily find someone to replace me, since, from Jacques Demy to Claude Chabrol, not to mention Louis Malle, Agnès Varda and Michel Deville, there should be no difficulty persuading a good film-maker to direct one of the episodes.

In any event, I hope that the coming year will provide us with an opportunity to get together, whether in Paris or in Warsaw.

Please accept my very warmest regards,

François Truffaut

1 – Polish director, born in 1926: *Kanal*, *Ashes and Diamonds*, *Man of Marble*, *Man of Iron*, *Danton*, etc.
2 – French television producer.

To Gilles Jacob *Paris, 16 February 1973*

My dear Gilles,

I prefer to send you this little note rather than ring you up, as I was told that your line was permanently engaged with colleagues of mine threatening to kill you, as well as your wife and children.[1]

Actually, I'm trying to locate an interview (of me by you), concerning the events of May 68 and the closure of the Cannes Festival, that appeared in a magazine, but I no longer know which. I hope you'll be able to assist me.

Hoping to see you very soon,

françois

1 – 'A humorous allusion by Truffaut to an estrangement between Claude Berri and myself following a review in *L'Express* that he had not appreciated. When he got over his fit of ill-temper, we became good friends again.' (Note by Gilles Jacob)

To Jean Gruault

April 73

My dear Jean,

I hope you will sit down before reading the copy of the letter that I have to send to Miss Guille; you are to blame for all of this; if you had succumbed to her advances, she would have been paid in kind and would have proved less grasping. To think of all that work – yours especially – for nothing. But I haven't had my last word: six months after the bitch's death, I'll be setting up the first shot of *L'Histoire d'Adèle*,

your friend,
françois

To Frances Guille[1]

from Paris, 10 April 1973

Miss Guille,

The sum of two hundred thousand francs (twenty million in old francs) which you have seen fit to demand as a future co-scenarist of *L'Histoire d'Adèle* (in addition to the thirty thousand new francs for the rights to your biography) is so disproportionate that it seems to me in defiance of all logic, convention and common sense.

We are therefore, Jean Gruault and I, shelving the project and regret it all the more bitterly as we have never encountered such a situation in our fifteen years in the cinema.

By the same post, I am obliged to inform Monsieur Jean Hugo of this fiasco, for which I hold you entirely responsible.

Let me express again, Miss Guille, my profound disappointment,

François Truffaut

1 – See note 4, letter dated [1971], p. 360.

To Jean-Pierre Aumont *11 April 73*

My dear Jean-Pierre,

I have just learned that you'll be away until the 26th and I didn't manage to call you back last week. In any event, I hope to show you the film,[1] our film, as soon as you return. The editing was done with care and sensitivity, the music is good, my impression is that I have left nothing undone. I know that the film makes an impact on people in the profession – a strong impact – the question-mark is how the public will react.

Since we finished shooting, you may be thinking that I have neglected or forgotten you, nothing of the kind: I watched you nearly every day on the editing table and the projection screen; very much more so than during the shoot when everything always happens so quickly, I discovered and analysed you, in slow motion, in reverse, at normal speed; as a result, I'm delighted at having obtained you for the role of Alexandre; you have the most beautiful male voice in the film, you are perfect in every scene (the best being the one in the car), your human qualities are evident and they make the role. All in all, the film rings true and is well acted. That, my dear Jean-Pierre, is what I wished to tell you today, call me as soon as you return,

love to Marisa[2] and you,

françois

1 – *La Nuit américaine.*

2 – Aumont's wife, the actress Marisa Pavan, born in 1932.

To Jean Hugo *12 April 1973*

Dear Monsieur,

I feel very guilty at not having kept in touch after you gave me such a warm welcome at Lunel, but I was immediately taken up with a particularly difficult film, *La Nuit américaine*, which I have only just completed.

I was very happy to have met Maître Trumeau,[1] even if the occasion, unfortunately, was a lawyers' meeting which ended with Miss Guille being so difficult and unreasonable that I have had to abandon the project of a film on the story of Adèle. The enclosed photocopy will show you what I mean. Naturally, in my heart of hearts, I continue to hope that, however long I may have to wait, I will be able to mend the broken or entangled threads.

I would like you to know that I am very grateful that you were, for your part, so well-disposed and responsive to our project. There was no disagree-

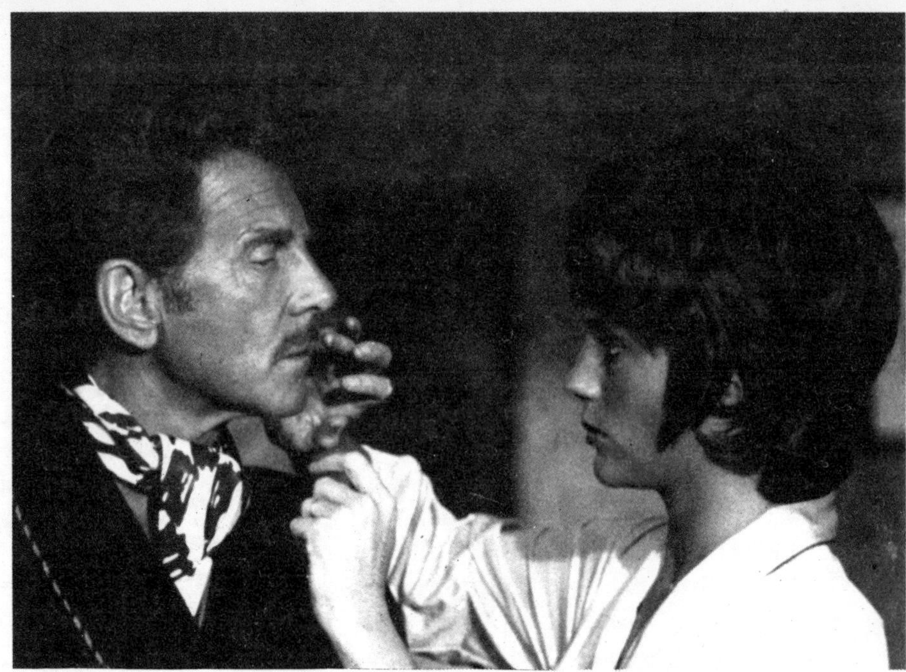

Jean-Pierre Aumont and Jacqueline Bisset in *La Nuit américaine.*

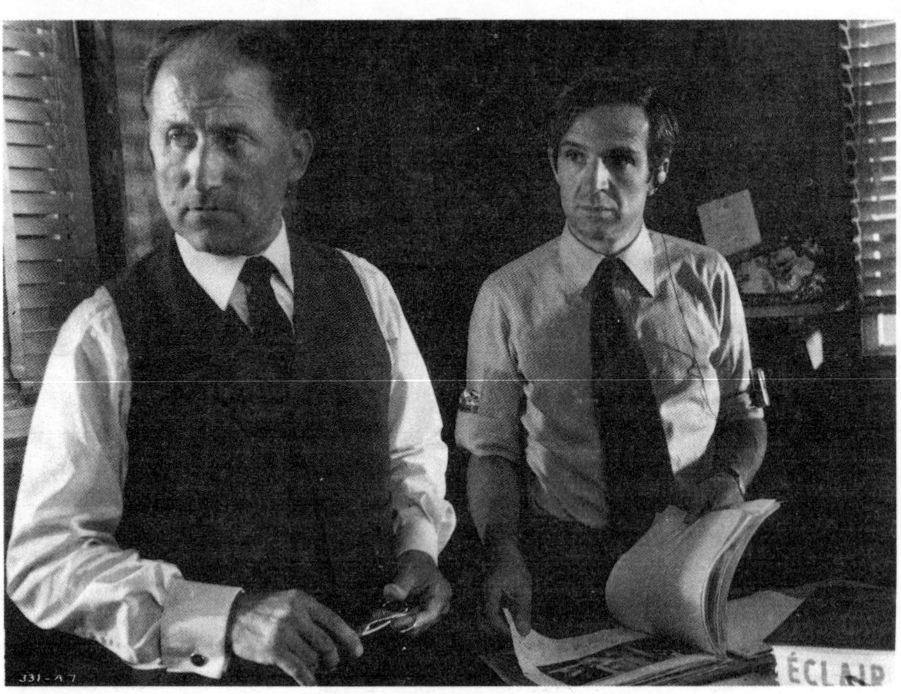

The producer and his director (Jean Champion and François Truffaut in the cast of *La Nuit américaine*).

ment between Maître Trumeau and ourselves, it was only Miss Guille who put an American spoke in our French wheel (I ought rather to say a Hollywood spoke!).

Please convey my kindest regards to Madame Hugo and your children and believe that I remain

Most respectfully yours,
François Truffaut

1 – Hugo's lawyer.

To an actor

Paris, 10 May 1973

My dear X—,

Before the release of *La Nuit américaine*, on which you worked, I have to tell you that, in the final cut, I was obliged to sacrifice your dialogue scene, when you tell me the story of the woman on the bench who commits suicide. The film was much too long and I had to bring it down to two hours.

That said, you are present throughout the film, in the numerous scenes of the shoot that I have kept, and with your various appearances you have created a whimsical character who stands out well and whom I consider very successful.

I wanted to forewarn you so that you wouldn't be too disappointed if you were to come and see the film at the Cannes Festival or else when it opens.

With my very best wishes, I remain

Yours sincerely,
François Truffaut

Jean-Luc Godard[1] to François Truffaut

[May 1973]

Yesterday I saw *La Nuit américaine*. Probably no one else will call you a liar, so I will. It's no more an insult than 'fascist', it's a criticism, and it's the absence of criticism that I complain of in the films of Chabrol, Ferreri,[2] Verneuil, Delannoy,[3] Renoir, etc. You say: films are trains that pass in the night, but who takes the train, in what class, and who is driving it with an 'informer' from the management standing at his side? Directors like those I mention make film-trains as well. And if you aren't referring to the Trans-Europ, then maybe it's a local train or else the one from Munich to Dachau, whose station naturally we aren't shown in Lelouch's film-train. Liar, because the shot of you and Jacqueline Bisset the other evening at Chez Francis[4] is not in your film, and one can't help wondering why the director is the only one who doesn't screw in *La Nuit américaine*. At the moment I'm filming something that will be called *Un simple film*, it will show in a simplistic manner (in your manner, in Verneuil's and Chabrol's, etc.) those who also make films, and just how these 'whos' make them. How your trainee continuity-girl numbers each shot, how the guy from Éclair[5] carries his equipment, how the old man from Publidécor paints Maria Schneider's backside in *Last Tango*, how Rassam's switchboard operator telephones and how Malle's accountant balances the books, and in each case we'll be comparing sound with image, the sound of the boom with the sound of Deneuve that it records, Léaud's number on the sequence of images with the social security number of the unpaid trainee, the sex life of the old guy from Publidécor with that of Brando, the accountant's own day-to-day budget with the budget of *La Grosse Bouffe*,[6] etc. Because of the problems of Malle and Rassam who produce expensive movies (like you), the money that was reserved for me has been swallowed up by the Ferreri (that's what I mean, no one prevents you from taking the train, but you prevent others) and I'm stuck. The film costs about 20 million and is produced by Anouchka and TVAB Films[7] (the company owned by Gorin[8] and me). Could you enter into co-production with us for 10 million? for 5 million? Considering *La Nuit américaine*, you ought to help me, so that the public doesn't get the idea we all make films like you. You aren't a liar, like Pompidou, like me, you speak your own truth. In exchange, if you like, I can sign over my rights to *La Chinoise*, *Le Gai Savoir* and *Masculin-Féminin*.

If you want to talk it over, fine,

Jean-Luc

1 – French director, born in 1930.
2 – Marco Ferreri, Italian director, born in 1928: *El Cochecito*, *L'Ape Regina*, *La Donna Scimmia*, *Dillinger è morto*, *Liza*, *Touchez pas la femme blanche*, *La Dernière Femme*, etc.
3 – Jean Delannoy, French director, very much of the old school, born in 1908.
4 – A Parisian restaurant.
5 – A film laboratory.
6 – Marco Ferreri's *La Grande Bouffe*.
7 – 'Tout va bien Films', named after Godard's film.
8 – Jean-Pierre Gorin, Godard's political mentor within the Groupe Dziga-Vertov and the co-director of *Tout va bien*.

To Jean-Luc Godard *[May–June 1973]*

Jean-Luc. So you won't be obliged to read this unpleasant letter right to the end, I'm starting with the essential point: I will not co-produce your film.

Secondly, I'm sending back to you the letter you wrote to Jean-Pierre Léaud: I read it and I think it's obnoxious. And because of that letter I feel the time has come to tell you, at length, that in my opinion you've been acting like a shit.

As regards Jean-Pierre, who's been so badly treated since the business with Marie and more recently in his work, I think it's obnoxious of you to kick him when he's down, obnoxious to extort money by intimidation from someone who is fifteen years younger than you are and whom you used to pay less than a million when he was the lead in films that were earning you thirty times as much.

Yes, Jean-Pierre has changed since *Les 400 Coups*, but I can tell you that it was in *Masculin–Féminin* that I noticed for the first time how he could be filled with anxiety rather than pleasure at the notion of finding himself in front of a camera. The film was good and he was good in the film, but that first scene, in the café, was a painful experience for anyone looking at him with affection and not with an entomologist's eye.

I never expressed the slightest reservation about you to Jean-Pierre, who admired you so much, but I know that you were bad-mouthing me behind my back, in the way that a guy might say to a kid, 'And your father, is he still pissed out of his mind?'

Jean-Pierre is not the only one to have changed in 14 years and if *A bout de souffle* and *Tout va bien* were to be screened one after the other, we'd all be dismayed and saddened to see how cynical and unadventurous the latter is by comparison.

I don't give a shit what you think of *La Nuit américaine*, what I find deplorable on your part is the fact that, even now, you continue to go and see such films, films whose subject-matter you know in advance will not correspond to either your conception of the cinema or your conception of life. Would Jean-Édern Hallier[1] write to Daninos[2] to take issue with him on his latest book?

You've changed your way of life, your way of thinking, yet, even so, you continue to waste hour after hour ruining your eyesight at the cinema. Why? In the hope of finding something that will fuel your contempt for the rest of us, that will reinforce all your new prejudices?

Now it's my turn to call you a liar. At the beginning of *Tout va bien* there is this phrase: 'To make a film one needs stars.' A lie. Everyone knows how determined you were to get J. Fonda[3] who was beginning to lose interest, when all your backers were telling you to take just anyone. You brought together those two stars of yours[4] the way Clouzot used to do: since it's their good fortune to be working with me, they ought to be content with a tenth of their normal salary, etc. Karmitz[5] and Bernard Paul[6] need stars, but not you, so it's a lie. And then we read in the newspapers: he had stars 'imposed' on him . . . Another lie, concerning your new film: you don't mention the very substantial subsidy you solicited, and obtained, from the state, and which ought to have been enough even if Ferreri, as you absurdly accuse him, spent the money that was 'reserved' for you. So, he thinks he can get away with anything, this wop who wants to take the bread out of our mouths, this immigrant worker, have him deported, via Cannes!

That's always been one of your gifts, setting yourself up as the eternal victim, like Cayatte, like Boisset,[7] like Michel Drach;[8] the victim of Pompidou, of Marcellin,[9] of the censors and the distributors with their eager little scissors, whereas in reality you've always contrived to have things work out just the way you want them to and when you want them to and above all you've always contrived to uphold your pure, incorruptible image, even if it should be to the detriment of someone as defenceless as, for example, Janine Bazin. Six months after the Kiejman business,[10] Janine had two of her programmes cancelled, an act of vengeance that was very cunningly deferred. Since Kiejman would not have contemplated talking about the cinema and politics without interviewing you, your role in this affair – and a role is what it was – consisted yet again in promoting your own subversive image, which explains the well-chosen little comment. The comment is made: either it's kept in and it's sufficiently sharp for no one to suspect you've gone soft or else it's cut out and everyone is over the moon: yes, decidedly, they say, Godard is Godard, he'll never change, etc.

Everything goes off like clockwork, the programme is cancelled and you remain on your pedestal. No one happens to notice that the comment is just another of your lies. If Pompidou is, as you claim, the 'director' of France, then it's the Communist Party and the unions that you abuse – by means (means too subtle for the 'masses') of periphrasis, antiphrasis and derision – in *Tout va bien*, a film originally intended for the widest possible public.

If I withdrew from the debate on *Fahrenheit 451*[11] at the same period, it was in an attempt to help Janine, not out of solidarity with you, which is why I didn't return your telephone call.

The fact remains that Janine was in hospital last month, she was knocked down by a car while making her last programme, she had to have an operation on her knee (she's had a limp since adolescence, etc.), so there she finds herself in hospital without any work and without any money and naturally without any word from Godard who will only step down from his pedestal to amuse Rassam every so often. And I can tell you: the more you love the masses, the more I love Jean-Pierre Léaud, Janine Bazin, Patricia Finaly[12] (and she's just out of a nursing-home and has had to pester the Cinémathèque over and over again for her six months' back salary) and Helen Scott whom you meet in an airport and cut dead, why, because she's an American or because she's a friend of mine? The behaviour of a shit. A girl from the BBC rings you up to ask if you'll say a few words on cinema and politics for a programme about me, I warn her in advance that you'll refuse, but that's not good enough for you, you hang up on her before she's even finished her sentence, the behaviour of an elitist, the behaviour of a shit, as when you agree to go to Geneva or London or Milan and you don't go, to startle people, to astonish them, like Sinatra, like Brando, you're nothing but a piece of shit on a pedestal.

For a while, following May 68, no more was heard of you or else it was all very mysterious: it seems he's working in a factory, he's formed a group, etc., and then, one Saturday, there's an announcement that you're going to speak on the radio with Monod.[13] I stay in the office to listen to it, in a sense just to know what you've been doing; your voice trembles, you seem very nervous, you declare that you're going to make a film called *La Mort de mon frère*, about a black worker who was ill and had been left to die in the basement of a TV factory and, listening to you, and despite the fact that your voice is trembling, I know: 1. that the story isn't true, or at any rate it didn't quite happen like that; 2. that you would <u>never</u> make such a film. And I say to myself: what if the poor guy has a family and his family is now going to live in the hope of the film being made? There wasn't a part for Montand in that film or Jane Fonda, but for a ¼ of an hour you gave the impression of 'doing the right thing', like Messmer[14] when he gives the vote to nineteen-year-olds. Phony. Poseur. You've always been a poseur, as when you sent a telegram to de Gaulle about his prostate, when you called Braunberger a filthy Jew over the telephone, when you said that Chauvet[15] was corrupt (because he was the last and only one to resist you), a poseur when you lump together Renoir and Verneuil as though they were the same thing, a poseur even now when you claim you're going to show the truth about the cinema, those who work in the background, who are badly paid, etc.

When you had a location, a garage or shop set up by your crew, and then you would arrive and say 'I don't have any ideas today, we won't shoot' and the crew would have to take it all back down again, did it never occur to you that the workers might feel completely useless and rejected, like the sound crew that spent a whole day in the empty studio at Pinewood waiting in vain for Brando?

Now, why am I telling you all this today instead of three, five or ten years ago?

For six years, like everyone else, I saw how you were suffering on account of (or for) Anna[16] and everything that was odious about you we forgave because of that suffering.

I knew you had seduced Liliane Dreyfus (ex-David) by telling her 'François doesn't love you any more, he's in love with Marie Dubois who's in his new film,' and I found that pitiful but touching, yes, why not, even touching! I knew you had gone to see Braunberger and said to him, 'Let me make the sketch that Rouch is supposed to shoot'[17] and I found that . . . shall we say, pathetic. I was strolling along the Champs-Élysées with you and you said to me, 'It seems *Bébert et l'Omnibus*[18] isn't doing well, serve it right' and I said 'Oh, come on now . . .'

In Rome, I quarrelled with Moravia because he suggested that I film *Le Mépris*;[19] I had gone there with Jeanne to present *Jules et Jim*, your latest film wasn't doing too well and Moravia was hoping to change horses in midstream.

It was also out of solidarity with you that I had a row with Melville who couldn't forgive you for having helped him make *Léon Morin prêtre*[20] and was looking to do you down. You, meanwhile, deliberately humiliated Jeanne and, to please Anna (after the business of *Eva*)[21] you made a ludicrous attempt to blackmail Marie-France Pisier[22] (Hossein,[23] Yugoslavia . . . over and over again . . . 'the wedding-ring'), etc. You cast Catherine Ribeiro, whom I had sent to you, in *Les Carabiniers*, and then threw yourself on her the way Chaplin throws himself on his secretary in *The Great Dictator* (it wasn't I who made the comparison) – I list all of that just to remind you not to forget anything in this film of yours that's going to be telling the truth about cinema and sex. Instead of showing X—'s arse and Anne Wiazemsky's[24] pretty hands on the window-pane, you might try it the other way around now you know that not only all men but all women are equal, including actresses. With every shot of X— in *Week-End* it was as though you were tipping a wink at your pals: this whore wants to make a film with me, take a good look at how I treat her: there are whores and there are poetic young women.

I'm telling you all of this because, as I have to admit, even though one could still detect, in certain statements you made, that selfsame posturing, now slightly tinged with bitterness, I really thought you had changed, at least that's what I thought <u>until</u> I read the letter you addressed to Jean-Pierre

Léaud. If you had sealed it, I would have given it to him without reading it and I would have regretted it, perhaps you wanted to give me the opportunity not to deliver it to him . . . ?

Today you're unassailable, everyone thinks you're unassailable, you're no longer the long-suffering swain, like everyone else you think you're better than everyone else and you know you think you're better than everyone else, you regard yourself as a repository of truth on life, politics, commitment, the cinema and love, it's all an open book to you and anyone who has a different opinion from yours is a creep, even if the opinion you hold in June is not the same one you held in April. In 1973, your prestige is intact, which is to say, when you walk into an office, everyone studies your face to see if you are in a good mood or whether it would be better to stay put in one's own little corner; on occasion you're prepared to laugh or smile; you call people *tu* now instead of *vous*, but the intimidation is still there, as well as the easy insult and the terrorism (that gift of yours for the backhanded compliment). What I mean is that I need have no worries on your account, in Paris there are still enough wealthy young men, with a chip on their shoulder because they had their first car at 18, who will be delighted to pay their dues by announcing: 'I'm the producer of Godard's next film.'

When you wrote to me at the end of 68, demanding 8 or 900 thousand francs which in fact I didn't owe you (even Dussart[25] was shocked!) and you added, 'In any case, we've nothing more to say to each other,' I took it in its absolutely literal sense: I sent you the dough and, apart from a couple of moments when we softened (you when I was unhappy in love, me when you were in hospital), I've felt nothing but contempt for you ever since – as when I saw the scene in *Vent d'est* showing how to make a Molotov cocktail and, a year later, you got cold feet the first time we were asked to distribute *La Cause du peuple* in the street . . .

The notion that all men are equal is theoretical with you, it isn't deeply felt, which is why you have never succeeded in loving anyone or in helping anyone, other than by shoving a few banknotes at them. Someone, maybe Cavanna,[26] once wrote: 'One should despise money, especially small change' and I've never forgotten how you used to get rid of centimes by slipping them down the backs of chairs in cafés. By contrast with you, I've never said a negative word about you, partly because you were being attacked stupidly and for mostly the wrong reasons, partly because I've always hated feuds between writers or painters, dubious scores being settled by means of open letters to the press, and finally because I've always felt you were both jealous and envious, even when things were going well for you – you're hyper-competitive, I'm almost not at all – and there was also on my part a certain admiration, I find it easy to admire, as you know, and a real desire to remain friends with you ever since you were upset by that remark I made to Claire Fischer about the way our relationship had changed after the army (for me) and Jamaica (for you). There are many things I don't state outright because I'm never completely sure that the contrary isn't just as true, but, if I now state outright that you are a shit, it's because, when I see Janine Bazin in hospital and read your letter to Jean-Pierre, there can no longer be any room for doubt. I'm not raving, I don't say that you are to blame for Janine being in hospital, but the fact that she is out of work, after ten years in television, is directly linked to you and you don't give a shit. Here you are, in 1973, as fond as ever of making grand gestures and spectacular announcements, as arrogant and dogmatic as ever, secure on your pedestal, indifferent to others, incapable of simply and unselfishly giving up a few hours of your time to help someone. Between your interest in the masses and your own narcissism there's no room for anything or anyone else. After all, those who called you a genius, no matter what you did, all belonged to that famous trendy Left that runs the gamut from Susan Sontag[27] to Bertolucci[28] via Richard Roud, Alain Jouffroy,[29] Bourseiller[30] and Cournot,[31] and even if you sought to appear impervious to flattery, because of them you began to ape the world's great men, de Gaulle, Malraux, Clouzot, Langlois, you fostered the myth, you accentuated that side of you that was mysterious, inaccessible and temperamental (as Scott would say), all for the slavish admiration of those around you. You need to play a role and the role needs to be a prestigious one; I've always had the impression that real militants are like cleaning women, doing a thankless, daily but necessary job. But you, you're the Ursula Andress of militancy, you make a brief appearance, just enough time for the cameras to flash, you make two or three duly startling remarks and then you disappear again, trailing clouds of self-serving mystery. Opposed to you are the small men, from Bazin to Edmond Maire[32] and taking in Sartre, Buñuel, Queneau, Mendès-France,[33] Rohmer and Audiberti, who ask others how they're getting on, who help them fill out a social security form, who reply to their letters – what they have in common is the capacity to think of others rather than themselves and above all to be more interested in what they do than in what they are and in what they appear to be.

Now, anything that can be written can also be said, which is why I conclude as you did: if you want to talk it over, fine,

françois

'If I had, like you, failed to keep the promises of my ordination, I would prefer it to have been for a woman's love rather than for what you call your intellectual development.' *Le Journal d'un curé de campagne.*

1 – French novelist and essayist, one of the founders of the theoretical journal *Tel Quel.*
2 – Pierre Daninos, French writer of humorous fiction, most famously *Les Carnets du Major Thompson.*
3 – Jane Fonda, American actress, born in 1937.
4 – The other was Yves Montand.
5 – Marin Karmitz, French director, producer and distributor, born in 1938: (as director) *Sept Jours ailleurs*, *Camarades* and *Coup pour coup.*
6 – French director (1930–80): *Le Temps de vivre*, *Dernière Sortie avant Roissy*, etc.
7 – Yves Boisset, French director, born in 1939: *Un condé*, *L'Attentat*, *Dupont Lajoie*, *Le Juge Fayard, dit 'le Shérif'*, etc.
8 – French director (1930–90): *On n'enterre pas le dimanche, Amélie ou le Temps d'aimer, Élise ou la Vraie Vie, Les Violons du bal*, etc.
9 – Raymond Marcellin, then the Minister of the Interior.
10 – The 'Kiejman business' concerned a television programme, 'Vive le cinéma', chaired by the lawyer Georges Kiejman and cancelled at the last minute because of its irreverence of tone.
11 – See the letter to the producers of *Les Dossiers de l'écran*, 27 June 1972, p. 377.
12 – Godard's secretary from 1963 to 1967.
13 – Jacques Monod, French biologist and winner of the Nobel Prize for Medicine (1910–76).
14 – Pierre Messmer, then Minister for the Armed Forces and later Prime Minister.
15 – Louis Chauvet, French film critic.
16 – Karina.
17 – For *Paris vu par* (1964).
18 – By Yves Robert (1963).
19 – *Le Mépris* was filmed by Godard in 1963.
20 – By Jean-Pierre Melville (1961).
21 – By Joseph Losey (1962).
22 – French actress, born in 1944: *L'Amour à vingt ans*, *Trans-Europ Express*, *Baisers volés*, *Cousin cousine*, *Barocco*, *Céline et Julie vont en bateau*, etc.
23 – Robert Hossein, French actor and director, born in 1927: (as director) *Les Salauds vont en enfer*, *Toi le vénin*, *Les Scélérats*, *Le Vampire de Düsseldorf*, *J'ai tué Raspoutine*, etc.
24 – French actress, born in 1949: *Au hasard Balthazar*, *La Chinoise*, *Out One*, *Theorem*, etc. She was Godard's companion for several years.
25 – Philippe Dussart, French production manager and producer, notably of Resnais's films.
26 – François Cavanna, French novelist and journalist, born in 1923.
27 – American novelist and essayist.
28 – Bernardo Bertolucci, Italian director, born in 1940: *Before the Revolution*, *The Conformist*, *Last Tango in Paris*, *1900*, *La Luna*, *The Last Emperor*, etc.
29 – French writer.
30 – Antoine Bourseiller, French stage and film director.
31 – Michel Cournot, French journalist and the director of one film, *Les Gauloises bleues.*
32 – French trade-union leader and politician.
33 – Pierre Mendès-France, French politician.

To Jean-Loup Dabadie

early June, Friday [1973]

My dear Jean-Loup,

I have only very recently realized the – richly deserved – importance which you have come to assume for producers and distributors in the profession, in the wake of several real and major successes.

Because of that, the proposition we made to Jean-Paul Faure[1] now strikes me as being unrealistic and unfair to you. I have no wish to take advantage either of our friendship or of your wish to work with me again. I have, moreover, lost a little money of late in projects that came to nothing and this has prompted me to be more cautious whenever the idea for a film might be considered slightly experimental. I'm not yet convinced that I would be capable of bringing off this film about children, which is why I don't want to tie myself in advance to a backer or producer or distributor, and so feel that I am tied.

What I am saying is that I didn't choose the right subject for a new collaboration between us and that I suggest each of us consider himself released from the obligation.

Either, on some future occasion, you write a script in the style of *Louise*[2] and offer me first refusal (if you regard it as being in my line) or else we agree on a precise subject with which both of us are happy and which would be conceived with certain stars in mind, and it would all go through the normal channels.

I think this way of going about it would make better sense than the rather vague arrangement I was offering you. In any event, the point of this letter being mainly to put you at ease, we ought to get together and talk things over; give me a ring, I'll be leaving Paris on 22 June for quite a long time.

Everything is going quite well with *La Nuit américaine*. I'm a very happy man at the moment; I hope you're happy too – the question, in your case, need only be posed as far as work is concerned.

Kiss Marie for me and, as for you yourself, a good, firm handshake should do the trick,

regards,
françois

1 – Dabadie's agent.

2 – *Chère Louise*.

To Gilles Jacob *Paris, 12 June 1973*

My dear Gilles,

Thank you for your note. I'm returning the two pieces you sent me concerning Cannes 1968.

Thank you for what you say about *La Nuit américaine*. The brief description of the film in the listings of *L'Express* is a bit dangerous as it risks making the public think that it's a documentary or else too intellectual. I don't know if it's feasible to change it during a first run. If it is, I think that would help the film. Word of mouth is better than the box-office, probably because of just this kind of ambiguity.

Let me wish both of you a lovely summer. See you soon,

your friend,
françois

To a journalist *Paris, 15 June 1973*

Dear Monsieur,

Here, very rapidly, are my answers to your questions:

1. There is no doubt that the movement away from studio filming coincided with the advent of the New Wave, which could only make an impression in the industry by aiming for both material and financial simplification at the same time as a greater sense of realism.

Simultaneously, or very soon afterwards, the studios, which were becoming increasingly expensive to run (in spite of the growing importance of television), naturally began to attract the attention of property speculators.

2. For a director, shooting in real exteriors presents certain difficulties in the preparation of a film (many locations will have to be scouted before one is chosen) as also in its actual shooting (if the set is too small, one places the camera where one can and not always where one would prefer). On the other hand, there are obvious advantages: the pleasant surprise one sometimes receives from an unexpected distribution of elements in a real exterior, the sense of reality lent by the glimpse of a courtyard in the background, etc., etc.

3. It is true that, with the closure of the studios, there has been a real change in film-making methods; the use of doubles for stars, for example, becomes a kind of anachronism in real interiors and the number of technicians has to be reduced, otherwise half the crew will spend their time hanging about on stairways.

I also agree that, since the use of colour became general, the number of disadvantages of systematically filming in real décors has increased unless, of course, one decides to film them as though one were in a studio: by repainting the walls, rearranging the furniture . . .

I do not share your opinion that shooting in real décors has become routine, but there has certainly been – again since the use of colour became standard practice – an insufficient control over the filmed image on the part of many directors. For example, when I see a street scene in a comedy, and half of the street is in shadow and the other half in sunlight, it seems to me that the comic force of the shot has been reduced by half.

There are many directors and cinematographers who think the way to make a beautiful composition of some natural vista is to have a green meadow fill two-thirds of the image and blue sky fill the other third, whereas, when it is projected, the sun is no longer the sun but simply a whitish or yellowish expanse through which can be seen the seams of the cinema screen, which is rarely as clean as it ought to be. In that particular case, instead of filming the sky, one has actually managed to diminish the dramatic value of an image by a mutilation of space.

It is my opinion, in any event, that it is not in a film's interest to be shot a hundred per cent on location, since there should always be an element of artifice. In the case of *A bout de souffle* which is probably the masterpiece of films shot entirely in real interiors and locations, its artistic homogeneity was guaranteed by the fact that the film was entirely post-synchronized and that particularity of sound created its style.

These are only a few reflections, there are many others that might be made as well.

To Helen Scott

Sunday 9 July 1973

Dear Scottie,

I am typing on an American keyboard, so there will perhaps be a few errors, excuse me.

I haven't heard anything from you since Madeleine has been in Cannes; I hope all is well on the avenue Hoche (not only with Lelouch) and at the office. I've heard that Picker[1] is leaving to set up as an independent producer, I hope I'm not mixing him up with Stanley Schneider who certainly is, but who will be producing films for Columbia.

My life first of all. It's more or less monastic, as I am exhausted by six hours of English every day and I have a very private and comfortable little bungalow here where I feel so at ease that I'm happy to stay curled up alone for days on end, today, for example, thanks obviously to the old black and white movies on TV. Every Saturday afternoon I go and see Renoir, he's very old and very tired, he refuses to walk, it's not that there's any real physical cause, he simply refuses, but he comes to life every afternoon when dictating his memoirs to a French secretary. Which reminds me, ask Christine to give you a 'Renoir–Bazin' in English, I'd like to have your opinion on the translation. Renoir, at any rate, was very pleased with that particular edition, which is more attractive than the French.

My visit to Hitchcock was more formal, lunch in his office at Universal, but also with Alma, who was on good form. Hitch is mulling over a new film project and is very impatient for the writers' strike to end. He's getting fatter and fatter, redder and redder, richer and richer. His old half-hour programmes are on TV every evening, sometimes two in the same evening. Universal has changed a great deal, there's now a hotel and lots of new buildings, all because of the guided tour for visitors with its make-believe films being made and its fake stuntmen, there's a whole Disneyland aspect to it which is very profitable and with which Hitch seems to be involved. I didn't see Peggy R., who was probably on holiday.

The big thing now is obviously Watergate, which I watched every morning (five days of *Dean's testimony*).[2] Even if one didn't completely understand it, it was absolutely fascinating and I read every word about it in the *Los Angeles Times*. It starts again this afternoon with Mitchell. A lot of people think the election will be declared null and void and that Nixon will be out within six months, others think he'll pull off something in the next 3 weeks to turn the situation to his advantage. In any case – to paraphrase the sort of joke that's going around – my holiday here is less expensive than if I'd gone to Spain.

My teacher, Michel Thomas, says he finds it harder to rid me of my faults than to teach me the correct forms. He's Polish and led a resistance cell in the exact spot where Claude Berri was hidden (he adores *Le Vieil Homme*).[3] He was tortured by Barbie and he went to the French consulate last year, on his own volition, to testify that he would recognize him if he saw him . . . He gave lessons to Montand during the Marilyn period, he taught French to Grace Kelly and Preminger and, more recently, English to Trintignant and Jacques Deray[4] (who was more gifted than Trintignant). He has never criticized me, his manner is a little like that of a psychoanalyst and he has the patience of an angel, but I can see he's astonished by how severely I'm blocked; the truth is that there is in me a refusal to learn which is as powerful as my wish to know. Sometimes, I catch myself looking at him with utter loathing while he asks me, in an almost tender fashion, to translate: 'JE NE

LUI AI PAS DIT QUE JE ME PRÉPARAIS A LE LUI OFFRIR PARCE QUE JE NE VOULAIS PAS QU'ELLE SACHE QUE J'ALLAIS L'ACHETER.'

With the vocabulary I already know, any normal person would have finished the day before yesterday (2 weeks of 30 hours), but I feel I'll need three times as many lessons. Anyway, he told me that he would make it his job to teach me and that I wouldn't leave here without being able to write, read, speak and even understand. Renoir, who speaks very well, admits that understanding is hardest and told me that lots of things escaped him in Dean's testimony.

I rarely go out, but I dined several times with Leslie Caron[5] and her very nice husband, a producer. They're planning to settle in Paris, Leslie can't bear the life here. I went to two parties. The first was given by a charming woman, a painter, Barbara Poe, ex-wife of the *script-writer*[2] James Poe. There was Eddie Albert[6] and his wife Margot,[7] an actress whom you may have heard of, Spanish by birth, she played in *Zapata*[8] with Brando and has done a lot of theatre work. One woman asked me, when the conversation turned to food pollution, 'Et en France, est-ce que vous mettez des préservatifs autour des légumes?'[9] It was a *nice party*,[2] everyone was a liberal and in favour of the city's new black mayor. And, actually, since I've been here, I haven't met anyone who voted for Nixon . . . Last night, another party, much more typical of Hollywood, given by young Peter Guber, the head of production at Columbia, exactly the character out of *What Makes Sammy Run?*:[10] a billiard-room with a ceiling made up of luminous posters for the Company, a barbecue on the lawn and later the screening of a comedy which I didn't watch as I was flirting with Buck Henry,[11] who's really very sweet. There was Herbert Ross[12] who made *The Last of Sheila*, Leo Jaffe, Stanley Schneider who is, as I said, going to settle out here, Guy Hamilton[13] and lots of other people whose names I didn't catch.

On weekdays, however, I don't go out, I see practically no one, I've even given up scouring the city for French newspapers, I write very little and never at length. I say that not to make you feel privileged! but to let you know that I'd be happy to hear from you even if I don't answer your next letters at such great length. At the start Michel Thomas had told me: 'There will be no homework, no lessons, nothing to learn by heart,' he ended by arranging tapes specially for me to listen to when I'm alone and which concentrate on the mistakes I make most frequently. Because of this, I no longer read a word of French and write as little as possible, except to the family. Even TV is bad for me since I never try to understand the dialogue of any film. Anyway, there you have it. I can see I'll have to continue studying, maybe in Paris, every morning at home throughout the year. I'm going to be spending quite a lot of time in America, two weeks in New York for the N.Y. festival, then 4 days in Boston immediately after, then Montreal, then a week in San Francisco and again in Los Angeles in the second half of October, all with the aim of doing as much as possible to promote *La Nuit américaine* over here, which at least will give some meaning to my two-year break (except if Saul Cooper[14] bankrupts Carrosse).

What I hope for now is a nice long letter from you, one that would take into consideration the fact that I haven't read a French newspaper in 2 weeks, which means that I would even be interested in the state of Pompidou's health. Perhaps, as you often did at that period, you spend your evenings out and at the Club Lelouch?

Goodbye, Scottie, I send you a tender kiss,

hope to hear from you soon,

françois

1 – David Picker, who was briefly president of Paramount.
2 – In English in the original letter.
3 – Berri's *Le Vieil Homme et l'Enfant* (1967).
4 – French director, born in 1929: *Rififi à Tokyo*, *La Piscine*, *Borsalino*, *Un papillon sur l'épaule*, etc. The film for which he and Jean-Louis Trintignant were required to learn English was the Franco-American co-production *Un homme est mort* (*The Outside Man*), shot in Los Angeles.
5 – French-born actress and dancer, born in 1931: *Lili*, *Daddy Long Legs*, *Gigi*, *Fanny*, *L'Homme qui aimait les femmes*, etc.
6 – American actor, born in 1908: *Roman Holiday*, *Oklahoma!*, *Attack!*, *The Roots of Heaven*, *The Longest Day*, *Seven Women*, etc.
7 – Correctly, Margo, and of Mexican, not Spanish, origin.
8 – Elia Kazan's *Viva Zapata!* (1952).
9 – A French-speaking person would produce the same unintentionally comic effect in English by saying 'And do you in America put protectives on vegetables?'
10 – By Budd Schulberg.
11 – American screenwriter and occasional actor, born in 1930.
12 – American director and choreographer, born in 1927: *Play It Again, Sam*, *The Turning Point*, *Pennies from Heaven*, *Footloose*, etc.
13 – British director, born in 1922: *An Inspector Calls*, *The Devil's Disciple*, *Goldfinger*, *Diamonds Are Forever*, *Live and Let Die*, etc.
14 – A United Artists executive.

To Guy Teisseire *[July 1973]*

My dear Guy,

I've corrected, clarified and pruned our interview[1] as carefully as possible. Don't be annoyed when you see what I've cut: *La Grande Bouffe*, the Cayatte film,[2] Michèle Mercier, every second reference to Bardot, and *La Maman et la putain*,[3] but I just <u>can't</u> do otherwise. The vitriol, *that was*

Place Stamp Here

cher Richard,
attention ! je ne peux
rien dire, mais cette
carte est écrite
à l'encre
sympathique,
à bientôt,
amitié,
françois

The Watergate Hotel
(pictured center)
IN THE RENOWNED WATERGATE COMPLEX
This non-convention hotel has magnificent views of the Potomac, the capital city and Kennedy Center.
2650 Virginia Avenue, N.W. Washington, D. C. 20037
Phone: 202—965-2300

'Dear Richard, careful! I can't say anything but this card was written in invisible ink, see you soon, yours, françois' (postcard to Richard Roud).

before![4] I have had too much good fortune to attack those who have been less lucky, it's as simple as that.

Even so, I think our conversation is lively, a little thin where *La Nuit américaine* is concerned, but interesting on the actresses. If you have to cut, I would prefer it to be large chunks rather than lots of small ones, and the paragraphs on TV, politics or books rather than those dealing with the cinema. Don't cut the brief appreciation of current French cinema, I think it's timely and accurate.

See you soon, in September,

yours,
françois

P.S. I would prefer you to cut from page 12 onwards, since the first part seems better to me.

1 – For *Ciné-Revue*.
2 – André Cayatte's *Il n'y a pas de fumée sans feu*.
3 – By Jean Eustache.
4 – In English in the original letter.

To Koichi Yamada[1]

Los Angeles, 17 July 1973

My dear Yamada,

This is a rather belated reply to your letter of 17 June, as I am in Los Angeles for several weeks.

I take English lessons daily and often visit Jean Renoir who, though very tired, nevertheless finds the energy to dictate his memoirs to a French secretary for three hours every day.

As far as publishing the screenplay of *La Nuit américaine* is concerned, we must give up the idea of having its publication coincide with the film's release, since I'm not yet ready to send you the material.

As for the novel entitled *La Nuit américaine*, I have to tell you that it has nothing to do with the film. Christopher Frank is an Englishman who lives and writes in France, and his novel, which coincidentally has the same title as my film, was published just as we finished shooting. In France, any potential misunderstanding was quickly cleared up by the press and I hope that the Japanese publisher won't lead the public into error, for example by using a still from the film on the book-jacket or anything along those lines.

I return to Paris in September and then, if you wish, I'll send you the screenplay of the film and a typed copy of the *Fahrenheit 451* diary.

I would especially like to hear more about the translation of Bazin's book on Chaplin, I hope it's going to be published.

Wishing you all the best, my dear Yamada,

françois

1 – Japanese film critic, born in 1938. It was meeting Truffaut in 1963 that determined his vocation; he has since translated Truffaut's books into Japanese (*Le Cinéma selon Hitchcock*, *Les Films de ma vie*, etc.) and contributed to *Cahiers du cinéma*, for which he has interviewed several major Japanese directors.

1974

To Simon Benzakein[1] *Paris, 10 March 1974*

My dear Simon,

Having returned to Paris, I can now give you my answer to the question of a possible remake of the film *Casablanca*.[2]

It is not my favourite Humphrey Bogart film, I have a far greater admiration for *The Big Sleep*[3] or *To Have and Have Not*.[4] Because of that, I should logically find the idea of directing a new version less intimidating, and I have not forgotten that the film has quite a French atmosphere.

I am aware, however, that American students have created a cult around the film, principally its dialogue, which they know by heart. There can be no doubt that most actors would feel as intimidated as I do and I cannot imagine Jean-Paul Belmondo or Catherine Deneuve being willing to step into the shoes of Humphrey Bogart and Ingrid Bergman. I realize that Americans tend to see these things rather differently.

I am not shocked by the idea of remaking a film, provided it has a very good, adult story which might be handled more explicitly today and that its title is not one that carries too much weight in the history of the American cinema.

If Warner Bros. really want me to direct a film for them, I suggest you send me a list of titles from which I might make a choice.

There you have my answer and I ask you to communicate it to Frank Wells.[5] In any case, I hope to meet him on 8 April at the Oscar ceremony, which I plan to attend in the company of Valentina Cortese (nominated for 'Best Supporting Actress') and my collaborator Suzanne Schiffman (nominated for best original screenplay).

Thanking you nevertheless for having thought of me for *Casablanca*, I remain very cordially yours,

François Truffaut

1 – Benzakein was at that period a producer at PECF, a subsidiary of Warner Bros.
2 – By Michael Curtiz (1943).
3 – By Howard Hawks (1946).
4 – By Howard Hawks (1944).
5 – An executive at Warner Bros.

To Nicolas Roeg[1]

Paris, 16 April 1974

My dear Nic,

Thank you very much for your letter of 5 April. As it nappens, you wrote it on the same day as I received the Oscar. Thanks again.

I am sending you a book which fascinated me and which, if I were an English director and not a pathetic little insular Parisian, I would have no hesitation in filming. I refer to *Father Figure*, by Beverley Nichols;[2] I'm sending you my copy of the French version, but I suppose it would make better sense for you to read it in English and, above all, I hope I'll have tempted you to make a film of it, one that would be both powerful and sincere, terrifying and yet somehow exalting, because of all the contrasts that are to be found in it.

I very much hope to see *Don't Look Now* in Paris soon and if not I'll arrange to see it in the course of my travels to New York and Los Angeles.

I know that at present, professionally, things are going well for you, thanks to the success of the film, and I am delighted, as are Suzanne Schiffman and Helen Scott who send you their very kindest regards.

Best wishes,
François

1 – English cinematographer (notably of *Fahrenheit 451*) and director, born in 1928: *Performance* (co-directed with Donald Cammell), *Walkabout*, *The Man Who Fell to Earth*, *Eureka*, *Track 29*, etc.
2 – An autobiographical memoir in which Nichols recounts how he tried to kill his father.

To Koichi Yamada

Paris, 22 April 1974

My dear Yamada,

Thank you very much for your letter of 15 April. It gave me great pleasure to read it. I can assure you that I do understand the problems currently faced by publishers (there is also a shortage of paper in New York and Paris, as in Japan) and I am also aware of the difficulties regarding the opening of *Une belle fille comme moi* in Japan: Bernadette is not the Mona Lisa[1] and I am not Leonardo da Vinci!!

By contrast, I hope that everything will go well with *La Nuit américaine* which Warner Bros. would prefer to open around July, probably after *The Exorcist*[2] which is a very big, important production for the company. I think Warner Bros. is planning to send Jacqueline Bisset to Tokyo to publicize the film. Anyway, we'll see . . .

Apart from that, I am at present putting the finishing touches to a collection of some of my reviews to which I have given the title of *Les Films de ma vie*.

Everyone in Paris is well. Let me know how you are from time to time,

affectionately yours,

françois

P.S. Jean Renoir has just finished a superb book of memoirs: *Ma Vie et Mes Films*. June publication. I'll send it to you.

1 – The exhibition of the Mona Lisa then being held in Tokyo enjoyed such an extraordinary success that the opening of *Une belle fille comme moi* in one small cinema had been completely ignored.

2 – By William Friedkin.

To Jean Collet[1] *[9 May 1974]*

My dear Collet,

I don't seem to be able to reach you, I hope my secretary hasn't been calling you at an old number. Why don't you call me, and come and have lunch with me before the holidays? If you write this book on my work, I can organize screenings of any film you like; I would prefer you not to speak of some of them from recent memory and others from a much vaguer memory; for my part, I have deliberately delayed the inception of this book for so long, no doubt because I wanted to feel I had ended the first period of my career, in short, I'm rather keen – so are you, obviously – for it to be The book.

For the Godard, thank you; I prefer, and I will obviously keep, the earlier version, you know why. Godard has fouled his own backyard, you'll know what I mean when you read Renoir's book *Ma Vie et Mes Films* (published by Flammarion in June), a masterpiece, even from a literary point of view.

Hoping to see you soon, dear Jean,

regards,

françois

1 – The film critic Jean Collet lectures on cinema at the Universities of Paris and Dijon. He is the author of *Jean-Luc Godard* (1963) and two books on Truffaut (1977 and 1985).

To Jean Gruault

Paris, 27 June 1974

My dear Jean,

Please find enclosed cheque no. 8696786 from the Crédit Lyonnais for 377 francs, representing 50% of the 754 francs that I have just received from Éditions G.P., with reference to the copyright of *L'Enfant sauvage*.

Hoping it arrives safely,

Yours,
françois

P.S. The sum is a modest one, but Lavarède circled the globe with very much less.[1]

1 – An allusion to Paul d'Ivoi's book *Les Cinq Sous de Lavarède* (*Lavarède's Five Pennies*), of which a film was made in 1938 with Fernandel.

To Koichi Yamada

Paris, 10 July 1974

My dear Yamada,

I received your letter of 1 July, for which thank you.

I'm sending you another copy of Jean Renoir's book, in case you might need it to have it read by a publisher, and I remind you that nothing should be done without first consulting Madame Doynel, Jean Renoir's secretary, or Flammarion.

Don't trouble yourself about *La Nuit américaine*. My objection to your subtitle, *A Love of the Cinema*, comes from the fact that, in France and America, we realized that, whenever articles or interviews explained the meaning of the title, it produced an effect of wariness among the public.

Despite the interest aroused by the film, many people decided against going to see it and, when asked why they had stayed away, they answered: 'We had the impression it was a very technical film, a documentary.' By contrast, whenever the public has gone to see the film, the reactions have been favourable. That's why it would be preferable to let them think it has a plot like any other, without attempting to explain the title.

There's something else I would like your opinion on. I've started jotting down notes for a possible film[1] about a man who makes a cult out of the dead and spends a lot of his time commemorating people he has known and loved who have died. I thought that in Japanese literature there might be lots of details on such a theme.

What I'm looking for above all are very precise, very concrete or physical details. I was thinking, for example, of the sensibility of that old writer who died a few years ago, two of whose books I had adored: *The Key* and *Diary of a Mad Old Man*.[2] If you could find some material along these lines and send it to me, I'd be very pleased.

It will probably have to be books written in Japanese, but if you were to make pencil notes in the margin beside the relevant passages, I'd be able to have them verbally translated in Paris. If you can't find anything, it's not a problem and, in any case, it's quite a long-term project.

Hoping for a letter from you soon, best regards,

françois

1 – *La Chambre verte.*

2 – By Junichiro Tanizaki.

To Jean Gruault

from Cannes, 21 July 1974

My dear Jean,

First of all, I hope you are impressed by my brand new portable typewriter; I call it the Christine II,[1] you know why. Please find enclosed the contract for *The Altar of the Dead*;[2] it's not exactly a million-dollar deal, but, as Berbert told you, this is a trial project and if, as I would like, the film does get made as a normal production, we can always draft a new one.

Before taking the plunge, I'd like you to plan out the structure of the whole narrative; think of it as an adaptation of a play, with four or five acts. The first part is a kind of prologue, leading up to the widower's (his name escapes me) remarriage. (Consult the lists of names in James's diaries to find names that are, if not French, then at least more neutral than the original ones, which are too English.)

The second part goes from the introduction of the second wife of the man he meets in the street to the meeting with the heroine. The third takes up from there to the completion of the chapel. The fourth act, from there until the death of the heroine's mother. And the fifth act is the ending.

Perhaps his devotion to his dead fiancée should be part of a gradually unfolding mystery, in which there is a real element of suspense – but without mystification. Don't forget that our main character has to be mysterious and charismatic and the best way of achieving such an effect is to have a couple of scenes in which he is talked about in his absence. If a character says 'I have a secret,' the immediate reaction is 'Who the hell does he think he is?', whereas if two other characters say of him 'There's a man with a secret,' then the spectator is intrigued and his attention is held. That's why, using lines from the book, I improvised the scene in *Jules et Jim* in which the two men discuss

François Truffaut and Koichi Yamada, 'my Japanese friend'.

her in her absence: 'Catherine is a force of nature . . . she's in a constant state of crisis, etc.'

I see the central relationship as being a bit like the one in *The Beast in the Jungle*, by which I mean, she's in love with him from the start (and she knows it), whereas he is in love with her but doesn't know it, probably because he doesn't know that one can fall in love twice in a lifetime. That is really one of our favourite themes: the permanent and the temporary.

The problem with James is that nothing is ever stated and film doesn't allow that kind of vagueness; we're going to have to explain everything, make everything clear, and we're also going to have to find a thousand ways of emphasizing what I call the privileged moments (like the scenes of book-burning in *Fahrenheit 451*). In this instance, the privileged moments are the religious ceremonies, the lighting of the candles, the rituals, all that sort of Japanese religiosity, which is our real reason for wanting to make the film. Then, still on the subject of privileged moments, the meetings of the hero and heroine; they never talk about love (except maybe in the 5th act) but we have to give the public the impression it's watching a romantic movie.

We'll probably need to invent a few additional characters; I propose: the hero's faithful servants, an old couple; two priests (we need two so that they can discuss the hero); two of his colleagues, for the same reason; and perhaps a caretaker near the chapel or the caretaker of the graveyard.

When the hero does anything strange, make sure it's emphasized and has a strong visual impact: it should be handled as though it were a thriller, to highlight the man's hidden life, his slight craziness (for example, if he wants to avoid meeting someone in the street, rather than just crossing the road as he would in a normal film, we might actually show him taking refuge in the stairwell of a building under construction).

That's all I can think of for now, particularly as I don't have a copy of the book at hand. I hope these notes don't contradict the notes I made in the margins of my copy.

If you need to speak to me, you can always call me here, in Cannes, boulevard Albert 1er, Résidence Saint-Michel: tel:38.19.95 (preceded by 15.93); you can reach me here every day at 2 p.m. and after 7 in the evening, until 7 July. Then you can write to me in Los Angeles until 15 September, which is Renoir's 80th birthday.

Beverly Hills Hotel
9641 Sunset Boulevard
Beverly Hills (California)

I will quite understand if you prefer to get on with it by yourself for the time being. I received the more or less definitive version of *Adèle* and am quite pleased with it, but we've still got five months to improve it.

Back to James. There's one story I like a lot called *The Friends of the Friends* (in the same collection as *The Jolly Corner*) and perhaps we could use some of it, for example the fact that, before they met each other, both the man and the woman lost someone they loved and in both cases they sensed that the person had died, at the very moment of death, though they themselves weren't present. It's a very interesting notion.

That's enough of my harassment, my dear Jean, for even if they are too big to sit on your lap, you must attend to your children nevertheless and also Ginette, that (young) Mother Courage.

Best wishes, then, to all the inhabitants of the most intelligent villa in the Villa Rimbaud (let's not have Gruault's silence[3] quite yet).

your old mate,
françois

1 – An allusion to the continuity person, Christine Pellé.
2 – *La Chambre verte*, directed by Truffaut in 1977, was inspired by three short stories by Henry James: *The Altar of the Dead*, *The Friends of the Friends* and *The Beast in the Jungle*.
3 – Jean Gruault never quite got the point of this mysterious postscript. It is, presumably, a reference to the fact that Rimbaud ceased to write at an early age and began trading arms in Abyssinia.

To Bernard Dubois[1]

from Los Angeles, 10 August [1974]

Dear Beryann,[2]

Please accept my apologies in advance for the numerous typing mistakes due to this Yankee keyboard.

I read your improved and expanded script[3] in the plane, very carefully.

1. The girl wearing tennis whites on the train; whether she's played by Lola or not, I think she deserves a close-up, from just below the waist or perhaps even closer in order to emphasize her vanilla ice-cream. (You could use the same angle and the same composition each time we see Lola and her ice-cream.)

3. The sentence: 'Yann, whom I recognize without ever having seen him' is amusing and intriguing, but what will it mean in the film? I think that this is one instance, and there are several, where you would do well to make the dialogue slightly less elliptical. Something like:
Bernard: Hello there. Are you Yann? I knew it.
Yann: And you're Bernard Dubois.
Bernard: Of course.[4]

It may seem heavy-handed to you, but each time I come across them, I think I should draw your attention to things which might not have quite the resonance for ordinary spectators that they have for you. So, to continue:

5. Your enthusiasm for long tracking shots makes me wonder how you are going to end scenes (those which need to come to a good full stop). Thus, at the end of scene 5, I suggest you let the two faces in balaclava helmets come full screen to black, so that you can reverse the process at the beginning of scene 6 (the chemist's shop). The scene in the chemist's needs a proper beginning, middle and end or it will look as though it's been patched up on the editing-table. 'Valium' is a little too opaque, I suggest 'I slipped her some Valium.' This whole scene in the chemist's would be much better if it were done in a whisper: try it out in rehearsal. At the end of the scene, to arouse the public's curiosity and avoid a documentary-style banality, I would show, in the reverse angle shot, some police cars or else have the sound of sirens on the soundtrack. After the phrase ' . . . my usual practice . . .', one might have the two characters breaking into a run.

8. If you don't get Jane Birkin, I'd suggest Bernadette Lafont who will have finished the Szabó and would certainly accept the part. So that it doesn't come as too much of a surprise, later, that she is a Cadillac salesgirl, I would recommend your inserting a line telling us she has found a job with Cadillac refrigerators (so that the name Cadillac has already been introduced). Then, I would make the following major change: rather than making the whole thing a question of sex, I would actually take it in the opposite direction: Marie-France might, for example, explain that she has given up her hotel room, or her bedsitter, to live in the convent; she could say, quite seriously and sincerely, that she believes she has found God and is tempted to become a nun but, before taking her vows – which is a decision which will change her whole life – she needs time to think things over and gradually move closer to God, etc. (You won't have any trouble guessing where I got this idea from.) The point is, as far as this character is concerned, that the spectator gets the wrong idea so that the following scene in the car, when she gives Bernard a blow-job – if I've understood correctly – will really come as a shock. OK? Also in scene 8, if Agathe were to drink too much, another character might say something like 'Be careful, Agathe, you're getting tipsy.' (In that way, we'll learn her name which we don't yet know.)

9. I didn't get any of the business about Bernard's suitcase, but I imagine it's clear as daylight to you.

10. When Yann arrives, there ought to be – five years on – something different about him. I suggest a false moustache, which he could remove, on camera, a little later in the scene, for example when he says: 'Nothing

happened, hashish, gamma . . .' When Bernard comes back and says he has come into some money, given that we saw his parents at the station, he should specify: 'I had a legacy from my only uncle, I was his only godson . . .', or something like that.

12. Marie-France, if you want, could explain that she has moved from Cadillac refrigerators to the cars of the same name, but you may – rightly – think it's a bit obvious . . . I suggest you raise a laugh (Lubitsch always used to say that a laugh was not to be sneezed at) by inserting a line for Bernard, while Marie-France is rummaging around out of shot: 'Yes, really, that's a very nice car . . .'

13. I hope you won't mind my pointing out that you two are the only people who know that it's Lola's mother. As far as we're concerned, she's just another woman; I don't suppose this matters, but you should be aware of it.

14. On Lola, use the same angle as with the girl in the train. Bernard should be holding the package the way a bishop carries the Sacred Heart of Jesus; the religious quality of this scene should be very strong (the principle being, as always, to emphasize the contrast with what will happen later and avoid documentary-style reportage).

15. The transition from 16 mm to Super 8 should coincide with the first thud of the sledge-hammer (also, you can save money by switching cars at this point and possibly using a battered old car that would cost you much less). Moreover, if you want to justify seeing the scene on television, there are two things you can do: a) you can show a television company van parking on the Place de la Concorde and the crew getting ready to shoot: b) you can show the scene on television, then pull back to reveal that we're in a dining-room with the very ironmonger who sold Bernard the sledge-hammer, astonished to recognize his customer, etc. At the end of the scene, whether you choose to end on Serge Marquand, a fat passer-by trying her luck, Bernard reading the small ads or the ironmonger bathing his feet in front of his TV, make sure you have a good final shot so that you can fade to black in camera. I think that is essential.

Between 17 and 17a I would add another scene, in a typewriter shop, with Bernard unable to decide which one to buy.

Salesgirl: I'd take that one if I were you.

Bernard: You advise me to take it!

Salesgirl: Yes.

Bernard: In that case, I *will* take it.

He grabs it and rushes out of the shop. The salesgirl is astonished. She rushes after him, trips and falls, then looks up at us. Close-up. The end.*

Then we are on the barge. I like the idea of the barge and I have faith in improvisation; I'm sure it will be very good.

18. Separate shot on Lola, seated using the special Lola angle to remind us of the two previous shots. Lola should wear the same dress from beginning to end, so should her mother.

20. Bernard Menez's entrance. Instead of having the ironmonger watching TV (15), perhaps you could do it with Menez, establishing quite clearly that he is a writer?

21. 'I'd love to know her mother' is too elliptical, I think. You need two or three lines playing on the word know to achieve the effect you want, otherwise the spectator won't note anything particular about the phrase.

22. This is a very disappointing scene. I don't think it works nearly as well as the rest. I can't quite put my finger on it, but I think the trouble is that we don't have any problem accepting the way Yann, Bernard, Agathe and Marie-France talk because they are all part of the same family, but when these two other women come into it, the whole business becomes a little too systematic; that's the trouble with arbitrary details like that. I do like the mother's last line but nothing much else. If you agree, then I would suggest you simply explain to the two women what you want from them and let them improvise their own lines. (I know Jacqueline Pierreux is capable of working in that way.) You may be afraid that the improvised dialogue will jar but I don't think it will, particularly as we are dealing with 'outside' characters. As it stands, the scene will probably annoy spectators and spoil the last part of the film; it's absolutely essential that you are satisfied with the way it fits into the scheme of the film; it should be a bit like winding up an alarm clock at the end of the narrative; ideally, it might seem to open up a new chapter in the film, even if the following scene contradicts this effect. Underlying what the mother is saying might be this idea: young man, after everything the three of us have been through together, your life will never be the same again.

22. Just a suggestion: if you don't like it, forget it. I imagine Bernard as being confused: should he change his way of life, etc. He goes to see a fortune-teller, almost in the open air, in a fairground; she is curtained off, but there is no ceiling (you won't need lights). The fortune-teller is completely straight with him: she can't help him because she herself has lost her handbag and can't think where it might be; she's lost her past, her present and future and, being honest with herself, she's going to have to change jobs . . . I think something like this ought to be inserted between the scene with the two women and the scene in the evening, with Agathe and the telephone.

23. Again, the dialogue is not clear enough. I suggest something like:

Bernard: 'Hello? Oh it's you, Lola, you've got exactly the same voice as your mother, etc.' And then, at the end, 'Please give your mother my regards.'

24. I don't much like the list of names, particularly that of Jean-Pierre Léaud. It looks too much like the *private jokes*[4] the New Wave was criticized for; just put in, oh, I don't know, Denis Berry instead of Jean-Pierre Léaud.

The end, the whole of scene 24, is interesting and looks promising, but not really disciplined enough, given that this is the end of the film; every word should count, there must be real emotion, born, then protected and nurtured, and growing in strength; Agathe's monologue must ring very true, which means lots of rehearsals and discipline.

25. I think the idea we discussed the other day, with Bernard grumbling that his son never calls him daddy, would be wonderful for this scene. The ending, the little boy in the car, I found very sad, which is probably what you wanted me to feel.

The script is much improved; the underlying theme of the search (the quest, as critics or blurbs put it) doesn't always come across as strongly or as clearly as I would wish, but I think that will remedy itself when you start shooting. People mustn't come out of the cinema wondering why anyone bothered to make the film, that's the only real danger and nothing else matters as much.

I want you to know that though, at first, the principal reason for my interest in this project was to help Jean-Pierre, it's now the film itself that interests me. If ever anything goes wrong because of Jean-Pierre, I'd advise you to make it anyway, either by replacing him, by improvising or whatever. *The show must go on.*[4] I know you'll be much too busy to reply and let me know how you are, but that's my hard luck. Even if you do get Jane Birkin, I think you ought to keep the name Marie-France because using an actor's real name never really works when the actor is well known. It's one of the less appealing aspects of New Wave folklore;** if, when Bernard has become a writer, on the barge, you need some brief scene, I suggest you have him tell, as though it were the plot of a novel, one of the stories Bernard told us in *L'Avance*; as far as I can remember, two of them were fairly self-contained and one of them was quite precise and funny; it might make a nice little interlude and bring us closer to the character because we will know more about what he wants to do.

As far as Jean-Pierre is concerned, he has worked with lots of different directors in lots of different ways, but I think he is at his best when he is quite valiant and sincere; nothing pretentious or snobbish but – I can't think of a better word to say what I mean – valiant, honest in his mistakes, well-intentioned and funny without trying to be. But that's enough for now or I'll start to encroach on Bernard's vision which is all the more precise by being autobiographical, more or less.

It only remains for me to wish you all the luck you deserve – you already have all the courage you need; I'll be back on 3 September.

See you, Yanard, all the best,
françois

*This scene could be shot from the street, through the shop window, but the dialogue would have to be audible.

**And, oddly enough, actors are always below par, less involved somehow, when their characters have the same name as they have.

1 – French director, born in 1945: *Les Lolos de Lola* and *Au bout du printemps*.
2 – An amalgam of two names: Bernard Dubois (the director) and Yann Dedet (his collaborator).
3 – *Les Lolos de Lola*: Les Films du Carrosse were involved in the production of this film, which starred Jean-Pierre Léaud.
4 – In English in the original letter.

To Bernard Dubois *11 August [1974]*

Dear Beryann Dudet,

How nice to be able to give sensible advice while languidly reclining beside the swimming-pool of a Hollywood hotel, I just can't resist! So here is your Uncle François's final word, and then I'll retreat into the shadows, I promise!

I reread your script this morning, looking for nits to pick, and of course I found some.

6. I am a little worried – not that I lose any sleep over it – about the transition from scene 6 to scene 7, from the conversation in the chemist's shop to its continuation beside the Seine; the point is that the spectator must be sure it is the same conversation, the same scene really; you will have to make up for the break in location by emphasizing the continuity of voice-patterns, the rhythm of the dialogue and probably even the same walking pace of the two friends.

8. During Marie-France's monologue I would make sure that – despite the need to save on stock – you have a fairly long silent shot of Bernard ogling Agathe; you may need it either to make the transition to the shot of M.-F. talking or to shorten her speech if the acting's not up to it or the film's too long.

10. The reference to Julien is rather off-the-cuff and my worry is that no one will notice it; couldn't you show some snapshots of the child in this

scene? Because your dialogue is 95% poetry and only 5% functional you are going to have trouble getting certain essential facts across. I mention this because I am extremely familiar with the problem myself. The same is true, in this same scene, concerning Yann's remark: 'I have a girlfriend who loves vanilla ice-cream.' You must make sure the remark makes its impact quite clearly within the context.

13. I keep coming back to the same old points: I think it would be helpful to find some gimmick for the costume worn by Lola's mother, maybe a sexy leopard-skin top or something like that to help us identify and recognize her easily . . . Or it could be, for example, a pair of glasses on a chain around her neck?

15. If you accept my idea of the theft of the typewriter in scene 17 or 17a, you'll have to find something else to come out of the boot of his car: what about some tins of cocoa?

17. I'm sure the barge is going to be very useful to the film, both in visual and purely human terms. If the improvised activity which we see relates to the realities of daily life on a barge (bringing water on board, dropping anchor, mooring, operating pulleys and levers), it will help the film and make its more arbitrary aspects easier to accept.

18. During Yann's monologue, I'm sure you've planned a long, silent shot of Bernard feasting his eyes on Lola. This will be very useful. I would make the last panning shot very long, to build up the tension. If it's too quick, it will resemble a wipe and people will think there's been a leap forward in time or space. If it's merely average speed, it will be banal and boring. But if it's very slow, it will keep audiences on their toes. A zoom would be ideal (unless you're allergic to them, which I would quite understand), because you could single out, at the end of the shot, the word HÔTEL and one of the bedroom windows.

19. Now, we're inside the hotel, which must come across very clearly, either by having the camera movement continue at the same rhythm as in the preceding shot, or by cutting away to the ROOM PRICE sign on the back of the door. It would be a pity to leave any lingering doubts in the spectator's mind: we are inside a hotel.

20. Again, thinking ahead to when you are editing, you should have a silent insert shot of Agathe continuing to fish – or doing something else – during the monologue of the bookish swimmer.

21. At Charlety, for the same reasons, a shot of Agathe, alone, reading *Ciné-Revue* before Lola arrives, would be nice and also useful. At the end of the scene, when Agathe says, 'Oh, now Julien's copying her too,' the point will be lost unless Lola (and the audience) already knows Julien (people may

even confuse him with Yann if he's just mentioned in passing, yes, I assure you, it happens. Think about it). To tell the truth, I think you'll have to bring Julien into the picture well before this, during the first scene on the barge (20). That's the best solution. Then he can be at Charlety too . . . playing on his own somewhere.

24. Still on the question of important lines of dialogue that might pass unnoticed, you must find some way of emphasizing Yann's: ' . . . To have a child by you, are you listening to what I'm telling you, Bernard, the mother wants to have a baby by you . . .', etc. Then, during Yann's long monologue, you ought to allow for a very visual silent shot of Agathe doing her exercises. This is a crucial scene and you must find a rock-solid way of doing it.

Between 24 and 25, *I am wondering*[1] whether you don't need to insert a quick little scene which would also serve to get rid of three of the principal characters: Lola, her mother and Menez (if you can't get Menez, there's always Serge Marquand, but he wouldn't be as good). I see a scene at the town hall. Both women, mother and daughter, are pregnant. The mayor – perhaps the same actor who played the ironmonger – wearing his official sash, could say: 'Do you, X, take one of these two women as your lawfully wedded wife? – Yes!' Then there would be a contest of courtesies between mother and daughter: 'You go first – No, mother, you go first' and so on. In the end, the mother might say; 'Come on, we'll sort it out among the three of us' and she would go and stand next to the groom; they would exchange rings, with the daughter standing between and behind them. If you don't like this idea, forget it. If it makes you think of something else, that's fine. I just think you need something between the barge and the zoo, to make the zoo scene more of an epilogue. Besides which, Lola and her mother are relatively important characters and it's no bad thing to give them a real ending. But where is Yann in all this?

26. I still think little Julien going off all on his own in a taxi is terribly sad; if the child is capable of it, perhaps he could do something a bit strange or a bit grown-up, once he is on his own in the cab, that would be interesting; he could, for example, give the driver his address and say: 'First go to the Pont de Grenelle; you can't take the rue de la Croix-Nivert because it's one-way, so if I were you I'd take the avenue de Malakoff and then the third turning on the left.' You see what I mean.

This time, I promise, I won't bother you again until 4 September. Make a good film,

all the best,
françois

P.S. If, despite all you've got to do, you can find the time to send me a brief reply, just to let me know you've received both my letters, that would be very nice. You could always give it to Janine, at Carrosse, she'll send it on with the mail from the office.

1 – In English in the original letter.

To Koichi Yamada, *Paris, 1 October 1974*

My dear Yamada,

I have your letter of 31 July in front of me and have only just returned to Paris.

Notwithstanding the great success of *The Exorcist*, I hope that *La Nuit américaine* has finally opened in Tokyo and I rely on you to keep me posted.

I had already read the books you mention, *The Sleeping Beauties*[1] and *Tales of the Rain and the Moon*[2] (which have just come out in paperback here) and they are, as you say, magnificent.

In fact, I certainly didn't explain to you properly what it is I'm looking for in connection with the cult of the dead. I remember, for example, that in *Diary of a Mad Old Man* the hero begins making a sketch of the statue which is to be placed on his tombstone; being besotted with his stepdaughter, he makes charcoal tracings of the young woman's feet in order to substitute them for his own on the future monument. That's the kind of idea that really interests me since it would be impossible to find its equivalent in Western literature.

I am well aware that this kind of research is rather complicated; don't put yourself out too much.

Jean-Pierre Léaud's Super 8 mm film was abandoned in favour of a 16 mm film in which he is the leading actor and which has been directed by a very talented young man, Bernard Dubois. The film is called *Les Lolos de Lola*; more translation problems looming on the Japanese horizon!

Very cordially yours,
françois

1 – By Yasunari Kawabata. 2 – By Akinari Veda.

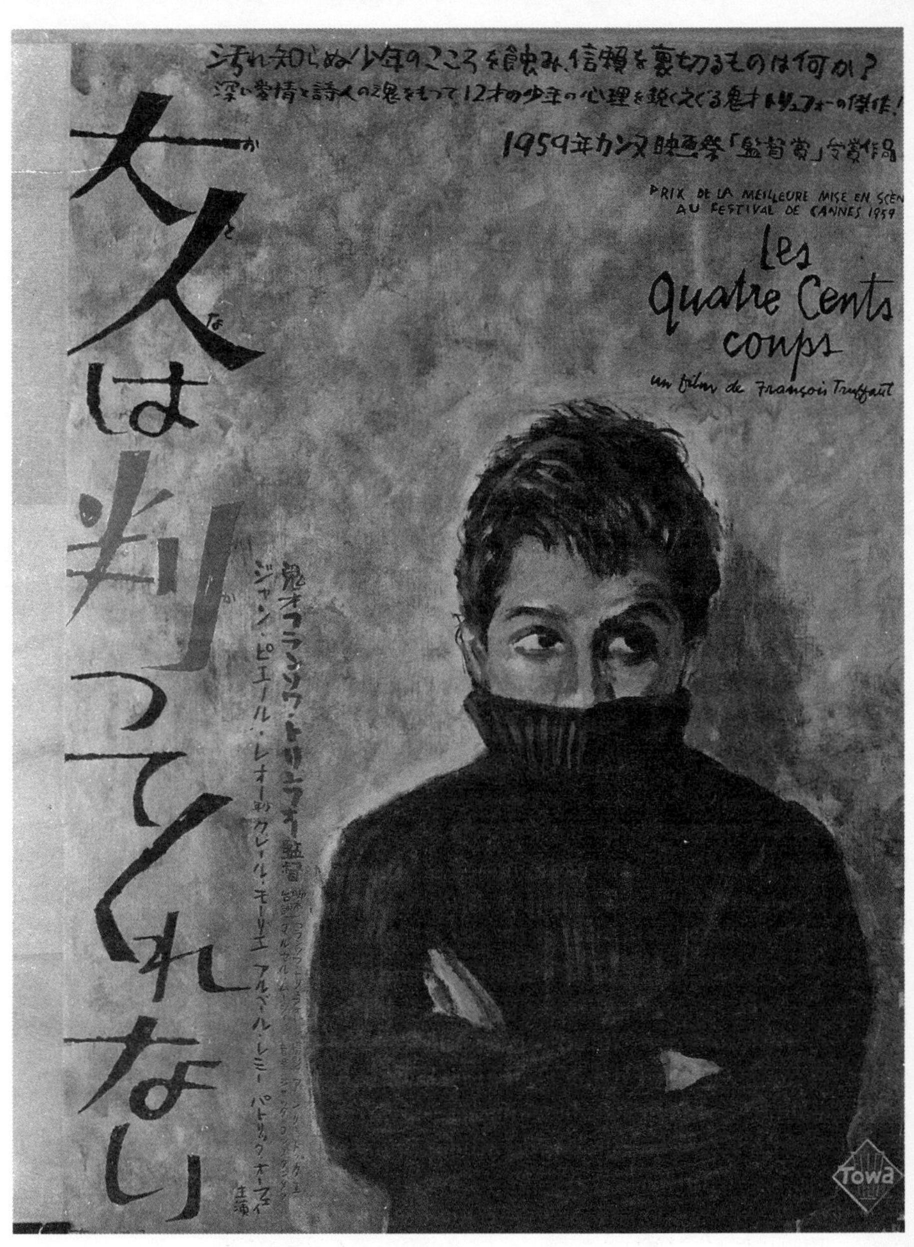

The Japanese poster for *Les Quatre Cents Coups*.

To Tay Garnett[1]

Paris, 9 October 1974

Dear Sir,

I have already sent your questionnaire[2] to Messrs René Clair, Jacques Tati and Costa-Gavras. I have received a note from René Clair informing me that he intends to reply.

I myself have started to fill in the questionnaire, but it will take me quite a while, as I wish to do it as carefully as possible, and I hope to send you my answers in two weeks' time.

Let me now ask you a question: do you want me to send this questionnaire – on your behalf as before – to other film-makers such as Philippe de Broca, Claude Lelouch, Claude Berri and Alain Resnais? If so, let me know as soon as you can.

In fond memory of our meeting at the Beverly Hills Hotel, I remain

Yours sincerely,
François Truffaut

1 – American director (1889–1977): *Her Man*, *One Way Passage*, *China Seas*, *Stand-in*, *Seven Sinners*, *The Postman Always Rings Twice*, etc.

2 – This questionnaire, sent by Garnett to a number of international film-makers, was eventually published in 1977 as *Learn from the Masters*.

To Nestor Almendros

Paris, 9 October 1974

My dear Nestor,

The other day, on the telephone, I forgot to speak to you about Florent Bazin. You met him last year and gave him some encouragement.

Since then, he has done an initial stint on Laszló Szabó's film *Zig Zag*, and I know the camera crew found him very satisfactory, so much so that everyone agreed he should be hired again for Claude Berri's current production, *Le Mâle du siècle*. I'd nevertheless very much like to have him with us on *L'Histoire d'Adèle*, if you have no major objection.

We have, at the Carrosse office, a small package for you, not very bulky but fragile, which you might like to collect next time you drop by.

Yours,
françois

To Maurice Cazeneuve[1] *Paris, 25 October 1974*

Dear Monsieur,

We are speeding up the preparation for my next film and it really would be impossible for me to come and have a talk with you on Sunday.[2] This week, in fact, I have received, from television producers, several propositions similar to yours but, feeling as I do that I should not spread myself too thin – with two films to shoot in 1974 – I prefer to keep my distance from this great upheaval.

If we had seen each other, there are two suggestions I would have made to you. The first: to recall Janine Bazin, since I sincerely believe, quite independently of my friendship with her, that the series *Cinéastes de notre temps* represented the best method of interesting TV viewers in the cinema. The second suggestion would be to produce the equivalent of *Le Masque et la Plume*, which is to say, simply have five or six critics arguing about the latest films, without showing a single extract, as the problem of extracts on television has never been solved and I believe that, in nine cases out of ten, a fragment of film isolated from its context is totally counterproductive.

These were the only two ideas to have crossed my mind, since I did not have the time to give the matter more attention.

I am very touched that you thought to approach me, but I also hope you will understand why I cannot become involved.

I wish you well on your own shoot[3] and on the whole new adventure of a third channel.

Yours very sincerely,
François Truffaut

1 – French television director, born in 1923.
2 – Cazeneuve had just been appointed director-general of a new (third) television channel, FR3, and wished to consult Truffaut on the policy it should adopt towards the arts.
3 – *Splendeurs et Misères des courtisanes*, a TV version of Balzac's novel.

To Louis Daquin[1] *Paris, 8 November 1974*

Dear Monsieur,

It was with much surprise and a little emotion that I received your letter; as it happens, I am currently collating and prefacing André Bazin's early articles, which were published in student magazines during the war, and, because of that, I find myself at the moment rather closer to you than you could have imagined; I see unfolding before me such film titles as *Nous les gosses, Le Voyageur de la Toussaint, Madame et le Mort, Premier de cordée,*[2] and quite naturally I have been assailed by images I thought I had forgotten, the most tenacious of which is one showing the platform of an overhead Métro.

That will explain the emotion, I come now to the surprise. This concerns the power you seem to think I possess, to the point where you believe that, with my support, you might be able to set up your project – well, I have to tell you, that is unfortunately not the case. Apart from two films co-produced and distributed by Hercule Mucchielli's company, Valoria, all my films in the last ten years have been financed by American studios: Columbia, Warners and United Artists. Each time I tried to interest a French company in one of my films (*Baisers volés* and *L'Enfant sauvage*), I failed, probably because the scripts did not appeal to them. Even with the Americans things have not always been easy: in order to be able to shoot *L'Enfant sauvage* in black and white, I was forced to give up my producer's percentage which was considerable, *La Nuit américaine* was accepted by Warners . . . after having been turned down by United Artists, and, for my next film – which tells the story of Victor Hugo's second daughter – the opposite has happened: Warners has refused and United Artists agreed.

My own company, Les Films du Carrosse, allows me to script each of my films, cast it and draw up the budget; the film being thus protected from external pressures, I find myself with total creative freedom. For reasons which you will understand, it's a method which is not appreciated by French financiers who do not like one to come asking only for money; on the other hand, it works better with American companies which are always on the look-out for French films that can be sold all over the world. These American companies are less concerned than the French with the question of the star-system, since today there exist only local stars and, within the framework of a reasonable budget, they are prepared to trust me, thanks also to the near-legendary gift for organization and attention to detail of Marcel Berbert who manages my company and each of our productions.

It is true – and this perhaps influenced your decision to write to me – that in recent years I was involved in the production of such films as *L'Enfance nue*,[3] *Ma Nuit chez Maud*,[4] *La Faute de l'abbé Mouret*[5] and two other films due to come out in 1975, but on each occasion there was a group of eight to ten co-producers, each of whom invested a sum of not more than six million with the risk of losing half; for Rohmer's film, for example, we were absolutely determined that it be made despite having been turned down by both television and the Avance sur Recettes.[6] I might add that, out of all the films we helped in this way, *Ma Nuit chez Maud* is the only one to have shown a profit . . .

If I have apprised you of these confidential details, it is to demonstrate to you that I am not the man you need. As regards your project, I have no wish to discuss in it depth, as I did not completely understand your intentions, but I agree with you that a screenplay does not make a film; it seems to me that the 40 million from the Avance ought to be enough to pay for the shoot if you were to decide to work in black and white and 16 mm, as was the case with a first-rate film which I have just seen called *Les Doigts dans la tête*;[7] if the prospect of black and white 16 does not appeal to you, I imagine that one of the television channels might be willing to co-produce (as with *Lancelot du lac*),[8] which would give you 35 mm and colour; you would also have to find a distributor without asking for too much money, someone like Nedjar[9] (C.F.D.C.).

In fact, rather than an artisan such as myself, you might turn to one of those fellow directors of ours who have managed to achieve the ideal, which is to say, be more or less directly responsible for the distribution of their own films: Claude Lelouch, Sergio Gobbi, Louis Malle, Claude Berri . . .

It is my very sincere hope that you will be able to make this film, since you must have had an extremely powerful interior motive to break your long silence; courage you possess, all you need is luck.

Yours sincerely,
François Truffaut

1 – French director (1908–80).
2 – Four films by Louis Daquin.
3 – By Maurice Pialat (1969).
4 – By Eric Rohmer (1969).
5 – By Georges Franju (1970).
6 – The system in France whereby films are financially aided on condition that the money is returned to the state if the film should prove commercially successful.
7 – By Jacques Doillon.
8 – By Robert Bresson.
9 – Claude Nedjar, French producer and distributor.

To Coluche[1] *[1974]*

My dear Coluche,

Though a little late, I would like to compliment you very sincerely and cordially on your show; I know that, in the rue de Berri, it was incomplete, but if you perform it again in its entirety, I would be very happy to come back and see it. I have not forgotten: a) our meeting with Claude Berri four years ago; and b) your card congratulating me on *L.N.A.*[2]

You have greater presence than ever before, which is essential if the moments of silence that you interpolate into your material are to make an impact; and, with a real sense of invention and impeccable timing, the emotion you are capable of generating is really quite complex.

I had a very enjoyable evening and so did my daughter;

yours very cordially,
François Truffaut

1 – French actor and variety star (1944–86): *Le Pistonné*, *L'Aile ou la Cuisse*, *Le Maître d'école*, *Tchao Pantin*, etc.

2 – *La Nuit américaine*.

To Marcel L'Herbier[1]

Paris, 11 December 1974

Dear Monsieur,

Your letter arrived at a curious moment, as I am in the process of editing and annotating a collection of André Bazin's articles on the French cinema during the war.

I have therefore just bought the book which has been written about you,[2] in order to extract some technical information concerning *L'Honorable Catherine*[3] and *La Nuit fantastique*.[4] Thank you for having sent me a second copy.

I am sorry that your memory of my negative articles has remained so vivid, since I have come to realize in rereading them – for another book – that my good reviews have stood the test of time far better.

For your information, the Oscar which I received – and to which I attach exactly the same importance as to a winning lottery ticket – was not awarded to me over Bergman's film, which had competed the previous year and lost out to Buñuel's *Le Charme discret de la bourgeoisie*.

If, as a critic, I was not invariably kind to you, do believe me when I say I regret it, and the various prefaces which I have recently written, for Bazin's books as well as my own, will, I hope, help to answer the questions which one cannot help asking oneself concerning the function of a critic, as soon as one becomes the object of the criticism of others.

Finally, with regard to the use of an extract from *Fahrenheit* in your anthology *Le Cinéma du Diable*, I am very happy to give you my permission. I believe, unfortunately, that there is a risk of complications, since I was only the salaried co-scenarist and director of the film, which was produced by Vineyard Productions for the American company Universal. I therefore think it will also be necessary to get the authorization of, on the one hand, Lewis Allen and on the other, Mr Lew Wasserman, the *big boss*[5] of Universal.

I haven't yet read Noël Burch's book in its entirety, but it seems to me first-rate and, if I have cause to regret that you have such a good memory, I would like to thank you for having sent me such a cordial letter.

Yours sincerely,
François Truffaut

1 – French director, (1888–1979): *L'Homme du large*, *L'Eldorado*, *Feu Mathias Pascal*, *L'Argent*, *Entente cordiale*, etc. When he wrote this letter to Truffaut, he was in his eighty-sixth year and almost blind.
2 – *Marcel L'Herbier*, by Noël Burch.
3 – Made in 1943.
4 – Made in 1942.
5 – In English in the original letter.

To Jean-Louis Bory *Paris, 11 December 1974*

Dear Jean-Louis Bory,

For some ten days now I have been mulling over a paragraph in your article 'Should we burn the Champs-Élysées?' without being able to digest it.

I had thought to suggest a meeting so that we might have a talk about it, I have opted instead for a letter, as I felt it would put you in a less awkward position.

The phrase which is causing me concern is the following: '. . . Truffaut, Chabrol, Demy and Rohmer have sold out to the system.'

If it concerned an appreciation, a value-judgement, I would obviously not have written, but the question is one of morality and no one likes to be called a bastard!

My dear Jean-Louis Bory, you and I have one point in common: we both enjoyed our greatest successes at the beginning of our careers.[1] You had the good fortune to become immediately a published and recognized artist, as I did. Since then, many of your books have been accepted by different publishers and because, from the very beginning, you demonstrated what you could do, no one has ever refused one of your manuscripts.

Let us suppose that one day you were to read in a newspaper: 'The true literature of today is to be found in manuscripts that were turned down by publishers, in books that were published at their authors' own expense and in mimeographed pamphlets: Genet fell silent in 1968; as for Sartre, Bory, Cayrol and Rezvani, they have sold out to the system.' Would you not think: 'This guy's got everything confused and mistakes form for content'?

You are not a 'marginal' author, you are a professional writer; your books are published because they are good, because you have a readership and because the hoped-for sales will enable the publisher's initial investment to be recouped. True or false? Even if, in station bookshops, they do not sell as well as Simenon or Guy des Cars,[2] your books are bought in drugstores and none the worse for that. True or false?

I may be mistaken, but I have the impression that, as a film director, I work in the same spirit as you do as a writer: we are free to choose our subject-matter, we handle it as we see fit and we send it out into the world.

The other day I heard you on television talking, in a very logical and uncynical fashion, about literary prizes and the dissemination of books: can you not apply the same clear-sightedness to the dissemination of films?

The best French film to have come out at the end of this year is *Les Doigts dans la tête*, I believe you are of the same opinion. The fact that it opened in a single cinema, the Racine, cannot be considered an honour for the film, it is, rather, a cause for dismay: by the beginning of January, the box-office returns will perhaps have recovered the distribution costs though it is by no means certain; what one would wish for *Les Doigts dans la tête* is that it might enjoy such a success at the Racine that Gourevitch[3] or Nedjar will decide to programme the film, before Christmas, in one of their sheds on the Champs-Élysées.

I have made thirteen films. A few were relatively successful, a few were relatively unsuccessful and three were total flops: *La Peau douce*, *La Sirène du Mississipi*, and *Les Deux Anglaises*. What exactly is it that you criticize me for: not having had enough failures or enough successes? Out of those thirteen films, which ones strike you as concessions to the system?

At the risk of being something of a bore, I'm now going to move into a long flashback to give you a rough idea of the course of my work in the last fifteen years. I discovered the cinema during the Occupation and Liberation and, following Jean Cocteau's advice: 'One should always sing in one's family tree', the films I make resemble those I liked. The films I liked, however, even when they were failures with the general public, like *La Règle du jeu* and *The Magnificent Ambersons*, had been shot in such a way as to be accessible to everyone. Since I had left school at 14, I could not logically aspire to the kind of intellectual pursuits of a Robbe-Grillet or of my friend Rivette. The stories I tell have a beginning, a middle and an end, even if I am quite aware that, in the final analysis, their interest lies elsewhere than in their plots.

I now begin my flashback.

Since you often seem to think that I have slid down the fatal slope (without your ever specifying the exact date), I would like to remind you that after *Les 400 Coups* (the village in which I was born, so to speak, on the night of the New Wave), I made *Le Pianiste* and *Jules et Jim* (I recently reread your enthusiastic review in *Arts*). Then came *La Peau douce*, good or bad, what's the difference, but after that *big*[4] fiasco at Cannes, there I was practically unemployed. An Italian producer offers me a small fortune to make one episode of a sketch film with Soraya and, what's more, he's prepared to buy the Italian rights to *La Peau douce*; I sleep on it, I meet the princess (who, I must say, was quite charming), then I turn it down. It is Antonioni who inherits Soraya from me.

Then I wander all over the place, my *Fahrenheit 451* script under my arm, nothing doing! Two years later, I reach the point where I can make the film provided I do so in London and in English. In the meantime I have turned down *Paris brûle-t-il?*,[5] *A la recherche du temps perdu*, Camus's *L'Étranger* and *Le Grand Meaulnes*, long live the system!

Then I made *La mariée était en noir*, *Baisers volés* (which almost didn't get made as the script was considered too insubstantial) and *La Sirène du Mississipi*. The latter film had been offered to me two years previously with Brigitte Bardot. I had adored the novel, but I had said, 'Bardot, out of the question. It will be Catherine Deneuve or no one.' I waited patiently in the wings and, as soon as the rights were available, I bought them with money lent me by Jeanne Moreau (long live true friends!) and I shot the film as I saw fit, good or bad, it was as I saw fit.

These problems are not widely known, as I don't like to speak of them in interviews; after all, the struggle for individual liberty is a part of life and I dislike the idea of playing on the sympathy of critics by telling them all about my difficulties with backers. Nor have I asked the State to subsidize me, and the only criticism I would make of Cocteau was that he tended to harp on too much about how 'France misunderstands its artists'! I now therefore have the reputation of a guy who always gets everything he wants, probably there's some truth in it and, one way or another, I can't complain. In any event, I feel totally responsible for the films I make, for their virtues and their flaws, and I never accuse the system. Back to where we left off.

Robert Dorfmann,[6] who wanted me to make a film for him, read my script for *L'Enfant sauvage* and said, 'I've always wanted to work with you and you bring me something absolutely impossible.' All right, I make the film with United Artists and, in order to do it my way and shoot it in black and white, I give up half my salary.

Then I made *Domicile conjugal* and there I'm quite willing to admit that it was not a 'necessary' film (well, not all that necessary) and that, for the first time in ages, I was ahead of the game because of the success of *Baisers volés*: nevertheless, I plead only half-guilty as *Baisers volés* had been rushed (because of the problems at the Cinémathèque) and my work with the actors went very much further in *Domicile conjugal*, a petit-bourgeois film, I quite agree!

Then came *Les Deux Anglaises*, a sorrowful film, possibly even wallowing in its own misery, but sincere, do believe me, to such a degree that I felt afterwards, as a real need, I had to compensate for it with a film that would be full of an almost feverish vitality, *Une belle fille comme moi*, which enabled me to go back to square one ('square one,' you're thinking, 'he said it, not me') with my Bernadette from *Les Mistons*.

Then I pulled myself together and came to terms with myself thanks to *La Nuit américaine* whose subject was, quite simply, my own reason for living. (You adore your mother, I hate mine, even now that she's dead, how could we ever have any two ideas in common?)

Since *La Nuit américaine* I have travelled, I have put together a book, *Les Films de ma vie* (early and recent articles), I have written prefaces for two books by André Bazin,[7] I have been turning down films again: *Le Petit Prince*[8] adapted from Saint-Ex and *La Vie de Scott and Zelda*[9] (oh yes) and I have finished various scripts intended for the three years that lie ahead.

Good or bad, my films are the ones I wanted to make and only those. I made them with the actors – known or unknown – whom I had chosen and whom I liked. If one day one of my projects is rejected, I'll go off and film it in Sweden or elsewhere. Since *Jules et Jim*, for example, I am regularly offered the chance to make films in America: the script of *Bonnie and Clyde* was written specially for me, but, after *Le Pianiste*, I no longer had any desire to film gangsters again; I am also aware that if all my personal projects were to come to nothing, I would end by accepting some of those commissions and the result would not necessarily be bad, but so far I have stood firm and I'm proud of the fact. One day I hope we'll have the chance to discuss the parallel adventure of films which get made and films which don't get made.

Please do not think me self-satisfied. I fully realize that, having the good fortune to be one of the twenty French directors who have freedom of choice, I ought to be more demanding and stringent.

I am aware that I am now at the half-way mark of my career and my greatest wish is to make a more complete success of the next thirteen films.[10] I know, for example, that I was wrong to be so fearful of the blank page and, because of that, I have adapted too many novels, especially American novels.

Oddly enough, it has become quite clear that (with the exception of *Jules et Jim*) my intentions have been better understood when I have filmed such original screenplays as *Les 400 Coups*, *Baisers volés*, *L'Enfant sauvage* and *La Nuit américaine* than when having filmed Irish and Goodis. I know that I still have a struggle ahead of me, but I can assure you that I will concentrate my efforts on the best way to make these films successful and not on any change, which would necessarily be an artificial one, in the choice of subject-matter.

In actual fact, I have never really chosen the subject-matter of any of my films. I let an idea enter my head, grow and develop there, I take notes and still more notes, and when I feel I have been possessed by it, then off we go.

It is in this manner that I am about to make a film on Adèle Hugo exactly five years after reading two pages on her by Henri Guillemin[11] in *Le Nouvel Observateur* (somewhere around February or March 1969).

A critic may be unable to accept as sincere this way of doing things – not from the dictates of choice or decision, but by a kind of progressive invasion of one's being; a writer, by contrast, cannot fail to have experienced it.

Now I am going to tell you about my projects.

L'Histoire d'Adèle H. (which, as I say, I start shooting in January) concerns Victor Hugo's second daughter, Adèle (as you can imagine, the name of Hugo did not exactly fire producers with enthusiasm). The film will be situated somewhere between *L'Enfant sauvage*, which is to say, a dramatization of real events, and *Les Deux Anglaises*, which is to say, an account of powerful and unrequited feelings.

Then, in July–August, *L'Argent de poche* [*Small Change*], a film centred on eight children, boys and girls, from birth to the age of twelve.

In 1976 I will make a film, not exactly on the subject of death, but on the dead, and the feelings we have about them. If it has to be shot in 16 mm and for television, then that's the way I'll do it, but first of all I'll try to make it in 35 mm and within the system, yes, 'fraid so.

Then I will film the story of a man, probably played by Charles Denner, who is overly obsessed with women.[12] I have still other projects, but I don't want to bore you much longer. I would simply like to have you accept the idea that I make these films exactly like you when you deliver a book to a publisher and he publishes it without asking you to add anything or cut anything or insist upon a misleading or lurid cover.

Having tried to demonstrate to you my 'whiter-than-whiteness' and the fact that I will always prefer one packet of my own brand of washing powder to two of another, I am now about to plead a case that really needs no defence because it concerns the 'whitest' of us all.

As long as ten years ago, Eric Rohmer decided to make his six *Contes moraux*. Between 1964 and 1966 he shot the first two in 16 mm, then *La Collectionneuse*. The fourth, *Ma Nuit chez Maud* was specially written for Jean-Louis Trintignant, who hesitated for two years before accepting, being finally moved by Rohmer's persistence and the fact that he refused to consider any other actor.

During that same period, the script of *Ma Nuit chez Maud* was turned down by the Avance sur Recettes and television: so we formed a group of seven co-producers and I went off to persuade Monsieur Contamine, who was then the director of U.G.C.,[13] to distribute the film, which as you know was the great success that *La Collectionneuse* had also deserved to be.

Then, imperturbably, Rohmer continued with his project: *Le Genou de Claire* and *L'Amour l'après-midi*.

Having completed the series, he has just spent three years: a) teaching cinema at Nanterre; b) directing a television programme on contemporary architecture; c) writing a university thesis on Murnau's *Faust* (200 pages) and brushing up his German in order to make his next film, based on Kleist, in the original language.[14]

Is that what you call 'selling out to the system'?

Unlike you or me, Rohmer has always refused to attend film festivals and he has never cared to appear on television: he is a man of unshakeable integrity, of a logical and rigorous intellect, yes, we have to accept this idea because it's true: the best French film-maker is both the most intelligent and the most sincere. His success is as well deserved as that of Ingmar Bergman, I hope you agree.

In any event, if you were one of those snobs who are capable of admiring a work of art only when it has been rejected by the general public, you would not have championed the cause of Eugène Sue, a populist writer who told poignant and exciting stories.

I am sending you this letter because, when you talk about films on *Le Masque et la Plume*, the way you describe them reminds me of a man whom I adored, Audiberti; I hope you also possess his good faith.

Yours very sincerely,
François Truffaut

1 – Bory's *Mon Village à l'heure allemande* and Truffaut's *Les Quatre Cents Coups*.
2 – Popular French novelist.
3 – Boris Gourevitch, French film exhibitor.
4 – In English in the original letter.
5 – Filmed by René Clément in 1966.
6 – French producer, born in 1912.
7 – *Le Cinéma de l'Occupation et de la Résistance* and *Le Cinéma de la cruauté*.
8 – Saint–Exupéry's book for children, filmed by Stanley Donen as *The Little Prince* in 1974.
9 – In fact, *Zelda*, Nancy Milford's biography of Zelda Fitzgerald.
10 – As it turned out, Truffaut was to make only eight more films.
11 – French writer and scholar, born in 1903, the editor of Victor Hugo's diaries.
12 – *L'Homme qui aimait les femmes* (*The Man Who Loved Women*) (1977), which did in the event star Charles Denner.
13 – French production and distribution company.
14 – *Die Marquise von O* (1976).

To Georges Delerue

Paris, 19 December 1974

My dear Georges,

I'm currently being unfaithful to you, but as it's with Maurice Jaubert, it's not precisely adultery, more like necrophilia.[1]

I'm sure that by the end of the year you will be completely immersed in your opera.

Please believe that I wish you and your wife every success in that great undertaking.

Your friend,
françois

1 – For *L'Histoire d'Adèle H.*, *L'Argent de poche*, *L'Homme qui aimait les femmes* and *La Chambre verte* Truffaut used pre-existent scores by Maurice Jaubert, who had died in 1940. Hence the reference to necrophilia.

1975

To Jean-Loup Dabadie *[16 January 1975]*

My dear Jean-Loup,

Forgive me for typing this letter, but when I use a felt pen my hand tires too quickly and I know I'm less elliptical on a typewriter.

Our shoot[1] is progressing very smoothly; Isabelle[2] is extraordinary and, as with Jeanne in the chalet in Alsace, I have the impression that the scenario is being improved instead of simply being recorded, which is so often the case, unfortunately. She is very disciplined and punctual, also very hard-working (we're filming in two versions: a set-up in French followed by the same set-up in English); like Jean-Pierre Léaud, she isn't keen on rehearsing and is only prepared to give of herself when the cameras are rolling, but then she gives so much of herself that one finds oneself filled with emotion, admiration and gratitude.

In reality, she escapes any categorization, I cannot compare her to anyone else and, because of that, she keeps me in a state of extreme tension, since she tends to ask a lot of questions which force me to question myself on the role of the actor. As far as I'm concerned, I am incapable of saying how the film will turn out – it will certainly be a strange and difficult one – but I know that I won't ever be quite the same again. That's all I can say after one week. She is, moreover, very much liked by the crew who would put up with her even if she were more temperamental, so convincing is her performance from the point of view of instinct and sensibility and the risks she's prepared to take. Of course, that fragile little girl is in reality possessed of incredible stamina. The role of Mrs Saunders (the landlady) is played by Sylvia Marriott, who played Mrs Brown, the mother of Anne and Muriel. *No problem.*[3] For the secondary roles, a lot of non-professionals, real Guernseyans (mainly for economic reasons, to economize on travelling and 'expenses', it seems all my films are shot in this way, probably because at the beginning they never seem very attractive, which is strange). I hope it will work, but I've never been too enamoured of the idea of blending the kind of truth produced by non-professionals (who act without projecting, as Bresson says) and that of professionals, who arrive at another kind of truth by another route.

My dear Jean-Loup, your silence since Christmas suggests to me that the idea of *Le Petit Roi*[4] doesn't interest you. The evening they showed *Roman Holiday* on TV, I thought: if Jean-Loup is watching this film, maybe he'll want to get going on *Le Petit Roi.* All right. I understand if you don't have a feeling for the subject. We had said, I had said, rather: for our next film, the initiative ought to come from you: Isabelle as a thief. For the moment, I'm not entirely convinced, but if I were to read a first draft or even a brief synopsis, I could come to a decision.

Well anyway, there's no hurry, let's talk about it again, when I return, at the end of March. I'd like to shoot *Le Petit Roi* in August 1976 (in case we're going to need several children as extras, which is likely). I know also from Catherine,[5] who has become with time a real and very great friend, that you were overworked and exhausted at the end of the year from having finished a number of different assignments.

Enough of this chatter. We still have two more weeks left of January; I take advantage of them to assure you that if I have no special wish for the Scheffer family – even if they lived in the rue Dabadie[6] – I do, on the other hand, wish every happiness, more precisely a continuation of the happiness they already possess, to the Dabadies of the rue Scheffer,

hoping to see you very soon, dear Marie, of whom only a single copy exists, and hoping to see you just as soon, dear Jean-Loup, one of five numbered copies (in Roman numerals).

your friend,
françois

Printed and bound in Guernsey, Thursday 16 January, at the Duke of Richmond Hotel where our exile[7] will come to an end around 10 March.

1 – Of *L'Histoire d'Adèle H.*
2 – Isabelle Adjani, French actress, born in 1955: *La Gifle*, *The Tenant*, *Barocco*, *Nosferatu*, *Subway*, *Camille Claudel*, etc.
3 – In English in the original letter.
4 – A project which was never filmed. The basic narrative idea – of a child who becomes king – derived from a celebrated Polish novel, Janusz Korczak's *King Mathias I*, as also from André Lichtenberger's *Le Petit Roi.*
5 – Deneuve.
6 – Jean-Loup and Marie Dabadie lived in the rue Scheffer.
7 – Truffaut is alluding to Victor Hugo's own exile in the Channel Islands.

'Of course, that fragile little girl is in reality possessed of incredible stamina . . .'
(Truffaut and Isabelle Adjani, *L'Histoire d'Adèle H.*)

To Bernard Gheur *St Peter Port, 24 January 1975*

My dear Bernard,

It was with great pleasure that I read your new book. I cannot possibly suggest any corrections, however, as I read it at a single sitting, carried along by the narrative, the way I watch certain films and become wholly engrossed by the plot, to the point where I forget the camera's existence.

There is, in any case, no doubt in my mind that you have become a professional writer. The subject-matter of your book awakened in me a number of dormant memories, but I couldn't help thinking of another director, Jean Eustache,[1] to whom I advise you to send it as soon as it's published, since your characters are extremely close to his. (Jean Eustache, c/o Les Films du Losange, 26, avenue Pierre-1er-de-Serbie, 75116 Paris.)

Thank you for letting me be the first to read the new book and good luck with your publishers.

Yours sincerely,
François Truffaut

1 – French director (1938–81): *Le Père Noël a les yeux bleus*, *La Maman et la Putain*, *Mes Petites Amoureuses*, *Une sale histoire*, etc.

To Ivry Gitlis[1] *St Peter Port, 2 February 1975*

My dear friend,

I am delighted at the thought that everything has been arranged and that we will soon be working together. The shoot[2] is going very well. Our young actress is very intense and the film will be tighter and more violent than the scenario and also, I hope, genuinely moving. I feel that you will be astonished, stimulated and above all very happy at the idea of playing opposite a partner such as Isabelle Adjani.

I find it hard to communicate with Claude Briac,[3] since we don't speak the same language, and that is why I preferred to write directly to you. I don't care for his suggestion that mention of your name on the credit titles should be preceded by 'With the participation of . . .', since, frankly, I find that both vulgar and meaningless. One acts in a film or one does not and, in the first instance, one is necessarily participating. I am quite aware that certain actors, wishing to distance themselves from their fellows (and losing sight of the fact that we'll all have equal billing in the cemetery), insist on having their names boxed off or followed by various odd phrases, such as 'in the role of So-and-So', but I must confess that such whims escape me.

In any case, apart from Isabelle Adjani, we have three excellent English actors in the film, and it would be an insult to them if I were to humour Claude Briac on this matter.

You are possessed of a strong and attractive personality and I am certain that, if acting appeals to you, we'll begin to see more and more of you on the screen. At which point you will be known as an artist with two distinct gifts.

The mesmerizer is an interesting part, and I promise that I will never forget you in the film's advertising, provided you agree to accept the same credit as Sylvia Marriott (who has made films for Walt Disney, King Vidor and myself, in *Les Deux Anglaises*), Bruce Robinson[4] (who has filmed with Franco Zeffirelli) and Joseph Blatchley[5] (a Shakespearean actor who is cast as the bookseller in our film and has just played the leading role in Tony Richardson's latest).[6]

I would have preferred to explain all of this to you in person, but I failed to reach you by telephone before you left for Italy.

The atmosphere of the shoot could not be more agreeable; the film will be four-fifths finished when you arrive, you will be very well received and it will all go off swimmingly.

See you very soon. Yours sincerely,
françois

1 – French violinist and composer, born in 1927. He has also written film music.
2 – Of *L'Histoire d'Adèle H.*, in which Ivry Gitlis plays the role of a magician.
3 – Gitlis's agent.
4 – In the role of Lieutenant Pinson. Robinson was later to write the script of Roland Joffé's *The Killing Fields* and direct *Withnail & I* and *How to Get Ahead in Advertising*.
5 – In the role of the bookseller Whistler.
6 – *Dead Cert*.

To Helen Scott *9, 10 February 1975*

My lovely big Scottie,

My typewriter is being shuttled back and forth from Christine's[1] bedroom (in the evening she types out the mail I dictate to her between the different set-ups) and my own suite whose snugness I'm sure you can imagine: a little bar, a fridge and a TV set that's been fixed up so that I can get the French Channel Two.[2]

The shoot progresses, it's difficult but there have been no real problems, and I think we're getting good results. Why difficult? Because of the two versions,[3] the rather stand-offish and uncooperative attitude of the people of Guernsey and no doubt because of the melancholy of the theme as well which generates a certain tension on the set; there are times when we find ourselves whispering all day long and it's only in the evening that we get our normal voices back. None of that does our work any harm and it's not uncommon to see the little make-up girls weeping behind the scenes while our young Adèle is performing.

The two young men I recruited from London (the bookseller and Lieutenant Pinson) are first-class, and the locals to whom we've given walk-on roles are acquitting themselves very well indeed.

We're all very tired and have lost weight, but it's a tiredness we like, and the technical crew is the best I've ever had; Bazin's son Florent is a member of the camera crew and everyone is delighted with him.

I'm pleased you're going to be translating my book; in a month you'll have the printed copy (it comes out at the end of March) and that will make your work easier. It seems obvious to me that the 1954 articles are very weak, those from 1955 a little less bad, those from 1956 respectable and those after that quite good; that means that I learned to write by writing; I have no worries on your account, I know it will all be smoothed out and put into an 'editorial' form which won't have any effect on its 'cinématique' aspect. Suzanne thinks only the first five pages will pose any problem and that afterwards the solutions you have found for them will cover the rest of the book. That seems logical to me.

With this typewriter I ought to be primed for a long letter, but the fact is that I don't have much to tell you; I have almost lost touch with Paris, apart from Madeleine and the children; I have no time to read newspapers, I'm not up to date on anything, except the fact that for once your friend Carné did not lunch alone.

Sunday morning:

I have a hangover, since I drank too much champagne last night in order to knock myself out and render myself senseless after a week that had been just too tough.

Nestor,[4] who takes everything literally, is very worried about your idea of opening an office on the Champs-Élysées: 'Doesn't Helen realize it could cost her more than she'll ever earn?' I reassured him as best I could.

Carrosse's private film society is going well; every week we screen two or three films in 16 mm: *Psycho*, *The Magnificent Ambersons*, *The Gold Rush*, *Fahrenheit*, *The Last Laugh*[5] and this evening *Les 400 Coups*. I'm waiting for and hope to receive 3 Buster Keatons.

I'm leaving you now, my dear Scottie, and beg you to excuse the dullness of this letter; I'm looking forward to seeing you again soon, because I miss you – even if you have the impression I neglect you when I'm in Paris – and I promise you I won't be staying in Guernsey nearly as long as Victor Hugo (yes, but he took Juliette with him, I can hear you say with gritted teeth).

I kiss you because I love you,

françois

1 – Christine Pellé, the continuity person on *L'Histoire d'Adèle H.*
2 – Truffaut was writing this letter from Guernsey in the Channel Islands.
3 – The film was being shot in both French and English.
4 – Almendros.
5 – F. W. Murnau's *Der letzte Mann* (1924).

To Jean-Loup Dabadie *on the eve of 1 May [1975]*

My dear Jean-Loup,

Here, a little belatedly, is my reply to your letter of 17 April.

Endlessly viewing and re-viewing Isabelle A.'s face on the Moritone screen, I feel it would be difficult for me to film it again for several years, certainly not before 1980. I think you'll understand what I mean when you see *Adèle H.* She has succeeded so well in making herself look old that she's going to have to reverse the process for her next roles, and, until her real age catches up with the age she appears in *Adèle*, I am not the man for the job. What's more, I'm convinced that she both needs and wants to experiment with other styles of direction.

You ought to see her again, talk to her about the project and together trace out the Identikit portrait of the ideal director for the film.

Would you like us to meet at the end of May to discuss other ideas?

Best wishes to Marie and Jean-Loup,

françois

To Paul Newman[1] *Paris, 26 June 1975*

Dear Paul,

Our meeting in New York last year had been so pleasant, and you were so friendly that I feel free to send you this little note.

I have heard that you are preparing a film about *Mandrake*[2] and I would like to draw your attention to a director you may not have thought of, though I feel he is ideal for such a project: I am referring to Alain Resnais.

The face of Isabelle A. (filming *Adèle H.*).

Since childhood, Resnais has had a passion for *Mandrake* and knows all it is possible to know about it. I also believe that if one does not want to disappoint the 'fans' of the famous comic strip, it would be important to use a director with a special talent for the visual and for stylization.

I can imagine the result of the collaboration between the excellent actor that you are and the author of *Last Year at Marienbad*.

If you have already made your choice or you find my suggestion strange, forget my idea, but not my admiration for your talent and my friendship for you.

François Truffaut

1 – Paul Newman, American actor and director (born 1925). This letter was written in English.
2 – The film was never made.

To Jean Gruault

21 November 75

My dear Jean,

I don't necessarily dislike misunderstandings, but I think it would be a pity if we let our friendship be undermined by a period of mutual silence for which I was originally responsible.

In the first place, there was my disappointment on reading *L'Autel des morts*, in the second place, your disappointment on seeing *Adèle* on the screen. As far as *L'Autel des morts* is concerned, I imposed a framework that proved too rigid for you to be able to invent and you did your best. I liked the script better on a second reading, I had it typed out and am now preparing to revise it with Suzanne before submitting the 4th version to you.

As for *Adèle*, I have to admit that your negative reaction was more sincere than I initially thought as many people have since reacted in the same way; Marcel Ophüls and his wife, for example, who went to see it in New York with the firm intention of liking it; not to mention such words as cold, frigid, and distant that have turned up in so many reviews. And after all you are perfectly within your rights to be disappointed by a film that you visualized differently from me. On my side, I will have a genuinely personal opinion on *Adèle* in 2 years' time when I'll be able to see the film again as though it had been made by someone else.

Regarding *L'Autel des Morts*, I wanted to change the title because I thought it might encourage us to be more inventive!

To finish with *Adèle*, here's proof that it's a film to be feared: Miss Guille (who had become Mrs Secor 1 or 2 years ago) died in her college at Wooster a week after seeing the film at the N.Y. Festival, of a heart attack.

My dear old Jean, I know you're happy working with Resnais;[1] I hope I'll see you again before a negress brings you to the rue Robert-Estienne,[2] I'm old, my arms are open to you,

your friend,
françois

1 – On *Mon Oncle d'Amérique*.
2 – Truffaut is alluding to the black woman who brings Adèle home at the end of the film and of whom the seventy-year-old Victor Hugo boasted that he had become the lover. 'She was my first negress,' he wrote in his diary.

To Gilles Jacob

21 Nov. 75

My dear Gilles,

You know I never try to lean on critics or their criticism. If *Adèle H.* didn't move you, then it was my fault, and no more need be said about it.

To refer to 'intellectual dishonesty'[1] twice in the same programme, that hurt me, for if, in the last ten years, I've refused to film *Le Grand Meaulnes*, *Un amour de Swann*, *L'Etranger*, *Zelda* and I don't know what else, it was precisely because I didn't want to deceive and disappoint the people who liked those books and had an image of them in their heads.

Adèle was 15 years older? So what? Kaspar Hauser after all was 15 years younger than Herzog's[2] version. A year ago everyone thought I was going to make a film about Madame Adèle Hugo, the mother, quite simply because no one knew Adèle, the daughter, not Gilles Jacob any more than Patrick Thévenon.[3] Since the beginning of September 75 every critic has become an expert on the Hugo family!

All right. The title card 'This story is authentic, it depicts incidents which occurred and characters who existed' was a suggestion by Jean-Loup Dabadie who rightly thought that, since the plot does not conform to a conventional dramatic structure and introduces all sorts of extravagant sequences, it was important from the beginning to angle the spectator towards the idea that, to put it simply, truth is sometimes stranger than fiction.

The same card appeared at the beginning of *L'Enfant sauvage*. I also remember the one from *Un condamné à mort s'est échappé*: 'This story is authentic; I offer it such as it is, without embellishment.' I can assure you, though, that if you read André Devigny's account (*Un condamné à mort s'est échappé*, Air du temps, Gallimard), you'll be surprised by the intellectual dishonesty of Bobby Bresson.

People are not idiots: they're quite aware that it isn't the real Lieutenant Fontaine,[4] the real Kaspar or the real Adèle on the screen!

What is true is that *Adèle H.* has divided the public in a very bizarre fashion, with some – quite numerous – spectators complaining of coldness, distance, frigidity and asceticism, while others talk of warmth, emotion and melodrama. I therefore recognize that there is something strange and lopsided about the film which I'll endeavour to analyse one day.

There, my dear old Gilles, you have the whole business. In America, where *La Gifle*[5] hasn't come out, our young actress has made an extraordinary impact, I'll send you the piece in the *New Yorker*, which is in my opinion the most profound (and obviously favourable!).

I've vaguely heard talk of the *Histoire d'O* problem,[6] my only regret is that these stories about the press are never made public; I hope you'll get another column, the one you've deserved since 'Saint Jean Vigo, Patron of Film Societies'[7]. I'd even go as far as to say: I'd rather be slated by Gilles Jacob any day than praised by, shall we say, Chapier![8]

your old friend,
françois

1 – 'This was an ill-chosen phrase uttered on the spur of the moment during a lively debate on the radio programme *Le Masque et la Plume*, an idiotically pedantic comment on the difference between Adèle Hugo's age and Isabelle Adjani's that I have always regretted.' (Note by Gilles Jacob)
2 – A reference to Werner Herzog's *Jeder für sich und Gott gegen Alle* (*The Enigma of Kaspar Hauser*) (1973).
3 – French journalist (for many years at *L'Express*) and writer.
4 – The protagonist of *Un condamné à mort s'est échappé*.
5 – By Claude Pinoteau and starring Isabelle Adjani.
6 – 'Jean-Jacques Servan-Schreiber, who was then managing director of *L'Express*, had not been well pleased by the fact that I wrote a negative review of *Histoire d'O*, a mediocre film to which the magazine had inexplicably devoted two of its covers. At the end of 1975 I was obliged to leave *L'Express*, of which I had been the film critic for five years.' (Note by Gilles Jacob)
7 – 'The title of an article on Vigo which I published in 1951 in a magazine called *Raccords*.' (Note by Gilles Jacob)
8 – Henry Chapier, French film critic and broadcaster.

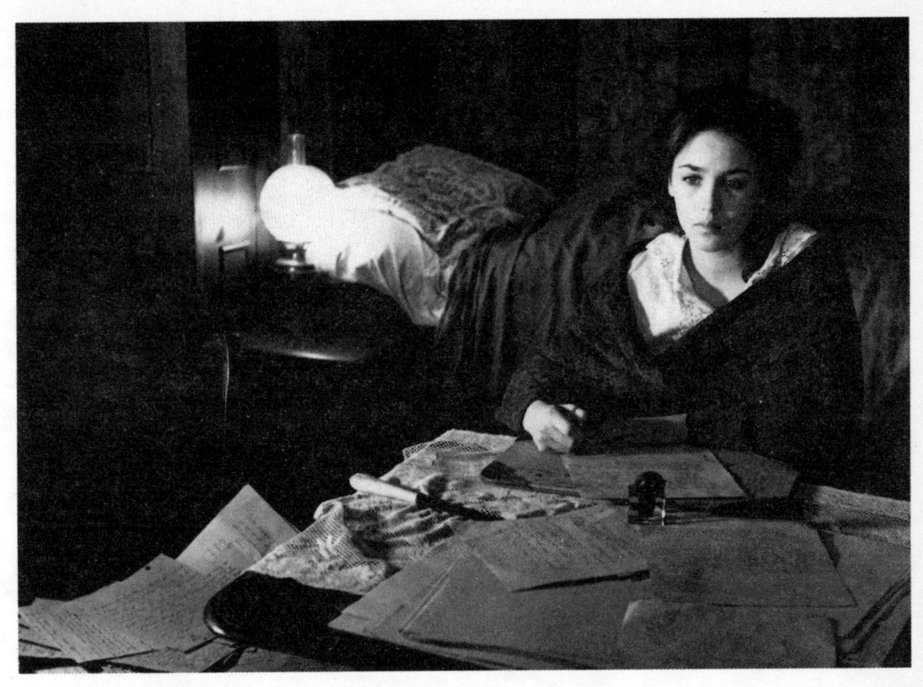

‘Our shoot is progressing very smoothly; Isabelle is extraordinary . . .’

1976

To Henri Langlois[1] *Paris, 4 February 1976*

My dear Henri,

The Cinémathèque Française has advertised the screening of *La Nuit américaine* on Sunday 8 February at 6.30. But the film is being shown on the same day in one of the cinemas run by Frédéric Mitterrand,[2] the 'Olympic 2'. I ask you therefore to cancel your screening, as you know my position on this matter.

I consider that the Cinémathèque strays from its proper vocation whenever it starts to compete with the commercial circuits or art-house cinemas. I'm depending on you to change your programme for Sunday, but, in my capacity as producer of *La Nuit américaine*, I am also writing to Warner Bros.[3] to make the same point.

Yours sincerely,
François Truffaut

1 – Co-founder (with Georges Franju) and Secretary-General of the Cinémathèque Française (1914–77).

2 – Film exhibitor, distributor and director (and nephew of the French President).

3 – Distributor of the film world-wide.

To Henri-Georges Clouzot[1] *6 February 1976*

My dear Georges,

Why not return to work, why not shout 'Action!'? I suppose that lots of people are trying to persuade you, I don't see why I should succeed; even so, I'd be happy to talk it over with you, if you have both the time and the inclination.

I've just completed the sound-mixing of my film,[2] I'm relatively free, I would be pleased to invite you to lunch or simply to have a chat, as you prefer.

Even from far away, I remain

Sincerely and faithfully yours,
François T.

1 – Clouzot, who was then 69, died the following year.

2 – *L'Argent de poche.*

To The Secretary-General of the CFDT[1]

Paris, 10 February 1976

Dear Monsieur,

Someone from the C.F.D.T. tried to contact me by telephone to ask me to comment on the fact that I signed the declaration in support of 'the programme for demoralization of the army'.

The reasons for my endorsement and support are as follows:

1. the unpleasant memories I have of my military service in Germany in 1951.

2. its consistency with the Appeal of the Hundred and Twenty-one which I signed in 1960.

Yours sincerely,
François Truffaut

1 – The Confédération Française Démocratique du Travail, the French social-democratic trade union.

To Liliane Dreyfus[1]

[10 February 1976]

My little Lili,

Your screenplay is first-class, superbly written and wonderfully well constructed (with the exception of the final image, which ought to be of the two leading characters Dani and Dominique rather than of some extras). Your girlfriend writes very stylishly. It all rather makes one think of a sequel to *Adieu Philippine*, 15 years on, with the difference that a man wouldn't have been able to write such good dialogue for 2 women, except for the Bergman of the marital comedies.

What you need is a good title. Unfortunately, the material is too good for the people of the Avance sur Recettes who have been conditioned to give money to anything literary and pretentious. You'll have to disguise the lightness of touch by adding after every number change 'Interior, automobile-evening, etc.' and every so often put in a few technical details, etc. Everyone will tell you it won't come to 90 minutes, whereas I'm sure it will, which is why it's so important to have it written as though it were a final version.

To interest a producer, what you have to suggest is an analogy with *A nous les petites Anglaises*[2] (with muscle-bound jocks instead of English nymphets!). You ought to show it to Albina,[3] Javal,[4] Beauregard and some TV people. A single casting error and the film is done for. Be careful, the dialogue is such that it wouldn't stand, it wouldn't survive, a jarring note.

Honestly, the film is very well written, nothing remains but to shoot it, with the kind of cameraman who will collaborate on the direction, like Pierre Lhomme,[5] and this time – not as with your last film – the absolute necessity of lots of rehearsals with the actors before the shoot, since the most important thing is the rhythm.

You have a good film there, Lili, don't do anything silly, out of haste or because you feel like helping out a friend or are over-tired; this script has to be protected like a baby,

love,
françois

1 – French actress and director (*Femmes au soleil*).
2 – By Michel Lang.
3 – Albina du Boisouvray, French producer and director (*Un film*).
4 – Bertrand Javal, French producer.
5 – French cinematographer, born in 1930. He has worked with Jean Eustache, Jacques Doillon, Jean-Paul Rappeneau, Jean-Pierre Melville, Robert Bresson, Claude Miller, James Ivory, etc.

To Jean-François Hauduroy

Paris, 26 February 1976

My dear Jean-François,

I would be very happy to have lunch with you, but in April, since until then I'll be taken up with *L'Argent de poche*.

So that you won't waste any time, here is the information relating to Peter Bogdanovich.

He is at present shooting a film, *Nickelodeon*, which deals with Hollywood's silent period.* He had a great deal of trouble raising the finance because of the resounding failure of his previous film.[1] I'll give you his address and I suggest you write to him using my name as a reference:

212 Copa de Oro Road
Bel Air
Los Angeles
California 90 024

I am certain he'll read your material (if it's in English).

I think, nevertheless, that an American script benefits from being presented by an agent. You have to remember that films like *Chinatown*[2] and *Three Days of the Condor*[3] make their way around Hollywood and are read by a dozen directors, actors and actresses before becoming the object of a deal. That may not bear much resemblance to what we at *Cahiers du cinéma* used to call the 'politique des auteurs', but it's what happens nevertheless!

My dear Jean-François, I take advantage of the occasion to offer you the American edition of a book which you like and which you let me read in French: *The Disenchanted*.[4]

Your friend,
françois

* Allan Dwan[5] is the historical consultant and will make an appearance in the film which stars Ryan and Tatum O'Neal, Burt Reynolds and Orson Welles.[6]

1 – *At Long Last Love.*
2 – By Roman Polanski.
3 – By Sydney Pollack.
4 – By Budd Schulberg.
5 – American director (1885–1981). Dwan made more than 400 films, the first in 1911 and the last, *The Most Dangerous Man Alive* (of which the film-within-the-film of Wim Wenders's *The State of Things* is supposedly a remake) in 1958.
6 – Neither Dwan nor Welles appeared in *Nickelodeon.*

To Richard Roud

Tuesday 27 April [1976]

My dear Richard,

Would you like to come and have dinner at my place, with a friend, on Monday evening, 3 May?

I apologize for pinning you down to a precise date, but I'm leaving Paris, in fact France and even Europe, the day after tomorrow, and for quite some time.

Naturally, I've invited Scottie. If you return during the weekend, you can reach me at 780.81.75.

Yours,
françois

The classroom of *L'Argent de poche*.

To Renée Saint-Cyr[1] *just before 1 May 76*

Dear Madame,

I very much liked your book, *Le Hérisson puni*. It's already several weeks since I read it and it has remained vividly etched in my memory. At first, when I discovered that it was the diary of a theatrical tour rather than a volume of memoirs, I had a slight sense of disappointment, which was, however, dispelled when I read it. Today I am full of admiration for you, the actress and the writer, full of resentment towards Jacques Daroy[2] . . . though, all things considered, I'm not so sure . . . it's especially thanks to him that your heart began to beat a little too rapidly, a little too strongly during the tour, when one could sense your anxiety growing.

My greatest hope, dear Madame, Mademoiselle Renée Saint-Cyr, is that the success of this book will encourage you to write another, it's in that hope that I am sending you this fan letter; you have much to say, you say it superbly well, with depth and grace, you must absolutely continue,

your very sincere admirer,
François Truffaut

1 – French actress, born in 1904: *Les Deux Orphelines*, *Les Perles de la couronne*, *Si Paris m'était conté*, *Le Monocle rit jaune*, etc.

2 – Jacques Daroy, French writer, producer and director, born in 1896.

To Serge Rousseau[1] *from Mobile, Alabama [1976]*

My dear Serge,

I adored Anny's[2] novel and, not having her address, I rely on you to forward this letter which she surely won't resent your reading before she does since it contains only praise and nothing at all salacious!

I continue to be im-Mobilised by the Spielberg film,[3] but I'm not wasting my time even though everything seems to take forever. I don't suffer from nerves when I act, I do it for my own and the crew's amusement, I'm not too sure I'm always good or above all capable of speaking lines other than my own. Nevertheless, they seem happy as I myself am on those days when we have a heavy shooting schedule; all the same, what perpetual frustration! Anyway, as I expected, there are lots of things I'm beginning to understand, from the temptation to nibble on chocolate to the pretence of sulking as a means of concentration, I find it all very amusing.

Do you like our new title: *L'Homme qui aimait les femmes*? I think it's more original than *L'Homme à femmes*:[4] with the latter, you have the impression you've already seen the film, right? In any case, the screenplay is progressing, it's getting thicker and more structured, Charles's face and voice are in my mind whenever I work on it.

How are Marie[5] and Dominique,[6] are you going on holiday with them? From when to when? If I ask, it's to satisfy my curiosity, but also to force you to write to me.

The star of the American film on flying saucers is Richard Dreyfuss, who is terrific; did you see him in *The Apprenticeship of Duddy Kravitz*?[7] My dear Serge, I like America but Los Angeles more than Wyoming or Alabama and I miss you, as well as our lunches at the Boulangerie. Let me know how you are, and also Marie, the Berris, Charles, Duperey the writer, Sagan the director[8], but not Lebovici[9] the publisher since you never see him.[10]

your friend, françois

1 – French actor, then agent, born in 1930. For Truffaut he played in *La Mariée était en noir* and *Baisers volés*.
2 – Anny Duperey, French actress, born in 1947. She had just published her first novel, *L'Admiroir*.
3 – Steven Spielberg's *Close Encounters of the Third Kind*. Spielberg had asked Truffaut to play the part of a French expert on Unidentified Flying Objects.
4 – I.e. *The Ladies' Man*.
5 – The actress Marie Dubois, who was married to Rousseau.
6 – Their daughter.
7 – By Ted Kotcheff (1974).
8 – The novelist Françoise Sagan had just directed her first film, *Les Fougères bleues*.
9 – Gérard Lebovici, French agent, producer and also publisher of books on the cinema.
10 – Truffaut is joking: Rousseau worked at the same agency as Lebovici.

To Claude de Givray and Bernard Revon[1] *7 June [1976]*

My dear friends,

Here is the Devil's Tower, the setting for most of the action of Steven Spielberg's film *Close Encounters of the Third Kind*, in which I play the role of a *French scientist*:[2] Claude Lacombe!

As far as our film *L'Agence Magic*[3] is concerned, I wanted to tell you: 1. to keep the details of the plot secret (already Helen Scott and J.-F. Stévenin[4] claim to know the story); 2. I ask you to create each of the characters as though it were a question of giving 5 or 6 major stars their best-ever roles. In actual fact, we'll be casting unknowns, but just imagine, as a guide, that: the automaton is Monty Clift, the mother, Joan Crawford, the daughter, Isabelle Adjani, the stepfather, a less distinguished Herbert Marshall. Then 2 or 3 very good parts that might be up for a Best Supporting Actor award. What we have to achieve is an extremely taut narrative, a tragedy unfolding against a sordid background; keep it slim and be careful of curves; don't write a scene just for the sake of a single detail, but group 10 details together in one good scene, even if it has to be a long one.

I hope I'm not getting on your nerves with these suggestions. I have such hopes of reading a good, almost perfect script in September. When you have no feeling for the dialogue of a scene, I'd prefer that you describe the conversation without putting it into direct speech: 'She tells him that she can't go on living without X and that she'll kill herself if Y doesn't manage to speak to Z.' O.K.?

It's within that kind of casual framework that I'm working at the moment with Suzanne on the script of *L'Homme qui aimait les femmes* which I'll shoot in October with Charles Denner.

I plan to shoot *L'Agence Magic* in 1977, I'm counting on you two to help me make a fine film: modest characters, grandiose emotions and above all individuals living their lives to the full.

1 – Truffaut's co-scenarists on *Baisers volés* and *Domicile conjugal*. The director had sent them an enormous postcard of the Devil's Tower in Wyoming.
2 – In English in the original letter.
3 – *L'Agence Magic* was the story of a down-at-heel variety tour in an unspecified African country, but Truffaut was thinking of changing the location to a small French town during the Occupation. Though the film was never made, it contained certain elements which were to reappear in *Le Dernier Métro*. The rights to the script were eventually bought by Claude Berri.
4 – Jean-François Stévenin, French actor and director, born in 1944.

To Gilles Jacob

Mobile, [July 1976]

My dear Gilles,

Since Jeanne Moreau has just one car in Paris and another in the Var, I'm pretty certain she won't have a garage to rent.[1] There have been various little hiccups in the course of our relationship; in spite of the affection and consideration we have for one another, I'm not mad about the idea of making such an enquiry, convinced as I am that the answer would be negative. On the other hand, I suggest you write to her yourself, 9, rue du Cirque, why not?

As you say, the festival entails ever greater risks, for everyone concerned, and I followed it, obviously from afar, yet attentively nevertheless, thanks to the newspapers that my secretary sent me.

I knew that Losey and Delon[2] were likely to be slaughtered, but I was convinced that Polanski[3] would come out of it well and that Gérard Blain,[4] as the nice-little-newcomer-who-deserves-to-be-encouraged, would have a triumph! Nothing of the kind!

It's become really impossible to predict. Rohmer[5] alone, or almost alone, did well out of the festival, but perhaps it was just a stay of execution. That's why, rightly or wrongly, I was so insistent on *La Nuit américaine* being screened out of competition.[6] It allowed everyone to say that if I had competed I would have won the Grand Prix, but, in fact, if I'd won the Grand Prix, the Rassam-Ferreri mafia (*La Grande Bouffe*) would have made me pay dearly for it. At Cannes everything comes down to tactics, to strategy.

Death in Venice[7] is endlessly screened in art cinemas because, in formal terms, it's an almost perfect film and one which has stood up well over the years; partly because of Mahler, but also because of a unity of tone in style and subject-matter, people like the film the way they like a record and they go and see it again and again. The year it went to Cannes,[8] however, the journalists (you were perhaps one of them, too bad, I'm telling you what I think) wanted to punish Visconti for having practically assumed the G.P.[9] was his for the asking, that's why they leapt on Losey's *The Go-Between* which benefited from the fact that it had arrived with no particular reputation. On the other hand, people seeing *The Go-Between* today for the first time tend to find it disappointing . . .

from Mobile, 17 July

I'm resuming this letter which, for all sorts of reasons, I interrupted two weeks ago.

Jeanne was a great success in Los Angeles (along with Viot,[10] Flot[11] and the others), but I was here, in this enormous hangar without any air-conditioning, with floodlights blazing away, etc. I know it's strong in Paris too, the heat, I mean.

I hope your son passed his bac; my elder daughter, Laura, passed with honours, which means she's free to choose her new school (she was at the Molière and has set her sights on Louis-le-Grand) with the idea of eventually taking a degree in literature; by making her a trainee continuity-girl on *L'Argent de poche*, I was hoping to persuade her to desert the groves of Academe for those of show-business, but . . . well, we'll see.[12]

I hope the sense of disenchantment expressed in your letter is only temporary. Your arguments against writing ('the French no longer read . . .') are impossible to take seriously. Raymond Guérin, Henri Calet and Henri Pollès are read by small groups of people who never stop passing their books around, they're wonderful writers who are completely ignored by the 'general public'. No one in America knows David Goodis, who died ten years ago, or Charles Williams, who committed suicide last year without receiving an obituary in a single newspaper. If you wish and need to write, then you do write, and that's all there is to it.

I'm a bit unhappy about this rambling, often disjointed, letter; the only thing I forgot to tell you is that we're working very hard, twelve hours a day. The film, originally budgeted at 11 million dollars, is now heading for 15 or 16 million, but I think it will be visually very striking, and the star, Richard Dreyfuss, is terrific. Whether your parking problem is solved or not, I wish you a very good year and my warmest regards to the whole Jacob family,

your old buddy,

françois

1 – 'I was in need of a parking space near the offices of the Cannes Festival.' (Note by Gilles Jacob)
2 – With *M. Klein*, screened at Cannes in 1976.
3 – With *The Tenant*.
4 – With *Un enfant dans la foule*.
5 – With *Die Marquise von O*.
6 – In 1973.
7 – By Luchino Visconti.
8 – 1971.
9 – The Grand Prix.
10 – Pierre Viot, then director-general of the Centre National de la Cinématographie.
11 – Yonnick Flot, a journalist at Agence-France-Presse, then director of Unifrance-Film.
12 – Laura Truffaut is now a professor of French literature at the University of California at Berkeley.

To Koichi Yamada *from Mobile, 22 July 1976*

My dear Yamada,

Thank you very much for your letter of 27 June. I'm very pleased you liked *L'Argent de poche*. I hope it will be a success in Japan, more so than *Adèle*, *L'Enfant sauvage* and *La Nuit américaine*, none of which enjoyed more than a 'succès d'estime'. It's not for the money that I express such a hope, even though that's important, but because I feel that the situation of my films is still rather shaky in Japan and that there's always the possibility of a distributor or exhibitor refusing to show one of them on the pretext that it's unlikely to make enough of a profit.

I owe my present freedom to America, and for quite some time now, since in France, as a rule, my films do only reasonably well, except for *L'Argent de poche*, the most successful since *Les 400 Coups*! But there, I've talked enough *'bizness'*.[1]

Yes, Pathé-Journal and Fox Movietone are anachronisms, intentionally so because of my memories . . . The young bride seen in the newsreel is my daughter Laura* (the elder), thus the mother of the little whistler. My younger daughter Eva plays the little girl who gets herself taken to the cinema.

So much the better if Major Enterprise is interested in translating the script. You can arrange all of that with Thérèse de Saint-Phalle. I wrote the book in the form of a novel so that children could read it more easily than a script. I wrote it during the editing, after the shoot itself, but for my next film, *L'Homme qui aimait les femmes*, I'm going to try and write the novel first to see if it then gives me any ideas about changing the screenplay! The leading role will be taken by Charles Denner surrounded by lots of unknown women.

Even here, in Mobile, I remain at your disposal to answer questions on *Les Films de ma vie*, since I've been given an office inside the immense hangar where we're shooting, and there's often a very long time to wait between shots. Let me know, too, how the reissued *Adèle* is doing! Very best regards.

françois

P.S. Don't fail to tell U.A. and Major Enterprise that the film is designed for families and children, even the book ought to be thought of as a children's book, for the holidays, etc.

*You saw her in the crew, she was the trainee continuity-girl!

1 – In 'English' in the original letter.

To Nestor Almendros *from Mobile, 26 July 1976*

My dear Nestor,

I hope you enjoyed working in Spain, I haven't had much information concerning the film,[1] since Suzanne was very vague. She told me, however, that for family reasons you weren't too keen on making Terry Malick's[2] new film. I told Bert Schneider,[3] who telephoned me here, that I wasn't sure about dates and that the question ought to be explored between you and Suzanne.

As you probably know, I play a French scientist in Steven Spielberg's new film, *Close Encounters of the Third Kind*; it's occasionally amusing, but very slow, very long, and I have to recognize that the vocation of actor has its painful side (or rather sides).

If you write to me, let me know whether or not *Adèle H* has opened in Spain, I can't understand this incredible delay. In any event, Hitchcock recently had the film screened for him, he liked it and you will, I imagine, be pleased to note that in the telegram he sent me he mentions the photography.

The Hungarian cinematographer Vilmos Zsigmond, who is doing the lighting for *Close Encounters*, also told me how much he admires you.

As Suzanne told you, we start shooting *L'Homme qui aimait les femmes* in mid-October, I'll hope you'll like the script; because we'll be shooting very slowly (4 or 5 shots a day), I'll have a lot of time to polish this new version.

A line or two from you would give me great pleasure, my dear Nestor, until we meet up again in October,

yours,
françois

1 – Vicente Aranda's *Cambio de sexo*, about a sex-change operation.
2 – Terence Malick, American director, born in 1945: *Badlands*, *Days of Heaven*. Almendros finally accepted the offer to work on the latter film and won an Oscar for his cinematography.
3 – The producer, along with his brother Harold, of *Days of Heaven*.

To Serge Rousseau *from Mobile, 29 July 1976*

My dear Serge,

Thank you for your letter from the Aude and all the news it contained. You don't mention whether you admired Huster[1] and Martine Chevalier in *Le Cid*. You don't give me any news of Isabelle, of Dudu (I read something about him in, I think, *Le Film français*), of Miou-Miou,[2] of Lelouch's film,[3] etc. In the depths of Alabama one is starved for news of Paris. Fortunately, my office sends me lots of letters and magazines . . .

Here, in Mobile, in the immense hangar where we're shooting (3 shots a day), I was able to acquire an office thanks to which I can spend nearly six hours a day on my own work (we work a twelve-hour day, with an hour's lunch break). I'm therefore now on the second version of *L'Homme qui aimait les femmes* and I'm even perhaps (shooting methods here give you a lot of leisure time) going to begin writing a novel which will coincide exactly with the screenplay, but in literary form, which might be published before the film comes out, even before it's finished. It's an exercise I find very amusing, anyway I'm going to try.

Normally, all going well, we ought to be able to respect the dates that were fixed (starting to shoot in mid-October), since delays here are made up by all the overtime they do; there has even been talk of making us work on Sundays . . . ! As I expected, I'm really discovering lots of things, behind the scenes, concerning the frame of mind of all sorts of people, not only actors, but I'd prefer to keep all of that for our conversations over lunch. I could also easily write a new version of *La Nuit américaine*, with a thousand quite different details.

What you tell me about Marie's[4] state of mind saddens me a little. You may tell her this or not, but I'm against the idea of her making *François le Champi*, given that we know in advance that it will have fewer viewers than some old Gilles Grangier[5] on the other channel. I've always felt an actor should do television only if he's forced to for his living or if he's offered a superb part that there's absolutely no chance of his ever doing in the cinema or if there's a first-rate director. I realize that Marie would tell me that what she needs, above all, is to act, but I suppose that our friend Chabrol, for example, would reply to his detractors by saying that he had a need to shoot every day.

Quite clearly, ours is a crazy profession where there's no such thing as justice; every day I meet Americans who tell me how good Marthe Keller is, how beautiful, intelligent, *very nice, charming girl*[6] and so on and so forth, and I adopt my neutral expression, which you certainly know, so as not to disappoint them. To come back to Marie, she will have to learn to be philosophical about those periods when she is 'resting'; anyway, all of that you know as well as I do, better even, since I know you to be capable of filling up all kinds of periods.

My typewriter has a life of its own, I have the impression of being chained to it as though to an animal and from now on, even for 48 hours, I lug it around with me everywhere, on planes. I hardly need tell you how impatient I am to read Anny's[7] new book. Why don't you suggest to Marie that she take up writing (again), but this time her memoirs, I mean of course provisional memoirs (obviously without any idea of publishing them, she's too young), but with the aim of preparing and assembling them for later? When I collated my reviews in *Les Films de ma vie*, I came to realize, for example, that in pieces on Rossellini or Rivette I had told stories and anecdotes which had completely slipped my memory only a few years later. It's a rather disturbing thing to find out. So I think Marie might relate her early career, her first TV play, the *Pianiste* shoot, her meeting with you (which was, I believe, during Leterrier's tests),[8] etc. Why not? It strikes me as more interesting than being a party to the demolition of George Sand![9]

Decidedly, sweet as you are, I have the feeling you aren't going to convey my lamentations to Marie, but, as you know her better than I do, I leave it up to you.

Out of all the examples you give me, I think the film with the best chance of being made is Joyce Buñuel's,[10] since she's a young woman who always achieves the goals she sets her sights on.

I suppose that Charles[11] has finished with Lelouch (let me know how things went) and started with Berri;[12] there too, he's on familiar ground, all he has to do is look as much like M. Langman as possible![13] (In *Le Cinéma de papa* – and elsewhere – I would obviously have preferred Charles to Yves Robert.) Did you know that, in fact thanks to Lelouch – exactly like Marthe Keller – Charles is quite known and liked here in America where *Toute une vie* (minus thirty minutes cut by Lelouch after Cannes) is called *And Now My Love*? The people here in Alabama are not exactly film buffs and the ones making the film with us, having heard that I had won an Oscar, have been coming up to congratulate me on *Un homme, une femme*, *Z* and, indeed, *And Now My Love*, but never on any of the films I've actually made . . . It's not too serious and, whenever I have three or four days off, I take a little trip to Los Angeles, which remains my paradise (artificial or not).

As an actor, I'm gradually coming to share the opinion of Jeanne Moreau, whom I think of constantly, about one's attitude towards the director and the crew and also towards one's work, which has to be treated as though it were a game, even when one has something difficult or unpleasant to do. Like every actor in every film ever made, I'll find myself saying, 'He never directed me, no one ever told me what to do,' and, in fact, it's both true and false. In any event, I find it very amusing to watch another director at work, and despite the huge differences (to give you an idea, his favourite French directors are Enrico[14] and Lelouch), to discover all kinds of points in common, or rather reactions in common. In any case, he really isn't pretentious, he doesn't behave like the director of the most successful film in the history of the cinema (*Jaws*), he's calm (outwardly so), very even-tempered, very patient and good-humoured. This film of flying saucers means a great deal to him, it's a childhood dream come true. In fact, the film is all special effects – a bit like Hitchcock's *The Birds* – the camera registers only what happens on the ground (we, the actors, respond to lighting effects) and there's always a mask on the upper part of the lens. That part of the shot will be added in the laboratory later: the sky, the clouds, the stars and those famous flying objects, which are getting larger and larger.

I don't know whether I've explained it very clearly, in any case, I suppose you'll go and see the film, as will Marie and Dominique, kiss them for me.

That's it for today, my dear Serge, I'm just as impatient as you are at the thought of our next lunch at the Boulangerie, what a calamity it would be if, when I returned, I found it had been turned into a jeans boutique!

lots and lots of love,

françois

1 – Francis Huster, French stage and film actor, born in 1947.
2 – See note 1, letter dated 25 September 1977, p. 472.
3 – *Si c'était à refaire.*
4 – Marie Dubois.
5 – French director, born in 1911. He made twelve films with Jean Gabin (*Gas-oil*, *Le Rouge est mis*, *Le Cave se rebiffe*, etc.).
6 – In English in the original letter.
7 – Anny Duperey.
8 – Film tests made by the director François Leterrier.
9 – The author of *François le Champi.*
10 – Luis Buñuel's daughter-in-law.
11 – Charles Denner, who had just finished shooting *Si c'était à refaire.*
12 – In *La Première Fois.*
13 – Claude Berri's father.
14 – Robert Enrico, French director, born in 1931: *Au cœur de la vie*, *Les Aventuriers*, *Tante Zita*, *Boulevard du rhum*, *La Cage aux Folles*, etc.

To Annette Insdorf[1]

from Mobile, 18 August 1976

Dear Mademoiselle,

Thank you for your letter which has cleared things up for me a little.

I found Dominique Fanne's book[2] very good and full of insights. Its sole flaw, I think, it that it is readable and comprehensible only for those who have seen each of my films as many times as she has – which is, when I think of it, perhaps not a flaw after all. It would be unfair of me to say that the book demoralized me, since, to be honest, I read it in proof while I was shooting *Les Deux Anglaises*, which is to say, at a moment when I was not in very good shape. Later, it seemed to me that, if I were to reread it more attentively, my work – which is more instinctive than intellectual – might suffer.

There also exists, on my part, an occasionally excessive respect for books. For all that I grant interviews without attaching any importance to them, I become nervous as soon as it's a question of a book. I have refused various proposals for interview-books (on the model of the Hitchcock) and biographies (too premature). That is why it is my wish that you complete your book without my participation. Obviously I will read it, but only once!

My schedule here has just been changed yet again. I leave tomorrow for Los Angeles where I will be spending no more than five days. Then Paris and Montpellier to prepare my next film.[3] Before the N.Y. Festival I will be returning to L.A. for five days' shooting and from there to Benares,[4] four

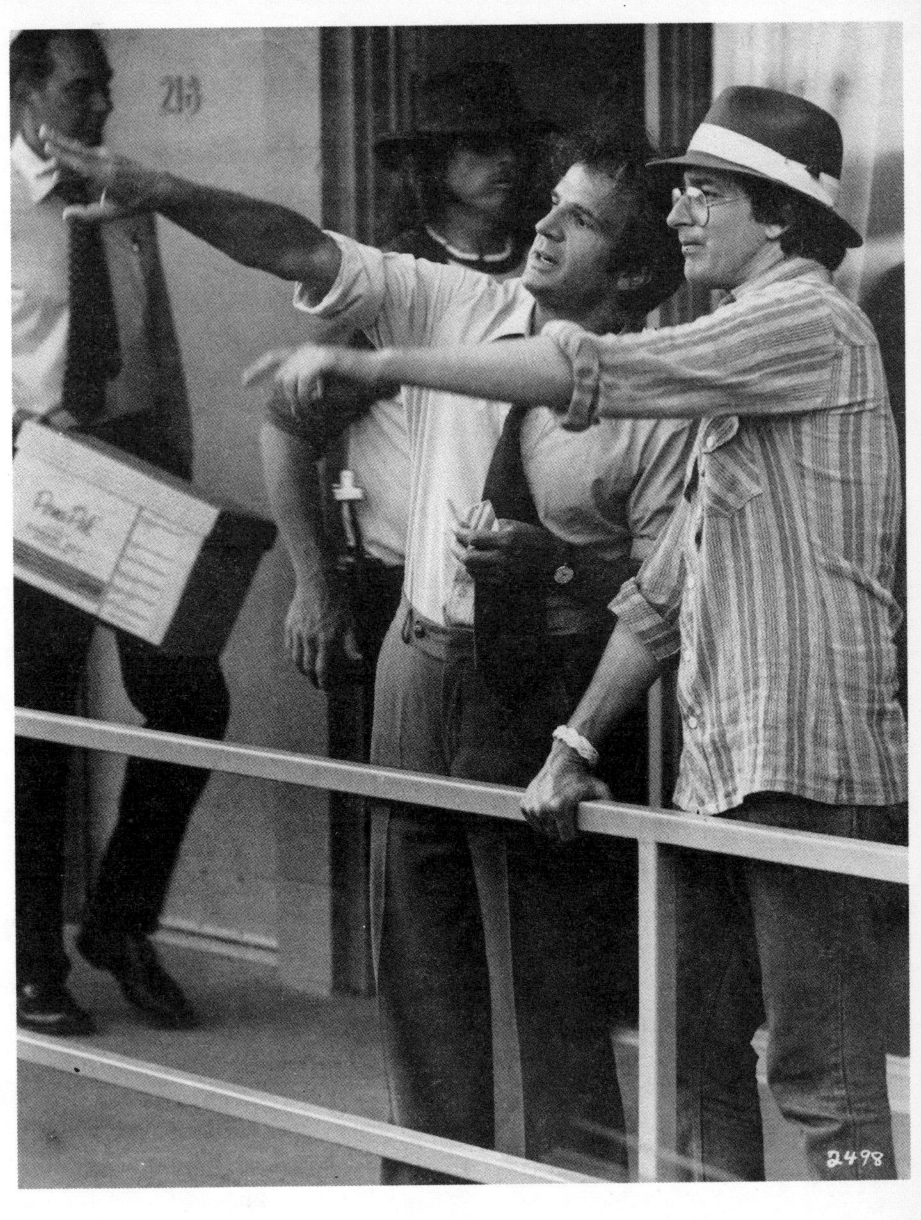

François Truffaut and Steven Spielberg (filming *Close Encounters of the Third Kind*).

days, then New York, five or six days, and it is there that I will see you, not at Yale.[5]

Forgive me for appearing a trifle finicky, I am, but a little less so under normal circumstances, which is to say, when I retain some control over my timetable.

yours truly,
françois

P.S. The 6 sections of your book seem to me an excellent choice and a very logical division. I will be in Paris from 24 August.

1 – American professor and journalist, born in 1950. As the author of *François Truffaut*, published in 1978 and considered by its subject to be the best book ever written on his work, Insdorf was to become a personal friend of the director.

2 – *L'Univers de François Truffaut*, published in 1972.

3 – *L'Homme qui aimait les femmes*.

4 – For the shooting of *Close Encounters of the Third Kind*.

5 – Where Insdorf taught.

To Jean Domarchi[1]

Paris, 24 September 1976

My dear Jean,

I never have any luck, since you always call me when I'm just about to leave on a trip.

I'm off to New York for ten days, and then I'll be in Montpellier until the end of the year for this new film, *L'Homme qui aimait les femmes*, whose ending, it seems, worries you.

I got the idea for that ending seventeen years ago while I was writing the dialogue of *Tirez sur le pianiste*.

Going even further back, I probably retained a vivid memory of having read about the miser Grandet's death[2] when he snatched the gold crucifix held out to him by the priest who was giving him extreme unction.

Decidedly, one never invents anything . . .

I'll be happy to lunch with you in January 1977, we'll speak about our friend Jacqueline Bisset.

Best wishes,
françois

1 – Professor of Law and Political Economy at Dijon University and at one time a regular contributor to *Cahiers du cinéma*.

2 – In Balzac's novel *Eugénie Grandet*.

Georges Desmouceaux (Claude de Givray's son) and Eva Truffaut (*L'Argent de poche*).

Truffaut and Rossellini. ‘Roberto, my Italian father . . .’

Alfred Hitchcock to François Truffaut[1] *October 20, 1976*

Dear François,

I do thank you for your handwritten letter.

In it, you tell me about your next film. What I want to know is how do you find the subject to make into pictures? At the moment, I am completely helpless in searching for a subject.

Now, as you realize, you are a free person to make whatever you want.[2] I, on the other hand, can only make what is expected of me – that is, a thriller or a suspense story and that I find hard to do.

So many stories seem to be about neo-nazis, Palestinians fighting Israelians and all that kind of thing.

And, you see, none of these subjects have any human conflict.

How can you have a comedy Arab? There is no such thing, or an amusing Israelite.[3] I describe these things because they come across my desk for consideration.

Some times I think that the best comedy or drama could be made right here in my office with Peggy, Sue and Alpha. The only difficulty about that idea would be that one of them would have to be killed off, which I would regret extremely.

Anyway, François, the best of luck to you on your next picture.

Kindest regards.

Yours affectionately,
Hitch

1 – This letter was written in English.

2 – It is paradoxical to find Hitchcock, at the height of his fame, complaining that he has become a prisoner of his own image and envying Truffaut his freedom.

3 – Probably a *lapsus* for 'Israelian', which is itself a mistake for 'Israeli'.

To Jonathan Rosenbaum[1] *9 Nov. 76*

My dear Jonathan,

Thank you for your last letter and your kindness with regard to the book on *Othello*.

I would be a hypocrite and would feel ill at ease if I did not tell you how sad I was when I read an article of yours in *Film Comment*[2] two months ago.

You don't like *Adèle H.* That is your privilege as a critic, as it is not to admire Isabelle Adjani. Except, why, when I asked nothing from you, did you say such nice things to me about *Adèle* in a letter written when you returned from New York?

With regard to my book, *Les Films de ma vie*, it contains several negative pieces: on Albert Lamorisse, Anatole Litvak, Jacques Becker (*Arsène Lupin*), Mervyn LeRoy and René Clément . . . Moreover, if I decided against publishing my negative criticisms of Yves Allégret, Jean Delannoy, Marcel Carné, etc., it is because these directors are now old men [. . .] and it would be needlessly cruel of me to hamper their efforts to continue working. It's a situation which you will understand better when you are a little older. That said, I accept your criticism of the book.

The writings of André Bazin: there, I really don't understand what it is you object to. The choice of texts? That was determined by what the publishers would accept or refuse and by the fact that Bazin himself had made a selection of his best articles for his book *Qu'est-ce que le cinéma?*. As I think I already told you in a previous letter, my aim in publishing Bazin's articles was a twofold one: to acquaint British and American film students with his work and also to help Janine Bazin who found herself in difficulties when French television cancelled her series of programmes *Cinéastes de notre temps*.

If I had written to you two months ago after reading your article, my letter would probably have been violent and unjust. Since then, my anger has subsided, but not a certain sadness, since I continue to feel that there was an incompatibility between the spirit of your article and the friendly tone of your letters. Dr Jonathan and Mr Rosenbaum?

In any event, I remain grateful for the care and attention with which you translated the Bazin–Welles; I hope the publishers conduct themselves in a more satisfactory fashion during the final stage of the project and I wish you the very best of luck,

Truffaut

P.S. I've been detained in Montpellier by the shooting of my new film, *The Man Who Loved Women*, it will therefore be impossible for me to come to the London Film Festival.

1 – American film critic and writer, born in 1943. He is the author of *Moving Places*, *Film: The Front Line 1984* and *Midnight Movies* (with J. Hoberman) and the editor of books on Rivette and Welles.

2 – An American film journal.

Jonathan Rosenbaum to François Truffaut[1] *12 November 1976*

Dear François,

I'm very sorry about the distress that my remarks in *Film Comment* have caused you. They have brought home to me Faulkner's remark that the critic addresses himself to everyone except the artist. My anger was chiefly directed against a particular critical climate in America, which included the reception of *L'Histoire d'Adèle H.* and Bazin – what I believed to be an essentially unreflecting attitude that overlooked too many things and accepted too much too easily. Frankly, I did not expect that you would read these remarks, and feeling relatively powerless, I did not believe that they would have much effect on anyone: they were a kind of protest against a myth – or what I believe to be a myth – that will surely outlast me.

I've just re-read my letter to you of last April 22nd, which ended by saying that I admired many things in *L'Histoire d'Adèle H.* (and was written about a month before I wrote those two paragraphs for *Film Comment*). I do admire many things about the film, and was not being insincere when I mentioned this in a letter. I admire it enough, in fact, to feel a very strong disappointment that it did not pursue some of its obsessional aspects further – something that I didn't mention in my letter because I felt it would have been rude in that context for me to say so. Whatever my misgivings about your recent work, the fact that I connect it with Chaplin's is – for me, at any rate – very high praise indeed. When I saw *L'Argent de poche* last week, I was struck by this relationship again, above all in the teacher's speech at the end, which reminded me a great deal of Chaplin's speech at the end of *The Great Dictator* – above all, because of its sincerity.

Perhaps the split that you see in my behavior – Dr Jonathan and Mr Rosenbaum – is based on what seems to me a kind of split in your own work. In much the same way, the 'real' Bazin for me is the Bazin who wrote the original Chavanne edition of *Orson Welles* more than the one who revised it by eliminating much of the theory and polemics and largely replacing it with information (much of it incorrect) taken from the French translation of Peter Noble's Welles book. And my misgivings about your publication of Bazin's texts – which I support in all other respects – is that it completely avoids problems of this kind, as if they didn't exist. In spite of your admirable desire for me to incorporate other writings by Bazin on Welles in the book, I feel that the book still represents Bazin's contribution incompletely, and I regret the absence of any acknowledgement in your introduction that much of what he eliminated from the Chavanne edition remains very important, theoretically as well as historically. In this respect, I felt that you were 'passing on' the book but not presenting it in the way that you present Welles' own work – which I feel that you do well and effectively. Perhaps I should have written to you about this at the time; shyness prevented me from doing so.

None of this, I should add, has anything to do with the help, encouragement and kindness that you have shown me in relation to the Welles book at every stage, all of which I continue to appreciate. And I can only express my regrets that my instinct as a critic conflicted with our own relationship, for whatever my misgivings about certain aspects of your work, I bear you no ill will. As someone whose own early criticism once led him to be barred from the Cannes Film Festival, I'm sure that you know a great deal more than I do about the perils and consequences of being an aggressive critic, but lately I've been discovering quite a few of these on my own.

Sincerely,
Jonathan Rosenbaum

1 – This letter was written in English.

To Jonathan Rosenbaum *Montpellier, 29 November 1976*

My dear Jonathan,

Thank you for your letter of 12 November, I was very touched by it. My only regret is that we didn't write to each other more often about Bazin's book on Welles. It was André S. Labarthe who put together the French edition, and my sole involvement was finding an American publisher, who accepted the book only on condition that I write a lengthy preface.

Bazin himself had revised the text of the Chavanne edition for a chapter on Welles in a book that was to be edited by Pierre Leprohon, and the project fell through.

If I had known that you regarded the Chavanne edition as superior, Janine Bazin and I would have given you the go-ahead to combine the two editions. Now it's too late.

I am unable to write at greater length, as I am shooting a film, but I remain

yours truly,
françois

1977

To Jean Collet

Paris, 22 March 1977

My dear Jean,

I reread your book and, as often happens with films, I appreciated it much more the second time.

I very much like the chapters on *L'Amour à vingt ans*, *La Peau douce*, *Baisers volés*, *Les Deux Anglaises* and *Adèle H.* I still have reservations about the chapter on *Jules et Jim*, but I would be hard pressed to explain why.

I've taken the liberty of correcting some factual errors.

Finally, I've compiled a few quotations which echo what you say in your foreword. I am sending them to you but you are obviously free to use all of them, some of them or none at all. In my opinion, the one by Ingmar Bergman could be used by Lherminier to launch the book (on either the front or the back of the cover, or as an epigraph . . . ?).

I hope you're happy with the illustrations. I'm amazed that Lherminier has agreed to publish such a massive volume, and I wonder what form it will take. You'll explain it all to me in person.

Would you like us to have lunch together on Monday the 28th? Let me know by phone.

Yours,
françois

P.S. I am not returning your manuscript; I'll give it back to you when we get together.

*Before I forget: I was astounded by the pertinence of the analogy between the photos thrown away by Franca[1] and the banknotes thrown away by Adèle. It had never occurred to me and I realize now that it must have been an unconscious memory.

*It sometimes happens, when I'm filming a shot, that I have that well-known sensation of reliving an experience, probably in just such a case as this.

1 – In *La Peau douce*.

To Charles Denner[1]

Paris, 29 March 1977

My dear Charles,

In answer to your request, here are a few guidelines which may assist you in interviews relating to our film.

I am all for the idea of not mentioning too often the fact that Bertrand Morane[2] is writing a book, since that would give the public the impression of a literary or intellectual film.

Though the character is very far from you (and from me), I have mentioned in every interview the fact that we had lunch together eighteen months ago, that I put the idea of the film to you and that it was therefore written specially with you in mind.

Many of the questions will focus on the character. Should he be regarded as positive or negative? I think the best answer was the one given by Brigitte Fossey:[3] 'He's just a man, etc.'

There will also be questions concerning feminism, what do you think of the ladies of the M.L.F.?,[4] etc. On that point, I feel our answer should be that we didn't seek to ingratiate ourselves with the M.L.F., but that the feminine characters, though numerous and episodic, are strong enough to hold their own with Bertrand Morane.

That's all I can see for the moment.

I have enclosed a press-book in which you will find, in a slightly altered form, the text you already know.

Perhaps it would also be a good idea for you to see the film again as soon as we've finished the sound-mixing, which will be in the week of the 11th to the 16th.

Finally, I'm sending you a photocopy of a charming letter from your little partner, Frédérique Jamet (the red dress, the blue dress). I have the feeling that a nice little postcard or letter from you would give her great pleasure; here is her address: 15, avenue Trudaine, 75009 Paris.

In the words of Claude Berri, the opening of the mine is on 27 April.[5]

Regards,
françois

P.S. I spoke to you of a very fine novel by François Darbon about a theatrical company on tour. I'll send it to you by the same post.

1 – Polish-born actor of French films, born in 1926: *Landru, Le Vieil Homme et l'Enfant, Le Voleur, La Mariée était en noir, Une belle fille comme moi, Z*, etc.

2 – Denner's character in *L'Homme qui aimait les femmes.*

3 – French actress, born in 1946: *Jeux interdits, Le Grand Meaulnes, Les*

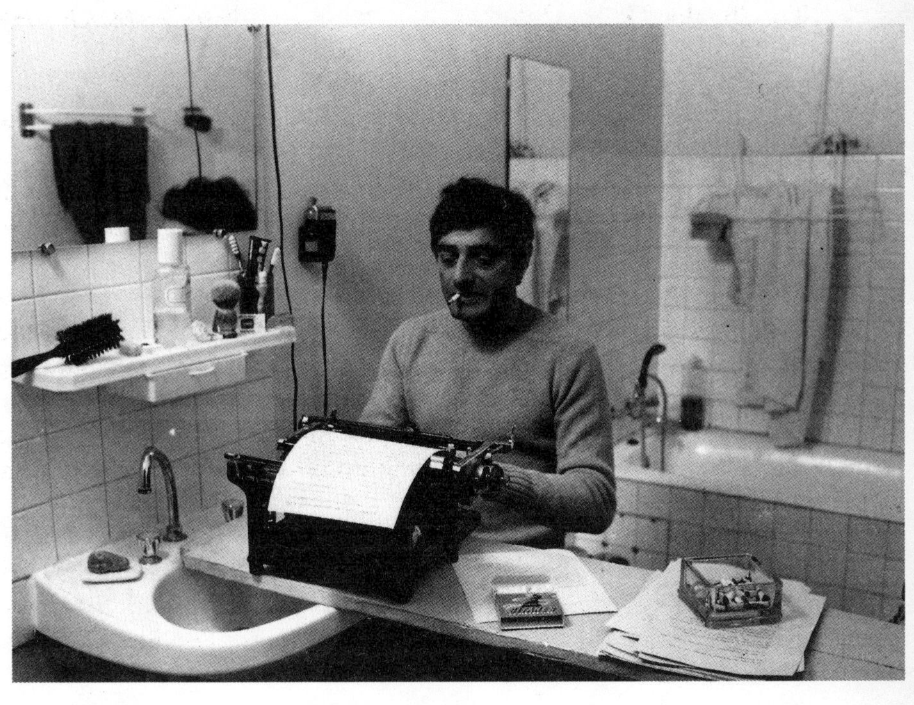

Charles Denner in *L'Homme qui aimait les femmes*.

Valseuses, *Le Bon et les Méchants*, etc., and *L'Homme qui aimait les femmes*.
4 – Le Mouvement pour la Libération des Femmes.
5 – Berri's phrase refers to the first public performance of a film, generally at 2.00 on a Wednesday afternoon, which is regarded by French producers as a crucial gauge of its subsequent career.

To Paula Delsol

12 April [1977]

Dear Paula,

Pending the release of your 3rd film (around 1992 . . . ?), allow me to congratulate you on *Ben et Bénédicte* which accords perfectly with *Une fille à la dérive*. The actors are perfect and well-directed, the ideas expressed on the screen are very much your own; I'm sure that the mimesis that exists between the actress[1] and yourself has already been pointed out to you. A single criticism, the sort that's supposed to make the praise sound more sincere, your heroine has less personality than you do. I like the idea that she doesn't complain or try to blame others for her own mistakes or weaknesses, but she just isn't as alive or as lively as you. This kind of reservation sometimes applies to my own films (*La Peau douce*) or Rohmer's (*L'Amour l'après-midi*), it comes from a certain modesty (yes!) on the part of autobiographical film-makers who fail to realize what it is about them that charms and intrigues other people.

Perhaps you don't agree? Let's talk it over at lunch some day, that's an invitation,*

love,
françois

*Ring me as soon as you're less harassed by the opening of your film. O.K.?

1 – Françoise Lebrun.

To Annette Insdorf

18 June [1977]

My dear Annette,

Thank you for your letter of 7 June. I was very pleased to hear from you. Richard Roud has requested *L'H.Q.A.L.F.*.[1] for the N.Y.F.F.[2] at the beginning of October. I'll be going with Scott, since I've put off my next shoot by a month. I'm having a lot of trouble with the script[3] (based, but this is confidential, on *The Altar of the Dead*). I have enclosed a little provisional synopsis. I will be playing the leading role, probably opposite Stacey Tendeter[4] (that's also confidential). We'll be shooting in Honfleur (in Normandy) around 15 October. So I decided to cancel the Truff. retrospective planned for Chicago in November.

It's true, I was thinking of making a film from *Confidence* and I haven't given up the idea . . . Jean Collet's book has come out; I'm sending it to you, without comment, you must judge for yourself. Not bad at all from the point of view of the illustrations.

Regarding your own book, do you think the quote by Ingmar Bergman might appear on the back of the book or on the dust-jacket?

As expected, the box-office figures of *L'H.Q.A.L.F.* are half-way between those of *Adèle* and *L'Argent de poche*, so we're pleased and relieved.

Here is my address from 1 to 31 July:

9936 Beverly Grove Drive,
Beverly Hills (Calif. 90210)
Tel.: (213) 275–14.54

Have you received all the books, records, stills and documents that you need? If not, let me know as soon as possible before the end of the month. I can bring some things in my luggage if I am going to see you in L.A. in July.

So there you have it, my dear Annette. I too have a very pleasant memory of your stay in Paris and our discussions. Oddly enough, my daughter Laura sent me, as a 'message from an anonymous admirer', the same postcard (the legs) that you sent to Josiane!

Goodbye, dear Annette, and lots of love,

françois

P.S. The best recent French film: Robert Bresson's *Le Diable, probablement*, his finest film in a long time. A sad event, the death of Roberto Rossellini.[5]

1 – *L'Homme qui aimait les femmes.*
2 – The New York Film Festival.
3 – Of *La Chambre verte.*
4 – In fact, it was to be Nathalie Baye.
5 – On 3 June 1977.

To Jean Mambrino *from Paris, 7 September 77*

My dear Jean,

Here is a copy of the script. *La Disparue* [*The Departed*] has become *La Chambre verte*. I'm sorry to have to disappoint you, but I didn't keep any of your dialogue, I couldn't speak it. Three abstract nouns in a sentence (if it's heard instead of read) impede the spectator's train of thought, which is why one has to use short sentences, etc.

Don't be discouraged. I am certain you could do a very fine adaptation of some novel or other, if you structured it well, and I hope you'll have a serious shot at it. My script isn't definitive but, such as it is, I feel more or less capable of acting and directing it; I will endeavour to improve and clarify the role of Cécilia during rehearsals before beginning the shoot proper (11 October). Nathalie Baye[1] will play Cécilia and Jean Dasté[2] Humbert.

There you have it, my dear Jean. If you don't feel totally discouraged after reading this new version, I would certainly welcome your suggestions, but I quite understand that your vision of the subject is different from mine. I see the 'obsessive' side of it (as with *Adèle*) and *you* see the 'luminous' side. In any event, I want the characters to be active, activist, not morose.

I hope that you had a pleasant time in Durban.

See you soon,

regards,
françois

1 – See note 1, letter dated end October 1978, p. 484.

2 – See note 1, letter dated 11 April 1978, p. 477.

To Miou-Miou[1] *Sunday 25 Sept. 77*

Dear Mademoiselle Miou-Miou,

Dear great lady of the present time, dear anti-Zitrone.[2] You are superb in Claude Miller's film[3] – depth, realism, emotion. I was not ashamed to shed tears while watching you; I also believe that you play the part so convincingly that even male spectators are liable to identify with you.

Please accept my admiration and, if I may be so bold, my friendship,

François Truffaut

P.S. I think the film is going to be very popular and have a long and successful run.

Jean Dasté and François Truffaut, actors in *La Chambre verte*.

1 – French actress, born in 1950: *Les Valseuses*, *La Marche triomphale*, *Josepha*, *Coup de foudre*, *La Lectrice*, etc.
2 – Léon Zitrone was a French television commentator with an often pompous delivery.
3 – *Dîtes-lui que je l'aime.*

To Georges Simenon[1] *from Honfleur, 23 November 1977*

Dear Monsieur,

I am a devoted admirer of your books of 'dictations' and I await them with impatience twice a year. To the two great subdivisions of your work, the psychological novels and the Maigrets, may now be added that of the 'dictations', which will constitute a third category.

In *A l'abri de notre arbre* you raise the question of a title that might describe this new style of book.

In the same way as you prefer to speak about 'little men' rather than 'great men', the term 'Memoirs' strikes you as being immodest, yet that's what they are after all or, more precisely, a cross between a private diary and a collection of memories. That is why I thought to offer you an overall title which might prove appropriate to your chronicle of moods, namely: *Mémoires élastiques* or else *La Mémoire élastique*.

It was a negative review of your novel *En cas de malheur* in *Le Canard enchaîné*[2] about twenty years ago that made me want to read the book; I greatly admired it and from that point on I became one of the silent majority of Simenonians.

Later, a Swiss friend of mine told me you had liked my first film, *Les Quatre Cents Coups*, and that gave me great pleasure. On two occasions I wondered whether I might adapt one of your books for the screen (*Trois Chambres à Manhattan* and *L'Horloger d'Everton*)[3] and both times I regretted not having dared.

I often speak about you with Jean and Dido Renoir whom I visit in Beverly Hills three times a year. They too adore your 'dictations', as I believe they have told you. In about ten days' time, I will be staying with them for a week and I know we will speak about *A l'abri de notre arbre*.

For your readers, Teresa has become a friend, I therefore wish both of you a happy new year beneath the shelter of your tree,

Yours cordially and faithfully,
François Truffaut

1 – Belgian novelist (1903–89).
2 – French satirical newspaper.
3 – Respectively filmed by Marcel Carné and Bertrand Tavernier (as *L'Horloger de Saint-Paul*).

To Rex Reed[1]

Paris, 28 November 1977

Dear Mr Reed,

I have just returned from Normandy, where I was shooting a new film, *The Green Room*, to find your letter of 15 November.

I plan to spend the Christmas holidays in Paris in the company of my elder daughter, Laura, who is eighteen.

Before Christmas she will have to undergo an operation on her foot which will immobilize her for two weeks. To entertain her, I plan to borrow and rent some 16 mm prints of films she is eager to see (and which I am eager for her to see), such as *Citizen Kane*, *The Big Sleep*, *The Lady Vanishes* and *Ugetsu Monogatari*.[2] For Christmas night, I will probably invite three or four handsome young men to entertain her, since, from a father's point of view, several boy-friends are safer than just one.

As Christmas presents, I will offer my friends books as I usually do and this year, preferably the new album of Fellini's drawings.

I hope I have answered your questions and apologize for having done so in French.

Yours sincerely,
François Truffaut

1 – American journalist and film critic: he had sent a number of film directors a questionnaire on 'How do you intend to spend Christmas?'

2 – By Kenji Mizoguchi (1953).

1978

To Annette Insdorf *Paris, 10 January 1978*

My dear Annette,

I wish you a happy new year and thank you for the superb Balthus catalogue.

I wonder if you received the letter I sent you from the Beverly Hills Hotel at the beginning of December.*

I wrote to you, among other things, that I was preparing to revise my article on Lubitsch,[1] but as it turns out I haven't been able to do the work.

My time is divided between editing *La Chambre verte* (the film will be finished by the end of March) and writing the script of *L'Amour en fuite* [*Love on the Run*], which will reunite Antoine Doinel, Claude Jade, Marie-France Pisier, Dani,[2] etc.

My agent, Don Congdon, tells me in his latest letter that he wishes to get in touch with you for various reasons, and I am very pleased that you'll be in contact with each other.

If you think my article 'Lubitsch Was a Prince' is sufficiently clear in its present form (in spite of some very *Cahiers du cinéma* in-jokes, which are probably untranslatable), then you have my go-ahead to send it to the editor of *American Film*, but not without <u>first</u> speaking to Don Congdon, since it's obviously he who co-ordinates and negotiates all questions relating to my literary rights in America.

Would you make sure, if you have revised the original translation of the text, that there's no risk of the official translator of *Films de ma vie* taking offence.

Perhaps it would be wiser not to put your name to the Lubitsch translation, Don Congdon will advise you on that.

Let me hear from you as soon as possible,

Affectionately yours,

Dear Annette, I send you my love and I have just this minute received your letter of 31 December. Thank you for the revisions. *Films <u>in</u> My Life* is perhaps more honest with regard to the public which might otherwise imagine it's a book on my own films!

As for Cartagena,[3] everything depends on United Artists N.Y., since they control the distribution of the film in South America with Spanish subtitles; there's nothing I can do for or against, where these territories are concerned.

Thank you also for *Take One*,[4] the interview is O.K. And finally, I'm sending you a few clarifications to improve the Lubitsch, since, for me, the publication of the article in a magazine that is clearly read by professionals in Hollywood deserves the greatest attention.

Thank you again, hoping to see you very soon,

françois

*I realize now that you didn't.

1 – Ernst Lubitsch, German-born director of German and American films (1892–1947): *Madame Du Barry*, *Die Bergkatze*, *The Student Prince*, *The Love Parade*, *Trouble in Paradise*, *The Merry Widow*, *Angel*, *Ninotchka*, *The Shop around the Corner*, *To Be or Not to Be*, etc.

2 – French singer and actress, born in 1944.

3 – The Cartagena Film Festival in Colombia.

4 – A Canadian film journal.

To Annette Insdorf

Paris, 15 February 1978

My dear Annette,

Thank you for your letter of 31 January.

I can't seem to decide between the two phrases concerning 'Lubitsch sweet cheese'.[1] I leave you to choose.

Thank you for the copy of *Take One*.

Frankly, as far as your contribution to the Lubitsch piece is concerned, I don't believe you should try to have your name on the translation (or even co-sign it), since all you did was correct it. It would be wiser not to risk offending Mayhew,[2] besides which we'll have occasion enough in the future to have our names associated (this does not constitute a marriage proposal!).

It's essential to have the article appear in *American Cinema* at the same time as the book is published and not several months before.

I've just finished *La Chambre verte* and I began to like the film during the editing. I think it's very sincere and quite intense. The first print with English subtitles will arrive in N.Y. at the beginning of May. Almendros and Jaubert[3] have excelled themselves!

Thanks again for Balthus and my birthday,

love,
françois

(I am sending you Jean Renoir's novel.)[4]

1 – From the article by Truffaut on Lubitsch, translated by Insdorf for *American Film*.
2 – Leonard Mayhew was the English translator of *Les Films de ma vie*.
3 – Truffaut is joking: Maurice Jaubert (whose music he used in the film) died in 1940. But the subject of the film in question, *La Chambre verte*, is precisely the cult of the dead and the notion that the dead are more alive than the living.
4 – *Le Cœur à l'aise*.

To Bob Balaban[1]

Paris, 11 April 1978

My dear Bob,

I very much liked the extracts from your diary that Steven gave me and, in spite of my poor command of English, every page made me laugh.

If I didn't speak of it to Richard Dreyfuss when I met him in London, it was only because I have a habit of not clearing up misunderstandings.

Richard said to me, 'Bob has written a really funny shooting diary' and I replied, 'Ah? Very good, very good.'[2]

It only means that I didn't want to disappoint Richard as he imagined he was telling me something I didn't know. (I hope you understand this mental reflex.)

In any case, I am very impatient to read the book when it's published and I send you my best wishes, also to Lynn and your little girl. Tell her to write my name on the first page of her dance card.[3]

Your friend,
françois

1 – The author of a diary of the shoot of Steven Spielberg's *Close Encounters of the Third Kind*.
2 – In English in the original letter; the previous quoted comment reads, 'Bob a écrit un shooting diary really funny.'
3 – Truffaut had sent, in the same spirit, two telegrams to Samuel Fuller's daughter Samantha. On her birth: 'Dear Samantha, already I love you. Truffaut.' When she was a year old: 'Dear Samantha, your suitor is waiting to take you to dinner when you are old enough. Love. Truffaut.'

To Jean Dasté[1]

Paris, 11 April 1978

My dear Jean,

Thank you for your note of 3 April. I hope your operation went well.

La Chambre verte is not shaping up as a major commercial success, but the film was very well received by the critics and I'm sure you've heard good things about it.

I'd very much like to see you the next time you're in Paris. My wish is to collaborate with you on a project that would concern what is called the History of the Cinema. This is the idea:

You and I will watch together, in a small screening room, *Zéro de conduite* and *L'Atalante*, after which, for two or three hours, I will ask you questions on your involvement in these two films. Perhaps you have the feeling that you have already said everything you have to say on the subject? Even so, I would like to try it, if you are agreeable.

Let me know what you think of the notion and accept my very best wishes,

françois

1 – French actor, born in 1904: *Boudu sauvé des eaux*, *Le Crime de Monsieur Lange*, *La Grande Illusion*, *Muriel*, *La Chambre verte*, *Une semaine de vacances*, etc., as well as the two Vigo films mentioned in the letter.

To François Porcile[1]

Paris, 8 May 1978

My dear François,

I have taken your advice, a little belatedly, and thanked Henri Storck[2] (and had the new record sent to him).

I am forwarding to you a copy of his reply, as it contains two or three pieces of information that will be of interest to you and also confirms something we already knew: Storck is a delightful man.

As you know, *La Chambre verte* has had good notices, but from the distributors' point of view the real title ought to be *La Chambre vide*![3]

Here, at Carrosse, we are busy on the preparation of *L'Amour en fuite* and I'm going to ask Georges Delerue to work with us.

And you, dear François? I hope you have started to revise your script. You are practically the only person capable of making a fiction film where the music would be both in the foreground and the background. I hope you will see the project through to its conclusion.

Regards to you and yours,
françois

1 – Musicologist of the cinema and musical adviser on *La Chambre verte*.
2 – Belgian producer and director, born in 1907.
3 – 'The Empty Room'.

To Annette Insdorf *[10 May 1978]*

Dear Annette,

Thank you for your letter of 4 May, the *American Film* article and the advertisement for your book. It all helps to boost my morale, which is not very high. The fact that *La Chambre verte* is doing very badly at the box-office is having an effect on me, a delayed effect but a very real one. The reviews were good but went on so much about DEATH that they've made the film as forbidding as, for example, *Johnny Got His Gun.*[1] The public is scared to go and see it.

Keep all of this to yourself, naturally, since the film still has a chance in N.Y. (after the next festival), in Scandinavia and Japan.

I'm not terribly happy with the script of *L'Amour en fuite* which I start shooting in 2 weeks. The novelty will be having 'real' flashbacks (*400 Coups – L'Amour à 20 ans – Baisers volés – Domicile conjugal*),[2] but, in trying to integrate them smoothly, we've come up with a wishy-washy script that will be very difficult to improve. Obviously, I'm going to do my utmost, but we'll also have to give some good scenes to Marie-France Pisier, Claude Jade and especially Jean-Pierre, and it's not easy. I've made too many films in the last 5 years (after *La Nuit américaine*), too many and too quickly. Les Films du Carrosse guarantees me a certain freedom, but it's very expensive and above all it prevents me from ever stopping and taking stock . Every month I turn down offers from Hollywood in order to avoid what happened to Wertmüller,[3] but one of these days, before I turn into a has-been, I'll end by letting myself be talked into it.

Certainly, to be honest, I have to confess that my morale was just as low when *Les Deux Anglaises* opened. So I'm sure I'll snap out of it, I hope. Forgive me for burdening you with such a hard-luck story. Maybe everything will go very well as soon as we start shooting. Most of the time it's letters from America that boost my morale, yours included, naturally. Thank you for *French Review*. Yes, I would like to read a few of the better reviews of *Les Deux Anglaises*.

Hoping for a letter from you very soon,

all my love and affection,
françois

1 – By Dalton Trumbo (1971).
2 – *L'Amour en fuite* used sequences from earlier films in the Antoine Doinel cycle.
3 – Lina Wertmüller, Italian director, born in 1928: *I Basilischi*, *Mimi Metallurgio Ferito nell'Onore*, *Film d'Amore e d'Anarchia*, *Pasqualino Settebellezze*, etc. Having become something of a cult director in the United States, she was signed by Warner Bros. to make four films in English. When the first of these, *The End of the World in Our Usual Bed in a Night Full of Rain* (1977), flopped both critically and commercially, the contract was terminated by mutual agreement, a blow from which her cult status never recovered.

To Jean Dasté

Paris, 1 June 1978

My dear Jean,

Thank you for your recent and most cordial letters.

I'm pleased you liked *La Chambre verte*.

Thank you for agreeing to let me interview you on your collaboration with Jean Vigo, but, for the moment, I don't envisage our meeting before the autumn, as I have just started a new film: *L'Amour en fuite* with Jean-Pierre Léaud.

It was a pleasure to see you again last night in *La Guerre est finie*.[1]

Wishing you a pleasant summer,

Yours,
françois

1 – By Alain Resnais (1966).

To Pierre Montaigne[1]

Paris, 26 June 1978

Dear Pierre Montaigne,

There was no question of my leaving your letter unanswered, as we are friends of old: on the other hand, I feel no particular obligation towards *Le Figaro* in which I am regularly insulted, often on a personal rather than a professional basis.

That, however, has nothing to do with my decision to shoot *L'Amour en fuite* without any publicity.

It's my belief that there has been too much talk about me in the newspapers, on radio and television since the beginning of the year, probably because of the concurrent release of *Close Encounters* and *La Chambre verte*. When you work in show business you have to let people forget about you from time to time and not hog the limelight.

I don't have the time to develop this idea and convince you that it's not a pose, but I'll do it when next we meet. I am not the only example of this as I understand that Stanley Kubrick and Patrice Chéreau[2] are also at present shooting films on virtually closed sets.[3]

In about ten days, I leave Paris to spend several weeks in California. *L'Amour en fuite* is due to come out in the first quarter of 1979, at which time I'll be happy to let you have priority for an interview, always assuming you bear me no ill will for my decision.

I wish you a pleasant summer; yours,
François Truffaut

1 – Film journalist on *Le Figaro*.
2 – French stage and film director, born in 1945: *La Chair de l'Orchidée*, *Judith Therpauve*, *L'Homme blessé*, etc.
3 – Respectively, *The Shining* and *Judith Therpauve*.

To Alain Souchon[1] *Monday 10 July 78*

Dear Alain,

Here is the dialogue for a few scenes in the film[2] involving mainly J.-P. Léaud and Dorothée[3] and also J.-P. Léaud and Monsieur Lucien. And, above all, the final scene and the 2nd monologue concerning the torn photo.

You may call Martine Barraqué, the editor, on 359.15.37. (*L'Amour en fuite*, Salle Ponthieu, 36 rue de Ponthieu). She knows all about it and will show you some extracts, either on the editing table or on the screen.

I am sure that you're busy writing a lovely song ('Ça coule sur ta joue' is very good). The character of Antoine Doinel is always on the run, always late, a young man in a hurry; the notion of flight is to be understood in every possible sense: time flying, always being projected into the future, always anxious (never content!), never calm, and also love flying out the window ('Ça coule sur ta joue') and also flight in movement; however much you try to flee from your problems, they're always right behind you, pursuing you, etc. There's the draughtsman's vanishing point . . . the laws of perspective . . . flight . . . Are women magical? Antoine should stop . . . fleeing . . . he should cherish the passing moment . . . cease to use every girl he meets as a means of settling accounts with his mother . . .

Too bad, for me, for you and for us, if I am confusing you with all these details . . . *Anyway, I trust you,*[4]

yours,
françois

1 – French singer and actor.
2 – *L'Amour en fuite.*
3 – French TV personality and actress, known simply as Dorothée.
4 – In English in the original letter.

To Jean-Louis Bory[1]

1 September 1978

Dear Jean-Louis Bory,

Torments that are like so many deaths, the sensation of being swallowed up in a black hole, of ceasing to exist, the unreality of faces glimpsed in the street, I've been through all of that and also the certitude that you will never be able to communicate to anyone else what it is that's going on inside you, the ground giving way under your feet, the unfeeling void.

I've been through all of that and it took me a year and a half to get over it before I found the spring that allowed me to bounce back, and three more years before I was capable of living normally again, which is to say, of offering my love unguardedly.

I am going to fold this letter, place it in an envelope and post it, but try to imagine that it has arrived rolled up inside a bottle. You are one of those who have the good fortune of being able to express the inexpressible and for whom the act of creation may be a means of survival. Never forget that.

I admired the courageous way you faced up to the sardonic Philippe Bouvard[2] when you presented *Ma Moitié d'orange*;[3] every week, on *Le Masque et la Plume*, you set an example of gallantry, gaiety and vitality. Because of that, I know that, one day, you will find the necessary strength to make your way back to the surface again, among us,

your very dear friend,
François Truffaut

1 – Truffaut wrote this letter on learning that Bory was suffering from a severe nervous depression. Bory, unfortunately, was unable to make his way 'back to the surface again', in Truffaut's phrase, and committed suicide a few months later.
2 – Popular French journalist and television personality, born in 1929.
3 – The book in which Bory for the first time spoke of his homosexuality.

To Alain Souchon

Paris, 19 September 1978

My dear Alain,

With no word from you, I console myself by watching TV, but eleven songs by Bécaud[1] for one by Souchon is hardly a fair exchange.

I trust you weren't offended by my objection to the word 'swallow'. In reality, it comes from the very mixed feelings I have about Walt Disney who sorely abused the analogy between humans and animals. That said, I'm well aware that by asking you to alter a couple of rhymes in your song I am behaving like the fashionable lady who criticized Van Gogh for having painted a Zouave.

Accordingly, I'll 'buy' your swallow, willingly and with no regrets.

I'm off to New York where I'll stay until the beginning of October but would you please, as soon as possible, ring Marcel Berbert at Films du Carrosse; he would like to have the name and phone number of your publisher so that Monsieur Bertrand de Labbey, who publishes my film music, can get in touch with him.

Hoping to see you soon, my dear Alain; let's not wait till the winter to have dinner together.

Regards,
françois

1 – Gilbert Bécaud, French singer.

To Jean Collet

Paris, 3 October 1978

My dear Jean,

I returned this morning from New York to find your letter.

It pains me to have to refuse you something, but it would be out of the question for me to obtain for you films which have not been distributed in Algeria.[1]

The films you cite were and are for sale and, if Algeria did not buy them, I don't see why we should lend prints which are themselves quite expensive and run a greater risk of deterioration with occasional screenings than with normal theatrical exhibition.

I've never had occasion to discuss this with you, but my position is that of a producer-director: which means that I reserve my gratitude for those countries which, because they buy my films, enable me to make others. When it's a question of intellectual or literary films, such as *Les Deux Anglaises et le*

Continent, for example, I can well understand that they might not interest certain socialist republics, but not *Les Quatre Cents Coups* or *L'Enfant sauvage*.

In any case, I don't have prints of my own, as they are all currently in distribution.

I know that the retrospective will now be incomplete, but I also know that you will understand my point of view.

Yours,
françois

P.S. Ditto for the Empress of Iran who wished to buy prints of each of my films that had been banned by her country's censor . . .

1 – For a Truffaut retrospective in Algiers.

To Koichi Yamada

Paris, 5 October 1978

My dear Yamada,

I left New York before your letter arrived. You were right to send a duplicate to Paris.

It will be impossible for me to come to Tokyo in December, as the sound-mixing of *L'Amour en fuite* begins on 22 November and will take two weeks. Then I have to be in Paris for my grandmother's birthday (ninety-six on 7 December!), then Nestor Almendros and I will be colour-grading the film in order to have a good print by around Christmas.

For me, there's no question of leaving Paris before the beginning of February and, from 15 February to 15 March, I have to be in America for the American Film Institute retrospective, to be held simultaneously in Los Angeles and Washington.

As soon as you have notification of the release date of *La Chambre verte*, I will arrange to keep myself free at that time to make the trip.

I'm sure Miss Takano as well as Mr and Mrs Kawakita[1] will understand how much better it will be for the film's Japanese career if I come specifically for the opening.

Let me know if, as they promised me, United Artists have put a print of the film at your disposal and also keep me informed of further developments.

I am sending you, by separate post, two copies of the original Henry James story in French and in English (*L'Autel des morts – The Altar of the Dead*) and I'll also be sending you as soon as possible the film's screenplay as it will appear in *L'Avant-Scène*.

Yours affectionately,
françois

1 – Naganasa Kawakita was the founder and president of Towa, which merged with Toho. His wife Kashiko, a celebrated cinéphile, is director of the Japan Library of Tokyo, which became, after her husband's death, the Kawakita Memorial Film Institute.

To Nathalie Baye[1]

[end of October 1978]

Dear Nathalie,

Don't let me down! Come with me to Milan, Thursday 15 November, to introduce *La camera verde* and present some prize or other to Olmi for *The Tree of Wooden Clogs*. It's the evening that will launch our funereal film in Italy. So don't let yourself be monopolized by 'The Three Broads' (as adapted by Michel Audiard)[2] and answer post-haste,

kisses,
françois

1 – French actress, born in 1948. With Truffaut she made *La Nuit américaine*, *L'Homme qui aimait les femmes*, and *La Chambre verte*, which is the film he refers to in this letter. Other films: *La Gueule ouverte*, *Une semaine de vacances*, *Le Retour de Martin Guerre*, *La Balance*, etc.
2 – An allusion to Chekhov's *Three Sisters*, which Nathalie Baye was playing on the stage. Audiard was a French screenwriter and director who specialized in slangy dialogue.

To Bernard Dubois

Paris, 13 November 1978

My dear Bernard,

I gave the matter a great deal of thought after the screening the other day and I decided not to 'speak' the role of the father in your film.

I am convinced that I am acting in everyone's best interests:

1. your film will be understood better;

2. the performance of Jean-Pierre (who is particularly moving in these scenes) will be seen to better advantage;

3. critics and film buffs will take the film more seriously, because it is a serious film and my participation might appear to be a private joke;

4. equally in my own interest, since, inasmuch as my speaking voice is

'Dear Nataloche . . .' Nathalie Baye and François Truffaut in *La Chambre verte*.

rather unusual, it is at least more acceptable when I am visible on-screen than when I am off (my voice-off narration in *Les Deux Anglaises et le Continent* was a contributing factor in that film's failure).

Do understand, my dear Bernard: the father's voice ought to be neutral and resonant, with the only oddity being the way the amplifier deforms it.

The voice of someone like Serge Rousseau would be ideal and I am almost certain that he would graciously consent to do it.

You might also make a test with your own voice, since the difference in ages would be disguised by the amplifier.

I agreed to play the role of the father because I saw it as a kind of joke in a jokey film, but, as it turns out, you have invested the project with a certain classicism, a certain rigour and seriousness, and it would be better to take this to its logical conclusion.

If the father's voice is a hundred per cent neutral (to the point where no one, emerging from the cinema, will think to ask who played the role), then the emotion expressed by Jean-Pierre (possibly helped at that moment by the fact that it was my voice which was answering him) will have a more profound effect on the public.

Films are babies and the world, in consequence, can be divided in two: what's good for the baby and what's not good for the baby.

It is in that spirit that I am writing you this letter.

Yours,
françois

To Olga Horstig-Primuz[1] *Paris, 13 November 1978*

Dear friend,

Do tell Bibi Andersson[2] from me that if I had a project for her, she would be the first to know, in any case before the newspapers.

I've noticed before that the Canadians have a tendency to spread false rumours and invent film projects, probably to gain publicity for their studios . . .

Unfortunately, no, I haven't any project for Bibi, I say unfortunately, because I very much admire the actress and I very much like the woman, whom I met in New York. Tell her to look me up if she's making a film or just passing through Paris.

I read systematically all the biographies of actors and I notice that they have one point in common whose very persistence can only mean that a truth is being stated, I refer to the tribute which all of them pay to Olga Horstig-

Primuz as friend and as agent. I hope that such a consensus of opinion makes you happy and above all that it will inspire you to write your memoirs.

Cordially,

françois

1 – Actors' agent.

2 – Swedish actress of numerous Bergman films, born in 1935.

1979

To Alain Souchon *[early January 1979]*

My dear Alain,

It's disgusting that we've let so many days go by, but, after all, you gave me the impression that you had made yourself at home on the stage of the Olympia and that you weren't about to move.

Aside from 'Toto 30 ans', I liked all your new songs, 'Le Dégoût' (harrowing, *very strong*),[1] 'La Cornemuse' (really inspired, a dream come true, a vast fresco), 'Lulu' (heartrending). When you're very serious, as when singing 'Le Dégoût', you begin to take on a resemblance to Jean Cocteau when he acted in *Le Baron fantôme*[2] (you're too young to have known it, but I can assure you it's a moving experience).

You are, in short, a very fine singer. I won't bother to list the press screenings of *L'Amour en fuite*, since they're held in the evening, usually 6.30 or 8.30, but the film has been better received than I expected, it's as though a thorn has been removed from my foot, life could be worse, I'm very fond of you,

Truffaut

P.S. Don't forget to thank Voulzy[3] from me, tell him thank you and bravo.

1 – In English in the original letter.
2 – By Serge de Poligny (1943).
3 – Laurent Voulzy, the co-author with Souchon of the song for *L'Amour en fuite*.

To Alain Souchon *[early January 1979]*

Dearalainsouchon,

To convince his publishers that he was a real writer, William Saroyan[1] told the staff of *Esquire* that he was going to send them *a short story, day by day*,[2] and he kept his word and succeeded in getting published. Am I going to have to write you a letter, day by day, to convince you, and your accomplice

Voulzy, that I am very happy, very happy with your song? The film is a letter, your song is the envelope for that letter; it envelops it. Doinel has always been in search of a family, he's happy to be sponging off Souchon. I was teasing you yesterday about being middle-aged at 30, it was simply a lack of humour on my part with regard to the question of growing old. 'Toto 30 ans' is also good, and I like 'Nouveau' and 'Papa Mambo' as well. André Gide's advice was: 'Doubt everything, but do not doubt yourself.' On Wednesday the 24th at 2.00 there is what Claude Berri calls 'the opening of the mine' at the Colisée and elsewhere . . . an invitation follows, my affection remains . . . and my gratitude,

françois

1 – American novelist and dramatist, born in 1908.

2 – In English in the original letter.

To Jacques Siclier[1] *[late January 1979]*

My dear Siclier,

If I didn't know you, I wouldn't write this letter. I'd content myself with being content![2] But we first met each other, when? About twenty, twenty-five years ago and I associate you with Teisseire, Gauteur,[3] Claude de Givray, all of them cousins of Doinel, and why not tell you the truth: after having had so many doubts during the five months I was editing, it's a real pleasure to find that I have been understood, yes, simply understood. It's true, I do feel close to Simenon's sensibility. Your paragraph on Monsieur Lucien shows that you responded to every shot, every line of dialogue and that you were even able to read what was concealed between the images as only Bazin could. Critics can say to their readers: 'go see it' or 'don't go see it', they are rarely capable of helping the director to pull himself together.

I won't thank you, but I will shake your hand,

warmly,
françois

1 – French film critic and journalist.

2 – Truffaut had just read Siclier's review of *L'Amour en fuite* in *Le Monde*.

3 – Claude Gauteur, French journalist and film historian.

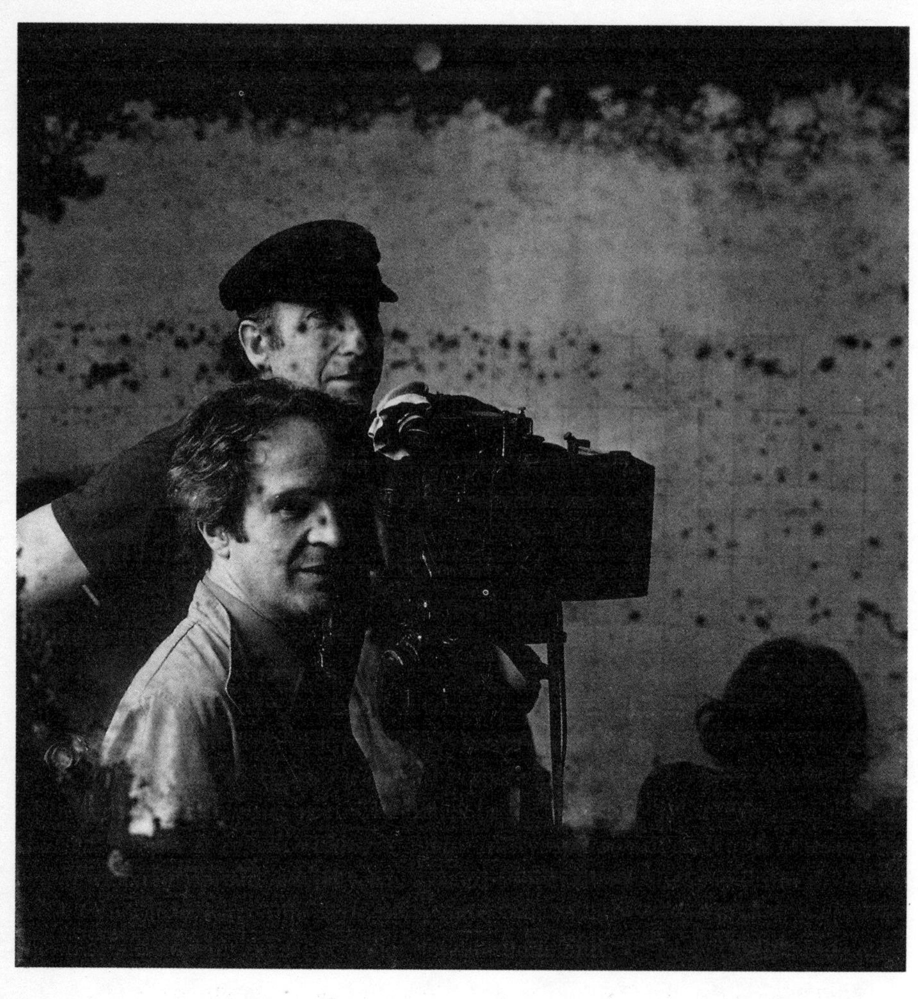

'. . . after having had so many doubts during the five months I was editing . . .': François Truffaut and Nestor Almendros, the cinematographer of *L'Amour en fuite*.

To Nathalie Baye *[February 1979]*

Dear Nataloche, 3 days before the Césars,[1] I'm hoping for you – not with all my heart, but with half of my heart, let's say with my left auricle:

'What do you mean by that?'

'By that, I don't mean much of anything,' as, not Ferrand,[2] but Pierre Dac[3] used to say.

So, fine, I send you my love, see you on Saturday, and I'm going to place a treble bet:

Léautaud
Léaud
Léotard[4]

1 – Nathalie Baye had been nominated for a César (the French Oscar) for her performance in Godard's *Sauve qui peut (la Vie)*.
2 – Ferrand was the name of the film director played by Truffaut in *La Nuit américaine*. He was deaf in one ear, and in this letter Truffaut is punning on the words for 'auricle' (*oreillette*) and 'ear' (*oreille*), as also on the word *entendre*, which means both 'to mean' and 'to hear'.
3 – Popular French humorist.
4 – Paul Léautaud was a French writer and diarist, much admired by Truffaut; Léaud is, of course, Jean-Pierre Léaud; and Léotard, the actor Philippe Léotard, who was at the time Baye's companion.

To Mario Soldati[1] *Monday [20 March 1979]*

My dear Mario,

The kind of friendly complicity we enjoyed on the Cannes jury in 1962 emboldens me to say: My dear Mario! I'm very happy to know that I will be seeing you again on Thursday, but I'd rather not wait until then to tell you that I cannot make a film version of *L'Épouse américaine*. I loved the book, I read it with real emotion, and I was infinitely touched by its precision of detail, but, as with *Un amour de Swann*, the story is told only 30% through action and dialogue, and 70% through the narrator's comments. Books like that are automatically disfigured by the cinema which chops them all up into slices of dialogue. My elder daughter enrols in Berkeley this coming autumn and you can imagine how, logically, I would have leapt at the chance of making a film nearby, but this adaptation seems to me to pose insurmountable problems without going into the (very delicate) matter of casting and the English language which I don't speak well, far from it . . . I am nevertheless genuinely moved that you thought of me to film your story; I am

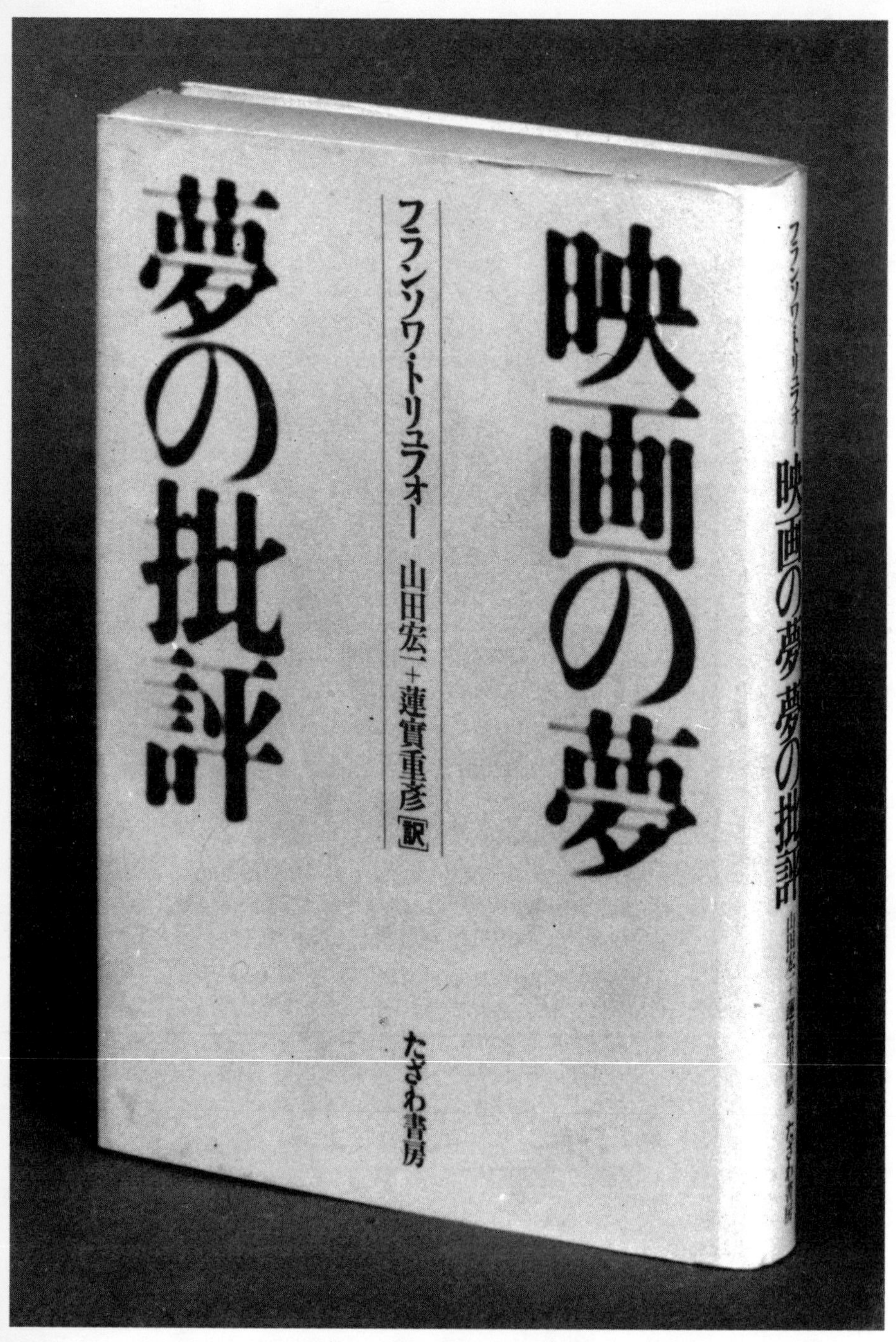

The Japanese version of *Les Films de ma vie*.

King Vidor, Frank Capra and François Truffaut.

sure you will find a practical solution to what is a very real problem and I am looking forward to seeing you soon,

friendly yours,[2]
françois

1 – Italian director and writer, born in 1906. His films include *Tragica Notte*, *Malombra*, *Quartieri Alti* and *Le Miserie del Signor Travet*.

2 – In English in the original letter, as were the preceding eight words.

To Éditions Gallimard

Paris, 22 March 1979

Dear Madame,

Though I am not quite sure of having properly understood what is expected of me, here is the statement intended for the new publicity campaign of the Série Noire:[1]

'Poets without meaning to be, artists who never use the word Art, the writers of the Série Noire are the submerged genius of American literature.'

If the verb are seems inadequate, it might be replaced with constitute or form.

I hope you will find this appropriate and remain

Yours faithfully,
François Truffaut

1 – A Gallimard imprint specializing in American thrillers.

To Robert Aldrich[1]

Paris, 26 April 1979

Dear Robert,

I was very pleased to receive your letter, especially as it gives me the opportunity to tell you how much I enjoyed your seminar in *American Film* a few months ago. I always wonder about the reasons that prompt actors and directors to lie when interviewed, and you, evidently, said the truth, all the truth on our craft which can be at the same time wonderful and cruel.

The incident at the Directors' Guild Screen Room is nothing to worry about. The fact is that screening conditions in Los Angeles are most of the time so perfect that I was very disappointed to find out that the Directors' Guild Theater could be the exception. For instance, it does not have double doors and, because of that, any time someone enters the theater during the screening, it causes a luminous impact on the screen as well as on the spectators. Furthermore, when I got in, they were showing Jean Vigo's masterwork, *Zéro de conduite*, and it hurts that such a film could not be treated better.

Again, the fact that it was in the Directors' Guild Theater accounts a lot for the way I reacted. In any case, this was not a happy period as it was the same week we had lost Jean Renoir . . . His wife, Dido, told me how much she was touched by the few words you had with her at the funeral.

Chances of life having brought us together, I hope that we will find happier circumstances to see each other.

I know your courage and your talent and I can only wish you the best of luck for the films to come.

Warmest regards,
françois

1 – American director (1918–83): *Apache*, *Vera Cruz*, *Kiss Me Deadly*, *The Big Knife*, *Attack!*, *Whatever Happened to Baby Jane?*, *The Dirty Dozen*, *Ulzana's Raid*, etc. Aldrich was, at the time, president of the Directors' Guild in Hollywood (directors take turn to preside) and Truffaut had written to the Guild to complain of the less than satisfactory conditions in which *Zéro de conduite* was screened there. This letter was written in English.

To Francis Veber[1]

Paris, 28 May 1979

My dear Francis,

Forgive me for having let several weeks pass without getting in touch with you. *Il était une fois un flic*,[2] which I took great pleasure in seeing again last night, finally got the better of my rudeness.

I very much liked *Coup de tête*,[3] but my interest as a spectator came to an end with the guy's big scene: 'Enjoy your meal, gentlemen,' since, from that point on, the waiter having had his revenge, there's no longer anything we particularly want to see happen and the character of the woman who was raped had not been sufficiently developed in the previous scenes to make us wish for a happy ending. But it's certainly a powerful film, well written and well told.

Then I went to the Girardot–Marielle comedy.[4] I haven't seen such a badly photographed film in years. On the other hand, the story interested me from beginning to end, I laughed a lot, thanks to the dialogue, and I think a blind man would have got as much pleasure out of it as I did since one can hardly see the protagonists' faces. But, I repeat, I liked the characters, the dialogue and the plot.*

As far as *Le Garde du corps*[5] is concerned, I consider it a first-rate idea, but I think I'll have to turn it down for the following reason: at the present time, the best actor for the part would be Patrick Dewaere[6] who, or so I am led to believe, has no wish to make a film with me. With Jacques Dutronc,[7] whom I admire enormously, it would be a different matter, but I have the impression that you wrote the script, consciously or not, with Dewaere in mind . . . ?

Otherwise, *Le Garde du corps* would interest me if the girl's role were as important as that of the hero, even to the point where certain scenes might be depicted from her point of view. I see there the possibility of a poetic, prestigious and moving character.**

I have just begun a script with Suzanne Schiffman on the period of the Occupation,[8] so my need for a project has lost something of its urgency, but not my wish to work with you and, if you aren't too busy, I'd be happy to see you again in order to exchange ideas.

Best regards,
françois

*Forgive me if I seem to be assuming the odious role of the critic again, the inspector of works, the nit-picker, but you did ask me to see these two films and talk to you about them from a professional angle.
**It seems to me that the heroine should be as important as Audrey Hepburn in *Roman Holiday*[9] and Maureen O'Hara in *The Quiet Man*,[10] to take two great films about a couple.

1 – French screenwriter and director, born in 1937: (as screenwriter) *Le Grand Blond avec une chaussure noire*, *Adieu poulet*, etc.; (as director) *Le Jouet*, *La Chèvre*, etc.
2 – By Georges Lautner (1972).
3 – By Jean-Jacques Annaud.
4 – Édouard Molinaro's *Cause toujours, tu m'intéresses*, starring Annie Girardot and Jean-Pierre Marielle.
5 – An idea Veber was proposing to Truffaut.
6 – French actor (1947–82): *Les Valseuses*, *Lili aime-moi*, *La Meilleure Façon de marcher*, *Préparez vos mouchoirs*, *Série noire*, etc.
7 – French singer and actor, born in 1943: *Antoine et Sébastien*, *L'important, c'est d'aimer*, *Mado*, *Violette et François*, *Sauve qui peut (la Vie)*, etc.
8 – *Le Dernier Métro*.
9 – By William Wyler (1953).
10 – By John Ford (1952).

To an American journalist

Paris, 20 July 1979

Dear Sir,

The two things that would make me happy during the 80s are:

1. for *The Magnificent Ambersons* to be restored to a complete, uncut version including the thirty minutes removed by the R.K.O. executives;

2. the publication of Jean Cocteau's secret diary, entitled: *Le Passé défini.*[1]

I trust that I have satisfied your curiosity and remain

Yours sincerely,
François Truffaut

1 – The first two volumes of *Le Passé défini* were published in France in 1983 and 1985; and subsequently in English as *Past Tense.*

To Jacques Doillon[1]

Paris, 13 September 1979

My dear Jacques,

Through my visits to the Institut des Sourds-Muets[2] in the rue Saint-Jacques, I have made the acquaintance of Janine Peyre, a teacher and more recently a screenwriter.

She has written a script, *L'Or du silence* (ex-*La Cage de verre*) whose protagonists are a young deaf-mute woman and a photographer with normal hearing.

This script struck me as very interesting and full of specific details of a type that simply cannot be invented.

By contrast, the American film *Voices,*[3] which opens this week and deals with the same theme, seems to me to demonstrate absolutely the wrong way of going about it. I saw only a few extracts.

I told Janine Peyre I felt you were the best director for her story and promised her I would contact you, even though I don't know what your projects are and cannot help suspecting you might be reluctant to film the story of an outsider, immediately after your very fine *Drôlesse* . . .

What do you think? Will you agree to read Janine Peyre's script? If so, let me know and I'll have it sent to you.

Kindest regards,
françois

P.S. On 31 of January 1963 you wrote to ask me for an interview for your student magazine, with its print run of 1000 copies. So you see, we're old pen-pals . . .

1 – French director, born in 1944: *Les Doigts dans la tête*, *Un sac de billes*, *La Femme qui pleure*, *La Drôlesse*, *La Pirate*, *La Vie de famille*, *Comédie*, etc.
2 – The Institute for the Deaf and Dumb.
3 – By Robert Markowitz.

To Jacques Doillon

Paris, 21 September 1979

My dear Jacques,

Don't worry: the rue Robert-Estienne hasn't yet become the rue Lauriston.[1] It was while I was looking for some documents to return to the Rossellini family that I came across your letters from 1963! I read them again with real pleasure, you have no cause to be ashamed of them.

As we go through life, we become a succession of different individuals, which is what makes books of memoirs so very strange, with an ultimate individual endeavouring to synthesize all his previous incarnations. Worst of all is the rereading of love letters. That's when one notices how one spends one's life setting oneself up to be hurt rather than doing the best for oneself.

I am sending you Janine Peyre's script. In my opinion, it's less likely to help you make up your mind than spending an hour at the Institut des Sourds-Muets or attending their annual dance, which is incredible in its gaiety and vitality.

Anyway, see for yourself and let me have your impressions and also your suggestions, if you yourself aren't interested, concerning which film-maker we might direct Janine Peyre to . . .

Kindest regards,
françois

1 – In which the Gestapo had its Paris headquarters during the Occupation.

To Richard Roud

Paris, 28 September 1979

My dear Richard,

Can you imagine the resentment I feel, knowing, while I'm cooped up in my office like Bokassa in his Caravelle, that the New York Film Festival is proceeding without me?

However, I've decided not to wait for your return to send you an amusing document[1] which clearly shows, concerning the Cinémathèque, that the post-Langlois period rivals that which preceded it and also that your book will never be completed.

I have in front of me your splendid programme, which enables me to follow your schedule day by day.

Do not fail to convey my best wishes to all your team.

Cordially,
françois

1 – This document is lost.

To Annette Insdorf

Paris, 19 October 1979

My dear Annette,

Thank you for your letter of 4 October. Thanks also for having arranged the transcription of the A.F.I.[1] seminar.

I take note of your interest in translating *Le Cinéma de l'Occupation*,[2] but, before informing my agent-friend Don Congdon of it, I'm going to wait until the contract with Stanley Hochman is signed. Personally, I'd be delighted with such a solution; since if the book is to be improved, there are certain decisions that have to be taken and certain additions that have to be made, and everything would be simplified by the fact that we know each other – not to mention my confidence in the quality of your work.

I've also taken note of your new address.

Next week Abel Gance will be 90 and, naturally, I plan to send him a friendly and respectful little greeting. I very much like his film on Beethoven[3] and I'm sure you'll get a great deal of pleasure out of seeing it several times.

It won't be possible for me to attend the conference in the Grand Duchy of Luxembourg, but I'm sure it will be very well organized, as I was there three months ago with Claude Jade, it was all very pleasant.

The shoot of my new film, *Le Dernier Métro*, will occupy me for thirteen weeks, from 28 January onwards, and then I'll have to keep a promise I made to take a few long trips (Australia and Venezuela), the film being ready to open in 1980.

Everyone at Carrosse is well.

I send you my love, dear Annette,

françois

P.S. Dear Annette, at Herlin Inc., 108 West 28th Street N.Y., you can find *More About All About Eve*[4] for $25 (no. 49 in the catalogue). Could you buy it for me? I'll reimburse you and my gratitude to you, which is already considerable, will become even greater.

1 – American Film Institute.
2 – A collection of articles by André Bazin.
3 – *Un grand amour de Beethoven* (1936).
4 – By Joseph L. Mankiewicz.

To Abel Gance[1] *[25 October 1979]*

Dear Monsieur Gance,

Here is the text of the telegram you would have received today had the post office not been on strike . . .

DEAR ABEL GANCE YOU LEFT THE STARTING-POST BEFORE THE BIRTH OF THE CINEMA AND IT IS OUT OF BREATH ATTEMPTING IN VAIN TO CATCH UP WITH YOU – STOP – A TELEGRAM CANNOT EXPRESS THE NINETIETH[2] OF WHAT WE ALL OWE YOU – STOP – I WISH YOU A TRIPLE BIRTHDAY WITH A ROLY-POLYCAKE[3] – STOP – A AS IN ADMIRATION A AS IN AFFECTION – YOUR FRANÇOIS TRUFFAUT

I am pleased to know that you will be at the Cinémathèque tonight, since it's a place we go to, almost always, with the impression of going to your home,

françois

1 – French director (1889–1981): *La Roue*, *Napoléon*, *J'accuse*, *Le Paradis perdu*, *Le Capitaine Fracasse*, *Cyrano et d'Artagnan*, etc.
2 – It was Gance's ninetieth birthday.
3 – Truffaut is alluding to two of Gance's technical innovations, the triple screen of *Napoléon* and Polyvision.

To Tanya Lopert *Thursday 8 November 79*

Dear Tanya,

Do you know whom I find moving in *La Fraîcheur de l'aube* which has aroused such Athenian raptures?[1] You? I'll tell you the name of the person whose smile is so contagious that it spreads through the auditorium and even lights up the usherettes' faces, it's Dudu.[2] I'll give you a thousand to one you won't guess the person I thought I knew from A (the Abbé Constantin) to Z (Constantin Gavras) and who took me by surprise in his role as a flibbertigibbet, yes, you've guessed, it was the ex-Ayatollah Komédie (Française), Pierre Dux,[3] with X as in Xtraordinary. The couturier from *Falbalas*[4] leaves us in no doubt that, on the beach, adventure lies just around the corner, in short, you are all at your best in this play whose warmth and beauty are worthy of Saroyan.

I send you my love, dear Tanya, and I won't tell you to keep your spirits up, since spirits are already high on both sides of the footlights,

yours affectionately,

françois

1 – Truffaut is referring to the success of the play (by the American Herb Gardner) at the Théâtre de l'Athénée in Paris.
2 – The actor André Dussolier.
3 – The actor Pierre Dux had formerly been director of the Comédie-Française.
4 – Raymond Rouleau, who played a fashion designer in Jacques Becker's *Falbalas* and was also the director of the play to which this letter refers.

To Jean Dewever[1]

Friday 23 Nov. 79

My dear Jean,

It makes me extremely proud that *Les Honneurs de la guerre* has now been added to the catalogue of Les Films du Carrosse and I was eager to tell you how much I admired it. It's a beautiful film that will never seem dated and I am certain that it has a better chance of being understood and appreciated by the new generation of filmgoers.

Sometimes I envy you for having had the courage to flee the asphalt jungle[2] of the Champs-Élysées, life must be more human in Roussillon,[3] one of these days I'll follow your example.

My very best wishes for the present and the future and, far away though I may be, my very warmest regards,

françois

1 – French director, born in 1927: *Les Honneurs de la guerre* (1960).
2 – Truffaut is alluding to the title of John Huston's gangster film of 1950.
3 – The region of France where Dewever lives.

To an insurance company

Paris, 23 November 1979

Monsieur,

I was indeed witness to an accident on the evening of 5 November 1979.

A car going up the avenue Marceau (coming from the place de l'Alma) went through a red light at the corner where the avenues Marceau and Pierre-1er-de-Serbie[1] meet, crashed into a taxi and badly damaged it.

Since the two cars had come to a halt in the middle of the crossroads, I approached to make sure that no one had been injured. It was when I saw the driver of the private car hurriedly removing the tricoloured rosette from the front of his dashboard (without concerning himself with the damage he had caused to the taxi or the condition of its passenger) that I came forward as a witness to the accident.

I do not draw well enough to be able to make a sketch of the position of the two vehicles, but there was no doubt at all that the taxi was proceeding correctly and that the private car, approaching at a very high speed, did not stop at the red light.

I naturally remain at your disposal in the event that I may be required to repeat this evidence.

Yours sincerely,
François Truffaut

1 – At that period Truffaut was living in the avenue Pierre-1er-de-Serbie.

To Annette Insdorf

[28 December 1979]

Dear Annette,

Your timing is terrific, as the book arrived on my table at Carrosse just in time for Christmas . . . Thank you for this postscript to our friendship. There's an atmosphere of preparation[1] in the rue Robert-Estienne, which is a hive of activity. Catherine D.[2] lost her father just last week, Maurice Dorléac, an actor since 1935. We still haven't found the empty theatre where we'll be shooting during the first month (February). The shoot, my longest since *F.451* and *Les 2 Anglaises*, will last 14 weeks and take us up to the beginning of May. For the record, let me run through the cast again: Catherine, G. Depardieu,[3] Sabine Haudepin,* Andréa Ferréol, Jean-Louis Richard, Heinz Bennent[4] (a German actor), Maurice Risch and perhaps Jean Poiret,[5] Paulette Dubost (Lisette in *La Règle du jeu*), Laszló Szabó and Christian Rist.[6]

Under the heading of private life: Marie de Poncheville[7] has married a young American writer-scenarist, my daughter Eva considers herself engaged to a publicist and psychoanalyst gentleman, Laura is in Paris at the moment and pleased to be here, but she'll be no less pleased to return to Berkeley where she is awaited by Steve Wong[8] who is finishing his first play while continuing to work at the Pacific Film Archives.[9]

Like everyone else I was disappointed by *Tess*,[10] but I thought *La Luna*[11] better than what has been said, and especially written, about it. Rohmer directed a theatrical production of Kleist's *Catherine de Heilbronn*, it was magnificent.

For a German publisher, I've written a long preface on H.-P. Roché for a French edition of his two novels, *J. et J.* and *Les Anglaises*. I'll have you read the text and you can tell me whether it would be a good idea to translate it for publication in America, perhaps for *French Review* . . . ?

Let me know how you're getting on with your research into the history of your family, and your father. If you aren't coming to France, are there certain magazines or books that you'd like to receive? Don't hesitate to ask.

I do hope I'll have a letter from you before I start shooting (on Monday 28 January) and I take the opportunity now of wishing you a terrific 1980,

with lots of love, dear Annette,

françois

*The little girl in *Jules et Jim*.

1 – For *Le Dernier Métro*.

2 – Deneuve.

3 – Gérard Depardieu, French actor, born in 1948: *Nathalie Granger*, *Les Valseuses*, *Stavisky*, *Maîtresse*, *Préparez vos mouchoirs*, *Mon Oncle d'Amérique*, *Jean de Florette*, *Manon des sources*, *Camille Claudel*, etc.

4 – German actor, born in 1922: *The Lost Honour of Katharina Blum*, *The Tin Drum*, etc.

5 – French actor, dramatist and director, best known as the author and (in the theatre) star of *La Cage aux Folles*.

6 – With the exception of Rist, all the actors mentioned by Truffaut appear in the film.

7 – French journalist and publisher, she appeared (as Marie Jaoul) in *La Chambre verte*.

8 – He later married Laura Truffaut.

9 – The Berkeley cinémathèque.

10 – By Roman Polanski.

11 – By Bernardo Bertolucci.

To Koichi Yamada *[December 1979]*

My dear Yamada,

As one grows older one becomes more and more afraid of travelling. Without you, my Japanese friend, I would never have come to Tokyo. Which would have been a pity, as this trip has been wonderful. Here is a little local currency, it isn't I who am giving it to you, it's Carrosse of which you are, after all, an associate. Whatever you do, don't go reporting it to the police! I too, once upon a time, was helped materially by people like André Bazin and Rossellini to do what I enjoy doing.

You have all my confidence and my friendship; happy new year for 1980,

françois

1980

To Jean-Claude Grumberg[1] *from Paris, 15 January 1980*

Dear Monsieur,

Had I seen *L'Atelier* two months ago, I would not have waited so long before calling you to the rescue.

Since last Friday the possibility of doing so has been going round and round in my head until at last Serge Rousseau encouraged me to speak to you.

Your Léon is sublime, he has everything that my Lucas lacks. Would you agree to kollaborate?[2]

Lucas Steiner will be played by Heinz Bennent, a very fine German actor (*The Tin Drum*)[3] who speaks French well without a guttural accent. The problem is that I don't know how to make him speak, I don't know how to make him come alive. For me there can be no doubt: the solution is to be found on the tip of your pen, which is decidedly better than mine. Suzanne S. and I worked for the dead,[4] would you like to help us interest the living?

Read the script, think about it, let me know what your answer will be.

You will always be able to reach me at Les Films du Carrosse, 5, rue Robert-Estienne (8^{e}), whose telephone number is 256.12.73 or 359.19.74 or again 359.26.46; in any event, I thank you for the two hours of reading and the two hours at the Gymnase[5] last Friday; when humour can be made to alternate with melancholy, one has a success, but when the <u>same</u> things are funny and melancholic at the same time, it's just wonderful,

yours,
François Truffaut

1 – French dramatist and screenwriter, who worked on the script of *Le Dernier Métro*.
2 – Truffaut's 'k' is a facetious reference to the period in which the film is set.
3 – By Volker Schlöndorff.
4 – In *La Chambre verte*.
5 – The Parisian theatre.

To Richard Roud *18 January 1980*

My dear Richard,

This is the first time I've let documents[1] as precious as these out of the Carrosse office. It's impossible for me to have them all photocopied, there are too many pages and we're tied up with the preparation of the film.[2]

I'm relying on you to be 'the dragon that guards over this treasure' (which was how Cocteau described Langlois) and not to mix these papers up with any others or mislay anything. Contrary to what you first supposed, I'm very happy at the idea of a book attempting to piece together the Langlois jigsaw. I have confidence in you and wish you the best of luck,

yours,
françois

P.S. A little gift: the latest and last novel by Renoir.

1 – Concerning Henri Langlois and the Cinémathèque.

2 – *Le Dernier Métro.*

To Jean-Claude Grumberg *Paris, 25 January 1980*

My dear Jean-Claude,

When I write letters on the eve of a new shoot, I have more or less the impression that I am dictating my will. You are therefore the executor of my last wishes (a less imperious word than 'commands').

In order to strengthen the character of Daxiat[1] and show him to be genuinely dangerous, I wish to add a scene that will be numbered 30b and have him in a radio studio giving his weekly talk on the subject of the Jews and homosexuals who are infesting the Paris theatres. When this scene comes to an end on the screen, the sound will continue for thirty seconds over a shot of the radio in Marion's dressing-room.

If we choose to work with pre-existent elements, then 'Daxiat's bulletin' might deal with the Comédie-Française, since we know he hopes to worm his way into it. It's with this in mind that I'm sending you a few pages of a book on the secrets of the Comédie-Française and, still with the same idea, a few pages of *Les Décombres*[2] and a very unambiguous little note from Darquier de Pellepoix.[3]

Don't worry: I start on Monday and have no intention of submerging you with notes and documents. I'll leave you to get on with it, but, in case you

need to reach me, I'll give you my private number, 723.67.74, where you'll find me any evening after 8.30.

françois

1 – The collaborationist theatre critic in *Le Dernier Métro* played by Jean-Louis Richard.

2 – By the pro-Nazi writer Lucien Rebatet.

3 – The High Commissioner for Jewish Affairs during the Occupation.

To Jean-Claude Grumberg *February 1980*

My dear Jean-Claude,

Thank you for the first batch of texts. I like them very much, I'm pleased that I decided to call upon your services and that you agreed to Léonise[1] Lucas.

I can't guarantee that I will adopt all your ideas. It may turn out that I'll keep only 30 or 50% of your dialogue, either because I prefer my own form of words or because I think it more suited to the two actors, but there is no longer any doubt in my mind that, thanks to you, the character of Lucas is going to become more complex.

I very much like the allusion to the sun and the rain, the brief misunderstanding over the 'bad news', the precise details about denunciations, the rat-trap, Montherlant being supposedly Jewish, the story of Goebbels as a film director, the phrase 'we always contrive to be pitied', the word 'convoyer'[2] and the awkward question of Jewish roles – in short, you are absolutely on the right track and I am impatient to see the rest.

What are you going to do about scene no. 38? Do you think you can make it stronger, more violent and more moving (even if it has to be longer)? As for Daxiat's speech in 30b, I slightly regret that you decided against relating it to the situation of the theatre in Paris. (I hope you're going to be stimulated by reading the book on the Comédie-Française.) It was you yourself who said to me, 'I would like to write a pastiche of an article by Daxiat.' To be sure, such a pastiche already exists in no. 93 . . .

You might like to know that this week I'll be filming no. 43, but I think it's all right as it is. If you should have a brilliant idea for it, there's absolutely no time to lose! Do you have a different conception of 64, in which the couple's relationship should develop a little more, I don't know in what direction, probably for the worse with an underlying feeling of bitterness? By contrast, no. 69 ought to be strengthened in that there should be a greater sense of excitement or exaltation in the run-up to the first night of a play, wouldn't you say? I think the conception of 73 is fine, but if you can improve it, so much the better.

During the performance, I must have several brief, silent insert shots of Lucas. Seeing him feverishly jotting down notes is not enough. If you can think of any silent, solitary things for him to do (but not masturbation, and yet . . .), so much the better. I sense there's something missing there.

I like 91 just as it is, but if, along the same lines, you are able to strengthen the cruelty, I say, yet again, so much the better! Ditto for 106.

No. 113: there, for the confrontation of Lucas and Bernard, I'm sure you'll find something better than we did. Perhaps it's in this scene that we should include the phrase about the rat-trap and the cheese or, better still, extend the image of the trap by developing it. The verbal duel between the two men might be sharper, more scathing, more aggressive, before reaching the punchline 'Do you love my wife?' (117)

My accomplice, Suzanne Schiffman, gets out of hospital tomorrow, but she won't be able to rejoin our shoot for another ten days. She will be staying with me during her convalescence and it's she who will be your contact starting from the middle of this week. If it would interest you, for the continuation of your work, to view a few of the scenes that have already been shot, she will be able to organize that for you.

I don't know if your vocal anxieties are psychosomatic, as they say these days, but I hope for your sake that you get your voice back very soon in all its strength and also your morale, which will return at the same time; this should be filed under the heading of: what business is it of mine!

I take the liberty of calling you Jean-Claude because you seem to me very much younger than I am.

With all my thanks and best regards,

françois

1 – To render him more like the character Léon in Grumberg's play *L'Atelier*.

2 – In the sense of 'convoying' Jews to a concentration camp.

To Charles Aznavour *8 April 80*

My dear Charles,

Le Pianiste was my second film, I was still at the stage when I didn't know a Nagra from a caméflex,[1] but it gave me a marvellous sense of security to have you on the set in front of me, at the centre of the screen, attentive and open-minded, meticulous and flexible, ordinary and unique, nervous and poetic. What a host of wonderful, beautiful memories, especially of the filming in the snow, but also what a host of people who have died since that adventure: Nicole Berger, Claude Mansard, Albert Rémy, Catherine Lutz,[2] Francis Cognary,[3] David Goodis!

You're a magnificent actor and, should the occasion arise, we'll work together again one of these days.

My current production (*Le Dernier Métro*) prevents me from coming to see and hear you at the Olympia, but I'll be thinking of you on 15 April and I wish you the very best and not only for that evening,

till we meet again Charles

yours,
françois

1 – The first is a tape recorder, the second a camera.

2 – Members of the film's cast.

3 – Truffaut's assistant director on the film.

To Gabriel Desdoits[1]

Paris, 18 April 1980

My dear Gabriel,

Thank you for your letter of 10 April and Mr Holton's proposition.

Nothing would give me greater pleasure than to see *Adèle H.* turned into an opera!

Since the insanity of Adèle Hugo (who died in 1916) was a kind of family secret, I was obliged, in order to make the film, to obtain the permission of her nephew, Jean Hugo, who is still alive and lives at Lunel. The screenplay was adapted by Jean Gruault and myself from the biography of Adèle by Miss Frances V. Guille, who therefore had a contract and a percentage in the film. Miss Guille died a few weeks after the film opened in New York and her beneficiary is her husband, Walter T. Secor.

Jan Dawson is a young English journalist who translated our French dialogue in order to assist us in establishing an English-language version of the film.

Helen Scott graciously collaborated on the publication of the book.

In my opinion, the only people who should be concerned materially and morally are Miss Guille (through Mr Secor), Jean Gruault and myself, but that's only one opinion, since, in this kind of undertaking, it's difficult to foresee every angle.

Moreover, it will be necessary to check that the contract with New World Pictures does not infringe on any of this.

There you have the situation, my dear Gabriel, and so that you may summarize it for your American correspondent, I am sending you by the same post copies of the six principal contracts.

Keep me informed of developments. I have every confidence in you as our agent in this matter and, if all works out for the best, we will take our seats side by side in the front row of the balcony on the opening night on Broadway.

Very cordially yours,
françois

1 – French film salesman based in New York.

To Georges Delerue

Paris, 23 April 1980

My dear Georges,

Your César[1] still awaits you on the mantelpiece of Marcel Berbert's office. As for its big brother from America, the Oscar, I suppose it was delivered to you in person.

I'd like you to know that everyone here at Carrosse is happy for you, as are those of us shooting *Le Dernier Métro*, though a little belatedly because of the time difference.

What I now want to propose to you is that you write the music for *Le Dernier Métro*. Originally, my plan was to use nothing but songs from the period of the Occupation, and several of these will be in the film, their presence justified by a street singer, three wireless sets, etc. The main ones are 'La Prière à Zumba', 'Bei mir bist du schön' and especially 'Mon Amant de la Saint-Jean', which will function as a kind of leitmotiv just as 'Que reste-t-il de nos amours?'[2] did in *Baisers volés*.

Now that we have reached the stage of the rough-cut, I realize that some real film music is required, because of certain silent effects, some disparate incidents which have to be linked up, a certain tension which has to be maintained, a rather mysterious atmosphere and a twofold love story.

Unlike *L'Amour en fuite*, it will have little narration: probably a minute at the beginning and two minutes near the end of the film, so there is room for music here and there, and often at the end of a scene in the manner of those wonderful few bars[3] which, in *La Nuit américaine*, round off the scene of Valentina Cortese opening the wrong door.

I leave Paris on Monday 28 April, but until then you can ring me either at the office or at home. I return from America on 13 May; Martine Barraqué, however, will be able to let you see the film in the week of 5 to 9 May, if you so wish.

We begin sound-mixing on 21 July, which means that the music could be recorded on the days following the 14th.

I impatiently await your answer in the hope that it will be affirmative and I sign myself, in any event, your friend,

françois

1 – For the score of *L'Amour en fuite*.
2 – By Charles Trenet.
3 – Also composed by Delerue.

To Guy Teisseire

Paris, 25 April 1980

My dear Guy,

The work schedule for *Le Dernier Métro* was so heavy that I preferred to have the set closed to journalists in order to get it finished in time. Which explains Pierre Montaigne's fit of rage, etc.

I found on my desk a note from Marcel Berbert concerning the magazine *V.S.D*. The memories we share as cinephiles are too strong and go back too far for me to be able to refuse you anything.[1]

I return from Los Angeles on 15 May and, from then onwards,* I'm at your disposal for a meeting, an interview or, better still, a Hitchcockian lunch.

Yours,
françois

P.S. *Or else when you return from Cannes if you're going or after you've written your 3rd novel if you're in the middle of it.

1 – No article subsequently appeared in *V.S.D*.

To Guy Teisseire

Monday 23 June 80

My dear Guy,

A setback in my work forces me to postpone our lunch on Wednesday. Since you're more difficult to reach than I am, why don't you call me so that we can fix up another date?

As I write this, three secretaries are searching for your most recent address and telephone number: are you Roger Thornhill or George Kaplan (with a strong hint of Vandamm)?[1]

My apologies for Wednesday, owing-to-last-circumstances-métro-beyond-my-control,

yours,
françois

1 – Roger Thornhill is the character played by Cary Grant in Hitchcock's *North by Northwest*; George Kaplan, the fictitious character (created by the secret service) for whom Thornhill is mistaken; Philip Vandamm, the character played by James Mason in the same film.

To Annette Insdorf

Paris, 26 June 1980

Dear Annette,

Thank you for your letter of 20 June 1980.

I am sending you the book of *Jules et Jim* care of Avon, but I confess that I haven't got any name to give you since the idea of the preface was mine alone.

Logically, it's my agent, Don Congdon, that I should be asking to take the necessary steps but he wouldn't understand why I am not asking for any money and, in any case, I'm very keen for you to translate it.

Congratulations on your sale to Macmillan in England. The photo of you with Robert Redford didn't bring a smile to my face, quite the reverse, as I imagined the sort of exchange that must have been made on the walls of your studio: 'I'll remove this one where I'm with that moron Truffaut and put sexy Redford in its place!'

I'm staying in Paris for the whole summer to put the finishing touches to *Le Dernier Métro*. We will definitely not be going to Venice and, as far as the New York Film Festival is concerned, that will be decided around 20 July.

Affectionately,
françois

P.S. At Avon, the only solution as far as I can see is to ask to speak to the person who edited *Jules et Jim* and *Les Deux Anglaises*, but if taking such a step makes you uncomfortable or doesn't seem natural to you, just forget it.

To Jean Aurel *[1980]*

My dear Jean,
No, it isn't

THE END OF THE MARQUISATE OF AUREL[1]

I am going to spend the night in Los Angeles and I return to Paris around 12 May. I'll be delighted if you're there, a Parisian, available for lunching, chatting and watching *Le Dernier Métro*, which in its present state is completely lopsided,[2]

yours,
françois

1 – This was a newspaper caption which Truffaut inserted in the original letter.
2 – Truffaut had great confidence in Aurel's opinion, which he often sought during the editing of his films.

To Georges Franju *Paris, 3 July 1980*

My dear Georges,

I am at present editing a new film, *Le Dernier Métro*, whose action takes place in Paris during the Occupation.

To justify the title and articulate the narrative in two or three places, I filmed a few shots of the Métro, but I cannot use any of them, as they are hopelessly contemporary: neon lighting, stations which have been redesigned and too many sources of light.

I viewed a great deal of footage in the Métro film library, but the same problems presented themselves.

I have, however, retained a very vivid memory of your film *La Première Nuit*[1] and have just seen it again with undiminished admiration. During the first ten minutes I noted three or four shots – less than thirty seconds in all – which would do perfectly if you were to allow me to use them. I am speaking, naturally, of shots full of anonymous passengers in which it is impossible to distinguish your two little protagonists, and of a lateral pan in which a train passes very quickly, like a streak of light . . .

Your producer, Anatole Dauman, has very kindly given me his permission, but it's obviously yours which matters to me and, concerning as it does the rather delicate question of unacknowledged quotation, I would perfectly

FRANÇOIS TRUFFAUT

Mon cher Jean,

non, ce n'est pas

LA FIN DU MARQUISAT D'AUREL

Je vais dormir à Los Angeles, je rentre à Paris vers le 12 Mai. Tant mieux pour moi si vous êtes là, parisien, disponible pour déjeuner, bavarder et regarder le dernier métro si brinquebalant dans son état actuel,

amitiés,

François

François Truffaut's handwriting (letter to Jean Aurel).

understand if you preferred to refuse: your film is a cinematic poem, not a documentary, you are not a director of stock shots but an artist.

I impatiently await your answer and, whichever it should be, remain

very cordially yours,
françois

Nevertheless, we might have a phrase in the credit-titles rendering unto Caesar . . .

1 – A short made in 1958.

To Anatole Dauman[1]

Paris, 7 July 1980

Dear friend,

With a generosity equal to your own, Georges Franju has allowed me to use a few shots from his *Première Nuit* in my *Dernier Métro*.

I would say that, in the final cut, we'll keep between forty-five seconds and a minute, but, to give ourselves some leeway in the editing, Martine Barraqué and I would like to duplicate between one minute thirty and two minutes of the internegative, corresponding to the threads that we would place in the print you have been kind enough to lend us.

It's time now for me to express my gratitude, since, thanks to you, there is one criticism that no one will be able to make: 'But why the devil did they call it *Le Dernier Métro*!'

Your friend,
François Truffaut

1 – French producer, born in 1925.

To Annette Insdorf

from Paris, 24 July 1980

Dear Annette,

Thank you for your letter of 4 July. We'll wait for the publisher's answer and, if it's negative, we'll resign ourselves to the fact that my Roché piece will just have to be put away in a bottom drawer or, more precisely, inside a file that I'll reopen the day film-making is forbidden me on medical grounds and I start writing my memoirs.

I adore Abel Gance, but I don't believe he is sufficiently rational for his wish to live in California to be anything other than a whim. After a week in

Barbet's house . . . or Luddy's[1] . . . or Coppola's,[2] or anyone else's, he'll want to return to France, take it from me. He receives a small pension from the government . . .

If someone has to pay for the airline ticket, it seems to me it ought to be Coppola since he bought (from whom? from Lelouch?) *Napoléon* which he's getting ready to release. Obviously, the main problem will be the nurse, a prerequisite for a man of 91. Last night I saw Gance on TV, he had really aged, he seemed almost blind, but mentally alert. I have no contact with the Société des Réalisateurs.[3] This whole escapade, if you think it desirable, ought to be arranged directly between Luddy–Coppola and Gance himself.

What's new, dear Annette? Nestor Almendros's book is remarkable.[4] I saw *Alien*[5] again, it's a really powerful film. Resnais's film[6] is a big success with the public, as is Tavernier's,[7] though in more modest proportions. *Positif*[8] has just published a splendid anniversary issue on Ophüls. Suzanne is working on the new film by Pascal Thomas.[9] Rohmer begins shooting in two weeks' time. Georges Delerue has written a fine score for *Le Dernier Métro*.

I very much hope to see you at the NYFF in early October. I spoke to Richard Roud this morning, I hope to be there for the closing days.

From the amateurism of my typing you will have guessed that Josiane[10] is on holiday.

I saw you on French television when they repeated the Hitchcock evening at the AFI. We were very good and I haven't forgotten how you saved me from ridicule by giving me a lesson in diction which outclassed the one in *Singing in the Rain*[11] ('Moses supposes his toeses are roses . . .'). Which reminds me, *The Rose*[12] isn't at all bad, anyway the woman[13] is brilliant.

Let me know in your next letter how your own work is progressing, your script and the study of the Holocaust.[14] I have a great admiration for your capacity for work, for the determination with which you cheerfully set yourself very precise goals, and all without any apparent effort, without any complaints, in short, the undaunted Annette I know you to be.

Give my regards to your parents when you see them. If they're suffering from the annual heatwave, remind them of Washington in the snow!

All my love,
françois

P.S. To come back to Gance. It's because of his 'gratifying' (the 'in' word) memory of Telluride[15] that Gance imagines he would be happier in California, but it won't take him long to realize that it's not the sort of country in which old people are treated with love and respect; I can't forget the loneliness of Renoir, who realized how happy he had been in Paris.

1 – Tom Luddy, formerly curator of the Berkeley Film Archives, then executive producer for Francis Ford Coppola.
2 – Francis Ford Coppola, American director, born in 1939.
3 – The Society of Directors.
4 – *A Man with a Camera.*
5 – By Ridley Scott.
6 – *Mon Oncle d'Amérique.*
7 – Bertrand Tavernier's *Une semaine de vacances.*
8 – A French film journal and immemorial rival to *Cahiers du cinéma.*
9 – *Celles qu'on n'a pas eues.*
10 – Josiane Couëdel, who was then production secretary at Les Films du Carrosse.
11 – Correctly, *Singin' in the Rain*, by Gene Kelly and Stanley Donen (1952).
12 – By Mark Rydell.
13 – Bette Midler.
14 – *Indelible Shadows, Film and the Holocaust*, published in 1983.
15 – A ski resort in Colorado which is also host to a chic film festival.

To Richard Roud

Paris, 4 August 1980

My dear Richard,

The latest news from the Cinémathèque is very depressing.

Alain Vannier spoke to me of Thursday 9 October[1] which strikes me as an excellent date. Whether or not we would have the closing night, I wanted the film to be shown near the end, primarily to let our friend Scott give full rein to her perfectionism.*

Catherine D. and I will be arriving on Sunday the 5th (I think Scott would like to come a few days earlier) and Catherine seems set on the Hotel Carlyle, but such questions of organization can easily be arranged between Scott and Catherine Verret.

As I recall, it was at the 1970 festival that we presented *Tristana* and *L'Enfant sauvage*. This anniversary prompts me to put myself forward as a candidate for the N.Y.F.F. of 1990.

My regards to all the festival's staff. See you very soon, my dear Richard,

yours,
françois

*Seriously, we'll only just be ready.

1 – For the screening of *Le Dernier Métro* at the New York Film Festival.

To a food columnist

Paris, 8 August 1980

My dear friend,

I have a very pleasant memory of the hour we had together on the radio, except that I thought it was much more recent.

I am sorry to have to disappoint you, but I am on such bad terms with food that I cannot answer your questionnaire.

Bruno Bettelheim explains that, with food, one has the same relationship as with one's mother, and I really believe that that's the case with me. The fact remains that an hour after a meal I am incapable of saying what I ate. It's the same thing in my work since, in twenty years, I have failed to discover the recipe that would enable me to make nothing but good films.

You will certainly have heard of those colleagues of mine who are also gourmets: Claude Chabrol, Bertrand Tavernier, Jean-Luc Godard, Alexandre Astruc.

I wish you every success for your book and remain

Yours faithfully,
François Truffaut

To Robert Fischer[1]

Paris, 8 August 1980

My dear Robert,

Thank you for your note, for the 'Filmprogramm' of *La Chambre verte* which is superb and for your letter of 26 June.

First of all, concerning the preface on Henri-Pierre Roché, even if it won't be appearing immediately, I wish to make an important change on page 17. This involves removing the names of Franz Hessel and Helen Hessel and replacing them by the initials F.H. and H.H.; for I have just learned that Helen Hessel is still alive (ninety-four years old) and that her son is ambassador to Switzerland. The keys to *Jules et Jim* must continue to remain secret.[2]

I therefore rely on you to make the change. If, some day, you can obtain any information on Franz Hessel's literary career (I think he died in the 40s), I would be very pleased.

I am still working on the editing of *Le Dernier Métro*, the film won't be ready for Venice, but it will open in Paris on 17 September and will be shown at the next New York festival.

I am sending you the publicity handout, but we haven't got any real stills yet for the press.

I'm pleased to know that you are hard at work on the book about the new German cinema and the film project on the Austrian actor.

I wish you good luck in your work.

Very best regards,
François Truffaut

1 – German film critic, born in 1954. He edited a number of Truffaut's books and was himself the author and translator of books on Hitchcock and the New German Cinema.

2 – Helen Hessel, the model for the character of Catherine in *Jules et Jim*, died in 1982. Her son gives a detailed account of his childhood and a description of his parents in a documentary film by Thomas Honickel on the background to *Jules et Jim*.

To Georges Delerue

28 August 1980

My dear Georges,

The film is finished, the music is terrific: it reinforces the romantic aspects, it adds mystery, it enhances the ending, in short, I'm delighted and I hope you'll be able to come to the première in Paris on 16 September.

yours,
françois

To Richard Roud

Paris, 3 September 1980

My dear Richard,

I'm taking advantage of a short trip by Nestor Almendros to give him some press handouts for the festival.

Since *Le Dernier Métro* doesn't have an American distributor yet, I hope there's someone on your staff who will be able to translate it or edit a little press-book. Perhaps I'm mistaken, perhaps that's the responsibility of the French Film Office?

The copy marked Richard Roud will show you to what extent the brochure can be reduced and simplified.

The first screenings of *Le Dernier Métro* have been extremely promising and I have almost no more worries about the kind of reception the film will have in France. I've invited Jean-Yves Mock[1] to the Paris première on 16 September.

Having parted company with Pascal Thomas,[2] Suzanne is now free to assist Helen, so the subtitled print will be ready on time.

Let me continue this disjointed monologue: I've taken the liberty of giving your New York address and telephone number to Madame Hortense Chabrier, who left Laffont to found her own publishing house. She's launching it with the new Erica Jong and she would be interested in having your Langlois.

Nestor Almendros's book is first-rate, perhaps you might suggest the name of an American publisher to him?

The N.Y.F.F. again: Gérard Depardieu and his wife will be joining our little expedition.

James Monaco[3] has asked me to take part in his 'Sunday Morning' programme, but I intend to offer him Catherine instead for the double reason that she is prettier to look at and her English is better.

Hoping to see you very soon, dear Richard,

best wishes,
françois

1 – French writer, born in 1928.
2 – On the shoot of *Celles qu'on n'a pas eues.*
3 – American film critic and writer.

To Jean Mambrino

25 Sept. 80

My dear Jean,

Thank you for your kind words and for the book of poems. I am not what you would call a good reader of poetry, but the beautiful little copy of *La Ligne du feu* sits on my desk and I often open it.

Let's get together at the end of the year, I'm off to America for a while; I am dog-tired but happy and send you my best wishes

françois

To Gérard Lebovici

Paris, 30 September 1980

My dear Gérard,

Jean-Paul Torok[1] was right: I have no intention of becoming typecast as Hollywood's notion of a French scientist.[2]

All the same, the proposition is pretty flattering when you consider that thirty-eight actresses were put forward for the feminine role and only two actors for the American role.

To have my vanity – in America, they would say my ego – completely satisfied I'd like a copy of Mr Samuelson's letter to be sent to Jean-Paul Belmondo. He will finally understand that he ought to have directed *La Sirène du Mississipi* while I would have been very good in the role of Louis Mahé.[3]

Since you want me to reply seriously, I suggest you send Mr Samuelson a list of the other actors handled by Artmedia who speak English with a 'pronounced' French accent.

In any case, this project seems to be an offshoot of the actors' strike in America, which is now apparently at an end.

Regards
françois

P.S. I am returning your documentation.

1 – French film critic.
2 – Truffaut is of course alluding to his role in *Close Encounters of the Third Kind*.
3 – Played by Belmondo in *La Sirène du Mississipi*.

To Robert Fischer

Paris, 24 October 1980

My dear Robert,

Thank you for your letter of 19 October.

I am sending you a second copy of Nestor Almendros's book to give to Hanser since, in my opinion, it might well be of interest to them.

I'm also sending you three copies of the script of *L'Amour en Fuite* and, as you requested, some material on *Le Dernier Métro*, and finally the two latest issues of *Cahiers du cinéma* which contain the interview with me.

I was very touched and very moved by the idea of receiving the documentation on Franz Hessel. His widow has just recently written to me and sent a beautiful photograph of herself from the period of her youth. She had rather hard features and was certainly less beautiful than Jeanne Moreau, but there's a strong personality there.

I'm also sending you the third (posthumous) novel by Henri-Pierre Roché, *Victor*, published by the Centre Beaubourg. I'll try and obtain another copy, but, until then, I suggest you lend it to your friend Charly Möller.

As regards your idea of publishing *La Mariée* and *La Sirène*, I will endeavour to help you. A similar project was considered then abandoned by an American publisher. The necessary transcription work was therefore undertaken, though perhaps never completed, and I'll try and find the texts again.

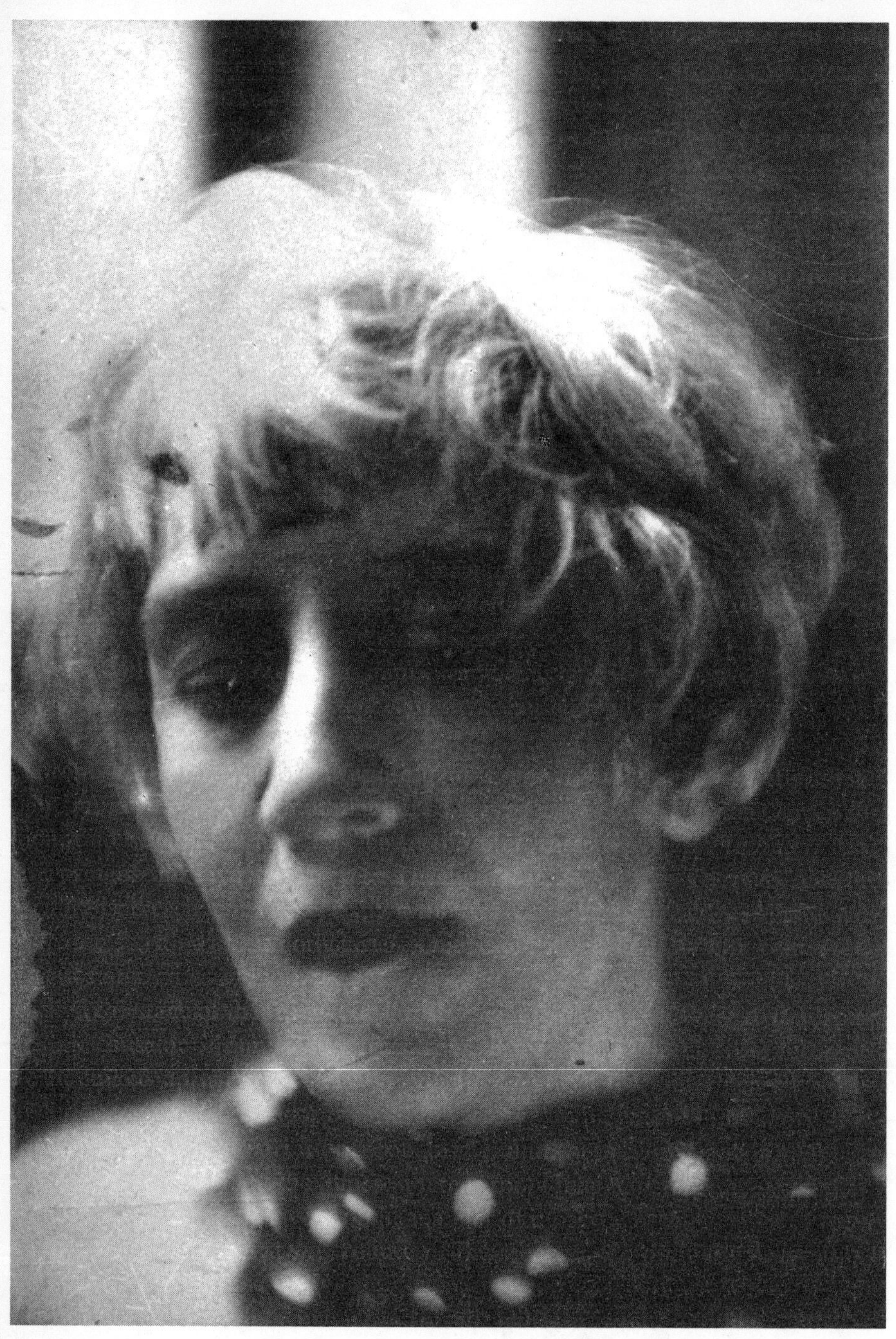

Helen Hessel, the real Catherine of *Jules et Jim*.

11.9.1980

Pour vous
cher François Truffaut
ce Document
qui date du Temps
de
Jules et Jim
affectueusement
Helen Hessel

'11.9.1980
For you dear François Truffaut this document which dates from the time of Jules and Jim
affectionately
Helen Hessel'

As far as *Jules et Jim* is concerned, if you succeed in publishing your edition of *Protocol*, of course you may use the preface in question.

I'm looking forward to receiving the Welles–Bazin in a month's time.

Yes, the reception that *Le Dernier Métro* has had in France, Belgium and Switzerland exceeds all our expectations, and I am therefore very pleased.

I am greatly touched by your devotion and hope that circumstances will bring us together soon.

I've arranged for Heinz Bennent to be artistic supervisor on the German version of *Le Dernier Métro* and, if all goes well, and I'm not shooting a new film, I'll come to Munich for the opening.

Regards,
françois

To Annette Insdorf

Paris, 12 November 1980

My dear Annette,

Thank you for your letter of 3 November.

Your *New York Times* interview is very good, but there are nevertheless three or four minor points that ought to be cleared up. As far as Suzanne is concerned, there's been a misunderstanding, it was she who argued for Bennent, saying that it must be possible for a Jewish character to be played by a non-Jewish actor.

In any event, dear Annette, there's no urgency, as the film hasn't been sold to America yet, though it probably will be before the end of the year. It's been selected by France as a candidate for the Oscars.

I was very pleased with the *Village Voice* article on homosexuality in my films and it ties in with my liking for *The Stunt Man*[1] and the looks exchanged by the male protagonists of that poetic and dreamlike film.

Paris awaits you on 4 December, I will be very happy to see you as soon as you arrive. I'll be in Israel from the 9th to the 13th.

Love,
françois

1 – By Richard Rush.

To Hervé Le Boterf[1] *14 Nov. 80*

Dear Hervé Le Boterf,

Twenty-five years ago we were neighbours in the offices of *Cinémonde*. I have just made a film, *Le Dernier Métro*, set in the world of the theatre during the Occupation. In the period when I was writing the screenplay, your book *La Vie parisienne sous l'Occupation* was of very great and constant help to me. I acknowledged my sources in the press-book, but no mention of my debt to you seems to have appeared in the newspapers. This little note is intended to convey to you my interest in everything you write, everything you publish, to convey to you, finally, my gratitude,

kindest regards,
François Truffaut

1 – French journalist and writer, born in 1921.

To Jean Aurel *4 Dec. 80*

My dear Jean,

Here is the photocopy of our oral skeleton[1] (that phrase really needs a drawing!).

It's a little bit too theoretical, but that doesn't worry me. If we succeed in structuring it correctly, the rest will follow, which is to say, flesh, life, humour and organization.

Make notes, think about it when you're driving, I'll ring you when I return around the 15th. After that, I intend to work sometimes with you, sometimes with Suzanne (and conceivably the 3 of us together), until we're satisfied with our story,

yours,
françois

1 – Truffaut, Aurel and Suzanne Schiffman were working on the screenplay of *La Femme d'à côté* (*The Woman Next Door*).

To Richard Roud *Paris, 16 December 1980*

My dear Richard,

Here is my proxy so that you can vote in my name at the General Assembly of the Cinémathèque.

Actually, I'm sure you don't need it to attend the meeting, but it's as good a way as any to tell you that I'm impatient to read your book.

I will in fact be back from Rome on 6 January and I will be happy to have lunch with you shortly after if you're in Paris. Merry Christmas,

yours,
françois

Catherine Deneuve and Heinz Bennent in *Le Dernier Métro*.

1981

To Annette Insdorf

Paris, 5 January 1981

My dear Annette,

Before anything else, I want to wish you a happy new year and I really feel that 1981 will turn out to be a kind of watershed in your professional life.

I'm sorry that some wretched hotel thief[1] should have been responsible for your premature departure. Thank you for all the material contained in your letter.

It's true, the review of *Le Dernier Métro* is more than just favourable, it's moving, and I'm delighted with it.

Your article on Jaubert is first-rate and I'm going to have two copies made of it for Madame Jaubert and François Porcile.

The only point of contention is the statement made by Rush.[2] When he declared for a fact that I knew *The Stunt Man* and had tried unsuccessfully to buy the rights, why did you not question him in greater depth or check the matter with me?

Even now, I still haven't read a novel in English. The first book I read in English was Selznick's *Memo*,[3] after taking a few weeks' lessons from Michel Thomas in Los Angeles in the autumn of 73.

I wrote the script of *La Nuit américaine* with Jean-Louis Richard in August 71 and I had started jotting down notes for the film as long ago as the *Sirène* shoot in December 68.[4] As you see, I'm quite meticulous about dates.

In 1963 Lewis Allen proposed *The Day of the Locust*[5] to me, but I preferred him to produce *Fahrenheit*.

I liked *The Stunt Man* (the film), but I'm a little annoyed at Rush's irresponsible statement, first because he must also have made it to other people besides yourself, and then because this kind of falsehood tends to be repeated from article to article as the years go by.

As far as my presence at the Oscar ceremony is concerned, it's a trifle premature, since I'm not certain yet whether I'll be nominated. The film will definitely be distributed in America by United Artists and I hope they'll make a good job of it.

Naturally, I'd be delighted to see you there. By separate post, I'm sending you a little gift: the screenplay of *Napoléon* as it was published in 1927. I think I'm right in saying that the second volume never came out, at any rate I've never seen it. I hope this book won't go astray.

In the hope of seeing you soon, dear Annette, I remain

very affectionately yours,

françois

1 – While staying in Paris, Insdorf had been robbed.
2 – Richard Rush, American director, born in 1930: *Psych-Out*, *Getting Straight*, *Freebie and the Bean*, *The Stunt Man*, etc.
3 – *Memo from David O. Selznick*, published in 1972.
4 – In fact, Truffaut shot *La Sirène du Mississipi* in the spring of 1969.
5 – Nathanael West's novel was filmed by John Schlesinger in 1975.

To Annette Insdorf

8 January 81

Dear Annette,

I find Rush's cavalier attitude hard to swallow and, rather than keep my recriminations to myself, I prefer to let you know my feelings on the matter, as you are my friend, the author of the best book on my work and a discreet confidante.

You must be aware that all film directors, whether famous or obscure, regard themselves as misunderstood or underrated. Because of that, they all lie. They're obliged to overstate their own importance.

You will certainly have noticed (I think in *American Film*) the unwarranted use which the director of *Fingers*[1] has made of the brief piece I wrote for my retrospective in Washington. I obviously never said, or wrote, that *Fingers* was one of the greatest American films of the sound period. Well, anyway, when Rush quotes Bergman and Kubrick (who must certainly have said something favourable, amicable and sincere about his work), there's every reason to suppose that he is exaggerating and that Bergman and Kubrick will be annoyed when they read it.

When we see each other, I plan to have a long talk with you on the question of influences and the distinction that one has to make between allusions and plagiarism, since these are matters of real importance.

To come back to Rush, what strikes me as possible, even probable, and wasn't mentioned in your interview, is that the commercial failure of *Day for Night* (despite the Oscar) must have had some bearing on the negative attitude taken by Warner Bros., the distributors of my film, with regard to

The Stunt Man. Also, there was the similarity between *Hooper*[2] and *The Stunt Man* which would have benefited from being clarified. In the presentation text that I wrote for the opening of *La Nuit américaine*, I did not conceal the sources of my inspiration: *Singin' in the Rain*, *8½*, *Le Schpountz*[3] and *The Bad and the Beautiful*,[4] though inspiration isn't the correct word as (except in the case of *Singin' in the Rain*) my aim was to contradict (or to complement) the above-mentioned films.

In your marvellous study of the film, you were right to mention *La Règle du jeu* as a latent influence, since I grew up with that film as with *Citizen Kane*.

Apart from *The Day of the Locust*, which I got Helen Scott to summarize for me, the only book I've ever been offered on the subject of moviemaking is *The Moviegoer*,[5] which I have in any case not read, that was in 1975, which is to say after *La Nuit américaine*, because, as you know, one is always offered material retroactively, i.e. biographies of women after *Adèle*, films with children after *Small Change*, etc.

Perhaps, dear Annette, my insistence on refuting Rush's statement will surprise you since not only is it not pejorative but it was presented merely as a titillating and even flattering piece of information. The truth is that directors don't only have friends and that their detractors, mean-minded hair-splitters, are only too happy to latch on to this kind of pseudo-factual argument to reinforce their own negative and derogatory theorizing. Just imagine a Jonathan Rosenbaum writing about *La Nuit américaine* again and making use of Rush's statement. So that you understand fully what I mean, I'm sending you a photocopy of the *Nouvel Observateur* review of *Le Dernier Métro*. It was written by Michel Mardore,[6] who has made a couple of disastrous films:[7] there was such a good atmosphere at the initial screenings that he doesn't dare attack head-on, but where the review is utterly treacherous is in its insinuations. To a certain extent it's my own fault: I didn't have to call the heroine of *La Disparue*[8] Héléna or stick a gamekeeper in the play. I'm sure you'll understand my frame of mind and forgive my pestering you with such a long letter.

There you have it. Seen you soon, dear Annette, and all my love,

françois

1 – James Toback.
2 – By Hal Needham. It also dealt with stuntmen.
3 – By Marcel Pagnol (1938).
4 – By Vincente Minnelli (1952).
5 – By Walker Percy.
6 – French film critic and director.
7 – *Le Sauveur* and *Le Mariage à la mode*.
8 – The title of the play which is staged in *Le Dernier Métro*.

To Bertrand Poirot-Delpech[1]

Monday 23 February 81

Dear Bertrand,

At the flea-market I came across this book,[2] it's for you. I haven't cut the pages, I thought that manipulating the paper-knife would be part of the pleasure.

yours,
françois

1 – French journalist and novelist.
2 – Enclosed with this letter was a book 'in praise of poverty' written by the father of the French President Valéry Giscard d'Estaing.

To Marcel Moussy

26 Feb. 81

My dear Marcel,

Thank you for your letter of 1 February. It was on precisely that day I decided that *Le Dernier Métro* was an old film and that it was time to begin a new one: which will be *La Femme d'à côté* with Depardieu, Fanny Ardant,[1] Henri Garcin, etc. starting in 3 weeks' time and due to come out in October.

I will, not 'would', be happy to see you again any time, between 15 June and whenever you go on holiday, we'll have a nice quiet chat. I know a young actress-cum-singer with a Mozartian voice and the physique to match, 27 years old, Arielle Dombasle,[2] one of Rohmer's actresses, do you think I should take the liberty of recommending her to Bluwal?[3]

love to the 2 of you,
françois

1 – French actress, born in 1949: for Truffaut she made *La Femme d'à côté* and *Vivement dimanche!* (*Finally Sunday!*).
2 – French actress, born in 1957 (Truffaut was mistaken about her age).
3 – Marcel Bluwal, French TV director.

To Hervé Le Boterf

27 February 1981

My dear friend,

For three months now, your letter has been keeping me company on my travels and time and again I've decided against replying to you from so far away and on a postcard. That's why I offer you such belated thanks, both for

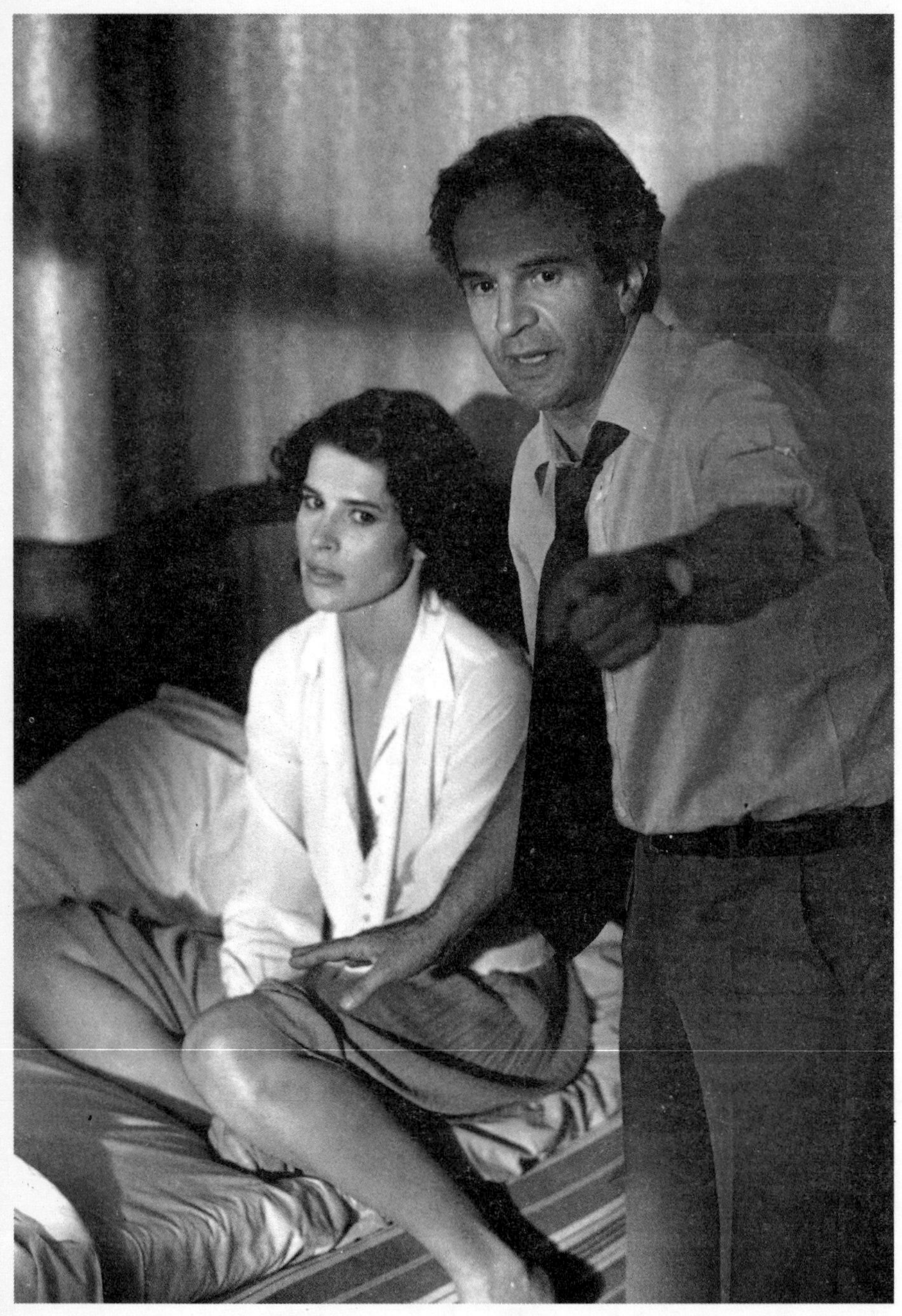

François Truffaut: a woman next to him (filming *La Femme d'à côté* with Fanny Ardant).

the letter and the books received (the Leslie Howard, the Fresnay, the Clift[1] and the Cooper[2]).

I've long followed your activity at France-Empire with great enthusiasm. If I did not make films, I would be a publisher. I would like to recommend some American books to you, but you know them all (the Swanson or *Swanson by Gloria S.* from Random House is very good).

As for myself, I decided, on the day after the Césars, to relegate *Le Dernier Métro* to the past and plunge in at the deep end next month: *La Femme d'à côté* with Gérard Depardieu and Fanny Ardant, a contemporary tale of passionate love. We'll finish shooting on Saturday 23 May, then ten days' holiday, and by mid-June we'll therefore be able, at long last, to have lunch together somewhere around the rue Bayard or the rue Marbeuf . . .

I've just turned 49, I'm still too young to think of writing my memoirs and above all I want to take advantage of my present good health to continue making films. Siclier's book on the 220 films of the Occupation[3] is not at all bad (out soon from Veyrier); but I found Pol Vandromme's *Le Vigan*[4] rather frustrating. Speaking of La Vigue,[5] the idea of giving you a part in one of my films appeals to me; I haven't even seen you act (or else I didn't recognize you?), we'll discuss it over an entertaining lunch,

hoping, then, to see you soon, yours very cordially,

François Truffaut

1 – Montgomery Clift.
2 – Gary Cooper.
3 – *La France de Pétain et son cinéma.*
4 – Robert Le Vigan, French actor (1900–1972): *Madame Bovary*, *La Bandera*, *Les Bas-Fonds*, *Quai des Brumes*, *Goupi Mains rouges*, *Golgotha*, etc.
5 – Le Vigan's nickname.

To Marcel Berbert *[early 1981]*

Dear Dr Dornez,[1]

We're on the look-out for a good actor to play your role. How would you feel about Marcel Berbert who has – already – been a doctor in *La Chambre verte*, a bookseller in *U.B.F.C.M.*,[2] an administrator in *Le Dernier Métro*, who is, in short, an actor of real experience?

There will be a little dialogue, just a little (not much more than in the present script), as most of the phrases will go to Philippe[3] and the monologues to Mathilde.[3]

The young director of the New Wave awaits an answer in Grenoble,

yours,

fr.

1 – The role in *La Femme d'à côté* that Truffaut is offering to Berbert.

2 – *Une belle fille comme moi.*

3 – A character in *La Femme d'à côté.*

To Jean-Loup Dabadie *3 March 1981*

My dear Jean-Loup,

Your Clara enchanted me as did the swell guys,[1] it's a superb screenplay, of a type that seems utterly heartfelt and requires a brain in excellent working order.

My desire to work with you is just as great as ever, but it has taken a paradoxical form. I don't want to come to you with a subject and then discuss it and talk around it and collaborate on it as I do with Gruault, Aurel and Suzanne, I would prefer the idea to come from you, I'd also like you to develop it and submit it to me, as at the period of *Chère Louise*.

Probably because of the prickly nature of our friendship, my feeling towards you is like that of an actor angling for a part but not liking to suggest anything, I want to be wanted and even seduced. If something along those lines strikes you as feasible, think about it. Naturally, my reference to *Chère Louise* was intended to be taken in the same spirit, what I'd prefer is a serious subject with some light relief rather than the other way round.

In the meantime, I'll be filming, for such is my destiny, *La Femme d'à côté* with Depardieu, Fanny Ardant, Henri Garcin, etc., a contemporary story of passionate love.

If you're busy, up to your ears in work, forget this letter (though my proposal is good for the whole decade), but don't forget that I am, even from afar,

your friend,
françois

1 – Truffaut is alluding to Jacques Monnet's film *Clara et les chics types*, which was scripted by Dabadie.

To Michel Boujut[1] *18 March 1981*

My dear Michel,

You will see from the two articles which I've unearthed that the notion of the young directors of the New Wave stabbing their elders in the back is a pure fabrication. It was from *Cahiers* that Gance, Pagnol, Guitry, Rossellini and Ophüls received the most sympathy and gratitude. Three months after the Cannes screening of *Les 400 Coups*, I became co-producer of *Le Testament d'Orphée* which every producer – starting with Raoul Lévy – had turned down. This is a private letter, and I have no wish to reply to attacks,[2] but I wanted you to be in full possession of the facts,

cordially,
françois

1 – French film journalist and writer, born in 1940.
2 – *Les Nouvelles littéraires* had published, alongside Boujut's interview with Truffaut on the subject of *La Femme d'à côté*, a polemical article by Alain Rémond whose basic argument was that the director had reverted to the stale conventions of the so-called *cinéma de papa* which, as a critic, he had once deplored.

To Annette Insdorf

Friday 20 March 81
(the 1st day of spring)

Dear Annette,

I start a new film in 8 days' time, in Grenoble (*La Femme d'à côté*), with Gérard Depardieu and Fanny Ardant, a love story. We'll finish shooting around 20 May, I won't be going to the States immediately after that, as Laura is coming to France at the beginning of June. Thank you for your 2 letters and the articles and bravo for *Cinématographe*.[1]

I liked *Raging Bull*[2] quite a lot and especially Rohmer's new film, *La Femme de l'aviateur*, which generates real suspense through its dialogue and is very well acted.

hoping to see you again soon, love, dear Annette,

françois

1 – The film journal of which Annette Insdorf had just been appointed New York correspondent.
2 – By Martin Scorsese.

To Robert Chazal[1]

Grenoble, 9 April 1981

My dear Robert,

We have known each other for twenty-five years and I have never challenged any of your judgements on my work, the fact that I used to write criticism myself having led me to respect the independence of critics.

Now that the Oscars have been awarded, I feel the need to let you know, privately, how hurt I was by the repeated references in *France-Soir* to a supposed hostility on the part of the Academy to France's selection of *Le Dernier Métro*.

My impression is that it all started with an anonymous article in *Le Film français*, which was then picked up by *Le Monde* and several times by *France-Soir* (unsigned), until your article on the day after the Oscars.

The only information I have on this matter can be summed up as follows:

From October until December 1980, Roger Corman[2] (New World Pictures), the American distributor of several of my films as well as, more recently, Resnais's *Mon Oncle d'Amérique*, attempted to obtain the distribution rights to *Le Dernier Métro* but did not make a sufficiently good offer. When he learned that our film had finally been bought by United Artists, he was furious and declared that the choice made by the French commission (*Métro* instead of *Mon Oncle . . .*) was 'political' rather than 'artistic'. The journalist who reported this statement in *Variety* added an ironic commentary to it by pointing out, precisely, that Corman had not succeeded in buying *Le Métro*!

That is, to my knowledge, the only material on which the journalist from *Le Film français* based his article, arbitrarily ascribing Corman's personal reaction to a 'group of members' of the Academy. When I returned from Canada, I could at that moment have had the error put right or asked for the situation to be clarified; if I didn't, it was because I loathe any form of polemics and also out of respect for a fellow film-maker like Resnais.

I find it unjustified and unjust that, by extrapolating from the ill-tempered reaction of one incensed distributor, the press has gradually come to attribute his dissatisfaction to 'certain members of the Academy', then to the Academy itself, then to practically the whole of America.

Allow me to inform you that, five years ago, a similar situation arose when the French committee for the Oscars chose *India Song*[3] over *L'Histoire d'Adèle H.* Even then, Roger Corman was already making the same kind of protest (he had bought *Adèle H.*!). His reaction, as it happens, might almost have seemed justified in retrospect, given that the Academy quite simply eliminated *India Song* after its first screening, which means that there was no French film among the nominations that year. So you see, there probably would have been more reason for controversy in the French press then than there was on the present occasion, when after all Resnais and I were both in with a chance. Five years ago, when Corman asked me to make a protest to Unifrance about the rejection of *Adèle H.*, I refused on the grounds that the decision should be respected and that Marguerite Duras had a right to her chance.

Obviously, none of this is very serious; I think you know me well enough, my dear Robert, to know that I accept both failures and successes with equal good humour, am capable of putting good and bad luck into a perspective where everything is relative.

Behind the insistent repetition of this false piece of information I believed I sensed a hostility to *Le Dernier Métro* that could not in any way have been anticipated from the long article you wrote when it opened. If you think that *Le Dernier Métro* deserved neither its prizes nor its popularity and that it has been scandalously overrated, say so openly, write it, that would hurt me less than the ostensibly neutral and objective dissemination of incorrect information.

Whether favourable or critical – and for the most part they have been generous – your reviews of my work have never caused me to doubt your loyalty, and that is why I wished to write this letter to you, a letter that will obviously be invalidated if, on this matter, you should happen to possess further information of which I am unaware.

Yours sincerely,
François Truffaut

1 – French film journalist and critic, born in 1912.
2 – American director, producer and distributor, born in 1926: (as director) *Machine-Gun Kelly*, *A Bucket of Blood*, *The Little Shop of Horrors*, *The Pit and the Pendulum*, *The Raven*, *The Masque of the Red Death*, *The Wild Angels*, *The Trip*, etc. He may also claim to have discovered such film-makers as Coppola, Scorsese, Bogdanovich, Dennis Hopper, Monte Hellman and Jonathan Demme.
3 – By Marguerite Duras.

Robert Chazal to François Truffaut *Paris, 14 April 1981*

My dear François,

Your letter from Grenoble has surprised and shocked me. It is true that mention was made several times of the various incidents and judgements surrounding the French selection for the Oscars (though there was no intention of singling out *Le Dernier Métro*). But far more was written in *France-Soir* about the qualities, value and place of *Le Dernier Métro* in current French cinema. I myself not only wrote the review that you know but declared, on numerous occasions (the Unifrance-Film Prize, the Césars, etc.), that *Le Dernier Métro* was one of the most accomplished and important films of the year. We were also the first to report that your film had had more than a million spectators in Paris.

I fail to understand how you can write: 'If you think that *Le Dernier Métro* deserved neither its prizes nor its popularity and that it has been scandalously overrated, say so openly, write it, that would hurt me less than the ostensibly neutral and objective dissemination of incorrect information.' That really is a gratuitous insult.

What you call the Corman incident was, as you well know, the subject not only of an article in *Le Film français* but also of rumours brought back from Hollywood by people who had just returned from there. It may be that we made too many allusions to it, but we spoke a lot about the Oscars, and the French hopes were naturally a priority.

I am sorry that you have taken offence, but I am very much sorrier that this has led you to question my loyalty to you. Yes, I repeat, I was deeply shocked by your letter.

That, of course, in no way lessens the interest that I take in your films nor the esteem that I have for their director.

A little sadly yours,
R. Chazal

To Robert Chazal *[25 May 1981]*

My dear Robert,

On returning from Grenoble I saw your rectification *vis-à-vis Le Dernier Métro*. It was reassuring, it demonstrated your sense of fair play and made me very happy; thank you for it and believe that I am

very cordially yours,
françois

To Koichi Yamada *Paris, 17 July 1981*

My dear Yamada,

I am happy to know that you received the Hitchcock stills and today I'm going to try and answer your letter of 29 June.

Unfortunately, I have no information on the film *Harmony Heaven*.[1] The title is not even cited in the excellent book by Maurice Yacowar: *Hitchcock's British Films*.

Nor have I any recollection of Hitchcock's appearance in *The Thirty-Nine Steps*.[2]

I find these queries of yours infinitely disturbing, as they make me aware of my failing memory. Twenty years ago, I would have been able to answer every one of them without having to consult a single book and with the same serene assurance as the famous Mr Memory.[3]

I am in fact very busy editing *La Femme d'à côté*, since the film has to be finished by September. The music will be recorded in London in mid-August.

Very confidentially, I can tell you that in September Gallimard is publishing a very important book by Simone de Beauvoir. It will be entitled *La Cérémonie des adieux* and its subject is the last ten years in the life of Jean-Paul Sartre.

I bring it to your attention as perhaps it would be a good thing for you to translate . . . but only after the Hitchcock!

Very affectionately yours,
françois

1 – Co-directed by Hitchcock, Eddie Pola and Edward Brandt (1929).
2 – In *The Thirty-Nine Steps* Hitchcock is to be glimpsed walking along a street.
3 – Mr Memory is a character in *The Thirty-Nine Steps*.

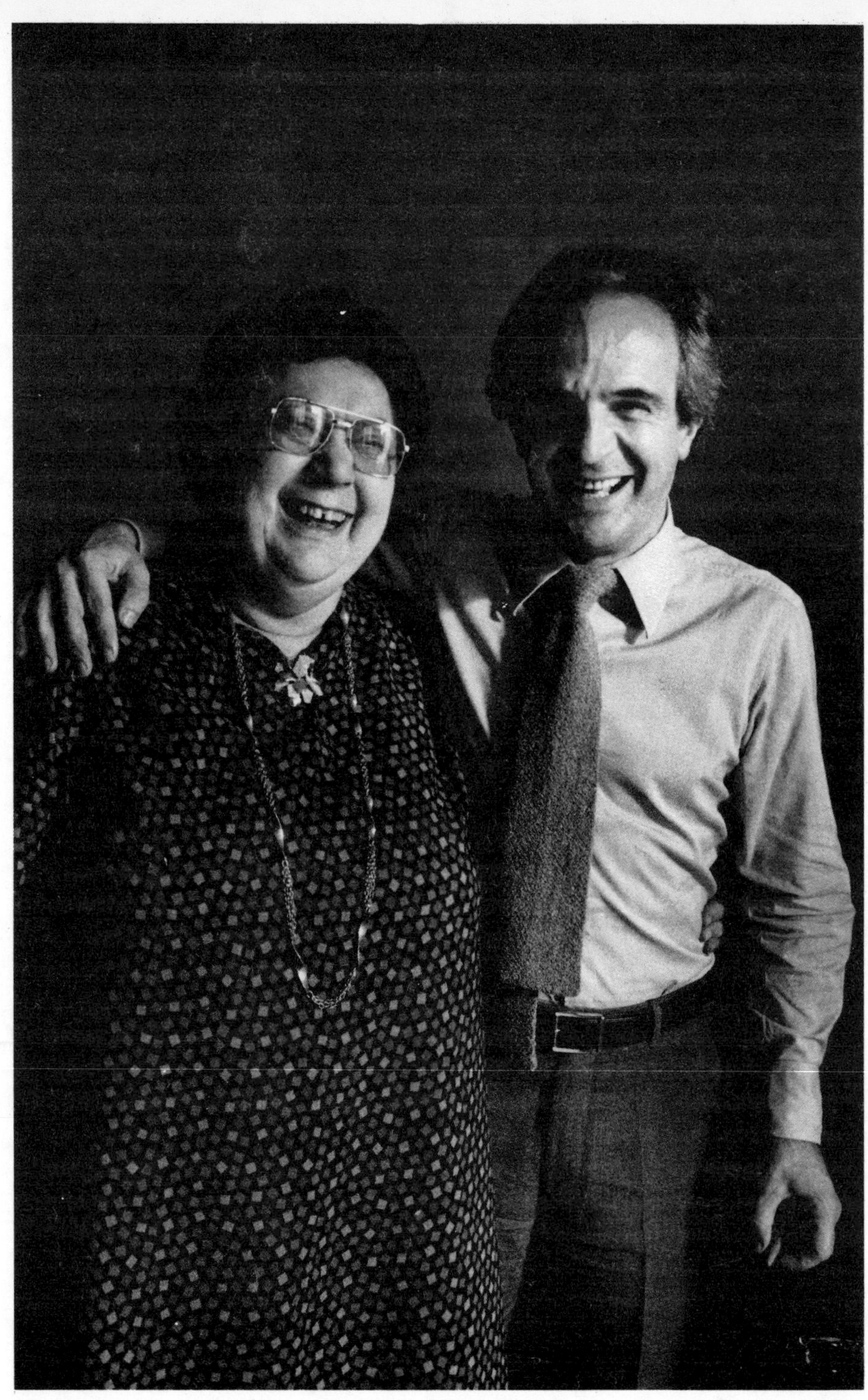

Helen Scott and François Truffaut.

1982

To Robert Lachenay *3 February 82*

Dear old Robert,

Call me at the office any morning around twelve and we'll get together. I've thought of an arrangement that will be to your advantage and won't cost Carrosse too much, concerning the film *Une visite*.[1] I'm very grateful to you for finding that forgotten reel of film, it confirms what a good friend you are, I have the impression that each of us will soon be able to say of the other: 'I've known him for 40 years!'

yours,
françois

1 – A 16 mm short film made by Truffaut in 1954 (photographed by Rivette and edited by Resnais).

To the Société des Réalisateurs de Films[1] *[3 March 1982]*

Dear Sirs,

Since becoming a member of the S.R.F. and receiving your bulletins, I have been suprised to note, here and there, a number of disobliging remarks on the subject of such colleagues of mine as G. Lautner,[2] Claude Zidi[3] . . . I do not know whether they are members of the S.R.F., but, in any event, if this vague impression that I have were to be confirmed – that they are being subtly discriminated against – then I would no longer regard it as the SOCIETY OF FILM DIRECTORS but as a SOCIETY OF CERTAIN FILM DIRECTORS, and I would no longer wish to belong to it.

François Truffaut,
director

1 – The Society of Film Directors.

2 – Georges Lautner, French director, born in 1926: *Le Monocle noir*, *Les Tontons flingueurs*, *Les Barbouzes*, *Galia*, *Le Pacha*, *Les Seins de glace*, etc. Lautner's mother was the actress Renée Saint-Cyr (see p. 447).

3 – French director, born in 1934: *Les Bidasses en folie*, *Les Fous du stade*, *La Moutarde me monte au nez*, *L'Aile et la Cuisse*, *Les Ripoux*, etc.

To Koichi Yamada

Paris, 23 March 1982

My dear Yamada,

In his last book Buñuel states that he puts all his faith in serendipity.

It so happens that your letter arrived while I was being interviewed by the people from *Pia*.[1]

I am dictating this letter quickly so that they can take it with them.

1. *Une visite* will leave by courier in a few days. As it's a completely silent film, it will pose no translation problems. Since the story is nevertheless a bit obscure, I've summarized the plot on the enclosed page, along with the credits. You must decide whether it would be a good idea or not to translate this synopsis and have it distributed before the screening.

2. Mr Hayashi[2] was very nice, but since I have to leave Paris tomorrow I refused to do a TV programme, since I will only be in Paris for twenty-four hours on 10 April before flying to Tokyo. As for Mr Nakamura, he struck me as being a real cinéphile.

3. If, on 16 April, you let him choose between *Histoire d'eau* and *L'Amour à vingt ans*, I would prefer *L'Amour à vingt ans* just as I'd prefer *Les Deux Anglaises* to *Une belle fille comme moi*.

4. I'll give you and Mr Hasumi[3] all the time you need, but I would nevertheless like to see the two Japanese films you regard as the best of the last two years.

5. The schedule for Friday 16 April will absolutely have to be arranged so that I can attend the reception for the President at the embassy,[4] since it really would be most uncivil of me not to go. I really think that scheduling the presentation of *La Femme d'à côté* on the same day as Mitterrand's reception at the embassy shows a lack of co-ordination. For the following day, Saturday the 17th, the coincidence of dates is not so serious, but it might be necessary to split up the signing session so that I'll be able to look in on the meeting with Jack Lang.[5]

6. The novel by Charles Williams that I hope to shoot in October is called in English *The Long Saturday Night* and in French *Vivement dimanche!* It will star Fanny Ardant.

7. Mademoiselle Josiane thanks you for thanking her.

your friend,
françois

P.S. I've just reread the Hitchcock contract. There is unquestionably money owing to you and Helen Scott. The first two days after my arrival we must set up an appointment with the publishing house of Shobun Sha Ltd (Katsuya Nakamura or Miss Hara). If we find ourselves in conflict with this publisher, perhaps we can obtain the services of a lawyer through Unifrance-Film-Tokyo or the consulate. I'm sending you photocopies of the contracts which will acquaint you with the situation. Don't let my aggressiveness worry you: we must not only rejoice in the book's success but fight to receive our fair share of it.

1 – A Japanese listings magazine.
2 – The editor of *Pia* and organizer of the 1982 Truffaut Festival in Tokyo.
3 – Shigehiko Hasumi, professor of French literature at the University of Tokyo, editor of a Japanese film journal and co-translator of Truffaut's books.
4 – François Mitterrand was making a state visit to Japan in April 1982.
5 – Mitterrand's Minister of Culture.

To Michel Boujut *[April 1982]*

My dear Michel,

Devastated by a terrorist bomb, the rue Marbeuf[1] looks like *Germany Year Zero*.[2] The post gets through nevertheless and with it has come, from America, a nice compliment to you, taken from some periodical for French teachers; the piece will certainly be of interest to you. I'm not alone in hoping that *Les Nouvelles littéraires*, like the famous presbytery, has lost nothing of its splendour;[3] I greatly admired the manner in which you confessed to having been a deserter and learned a lot from it.[4]

Keep your spirits up and good luck,

yours,
françois

1 – Only yards aways from Les Films du Carrosse.
2 – By Roberto Rossellini (1947).
3 – Truffaut is alluding to (and misquoting) a famous phrase, much admired by the Surrealists, from Gaston Leroux's *Le Mystère de la chambre jaune* (*The Mystery of the Yellow Room*): 'Le presbytère n'a rien perdu de son charme ni le jardin de son éclat.'
4 – Boujut had been interviewed in *Les Nouvelles littéraires* on the reasons for his desertion during the Algerian War.

To Marcel Moussy

23 April 1982

My dear Marcel,

After the explosion of a terrorist bomb the rue Marbeuf looks like the Berlin of *Germany Year Zero*. Your piece on René Clair pleased me, or should I say moved me, very much.

I cannot join the S.A.C.D.[1] or any other commission, any other panel; I've even asked the Fédér. internat. des c. clubs[2] to let me resign as president before the end of the year.

I would be happy for the two of us to collaborate again, but on a subject suggested by you. As for recommending you to my colleagues, I'm very willing to do so, especially now that your letter gives me the go-ahead. What you tell me of socialist television is depressing, worse than I imagined; keep your spirits up and above all better luck, all my love to Yvonne and you,

françois

1 – Société des Auteurs et Compositeurs Dramatiques (Society of Authors and Composers).

2 – Fédération Internationale des Ciné-Clubs (International Federation of Film Societies).

To Jim Paris[1]

Paris, 3 May 1982

My dear Jim,

No, I wasn't surprised by your letter and I think I knew, obscurely, that my corrections and additions might cause a problem.[2]

You have my permission to cut the paragraph on Charles Spaak[3] as well as the list of writers who were 'travestied'.

No, I don't see the preface as a 'tribune in which to expound my ideas', but I do feel that the polemical work engaged in by *Cahiers du cinéma* during the 50s has not always been correctly understood in America, any more than the notion of the 'politique des auteurs'. I have no wish to reopen the debate in the preface to your book, which is fundamentally a work of reconciliation, but I wanted to avoid this kind of comment being made: 'Well, well, in his preface to Jim Paris's book, Truffaut praises the kind of films that he and his friends attacked when they were critics.'

Nowadays, I have a rather dispassionate attitude to all of these matters and I can assure you that, when I watch a film by Duvivier, René Clair, Grémillon[4] or Autant-Lara on television, it is in the hope of liking it and having a 'pleasant surprise'. Unfortunately, nine times out of ten, I am disappointed and find myself with the same objections as before. These relate mainly to the representation of love, the female characters, the antibourgeois *statements*,[5] the absence of children and above all the falseness of the dialogue. When *Nous sommes tous des assassins*[6] was screened on television, I asked a young woman to watch it with me. At the beginning of the film, when we are shown the people who are going to make up the jury, I asked her to guess which of the jurors would be favourable to the defendant and which would be against, and she at once guessed correctly, so stereotyped were the characters (and the actors who played them).

The revolt, to use a very grand word, of *Cahiers du cinéma* was more moral than aesthetic. What we were arguing for was an equality of observation on the part of the artist *vis-à-vis* his characters instead of a distribution of sympathy and antipathy which in most cases betrayed the servility of artists with regard to the stars of their films and, on the other hand, their demagoguery with regard to the public.

I hope we'll have the opportunity one day of having a talk about this with examples and comparisons.

That said, I agree with you that there is no need to overload my preface, particularly as, were I to launch into an analysis of what it was that shocked us in the French cinema, I would have to analyse systematically the work of film-makers I admire, which would mean encroaching on the book itself, pointlessly so since your own comments on these films are for the most part first-rate.

When your letter arrived the other day, I desperately wanted to make myself better understood and wrote a new version of the passage that worried you. I soon realized that this new section would unbalance the text without satisfying either of us. I am therefore sending it to you, solely for your information, not to have it inserted.

For the final and definitive text I accept the solutions you propose in your letter. I am pleased that you are keeping the remark on the idea of children being sacrificed, relegated to the background.

Let's now regard this preface as finished; if you wouldn't mind, please send me a copy of the text when you have translated it. Excuse me for having created problems for you and please do not doubt my admiration for the great job you are doing.

Your friend,
François Truffaut

1 – American writer and critic.

2 – 'Truffaut wrote the preface to my book *The Great French Films* (Citadel Press, 1983). After criticizing the practitioners of

"psychological realism", he continued with a personal attack on Charles Spaak. As I intended to include seven films written by Spaak, I asked François to limit his comments to a few general observations to prevent the reader from questioning my own judgement, and this he graciously consented to do.' (Note by Jim Paris)

3 – Belgian-born screenwriter of French films (1903–75).

4 – Jean Grémillon, French director (1901–59): *Gardiens de phare*, *La Petite Lise*, *Gueule d'amour*, *L'Étrange Monsieur Victor*, *Remorques*, *Pattes blanches*, etc.

5 – In English in the original letter.

6 – By André Cayatte (1952).

To Marcel Moussy

Paris, 17 May 1982

My dear Marcel,

A filthy cold prevented me from replying to you sooner.

The Lacour project[1] seems to me first-rate. They ought to give a medal to that guy who's got the courage to tell real stories with characters, twists and turns and last-minute reversals.

Now, I don't envisage putting my finger in this particular pie, as I'm incapable of filming power relationships between men. Perhaps because I was an only son . . . Thanks to that, I enjoy watching them and adore Clouzot's films or Polanski's.*

Anyway, the producer whose name you mentioned did well to buy the rights to the novel and I hope you'll remain involved with the project.

Yours,
françois

*Reading over what I've just written, I can see that this sentence isn't clear; let's say that my preference is for filming women, children and, in the background, men between whom there is no real conflict. Which doesn't mean that I can't admire *The Master of Ballantrae* or *Le Rire de Caïn*.

1 – An adaptation of José-André Lacour's novel *Le Rire de Caïn* was written and directed by Moussy for French television.

To Macha Méril[1]

circa *25 May 1982*

Ma chère
Ma cha,

Obviously, if I hadn't made *La N. Am.*,[2] I would have grasped at the rights to *La Star*[3] like a drowning man grasping at a lifebuoy, but I've got no worries on your behalf: the film is written – and well written – with so many precisely rendered sensations, so many vivid observations, an equal weight given to important things and small details which is how we recognize an artist, that a director (why not a 'directress'?) will certainly turn up, and soon, to shout 'Action!'

Usually, actors/tresses who write books (I read them all voraciously) barely mention the realities of a film shoot, as though they had drifted through it without noticing them; you're different; one is absolutely convinced that you observed everything, understood everything and that you weren't interested only in yourself, but also in the budget, the work schedule and all the rest. I have nothing to say to Grasset, but to Macha of whom I still have a few images from 1966, images as tender as only memories can be, I freely express my admiration and my undying affection,

françois

1 – French actress, born in 1940: *Une femme mariée*, *Nous ne vieillirons pas ensemble*, *Les Uns et les Autres*, *Beau-Père*, etc.

2 – *La Nuit américaine*.

3 – Macha Méril's *La Star* had just been published by Éditions Grasset.

To Jean-Louis Trintignant[1]

Paris, 9 July 1982

My dear Jean-Louis,

This film, *Vivement dimanche!*, will tell the story of a secretary playing amateur sleuth in order to clear her boss, who has been falsely accused of several murders.

Fanny Ardant will play the secretary and the part I am offering you is that of her boss, Julien Vercel, the director of an estate agency in a town like Hyères or Sète.

Nestor Almendros will be director of photography and the film will be made in black and white; we'll perhaps shoot a few scenes in the Victorine studios, which would then serve as our headquarters.

The shoot is due to commence at the beginning of November and will last about eight weeks.

What else can I tell you? You have before you the third version of the script, there are one or two still to come since both the story and the characters might be improved, but the difference will be one of degree rather than of kind. The story being what it is, the characters being what they are, what we've got to get up on the screen is humour and charm, and the various contributions should remain invisible.

If you say to me: 'Dear François, as I told you at Pézenas, I am extremely keen to work with you, but I would prefer to wait for a part that's more this or more that . . .', I will fully understand and, for you as for myself, it will only be a pleasure deferred.

If, on the other hand, you choose this part as you might choose a pair of shoes, your feet will not hurt, as we'll tread lightly and softly, as though wearing moccasins.

When you've read the scenario, I suggest you ring me at Rochegude (very near Bollène) or come and have lunch since you're just a short drive away, I believe,

your friend,
François Truffaut

1 – French actor and director, born in 1930: (as actor): *Et Dieu créa la femme*, *Le Combat dans l'île*, *Un homme et une femme*, *Z*, *Ma Nuit chez Maud*, *The Conformist*, etc.

To Jean-François Hauduroy *27 August 1982*

Dear Jean-François,

We missed one another in June and, since then, a new screenplay has been born, the adaptation of a Série Noire thriller, *Vivement dimanche!*, already in preparation; we film at the end of October, in the Midi, with Fanny Ardant and Trintignant, in black and white, I hope.

As for the Indians, the answer is negative. The virus of fiction has definitively killed off the documentary as far as I'm concerned.

I'm pleased that you liked *La Femme d'à côté*, it's an extremely simple film, with perhaps a Becker-like quality recalling *Falbalas*, well-meaning characters caught up in a romantic passion. Work has prevented me from going to America this year, which I regret a little; I hope, some day soon, to see your name on the credit titles of a film, I remember *Mon Oncle Benjamin* with real pleasure; what's more, it's a pity not to have your interesting study of Simenon shown on television. My very best wishes to you and your wife,

françois

To Robert Fischer *Paris, 3 September 1982*

My dear Robert,

Here I am in Paris again.

I hope you received the material I sent you at the beginning of August.

For myself, I'd like to thank you for the programmes of *La Femme d'à côté*.

Naturally, you have my approval on the collage of articles which you did for *Le Dernier Métro*.

I give you full authorization on *L'Homme qui aimait les femmes*. The American director Blake Edwards is planning to remake the film a few years from now!

I would be happy, when they come out, to receive the German editions of *Jules et Jim* and *Les Deux Anglaises*.

I've read the texts that Professor Witte gave me concerning Helen Hessel, and I had the pleasure of receiving, some months ago, one or two letters from her as well as a very beautiful photograph. I believe she is now quite incapable of either speaking or writing as her earthly existence is drawing to a close.

Let me know if you received the issue of *Cahiers* on Orson Welles and the Gallimard edition of *Les Deux Anglaises*.

I am sending you *The Long Saturday Night* on which my next film is based, but, except for the beginning and end of the book, everything has been changed.

I start shooting in November, but, until then, I am at your disposal to send you any material you might need.

Very cordially yours, see you soon,
françois

To Gérard Lebovici[1] *Paris, 9 September 1982*

My dear Gérard,

The Venice Festival has just awarded the Golden Lion to *The State of Things* which Wim Wenders directed in black and white.

Every year, somewhere in the world, a director, taking advantage of his creative freedom, chooses a film in black and white and, almost every time, the film constitutes an event: *The Last Picture Show*, *Papillon*, *Manhattan*, *Raging Bull*, *Veronika Voss*, *The Elephant Man*.[2] Each of these works demonstrates that a film in black and white is, in any case, a film 'in colour', since it displays, between the black and the white, an infinity of greys which make it subtler and richer.

It was with my black and white film, *L'Enfant sauvage*, that I first teamed up with Nestor Almendros, and it's him I have asked to do the black and white photography of *Vivement dimanche!*, which I'm going to shoot in November.

Vivement dimanche! will attempt to recapture the mysterious, nocturnal, glittering atmosphere of those American comedy thrillers that used to enchant us. I believe that the use of black and white will help us revive their bygone charm, I believe above all that no one in the world will ever succeed in convincing me that black and white is less cultural than colour!

Colour was generalized, systematized, made virtually obligatory by the gutlessness of a nervous industry that was unable to peddle its standardized productions except in the form of packages, but this absurd – unwritten – law should not concern films which are directed with care and performed by artists who are known and admired both at home and abroad.

Films are not cans of baked beans. Like people, they've got to be conceived, received and scrutinized one by one.

That's my point of view, dear Gérard, one that I am sure you share and one that you will be better able than I to justify to our partners.

Yours,
françois

1 – In 1982 Gérard Lebovici was a producer at Soprofilms. He was worried – he or the TV channel Antenne 2, which was to co-produce *Vivement dimanche!* – by Truffaut's determination to make the film in black and white.

2 – Respectively by Peter Bogdanovich, Franklin Schaffner, Woody Allen, Martin Scorsese, Rainer Werner Fassbinder and David Lynch. Truffaut, however, was mistaken about *Papillon*, which was shot in colour.

To Richard Roud

Paris, 16 September 1982

My dear Richard,

As I said to you on the telephone, I was fascinated, enlightened and touched by your book.[1] It also brought back a number of memories, which is why it gave me so much pleasure to write, perhaps a little too quickly, this (overlong) preface.

Perhaps you remember, when you spoke to me of the 'editorial' demands being made by your publisher, that I was all for the meticulous approach which results in American books being better, more professionally, edited than ours. I wouldn't think of contradicting myself now and I trust that, even before you undertake the translation of my preface, you'll have no hesitation in criticizing or shortening or rearranging it. After the last week in October, I'll be unavailable (for nine weeks), but, until then, I am at your disposal to revise this or that paragraph, this or that page . . .

I think, for example, that the lengthy comparison between Langlois and de Gaulle could easily be cut.

Anyway, read it through yourself and let me know your feelings about it as soon as possible. I hope everything will go well with the New York Film Festival and that the sponsors will have renewed, and in my opinion fully deserved, confidence in you.

Our Scott has been rather troubled by pains that have kept her in bed for a week, after a short stay in the American Hospital; I'm vague, but so is she, and if the threatened organ is the heart, it would be exaggerating to speak of a heart attack. In any case, she has stopped smoking, she eats nothing but grapefruit 'just when lots of friends were ringing up to invite me out to dinner'. It's the same old tune, the same old words, the same old refrain.

There you have it, my dear Richard, now let's have news of you,

hoping to see you soon,

françois

1 – *A Passion for Films.*

To Jean-Pierre Brossard[1] *Paris, 23 September 1982*

Dear secretary-general and friend,

When I accepted the presidency of the F.I.C.C. in 1979, it was understood that the mandate would be for two years. By request of the delegates who met in Lisbon in 1981, that mandate was renewed, though I made it clear that I wished to step down as soon as the procedures for a new election had been established.

Not having sought it in the first place, I confess that I would have refused such an honour had I had any suspicion of the displeasure, never publicly expressed but for me quite patent, that my election would cause among various French officials of the Fédération.

Several of my letters to them have gone unanswered and I have occasionally had the impression of being confronted with an administrative wall similar to that erected by certain ministries and TV channels: failing to acknowledge receipt of letters so that nothing gets put in writing.

To be absolutely honest, I must add that, if I have met with hostility from several of my countrymen, my relations with foreign delegates have been much more cordial and, thanks to being president, I have made new friends from every corner of the globe.

I should finally like to confirm that, as my work is taking up more and more of my time, I wish to be relieved of my duties as soon as possible and that under no circumstances will I be a candidate at the next election.

Yours sincerely,
François Truffaut

1 – Secretary-general of the Fédération Internationale des Ciné-Clubs.

To a journalist

Paris, 30 September 1982

Dear Madame,

In reply to your letter of 23 September, I have to inform you that I seldom eat at the Coupole[1], being both professionally and socially a man of the Right Bank.

Nevertheless, I have lunched on occasion at the Coupole, for example with Jean-Paul Sartre at the period when we were preparing together a series of television programmes that were immediately cancelled by Jacques Chirac, who was then Prime Minister.

What I appreciate at the Coupole is the kind of anonymity engendered by the large number of tables and customers, even if, conversely, having had poor hearing since my childhood, I find it hard to bear the noisy atmosphere, comparable only to that of Victoria Station at six o'clock in the evening.

I hope that I have satisfied your quite legitimate professional curiosity and remain

Yours respectfully,
François Truffaut

1 – A perennially fashionable Left Bank restaurant.

To Richard Roud

Paris, 22 October 1982

My dear Richard,

I am sending this note both to your Broadway office and your Paris apartment.

Rereading the last part of your book, I've come to regret not having mentioned in my preface the importance of the role played by Jean Riboud.

Which is why I have reworked page 9[1] in order to include it.

Furthermore, you must not hesitate to cut the sentence concerning Céline and Proust, which, I agree, serves no useful purpose.

This note allows me now to leave for my shoot[2] with a relatively clear conscience. Hoping to see you very soon,

yours,
françois

P.S. A photo of H.L.[3] visiting the set of *L'Enf. sauvage*.

P.9: 'The struggle was carried out on all fronts, in the streets, in offices, on the phone. We inundated the newspapers with our articles and *communiqués*. They were at first favourable to our cause, but then became more and more intimidated by the government. Several hundred directors, from Chaplin to Kurosawa, from Satyajit Ray to Rossellini, sent telegrams to *Cahiers du Cinéma* – very active in this struggle – threatening to withdraw their films from a Cinémathèque deprived of Langlois. Finally, as Richard Roud explains so well, the government had to give in, not only because of the pressure of the *cinephiles* but also thanks to the effective action behind the scenes of some powerful men, the most important of whom was Jean Riboud, chief operating officer of the multinational Schlumberger company and a friend of the arts. Once Langlois was reinstated, we could get some sleep again and go back to our own work.'

1 – The text is reproduced here.
2 – Of *Vivement dimanche!*
3 – Henri Langlois.

Fanny Ardant, 'the "secretary turns private eye" type of plot' (*Vivement dimanche!*).

1983

To Sarah Racine-Freess[1]

Sat. 26 Feb. 1983

Dear Sarah,

Welcome among us. As you will discover, it won't be fun and games every day, but even so . . . Sometimes life is a slice of bread and butter, other times a slice of bread and . . . In either case, though, you've just got to eat it up.

Since I can already foresee the queues forming, I'm asking you without further delay to reserve for me the 1st Wednesday of March 1996. I'll take you to see a film forbidden to under-13s, and then we'll go and have an ice-cream at Angélina's,[2] is it a deal?

With all my affection, dear Sarah, I bestow on you a kiss,

françois

1 – Claudine Bouché had been Truffaut's editor at the beginning of his career. In February 1983 her daughter gave birth to the baby to whom this letter is addressed.

2 – A fashionable Parisian tea-room.

To Jean Gruault

Brussels, March 1983
during the writing of 00–14[1]
and the filming of Benvenuta

My dear old chum,

We're leaving (it's half-past twelve) for the Sheraton to see the books and have lunch.

At about 4.00 we're going to the Vendôme to see Zinnemann's *Five Days One Summer*. We'll be back by about 6.30, and Fanny[2] will go and have her hair done, I'll stay here where we'll have dinner when she returns; I hope you'll join us at some point during the day. Fanny was pleased to have spoken to Resnais, kisses from both of us,

fr.

1 – The script on which Gruault and Truffaut were collaborating when Truffaut fell ill. Having admired Bergman's *Fanny and Alexander*, Truffaut similarly wished to

combine a film and television series. The working title, *00–14*, refers to the fact that the narrative was to have extended from 1900 to 1914.

2 – Fanny Ardant was at that moment acting in André Delvaux's film *Benvenuta*, being shot in Brussels.

To Jean Aurel

15 March 83

My dear Jean,

I'll be back from Belgium, where Fanny is making a film with André Delvaux, around 28 March. I haven't forgotten you and we'll speak then about *La Fille sur téléphone* and try to tell the story from the point of view of characters other than the heroine; it would be a pity to give up now . . . At the moment Delerue is busy on *Vivement dimanche!* (50 minutes of music). At the beginning of April I'll invite you to see the film again before the sound-mixing, scheduled for 2 May, but we'll continue to work calmly, without rushing things. Well then, it's a date, lunch in 2 weeks,

yours,
françois

To Nestor Almendros

15 March 83

My dear Nestor,

Here's the little piece I wrote on 'Why *Vivement dimanche!* is in black and white'. For the final version of the press-book I'd prefer to replace this text with yours, which will certainly have more documentation and be better for the press. That said, if there are 2 or 3 sentences in my text that can be inserted into yours, don't hesitate to extract them and use them as you will. I return from Belgium on the 25th. Will you come to the screening on Monday the 28th? There will be Gérard Lebovici, Serge Rousseau, Scott, Berbert, Vannier and the publicist; give me your piece then, if it's ready.

I hope you're in good health and that everything is going well for you.

regards,
françois

P.S. At L.T.C., the other morning, the beauty of your photography was unmistakable.

To Evelyne Bouix[1] *from Paris, 12 April 1983*

Dear Mademoiselle,

I really admired your performance in *Edith et Marcel.*[2] Audiences will certainly be appreciative, but they will have no conception of the work involved; they will think it was sufficient for you, when filming started, to step into Piaf's shoes and step out of them again on the last day, whereas in reality you would have had to make the effort a thousand times to adapt yourself, every day, before every shot. The result on the screen is amazing.

Like Piaf, you resemble the mime Baptiste, like hers your face has its own natural pathos. As always in Claude's films, you had to contend with a co-star in the form of the camera – I write this sentence with a smile of admiration – and you succeeded in making it dance to your tune the way an Indian dancer charms the snake which envelops her in its coils.

The Piaf–Cerdan romance is quite unusual, it shows that there is no incompatibility between love that is calculating and love that is sincere; it makes for an extraordinarily touching couple.

I am sure that 1983 will be a memorable year for you for at least two reasons,[3] I wish you the best of luck for everything to come and I rely on you to convey to Claude my compliments and my regards,

Yours truly,
François Truffaut

1 – French actress, born in 1953: *Les Uns et les Autres, Les Misérables, Edith et Marcel, Partir, revenir*, etc.

2 – By Claude Lelouch.

3 – The film's release and the birth of her and Lelouch's daughter, Salomé.

To Serge Rousseau *Tuesday 12 April 83*

My dear Serge,

In reply to your request concerning the possible subject of a film for J.H.,[1] here is, by the author[2] of *Maria Chapdelaine* and *Monsieur Ripois et la Némésis*,[3] a novel about a pugilist, *Battling Malone*, a trifle thin, a trifle dated, but interesting and containing among the leading roles – by a stroke of luck – that of a well-bred young woman, the hero's patroness.[4] Hémon died in 1913, the book is therefore in the public domain, his daughter is an elderly lady living in Saint-Malo, at least I hope for her sake she is . . .

Enjoy it, regards,
françois

1 – Johnny Hallyday, French singer and actor.
2 – Louis Hémon.
3 – From which novel René Clément made a film in 1954, *Knave of Hearts*, with Gérard Philippe, Valerie Hobson and Joan Greenwood.
4 – Hallyday's companion was the actress Nathalie Baye.

To Jean-Loup Dabadie

12 April 83

My dear Jean-Loup,

Your project about two men living together is certainly interesting, but it's not for me. Even so, the desire to work together is mutual, as you know. You will see, in Resnais's film *La Vie est un roman*, Fanny Ardant in her romantic manner. At the end of May, if you're in Paris, I'll show you the same actress playing a Katherine H.[1] role in a comedy thriller (the 'secretary turns private eye' type of plot). If these two roles suggest a third to you, or might suggest the possibility of such, then it would be marvellous if we launched into it together; take all the time you need to think about it and accept the very best wishes of your (already) old friend,

françois

P.S. To think that I don't even know your present address.

1 – Hepburn.

To Guy Marchand[1]

28 April 83

My dear Guy,

Every time I see you I'm bowled over: what a man, what an actor, but with *Coup de foudre*[2] you've risen even further in my estimation. One of these days, I'll have a script for you, but it will be the leading role or nothing.

The idea has taken root, I'm going to let it mature and, when the time comes, I'll get it down on paper and then into the postbox for you to read it,[3]

so, congratulations again for every film, every role, every performance, I know you must be a happy man,

yours,
françois

1 – French singer and actor, born in 1937: *Boulevard du rhum, Une belle fille comme moi, Cousin, cousine, Loulou, Coup de torchon*, etc.

2 – By Diane Kurys (*At First Sight*).
3 – Truffaut was thinking of casting Marchand as a man leading a double life: a perfumer by day, a ladykiller (in the literal sense) by night.

To Jean Gruault

Paris, 26 May 1983

My dear old Jean,

I leave for Rome tomorrow morning and, naturally, I'm taking with me the first two parts of *00/14* to tighten them up for the cinema version.

As for the scenes that have been cut, I'll put them safely away for the television version, if it works out . . .

I hope that by my return, on 7 June, I'll find on my desk not the whole script, but what we may call the second third. At first I was irritated by G.B.'s taking the initiative, now I feel motivated to pursue our project to its conclusion.

Model yourself after Balzac, slip on an old dressing-gown, drink thirty cups of coffee a day so that you'll be able to write the words 'The End' a few hours before the 14 July dance at the Villa Rimbaud.

Love,
françois

To Alain Souchon

June 83

My dear Alain,

In *L'Été meurtrier*,[1] you are very good* and it would appear that it isn't the first time,[2] you have therefore nothing to worry about. As for working together some day, why not, I'd like that as well; first of all, though, what we need is a good story with a good part for you. For the moment, I'm at work though not on a film, but that won't be for long. When you are offered something, ask yourself 3 questions: 1. Is it a good part? 2. Will it be a good film? 3. Am I well paid? You can invert 2. and 3., but remain firm on 1. But you're already aware of that, you know it without being told; I think Cocteau would have been happy to know you, as I am myself.

best wishes,
françois

*Very good, really very good.

Fanny Ardant, François Truffaut, Suzanne Schiffman, Christine Pellé and Florent Bazin (filming *Vivement dimanche!*).

1 – By Jean Becker.
2 – Souchon also appeared with Catherine Deneuve in Claude Berri's *Je vous aime*, a film that Truffaut had probably not seen.

To Koichi Yamada

Paris, 7 June 1983

My dear Yamada,

Thank you for your letter of 29 May and the clarifications relating to the delayed contract for *Les Films de ma vie*.

As far as the Hitchcock book is concerned, I think that your assessment of 23,000 copies is too modest and that the Japanese edition could well approach 30,000 copies by the end of 1984, and here is why:

Patricia Hitchcock has finally signed over to Universal (C.I.C.) the rights to *The Man Who Knew Too Much*, *Rear Window*, *Vertigo*, *The Trouble with Harry* and *Rope*. These five films are going to be distributed all over the world and it's likely that the first three will do as well at the box-office as some of the big American movies of today. It's a major event.

I suggest, either that you contact the press and publicity office at Universal, or have four or five copies of our book sent to them so that we can be sure they will use it in their press handouts. It's all going to happen very quickly.

I remain at your disposal to answer all the questions you might have concerning *Fahrenheit 451*. I know that there was an American edition (at least in part) of the journal[1] at the period when Andrew Sarris was bringing out an American edition of *Cahiers du cinéma*. On the other hand, the journal has never been published in book form in America, but doubtless it will be one day.

I have nothing against the idea of appearing in a Japanese commercial provided the product is not one I disapprove of, like alcohol, for example! Being less well known than an actor, I don't think it can do me any harm. Anyway, we'll see.

Vivement dimanche! hasn't been sold to Japan yet. We had a serious problem with the optical transfer of the music, so the first screenings for buyers won't be held for another month.

I'm sending you the two posters which we recently made for Cannes.

I often think about what might be the best way to thank you for everything you've done for me and I want you to know that a return airline ticket from Tokyo to Paris will be at your disposal this autumn, preferably from October onwards, since I won't be in Paris very much before then.

In the meantime, don't fail to let me know what books and magazines you need. You're going to receive André Bazin's book *Le Cinéma français de la*

Libération à la Nouvelle Vague. Would you like some more *Avant-Scènes*[2] on *Le Dernier Métro*?

Regards,
françois

1 – Truffaut's journal of the *Fahrenheit 451* shoot, which Yamada was translating.

2 – The film magazine *L'Avant-Scène du Cinéma*.

To Bernard Gheur *26 July 83*

Dear Bernard,

Your book seems to me very fine, I scanned it thoroughly rather than read it, as:

– exhausted, I'm resting in Honfleur
– I have a film coming out in 2 weeks
– I'm working on a splendid new edition of the Hitchcock book
– and above all, I am expecting a child[1] any time now.

That explains my silence, but, above all, be assured of my friendship,

françois

1 – Joséphine, the daughter of Truffaut and Fanny Ardant.

To Annette Insdorf *Wednesday 3 August 83*

My dear Annette,

Bravo for *Indelible Shadows*, it's a very fine book, extraordinarily instructive and very well argued. No longer will anyone be able to write about the cinema pertaining to that period – the darkest and most dramatic of the 20th century – without referring to your important and exemplary work. I am sure you have heard nothing but good things said about it since it was published and that this will encourage you to write a third book. Dear Annette, I won't be coming to New York this year, mainly because I'm expecting a baby; Fanny Ardant won't be coming either and for the same reason! (I preferred to let you know in writing before the rumour-mongers get to work.) It's therefore a rather euphoric François who congratulates you and sends you his love,

françois

To Jean Collet

5 August 1983

My dear Jean,

Your piece on Hitchcock is first-rate, it arrived at the right moment, as I've just been writing the final chapter of a new edition of the Hitchbook, a de luxe edition, for 1 month now to the point where I've been dreaming about it at night, it was no joke.

I'm only briefly in Paris for a few interviews and I'm returning to Normandy, since a child (not a screenplay, a real baby) is due to be born at the beginning of October, oh yes.

So, we'll finally succeed in seeing each other at that moment, certainly I hope so; even now people often talk to me about your programme, always favourably. I hope you are happy,

your friend,
françois

To Richard Roud

Paris, 11 August 1983

My dear Richard,

This is a postscript to my letter of last week.

Thanks to you, I've now made peace with Mary Meerson who, enchanted with your book and also with my preface, invited my colleagues and myself to a private dinner-party last night, following the première at the Cinémathèque of *Vivement dimanche!*

Still on the subject of your book, I'm impatient to receive a few copies (one with a dedication from you would be terrific) so that some of my overseas correspondents (in Japan for example) might know of its existence. Another thing: when is the French edition? Will you authorize me to have it read by Paul Fournel, the new boss of Ramsay, who is republishing, very sumptuously, my Hitchcock in October and who seems very dynamic?

I made lots of notes while rereading your book. Some of these you might find useful, for example this definition of Langlois by Cocteau: 'The dragon who guards over the treasure', or else the certainty I now have concerning the Antibes Festival (which unfortunately I didn't attend). The secret film that wasn't announced and was screened in the open air beneath the ramparts was Chaplin's *A Woman of Paris*.

As far as the uncut version of *Les Deux Anglaises* is concerned, it won't be ready before the autumn, as it represents quite a lot of work, and the addition to my family will detain me in Normandy for another month. If you still want to show this version next year (with English subtitles throughout, naturally), there's absolutely no problem and we might, with this in mind, co-ordinate our plan of action with Linda Beath[1] who will almost certainly be the film's next distributor in the United States.

I hope your 20th festival will be a dazzling success and I look forward to seeing you again soon,

'bye, my dear Richard, and my very warmest regards,

françois

1 – New York film distributor (Spectrafilm).

To Richard Roud *9 Sept. 83*

My dear Richard,

Before going into the American Hospital to have my skull opened up (I had a cerebral haemorrhage while on holiday in Honfleur), I want to wish you good luck in everything, to apologize for being at present incapable of helping in the promotion of your fine book and, above all, to express my gratitude for the almost annual party of which I was the beneficiary and you the ringmaster; see you again soon, I hope,

your friend,
françois

To Robert Fischer *Paris, 9 September 1983*

My dear Robert,

I am writing to you just before entering the American Hospital for an operation following a vascular accident that happened to me during my holiday (a cerebral haemorrhage!).

That is why I probably won't be able to exchange any more letters with you before the end of October, which is to say, after my convalescence.

First of all, I want to thank you for having sent me the amazing Hitchcock bibliography. I, in my turn, am sending you an additional document which I was given in 1962. If you find it interesting, I suggest you make a photocopy of it for Herr H. J. Wulff and offer it to him on my behalf.

Thanks also for your letter of 2 September and for the kind things you say about *Vivement dimanche!* I cannot suggest a title to you, as I don't have a sufficient feel for German. I know that the Italians and the English have decided to adopt a literal translation of the French title, but I believe the Americans are planning to call the film *Confidentially Yours*, after rejecting a title that seemed to me not too bad: *Female Investigator*.

In answer to your question, I don't detest *The Woman in the Raincoat*, but I am not the best judge.

For the last four or five years I have been buying back the world rights to my book on Hitchcock and I am astonished never to have received any royalty statements from Hanser.[1]

Do you suppose the Hanser edition is out of print? This matters to me, since, next month, the French publisher Ramsay is bringing out a new, extremely sumptuous and magnificently illustrated version for which I have written a new introduction and, most important, a sixteenth chapter covering Hitchcock's last years.

I'll send you a copy of this edition as soon as possible and I'd naturally be very happy for it to be published in Germany.

I am unable to answer your question on the transcription of the programme *La Leçon de cinéma*,[2] since I never received a copy of the script. You would have to write to Jérôme Prieur at I.N.A.[3]

As far as *Mata-Hari* is concerned, I've bought back the negative (thanks to the success of *Le Dernier Métro*), but I don't have the right to distribute the film until 1985.

Of all my films, one alone was massacred, amputated and truncated because of its commercial failure: *Les Deux Anglaises et le Continent*. When my convalescence is over, I'm going, along with my editor Martine Barraqué, to set about reconstructing the uncut version. Then my hope will be that this uncut version receives a wide release. I believe it came to about 135 minutes. Can you tell me if the version released in Germany was the short or the long one? Can you perhaps check by consulting the script as it was published in *L'Avant-Scène*?

My dear Robert, even if I cannot write to you before the end of October, I would be happy to read anything you might wish to write to me.

Thank you for the work you are going to do on *Vivement dimanche!* and believe me when I say that I will always be your friend,

hoping to see you soon, affectionately,

françois

P.S. Recently I liked Diane Kurys's *Coup de foudre*, Fassbinder's *Bollweiser* and, on video, something I'll never tire of, *Limelight*,[4] sublime. I wrote the preface to Richard Roud's biography of Langlois (Viking Press, N.Y.), but unfortunately I don't have a copy to send you.

1 – The book's German publisher.
2 – A television programme produced by Jean Collet and directed by José Bersoza.
3 – L'Institut National de l'Audiovisuel.
4 – By Charles Chaplin (1952).

To Koichi Yamada

9 Sept 83

My dear Yamada,

Tomorrow, I enter the American Hospital for an operation inside my head (it's for a congenital aneurism which brought on a cerebral haemorrhage last month in Honfleur). My morale is high, but, should things turn out badly, I want to convey to you my thanks, my affection and my desire that you will always be my representative-translator-friend-alter ego-my Japanese brother in a word. If all goes well, I'll be able to write you again in October, by which time I'll be the father of a little child, the one that Fanny Ardant is expecting; goodbye, dear Yamada, till we meet again, yes, till we meet again, I very much hope that we shall

love,
françois

1984

To Annette Insdorf *16 January 84*

Dear Annette,

It was a pleasure hearing you on the phone, your proposal to have the interview read to me is very kind, I appreciate it. In confidence let me tell you that I leave tomorrow for the Colombe d'Or at Saint-Paul-de-Vence: 93 (Alpes-Maritimes) 32–80 where we'll be, Fanny and I, until 26 January. If you wish, you may add this to our interview: on 12 September last, I was operated on for an aneurism of the brain, but film criticism was 20 years ahead of conventional medicine, since, when my 2nd film, *Tirez sur le pianiste*, came out, it declared that such a film could only have been made by someone whose brain wasn't functioning normally!

Two months after Joséphine's birth, Fanny Ardant triumphed on the stage when she replaced (in 4 days, at the last minute) Isabelle Adjani, who had suffered a breakdown in Strindberg's play *Miss Julie*. At present, she's getting ready to work with Alain Resnais again on 20 February: *L'Amour à mort*.

What else can I add? I've begun to go to the cinema again. I liked Fellini's film about the liner,[1] a French film, *Vive la sociale*,[2] which won the Vigo prize, and also *Zelig*,[3] not only because of the black and white.

Here, dear Annette, still in confidence, which is to say just for you, is my home number in Paris where you can reach me from 26 January: 723-82-90.

May this year 84 grant us the opportunity to see each other again and have a long chat, that's my wish dear Annette and I send you all my love,

françois

1 – *And the Ship Sails On.*
2 – By Gérard Mordillat.
3 – By Woody Allen.

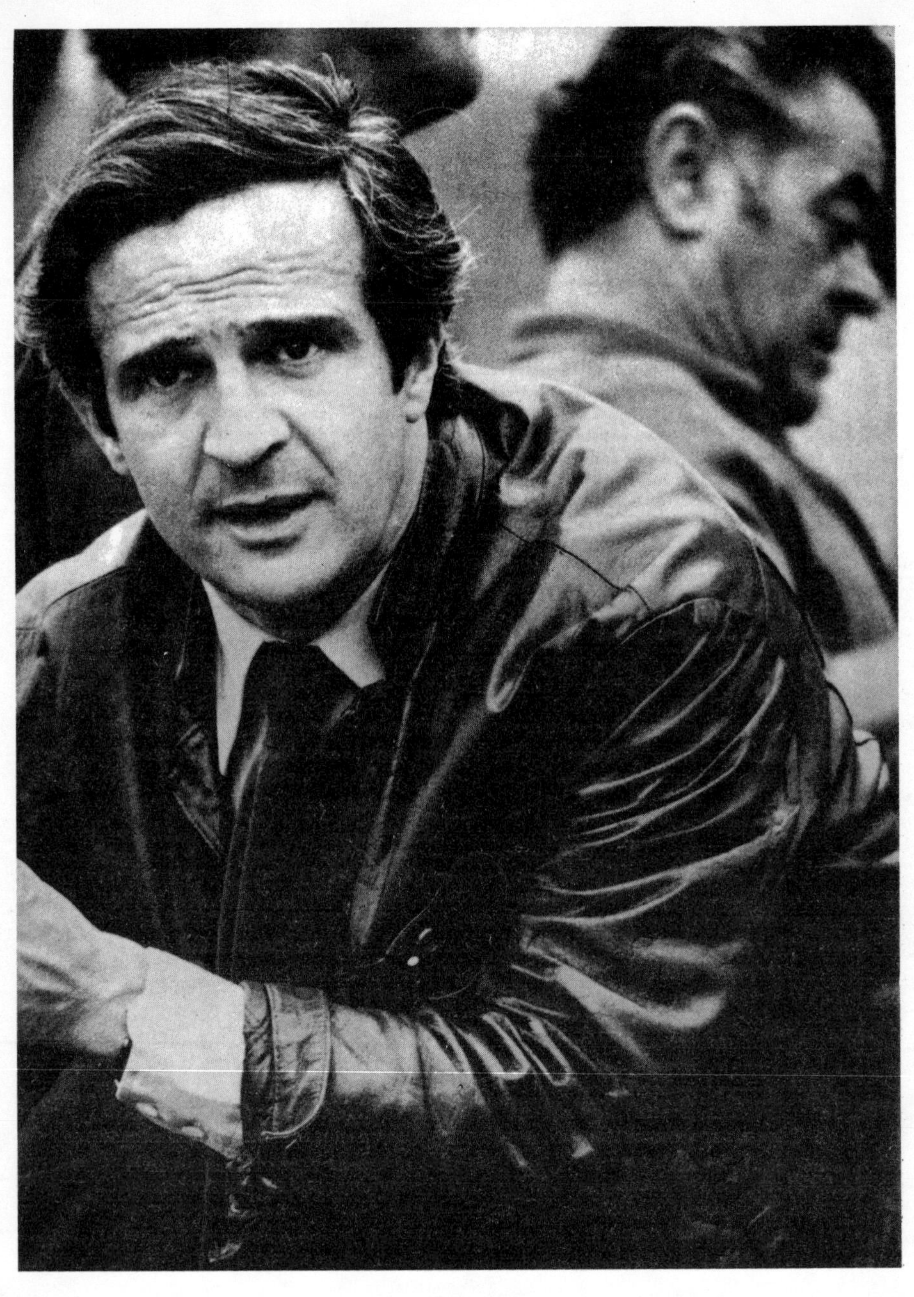

François Truffaut died in hospital on 21 October 1984.

'Out of all of that,
something
nevertheless will remain,
a trace,
a testament,
a rectangular object,
320 bound pages.
What we call a book.'

L'Homme qui aimait les femmes

Chronology

The quotations are from François Truffaut.

1932 Birth of François Truffaut on 6 February, in Paris. His father, Roland Truffaut, is an architect; his mother, Janine de Monferrand, is a secretary at *L'Illustration*. 'I lived near Pigalle, in the rue Henri-Monnier . . .'

1946 After dropping out of school, François Truffaut works as a labourer, copy-boy and welder. 'I started working when I was fourteen and a half, so that in fact my adult life began earlier than most . . . There were periods when I ran away from home and lived like a vagrant, then eventually I felt there was an urgent need for me to work . . .'

He borrows money to found a film society, the Cercle Cinémane, of which only one session is held. He makes the acquaintance of André Bazin.

Having run away from home again, he is placed in an observation centre for delinquents at Villejuif.

1948 Thanks to Bazin, who is the journal's film editor, he works for *Travail et Culture*.

1950 He writes his first articles for *Elle* and *La Gazette du cinéma*. He enlists in the army following an unhappy love affair and also because he had sold all the books belonging to his friend Robert Lachenay without telling him. 'I was only eighteen, I still had two years to go before doing my military service, it was the period of the war in Indo-China and I enlisted. I wanted to enlist for only two years, but the war was going so badly at that stage . . .' He is stationed in northern Germany in an artillery regiment. Absence without leave: he is charged with desertion. Military prison. Bazin explores every possible avenue to have him released. Truffaut is finally discharged on grounds of 'personality disorder'. He lives for two years with André and Janine Bazin, at Bry-sur-Marne.

1953 He works for a few months in the film unit of the Ministry of Agriculture, then joins *Cahiers du cinéma*.

1954 Publication of his article 'Une certaine tendance du cinéma français' (in *Cahiers du cinéma* no. 31). He becomes a contributor to the magazine *Arts* and directs his first short film, *Une visite*.

1956 He becomes Roberto Rossellini's assistant: 'In a sense he took the place of Bazin, during the transition between the period of criticism and the period of creation . . .'

1957 Having set up his own production company, Les Films du Carrosse, he makes *Les Mistons*, a short with Bernadette Lafont and Gérard Blain. On 29 October he marries Madeleine Morgenstern.

1958 10 November 1958 to 9 January 1959: filming of *Les Quatre Cents Coups* with Jean-Pierre Léaud. 'I clearly remember Rivette saying to me, "We're going to make films, we all agree, we're all going to make films." ' Death of André Bazin just one day after Truffaut starts shooting *Les Quatre Cents Coups*.

1959 22 January: birth of Laura Truffaut.

30 November 1959 to 22 January 1960: filming of *Tirez sur le pianiste* with Charles Aznavour and Marie Dubois. 'As regards *Tirez sur le pianiste*, which is adapted from a novel by David Goodis, a single image prompted me to make the film; it was in the book: a road sloping downhill in the snow, the car descending, its engine silent. That was all.'

1961 He produces Claude de Givray's film *Tire-au-flanc*, in which he plays the role of a soldier reading *Werther*.

10 April to 28 June: filming of *Jules et Jim* with Jeanne Moreau, Henri Serre and Oskar Werner. 'In my twenty years of making films, the shoot of *Jules et Jim* has remained, thanks to Jeanne Moreau, a luminous memory, the most luminous of all.'

29 June: birth of Éva Truffaut.

He films *Antoine et Colette*, one of the sketches of *L'Amour à vingt ans*, with Jean-Pierre Léaud.

1963 21 October to 30 December: filming of *La Peau douce* with Françoise Dorléac and Jean Desailly: 'A story, told in quite meticulous detail, of adultery . . .'

1966 12 January to 22 April: filming of *Fahrenheit 451* with Oskar Werner and Julie Christie. 'But, one day, one of the firemen begins reading a book and wonders why he has to burn it – the whole film is there.'

He publishes *Le Cinéma selon Hitchcock* after four years of working on it with Helen Scott.

1967 16 May to 10 November: filming of *La Mariée était en noir* with Jeanne Moreau. 'In fact, I was excited by one idea: making a love film without a single love scene.'

1968 5 February to 28 March: filming of *Baisers volés* with Jean-Pierre Léaud and Claude Jade. '. . . a film which aspires to resemble a song'.

The Langlois affair: Truffaut organizes the Comité de Défense de la Cinémathèque Française.

1969 2 February to 7 May: filming of *La Sirène du Mississipi* with Jean-Paul Belmondo and Catherine Deneuve. 'I defy anyone to close William Irish's fine novel *Waltz into Darkness* without thinking, "Ah! Catherine Deneuve would be wonderful in that part!" '

July to September: filming of *L'Enfant sauvage* with Truffaut himself and Jean-Pierre Cargol. 'What is natural to us we inherit, but our cultural selves can only be shaped by education. Hence the importance of that education and why it's such a beautiful theme.'

1970 21 January to 18 March: filming of *Domicile conjugal* with Jean-Pierre Léaud and Claude Jade.

Publication of *Les Aventures d'Antoine Doinel.*

1971 20 April to 5 July: filming of *Les Deux Anglaises et le Continent* with Jean-Pierre Léaud, Kika Markham and Stacey Tendeter. 'Two English sisters in love with a Frenchman whom they call "the Continent" and whom they greet by saying "Bonjour, la France!" '

He edits and prefaces André Bazin's book on Jean Renoir.

1972 14 February to 12 April: filming of *Une belle fille comme moi* with Bernadette Lafont, André Dussolier and Guy Marchand. 'Suddenly I decided to send myself up . . .'

1973 22 September to 3 May: filming of *La Nuit américaine* with Jean-Pierre Aumont, Jean-Pierre Léaud, Jacqueline Bisset and Truffaut himself. 'There is a nostalgia for the sort of films that aren't afraid to tell a story, that aren't afraid of melodrama and that aren't afraid to be judged.' Oscar for Best Foreign Film.

1975 8 January to 21 March: filming of *L'Histoire d'Adèle H.* with Isabelle Adjani and Bruce Robinson. 'All I can say is that, since I am decidedly incapable of making films "against", I will continue to make films "for" and that it's with the same kind of love that I love Antoine Doinel, Catherine, Montag, Julie, Muriel Brown, Victor and Adèle H.'

17 July to 9 September: filming of *L'Argent de poche*. 'The idea was to make the public laugh, not at the children's expense, but with them . . .'

Publication of *Les Films de ma vie.*

1976 Publication of *L'Argent de poche*, a novelization of the film.

May to August: Truffaut is in the United States to play the role of the scientist Claude Lacombe in Steven Spielberg's *Close Encounters of the Third Kind*. Spielberg: 'I needed a man with the soul of a child . . . That's how I saw Truffaut . . . He resembles all the children in his films.'

19 October 1976 to 5 January 1977: filming of *L'Homme qui aimait les femmes* with Charles Denner. 'Bertrand's passion was an exclusive one: woman, women, all women.'

1977 11 October to 25 November: filming of *La Chambre verte* with Nathalie Baye and Truffaut himself. 'It seemed to me that, if I were to play the part, I would obtain the same difference as when, dealing with my mail at the office, I dictate certain letters to be typed and write others in my own hand. *La Chambre verte* is like a letter written by hand.'

1978 29 May to 5 July: filming of *L'Amour en fuite* with Jean-Pierre Léaud, Claude Jade and Marie-France Pisier. 'The principle of the film: everyone tells stories to everyone else.'

1979 Truffaut is appointed president of the International Federation of Film Societies.

1980 28 January to 16 April: filming of *Le Dernier Métro* with Catherine Deneuve, Gérard Depardieu and Heinz Bennent. 'I wanted to satisfy three desires: to show a theatre backstage, evoke the atmosphere of the Occupation and give Catherine Deneuve the role of a responsible woman.'

1981 1 April to 15 May: filming of *La Femme d'à côté* with Fanny Ardant and Gérard Depardieu. 'A couple worthy of the cinema, two larger-than-life figures, the blond and the brunette, a man who appears simple but is in fact complicated, a woman who appears complicated but is as simple as saying goodbye.'

1982 4 November to 21 December: filming of *Vivement dimanche!* with Fanny Ardant and Jean-Louis Trintignant. 'Every story is a tall story, but that doesn't matter if one's pleasure is all the more intense. Pleasure should be more intense than analysis.'

Preface to Dudley Andrew's book *André Bazin*.

1983 Truffaut works throughout the summer on the final chapter of *Hitchcock–Truffaut*. Following his collapse, he is hospitalized in August for a series of tests, then undergoes an operation on 12 September.

28 September: birth of Joséphine, the daughter of François Truffaut and Fanny Ardant.

1984 Publication of the definitive version of *Hitchcock–Truffaut*.

François Truffaut is hospitalized on 28 September, at the American Hospital in Neuilly-sur-Seine, and dies there on 21 October.

Photographic credits

The photographs and documents which illustrate this book are published by kind permission of Les Films du Carrosse and: *Cahiers du cinéma*: p. 89; Huffschmitt Collection: p. 325; *Elle* and Y. Maton: p. 560; Jacques Kirchmeyer: p. 160; Kobal Collection: pp. 248, 294, 298, 382, 457, 485; Magnum: p. 353; Robert Lachenay: pp. 10, 32. All rights reserved: pp. 326, 568.

Index of Correspondents

Adam, Jean-François, 335
Aldrich, Robert, 494
Almendros, Nestor, 363–4, 373, 418, 452, 556
Aumont, Jean-Pierre, 374, 381
Aurel, Jean, 513, 525, 556
Aznavour, Charles, 134, 170, 206, 217, 508

Balaban, Bob, 476
Baum, Ralph, 81
Baye, Nathalie, 484, 491
Beauregard, Georges de, 142
Benzakein, Simon, 401
Berbert, Marcel, 363, 533
Bercholz, Joseph, 163
Bessy, Maurice, 77, 243
Bitsch, Charles, 95, 96, 98, 100, 104, 107, 109, 113, 116, 304, 334
Bory, Jean-Louis, 322, 423, 481
Bouix, Evelyne, 557
Boujut, Michel, 534, 543
Brossard, Jean-Pierre, 551
Brusati, Franco, 244
Buñuel, Luis, 225

Cazeneuve, Maurice, 419
Chazal, Robert, 535, 538
Clouzot, Henri-Georges, 252, 442
Collet, Jean, 403, 465, 482, 563
Coluche, 421
Congdon, Don, 210, 246, 296
Costa-Gavras, 334
Cravenne, Georges, 307

Dabadie, Jean-Loup, 362, 365, 368, 392, 430, 436, 534, 558
Daquin, Louis, 419
Dasté, Jean, 477, 479
Dauman, Anatole, 515
Delerue, Georges, 429, 510, 519
Delsol, Paula, 241, 468
Denner, Charles, 466
Desdoits, Gabriel, 509
Dewever, Jean, 501
Diamantis, Roger, 355
Doillon, Jacques, 497, 498
Domarchi, Jean, 458
Doniol-Valcroze, Jacques, 342
Dreyfus, Liliane, 443
Dubois, Bernard, 408, 413, 484
Duhamel, Marcel, 200

Eisner, Lotte, 131

Ferry, Odette, 87, 292, 293, 369, 373
Fischer, Robert, 518, 521, 549, 564
Florey, Robert, 378
Franju, Georges, 132, 513

Gance, Abel, 500
Garnett, Tay, 418
Gheur, Bernard, 284, 302, 340, 345, 346, 347, 433, 562
Gitlis, Ivry, 433
Givray, Claude de, 448
Givray, Lucette de, 327
Godard, Jean-Luc, 385
Gruault, Jean, 337, 362, 375, 380, 404, 405, 438, 555, 559
Grumberg, Jean-Claude, 504, 505, 507
Guille, Frances, 380

Hakim, Robert, 301
Hauduroy, Jean-François, 315, 444, 548
Hitchcock, Alfred, 177, 199, 283, 289, 299, 309, 317, 324
Horstig-Primuz, Olga, 486
Hugo, Jean, 360, 381
Huntley, John, 299

Insdorf, Annette, 456, 468, 474, 475, 478, 499, 502, 512, 515, 524, 528, 529, 535, 562, 567

Jacob, Gilles, 312, 315, 336, 337, 338, 379, 393, 439, 449
Jones, Elinor, 251, 274

Lachenay, Robert, 1, 2, 4, 7, 13, 14, 15, 17, 18, 21, 22, 27, 29, 30, 35, 40, 42, 44, 45, 48, 50, 52, 54, 55, 56, 57, 58, 59, 60, 62, 63, 64, 66, 67, 68, 69, 70, 71, 73, 74, 76,

77, 84, 104, 106, 118, 119, 120, 131, 230, 541
Laffont, Robert, 176
Langlois, Henri, 442
Le Boterf, Hervé, 525, 531
Lebovici, Gérard, 520, 549
Ledoux, Jacques, 305
Lelouch, Claude, 341
L'Herbier, Marcel, 422
Lherminier, Pierre, 162, 313
Lopert, Tanya, 345, 500
Louis, Théodore, 305

Mahias, Lydie, 342
Malle, Louis, 154
Mambrino, Jean, 82, 88, 165, 470, 520
Marchand, Guy, 558
Méril, Macha, 546
Miou-Miou, 470
Mocky, Jean-Pierre, 147
Montaigne, Pierre, 479
Moullet, Luc, 85, 86, 93, 316
Moussy, Marcel, 120, 121, 123, 124, 126, 127, 128, 531, 544, 546

Newman, Paul, 436

Oury, Gérard, 282

Paris, Jim, 544
Peyrefitte, Alain, 211
Poirot-Delpech, Bertrand, 531
Pons, Maurice, 103, 114, 116
Porcile, François, 477

Racine-Freess, Sarah, 555
Reed, Rex, 473
Régent, Roger, 308
Revon, Bernard, 448
Rezvani, Danièle, 263, 291, 330
Rezvani, Serge, 263, 291, 330
Roeg, Nicolas, 402
Rohmer, Eric, 33, 34, 78, 83, 90, 91, 92, 101, 367
Rosenbaum, Jonathan, 461, 464
Ross, Lillian, 354
Roud, Richard, 328, 346, 445, 498, 505, 517, 519, 526, 550, 552, 563, 564
Rousseau, Serge, 447, 453, 557

Saint-Cyr, Renée, 447
Scott, Helen, 137, 144, 148, 155, 158, 161, 166, 171, 175, 180, 182, 189, 194, 201, 204, 207, 208, 212, 218, 220, 223, 226, 228, 231, 234, 236, 241, 243, 245, 247, 255, 258, 260, 264, 268, 269, 275, 276, 278, 288, 332, 371, 394, 434
Siclier, Jacques, 489
Simenon, Georges, 472
Soldati, Mario, 491
Souchon, Alain, 480, 482, 488, 559
Stéphane, Nicole, 250

Teisseire, Guy, 286, 324, 397, 511
Trintignant, Jean-Louis, 547

Verber, Francis, 495
Vecchiali, Paul, 347
Vilar, Jean, 266

Wajda, Andrzej, 379
Walton, Tony, 287

Yamada, Koichi, 399, 402, 404, 416, 451, 483, 503, 538, 542, 561, 566

To a Danish correspondent, 146
To a food columnist, 518
To a future ex-film-maker, 168
To a petitioner, 372
To a screenwriter, 144
To a student of IDHEC, 313
To an actor, 383
To an admirer of Georges Brassens, 272
To an agent, 316
To an American journalist, 497
To an aspiring screenwriter, 155
To an insurance company, 501
To Editions Gallimard, 494
To *France-Observateur*, 177
To journalists, 132, 393, 552
To the Centre National de la Cinématographie, 304
To the organizer of a film society, 134
To the President of the High Court, 350
To the producers of *Les dossiers de l'écran*, 377
To the Secretary-General of the CFDT, 443
To the Société de Réalisateurs de Films, 541
To young screenwriters, 136, 285

Madame Bigey to Robert Lachenay, 25
Robert Lachenay to François Truffaut, 37
Max Ophüls to François Truffaut, 82
Helen Scott to François Truffaut, 254
Jean-Luc Godard to François Truffaut, 383
Alfred Hitchcock to François Truffaut, 461
Jonathan Rosenbaum to François Truffaut, 463
Robert Chazel to François Truffaut, 537

General Index

A bout de souffle, 139, 142, 156, 186, 385, 394
Adam, Alfred, 29, 30
Adam, Jean-François, 336n
Adam's Rib, 22
Adieu Philippine, 165, 167, 196, 443
Adjani, Isabelle, 429–31, 436–7, 440–1, 448, 453, 461, 567
Agence Magic, L', 448–9
Albert, Eddie and Margo, 396
Albicocco, Jean-Gabriel, 194
Aldrich, Robert, 87, 98, 100, 495n
Alexandre, Aimée, 64n, 70
Alien, 516
Allégret, Yves, 17n, 462
Allen, Jay Presson, 232, 238, 250, 255, 259, 261
Allen, Lewis, 219, 223, 228, 229, 232, 234, 236, 242, 244, 249, 251, 255, 258–9, 260, 261, 262, 264–5, 269, 270, 276, 277, 279, 288, 422, 528
Almendros, Nestor, 364n, 435, 475, 483, 490, 516, 519, 520, 521, 547, 550
Alphaville, 266n, 280
Amant de cinq jours, L', 161
Amants, Les, 123
Amants de Teruel, Les, 207
Amérique Vue par un Français, L', 138, 139
Amore, 101
Amour à la chaîne, L', 281
Amour à Mort, L', 567
Amour à vingt ans, L', 167, 172, 181, 188, 193, 196–7, 209, 214, 216, 262, 379, 465, 478, 542
Amour de Swann, Un, 250–1, 439, 491
Amour en fuite, L', 474, 478, 479, 480, 483, 488, 510, 521
Amour fou, L', 336
Amour l'après-midi, L', 365n, 428, 468
Andersson, Bibi, 486
Andress, Ursula, 287, 390
Anna la bonne, 150
Anne and Muriel, see Deux Anglaises et le Continent, Les
Année dernière à Marienbad, L', 151, 161, 166, 173, 186, 438
A nous les petites Anglaises, 444
Antonioni, Michelangelo, 168, 425
Apollinaire, Guillaume, 57
Apprenticeship of Duddy Kravitz, The, 448
Aragon, Louis, 155
Arasca, Célou, 43
Archer, Eugene, 180, 210, 221, 288
Archibaldo de la Cruz, 94
Ardant, Fanny, 272n, 531–5, 542, 547, 548, 554, 555, 556, 558, 560, 562, 566–7
Argent de poche, L', 427, 443n, 444, 446, 450, 451, 459, 463, 469, 530
Artists and Models, 87
Ascenseur pour l'échafaud, 123
Astruc, Alexandre, 24, 104, 151, 152, 518
Atalante, L', 477
Atelier, L', 504, 508n
Attack, 93, 98, 112
Auber, Brigitte, 177
Aubriant, Michel, 77
Audiard, Michel, 484
Audiberti, Jacques, 61n, 164, 172, 281, 292, 330, 390, 427
Auffay, Patrick, 138, 167
Au hasard Balthazar, 282
Aumont, Jean-Pierre, 374, 375n, 382
Aurel, Jean, 90, 91, 159, 173n, 270, 334, 364, 514, 525n, 534
Aurenche, Jean, 98, 117
Auriol, George Jean, 35n, 39
Aussi longue absence, Une, 159, 162, 207
Autant-Lara, Claude, 27, 94n, 98, 296n, 309n, 544
Avedon, Richard, 149
Aventures d'Antoine Doinel, Les, 355, 359, 361
Aventures d'Arsène Lupin, Les, 462
Aymé, Marcel, 40n, 62n, 365
Aznavour, Charles, 132, 134n, 167, 194, 205, 206n, 209, 216, 239, 357

Baby, Yvonne, 313, 337n, 338
Bachelor Party, The, 104
Bachman, Gideon, 189
Bad and the Beautiful, The, 530
Bad Seed, The, 93

Baie des anges, La, 255
Baisers volés, 286n, 311, 315, 317, 322, 327, 330, 333, 358–9, 420, 425–6, 465, 478, 510
Bal, Walter, 373
Balcony, The, 221, 232
Ballad of a soldier, 163
Ballon rouge, Le, 154
Balthus, 183, 184, 359, 474
Balzac, Honoré de, xi, 1, 43, 49, 57, 64, 69, 71, 72, 559
Bande à part, 241n, 257
Bar, Jacques, 229, 233, 234
Barbie, Klaus, 395
Bardèche, Maurice, 64n, 73
Bardot, Brigitte, 108, 109n, 159, 258, 260n, 338, 397, 425
Baron fantôme, Le, 308, 488
Barraqué, Martine, 480, 510, 515, 565
Barrault, Jean-Louis, 114
Bas-Fonds, Les, 27
Bates, Alan, 338
Baudelaire, Charles, 152
Baum, Ralph, 81n
Baye, Nathalie, 469n, 470, 484n, 485, 558n
Bazin André, xiv-v, 17, 19, 28, 31, 41, 42, 50, 57, 58, 60, 61, 62, 65–8, 72, 82, 91, 95, 96, 111, 112, 119, 196, 314, 347, 367, 390, 419, 422, 426, 462–4, 489, 500n, 503, 561
Bazin, Florent, 76, 418, 435, 560
Bazin, Hervé, 45
Bazin, Janine, 72, 100, 281, 314, 316, 367, 377, 386–7, 390, 419, 462, 464
Beath, Linda, 564
Beauregard, Georges de, 444
Beau Serge, Le, 113n, 117, 118, 123
Beauvoir, Simone de, 240n, 351, 353, 539
Bécaud, Gilbert, 482
Becker, Jacques, 139, 141n, 462
Bed and Board, see Domicile conjugal
Bel Age, Le, 139
Bel Geddes, Barbara, 185
Belle de jour, 338
Belle fille comme moi, Une, 356n, 364, 368, 370, 372, 375, 402, 426, 542
Belles de nuit, Les, 121
Belmondo, Jean-Paul, 180, 189, 195, 222, 229, 257, 301, 322, 338, 359, 401, 521
Benedetti, Nelly, 220, 227, 229
Ben et Bénédicte, 468
Benjamin, 315, 322
Benjamin, René, 73
Bennent, Heinz, 502, 504, 524, 527
Benton, Robert, 252, 275
Benzakein, Simon, 401n
Berbert, Marcel, 161, 202, 207, 219, 222, 245, 246–7, 262, 275, 328, 375, 404, 420, 482, 510, 511, 533, 556
Bercholz, Joseph, 164n
Bergen, Candice, 371
Berger, Nicole, 117, 170, 208, 357, 509
Bergman, Ingmar, 91, 93n, 172, 221, 256, 257, 314, 336, 422, 427, 443, 465, 469, 529
Bergman, Ingrid, 82, 101, 276, 278–9, 401, 435
Bernanos, Georges, 49
Bernard-Aubert, Claude, 150
Berri, Claude, 333, 363n, 371, 380n, 395, 418, 421, 448, 455, 466, 489, 561n
Berry, Denis, 412
Berry, Jules, 95
Bertolucci, Bernardo, 390, 503n
Bessy, Maurice, 95, 133, 378
Bettelheim, Bruno, 518
Bigey, René, 119n, 125, 357
Bigger Than Life, 93, 95, 96, 97
Big Knife, The, 98, 100, 101–2, 114
Big Sleep, The, 401, 473
Billard, Pierre, 312, 340
Birds, The, 178, 179, 184, 192, 199, 200, 212–14, 216, 218–19, 222, 300, 455
Birkin, Jane, 409, 412
Bisset, Jacqueline, 374, 382, 384, 402, 458
Bitsch, Charles, 92, 106, 109n, 110
Bitter Victory, 114
Blain, Gérard, 105, 107–11, 450
Blanchar, Pierre, 113
Blatchley, Joseph, 434
Bleu d'outre-tombe, Le, 138
Blue Angel, The, 19
Blue Gardenia, The, 93
Bluwal, Marcel, 123, 531
Bob le flambeur, 123
Boetticher, Budd, 93, 94
Bof, 366
Bogart, Humphrey, 401
Bogdanovich, Peter, 207, 444, 550n
Boisrouvray, Albina du, 444
Boisset, Yves, 386
Bollweiser, 565
Bonjour Monsieur La Bruyère, 97
Bonnes Femmes, Les, 140
Bonnie and Clyde, 233, 234, 238, 240, 242, 244, 251–2, 274–5, 426
Bord, Renée, 189
Bory, Jean-Louis, 324n, 423, 481n
Bost, Pierre, 98
Bouché, Claudine, 233, 234, 555n
Bouix, Evelyne, 557n
Boulanger, Daniel, 358
Boulevard, 138
Bouquet, Michel, 358, 359
Bourgeois, Jacques, 24
Bourseiller, Antoine, 390

Bouvard, Philippe, 481
Bracker, Milton, 151, 159
Bradbury, Ray, 132n, 145, 179, 180–1, 185, 187, 195, 247, 296–7
Brando, Marlon, 387, 388, 396
Brasillach, Robert, 64, 73
Brassens, Georges, 272
Brasseur, Claude, 239
Brasseur, Pierre, 7, 25n
Braunberger, Pierre, 28, 91, 95n, 97, 108, 116–17, 127, 145, 155, 165, 172, 209, 343, 387, 388
Brel, Jacques, 375
Bresson, Robert, 16, 17, 18, 89, 106n, 112, 140, 257, 282, 421n, 430, 440, 469
Briac, Claude, 432–3
Brialy, Jean-Claude, 101, 106, 117, 140, 334, 360
Bride Wore Black, The, see Mariée etait en noir, La
Bridge over the River Kwai, The, 280
Brierre, Christine, 258, 364, 371
Brierre, Jérôme, 204, 205, 260
Brigitte et Brigitte, 316
British Film Institute, 299
Broca, Michèle De, 371
Broca, Philippe De, 148, 161, 164n, 239, 260n, 282, 362, 363n, 366, 418
Brook, Peter, 159, 221
Brooks, Richard, 91, 100
Brulé, Claude, 133
Brusati, Franco, 244n
Buñuel, Joyce, 455
Buñuel, Luis, 93, 226n, 241n, 260, 305, 340n, 390, 422, 542
Burch, Noël, 422
Burglar, The, 185, 192, 229
Burmese Harp, The, 95
Burr, Raymond, 300
Bus Stop, 93, 97, 98, 101

Cagney, James, 171, 206
Cahiers du cinéma, 17, 77, 78–80, 82, 85, 90, 91, 92, 98, 100, 101, 104, 118, 167, 177, 184, 191, 219, 256, 258, 262, 276, 297, 322n, 342, 445, 521, 534, 544–5, 549, 553, 561
Calder, John, 195
Calef, Henri, 343
Calet, Henri, 450
Camera obscura, 219, 279
Camp, Yvette, 307
Camus, Albert, 176, 263, 313, 424
Camus, Marcel, 132, 151, 154n, 156
Candide, 151
Capra, Frank, 493
Carabiniers, Les, 183
Carbonnaux, Norbert, 105, 151
Carlo-Rim, 97
Carné, Marcel, 25n, 56n, 109n, 159n, 434, 462, 472n
Carol, Martine, 29
Caron, Leslie, 396
Carroll, Madeleine, 300
Cars, Guy des, 424
Cartacalha, 308
Carton, Pauline, 112
Casablanca, 401
Cassavetes, John, 156
Catherine the Great, 311
Cause du peuple, La, 350–1, 389
Cavanna, François, 389
Cayatte, André, 113, 159, 238, 386
Cayrol, Jean, 199n, 423
Ceccaldi, Daniel, 223
Cela s'appelle l'aurore, 93
Céline, Louis-Ferdinand, 553
Centre National de la Cinématographie, 201, 304
Cerdan, Marcel, 557
Ce sacrée Amedée, 112
Ce soir ou jamais, 165
Chabrier, Hortense, 520
Chabrol, Claude, xv, 83, 88, 91, 105, 107, 111–12, 117n, 118, 123, 131, 140, 147, 164, 177, 188, 191, 195, 201, 209, 363n, 379, 383–4, 423, 454, 518
Chambre verte, La, xv, 345n, 405n, 408n, 469n, 470, 471, 473–5, 477–80, 483–4, 533
Champion, Jean, 375, 382
Chapier, Henry, 440
Chaplin, Charlie, 14, 105, 283, 321, 367, 388, 400, 463, 553, 563, 566n
Charensol, Georges, 340
Charles, Pauline, 226
Charlotte et Véronique, 117
Charme discret de la bourgeoisie, Le, 422
Chauvet, Louis, 95, 387
Chayefsky, Paddy, 257
Chazel, Robert, 537n
Chenille, André, 13, 16, 17, 19, 28, 29, 42, 48, 55
Cheray, Jean-Louis, 117
Chéreau, Patrice, 480
Chère Louise, 362, 392, 534
Chéri-Bibi, 59
Chevalier, Martine, 453
Chienne, La, 22
Chiens perdus sans collier, 111
China, 27
Chinatown, 445
Chinoise, La, 384
Chirac, Jacques, 552
Christie, Julie, 279, 287, 294
Churchill, Sarah, 47

Ciampi, Yves, 162n, 163
Cid, Le, 453
Cinéma de papa, Le, 362, 455
Cinémane film society, xiv, 14n, 42, 68
Citizen Kane, 340n, 473, 530
Citron, Herman, 292, 295
Clair, René, 72, 105, 121, 126n, 153n, 173n, 272n, 418, 544
Clara et les Chics Types, 534
Clément, René, 29, 93, 98, 173, 239, 251, 296n, 428n, 462, 558n
Cléo de 5 à 7, 165, 167, 176
Clift, Montgomery, 448, 533
Cloche, Maurice, 22
Close Encounters of the Third Kind, 445n, 448, 448n, 452, 457, 480
Clouzot, Henri-Georges, 17n, 150, 153n, 254n, 257, 390, 443n, 546
Cocteau, Jean, ix, 13, 18, 30n, 54, 72, 87, 104, 106n, 121, 124n, 139, 150, 279, 280, 307, 424, 425, 488, 497, 505, 559, 563
Coeur battant, Le, 159
Collectionneuse, La, 427
Collector, The, 264, 268, 270
Collet, Jean, 403n, 469, 566n
Colpi, Henri, 159n, 162
Coluche, 421n
Condamné à mort s'est échappé, Un, 104, 439
Condition humaine, La, 374
Congdon, Don, 180, 186, 202, 206, 211n, 215, 249, 254, 258, 269, 270, 282, 333, 347, 474, 499, 512
Constantine, Eddie, 146, 149, 265
Contrebandières, Les, 316
Cooper, Saul, 397
Coppola, Francis Ford, 516
Corbeau, Le, 16, 252, 254
Corman, Roger, 536, 538
Corniaud, Le, 282–3
Cortese, Valentina, 374, 401, 510
Costa-Gavras, 335n, 418, 500
Cottafavi, Vittorio, 86, 176
Couëdel, Josiane, 517, 542
Countess from Hong-Kong, A, 367
Coup de berger, Le, 97, 107
Coup de foudre, 558, 565
Coup de tête, 495
Couple, Un, 147, 148
Cournot, Michel, 331, 390
Cousins, Les, 123
Cousseau, Jacques, 118, 127
Coutard, Raoul, 208, 214, 220, 307
Cranes Are Flying, The, 124
Cravenne, Georges, xiii, 307, 308n
Cravenne, Robert, 204
Crawford, Joan, 448
Créatures, Les, 282
Crin blanc, 107
Crowther, Bosley, 149, 188, 214

Dabadie, Jean-Loup, 364, 367n, 439, 534n
Dac, Pierre, 491
Dakota Incident, 112
Dani, 374, 474
Daniel-Norman, Jacques, x
Daninos, Pierre, 385
Daquin, Louis, 309n, 419–20
Darach, Brad, 186
Darbon, François, 466
Daroy, Jacques, 447
Dassin, Jules, 156
Dasté, Jean, 470, 471, 477n
Daudet, Alphonse, 4n, 61n, 63
Dauman, Anatole, 513
Davis, Richard, 145, 206
Dawson, Jan, 509
Day, Doris, 171, 206, 300
Day for Night, see Nuit américaine, La
Day of the Locust, The, 528, 530
Dean, James, 87, 101, 111, 146
Death in Venice, 450
Decaë, Henri, 123
Decugis, Cécile, 108, 138
Deep Water, 279
Delannoy, Jean, 91, 113n, 153n, 162n, 383, 462
De Laurentiis, Dino, 243, 244
Delerue, Georges, 151, 165, 240, 364, 366, 477, 511n, 516, 556
Delon, Alain, 338, 449
Delorme, Danielle, 152
Delsol, Paula, 112, 241n
Delvaux, André, 306, 556
De Mille, Cecil B., 94
Demoiselles de Rochefort, Les, 282
Demongeot, Catherine, 154
Demonsablon, Philippe, 96
Demy, Jacques, 139, 142, 151, 156, 158, 161, 164n, 238, 255–6, 260, 282, 355, 379, 423
Deneuve, Catherine, 282, 322, 327, 336, 338, 359, 384, 401, 425, 431, 502, 517, 520, 527, 561n
Denner, Charles, 358, 368, 427, 449, 452, 455, 466n, 467
Depardieu, Gérard, 502, 520, 531, 533, 534–5
Deray, Jacques, 395
Deréal, Colette, 127
Dernier Métro, Le, 354n, 496n, 499, 504n, 507n, 509–13, 515, 517n, 518–19, 521, 524, 525, 527, 528, 530–1, 533, 536–8, 549, 562, 565
Desailly, Jean, 220, 227, 229

Desdoits, Gabriel, 204, 510n
Desert of the Tartars, The, 176
Deutschmeister, Henry, 205, 207, 209, 214
Deux Anglaises et le Continent, Les, 356, 363, 364, 366, 373, 375, 424, 426, 427, 434, 456, 465, 478–9, 482–3, 503, 512, 542, 549, 563, 565
Devigny, André, 439
Deville, Michel, 165, 316n, 379
Devil's Eye, The, 172
Devos, Raymond, 363
Dewaere, Patrick, 496
Dewever, Jean, 501n
Dhéry, Robert, 187
Diable au corps, Le, 295
Diable, probablement, Le, 469
Dialogue des Carmélites, Le, 138, 139
Diamantis, Roger, 359n
Diary of a Chambermaid, see *Journal d'une femme de chambre, Le*
Diderot, Denis, 57, 282
Diener, David, 187, 193
Dimanches de Ville d'Avray, Les, 196, 207
Disney, Walt, 434, 482
Dîtes-lui que je l'aime, 472
Divorce Italian Style, 232
Djurka, 305, 330
Doigts dans la tête, Les, 424
Doillon, Jacques, 421n, 498n
Domarchi, Jean, 93, 95, 96, 97, 100, 109, 458n
Dombasle, Arielle, 531
Domicile conjugal, 307n, 338, 340, 359, 362n, 425, 478
Don't Look Now, 402
Donat, Robert, 300
Doniol-Valcroze, Jacques, 87, 91, 93, 94, 95, 100–1, 105, 112, 119, 150, 152, 159n, 314, 334, 342
Dorfmann, Robert, 282, 425
Doris, Pierre, 365
Dorléac, Françoise, xv, 220, 227, 228, 232, 254, 282, 345, 357
Dorléac, Maurice, 502
Dorothée, 480
Dostoevsky, Feodor, 54
Douce, 27, 308
Douchet, Jean, 333
Downhill, 299
Drach, Michel, 386
Dragueurs, Les, 147
Dreyer, Carl, 95, 262, 305
Dreyfus, Liliane, 388, 444n
Dreyfuss, Richard, 448, 451, 476
Drôlesse, La, 497
Dubois, Bernard, 413n, 416
Dubois, Marie, 357, 388, 448, 454
Dubost, Paulette, 502
Duhamel, Marcel, 151, 201n
Duhour, Clément, 107
Du Maurier, Daphne, 184
Duperey, Anny, 447, 448, 454
Dupuis, Claudine, x
Duras, Marguerite, 61n, 152, 536
Dussart, Philippe, 389
Dussolier, André, 500
Dutronc, Jacques, 496
Duvivier, Julien, 8n, 28, 56n, 138, 544
Dux, Pierre, 500
Dwan, Allan, 94, 445

Easy Virtue, 299
Eclipse, The, 201
Edith et Marcel, 557
Edwards, Blake, 549
8½, 220, 530
Eisenstein, Sergei Mikhailovich, 259
Eisner, Lotte, 95, 131n
El, 226
Elena et les Hommes, 93, 98, 101
Elephant Man, 549
Enclos, L', 161, 166
En effeuillant la marguerite, 108
Enfance nue, L', 420
Enfant sauvage, L', 257, 271, 279, 289, 337, 338, 340, 346–9, 360, 364, 373, 404, 420, 425, 426, 439, 451, 483, 517, 550, 553
Enfants du Paradis, Les, 24
Enfants terribles, Les, 123, 251
Enigma of Kaspar Hauser, The, 439–40
Enrico, Robert, 455
Epouse américaine, L', 491
Et Dieu créa la femme, 97
Et mourir de plaisir, 148
Etaix, Pierre, 316
Eté meurtrier, L', 559
Etranger, L', 176, 424, 439
Eustache, Jean, 399n, 433
Eva, 161, 201, 205, 207, 255, 388
Exorcist, The, 402, 416

Fahrenheit 451, xiii, 132n, 145, 148–9, 153, 173, 179, 180, 185, 189, 195, 202–10, 214, 216, 221, 228, 234, 236, 239, 243, 246–7, 251, 260–1, 262, 264, 266, 268, 274–5, 277, 279, 280, 284, 287, 290, 291, 296–7, 309, 330, 334, 351, 358, 377, 386, 399, 407, 422, 425, 435, 528, 561
Faisons un rêve, 18
Falbalas, 548
Fallet, René, 19
Fanne, Dominique, 456
Fant, Kenne, 256
Farceur, Le, 148, 151, 161

Fassbinder, Rainer Werner, ix, 550n, 565
Faulkner, William, 463
Faure, Élie, 64
Faure, Jean-Paul, 392
Faust, 428
Faute de l'abbé Mouret, La, 420
Favalelli, Max, 95
Fear, 101
Fear Strikes Out, 118
Félix, Louis, 112
Fellini, Federico, 105, 221, 473, 567
Femme d'à côté, La, 525n, 531–5, 539, 542, 548–9
Femme de l'aviateur, La, 535
Femme est une femme, Une, 161, 197, 207
Femme mariée, Une, 265
Femme seule, Une, 151
Ferme aux loups, La, 308
Fernandel, 113, 404n
Ferreri, Marco, 383, 384, 386, 450
Ferry, Odette, 88n, 177, 202, 290, 311, 317
Figueroa, Gabriel, 54
Fille à la dérive, Une, 468
Films du Carrosse, Les, 112, 116, 118, 119, 166, 167, 187–8, 195, 220, 249, 262, 265, 270, 278, 301n, 328, 363, 397, 413n, 418, 420, 435, 477, 478, 482, 499, 501, 503, 504, 510, 541, 543n
Finally Sunday!, *see Vivement dimanche!*
Finaly, Patricia, 387
Fin du voyage, La, 193
Fingers, 529
Fischer, Claire, 390
Fischer, Robert, 519n
Five Days One Summer, 555
Flamand, Georges, 128
Flamment, Georges, 22
Flaud, Jacques, 117
Florey, Robert, 378n
Flot, Yonnick, 450
Fonda, Jane, 229, 386, 387
Fontaine, Joan, 327
Ford, Glenn, 27
Ford, John, 22n, 100, 108, 496n
Forêts, Louis-René des, 152
Forty-First, The, 104
Fossey, Brigitte, 466
Four Hours, 290
Four Hundred Blows, The, *see Les Quatre Cents Coups*
Fournel, Paul, 563
Fraicheur de l'aube, La, 500
Française et l'Amour, La, 148
Francen, Victor, 113
François le Champi, 454
Franju, Georges, 105, 132n, 176, 280, 421n, 442n, 515
Frank, Christopher, 399
Frankel, Dan, 139, 172
Frankenheimer, John, 223n
French Film Office, New York, xv, 178, 194, 227n, 258, 261, 282, 519
Frenzy, 317–22, 324, 373
Fresnay, Pierre, 59, 533
Frey, Sami, 239
Friendly Persuasion, 163
Fuller, Samuel, 100, 476n
Furlaud, Maxime, 181, 184, 186
Furst, Renée, 242

Gabin, Jean, 56, 306
Gai Savoir, Le, 384
Gance, Abel, 118, 309n, 316, 341, 499, 500n, 515, 516, 534
Garcin, Henri, 531, 534
Garde du corps, Le, 496
Garnett, Tay, 418n
Gaulle, Charles de, 203, 260, 387, 390, 551
Gauteur, Claude, 489
Gégauff, Paul, 139
General, The, 316
Genet, Jean, ix, 35, 40n, 47, 49, 55, 60, 64, 76, 140, 423
Genou de Claire, Le, 428
Génovès, André, 362
Géraldy, Paul, 46
Géret, Georges, 260, 266
Germany Year Zero, 543, 544
Gervaise, 93, 97
Gheur, Bernard, 285n
Gide, André, 49, 54, 89n, 292, 489
Gifle, La, 440
Gilmore, Noelle, 186, 192, 194
Giono, Jean, 59, 63, 251n
Gitlis, Ivry, 434n
Givray, Claude de, 108, 119n, 126, 139, 141n, 146, 149, 155, 158–9, 161, 164, 166, 172, 205, 245, 256, 260, 270, 276, 281, 286n, 328n, 449n, 489
Givray, Georges de, 328, 459
Givray, Lucette de, 137, 145, 153, 173, 182, 188, 201, 207, 209, 215, 226, 228, 232, 245, 256, 257, 261, 275, 281
Glenn, Pierre-William, 365n, 373
Go-Between, The, 450
Godard, Jean-Luc, 92, 96n, 117n, 119, 137n, 138, 140, 150, 152, 153, 158, 161, 162n, 164, 165, 167, 168, 214, 216, 219, 222, 226, 239, 247, 251–3, 265, 278–80, 288, 312, 325, 383–91, 403, 518
Gold Rush, The, 435
Goodbye Mr Chips, 4
Goodis, David, 132, 145, 149, 151, 180, 185, 187, 192, 200–1, 229, 257, 426, 451, 509
Gorgeous Bird Like Me, A, *see Belle fille*

comme moi, Une
Gorin, Jean-Pierre, 384
Graetz, Paul, 117, 295
Grande Bouffe, La, 384n, 397
Grand Élan, Le, 308
Grandes Personnes, Les, 159, 161
Granelli, Mireille, 101
Grangier, Gilles, 454
Grant, Cary, 177, 265, 512n
Great Dictator, The, 321, 388, 463
Green Room, The, see Chambre verte, La
Greene, Graham, 27
Grégor, Nora, 24
Grémillon, Jean, 544
Grenier, Cynthia, 173
Grimblat, Pierre, 145, 149, 233
Gruault, Jean, 256, 271, 279, 289, 338n, 360, 380, 509, 534
Grumberg, Jean-Claude, 504n
Guber, Peter, 396
Guendalina, 104
Guérin, Raymond, 450
Guerre est finie, La, 282
Guille, Frances V., 360, 380, 381, 383, 438, 509
Guillemin, Henri, 427
Guitry, Sacha, 17n, 21n, 45n, 72, 109n, 118, 534
Guns in the Trees, 186

Hakim, Robert and Raymond, 301n, 338
Hallier, Jean-Edern, 385
Hallyday, Johnny, 557
Hamilton, George, 265
Hamilton, Guy, 396
Hanin, Roger, 281
Harmony Heaven, 538
Harvey, Cyrus, 180, 186, 193
Hatari, 210
Haudepin, Sabine, 229, 502
Hauduroy, Jean-François, 139, 315n
Hawks, Howard, 8n, 78n, 100, 210n, 213, 256, 401
Hayden, Sterling, 281
Hayward, Susan, 51
Hedren, Tippi, 213
Henry, Buck, 396
Hepburn, Audrey, 496
Hepburn, Katharine, 22, 558
Hermantier, Raymond, 28
Herrmann, Bernard, 199, 290
Herzog, Werner, 439
Hessel, Franz, 518, 521
Hessel, Helen, 266, 518, 521, 522–3, 549
High and the Mighty, The, 101
Highsmith, Patricia, 279
Hiroshima mon amour, 140, 149, 153, 156, 335, 354
Histoire d'Adèle H., L', 360n, 375, 380, 408, 418, 427, 430, 436, 438–40, 451, 452, 461–3, 465, 469, 509, 530, 536
Histoire de Vasco, 114
Histoire d'O, 440, 542
Hitchcock, Alfred, xii, xv, 88, 89, 91, 94, 100, 166, 179–180n, 181–4, 187–8, 189, 191–7, 199–200, 202, 205, 207, 209, 213, 215, 218–19, 222, 226, 228, 231, 240, 243, 246, 247, 254–5, 258, 261, 265, 268–9, 270, 276–7, 282–4, 288–90, 292–3, 295, 296, 299, 326, 348, 369, 373, 395, 452, 538, 543, 563
Hitchcock, Alma, 202, 348, 395
Hitchcock, Patricia, 561
Hitler, Adolf, 29, 58, 166, 321
Holt, Jany, xii
Homme au crâne rasé, L', 306
Homme de Rio, L', 238
Homme et une femme, Un, 455
Homme qui aimait les femmes, L', 428n, 447, 452, 453, 458, 462, 467, 469, 549
Honneurs de la guerre, Les, 501
Honorable Cathérine, L', 422
Hooper, 530
Horstig-Primuz, Olga, 487n
Hossein, Robert, 388
House of Strangers, 51
House of the Angel, The, 104
Howard, Leslie, 533
Hughes, Robert, 173
Hugo, Adèle, 360n, 427, 439, 509
Hugo, Jean, 360, 380, 509
Hugo, Victor, xi, 360n, 420, 427, 436, 439n
Huntley, John, 299n
Hussards, Les, 85
Huster, Francis, 453
Huston, John, 94, 259

IDHEC, 280
Il était une fois un flic, 495
India Song, 536
Inge, William, 222
Insdorf, Annette, 458n
Irish, William, 233, 246–7, 322, 334, 426, *see also* Woolrich, Cornell
Isabelle a peur des hommes, 116

Jacob, Gilles, 312n, 440
Jade, Claude, 327, 328, 474, 478, 499
Jaffe, Leo, 396
James, Henry, 405, 408
Jamet, Frédérique, 466
Janus Films, 195, 207, 218, 232, 377
Jaubert, Maurice, 429, 475, 528
Javal, Bertrand, 444
Jaws, 455
Jeannel, Alain, 108

Jeanson, Henri, 127
Jelinek, Henriette, 330
Joan of Arc at the Stake, 78
Joe Macbeth, 91
Johnny Got His Gun, 478
Johnny Guitar, 281
Joli Mai, Le, 211–12
Jones, Elinor, 238, 249
Jong, Erica, 520
Jouffroy, Alain, 390
Journal d'un curé de campagne, Le, 16n, 17, 19, 391
Journal d'une femme de chambre, Le, 116, 226n, 239, 260
Judgment at Nuremberg, 166, 173
Juin, Georges, 21
Jules et Jim, 145, 148, 153, 155, 156, 159, 161, 162, 163, 166–7, 169, 172, 174, 175, 177, 183, 186, 189, 193, 195, 201, 209, 215, 220, 232, 261, 262, 266, 271, 281, 343, 360, 377, 388, 405, 424, 426, 465, 503, 512, 518, 522–4, 549
Jürgens, Curd, 113
Juste avant la nuit, 362
Jutra, Claude, 139, 150, 276

Kael, Pauline, 266
Kalatozov, Mikhail, 124
Karina, Anna, 158, 165, 186, 239, 281, 282, 388
Karmitz, Marin, 391
Kast, Pierre, 111, 141n, 150, 151, 152, 164
Kawakita, Naganasa and Kashiko, 483
Kazan, Elia, 87
Keigel, Léonard, 107
Keller, Marthe, 371, 454, 455
Kelly, Grace, 327, 395
Kennedy, John Fitzgerald, 226, 336
Kiejman, Georges, 377, 386
Killer is Loose, The, 93
Kipling, Rudyard, 52
Klee, Paul, 312
Klossowski, Pierre, 358, 359
Korda, Michael, 258, 282, 292, 295, 322
Kramer, Stanley, 166, 173, 213
Kubrick, Stanley, 257, 480, 529
Kurosawa, Akira, 553
Kurys, Diane, 559n, 565
Kyrou, Adonis, 93

Labarthe, André S., 93, 96, 371, 377, 464
Lachenay, Robert, xii, xiv, 108, 113, 122, 125, 205
Lâches vivent d'espoir, Les, 150, 159
Lacour, José-André, 546
Lady Vanishes, The, 373, 473
La Fayette, 201
Laffont, Robert, 27, 176n, 178, 191, 292–3, 295, 299, 300, 312
Lafont, Bernadette, 106n, 107–8, 110, 111, 305, 364, 365, 369, 370, 371, 402, 409, 426
Laforêt, Marie, 194
Lamorisse, Albert, 109n, 139, 151, 154n, 462
Lancaster, Burt, 222
Lancelot du lac, 421
Landau, Ely, 214
Landru, 209
Lang, Fritz, 14, 22n, 92, 93, 100
Lang, Jack, 542
Langlois, Henri, 95, 131, 132n, 318, 322–5, 327, 343, 390, 442n, 505, 551, 553, 563, 565
Lapierre, Marcel, 64, 73
Lapointe, Boby, 194, 272
Largemains, Bernard, 58n, 104
Lassalle, Martin, 140
Last Laugh, The, 435
Last Métro, The, see Le Dernier Métro
Last of Sheila, The, 396
Last Picture Show, The, 549
Last Tango in Paris, 384
Lattuada, Alberto, 106
Laughton, Charles, 180
Laurent, Agnès, 105
Laurent, Jacques, 91
Laurie, Piper, 239
Lautner, Georges, 496n, 541
Leáuaud, Paul, 491n
Léaud, Jean-Pierre, ix, 138, 170, 172, 181, 184, 205, 233, 257, 279, 289, 305, 311, 328, 355, 356, 364, 374, 384, 385, 387, 388–9, 390, 412, 413n, 416, 430, 478–80, 484–6
Le Boterf, Hervé, 525n
Lebovici, Gérard, 306, 330, 362, 364, 366, 448, 550n, 556
Lebrun, Françoise, 467n
Ledoux, Jacques, 305n
Lefèvre, René, 112
Lelouch, Claude, 312, 342n, 371, 383, 397, 418, 421, 453, 455, 516, 557
Léon Morin prêtre, 388
Leopard, The, 222
Léotard, Philippe, 491
Lépicier, Eugène, 265, 280, 288–9
Leprohon, Pierre, 313–14, 464
LeRoy, Mervyn, 93, 462
Lesaffre, Roland, 109
Lesage, Janine, 85, 97
Leterrier, François, 454
Le Vigan, Robert, 533
Levine, Joseph E., 199n, 214, 222
Lévy, Raoul J., 145, 148–9, 153, 201, 247, 279, 535

Lewenstein, Oscar, 275, 281, 292
Lewis, Jerry, 365
L'Herbier, Marcel, 313n, 374, 422n
Lherminier, Pierre, 163n, 465
Lhomme, Pierre, 444
Liaisons dangereuses, Les, 173
Libert, Nadine, 221, 232, 281
Lifeboat, 101, 290
Limelight, 565
Litvak, Anatole, 264, 462
Lodger, The, 218
Logan, Joshua, 94, 101
Lola, 139, 142, 151, 156, 158, 159, 161, 167, 197, 207, 355
Lola Montès, 81
Lolos de Lola, Les, 413n
Lombard, Carole, 287
Long Saturday Night, The, 549
Lonsdale, Michel, 327
Lopert, Tanya, xv, 345n
Lord of the Flies, 221
Losey, Joseph, 391n, 449–50
Lost Patrol, The, 22
Louis, Théodore, 307n
Love Me or Leave Me, 171, 206
Love on the Run, see Amour en fuite
Lubitsch, Ernst, 410, 474–5
Luccioni, Micheline, 97
Luddy, Tom, 516
Lumet, Sidney, 180, 186, 215
Lumière, Louis, 108
Luna, La, 502
Lust for Gold, 27

M comme Mathieu, 336
MacCartney, Filgate Terence, 221, 225, 228
MacGregor, Duncan, 187, 193, 197, 214, 221
McLaren, Norman, 167
Madelin, Louis, 46
Magnificent Ambersons, The, 424, 435, 497
Mahias, Lydie, 342n
Maire, Edmond, 390
Mâle du siècle, Le, 418
Malick, Terence, 452
Malige, Jean, 107, 112, 241
Malle, Louis, 123, 124n, 152, 153n, 189n, 258, 313n, 325, 343, 379, 384, 427
Mallet, Françoise, 71
Malot, Hector, 285
Malraux, André, 33, 145, 152, 322n, 341, 390
Malraux, Florence, 151, 152, 355
Maman et la Putain, La, 397
Mambrino, Jean, xiii, 83n
Mandrake, 436, 438
Manhattan, 549
Mankiewicz, Joseph L., 52n, 100, 141n, 500n
Mann, Daniel, 87, 88n
Mann, Delbert, 88n, 106n
Ma Nuit chez Maud, 420, 427–8
Man on the Run, 27
Man Who Knew Too Much, The, 300, 324, 561
Man Who Loved Women, The, see Homme qui aimait Les femmes, L'
Man with the Golden Arm, The, 96, 102
Marais, Jean, 29
Marcabru, Pierre, 193
Marcellin, Raymond, 386
Marchand, Guy, 369n, 558n
Marcorelles, Louis, 98n, 316
Mardore, Michel, 367, 530
Mariano, Luis, 366
Marie-Antoinette, 89
Mariée était en noir, La, 246, 249, 255, 275, 277, 281, 291–2, 307, 309–11, 315, 322, 324, 327, 330, 334, 355, 357, 358, 425, 521
Mari à prix fixe, Un, 281
Marker, Chris, 211–12
Marlier, Carla, 264n, 267
Marnie, 213, 222, 231, 259, 284, 290, 295, 296, 300
Marquand, Serge, 415
Marriott, Sylvia, 430, 434
Mars, François, 24, 42
Marshall, Herbert, 448
Masculin-Féminin, 384, 385
Mason, James, 22, 97, 512n
Master of Ballantrae, The, 546
Mata-Hari, 204–5, 209, 243, 244, 245, 256, 261, 265, 274, 565
Maternati, Jo, 180, 187, 193, 196–7, 234, 249
Matisse, Pierre, 183
Maupassant, Guy de, 103
Mauriac, Claude, 24, 59, 61, 73
Mauriac, François, 25n, 47
Maurier, Claire, 128
Mayhew, Leonard, 475
Mayniel, Juliette, 147
Meerson, Mary, 131, 563
Mekas, Jonas, 186
Mélangite, La, 151
Melville, Jean-Pierre, 117n, 124n, 207, 343, 388
Mendès-France, Pierre, 390
Menez, Bernard, 415
Mépris, Le, 219, 222, 238, 388
Mercier, Michèle, 343, 357, 397
Méril, Macha, 547n
Messmer, Pierre, 387
Mezzrow, Mezz, 54
Micha, René, 340

Mickey One, 241n
Midler, Bette, 517n
Miller, Arthur, 181
Miller, Claude, 258n, 470
Miller, Henry, 200
Mimieux, Yvette, 239
Mingus, Charlie, 150
Miou-Miou, 453, 470, 472n
Mississippi Mermaid, *see Sirène du Mississipi, La*
Miss Julie, 567
Mistons, Les, 105, 109–11, 114–19, 355, 370, 426
Mitterrand, François, 542
Mitterrand, Frédéric, 442
Moby Dick, 93
Mock, Jean-Yves, 519
Mocky, Jean-Pierre, 148
Moderato Cantabile, 159, 163
Moguy, Léonide, 203
Moinot, Pierre, 322–3
Molinaro, Edouard, 161, 164n, 496n
Möller, Charly, 521
Mon Oncle, 127, 146, 154
Mon Oncle d'Amérique, 536
Mon Oncle Benjamin, 548
Monaco, James, 520
Monferrand, Janine de, xiii, xviii, 13, 271
Monod, Jacques, 387
Monroe, Marilyn, 395
Monsieur de compagnie, Un, 259
Monsieur Ripois, 295
Monsieur Sorge, 161
Montaigne, Pierre, 480n, 511
Montand, Yves, 282, 387, 391n, 395
Montez, Maria, 374
Montherlant, Henri de, 39, 40n, 507
Morand, Paul, 202
Moravia, Alberto, 188, 388
Moreau, Col. Albert, 50
Moreau, Jeanne, 138, 149, 151, 152–3, 158, 161, 165, 166, 173, 183, 201, 205, 208, 221–2, 226, 227, 242, 245, 248–9, 251, 258, 261, 263, 266, 275, 279, 281, 291–2, 307, 309–11, 316, 330, 358, 366, 388, 425, 430, 449, 455, 521
Moreau, Jérome, 138, 139
Moreno, Dario, 108
Morgan, Michèle, 29
Morgenstern, Ignace, 121, 123, 139, 146, 158, 161, 223n
Morgenstern, Madeleine, 98, 100, 107, 109, 115n, *see also* Truffaut, Madeleine
Morlay, Gaby, xii
Mort de Belle, La, 161, 203
Mort du cygne, La, 202
Mort en ce jardin, La, 93
Morte Saison des amours, La, 151, 159
Moskowitz, Gene, 95
Moullet, Luc, 85n, 95, 96
Mountain Eagle, The, 299
Mourre, Michel, 15, 17, 18, 24
Moussy, Marcel, 121n, 130, 139, 140, 180–1, 202, 204, 256
Moussy, Yvonne, 127, 130
Mr Arkadin, 102
Mulligan, Robert, 118
Muriel, 196, 219, 227, 335
Murnau, F. W., 87, 93n, 111, 428, 436n
Mystère Picasso, Le, 91

Napoléon, 341, 516, 529
Nedjar, Claude, 421
Newman, David, 252, 275
Newman, Paul, 173, 181, 438n
Nichols, Beverley, 401
Nichols, Mike, 371
Nickelodeon, 444
Nietzsche, Friedrich, 59, 63
Night of the Hunter, The, 101
Nixon, Richard, M., 395, 396
Noble, Peter, 463
Nosferatu, 111
North by Northwest, 265, 309, 512n
Notorious, 324
Notte, La, 166, 173
Nourissier, François, 101–2
Nous sommes tous des assassins, 545
Nuit américaine, La, 363n, 374, 374n, 375, 381, 383–5, 392, 393, 397, 399, 402, 404, 416, 420, 422, 426, 442, 450, 451, 454, 478, 510, 528–9, 530, 546
Nuit et Brouillard, 92, 95, 101, 199n
Nuit fantastique, La, 422
Nuit porte conseil, La, 14

Odets, Clifford, 115n
Odette, 47
Oeil pour oeil, 113
Ogre of Athens, The, 95
O'Hara, Maureen, 496
Okada, Eija, 153n
Okasan, 78
Olmi, Ermanno, 210n, 484
O'Neil, Ryan and Tatum, 445
On the Beach, 213
00/14, 559
Ophüls, Marcel, 139, 151, 164, 168n, 438
Ophüls, Max, 78, 81–2, 101, 103, 105, 139, 516, 535
Orfeu negro, 154, 163
Orphée, 54, 105
Os Bandeirantes, 151, 159
O'Toole, Peter, 206n, 243, 250, 311
Ours, L', 159
Oury, Gérard, 283n

Pabst, Georg Wilhelm, 33–4
Pagliero, Marcel, 14
Pagnol, Marcel, 534
Painlevé, Jean, 111
Palance, Jack, 97
Papillon, 549
Paradine Case, The, 311
Paradis perdu, 308
Parapluies de Cherbourg, Les, 238, 242
Parinaud, André, 105, 112
Paris, Jim, 545n
Paris nous appartient, 122, 127, 136, 138, 139–40, 143, 146, 150, 166, 167, 171, 192, 210
Partie de plaisir, Une, 139
Pascal, Blaise, 61, 62, 63
Pasolini, Pier Paolo, 328
Passage du Rhin, Le, 159
Pathé, Ariane, 15, 17, 24
Paul, Bernard, 386
Peau douce, La, 219–21, 223, 225, 227–8, 231–2, 234, 236–7, 240, 242, 244, 252, 255, 256–7, 260–1, 271, 357–8, 377, 424–5, 468
Péguy, Charles, 43, 46
Pellé, Christine, 408n, 436n, 560
Pellepoix, Darquier de, 505
Penn, Arthur, 186, 188, 221–2, 239, 259, 264
Pepin, André, 167, 172, 218–19
Pépita, 27
Perkins, Anthony, 300, 317
Perret, Pierre, 369
Petit Soldat, Le, 140, 146, 150, 153, 186, 209
Petite Voleuse, La, 257, 289
Peyre, Janine, 497, 498
Peyrefitte, Alain, 212n
Philipe, Gérard, 295
Phillips, Stephanie, 244
Piaf, Edith, 372, 557
Pialat, Maurice, 366, 371, 421n
Picker, David, 394
Picnic, 222
Picture of Dorian Gray, The, 16
Piéral, Armand, 27, 176
Pigaut, Roger, 152
Pingaud, Bernard, 313
Pisier, Marie-France, 388, 474, 478
Plaisir, Le, 103
Poe, Edgar Allan, 152
Poe, James and Barbara, 396
Pointe courte, La, 102
Poiret, Jean, 502
Poivre, Annette, 24
Polanski, Roman, 282, 445n, 450, 503n, 546
Poldès, Léo, 16n, 19, 70
Pollès, Henri, 450
Pompidou, Georges, 384, 386, 397
Poncheville, Marie de, 502
Pons, Maurice, 103n, 111, 355
Ponti, Carlo, 222
Porcile, François, 478n, 528
Porteuse de pain, 22
Posto, Il, 210
Pottier, Richard, 29
Poujade, Pierre, 108, 133
Prasche, Françoise, 149
Première Nuit, La, 513, 515
Preminger, Otto, 98n, 180, 184, 204, 395
Prévert, Jacques, 16n 46, 49, 71, 74, 283
Prieur, Jérôme, 565
Princesse de Clèves, La, 161
Proie pour l'ombre, La, 159
Proust, Marcel, 43, 45, 46, 49, 64, 250, 553
Psycho, 213, 300, 317, 435
Pyramide humaine, La, 159

Quai des Orfèvres, 252
Quatre Cents Coups, Les, ix, 2, 119n, 120n, 121n, 125, 128n, 131, 132, 136, 137, 138, 156, 158, 159, 162, 172, 177, 184, 272n, 311, 342, 355–7, 377, 385, 417, 424, 426, 435, 451, 472, 478, 483, 535
Quelle joie de vivre, 173
Queneau, Raymond, 148, 167, 172, 390
Quiet Man, The, 496

RRRR, 284, 290
Racine-Freess, Sarah, 555n
Radiguet, Raymond, 63, 90n
Raging Bull, 535, 549
Raimu, 38, 111
Rassam, Jean-Pierre, 333, 384, 387, 450
Raw Deal, 27
Ray, Nicholas, 87, 94, 97, 100, 107, 114, 282n
Ray, Satyajit, 553
Rear Window, 199, 300, 561
Rebecca, 245, 311
Rebel Without a Cause, 97
Recréation, La, 161
Redford, Robert, 512
Reed, Rex, 473n
Régent, Roger, 309n
Règle du jeu, La, 22, 24, 47, 52n, 424, 530
Reggiani, Serge, 355
Régnier, Max, 38
Reichenbach, François, 141, 233
Religieuse, La, 57, 282
Rémy, Albert, 127, 223, 509
Renoir, Claude, 28
Renoir, Dido, 472, 495
Renoir, Jean, 22, 27, 30, 41, 47, 52n, 55, 90, 94n, 101, 114, 185, 202, 213, 279,

281, 313–14, 323, 374, 383, 387, 395, 396, 399, 403, 404, 407, 472, 495, 516
Renoir, Pierre, 28
Repos du guerrier, Le, 196
Resnais, Alain, 42, 86, 105, 142n, 149, 150, 151, 152, 167, 171, 172, 176, 186, 193, 196, 227, 256, 257, 280, 282, 323, 335, 366, 418, 436, 438, 516, 536, 541n, 555, 558, 567
Revon, Bernard, 286n, 328, 448n
Reynolds, Burt, 445
Rezvani, Danièle, 267
Rezvani, Serge, 263–4, 267, 272n, 423
Ribeiro, Catherine, 388
Riboud, Jean, 553
Rich, Claude, 327, 358
Richard, Jean-Louis, 204–5, 219, 225, 238, 247, 264n, 267, 276, 279, 289, 364, 502, 528
Richardson, Tony, 217n, 233n, 275–6, 281, 311, 434
Rire de Caïn, Le, 546
Rivette, Jacques, 35, 62, 69, 76, 77, 88–90, 92, 94, 119, 128n, 136–7, 139, 141n, 165, 172, 214, 282, 314, 334, 336, 424, 454, 541n
Robbe-Grillet, Alain, 149, 424
Robbins, Jerome, 158
Robert, Yves, 128
Robertson, Peggy, 199–200, 202, 205, 207, 283, 288–9, 292, 395
Robinson, Bruce, 434
Robinson, Edward G., 1, 22
Roché, Henri-Pierre, 195, 266, 360, 503, 515, 518, 521
Roeg, Nicolas, 402n
Rohmer, Eric, 21n, 36, 88, 109, 111, 112, 118, 119, 131, 188, 191, 314, 364, 390, 420, 423, 427, 450, 468, 502, 516, 531, *see also* Schérer, Maurice
Roman d'un tricheur, Le, 230
Roman Holiday, 496
Ronde, La, 259
Rope, 221, 245, 561
Rose, The, 516
Rose Tattoo, The, 87
Rosenbaum, Jonathan, 462, 530
Ross, Herbert, 396
Ross, Lillian, 228, 354n
Rossellini, Roberto, 78, 82, 83, 84, 90, 92, 97, 98, 100–1, 108, 183, 188, 213, 276–80, 454, 460, 469, 503, 534, 543n, 553
Rouch, Jean, 159n, 388
Roud, Richard, 216, 330n, 390, 398, 468, 519, 553, 565
Rousseau, Jean-Jacques, 47, 57
Rousseau, Serge, 364, 366, 448n, 486, 504, 556
Roy, Jules, 172
Rozan, Micheline, 207, 209, 266
Rozier, Jacques, 139, 165
Rucart, Marc, 70, 72, 74
Ruses du diable, Les, 347
Rush, Richard, 524n, 528–30

Sachs, Maurice, 27
Sadoul, Georges, 73, 95n, 313
Saga of Anahatan, 101
Sagan, Françoise, 152, 448
Saint, Eva Marie, 265
Saint-Cyr, Renée, 447n, 541n
Saint-John, Kitty, 239
Saint-Tropez Blues, 140, 159
Salaire de la peur, Le, 252
Salinger, J. D., 211, 214, 354
Samuels, Charles Thomas, 369, 371, 373
Sand, George, 454
Sang d'un poète, Le, 54
Saroyan, William, 488, 489n, 500
Sarris, Andrew, 288, 561
Sartre, Jean-Paul, 19, 55, 57, 60, 150, 152, 240n, 316, 350–1, 353, 390, 539, 552
Sautet, Claude, 152
Sauveur, Le, 365
Scarabée d'or, Le, 167, 193, 196
Scarlet Street, 22
Schaffner, Franklin, 550n
Schell, Maria, 93, 97
Schérer, Maurice, 18, 19, 24, 42, 62, 88–90, 95, 97, 98, *see also* Rohmer, Eric
Schiffman, Guillaume and Matthieu, 356
Schiffman, Suzanne, 237, 332, 401, 402, 449, 452, 496, 508, 516, 519, 524, 525, 534, 560
Schneider, Bert, 452
Schneider, Betty, 128, 137
Schneider, Maria, 384
Schneider, Romy, 257
Schneider, Stanley, 394
Schpountz, Le, 530
Schroeder, Barbet, 364n
Scob, Edith, 132
Scott, Helen, xii, xv-vi, 141n, 145, 178, 190, 211, 252, 274, 276, 284, 289–90, 293, 295, 299, 327, 346, 387, 402, 448, 468, 509, 517, 519, 530, 540, 543, 551, 556
Seavers, Dick, 207, 227, 234
Seavers, Janet, 207
Secor, Walter T., 509
Selznick, David O., 178, 528
Sennett, Mack, 150
Senso, 102
Sentimental Education, 377
Sept Péchés capitaux, Les, 163, 164n
Sergeant York, 8

Servais, Jean, 29
Seven Arts, 181
Seyrig, Delphine, 357, 358
Shadow of a Doubt, 317
Shadows, 156
Shoot the Pianist, see Tirez sur le pianiste
Siclier, Jacques, 96, 489n, 533
Siegel, Don, 94
Siegel, Liliane, 371
Signoret, Simone, 152
Si jolie petite plage, Une, 16
Silence de la mer, Le, 116, 123, 251
Sills, Stephanie, 261, 269
Simenon, Georges, 49, 313, 424, 472n, 489, 548
Simon & Schuster, 178, 181, 187, 191, 195, 210, 216, 228, 231, 234, 258, 269, 292, 295, 296, 297, 320, 327, 347
Simon, Michel, 22
Sinatra, Frank, 209, 387
Singin' in the Rain, 516, 530
Sirène du Mississipi, La, 301, 328, 330, 334, 335, 337–9, 347, 359, 424, 425, 521, 528
Siritsky, Jo and Sammy, 172, 186, 213, 229, 311
Skolimowski, Jerzy, 305
Slightly Scarlet, 96
Small Change, see Argent de poche
Smic, Smac, Smoc, 365
Smiles of a Summer Night, 102
Soft Skin, see Peau douce, La
Soldati, Mario, 22n, 494n
Something to Live for, 94
Sontag, Susan, 390
Soraya, 243, 244, 245, 425
Souchon, Alain, 481n, 482, 489, 561n
Spaak, Charles, 544
Spellbound, 245, 290
Spiegel, Sam, 260, 264–5, 268–9, 270
Spielberg, Steven, 447, 448, 452, 457
Stalin, Svetlana, 312
Stamp, Terence, 206n, 264, 268, 270–1, 274
Star, Harrisson, 256, 259, 259n, 262
Star, La, 546
State of Things, The, 549
Stéphane, Nicole, 251n
Stévenin, Jean-François, 448
Stevens, George, 94, 259
Stewart, Alexandra, 239, 274, 374
Stewart, James, 300
Stolen Kisses, see Baisers volés
Storck, Henri, 477
Story of Adèle H., The, see Histoire d'Adèle H., L'
Strangers on a Train, 317
Stravinsky, Igor, 312
Stroheim, Erich von, 58, 101
Stunt Man, The, 528, 530
Suddenly Last Summer, 139
Sue, Eugène, 428
Summer with Monika, 92, 93
Sutherland, Elizabeth, 181, 187, 197, 208, 210–11, 215, 227, 231, 234
Szabó, Laszló, 409, 418, 502

Tarnished Angels, The, 126
Taste of Honey, A, 216
Tati, Jacques, 105, 128n, 187, 282, 418
Tavernier, Bertrand, 472n, 516, 518
Taxi pour Tobrouk, 161
Taylor, Rod, 213
Tcherina, Ludmilla, 208
Teisseire, Guy, 286n, 489
Temps Chaud, 116–17, 127
Tendeter, Stacey, 469
Tenth Victim, The, 287
Terrain Vague, 159
Tess, 502
Testament d'Orphée, Le, 138, 166, 535
Testament d'un cancre, Le, 284
Thamar, Tilda, x, 112
Thibaudat, Claude, 4, 13, 42
Thirty Nine Steps, The, 265, 300, 373, 538
Thomas, Michel, 395, 396, 528
Thomas, Pascal, 516, 519
Thomas l'Imposteur, 280
Three Days of the Condor, 445
Tin Drum, The, 504
Tire-au-flanc, 60, 139, 149, 153, 155, 158, 161, 166, 167, 186–7, 193, 200
Tirez sur le pianiste, 121n, 134n, 136, 140, 144, 147, 151, 155, 157, 159, 166, 172, 185, 186–9, 192, 209, 216, 247n, 257, 262, 343, 357, 377, 424, 454, 458, 508, 567
To Be or Not to Be, 287
To Catch a Thief, 177
To Have and Have Not, 78, 401
Tom Jones, 233, 238, 280
Toni, 91
Topaz, 324, 327
Torn Curtain, 284, 288, 290, 295, 296, 299–301
Toro, vie d'un matador, 95
Torok, Jean-Paul, 520
Tout l'Or du monde, 173
Tout va bien, 385, 386
Toute une vie, 455
Tracy, Spencer, 22
Train, The, 239
Traversée de Paris, La, 93
Tree of Wooden Clogs, The, 484
Trenet, Charles, 113n, 272, 363, 511n
Trial, The, 196, 205, 207
Trintignant, Jean-Louis, 395, 427, 548, 548n

Tristana, 517
Trou, Le, 138, 139
Trouble With Harry, The, 102, 561
Truffaut, Eva, 157n, 201, 203, 204, 216, 225, 231, 234, 238, 244, 245, 247, 256, 257, 260, 356, 365, 452, 459, 502
Truffaut, Joséphine, 562n
Truffaut, Laura, 138, 144, 149, 156, 161, 201, 203, 204, 216, 225, 231, 234, 238, 244, 245, 247, 256, 257, 260, 279, 327, 356, 365, 450, 451n, 452, 469, 473, 491, 502, 535
Truffaut, Madeleine, 117, 119, 124, 126, 127, 130, 146, 155, 161, 166, 175, 181, 182, 193, 201, 204, 209, 210, 216, 225, 231, 234, 236, 242–5, 247, 256, 260, 270, 291, 327, 371, 394, 433, *see also* Morgenstern, Madeleine
Truffaut, Roland, xiii-iv, xviii, 271
Trumeau, Maître, 381, 383
Tushingham, Rita, 217n

Ugetsu Monogatari, 473
Ulmer, Edgar G., x, 85, 86, 87, 93

Vadim, Roger, 98n, 101, 114, 153n, 159, 164n, 172, 197, 260n
Van Gogh, Vincent, 482
Vandromme, Pol, 533
Vannier, Alain, 517, 556
Varda, Agnès, 102n, 151, 158, 165, 167, 176, 282, 379
Vecchiali, Paul, 347, 350
Véga, Claude, *see* Thibaudat, Claude
Vent d'est, 389
Vérité, La, 148, 150, 151
Verneuil, Henri, 127, 153n, 162n, 383–4, 387
Vernon, Anne, 98, 100, 101
Veronika Voss, 549
Vertigo, 199, 561
Vian, Boris, 58
Vidal, Gore, 277
Vidor, King, 434, 483
Vie conjugale, La, 240n
Vie est un roman, La, 558
Vie privée, 183
Vieil Homme et l'Enfant, Le, 395
Vigo, Jean, 14, 108, 440, 479, 495
Vilar, Jean, 268n
Vilmorin, Louise de, 71, 360
Viot, Pierre, 450
Visconti, Luchino, 223n, 450
Visite, Une, 541
Viva Maria, 260n, 264n
Viva Zapata!, 396
Vive la sociale!, 567
Vivement dimanche!, 272n, 531n, 547, 548,550, 554, 556, 560–1, 563–5
Vivre sa vie, 186, 196, 199n, 202, 214, 219, 222
Vlady, Marina, 222
Voices, 497
Voulzy, Laurent, 488, 489
Voyage en ballon, Le, 139, 151, 156, 159

Wajda, Andrzej, 168n, 379n
Walton, Tony, 288n
Waltz into Darkness, 322
Wasserman, Lew, 233, 422
Week-End, 388
Weekend at the Waldorf, 7
Welles, Orson, 40n, 196, 445, 463–4, 549
Wenders, Wim, 445n, 549
Wendkos, Paul, 229
Werner, Oskar, 149, 165, 206n, 208, 288, 298, 309
Wertmüller, Linda, 478
What Makes Sammy Run?, 396
What's New, Pussycat?, 287
While the City Sleeps, 93n
Wiazemsky, Anne, 388
Wiesel, Élie, 145, 153, 186
Wild Child, see Enfant Sauvage, L'
Wild Palms, The, 210, 221
Willens, Bernie, 222
Williams, Charles, 247, 451, 542
Williams, Tennessee, 87
Winston, Arthur, 214
Wizard of Oz, The, 7
Woman Next Door, The, see Femme d'à côté, La
Woman of Paris, A, 563
Wong, Steve, 502
Wood, Sam, 6n, 54, 68
Woolrich, Cornell, 240, *see also* Irish, William
Wright, Elinor, 233
Wrong Man, The, 177, 178, 192
Wyler, William, 17n, 163n, 259, 264, 270, 496n

Yacowar, Maurice, 538
Yamada, Koichi, 400n, 406
Yeux sans visage, Les, 132, 139

Z, 334, 455, 500
Zanuck, Darryl, 204
Zazie dans le métro, 148, 151, 154, 156
Zeffirelli, Franco, 434
Zelig, 567
Zéro de conduite, 477, 495
Zidi, Claude, 541
Zig Zag, 418
Zinnemann, Fred, 555
Zitrone, Léon, 470
Zsigmond, Vilmos, 453